AIR COMBAT LEGENDS
VOLUME ONE

Supermarine Spitfire
Messerschmitt Bf 109

AIR COMBAT LEGENDS
VOLUME ONE

Supermarine Spitfire
Messerschmitt Bf 109

General Editor
David Donald

AIRtime Publishing Inc.
United States of America

Published by AIRtime Publishing Inc.
120 East Avenue, Norwalk, CT 06851
Tel (203) 838-7979 • Fax (203) 838-7344
email: airpower@airtimepublishing.com
www.airtimepublishing.com

© 1996, 1997, 1998, 1999, 2004 Aerospace Publishing Ltd.
© 2001, 2002, 2004 AIRtime Publishing Inc.
Photos and illustrations are copyright of their respective owners

ISBN 1-880588-74-9

Editors
  David Donald, John Heathcott and Daniel J. March

Authors
  David Donald, Paul Ludwig, Dr Alfred Price

  Additional material by John Heathcott and Daniel J. March

Artists
  Mike Badrocke, Chris Davey, Keith Fretwell, Malcolm Laird,
  Tim Maunder, John Weal, Iain Wyllie

Jacket Design
  Zaur Eylanbekov

Controller
  Linda DeAngelis

Operations Director
  E. Rex Anku

Retail Sales Director
  Jill Brooks

Sales Manager
  Joy Roberts

Publisher
  Mel Williams

PRINTED IN SINGAPORE

To order more copies of this book or any of our other titles call toll free
within the United States 1 800 359-3003, or visit our
website at: *www.airtimepublishing.com*

Other books by AIRtime Publishing include:
  United States Military Aviation Directory
  Carrier Aviation Air Power Directory
  Superfighters The Next Generation of Combat Aircraft
  Phantom: Spirit in the Skies Updated and Expanded Edition
  Tupolev Bombers
  Black Jets
  Century Jets

New books to be published during 2004 include:
  Russian Military Aviation Directory Vols 1 and 2,
  Air Combat Legends Vol. 2, Modern Battlefield Warplanes,
  Warplanes of the Fleet

Retail distribution via:

Direct from Publisher
AIRtime Publishing Inc.
120 East Ave., Norwalk, CT 06851, USA
Tel (203) 838-7979 • Fax (203) 838-7344
Toll-free 1 800 359-3003

USA & Canada
Specialty Press Inc.
39966 Grand Avenue, North Branch
MN 55056
Tel (651) 277-1400 • Fax (651) 277-1203
Toll-free 1 800 895-4585

UK & Europe
Midland Counties Publications
4 Watling Drive
Hinckley LE10 3EY
Tel 01455 233 747 • Fax 01455 233 737

INTRODUCTION

This unique book is based on highly detailed reports first published in *Wings of Fame* and *International Air Power Review*. They profile the development, service history and technical aspects of the Supermarine Spitfire and Messerschmitt Bf 109 – two of the best-known and most successful fighters ever built, and two of the bitterest rivals that have ever entered combat.
For ease of reference, a comprehensive index is provided.

AIR COMBAT LEGENDS
VOLUME ONE
Supermarine Spitfire
Messerschmitt Bf 109

CONTENTS

By combining superb aerodynamics with one of the best aero-engines ever produced, R. J. Mitchell and his Supermarine team created a pure thoroughbred fighter which became an enduring legend. The Spitfire was the first aircraft that could tackle the hitherto all-conquering Messerschmitt Bf 109, and when the two met head-to-head in the summer of 1940 the result was one of the epic battles of history, and the first major upset to Hitler's plans for a German Empire. For the rest of the war the Spitfire remained the RAF's premier air-to-air fighter, and it lives on as the most poignant symbol of Britain's resolve and resistance, notably during the dark days when the nation and its Commonwealth was all that stood between freedom and Nazism. Here the story of the Merlin-powered land-based fighters is told.

Supermarine SPITFIRE (Merlin-engined variants)

One of Charles Brown's famous wartime air-to-air colour images features a Spitfire Mk VB, the personal mount of the commander of No. 222 Squadron, RAF sometime in late 1941/early 1942. The Rolls-Royce Merlin of another No. 222 Squadron aircraft coughs into life (inset). The development of the Merlin, the most successful inline piston engine of Allied design of the World War II period, was inextricably bound up with that of the Spitfire, one of several important aircraft to use the powerplant.

Supermarine Spitfire

Reginald Joseph Mitchell, born 20 March 1895, served his engineer apprenticeship with Kerr, Stuart and Co. of Stoke-on-Trent, a builder of steam locomotives. Though he witnessed K5054's first flights, Mitchell died on 11 June 1937 after a long illness, aged just 42.

The classic elliptical wing shape of the Spitfire, as epitomised by this Mk VB (below right), remained constant throughout the development life of the 'Merlin Spitfires'. Mk XVIs, the last of which appeared in mid-1945, were the final Merlin-engined variants. The classic lines of the early Spitfire marks began to change when a Mk VIII was fitted with a 'rear-view fuselage' in 1943. This was to become a feature of late-build Mk IXs and Mk XVIs and was one of very few major structural changes made to the 'Merlin Spits' during their production life. This Mk XVI (below) was the personal mount of ACM Sir James Robb, seen here on the occasion of his last flight in the aircraft on 21 September 1951, the year in which the last Merlin-engined RAF aircraft were retired.

Supermarine's Spitfire made its maiden flight in March 1936. In May 1949 the last Seafire Mk 47 was delivered to the Royal Navy, ending a production run of 22,000 aircraft all stemming from that same basic design. The intervening 13-year period included the hardest-fought, and technically the most innovatory, war ever fought. In the history of aviation no other design was developed so continuously, so aggressively, so thoroughly or so successfully as that of the Spitfire. The fighter entered service at the end of the biplane era and it remained in front-line service well into the jet age. To keep up with the changing range of threats and requirements, Reginald Mitchell's basic design underwent a protracted programme of incremental improvements. Compared with the prototype, the Seafire 47 had more than twice the engine power, and its maximum take-off weight was more than doubled. Its firepower was increased by a factor of five, its maximum speed was increased by a quarter and its rate of climb was almost doubled. This account covers the development of the Merlin-powered fighter variants of the Spitfire, from the prototype to the Mk XVI. A further part will cover the development and service career of the Griffon-powered fighter variants, and the Seafire. The parallel development of reconnaissance variants of the Spitfire has been covered in detail elsewhere.

By the early 1930s Reginald Mitchell, the chief designer of the Supermarine Aircraft Company, had established a formidable reputation for creating high-speed floatplanes. His Supermarine S.5 won the Schneider Trophy competition in 1927. His S.6 won it in 1929. In 1931 the Supermarine S.6B won the trophy outright for Great Britain and later raised the World Air Speed record to 407 mph (655 km/h).

The Spitfire prototype, K5054, was followed by about 40 different variants (including Griffon-engined aircraft and Seafires). Total production amounted to over 22,000.

This period saw rapid advances in aviation technology. The highly supercharged engine, the variable-pitch propeller, the streamlined all-metal airframe, the cantilever monoplane wing, the enclosed cockpit and the retractable undercarriage all appeared about this time. Each of them promised to give an improvement in aircraft performance.

In 1931 the fastest fighter in the Royal Air Force was the Hawker Fury, which had a maximum speed of 207 mph (333 km/h) – about half as fast as the Supermarine S.6B. In its quest for a fighter with a better performance, in 1931 the Air Ministry issued Specification F.7./30. This called for an interceptor fighter with the highest possible rate of climb and the highest possible speed above 15,000 ft (4573 m).

Type 224

Seven companies entered the competition, resulting in five biplane and three monoplane fighters. Reginald

Schneider Trophy

Supermarine's first Schneider Trophy design was a flying-boat. Although the American Curtiss CR-3 biplane floatplanes had scored an emphatic victory in the 1923 contest, Mitchell produced a number of flying-boat proposals, the most promising of which received Air Ministry backing. Powered by a Rolls-Royce Condor and known as the Sea Urchin, the aircraft had a predicted top speed of 200 mph (322 km/h), but problems with the engine transmission system led to its cancellation. Supermarine's next project was as radical as the Sea Urchin was apparently outdated. The S.4 cantilever monoplane of 1925 started a trend in aircraft design that was followed for 20 years. Though the S.4 project was beset with problems, its refined successor, the S.5 (powered, like the S.4, by a Napier Lion engine), took the RAF's High Speed Flight to first and second places in the 1927 Trophy race. For the 1929 contest, Mitchell needed more power to meet the challenge presented by Supermarine's main rivals, the Italian Macchis. Rolls-Royce agreed to supply their new R engine and in doing so laid the foundations for a long relationship between the two companies. A Rolls-powered S.6 went on to beat a Macchi M.67 across the line that year; in 1931 Britain took the Trophy outright and unchallenged with the 2,350-hp (1752-kW) S.6B.

Above: In this scene off the Isle of Wight on 6 September 1929 can be seen the High Speed Flight's winning S.6 (racing number 2) and third-placed S.5 (number 5), along with Italy's two Macchi M.67s and an M.52R moored in the Solent. The S.5 (serialled N219) was the same aircraft that had finished second in the 1927 race.

N247 was the winning S.6 of 1929. Its R engine was rated at 1,900 hp (1417 kW) in the S.6, 1,000 hp (746 kW) more than the Napier Lion in the S.5. By the time the S.6B was ready for the 1931 race, it had 2,350 hp (1752 kW) available.

Mitchell's first attempt at fighter design, the Supermarine Type 224, made its maiden flight in February 1934. A monoplane with all-metal construction and a supercharged engine, it was conservative in appearance and retained a fixed undercarriage and open cockpit. Powered by a 680-hp (507-kW) Goshawk engine, its maximum speed was only 228 mph (367 km/h). The Gloster SS.37, a classic fabric-covered biplane with a maximum speed of 242 mph (390 km/h), won the competition and later went into service as the Gladiator.

Once the Type 224 was flying, Mitchell saw several ways in which he could improve his design. He persuaded his company to provide initial financing for a more advanced fighter powered by the new Rolls-Royce PV 12 engine (later named the Merlin). The Air Ministry expressed interest in the projected fighter and drew up a new specification, F.37/34, to fund the construction of a prototype.

An oft-repeated myth has it that the Spitfire was 'developed from' the Supermarine racing floatplanes. This is simply not true. Mitchell certainly had learned a great deal about high-speed flight from his racing floatplane designs, but it is quite a different matter to say that the Spitfire was 'developed from' them. The two types of aircraft were intended for completely different roles. There was not a single component of any significance in the Spitfire that resembled its counterpart in the racing seaplane.

'Spitfire' was the name suggested for the Type 224, built to Air Ministry Specification F.7/30. With an inverted gull wing and fixed undercarriage, the Type 224 was hampered by the evaporative cooling system used by its 600-hp (447-kW) Rolls-Royce Goshawk engine. As a private venture, the company redesigned the aircraft around Rolls's new PV.12 engine as the Type 300. Impressed, the Air Ministry wrote Specification F.37/34 around the new design and funded a prototype – K5054, the first true Spitfire.

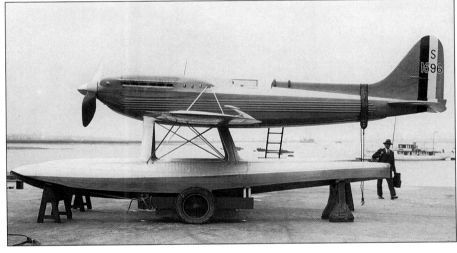

On 5 March 1936 the Supermarine F.37/34 made its maiden flight from Eastleigh airfield near Southampton, with chief test pilot 'Mutt' Summers at the controls. From the start it was clear that Mitchell's new fighter was altogether more effective than its predecessor. At the suggestion of the Vickers parent company, the new fighter was named the 'Spitfire'. We know that Reginald Mitchell had no part in the choice of that name. When the gifted designer learned of it he commented, "It's the sort of bloody silly name they would give it!"

The Spitfire became available just as the Royal Air Force had an urgent need of a high-performance modern fighter. In Germany the newly reformed Luftwaffe was building its

Supermarine S.6B S1596, sister aircraft of the outright winner of the Schneider Trophy in 1931, was flown by Flight Lieutenant George Stainforth to a 407.5-mph (655.81-km/h) world absolute air speed record on 29 September 1931.

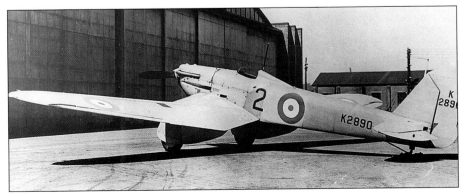

K5054 first flew on 5 May 1936 and over the next three years accumulated about 260 hours flying time. By October 1938 gun heating trials were complete and K5054's part in the development of the Spitfire had effectively come to an end. The aircraft was flown to Farnborough and employed as a 'high-speed hack' aircraft and in the planning of the world air speed record attempt in the 'Speed Spitfire'. Its flying career finally came to an end on 4 September 1939, the day after war was declared on Germany, when Flt Lt 'Spinner' White was killed when the aircraft nosed over onto its back in a landing mishap. The aircraft was not repaired.

Above: During the three days after the prototype's first flight, undercarriage fairings were fitted. Complicated and prone to malfunction, they were later simplified, the new arrangement becoming standard on production Spitfires. Note also the course pitch propeller.

Above: The F.37/34 prototype at Eastleigh is seen a few hours before its maiden flight. At this stage the aircraft was unpainted, its unfaired main landing gear was locked down and its 990-hp (738-kW) Merlin C engine drove a fine pitch propeller. Captain J. 'Mutt' Summers, Vickers's chief test pilot, undertook the first flight.

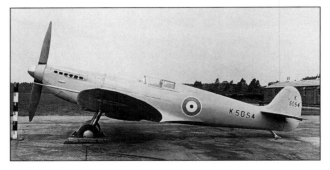

Right: By May 1936, F.37/34 had been named Spitfire (it was briefly known as the 'Spitfire II', the Type 224 being 'Spitfire I') and had been finished in a high-gloss blue-grey paint scheme. The long pitot tube on the wing was fitted for initial trials and was later replaced with a smaller example.

strength rapidly. Its new monoplane fighter type, the Messerschmitt Bf 109, was in large-scale production. To meet the growing threat, in June 1936 the British government signed a contract for Supermarine to produce 310 Spitfires.

In July 1936 the prototype of the new fighter completed its initial service trials at Martlesham Heath. Its maximum speed was 349 mph (562 km/h) at 16,800 ft (5122 m), and it could reach 30,000 ft (9145 m) in 17 minutes.

Most aspects of the Spitfire's flight trials went smoothly. In December 1936 the prototype resumed flying after the installation of its armament of eight Browning 0.303-in (7.7-mm) machine-guns. The initial firing trials with these weapons took place over the North Sea in March 1937, with the aircraft flying at 4,000 ft (1220 m). All eight guns fired their full complement of ammunition with no stoppages. A few days later the prototype went to 32,000 ft (9755 m) to fire the guns at high altitude. In the climb most

of the weapons had frozen solid, and the test was a complete failure. One gun fired 171 rounds, another fired eight rounds, one fired four rounds and the remaining five guns refused to fire at all. That was bad enough, but when the Spitfire touched down at Martlesham Heath the shock of the landing released the breech blocks of three weapons. Each loosed off a round in the general direction of Felixstowe, fortunately without hitting anyone.

Frozen guns

In the months to follow, Supermarine engineers tried various schemes to prevent the guns freezing, using progressively greater amounts of hot air ducted the radiator under the starboard wing. It proved a long process, however. When the first production Spitfires were delivered to the Royal Air Force in the summer of 1938, their guns still would not fire reliably at high altitude. At a meeting of the Air Council, Marshal of the Royal Air Force Sir Cyril Newall, the Chief of Air Staff, commented: "If the guns will not fire at heights at which the Spitfires are likely to encounter enemy bombers, the Spitfires will be useless as a fighting aircraft."

K5054's first major accident took place on 22 March 1937 when Flying Officer Sam McKenna made a forced landing after experiencing engine trouble. Between August and December 1936, the aircraft was grounded for modifications, including the installation of a 1,045-hp (779-kW) Merlin F engine and eight 0.303-in Browning machine-guns. It took 10 months to devise a heating system to prevent the guns from freezing at altitude.

It took until October 1938, more than a year and a half after the problem was first revealed, to devise an effective system to prevent the guns freezing. That month, a service pilot climbed the prototype to 32,000 ft (9756 m) and fired the contents of all eight ammunition boxes, without a single stoppage. From then the gun-heating modification was incorporated in all Spitfires on the production line.

Spitfire enters service

In August 1938, 29 months after the maiden flight of the Spitfire, No. 19 Squadron at Duxford was the first service unit to receive the new fighter. By December it had its full complement of aircraft, and was followed by other squadrons that began to convert to the type.

On 3 September 1939, when Great Britain entered the war against Germany, the RAF had taken delivery of 306 Spitfires. Of these, 187 were serving with 11 Fighter Command squadrons (Nos 19, 41, 54, 65, 66, 72, 74, 602, 603, 609 and 611). A further 71 Spitfires were held at maintenance units, ready for issue to replace losses. Eleven Spitfires served as trials machines, either with the makers or at service test establishments. One Spitfire was temporarily allocated to the Central Flying School, for use by those writing the Pilot's Notes on the aircraft. The remaining 36 Spitfires had been lost in accidents.

The Spitfire went into action against enemy aircraft for the first time on 16 October 1939. On that day nine Junkers Ju 88s of Kampfgeschwader 30 attacked Royal Navy warships in the Firth of Forth. Nos 602 and 603 Squadrons, based at Drem and Turnhouse, respectively, scrambled to engage the raiders. Flight Lieutenant Pat Gifford of No. 603 Squadron shot down one bomber and Flight Lieutenants George Pinkerton and Archie McKellar of No. 602 Squadron destroyed another. Fighters of No. 603 Squadron engaged another Ju 88 and shot out one of its engines, but it escaped out to sea.

In the months that followed, Spitfires had sporadic encounters with individual German bombers, minelayers or reconnaissance aircraft. For the most part, however, this was a period of expansion of the force and of training for the battles to come. By the beginning of May 1940 another eight squadrons (Nos 64, 92, 152, 222, 234, 266, 610 and 616) had received Spitfires, to bring the strength of the force to 19 squadrons.

The Spitfire was designed primarily as a short-range home defence bomber-destroyer. Mitchell had not intended that it should engage enemy fighters, and during the so-called 'Phoney War' it never had to. All of that came to

an abrupt end during May 1940, when the German army launched its powerful Blitzkrieg offensive against France, Holland and Belgium.

Spitfire fighters mounted their first operation over Europe on 12 May 1940. Six aircraft of No. 66 Squadron, accompanied by a similar number of Defiants of No. 264 Squadron, flew from airfields in East Anglia on a sweep over Holland. The force engaged a Ju 88 and inflicted some damage before it escaped inland. On the following day the two units flew a similar patrol, and for the first time Spitfires went into action against Messerschmitt Bf 109s. During a short but sharp engagement, four Ju 87s and a Bf 109 were shot down in exchange for five Defiants and a Spitfire.

The first encounter

The Spitfire first encountered German aircraft *en masse* on 21 May 1940. By then, the rapid German advance into Belgium and France brought the war within range of Fighter Command units based in Kent. In the days that followed, Spitfires and Hurricanes flew numerous sorties to cover the evacuation of Allied troops from Dunkirk. Both sides suffered losses during the fierce air battles fought around the port. When the evacuation ended on 3 June 1940, Fighter Command had lost 72 Spitfires — nearly one-third of the front-line strength of these aircraft. It was

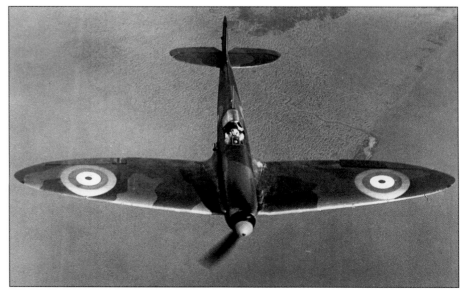

Supermarine Spitfire

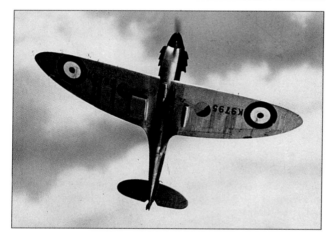

On 3 June 1936 the Air Ministry placed the first order for 310 Spitfire Mk Is at an agreed cost of £1.395 million (though delays associated with manufacture of the wing leading edge pushed this price up to £1,870,242). With this substantial order, Supermarine, a relatively small company, faced an immediate production capacity problem. Eventually, two factories at Woolston and Itchen (both near Southampton) were equipped to produce the new fighter, final assembly taking place at Eastleigh. Despite initial opposition from Supermarine, much use was made of sub-contractors such as Folland, General Aircraft, Pobjoy and Westland. In September 1940 the two Southampton works were badly damaged by enemy bombs and production was then dispersed around 65 different factories in southern England. As well as the assembly line at Eastleigh, others were established at High Post, Keevil, Henley and Aldermaston. Apart from Supermarine, the other Spitfire manufacturers were the Castle Bromwich Aircraft Factory (CBAF), established by the Morris motor car manufacturer Lord Nuffield, Westland and Cunliffe-Owen. Meanwhile, the first Spitfire order was followed by two more for 200 and 450 aircraft for Supermarine, plus an order for 1,000 Mk II aircraft placed with CBAF in April 1938. Thus, by the time war had been declared, the RAF had ordered 1,960 machines.

Above: Taken at one of the two Supermarine factories near Southampton, this photograph shows Mk Is prior to their movement to Eastleigh for the fitting of wings and engines during final assembly.

Right: The classic elliptical wing outline of the Spitfire is seen in K9795, the ninth aircraft off the Supermarine production line.

The 78th and subsequent production Mk I airframes, exemplified by P9450, the 601st Mk I (below), were fitted with a de Havilland three-bladed, two-speed variable-pitch propeller (de Havilland's constant-speed unit was not fitted to aircraft until mid-1940). Earlier aircraft, like the first production example (right), had a wooden fixed-pitch airscrew designed to perform most efficiently at service altitude. Other changes introduced during early production included the blistered cockpit canopy (to increase headroom), an improved radio (R/T) mast behind the cockpit and the glass plate 'bulletproof' windscreen.

as well the operation ended when it did, for the RAF had no choice but to accept this punishing loss rate as long as the evacuation continued; there could be no thought of abandoning the Royal Navy and the Allied troops to the mercies of the Luftwaffe.

Improvements to the Mk I

Between the entry into service of the Spitfire I, and the late spring of 1940, the fighter underwent a continuous process of modification. As a result of these changes, during the Battle of Britain the Spitfire was a considerably more effective fighting machine than it had been two years earlier.

One of the first major changes made to the Spitfire was to fit a more effective airscrew. Fighters of the initial production batch used a two-bladed fixed-pitch wooden airscrew. The pitch setting was a compromise between coarse pitch for high speed, and fine pitch for good acceleration at operation. As a result, there were power losses at both extremes of the performance envelope. The 78th and subsequent production aircraft were fitted with de Havilland three-bladed two-pitch metal airscrew with two settings, one for low speed and one for high speed.

Performance increase

The new airscrew gave a useful improvement in performance. It reduced the still-air take-off run from 420 to 320 yd (384 to 292 m). It also increased the maximum speed from 361 to 365 mph (581 to 587 km/h) at 20,000 ft (6100 m), and raised the service ceiling from 31,000 to 34,400 ft (9450 to 10490 m). Shortly before the Battle of Britain there was a crash programme to fit constant-speed propellers (either the Rotol or the de Havilland type) to all front-line Spitfires. The constant-speed mechanism automatically adjusted the pitch of the blades to provide the optimum setting, so that the engine was always run at its most efficient speed of around 3,000 rpm. This modification gave a substantial improvement in the fighter's rate of climb, and made it easier to handle in combat.

During the spring of 1940, supplies of 100 octane petrol became available. The RAF modified the engines of front-line aircraft to use this fuel, instead of the 87 octane fuel used previously. The new fuel gave improved performance at heights up to the engine's full-throttle altitude (16,500 ft/5030 m). The higher octane fuel allowed an increase in supercharger boost from +6 lb to +12 lb, which the pilot could select by pushing the throttle 'through the gate' to the fully forward position. This emergency power setting

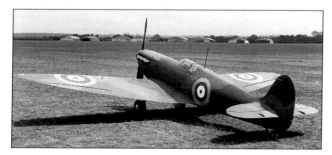

Above: This is Duxford on the occasion of No. 19 Squadron's Press Day in May 1939. Of interest in this photograph are the flat-topped canopies fitted to the second and fifth aircraft, the rest having the later bulged canopy, and the 'WZ' codes used by No. 19 from late 1938 to 1939.

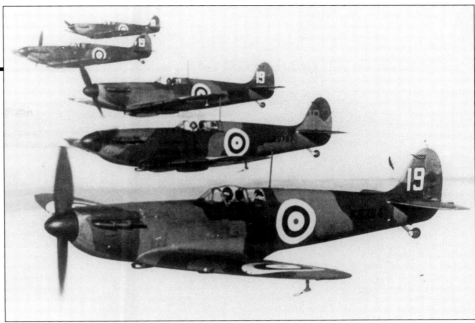

Above: This was among the first official air-to-air photographs taken of the new aircraft, on 31 October 1938 from aboard an RAF Blenheim. The lead Spitfire was flown by Sqn Ldr Henry Cozens. Initially, No. 19's aircraft carried the unit's number on their tailfins.

Service entry, 1938

No. 19 Squadron, RAF had always been a single-seat fighter squadron. Formed from the nucleus of No. 5 Reserve Squadron, the unit was formed and equipped with BE.12s in June 1916. However, the BE.12s proved unsuitable as fighters and were replaced by Spad VIIs from December. In June 1918 Sopwith Dolphins were employed, serving until the unit was disbanded in 1919. No. 19 was based at Duxford, Cambridgeshire upon reformation in 1923, as a fighter flight attached to No. 2 Flying Training School. It achieved full squadron status on 1 June 1924, equipped with Sopwith Snipes. Grebes, Siskins, Bulldogs and Gauntlets were among the squadron's equipment in the 1920s and 1930s, before becoming the first unit to fly the Spitfire from August 1938. No. 66 Squadron, formed at Duxford from 'C' Flight of No. 19, followed in November.

put a great strain on the engine, however, and it could be used for a maximum of five minutes only. The new facility increased the fighter's maximum speed by 25 mph (40 km/h) at sea level and 34 mph (54 km/h) at 10,000 ft (3000 m). It also gave a useful improvement in climbing performance between sea level and the full-throttle altitude.

The early production Spitfires carried no armour protection for the pilot or vulnerable parts of the aircraft. The value of such protection soon became clear, though there were limits to the amount that could be carried without incurring an unacceptable weight penalty. To protect the pilot's head from rounds coming from ahead, a thick slab of laminated glass was mounted on the front of the windscreen. Also, the upper fuel tank received a 3-mm (0.12-in) thick cover of light alloy, to deflect small calibre rounds striking at a shallow angle. Later, a 73-lb (33-kg) sheet of steel plate was fitted behind the pilot's seat to protect his head and back against rounds fired from behind.

Early in 1940, Spitfires were fitted with IFF (Identification Friend or Foe) equipment. This transponder produced a distinctive coded response on British radar screens, thereby providing positive identification in confused tactical situations. The facility greatly improved the quality of British fighter control during the large-scale actions that summer.

Putting on weight

The first production Spitfire I tipped the scales at 5,819 lb (2639 kg) and its maximum speed was 362 mph (583 km/h) at 18,500 ft (5640 m). In the summer of 1940 the all-up weight of a fully modified Mk I Spitfire was about 6,150 lb (2789 kg) and its maximum speed was about 350 mph (563 km/h) at 18,500 ft (5640 m). Yet, as has been said, despite the drop in maximum speed, the later aircraft were more potent fighting machines than those built initially.

Although the 0.303-in (7.7-mm) Browning gun was reasonably efficient against unarmoured aircraft, it was

With unusual grey serial numbers, this aircraft carries the markings of No. 66 Squadron, the second unit equipped with the type. This machine is equipped for gunnery practice with a gun camera fitted atop the starboard wing. During this period (early 1939), the serial number was not often carried. When it was displayed, it tended to be applied in small black figures on the tail fin.

First squadron

Spitfire Mk I
Delivered to No. 19 Sqn on 27 September 1938, K9795 was the 10th production Spitfire. The unit's number was carried on the tail; the colour varied according to the flight with which the aircraft flew. A white '19' is believed to have denoted '19' the squadron commander's aircraft. 'High visibility' markings were hurriedly replaced by more sombre marks after the Munich Crisis.

Troublesome cannon

Above: This frontal view of K9787 shows the arrangement of the eight Browning machine-guns with which most Spitfire Mk Is were equipped. These weapons had their own fair share of problems; using them at altitude was impossible until a satisfactory method of gun warming was devised.

relatively ineffective in penetrating armour or puncturing self-sealing fuel tanks. The obvious answer was to change to a heavier-calibre weapon, and the RAF had already selected the French 20-mm Hispano Suiza Type 404 cannon. In July 1939 the prototype cannon Spitfire, fitted with two Hispano Suiza-manufactured weapons, underwent tests at Martlesham Heath. During its firing trials in the Spitfire, the cannon suffered frequent stoppages. The weapon functioned reliably in the French Morane 406 fighter, where it was mounted on top of the engine and fired through the propeller hub. That produced a rigid installation, in which the mass of the engine absorbed the hefty recoil forces. In the Spitfire, in contrast, the cannon were placed in less rigid mountings in the wings. If the British fighter was pulling *g* at the time of the firing, the wings flexed and rounds were liable to misfeed, causing a stoppage. If the cannon on one side jammed, the unbalanced recoil forces on the other side made accurate aiming almost impossible. In the spring and early summer of 1940, RAF engineers devised a series of changes which appeared to resolve the problem. A small batch of Spitfires, each armed with two British-built Hispano 20-mm cannon and designated Mk IBs, entered service with No. 19 Squadron in June 1940.

Below: Spitfire Mk I L1007 became the Hispano Suiza 20-mm cannon-armed prototype in June 1939 and was tested at Martlesham Heath the following month. Though lighter than the Browning-armed Mk I, the Mk IB (as service examples were known) was no faster due to the extra drag caused by the cannon installation. The first Mk IBs used just two guns but this was deemed insufficient for combat. Later aircraft with the 'B' wing featured two pairs of Brownings outboard of the cannon.

Battle of Britain

The Battle of Britain has been covered in great detail in numerous other publications, so this account is restricted to an outline of the salient features of the Spitfire's performance during that epic action.

The RAF had expected great things from its cannon-armed Spitfires, but when No. 19 Squadron went into action in August 1940 the weapon's performance was abysmal. During the combat on 16 August, both cannon functioned properly on only one out of the seven Spitfires that engaged the enemy. On 19 August it was none out of three, on 24 August it was two out of eight and on 31 August it was three out of six. Following these embarrassing failures the squadron's commander, Squadron Leader R. Pinkham, complained to his superiors: "In all the engagements so far occurring it is considered that had the unit

'Speed Spitfire'

The possibility of building a Spitfire for an attempt on the world landplane speed record was mooted in the summer of 1937. At that time the Hughes H-1, flown by millionaire Howard Hughes, held the record with a speed of 567.115 km/h, not much more than the maximum speed of the prototype Spitfire – around 562 km/h (though the latter was achieved at altitude and speed record flights were restricted to 75 m altitude; K5054 was only capable of 467 km/h at sea level). Modifications would therefore be necessary, but it was felt that speeds of over 567 km/h were well within the Spitfire's capabilities. K9834, the 48th production Mk I, was taken from the production line and fitted with a Merlin II (Special) running on special fuel and rated at 2160 hp (1611 kW) for take-off. Driving a four-bladed fixed-pitch

propeller, the engine also required a modified cooling system. Meanwhile, in November 1937, the existing speed record was raised by a modified Messerschmitt Bf 109 V13 to just under 611 km/h, and in June 1938 the Heinkel He 100 V2 had set a closed-circuit record of 634.59 km/h. The 'Speed Spitfire', as it was known, first flew on 10 November 1938, but by December the Air Ministry, convinced that the He 100 was about to take the record to about 725 km/h, decided to proceed only with the research and development aspects of the project. Flight testing continued into 1939, a top speed of 656.5 km/h being attained. By the end of March the He 100 V8 had touched 746.6 km/h and in April the Me 209 V1 took the record to 755.14 km/h, well beyond the abilities of the Spitfire at the time.

Above: Finished in a coat of highly polished dark blue paint with a silver 'lightning stripe', the 'Speed Spitfire' carried the manufacturer's Class 'B' registration N.17. Notable features of the aircraft were its more streamlined cockpit canopy, a slightly reduced wing span with more rounded wingtips, and the large wooden four-bladed propeller.

Below: The 'Speed Spitfire', seen at Eastleigh in early 1939, has a towing dolly under the tail and has had the radiator fairing under the starboard wing removed.

Left: By November 1940, K9834 had been fitted with a Merlin XII engine and a standard cooling system. In this form it was delivered to the RAF's Photographic Reconnaissance Unit (PRU) at Heston as a 'hack' aircraft. The aircraft is pictured here in March 1942, by which time it had been fitted with a PR-type curved windscreen and an early Mk I-type cockpit canopy. K9834 survived the war, only to be scrapped in June 1946.

Night-fighters

A night-fighting role was always envisaged for the Spitfire, even though the narrow track of the type's undercarriage made it unsuitable for night-time operations, except in bright moonlight. The Luftwaffe began small-scale night bombing of British targets on 5 June 1940; the first large attack came on the night of 18/19 June. From this date day-fighter squadrons, including those equipped with Spitfires, were assigned night patrol sorties, so-called 'cat's eyes' patrols, which were entirely reliant on moonlight and/or the skills of searchlight operators to hold a target in their beams long enough for a fighter to 'get a shot off'. There were a number of successful engagements during the second half of June, but the Luftwaffe soon learned its lesson and flew its bombing missions at higher altitudes, beyond the range of searchlights. Overall, night victories were few and 'kills' by Spitfire pilots even fewer. Modifications made to the aircraft involved in these primitive night interceptions were minimal. To shield the pilot's eyes from the glare of the exhausts during night flying, Spitfires were often fitted with 'blinkers' in front of the cockpit.

been equipped with eight-gun fighters it would have inflicted far more severe losses on the enemy. It is most strongly urged that until the stoppages at present experienced have been eliminated, this squadron should be re-equipped with Browning gun Spitfires."

Headquarters Fighter Command accepted Pinkham's suggestion, and early in September the unit exchanged its cannon fighters for normal eight-gun Spitfires. The Hispano-armed Spitfire played no further part in the Battle of Britain.

Inadequate weapons

Because of these initial problems with the Hispano cannon, during the Battle the Spitfires and Hurricanes had to fight with a weapon that was inadequate against multi-engined bombers. There are several well-documented instances where German bombers regained friendly territo-

ry after taking more than 100 hits from 0.303-in (7.7-mm) ammunition. To achieve that concentration of hits probably meant that at least two British fighters had fired most of their ammunition into the bomber from short range.

The survivability of the German bombers was much enhanced by the self-sealing fuel tanks developed following combat experience in the Spanish Civil War. The light alloy tanks had a 1-cm (0.39-in) thick covering comprising alternate layers of vulcanised and non-vulcanised rubber. Surrounding the whole was an outer covering of leather. When a rifle-calibre round hit the tank it passed easily through this covering. When fuel started to leak through the hole, the petrol set up a chemical reaction with the non-vulcanised rubber, which caused the latter to swell and seal the hole. The carriage of fuel in self-sealing tanks saved many a German bomber from the fiery end that would otherwise have been its fate.

No. 72 Squadron was one of the units involved in the limited Spitfire night operations during mid-1940. Prior to being thrown into the fray over southeast England, the squadron was based at Acklington, with a night-fighter flight detached to Woolsington (today Newcastle Airport). On 27 June Flying Officer Thompson brought down a Ju 88 which had been caught in searchlights, one of the few Spitfire night kills.

Early Spitfire victors

Spitfire Mk I
Flt Lt George Denholm, a flight commander with No. 603 'City of Edinburgh' Sqn, was among the Spitfire pilots in action on 16 October 1939, the day of the first successful engagement of a Luftwaffe bomber by the RAF. Denholm shared in the downing of a Heinkel He 111 and on 17 March damaged a Dornier Do 17 before being shot down in this aircraft, L1067. He later commanded No. 603 Sqn.

Spitfire Mk I
N3173/KL-N was flown by Plt Off Colin Gray of No. 54 Sqn when he claimed his first victory, a Bf 109E near Dunkirk on 24 May 1940. His Spitfire received major battle damage in the process, but Gray managed to nurse it back to Hornchurch. Plt Off Gray went on to become New Zealand's top-scoring pilot of the war, with 27 individual 'kills', all achieved on Spitfires.

Spitfire Mk I
Named *Kiwi*, N3183 was the aircraft in which New Zealander Plt Off Alan Deere of No. 54 Sqn downed aircraft on consecutive days (24 and 25 May 1940) while covering the Dunkirk evacuation. During this action he was credited with seven victories in just five days. N3183 was shot down on 9 July; its pilot, Plt Off A Evershed, was killed.

Before the outbreak of World War II, there was considerable interest from various foreign powers in acquiring Spitfires. One of the first interested parties was Japan, in early 1937. Mitsubishi hoped to purchase a single example; had the deal gone through, the implications for a Pacific war could have been enormous. Orders were placed by, or licences granted to build Spitfires to, Belgium, Turkey, Holland, Yugoslavia, Switzerland, Lithuania and Estonia. The latter placed the first order, for 12 aircraft, in February 1939. Greece also ordered 12 and Portugal 15. France requested an example in early 1939 and, as an important friendly country, moved up the queue. Delivered to the Armée de l'Air in July 1939 it was the only Spitfire delivered overseas before the war. (One other Spitfire was packed for shipment to Poland in July 1939, but was diverted to Turkey after the Polish surrender. In June 1940 two aircraft of a Turkish order for 15 were also shipped.)

Not an export, but a Spitfire overseas none the less. Mk I L1090 was shipped to Canada soon after the war broke out and in May 1940 was flown for comparison against the USAAC's Curtiss XP-40 fighter prototype (in background, left) from the RCAF base at Uplands. Back on RAF charge by August, L1090 became an instructional airframe and was eventually written off in 1944.

Had a large numbers of cannon-armed Spitfires and Hurricanes been available to fight in the Battle, and had the cannon performed reliably, it is interesting to speculate how much more effective Fighter Command would have been. As it was, by resorting to 'overkill' on several occasions, the British fighters caused sufficiently heavy losses to the enemy bombers to force the Luftwaffe to abandon its daylight attacks on England.

Spitfire versus Hurricane

In recent years there has been controversy regarding the relative effectiveness of the Spitfire and the Hurricane during the Battle. As mentioned above, with their rifle-calibre machine-guns both types were deficient in firepower when they engaged enemy bombers. During the large-scale actions, Spitfires and Hurricanes achieved victories approximately in proportion to the number of each type taking part. The Spitfire's superior performance and its smaller size meant it was less likely to take hits, however. In major actions the Spitfires suffered an average loss rate of around 4 per cent of those engaging, while Hurricane losses averaged around 6 per cent.

Due to their lower rate of attrition, the Spitfire units spent more days in action than those equipped with Hurricanes. On average, a Spitfire unit spent nearly 20 days in action during the Battle before it had to be withdrawn to reform. That compared with under 16 days for the fully-engaged Hurricane squadrons (the four Hurricane units that played little part in the action are not included in this calculation). With more days in action, the individual Spitfire units were able to gain more victories. The 19 Spitfire squadrons taking part in the Battle are credited with 521 victories, an average of just over 27 per unit. The 30 fully-engaged Hurricane squadrons are credited with 655 victories, an average of just under 22 per squadron. In combat the average victory-to-loss ratio for Spitfire units was 1.8:1, while that for fully-engaged Hurricane units was 1.34:1.

During the summer and autumn of 1940, work to cure the failings of the Spitfire's cannon installation continued at the highest priority. Only near the end of 1940, too late to play a major part in the Battle of Britain, were the problems finally eradicated. Yet even when the cannon did work properly, another problem remained. The 60-round magazine fitted to each Hispano weapon contained sufficient ammunition for only five seconds' firing. That was judged insufficient for normal air-to-air combat. Accordingly, the next batch of Spitfire IBs carried a mixed armament of two Hispano cannon and four 0.303-in (7.7-mm) machine-guns. It proved a good compromise, and in November 1940 No. 92 Squadron re-equipped with the new variant. To differentiate these aircraft from the rest of the Mk Is armed with eight machine-guns, the latter were redesignated as Mk IAs.

In June 1940, after lengthy delays, the huge Nuffield factory at Castle Bromwich near Birmingham at last began large-scale production of the Mk II Spitfire. Externally the new variant looked like the late-production Mk I, the main difference being the Merlin 12 engine developing an extra 110 hp (82 kW). The increase in power gave the Mk II a slight edge in maximum speed and climbing performance, compared with its predecessor.

In August 1940 the first Spitfire IIs were delivered to No. 611 Squadron based at Digby. In the following month Nos 19, 74 and 266 Squadrons also received the new

With a serial in the HK-range, usually reserved for impressed and captured aircraft, this Spitfire has an interesting history. It was one of the two Spitfire Mk Is (P9566 and P9567) shipped to Turkey in June 1940. Both finished up at the fighter training school at El Ballah, Egypt in 1942, carrying the serials HK854 and HK856.

Armée de l'Air Mk I

Spitfire Mk I
Finished in RAF colours and carrying the manufacturer's B-class marking N.21, the 208th production Spitfire Mk I first flew on 25 May 1939. Flown across the Channel on 18 July, the aircraft was given the serial '01' and evaluated by French pilots who attained 363 mph (584 km/h) during tests. Though French reports suggested the aircraft was burnt by the authorities, photographs apparently taken after its discovery by German forces in Orléans in 1940 suggested otherwise.

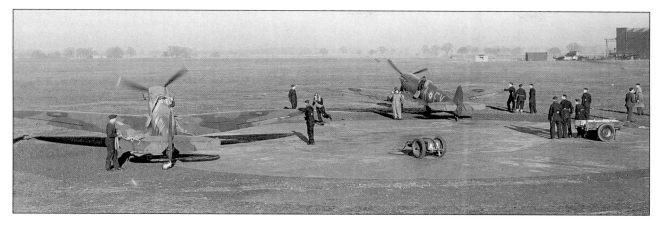

variant. The Mk II replaced the Mk I in several units, and the squadrons operating the newer variant concentrated in the southeast corner of England where the fighting was heaviest.

The initial batches of Spitfire IIs were armed with eight machine-guns. Later, small numbers were produced with the two cannon and four machine-gun armament and designated Mk IIBs. As with the Mk I, when that happened the machine-gun-armed machines were redesignated as Mk IIAs.

On the offensive

Early in 1941 RAF Fighter Command went over to the offensive. The new C-in-C, Air Chief Marshal Sir Sholto Douglas, termed the policy one of 'leaning forward into France' with the aim of drawing the Luftwaffe into action. On 9 January 1941 three squadrons of Spitfire Is flew an offensive sweep over northern France. The German fighter controllers chose to ignore the incursion, however, and it passed off without incident. The lesson was clear: sweeps by fighters alone would not bring the enemy into action. Like Fighter Command in the Battle of Britain, the Luftwaffe did not feel the necessity to engage sweeps by fighters flying alone.

On the following day the RAF made a more ambitious attempt to draw German fighters into action. The new type of operation, codenamed Circus, was centred around six Blenheim bombers attacking an ammunition dump near Calais. Seven squadrons of Spitfires and four of Hurricanes, a total of 103 fighters, escorted the bombers. This time there were scrappy fighter-versus-fighter actions and a Hurricane and a Spitfire were destroyed. German fighters suffered no losses.

In the weeks that followed, the Circus operations became a regular feature. For example Circus No. 5, on 26 February, involved an attack by 12 Blenheims on Calais harbour. The escorting force on that occasion comprised two squadrons of Hurricanes and four of Spitfires. Following 20 minutes behind came the Spitfire IIs of Nos 54 and 64 Squadrons, with the intention of engaging enemy fighters drawn up by the earlier incursion. One Spitfire in the follow-up force was shot down, the only aircraft lost on either side during the action.

The Mk V

During February 1941 the Spitfire V, the next major fighter version, made its appearance. The initial production aircraft were powered by the Merlin 45 engine which developed 1,515 hp (1130 kW) at 11,000 ft (3353 m) using +16 lb boost. The additional power gave it a substantial performance advantage over the Mk II. Apart from the new engine the other changes were relatively minor, and the new variant easily replaced the Mks I and II on the production lines. A few Mk VAs were built with eight 0.303-in (7.7-mm) machine-guns, but the majority were Mk VBs armed with the armament of two 20-mm cannon and four 0.303-in machine-guns.

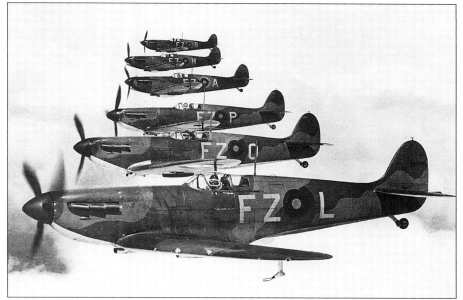

A well-known photograph, taken just before the beginning of the war, of a well-known pilot and his charges. Spitfire Mk I K9906/'FZ-L' was allocated to Flg Off Robert Stanford Tuck upon delivery to No. 65 Squadron from the Supermarine factory in March 1939. Tuck became one of the first pilots to be credited with five victories. In April 1940, K9906 was transferred to No. 64 Squadron. After the Battle of Britain and a period with an Operational Training Unit (OTU), it was converted to PR.Mk III Type C standard and eventually struck off charge in May 1943.

The most ambitious daylight incursion by the RAF during 1941 took place on 12 August. An attacking force of 54 Blenheims delivered a low-altitude strike on the electricity-generating plants at Knapsack and Quadrath in western Germany. Six squadrons of Spitfires – Mks II, IIB and V – and one of Whirlwind twin-engined fighters provided close escort during the initial phase of the penetration. Five squadrons of Spitfires flew down the bombers' route almost to the limit of their radius of action, orbited for five minutes and then headed for home. The withdrawal cover force comprised three squadrons of Spitfire IIs and

RAF Fighter Command lost 72 Spitfires, nearly a third of its front-line strength, covering the evacuation of the British Expeditionary Force (BEF) through Dunkirk during late May and early June 1940. This represented the first large-scale commitment of Spitfires into combat. This machine was shot down on 6 June.

Above: No. 41 Squadron was among the units that formed No. 11 Group, Fighter Command in defence of London and southeastern England.

Above: No. 616 Sqn 'scrambles' from Kenley. For several months this unit and No. 92 Sqn shared the same 'QJ' code letters, leading to considerable confusion, especially among post-war historians.

Battle over Britain

The 310 aircraft in the first Spitfire Mk I order were all delivered by September 1939. A further order for 200 was placed in April; the last of them had been built by Supermarine by August 1940. In early July RAF Fighter Command's total assets were 347 Hawker Hurricanes, 199 Spitfires, 69 Bristol Blenheim night-fighters and 25 Boulton Paul Defiants. The Spitfires were all Mk Is equipping 19 squadrons, of which 14 were combat ready. Another 83 aircraft were listed as unserviceable. These statistics give some idea of the attrition rates suffered in training as well as combat. On 8 August the main Luftwaffe assault began and by 18 August 1940, the day on which the greatest number of aircraft were destroyed, 348 Spitfires were on strength, representing about a third of Fighter Command's modern single-engined fighters. Of these, 276 were serviceable.

Spitfire deployment, 14 September 1940

(Unless indicated, all units were equipped with Mk Is)

No. 10 Group		No. 12 Group	
No. 152 Sqn	Warmwell	No. 19 Sqn	Fowlmere
No. 234 Sqn	St Eval	No. 64 Sqn	Leconfield
No. 609 Sqn	Middle Wallop	No. 74 Sqn	Coltishall (Mk IIs)
		No. 266 Sqn	Wittering (re-equipping with Mk IIs)
No. 11 Group		No. 611 Sqn	Digby (Mk IIs)
No. 41 Sqn	Rochford	No. 616 Sqn	Kirton-in-Lindsey,
No. 66 Sqn	Gravesend		Ringway
No. 72 Sqn	Biggin Hill		
No. 92 Sqn	Biggin Hill	No. 13 Group	
No. 222 Sqn	Rochford	No. 54 Sqn	Catterick
No. 602 Sqn	Westhampnett	No. 65 Sqn	Turnhouse
No. 603 Sqn	Hornchurch	No. 610 Sqn	Acklington

three more operating the Mk II (Long Range) version. German fighter and flak units reacted vigorously to this bold incursion, shooting down 10 Blenheims and inflicting damage on several others. Four Spitfires were lost.

Throughout 1941 the production of Spitfires increased steadily, allowing a major expansion of the force. From 19 Spitfire squadrons at the end of the Battle of Britain, Fighter Command moved to 46 squadrons equipped with Spitfires at the end of 1941.

Although the Mk V performed significantly better than earlier variants, it was outclassed by the Focke-Wulf Fw 190 which appeared in the autumn of 1941, providing the RAF with perhaps its biggest shock of the war. Fortunately for RAF Fighter Command, however, the new German fighter initially suffered engine overheating problems and was restricted in its operations. Also, the Luftwaffe was heavily committed on the Eastern Front, and could retain only a small force of fighters in the west. The Circus operations continued, although at a reduced frequency and at heavier cost than before.

The Mk V

The initial production versions of the Spitfire V, the VA and the VB, used Mk I and Mk II airframes with the minimum of change necessary to accommodate the Merlin 45 engine. The extra weight of the new engine and additional items of equipment reduced the fighter's strength factors, however. To restore them, the Mk V airframe was redesigned at several points to strengthen the structure. It was also fitted with the so-called 'Universal' wing, with provision to carry eight 0.303-in (7.7-mm) machine-guns, two 20-cannon and four machine-guns, or four 20-mm cannon. In practice, most aircraft carried the same armament as the Mk VB – two cannon and four machine-guns – although a few were fitted with four 20-mm cannon armament. The new sub-variant, designated the Mk VC, appeared in October 1941.

Left: Spitfires peel to port for the camera. Though the type had a marginal performance edge over the Bf 109 at altitude, it usually met its foe while climbing to intercept a bomber stream. At lower altitudes the two designs were on a par.

Right: This scene at Hornchurch sometime during the summer of 1940 features Spitfires of No. 222 Squadron ('ZD' codes) and No. 603 Squadron ('XT'). The steamroller in the background was used to flatten filled-in bomb craters.

Powerplant
The first 74 Spitfire Mk Is were powered by a Merlin II rated at 900 hp (671 kW) for take-off and 1,060 hp (790 kW); the rest had a Merlin III of similar rating. Fitted with a float carburettor, these engines were prone to 'cutting out' in negative g flight. To follow a diving enemy fighter a Spitfire was therefore obliged to perform a half-roll. It was not until December 1941 that a 'negative g' carburettor was tested by Rolls-Royce. They became standard on Merlin 50s fitted to late-build Spitfire Mk Vs.

Markings
Finished in the standard Dark Earth/Dark Green camouflage worn by the type since its introduction, this aircraft sports a standard 27-in (68.6-cm) fin flash, Type A fuselage roundels (with a yellow outer ring), Type B upper wing roundels and grey codes. During 1939 aircraft serial numbers were painted out on squadron aircraft for security reasons, but this appears not to have been a rigid rule; from early 1940, serials were left on service machines.

Night victories
On the moonlit night of 18/19 June 1940, during the first major night raid on England by the Luftwaffe, Flt Lt Adolf 'Sailor' Malan shot down two He 111s of KG 4 in quick succession in this aircraft. This remarkable feat was only possible with the help of searchlights, and earned Malan a Bar to his Distinguished Flying Cross.

Performance
Early Mk Is had a maximum speed of 362 mph (583 km/h) at 18,500 ft (5640 m) and were able to reach 20,000 ft (6100 m) in 9 minutes 25 seconds. Late-production machines were heavier due to the addition of armour and new equipment such as the coded IFF system. This brought top speed down slightly to 353 mph (568 km/h) at 20,000 ft (6100 m).

Spitfire Mk I versus Bf 109
During the Battle of Britain most of the fighter-versus-fighter combats took place in the height band 13,000 to 20,000 ft (3963 to 6100 m), because that was where the German bombers usually flew. At that altitude the Spitfire Mks I and II were about equal to the Bf 109E in capability. In the fleeting air combats that were the norm, tactical initiative far outweighed the relatively small performance differences between the two fighter types.

Spitfire Mk I
No. 74 Squadron
August 1940

No. 74 Squadron, RAF was based at Rochford and Hornchurch during the early phase of the Battle of Britain, before being withdrawn north to Kirton-in-Lindsey in mid-August. This aircraft, K9953, was on strength with No. 74 until at least early August, flown by the the unit's CO, Sqn Ldr D. F. 'Sailor' Malan, DFC and Bar, the South African ace who was instrumental in changing Fighter Command's tactics. In September, the unit re-equipped with Spitfire Mk IIs.

Gas detection
Fears that the enemy's arsenal might include gas (as it had in World War I) prompted the application of a painted gas detection square on the upper surface of the port wing. It changed colour if gas was present in the air.

Armour
As the value of its protection became clear, armour was fitted around the upper fuel tank and behind the pilot's seat. This aircraft would also have had a thick laminated glass slab fitted to the front of its windscreen.

Undersurface markings
This aircraft wears the so-called 'Night and White' undersurface colours introduced, with variations, in late 1938/early 1939 and made the official standard from 27 April 1939 until 6 June 1940. From early June 1940 Sky was the standard undersurface colour but, with the frenetic pace of operations, application to service aircraft was a drawn-out process.

Armament
While the bulk of the Spitfire Mk Is, including this one, were fitted with eight 0.303-in machine-guns, the limitations of rifle-calibre ammunition against aircraft with armour and self-sealing fuel tanks were all too obvious. A small number of Spitfire Mk IBs (Browning-equipped aircraft were eventually redesignated Mk IAs) entered service with No. 19 Squadron in June 1940.

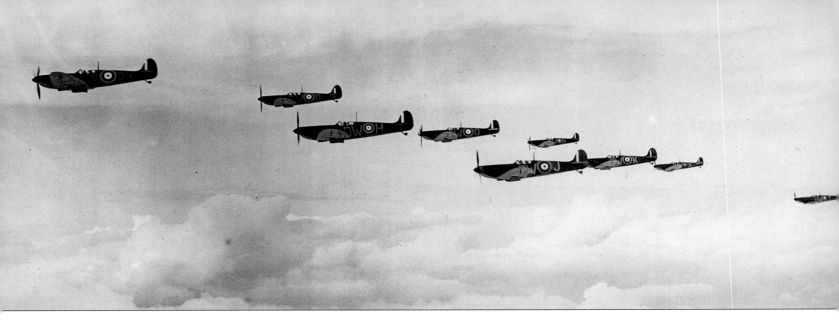

The Pressurised Mk VI

After the Battle of Britain there were fears that the Luftwaffe might be about to introduce new bomber types able to attack from altitudes above 30,000 ft (9150 m). To meet this perceived threat, a high-altitude interceptor version of the Spitfire was developed, the Mk VI. Based on the Mk V, the Mk VI was the first RAF aircraft to enter service fitted with a pressure cabin. The Merlin 47 engine fitted to this variant had an additional blower to supply air to the pressurised cabin, giving a pressure differential of 2 psi (13.79 kPa). Thus, when the fighter was at its maximum altitude of 37,000 ft (11280 m), the equivalent altitude in the cabin was 28,000 ft (8536 m). The Mk VI also had an extended-span wing with pointed tips, giving an additional 6.5 sq ft (0.6 m²) of wing area. In the event, the high-altitude bombing threat never materialised, and production

of this variant ceased after the initial order for 100 was completed.

Early in 1942 the Spitfire faced a new challenge. Britain's strategy in the Mediterranean hinged on the use of Malta as a base from which to interdict the Axis supply routes to Africa. Yet the besieged island was taking a fearful pounding from German and Italian bombers, and its continued

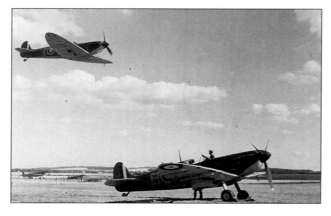

Battle of Britain colours

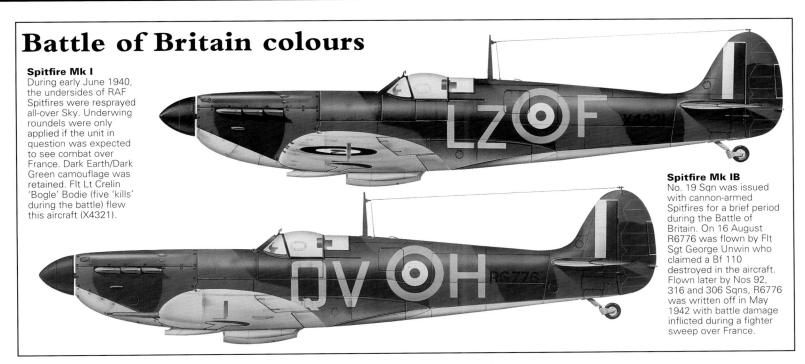

Spitfire Mk I
During early June 1940, the undersides of RAF Spitfires were resprayed all-over Sky. Underwing roundels were only applied if the unit in question was expected to see combat over France. Dark Earth/Dark Green camouflage was retained. Flt Lt Crelin 'Bogle' Bodie (five 'kills' during the battle) flew this aircraft (X4321).

Spitfire Mk IB
No. 19 Sqn was issued with cannon-armed Spitfires for a brief period during the Battle of Britain. On 16 August R6776 was flown by Flt Sgt George Unwin who claimed a Bf 110 destroyed in the aircraft. Flown later by Nos 92, 316 and 306 Sqns, R6776 was written off in May 1942 with battle damage inflicted during a fighter sweep over France.

survival was in question. Malta's main air defence comprised a small force of Hurricanes, which were no match for the Bf 109Fs that the Luftwaffe had deployed to the theatre.

Spitfire to the defence of Malta

The obvious solution was to deliver a number of Spitfire Vs to the island, but there was no simple way of doing this. Malta lay 1,100 miles (1770 km) east of Gibraltar, far beyond the Spitfire's normal ferry range. With the Axis naval and air blockade in place, it was almost impossible to deliver the fighters by merchant ship. The Hurricanes already on Malta had been transported half way by aircraft-

carrier, then they had taken off to fly the rest of the way to the island. From the nearest feasible flying-off point to Malta was 660 miles (1062 km), or about as far as from London to Prague. And that was still beyond the normal ferry range of the Spitfire.

For the Malta delivery operation, Supermarine designed a 90-Imp gal (410-litre) drop tank to fit under the fuselage of the Spitfire. Other modifications were necessary if the Spitfire was to operate successfully in the dusty conditions of the Middle East. Dust and sand entering the engine through the carburettor intake caused excessive wear, and would drastically reduce the life of the engine. To prevent this, a filter unit was mounted in front of the intake, in a beard-like fairing under the nose.

The first delivery of Spitfires to Malta took place on 7 March 1942, when 15 took off from HMS *Eagle* and flew to the island. Before the end of the month, the carrier completed two more delivery runs, to bring to 31 the number of Spitfires that reached the island.

The Spitfires arrived in the nick of time, for the Luftwaffe had stepped up its onslaught in preparation for the planned invasion of Malta. Heavily outnumbered, the Spitfires were pitchforked into a desperate battle for survival in which they took heavy losses. In April 1942 the US Navy carrier *Wasp* launched another 47 Spitfires for Malta,

Far left: Having marked the location with a smoke flare, the pilot of this Spitfire ASR.Mk II drops a dinghy to a hapless airman. These aircraft were fitted with Merlin XXs rated at 1,240 hp (925 kW) in place of the usual Merlin XII and a rack under the port wing for the carriage of marker bombs. Flare chutes on the underside of the aircraft carried rescue packs (comprising a dinghy and rations). This aircraft appears to have been converted from a cannon-armed Mk IIB. From mid-1944, Nos 276 and 277 Squadrons were equipped with Spitfire Mk Vs.

Air-Sea Rescue Mk IIs

During 1943, just over 50 Spitfire Mk IIs were converted as air-sea rescue aircraft for use mainly over the English Channel and Thames Estuary. Originally designated Mk IIC, these aircraft were redesignated Spitfire ASR.Mk IIs to avoid confusion with Spitfire fighters fitted with the 'C' wing. Nos 276 and 277 Squadrons, RAF were the main users of the ASR aircraft, though other rescue units (Nos 275, 278 and 282 Squadrons) were able to draw from a pool of these aircraft as necessary. 'AQ' was the code of No. 276 Squadron.

This is a Spitfire Mk IIA (long range) of No. 118 Squadron. The 40-Imp gal (182-litre) drop tank is visible on the port wing. The variant saw considerable use until the autumn of 1941, when the appearance of the Fw 190 brought an end to its activities.

Early in the war Supermarine made efforts to improve the Spitfire's limited radius of action. The drop tank was one possibility, but this was still an unproven concept and no such tank had been developed for any other British fighter. With the beginning of offensive sweeps and bomber escort missions over northwest Europe, early in 1941, the requirement became more urgent. About 60 Spitfire IIs were modified with a 40-Imp gal fixed tank fitted under the port wing, and were designated the Mk II (LR). Compared with the standard Mk II, the long-range version was 26 mph slower and took 2 minutes 48 seconds longer to climb to 20,000 ft; its low-speed handling characteristics were far less pleasant. However, with nearly half as much fuel capacity again as the standard Mk II, the long-range variant proved useful as a bomber escort. Several units flew this variant in combat from the spring of 1941 and Nos 19, 66, 118, 152, 222, 234, 501 and 616 Sqns have been identified as operating it at one time or other. When these squadrons moved to southeast England, they took over the Long Range Mk IIs from the units being withdrawn.

Operation Sunrise

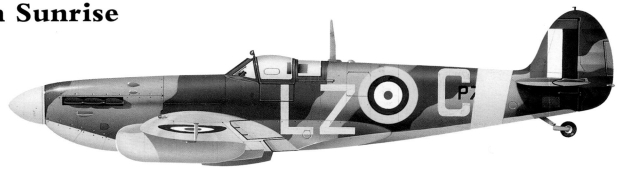

Spitfire Mk IIA(LR)
This aircraft of No. 66 Squadron – with those of Nos 152 and 234 Sqns – provided escorts for Operation Sunrise the daylight attack on the German battlecruisers *Scharnhorst* and *Gneisenau* and the heavy cruiser *Prinz Eugen* in Brest harbour on 24 July 1941.

Right: Once Mk III development had ended, N3297 was fitted with normal-span wings and handed over to Rolls-Royce at Hucknall as a testbed aircraft. When it was next flown, in September 1941, it was a very different machine. A two-speed, two-stage Merlin 61 with multi-ejector exhausts had been installed, along with a four-bladed Rotol propeller to absorb the new engine's extra power. Trials with the re-engined machine at Boscombe Down began in January 1942 and demonstrated great performance improvements compared to earlier aircraft, laying the foundations for the Mk VII/VIII/IX series aircraft. Note that the retractable tailwheel fitted to N3297 when it was converted to Mk III status has been retained.

Below: Results of the service trials conducted with the Mk III prototype were reported to Air Marshall Dowding, C-in-C Fighter Command at the end of July 1940. He forwarded them to the Air Ministry, drawing attention to two "serious disadvantages in an otherwise excellent aircraft." They were its long landing run which, Dowding suggested, would prevent the aircraft from being used for night operations, and its square wingtips. The latter made the aircraft more difficult to differentiate from a Messerschmitt Bf 109, thought the Air Marshall. Accordingly, N3297 was to be fitted with Spitfire Mk I wings, but in the event they were not fitted until after Mk III development had been abandoned.

and all except one arrived. The air fighting was so fierce that after a few days most of these fighters had been destroyed in the air or on the ground.

The next operation to resupply Malta with Spitfires, Operation Bowery, was the largest of them all. Shortly after dawn on 9 May, *Wasp* and *Eagle* arrived within range

Stillborn Mk III

Differences between the Mk I and Mk II were relatively few; the Mk III was the first attempt to seriously improve the Spitfire's design. The most important changes were the installation of a 1,390-hp (1036-kW) (for take-off) Merlin XX equipped with a two-speed supercharger that offered improved performance at all altitudes, 'clipped' 9.3-m wings and a retractable tailwheel. On 16 March 1940 N3297, the only true Mk III (a second prototype, W3237, was a converted Mk V), was flown for the first time by Jeffrey Quill. It was intended that the Mk III would replace Mks I and II on the production line; orders were placed for 1,000 examples, but circumstances eventually led to their cancellation. Merlin XXs were in big demand, especially for the Hurricane Mk II, and development of the single-speed, two-stage Merlin 45 was about to overtake the Merlin XX.

'Eagle' Squadron

Spitfire Mk IIA
Plt Off William Dunn was the first pilot from an 'Eagle' squadron (manned by American volunteers) to score five victories and, therefore, the first American ace. His fourth and fifth victories were made in this aircraft (P7308) of No. 71 Sqn while escorting a force of Blenheims attacking the steel works at Lille.

and launched a total of 64 fighters. Sixty reached the island, which would be sufficient to change the course of the battle. Never again would the island be in such peril as it had been during the first week in May 1942. In the months that followed, Royal Navy carriers mounted eight more operations to launch Spitfires for Malta, delivering an average of 29 fighters on each.

Carrier escort

The use of aircraft-carriers to deliver fighters to Malta was an enormously expensive business, however. Each time these valuable warships put to sea, it was necessary to lay on a major fleet operation to protect them. At the request of the Air Ministry, Supermarine engineers were working on one of the most difficult challenges they were ever asked to face: to devise a way to extend the Spitfire's ferry range to 1,100 miles (1770 km), sufficient for it to fly from Gibraltar to Malta in a single hop. The solution was to fit a huge 170-Imp gal (772-litre) drop tank under the fuselage, a 29-Imp gal (132-litre) auxiliary tank in the rear fuselage and an enlarged oil tank under the nose. For the flights all non-essential equipment was removed from the fighter, and its armament was reduced to two 0.303-in machine-guns for self-protection. During October and November 1942, 17 modified Spitfires set out from Gibraltar to make the

The RAF began offensive sweeps over France in December 1940 as Fighter Command 'leant forward into France', and 'Circus' and 'Ramrod' bombing missions began the following month. No. 452 Squadron, RAAF, equipped with Mk IIs, was among the many Spitfire units to take part in these attempts to lure the Luftwaffe into battle.

lengthy flight to Malta; all except one made it. That distance was about as far as from London to St Petersburg, a remarkable feat for an aircraft originally designed as a short-range interceptor. Upon arrival on Malta, the fighters had

Mk V's debut, 1941

Right: X4257 (with 'Keep Out' chalked behind the cockpit to deter the curious) started life in August 1940 as a Mk IB aircraft, and later that month became the first Spitfire to be fitted with a standard 'B' wing (as opposed to twin cannon armament originally fitted to Mk IBs). In February 1941, Rolls-Royce at Hucknall fitted a Merlin 45, the aircraft becoming a Mk VB. Later in the year it was issued to No. 92 Squadron, the first unit to fly Mk Vs, for service trials. A crash suffered by this aircraft on 19 March after engine failure pointed to weaknesses in the de Havilland constant-speed propeller, which proved liable to freezing at altitude. This led to the adoption of the Rotol design, subsequently fitted to many Mk Vs. Around 150 other Mk Is and IIs were re-engined to Mk V standard to supplement new production.

Left: At the request of USAAF commander Major General 'Hap' Arnold, two Mk VAs (R7347 and W3119) were shipped to Wright Field, Ohio during the summer of 1941. W3119 was transferred to NACA at Langley for an analysis of its flying qualities. An early Mk VC, AA963, followed in February 1942 aboard SS Evanger and was publicly displayed in Chicago in May. Here it is seen tied down at Wright Field, minus its wheels. AA963 was fitted with a DH propeller.

Right: No. 81 Squadron had a much varied history during World War II. After taking its Hurricanes to Russia with No. 151 Wing in 1941, the unit returned to Britain and reformed as part of the Hornchurch Wing with Spitfire Mk VBs, seen here. Engaged in sweeps over France, these aircraft carried the standard temperate RAF fighter camouflage scheme applied from May 1942. In late 1942 No. 81 stood down in preparation for overseas deployment, reforming in North Africa with Mk VCs. They were on strength only briefly, being replaced by Mk IXs during 1943. Towards the end of the year, No. 81 moved again, this time to the Far East with Mk VIIIs, which it flew until mid-1945, when they were replaced by Republic Thunderbolt Mk IIs.

Right: This view of a No. 92 Squadron Mk VB (converted from Mk IB R6923) shows the main recognition feature of the Mk V – the circular-section oil cooler under the port wing. On Mk I and II aircraft this had a half-moon section.

Above: In November 1941 there were fears that the Luftwaffe might resume its large-scale night attacks on Britain. Nos 65 and 111 Squadrons were temporarily assigned to the night-fighter role, their Spitfire VBs being painted matt black overall. It was intended that the Spitfires would intercept raiders illuminated by searchlights, and the units underwent training for the new role. In the event, the threat failed to materialise, and the squadrons reverted to their previous day-fighting role.

Below: A section of 'B' Flight, No. 122 Squadron leaves the ground at Fairlop, one of Hornchurch's satellites, during the summer of 1942. During August 1942, the unit's Spitfires were heavily involved in the abortive Dieppe landings, taking off at dawn on 19 August to cover the Allied landings. Its pilots spent an average of 7 hours 40 minutes in the air that day and claimed a Do 217 shot down and another two damaged, but, overall, the RAF's fighter cover proved inadequate.

Above: A No. 412 Squadron, RCAF Mk VB 'beats up' a ground position during an exercise. As well as 'Circuses', No. 412 (equipped with Mk VBs from October 1941) was also engaged in 'Rhubarbs' (small-scale fighter and fighter-bomber raids on targets of opportunity), 'Ramrods' (similar to a 'Circus', but with destruction of a target as the primary aim) and 'Rodeos' (fighter sweeps). The unit re-equipped with Mk IXs in October 1943.

Overseas deployment

The Mk V was the first Spitfire variant to be sent overseas and was widely deployed in Europe, the Mediterranean, the Far East and the southwest Pacific.

Right: AB320 was the first Mk VB intended for overseas issue fitted with the Vokes filter on the production line. Most Mk Vs built after July 1941 were 'tropicalised'. This aircraft also carries a 90-Imp gal (409-litre) belly-mounted drop tank of the type used on the relief flights to Malta from aircraft-carriers.

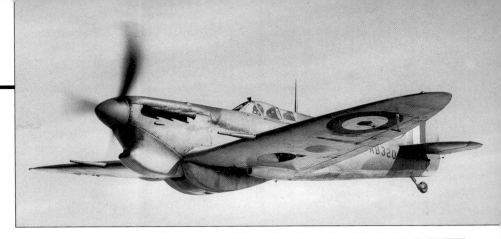

Below: Ordered as a Mk I, but delivered as a Mk VA (only 94 of which were built), X4922 was the airframe selected for the trial installation of the Vokes tropical air filter in April 1941. Built with a Merlin 45 engine installed, X4922 was later re-engined with a Merlin 46 and was struck-off charge in late 1944.

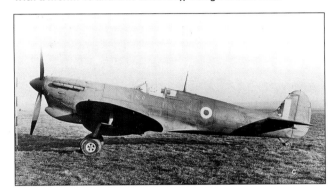

the extra tanks removed and the rest of the armament fitted, to restore them to normal operational configuration.

The Mk V spreads its wings

Following those initial overseas deliveries of Spitfire Vs to Malta, others went to units in Egypt. When Allied troops moved into northwest Africa in November 1942, Mk Vs of the RAF and the US 12th Air Force provided air cover for their advance. Southeast Asia was next to receive these fighters. In each of those theatres, the Spitfires' arrival enabled the RAF and its allies to secure air superiority.

The only war theatre where the Spitfire failed to live up to its high reputation was that of Australia. In January 1943, three squadrons of Spitfire VCs arrived in the Northern Territory to provide a defence against attacks by Japanese aircraft. No. 54 Squadron was based at Darwin airport while Nos 452 and 457 Squadrons went to the nearby airfields at Strauss and Livingstone.

On 1 February, No. 1 Fighter Wing, RAAF became operational. The unit first went into action on 6 February, when two Spitfires of No. 54 Sqn engaged and shot down a Mitsubishi Ki-46 reconnaissance aircraft. The fast, high-flying 'Dinahs' had cruised over the area at will photographing targets, but from then their lives became much more difficult.

The defenders had problems of their own, however. Their airfields, in a remote corner of Australia, lacked the equipment to support sustained combat operations. As well as shortages of spare parts, there were problems with the Spitfires themselves. The fighter had never previously operated in a true tropical environment close to the equator. On the ground, the aircraft had to face extremely high temperatures and high humidity. At altitude, the Spitfires encountered air temperatures somewhat lower than any they had previously encountered. Those very low temperatures caused repeated failures of the constant-speed units (CSUs). The CSU controlled the pitch of the propeller blades,

Above: Tropicalised Mk VBs await spinners for their Rotol propellers and cannon for their wings prior to being issued to squadrons in the Mediterranean. Some have belly-mounted drop tanks for the inevitable ferry flight to their intended base in either Malta or North Africa. The broader blades of the Rotol constant-speed propeller can be seen in this view.

Below: In profile, the modified fairing around the nose-mounted oil tank was evident. The aircraft's guns were removed during ferry flights, save for two 0.303-in (7.7-mm) Brownings.

From Gibraltar to Malta

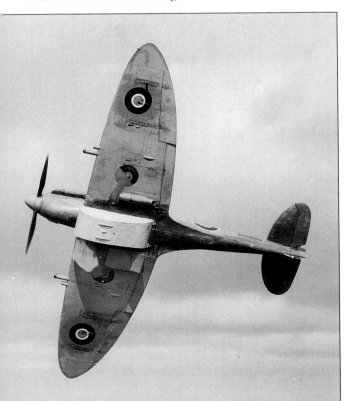

Left: As an alternative to the expensive use of aircraft-carriers to ferry Spitfires to Malta, Supermarine engineers were asked to extend the Spitfire Mk V's range to 1,100 miles (1770 km) to allow flights directly from Gibraltar to Malta. To this end, Mk VC BR202 was test flown with this huge 170-Imp gal (773-litre) belly tank and a 29-Imp gal (132-litre) auxiliary tank in the rear fuselage. To provide sufficient oil for the Merlin engine on such a long flight, a larger oil tank was fitted under the nose.

Above: Though this Mk VC, in the process of being craned aboard Wasp, appears to have 'clipped' wings, it is unlikely to have been flown from the carrier in this condition. Once aboard, it would have been reunited with its missing components before it was flown off when the carrier reached the Algerian coast.

Operation Bowery

Representing the first deployment of Spitfires overseas, the reinforcement of Malta began in March 1942. Three groups of Mk VBs, totalling 31 aircraft, were flown the 660 miles (1062 km) from the carriers HMS *Eagle* and *Argus* to the island, whose defence against Luftwaffe Bf 109s was entrusted to outclassed RAF Hurricanes. Forty-six Mk VCs followed in April, flown from the US carrier *Wasp* by pilots from Nos 601 and 603 Squadrons. The biggest of these operations was codenamed Bowery and took place on 9 May, when 60 aircraft were successfully delivered.

Above: With HMS Eagle in the background, two deck crewmen on USS Wasp sit on the tailplane of a Spitfire Mk VC as its engine is run up. One of the ship's own aircraft, a Grumman Wildcat, can be seen in the foreground.

Spitfires were crammed into Wasp's hangar deck en route to Malta. Operation Bowery was by no means the end of the reinforcement effort, as Royal Navy carriers Argus, Furious and Eagle continued to ferry aircraft to the beleaguered island until October. By the end of the month some 367 Spitfires had been delivered and issued to Nos 126, 185 and 249 Squadrons.

Above: His aircraft (with the name Bob's the Boss chalked on its engine cowling) held by deck crew, an RAF pilot does his pre-flight checks before departing for Malta.

Left: As Wasp's crew look on, another Spitfire leaves the ship's decks for Malta. No sooner had the aircraft arrived than they were pitched into the battle against Luftwaffe Bf 109s. The first aircraft delivered were finished in Dark Earth/Middle Stone desert camouflage. Later shipments wore standard RAF temperate day fighter colours (Ocean Grey and Dark Green) as they spent much of their time on patrol over the Mediterranean rather than the desert.

continually adjusting their angle so that the engine ran at its most efficient speed of 3,000 rpm. At the very low temperatures the oil in the CSU was liable to congeal, causing the propeller blades to move into fully fine pitch. When that happened, engine rpm raced uncontrollably to around the 4,000 mark. With the Merlin threatening to shake itself to pieces, the pilot had to shut it down immediately. Then he had either to bail out or make a forced landing. Several Spitfires based in northern Australia were lost to CSU failures.

Australian attacks

Spitfires first engaged a major Japanese attack on 2 March 1943. Nine Mitsubishi G4M 'Betty' bombers attacked Coomali, escorted by 21 Mitsubishi A6M 'Zeke' fighters. Twenty-six Spitfires were scrambled to engage the raiders, but, due to problems with ground control, several fighters failed to intercept. Like those in the Battle of Britain, the actions fought over northern Australia were characterised by heavy overclaiming by both sides. The defenders claimed two A6Ms and a Nakajima B5N 'Kate' single-engined bomber destroyed, and a B5N damaged. Japanese records show that no B5Ns took part in the action; almost certainly those claimed hit were A6Ms. For their part, the

Right: Recently arrived Mk VBs are seen on a landing ground in Libya. AB326 was one of many Spitfires shipped to Takoradi on the Gold Coast, West Africa and to Casablanca, French Morocco for assembly and ferrying across the continent to their prospective squadrons.

Left: In a flooded dispersal, a Mk V of the 5th Fighter Squadron, 52nd Fighter Group, USAAF stands next to a stack of fuel tanks. Transferred from the 8th AF to the 12th AF in late 1942, the 52nd FG found tropicalised Mk Vs waiting for them in Gibraltar. Soon in action in Algeria, the 52nd finished the war in Italy.

Above: Army and RAF personnel hastily refuel and rearm a Mk VC on Malta during the defence of the island. Initially, a shortage of 20-mm cannon ammunition forced the removal of a pair of the four Hispanos fitted to these aircraft. This machine appears to have had its inner pair of cannon removed in this way.

Japanese claimed the destruction of three defending fighters, reported as 'P-39s and Buffalos'. In fact, neither side lost any aircraft in the encounter.

The next major Japanese incursion was on 15 March, when 19 G4Ms attacked Darwin escorted by 26 A6Ms fighters. Twenty-seven Spitfires took off to intercept and there was a fierce engagement around the bombers. The defenders claimed nine attackers destroyed, four probably destroyed and six damaged. In fact, no G4Ms were lost – though eight were damaged. One A6M fighter was lost. The raiders claimed the destruction of 11 defending fighters, and the probable destruction of five more; in truth, four Spitfires and two pilots were lost.

Above: While Malta was being reinforced, No. 145 Squadron became the first unit to fly the Spitfire in the Western Desert. The unit's aircraft were shipped from Britain to Takoradi, assembled and flown to Egypt. The first two aircraft arrived there in May 1942.

Below: No. 417 Squadron, RCAF formed in England in 1942 and was quickly posted to the Middle East. Flying with cockpit canopies open in the heat, a section of the unit's Mk VCs patrols over open desert.

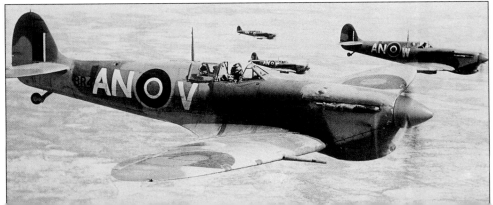

Above: Spitfire Mk VCs of No. 2 Squadron, SAAF fly in line-astern over the Adriatic. Armed with four 20-mm Hispano cannon, No. 2's aircraft were based in Sicily and Italy during 1943. With minimal fighter opposition in Italy, Spitfire units spent much of their time on ground-attack duties, often carrying up to 500 lb (227 kg) of bombs. A less publicised role performed by Mk Vs in the Mediterranean was high-altitude interception. In 1942, the Aboukir MU modified two Mk VCs, removing much equipment and all armament. Two 0.5-in (12.7-mm) Browning guns, extended wingtips and a specially tuned Merlin 46 were installed. Two Luftwaffe Ju 86P reconnaissance aircraft were downed by these aircraft.

Above: Bomb-laden Spitfire Mk VCs of No. 2 Squadron, SAAF overfly the Sangro River in eastern Italy en route to a target during the Italian campaign.

Below: As the Allies occupied Sicily and moved north through the Italian mainland, they occupied and made use of captured Italian airfields. This Mk VC, fitted with twin cannon and four Brownings, wears the codes of No. 43 Squadron and shares the dispersal at Comiso, Sicily with Spitfires of later marks, probably Mk VIIIs.

Following another lull, the raiders returned on 2 May. This time the Japanese force comprised 18 G4Ms and 26 A6Ms. Thirty-three Spitfires scrambled to engage the attackers, but five suffered technical failures and had to return early. The action developed into a running battle around the bombers and continued some way out to sea. The defenders claimed seven enemy planes destroyed, four probably destroyed and seven damaged. In fact, all the raiders regained their base, though seven G4Ms and seven A6Ms had suffered damage. Five Spitfires were lost or probably lost due to enemy action.

For the defenders, worse followed when the Spitfires headed for home after breaking off the action. The Merlins had run for long periods at high throttle settings, leading to four cases of engine or CSU failures. A further five Spitfires ran out of fuel on the way home. Altogether, 14 Spitfires failed to regain their airfields after the engagement, and three pilots were posted missing. Of the aircraft that force-landed, one was later recovered intact, three were stripped for spare parts where they lay and the rest had to be written off.

There were further Japanese attacks on 9 and 28 May. During the latter action, Spitfires claimed three bombers shot down for the loss of two of their own. The actual

Above: Pilots from No. 601 'County of London' Squadron, RAuxAF were among those to fly Spitfires to Malta from USS Wasp in April 1942. This formation of No. 601 Squadron Mk VBs is led by Wg Cdr Ian Gleed in the aircraft, AB502, in which he was shot down and killed on 16 April 1943. Note his use of personalised codes, a privilege usually only accorded to RAF wing leaders.

Below: 'Yellow 14', a MG 151 20-mm cannon-armed Bf 109G-6/R6 Trop of JG 53, was abandoned at Comiso in late summer 1943. Spitfire Mk Vs struggled against these late model aircraft; the Mk VIII was more of a match.

Tactical reconnaissance

Spitfire LF.Mk VB
EP688 wears the colours of No. 40 Squadron, SAAF in late 1942. 'Clipped' wings, probably modified at No. 103 MU, and an 'Aboukir' filter are fitted. The red parts of the roundel and fin flash have been repainted orange, a feature of No. 40 Squadron's aircraft. Another feature peculiar to this unit was its code presentation: red with a white outline.

For fighter-reconnaissance duties No. 40 Squadron operated a number of suitably equipped LF.Mk VBs, sometimes referred to as 'FR.Mk VBs'. As well as 'clipped' wings the aircraft sported an oblique F.24 camera behind the cockpit on the port side of the aircraft and were specially prepared for the role. The latter involved taping over wing and skin joints and polishing the aircraft to help achieve the highest possible speed. So-equipped, these aircraft moved forward with the British 8th Army after the Battle of El Alamein in November 1942.

Left: A Spitfire Mk VC of No. 54 Squadron, RAF is pictured at Darwin, Northern Territory, Australia in March 1943. The fighter had not previously operated in a true tropical environment facing high humidity and extremely high temperatures on the ground, and very low air temperatures at altitude. They caused severe problems, the most serious of which was the repeated failure of constant-speed units (CSUs). These problems were cured in the Mk VIII, which replaced the Mk VCs. No. 54 Sqn was one of three RAF squadrons to join the RAAF units deployed to Australia for defence of that country. The others – Nos 548 and 549 – were formed in Australia in 1944 and flew Mk VIIIs exclusively. Both units disbanded in 1945.

Japanese loss was two G4Ms shot down, and a third crash-landed near its base on Timor. Despite several claims, this was the first occasion on which a G4M had fallen to the Spitfires' guns.

Between then and the end of September, Japanese bombers carried out another five escorted attacks, incurring light losses during each. The lack of facilities at the airfields, and the general shortage of spare parts, reduced several Spitfires to a poor condition. Following action on 6 July, Squadron Leader Eric Gibbs, commander of No. 54 Squadron, had reported to his superiors: "Chiefly owing to the deplorable state of so many of our aircraft, for which no replacements have been forthcoming for months past, we were able to muster only seven Spitfires in the initial attack. Of the remaining four which were scrambled to intercept, one left the formation before the attack with a severe Glycol leak and subsequently force-landed, and three were unable to keep up. We lost two aircraft. Both pilots safe."

At the end of September the daylight raids ceased, giving way to occasional night attacks until they too ended after 12 November. Some published accounts have stated that the heavy losses the Spitfires inflicted had forced the raiders to cease their attacks; however, new research makes it clear that this was not the case. Throughout the series of attacks the Japanese losses had been remarkably light. The raids on Australia ended when they did because the experienced units were required elsewhere, after the war in the Pacific had taken a turn for the worse for the Japanese.

Above: Until their existence was made public, Spitfires supplied to Australia were referred to by the codename 'Capstan', after a brand of cigarette. The Spitfire's short range made the type unsuitable for patrolling the vast areas in the north of Australia.

'Clipped'-wing Mk Vs

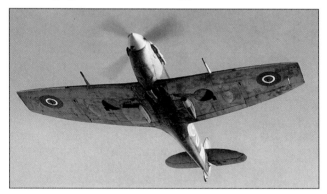

Left: Most LF.Mk VBs, with their Merlin 45Ms that produced peak power at low level, were built with or later fitted with 'clipped' wings to improve their roll rate 'on the deck'. This view of AA937, with the Air Fighting Development Unit in 1943, illustrates the aircraft's plan view.

Above: Officially captioned as depicting the Spitfires that escorted General Montgomery's aircraft as it returned to England in May 1943, this photograph shows Mk VBs of No. 303 Squadron. Having been engaged in bomber escort duties and sweeps over occupied Europe since 1941, the unit received long-awaited Mk IXs the following month.

Left: This immaculate Mk VB, serialled BL479, served with No. 316 'City of Warsaw' Squadron for just two months before transfer to another Polish unit, No. 308 Squadron. Significant numbers of standard Mk VBs and VCs were equipped with 'clipped' wings, in both the European and Mediterranean theatres.

Supermarine Spitfire F.Mk VC
No. 2 Squadron, No. 7 Wing,
South African Air Force, Desert Air Force
Italy, late 1943/early 1944

Engine and propeller

The Spitfire Mk V was created by installing the Merlin 45 into the basic Mk I or II airframe, with the engine mounts strengthened to take the heavier powerplant. Nine variants of this engine were fitted to Mk V series aircraft: the 45 and 46 (VA, VB, VC), 50, 50A, 55, 56 (VC), 45M, 50M and 55M (LF.Mk VB). The 45 was the basic 'single-speed, two-stage' engine, the 46, 50A and 56 were optimised for high-altitude performance with slightly larger supercharger impellers, and the 45M, 50M and 55M were low-level engines with cropped impellers. The 50 series and later engines were fitted with diaphragm-type anti-*g* carburettors, while the 55 and 56 featured a two-piece cylinder block. As can be seen, Mk VCs could be fitted with one of six different Merlins, and this was true of 'tropicalised' aircraft though it would appear that most of the latter had Merlin 46s installed in the factory. If an airframe survived long enough to see an engine change, it could easily leave a maintenance unit with a different mark of Merlin fitted.

Whereas the Spitfire Mk I had flown with a variety of propeller types – two-bladed fixed-pitch and three-bladed two-position or constant-speed – all production Mk Vs were fitted with either a de Havilland or Rotol constant-speed design. Two types of de Havilland airscrew were in use on the Mk V: the 20° unit and the Hydromatic. The DH 20° constant-speed propeller (with wooden blades), as used on the Mk I, was prone to the congealing of oil within the propeller's constant-speed unit (the CSU, which controlled the pitch of the blades) at altitude, a situation which led to a number of accidents, especially in RAAF aircraft operating in the tropical climates of northern Australia. There were moves to switch Mk V propeller production entirely to a four-bladed metal unit, but doubts arose about the supply of metal blades, which were in demand elsewhere. A four-bladed Jablo unit was also trialled but, in the event, both were abandoned. As an interim measure, three-bladed Jablo Rotol units were diverted from Hurricane production, though the bulk of Spitfire Mk Vs were so-equipped. Rotol propellers were identifiable by their longer, more pointed spinners and broader blades.

Camouflage and markings

Little variation from the RAF desert camouflage scheme was seen on RAF, Commonwealth and USAAF Spitfires in the North African/Mediterranean theatres. Dark Earth and Middle Stone upper surfaces and an Azure Blue underside were standard. Code letters were usually white with serial numbers stencilled in black. National markings were as applied to Spitfires in northern Europe during this period and comprised Type C1 fuselage roundels, Type B wing upper surface wing roundels, Type A underwing roundels and the standard fin flash, as introduced in 1942. On some SAAF Spitfires (including those of No. 40 Squadron), orange replaced red in these markings. An Insignia Red propeller spinner was a USAAF Mediterranean Theatre of Operations (MTO) marking widely adopted by RAF and Commonwealth units from late 1943.

No. 2 Squadron, SAAF

Having arrived in Egypt from Kenya (where the unit flew Furies, Gladiators and Hurricanes), No. 2 Squadron (motto: 'Upwards and Onwards') assembled at Sidi Haneish in July 1941. Training on Curtiss Tomahawk Mk IIBs was followed by sweeps over the Western Desert. From April 1942 conversion to Kittyhawks (Mk Is and later, though briefly, Mk IIIs) took place, bomber escort sorties being added to the squadron's duties until the Desert Air Force was equipped with Spitfires for the escort role. No. 2 thus concentrated on ground-attack work, providing air support for the Eighth Army during its advance through Libya after El Alamein. In the final months of the North African campaign, the squadron made raids in the battle area and attacked Axis lines of communication, bases and airfields in Tunisia.

Spitfire Mk Vs arrived in July 1943, a month before No. 2 moved to Sicily. Operational again from 23 August, the squadron moved to the Italian mainland and occupied newly-captured airfields during September. Spitfires provided fighter cover for the advancing Allied armies, until the lack of enemy air activity allowed them to concentrate on ground-attack missions for the remainder of the war. Though flown intensively, the Spitfire Mk Vs were on charge with No. 2 for just eight months. Spitfire Mk IXs arrived in February 1944, the unit remaining in Italy for the rest of the war in Europe. A few North American Mustang Mk IVs were taken 'on charge' in June 1945, but on 12 July the squadron's personnel left Tissano airfield en route for South Africa.

In all, 10 SAAF squadrons were equipped with Spitfires at one time or another during the war. They were Nos 1, 2, 3, 4, 7, 9, 10, 11, 40 and 41, all of which flew Mk Vs and IXs, though No. 1's use of Mk IXs was brief and the unit also flew Mk VIIIs. No. 40 Squadron also flew PR.Mk XIs briefly towards the end of the war. Almost all eventually served in Italy, Nos 9, 10 and 41 having been based exclusively in North Africa and the eastern Mediterranean. Nos 9 and 10 flew their Spitfires in sweeps over Crete in December 1944, No. 41 having disbanded during November.

The springbok marking on the tail of this aircraft is that of No. 7 Wing, SAAF which, by mid-1944, formed part of the Desert Air Force with No. 3 Wing, SAAF, and three RAF wings.

From fighter to 'Spitbomber'

From the earliest days of the Spitfire's career, the lack of hitting power of its eight rifle-calibre Browning machine-guns (in what later became known as the 'A' wing) had been a cause for concern. It was remedied by the installation of two Hispano 20-mm cannon with four Browning 0.303-in (7.7-mm) machine-guns. This armament fit (known as the 'B' configuration) was trialled in a small number of Spitfire Mk Is during the later stages of the Battle of Britain and, after major teething problems were solved, became the standard armament on early production Mk Vs.

Later, with the introduction of the 'C' (or 'universal') wing, it became possible to arm a Spitfire with either 'A' or 'B' armament or up to four of the Hispano weapons, each supplied with 120 rounds of ammunition. In practice, most Mk VCs were fitted with 'B' wing armament; the four-cannon arrangement was installed in considerably fewer aircraft. The first 'four-cannon' Spitfires were delivered to Malta during 1942, but were initially forced to operate with just two cannon installed due to a shortage of 20-mm ammunition. The four-cannon configuration also had its detractors among pilots concerned about the weight penalty it imposed (the all-up weight of a Mk VC with four cannon was some 800 lb/363 kg more than that of a Mk VA), but in theatres where fighter opposition was light, the extra firepower was useful in the ground-attack role. These aircraft were converted to carry four cannon, having left the factory with 'B' armament installed. Ports for the machine-guns remained, covered with doped red fabric, the redundant Brownings having been removed.

In late 1942, Air Vice-Marshal Sir Keith Park, AOC Egypt and Malta, wrote to the Air Ministry requesting the urgent production of bomber conversion kits for Spitfire Mk VCs. Fighter sweeps over enemy airfields on Sicily were ignored, he wrote, as he explained how flying trials had been carried out in North Africa (by Nos 126 and 249 Squadrons, RAF) with a 250-lb (113-kg) bomb under each wing or a 500-lb (227-kg) bomb under the fuselage. Thus, during 1943, Supermarine developed its own version for production. So-equipped, the Spitfire Mk VC was a potent fighter-bomber, especially when equipped with clipped wingtips which improved roll rate and thus low-level manoeuvrability.

Most LF.Mk VBs, as well as a number of F.Mk VBs and F.Mk VCs, were delivered to the Middle East with clipped wings, which reduced the aircraft's span by 4 ft 8 in (1.42 m). Many other Spitfires were modified in-theatre by No. 103 MU at Aboukir. These latter aircraft featured wooden wingtip fairings, which were of a slightly more rounded shape than the standard metal examples fitted in the UK.

Airframe improvements

The first Mk Vs were simply Mk I airframes allied to the more powerful Merlin 45 engine. Refinements originally intended for the Mk III were incorporated later in the Mk VC. They included a strengthened undercarriage with the wheels set 2 in (5 cm) further forward to help reduce the Spitfire's propensity for 'nosing over' on soft or rough airfields, and the 'C' or 'Universal' wing. The 'C' wing was much stronger than that fitted to the Mk VB and enabled the variant to take full advantage of the extra power provided by the Merlin 45 and its derivatives. Other detail changes included the installation of an innovative windscreen de-icing system, improved hood jettisoning and the addition (on some aircraft) of two wing stiffeners above the wheel well in each wing.

In order to address the Spitfire's inherent range deficiencies, belly-mounted drop tanks were developed for the Mk V. After initial jettisoning problems were solved, over 300,000 examples were produced (for Mk Vs and later variants); most were of 30-Imp gal (136-litre) or 45-Imp gal (205-litre) capacity. An even larger 90-Imp gal (409-litre) tank was used for ferry flights.

Mk V production

Official records are unclear regarding the exact number, but around 6,500 Mk Vs were built at the Castle Bromwich Aircraft Factory, at Supermarine's dispersed factories and by Westland Aircraft. Additionally, about 180 Mk Is and Mk IIs were converted by installing Merlin 45s. Spitfire Mk VCs were built by all three manufacturers – 478 by Supermarine, 1,486 by the CBAF and 495 by Westland. The exact identity of this aircraft is unknown, repainting of its code letter having obliterated its serial number, though other similar aircraft on charge with No. 2 Squadron, SAAF came from production batches built by the CBAF in late 1942/early 1943.

During 1942, prefix letters were added to official RAF aircraft Mark numbers to indicate the aircraft's intended role. Thus, the Mk VC became the F.Mk VC. Most Mk Vs used the 'F' prefix, variations from this being applied only where a change in role was accompanied by a major change to the aircraft. Therefore, Mk VBs optimised for low-level operations and fitted with Merlin 45Ms (or the equivalent) became LF.Mk VBs.

Tropical modifications

In order to cope with the harsh conditions of the Western Desert and tropical regions, a number of modifications were made to Spitfires destined for overseas theatres. Proving trials took place during January 1942, most Mk VCs being so-equipped on the production line and a large number of Mk VBs being retrofitted. On the line, these 'tropicalised' aircraft were distinguished by the large Vokes Aero-Vee filter under the chin, but this concealed more than 20 other modifications, all covered by the RAF technical order known as Mod 411. They included fitting a larger oil tank, the addition of attachment points for three types of external fuel tank, provision of a desert survival kit (including a 1.5-Imp gal/6.8-litre water tank, an emergency tool kit and rations) and repainting the aircraft in appropriate camouflage. However, the Vokes filter seriously reduced the Spitfire Mk V's climb and speed performance. A comparison with a standard Mk VB showed an increase in time to 20,000 ft (6096 m) of 1 minute 24 seconds and a top speed at that altitude reduced by 11 mph (18 km/h). To reduce drag and thus address the speed problem, No. 103 Maintenance Unit at Aboukir, Egypt designed the new, more compact Aboukir filter, which was also lighter, offered improved filtration and could be used in temperate climates (with the filter element removed). They were retrofitted to numerous Mk Vs in the North African/Mediterranean theatre. It also served as the basis for the Vokes filter fitted later as standard to the Spitfire Mk VIII and to Mk IXs serving in the Mediterranean.

Control surfaces

Pilots of the early Spitfire Marks expressed concern about the need to apply high aileron-stick forces when banking at high speed during combat. Much experimentation took place with servotabs and modified aileron aerofoil shapes, culminating in several months of wind tunnel testing at the National Physics Laboratory. Early in 1941, the problem was solved relatively simply, by replacing the Frise-type ailerons' fabric covering with metal. A sharper trailing edge was also incorporated, and the new ailerons were introduced on production aircraft from mid-1944 on late-production Mk VBs and most VCs.

In an attempt to provide better deceleration during air-to-air combat and better performance as a dive-bomber, dive brakes were trialled on Mk VBs. Split trailing-edge flaps and the Youngman bellows brake (as used on the Beaufighter) were separately test flown. However, neither provided the necessary 1g deceleration required at 400 mph (644 km/h).

Above: With a fighter shortage at home and concern at **USAAF HQ** that aircraft like the Bell P-39 and Curtiss P-40 were inferior in performance to their expected German adversaries, Spitfires were requested to equip the fighter groups arriving in Britain in 1942, despite the fact that the RAF's Mk Vs were struggling against new Bf 109 and Fw 190 variants. This formation comprises Mk Vs of the 109th (coded 'VX') and the 12th ('RS') Reconnaissance Squadrons of the 67th Reconnaissance Group. As well as various support tasks, the 67th RG took part in fighter sweeps with RAF units.

Spitfires for the USAAF

From mid-1942, 'reverse Lend-Lease' arrangements saw about 600 Spitfires made available to the USAAF, Mk Vs initially equipping the three squadrons of the 31st Fighter Group in June. With the similarly equipped 52nd FG, the 31st flew with the US 8th Air Force until October, when they were assigned to the 12th Air Force for Operation Torch, the Allied landings in North Africa. In September 1942, the three RAF 'Eagle' squadrons (equipped with Spitfires Mk Vs) were transferred to the 8th AF as the 4th FG. Also within the 8th Air Force, the 67th Observation (later Reconnaissance) Group (with four squadrons) employed Mk Vs for support duties and to fly fighter sweeps, while the 350th FG and the 496th Fighter Training Group had a limited number for training purposes. For Operation Torch, the 31st and 52nd FGs received tropicalised Mk Vs; once these units reached Italy in 1943, they received a few Mk VIIIs and IXs before transferring to the 15th Air Force and re-equipping with P-51 Mustangs. From November 1943, PR.Mk XIs equipped three of the four squadrons of the 7th Photographic Group.

Lima Challenger, a presentation aircraft 'donated' by a resident of the Peruvian capital, was on strength with the 307th Fighter Squadron, 31st Fighter Group at Merston in August 1942. Eighth Air Force Spitfire Mk Vs were finished in RAF temperate colours. The aircraft's RAF serial number was applied in small figures on the tail.

For the reasons outlined above, the Spitfire Mk V failed to quell the attacks on Northern Australia. By the time the fighter's failings became known and had been reported to its makers, the series of raids had come to an end. The Mk V's successor in that theatre, the Mk VIII, incorporated modifications which overcame the problems encountered over Darwin.

Back in the summer of 1941, Rolls-Royce engineers had begun bench testing of a Merlin 45 engine fitted with two supercharger blowers in series, one feeding into the other. Between the outlet of the first blower and the inlet of the second was an intercooler, to reduce the temperature of the

charge and so increase its density. The additional components added about 200 lb (90 kg) to the engine's weight and increased its length by 9 in (22 cm). Those differences were sufficiently small to allow the new engine to be fitted into the Spitfire airframe without major structural changes. The version of the new engine for use in fighters was designated the Merlin 61.

The engine company fitted an early Merlin 61 into the Spitfire III prototype, then serving as a testbed. Apart from a four-bladed propeller to absorb the extra engine power, the main external change was an enlarged radiator under the port wing to cool the liquid from the intercooler. The

'Mighty 8th' Spitfires

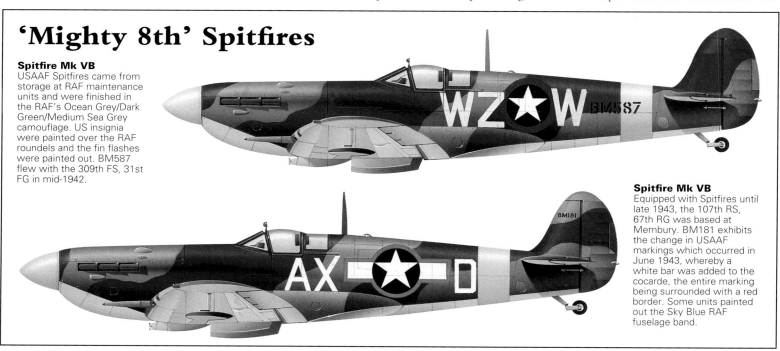

Spitfire Mk VB
USAAF Spitfires came from storage at RAF maintenance units and were finished in the RAF's Ocean Grey/Dark Green/Medium Sea Grey camouflage. US insignia were painted over the RAF roundels and the fin flashes were painted out. BM587 flew with the 309th FS, 31st FG in mid-1942.

Spitfire Mk VB
Equipped with Spitfires until late 1943, the 107th RS, 67th RG was based at Membury. BM181 exhibits the change in USAAF markings which occurred in June 1943, whereby a white bar was added to the cocarde, the entire marking being surrounded with a red border. Some units painted out the Sky Blue RAF fuselage band.

Fighting floatplanes

After Norway was attacked in April 1940, the RAF's campaign in defence of the country was hampered by the lack of suitable airstrips. Looking for solutions to the problem, the Air Ministry discussed the possibility of fitting floats to Hurricanes and Spitfires. To this end, a Spitfire Mk I (R6722) was fitted with a set of floats designed for the Blackburn Roc seaplane fighter and a scale model of a float-equipped Spitfire Mk III was tested. However, before the Mk I floatplane was completed, the Norwegian campaign ended. With the Battle of Britain looming, the urgent need for fighters saw R6722's conversion back to landplane standard. The floatplane fighter idea was dropped until 1942 when, after Japan entered the war, the idea was re-examined. This time three Mk Vs were fitted with floats designed by Supermarine and built by Folland. After trials the aircraft were declared combat-ready and shipped, not to the Pacific, but to Egypt in October 1943. From a concealed base on an unoccupied island in the Dodecanese group in the eastern Mediterranean, the Mk V floatplanes were to intercept German Ju 52 transports resupplying bases in the islands. However, after German troops and the Luftwaffe forced the British from the islands of Kos and Leros in October 1943, the plan had to be abandoned.

modified aircraft had an oblong-section radiator housing of similar external shape under each wing. The port housing contained the oil cooler radiator and part of the main coolant radiator; the starboard housing contained the other part of the main coolant radiator and the intercooler radiator.

The two-stage supercharger gave greatly increased engine power at high altitude. The Merlin 45 with the single-stage supercharger developed about 720 hp (537 kW) at 30,000 ft (9150 m). At that same altitude, the same basic engine with the two-stage supercharger developed about 1,020 hp (760 kW).

The Mk III with the experimental Merlin 61 installation began flight trials in the autumn of 1941, and initially there were problems getting the intercooler plumbing to work properly. By the end of 1941 the new engine was working satisfactorily, and revealed a huge improvement in the fighter's performance. Its maximum speeds were 391 mph (630 km/h) at 15,900 ft (4850 m), 414 mph (666 km/h) at 27,200 ft (8290 m) and 354 mph (570 km/h) at 40,000 ft (12200 m). The modified Spitfire's rate of climb far outstripped that of the Mk V, and its service ceiling was estimated to be 41,800 ft (12745 m).

Above: The first Mk V conversion was W3760. As originally converted this aircraft had a Vokes tropical filter fitted, a normal shaped fin above the fuselage and no armament. In light of experience during early flights, a revised fin was fitted later, along with a Mk IX-type filter and cannon armament. Four-bladed propellers were fitted to all Mk V floatplanes.

Above: In addition to the three Mk V floatplanes, one LF.Mk IXB was converted to a similar standard with a view to using the type in the Pacific theatre. During trials it demonstrated a top speed only 30 mph (48 km/h) less than that of the landplane. Conversion of a Mk VIII had been considered initially. Pictured during trials in summer 1944, MJ892 was converted back to landplane standard when the idea was dropped.

Left and below left: After the Dodecanese operation was abandoned, the Spitfire Mk Vs were assembled and flown from Great Bitter Lake in Egypt. By November they were in Alexandria and had been returned to Britain by the summer of 1944. All were struck off charge in December.

Below left: Folland Aircraft converted the second and third Mk V floatplanes, EP751 and EP754. The best speed attained by these aircraft during trials was 324 mph (521 km/h) at 19,500 ft (5944 m), considerably less than that of the land-based variant. The floats' detrimental effect on the top speed of the floatplane fighter was always seen as a major drawback of the concept, especially if they were to encounter land-based opposition. It was this that ultimately brought an end to plans for Folland Aircraft to convert 12 more Mk Vs for use in the Pacific war.

As an aerodynamically 'clean' design, the Spitfire was chosen for a series of high-speed diving trials at Farnborough in spring 1944. They investigated aircraft handling at speeds approaching the sound barrier. On 17 April, Sqn Ldr 'Marty' Martindale dived his PR.Mk XI EN409 from 40,500 ft (12344 m), reaching a true airspeed of 606 mph (975 km/h) or Mach 0.89 when the entire propeller and reduction gear was ripped from the aircraft. Martindale skillfully glided EN409 20 miles (32 km) to a safe landing.

'Camera Spits'

Suitably modified with camera equipment, extra fuel and, in some cases, cabin pressurisation, the Spitfire was the ideal high-speed 'PR' platform. Initial modifications were based on Mk Is, but the PR Spitfire evolved into a specialised sub-family, culminating in the PR.Mk XI in terms of Merlin-powered aircraft. Operating at extreme range, PR Spitfires undertook both low- and high-altitude work in extremely dangerous circumstances.

An oblique camera port behind the cockpit indicates the low-level 'dicing' role for which the PR.Mk VII (originally the PR Type 'G', then PR.Mk IG) was intended. Some were camouflaged, though most were finished in very pale pink.

Above: For low-level armed reconnaissance work, the PR.Mk XIII was introduced in early 1943. Converted from Mk I or V fighters or PR.Mk VIIs, the 26 Mk XIIIs featured a 'low-level' Merlin 32 and four 0.303-in (7.7-mm) machine-guns in the outer wings for self-defence.

Below: The intake below the exhaust ports on the starboard side of this aircraft indicates that cabin pressurisation was fitted to this aircraft, a PR.Mk X. Effectively a high-altitude, pressurised version of the PR.Mk XI, the Mk X entered service after the latter type and was not as popular with pilots, as visibility from its heavy Perspex canopy was poor. Only 16 were built, entering service with Nos 541 and 542 Squadrons from May 1944.

Introduced as a counter to the mounting losses suffered by PR Spitfires at the hands of Fw 190s and new Bf 109 variants, the Spitfire PR.Mk Xs and Mk XIs (above) were virtually immune to fighter interception until the spring of 1944, when the first of the Luftwaffe's jet fighters entered service. Both were powered by Merlin 60 series engines.

Three new Spitfire versions

The successful combination of the Merlin 61 engine and the Spitfire airframe came at an opportune time. As mentioned above, the Spitfire V was no match for the Fw 190 fighter which entered service in the autumn of 1941. The new engine was rushed into production and formed the basis for three important new Spitfire variants: the Mk VII, the VIII and the Mk IX.

The Mk VII was a dedicated high-altitude interceptor variant, with a pressurised cabin like that fitted to the Mk VI, and the same extended-span wing. With the additional power at high altitude, it promised to be far more effective

Left: This work-stained, Rotol propeller-fitted aircraft, ordered as a Mk I fighter, served as a PR.Mk III and later as a PR.Mk VI. The former was the first long-range PR variant, with extra fuel in the fuselage and in a small blister tank under the port wing. This was counterbalanced by two small cameras in a blister on the opposite wing.

In 'PR blue'

Spitfire PR Type 'F' (PR.Mk VI)
Ordered as a Spitfire Mk I, X4498 was converted to PR Type 'C' (Mk III) standard shortly after completion and in 1942 had a Merlin 45 fitted to become a Type 'F'. It is finished in the colours of No. 3 Photo Reconnaissance Unit at RAF Oakington, July 1941.

Unsuccessful Mk VI

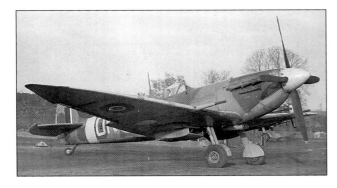

Left: Answering a perceived threat from high-altitude bombing by the Luftwaffe, the Mk VI was developed from the Mk V with a pressurised cabin, extended wingtips and a high-altitude Merlin 47 driving a four-bladed propeller. However, once in service it was unable to fight above 35,000 ft (10668 m). Mk VII BR579 was a No. 124 Squadron aircraft.

Above: Only two squadrons were fully equipped with Mk VIs and their successes were few. A number of other units used the type during brief stints based in the Orkneys and Shetlands while being rested. Six aircraft were also shipped to Egypt to join Mk VCs specially modified for high-altitude interception, but they failed to match the latter's performance.

than its predecessor. To permit a high-speed climb to altitude, perhaps followed by a long tail chase, the Mk VII had increased fuel tankage. Two extra fuel tanks were built into the wings, increasing the total internal fuel capacity to 124 Imp gal (563 litres). The airframe was redesigned and strengthened to cope with the extra weight and, to reduce drag, the tail wheel was made to retract. The second of the new variants, the Mk VIII, was a general-purpose fighter incorporating most features of the Mk VII except for the pressurised cabin.

The redesign work on the airframes of the two variants, and the retooling of production lines to build them, took several months. As a result, neither the Mk VII nor the Mk VIII became available in quantity until the middle of 1943.

With its Spitfire V units hard-pressed by Fw 190s when-

ever they ventured over northwest Europe, Fighter Command could not afford to wait that long. Its urgent need was for an interim Spitfire variant powered by the Merlin 61, able to engage the Fw 190 on equal terms. And it was wanted quickly. The stopgap variant became the Spitfire IX, essentially a Mk VC with the minimum of modification necessary for it to take the new engine. There was no attempt to restress the airframe of the Mk IX to

Repair and salvage

Below: Newly overhauled Spitfire Mk Vs at Westland's Ilchester plant await delivery to squadrons. W3127, nearest the camera, was built in 1941 and visited Westland twice for repair and/or modification during its career, finishing up at the Central Gunnery School before being reduced to instructional airframe status in 1946.

Above: Spitfire Mk Vs (including a USAAF example) and at least one PR.Mk XI share a large hangar with Hawker Hurricane Mk IIs at a maintenance unit (MU) 'somewhere in North Africa', possibly Aboukir, Egypt. No. 103 MU at Aboukir was responsible for reconditioning as many as 140 Allied aircraft per month during the height of the desert war.

Below: Inside Westland's Ilchester plant, at least 20 Spitfires (mainly Mk Vs), their old unit codes painted out, undergo refurbishment. This major undertaking was tackled by several companies.

Below: In every theatre, RAF repair and salvage units performed vital work behind the lines, recovering damaged airframes for potential repair and return to service. Here a Bedford/'Queen Mary' combination rescues an unserviceable Spitfire Mk V near the Tunisian front, probably in 1942.

Above: A Spitfire Mk VII of No. 131 Squadron is pictured in the spring of 1944 when the unit was based at Culmhead. The upper surfaces were painted in the light grey high-altitude camouflage, with toned-down national markings on the fuselage, tail and top surface of the wings. There were no markings under the wings.

Above: Distinguished from the Mk VI by its retractable tailwheel, the Mk VII was a much improved aircraft. As well as a more powerful Merlin 60 series engine, the Mk VII had more fuel capacity, improved cabin pressurisation and 'C' wing armament. EN474, seen here flying in the US, was one of 140 Mk VIIs built by Supermarine and was shipped across the Atlantic in April 1943. Coded as (foreign evaluation airframe) 'FE-400', it was assessed by the USAAF. It survived the war, to be displayed at the National Air & Space Museum, Washington, DC.

AB450 was built in August 1942 as a Mk VB and was immediately converted to become the Mk VII prototype. In September it was issued to the High Altitude Flight at Northolt, set up to combat high-flying Junkers Ju 86P bombers, and was absorbed in early 1943 by No. 124 Squadron. Here it was painted PR Blue with Medium Sea Grey undersides. Apparently fitted with a 'C' wing, its guns had been removed at this point.

Boulogne, proceeding towards French coast. We dived down on them and I attacked an Fw 190 from astern and below, giving a very short burst from 300 yd. I was forced to break away as I was crowded out by other Spits. I broke down and right and caught another Fw as he commenced to dive away. At 14,000 ft approx I gave a burst of cannon and M/G, 400 yd range hitting E/A along fuselage. Pieces fell off and E/A continued in straight dive nearly vertical. I followed E/A down to 5,000 ft over Boulogne and saw him hit the deck just outside the town of Boulogne and explode and burn up. Returned to base at 0 ft."

Although Kingaby's victory attracted little attention at the time, it marked a significant turning point for Fighter Command. It was the first occasion when the Spitfire had engaged the feared Fw 190 on equal terms. For the Luftwaffe, that engagement marked the beginning of the end of the air superiority it had established over northwest Europe nearly a year earlier.

Spitfires had their hardest day's fight, ever, on 19 August 1942. On that day British and Canadian troops carried out amphibious landings at and beside the port of Dieppe in northern France. Forty-eight squadrons of Spitfires supported the landings, 42 with Mk Vs, two with Mk VIs and four with the new Mk IXs. These units flew 171 squadron-sized patrols totalling 2,050 sorties (out of a grand total of 2,600 sorties flown by all Allied aircraft involved in the operation). Also during that action, the Spitfire squadrons suffered their heaviest single day's loss ever: 59 aircraft lost to enemy action out of a total Allied loss of 97.

In the months that followed, many more home-based units re-equipped with the Mk IX, and it became the most-used fighter type in the theatre.

Combat in the stratosphere

A few days after the Dieppe action, the Luftwaffe opened a new phase in its air attack on England. The so-called Hohenkampfkommando (High Altitude Bomber – Detachment), with a strength of two Junkers Ju 86R bombers, began operations from Beauvais in northern France. Powered by two turbo-supercharged diesel engines with

compensate for the increase in all-up weight. Pilots were warned of the dangers of overstressing the new variant in combat.

The Mk IX in service

In July 1942, No. 64 Squadron at Hornchurch became the first unit operational with the Spitfire IX. On 30 July, Flight Lieutenant Donald Kingaby gained the first victory in the new variant. Afterwards, he reported: "I sighted approximately 12 Fw 190s 2,000 ft below us at 12,000 ft just off

This Spitfire Mk VII of No. 131 Squadron was pictured in June 1944. By then the aircraft had been repainted in normal day fighter camouflage and carried invasion stripes. The pointed tip of the extended-span wing is evident, as is the additional air scoop on the starboard side of the engine that provided air for the cabin pressurisation blower.

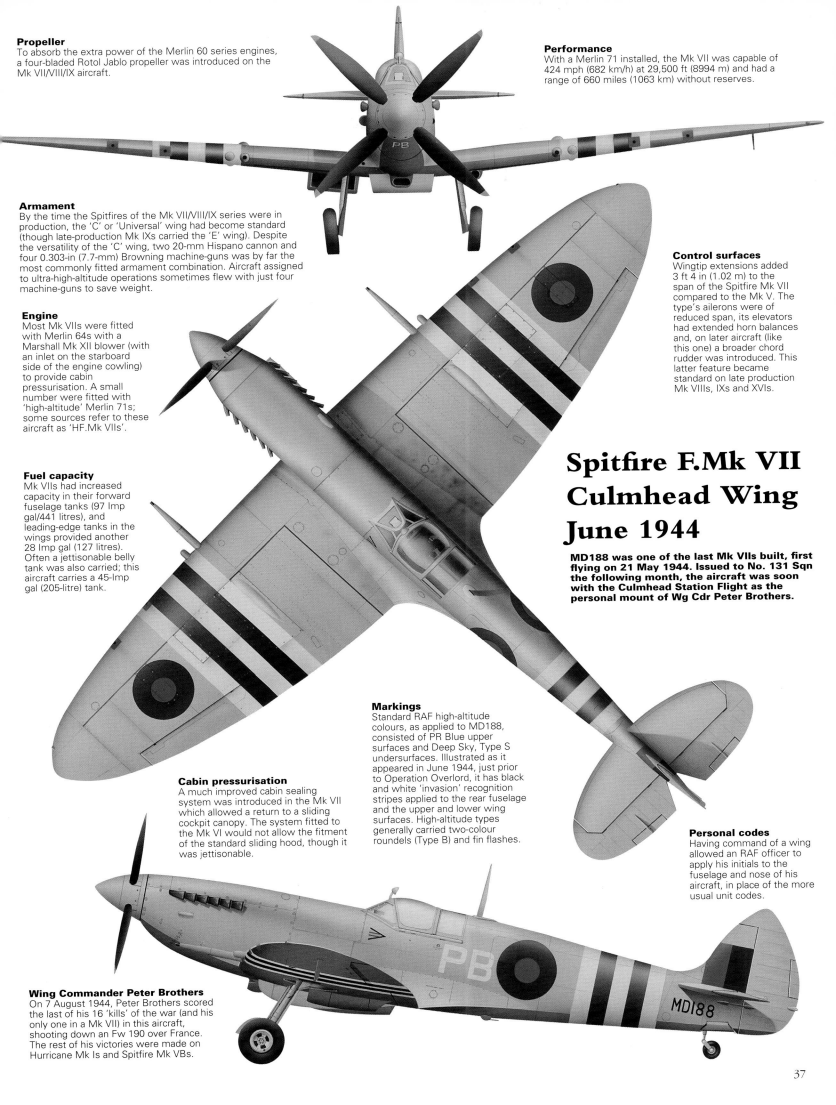

Propeller
To absorb the extra power of the Merlin 60 series engines, a four-bladed Rotol Jablo propeller was introduced on the Mk VII/VIII/IX aircraft.

Performance
With a Merlin 71 installed, the Mk VII was capable of 424 mph (682 km/h) at 29,500 ft (8994 m) and had a range of 660 miles (1063 km) without reserves.

Armament
By the time the Spitfires of the Mk VII/VIII/IX series were in production, the 'C' or 'Universal' wing had become standard (though late-production Mk IXs carried the 'E' wing). Despite the versatility of the 'C' wing, two 20-mm Hispano cannon and four 0.303-in (7.7-mm) Browning machine-guns was by far the most commonly fitted armament combination. Aircraft assigned to ultra-high-altitude operations sometimes flew with just four machine-guns to save weight.

Control surfaces
Wingtip extensions added 3 ft 4 in (1.02 m) to the span of the Spitfire Mk VII compared to the Mk V. The type's ailerons were of reduced span, its elevators had extended horn balances and, on later aircraft (like this one) a broader chord rudder was introduced. This latter feature became standard on late production Mk VIIIs, IXs and XVIs.

Engine
Most Mk VIIs were fitted with Merlin 64s with a Marshall Mk XII blower (with an inlet on the starboard side of the engine cowling) to provide cabin pressurisation. A small number were fitted with 'high-altitude' Merlin 71s; some sources refer to these aircraft as 'HF.Mk VIIs'.

Spitfire F.Mk VII Culmhead Wing June 1944

MD188 was one of the last Mk VIIs built, first flying on 21 May 1944. Issued to No. 131 Sqn the following month, the aircraft was soon with the Culmhead Station Flight as the personal mount of Wg Cdr Peter Brothers.

Fuel capacity
Mk VIIs had increased capacity in their forward fuselage tanks (97 Imp gal/441 litres), and leading-edge tanks in the wings provided another 28 Imp gal (127 litres). Often a jettisonable belly tank was also carried; this aircraft carries a 45-Imp gal (205-litre) tank.

Markings
Standard RAF high-altitude colours, as applied to MD188, consisted of PR Blue upper surfaces and Deep Sky, Type S undersurfaces. Illustrated as it appeared in June 1944, just prior to Operation Overlord, it has black and white 'invasion' recognition stripes applied to the rear fuselage and the upper and lower wing surfaces. High-altitude types generally carried two-colour roundels (Type B) and fin flashes.

Cabin pressurisation
A much improved cabin sealing system was introduced in the Mk VII which allowed a return to a sliding cockpit canopy. The system fitted to the Mk VI would not allow the fitment of the standard sliding hood, though it was jettisonable.

Personal codes
Having command of a wing allowed an RAF officer to apply his initials to the fuselage and nose of his aircraft, in place of the more usual unit codes.

Wing Commander Peter Brothers
On 7 August 1944, Peter Brothers scored the last of his 16 'kills' of the war (and his only one in a Mk VII) in this aircraft, shooting down an Fw 190 over France. The rest of his victories were made on Hurricane Mk Is and Spitfire Mk VBs.

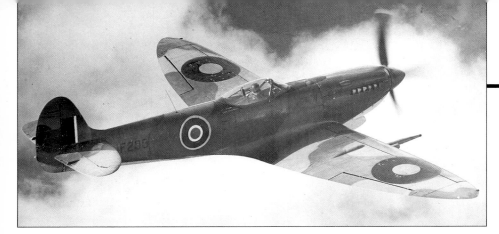

Merlin 61 power

Significant as the first Spitfire fitted with a bubble canopy, Mk VIII JF299 flew in this form in mid-1943. Flown by experienced pilots at the Air Fighting Development Unit, Duxford, the modified aircraft was very well received. As it did not adversely effect the aircraft's performance the 'rear-view fuselage' was applied to late wartime production Mk VIIIs, IXs and XVIs, as well as Griffon-engined Mk XIVs.

nitrous oxide injection, the new German bomber delivered attacks from altitudes above 40,000 ft (12200 m). Its puny load was a single 550 lb (250 kg) bomb, its maximum speed was little over 200 mph (320 km/h) and it lacked defensive armament. However, there were good grounds for believing that the bomber's excellent altitude performance would keep it beyond the reach of the defences. Obviously, the raids could not inflict much in the way of damage, but with Germany's own cities coming under increasingly heavy attack, the high-flying bombers would score useful propaganda points by delivering daylight attacks against which the British defences were shown to be impotent.

The first Ju 86R raid attack took place on 24 August 1942, when one aircraft bombed Camberley and the other bombed Southampton. Fifteen Spitfire Vs were scrambled but none reached a firing position. During the next two and a half weeks, the Ju 86Rs flew another 10 sorties over Eng-

land, all without encountering effective fighter interference.

The high-flying bombers' spell of invulnerability was fast drawing to a close, however. Fighter Command formed a new fighter unit, the Special Service Flight based at Northolt, to counter the menace. Two Spitfire IXs were expressly prepared for high-altitude operations. They were fitted with specially tuned Merlin 61 engines with a slightly higher reduction gear, and lightened by the removal of armour, the four machine-guns and all other unnecessary items of equipment.

Right: Spitfire Mk VIIIs of the 308th Fighter Squadron, 31st Fighter Group, 12th Air Force are seen at Castel Volturno, Italy, early in 1944. Fifty-five Mk VIIIs operated alongside Mk Vs with the 308th; other squadrons of the 31st FG flew Mk Vs and IXs.

Right: No. 145 Squadron, the first unit to be equipped with Mk Vs in North Africa, became the first Mk VIII unit in June 1943, based at Malta. Seen at Fano, Italy in November 1944, this aircraft carries No. 145's 'trademark' white-outlined codes, has had its fuselage band (and part of its serial number) painted out and carries a 500-lb (227-kg) bomb.

Below: AVM Harry Broadhurst, AOC Desert Air Force (the youngest AVM in the RAF at 38 years old) taxis his personally coded Mk VIII past the remains of airship hangars at Taranto, Italy in the summer of 1943. Having become privy to the 'Ultra' secret, the Allies' successful breaking of the German 'Enigma' code, Broadhurst was, by this stage, forbidden from flying on operations. His aircraft has extended wingtips, of the type applied to Mk VIIs and fitted to early production Mk VIII aircraft. Four Merlin variants were fitted to Mk VIIIs. Standard F.Mk VIIIs had either a Merlin 61 or 63. From late 1942, role prefixes were officially applied, but not always used – 'LF' for aircraft with the 'low-level' Merlin 66 fitted; 'HF' for Merlin 70-fitted, high-altitude examples.

Left: The entire production run of Mk VIIIs was delivered to units based overseas. This example belonging to No. 417 Squadron, RCAF is pictured at Venafro in Italy in the summer of 1944. Earlier this aircraft had served with the US 31st Fighter Group, and when the latter converted to P-51s it was returned to the RAF.

Replacing SEAC Mk Vs

Below: Spitfires were first deployed to the Far East in late 1943, when Mk VCs replaced Hawker Hurricanes in Nos 136, 607 and 615 Squadrons, RAF on the Burma front. They were ultimately replaced by Mk VIIIs. The Indian Air Force also flew Mk Vs and VIIIs in the India-Burma theatre. Few photographs of the IAF's Mk VIIIs exist; here, personnel service a No. 8 Squadron aircraft in Burma, 1945.

Above: RAF personnel of No. 81 Squadron show their extended wingtips-fitted Mk VIIIs to local people at Imphal. No. 81 was one of the first two units equipped with the Mk VIII in the Far East in late 1943. Finished in the Dark Green/Dark Earth camouflage applied to South East Asia Command (SEAC), with Blue/Sky Blue roundels, these aircraft lack the broad white recognition stripes applied later to SEAC aircraft. Red was removed from the markings carried by Allied aircraft in the Far East to avoid confusion with Japanese aircraft.

Left: No. 607 'County of Durham' Squadron Mk VIIIs rest at Imphal as a USAAF B-25 prepares to take off in the background. Though encounters with the enemy were initially rare, by mid-1944 these aircraft were engaged in the fight for air supremacy with the Japanese army. From early 1945 the unit turned to the fighter-bomber role, supporting Allied armies in Burma.

On 12 September a Ju 86R headed across the English Channel for yet another attack, but this time the defenders were ready. Pilot Officer Emanuel Galitzine took off from Northolt in one of the specially modified Mk IXs. He climbed to 40,000 ft (12200 m), heading southwest under radar control. As he neared the Isle of Wight he caught sight of the German bomber, slightly higher and to starboard. At about the same time that the crew of the Junkers saw him, the pilot jettisoned the bomb and selected full power in an attempt to outclimb the interceptor. The much-lightened Spitfire climbed more quickly, however, and Galitzine moved into an attacking position above and behind his quarry. "I positioned myself for an attack and dived to about 200 yd astern of him, where I opened up with a three-second burst. At the end of the burst my port cannon jammed and the Spitfire slewed round to starboard; then, as I passed through the bomber's slipstream, my canopy misted over."

It took about a minute for the Spitfire's canopy to clear, then Galitzine closed in for another attack on the Ju 86R which was now heading south and trying to escape out to sea. By clever manoeuvring, the bomber crew avoided that attack and the two that followed. At one stage in the action the pair exceeded 43,500 ft (13260 m), but then the Junkers entered a patch of mist and Galitzine lost contact. Running short of fuel, he broke off the action.

SEAC ace at Imphal

Spitfire LF.Mk VIII
In this aircraft Australian Flt Lt Wilfred Goold shot down a Nakajima Ki-43 'Oscar' and damaged two others over Palel on 18 May 1944. 'AF' was the code of No. 607 Sqn, RAF then based at Imphal. Goold shot down five Japanese aircraft in total. All were 'Oscars' claimed while in India with No. 607 Sqn.

Australian Eights

Above: This formation of Spitfire VIIIs of No. 548 Squadron operated from Darwin, northern Australia, early in 1945.

Right: With grey exhaust stains caused by a lean running engine, a Mk VIII of No. 79 Squadron, RAAF is pictured at Biak, New Guinea, in April 1945. From September 1944 HF.Mk VIIIs began to arrive in Australia; they carried serial numbers in the A58-6xx series.

Above: Mk VIIIs of No. 452 Squadron, RAAF are seen at Sepinang airstrip, Borneo in early August 1945. 'Ace of Spades' markings on the tails of these aircraft indicate its inclusion in No. 80 Wing, RAAF.

The Ju 86R landed at Caen bearing scars from the action: a single hole above and below the port wing, where a 20-mm armour-piercing round had passed clean through the structure. Obviously, the new bomber was not immune from fighter attack at high altitude, and the operations by the Hohenkampfkommando came to an abrupt halt. The action on 12 September 1942 was the highest-altitude combat fought during World War II.

Spitfire Mk IXs in North Africa

Towards the end of 1942, the Luftwaffe moved a Gruppe of Fw 190s to Tunisia. Initially confronting Spitfire Vs and fighters of lower performance, the German unit was for a time able to secure temporary air superiority over selected parts of the battle area. Then, as over northwest Europe, the RAF countered by moving Spitfire IX units into the area. No. 81 Squadron went into action with them in January 1943, followed soon afterwards by No. 72 Squadron. Another important addition was the Polish Fighting Team, a 16-pilot volunteer unit equipped with Mk IXs. Led by Squadron Leader Stanislaw Skalski, it included several other aces including Karol Pniak, Waclaw Krol, Eugeniusz Horbaczewski and Kazimierz Sporney. At the same time, the US 31st and 52nd Fighter Groups also received some Mk IXs and flew them alongside their Spitfire Vs.

The Mk IXs quickly restored air superiority, and assisted in the tightening of the air and sea blockade of Axis supply

RAAF wing leaders

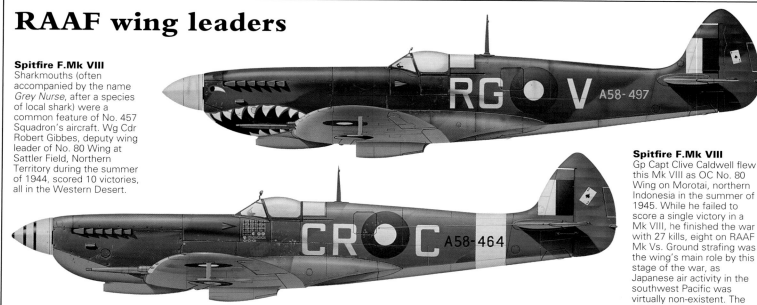

Spitfire F.Mk VIII
Sharkmouths (often accompanied by the name *Grey Nurse*, after a species of local shark) were a common feature of No. 457 Squadron's aircraft. Wg Cdr Robert Gibbes, deputy wing leader of No. 80 Wing at Sattler Field, Northern Territory during the summer of 1944, scored 10 victories, all in the Western Desert.

Spitfire F.Mk VIII
Gp Capt Clive Caldwell flew this Mk VIII as OC No. 80 Wing on Morotai, northern Indonesia in the summer of 1945. While he failed to score a single victory in a Mk VIII, he finished the war with 27 kills, eight on RAAF Mk Vs. Ground strafing was the wing's main role by this stage of the war, as Japanese air activity in the southwest Pacific was virtually non-existent. The white rear fuselage band was an identification marking carried by Morotai-based aircraft during this period.

Doubt exists regarding the true identity of this aircraft. Though Gp Capt Caldwell recorded this machine as A58-464 in his log book, it has been ascertained that its actual identity was lost when the white band was painted on the rear fuselage, obscuring the serial number which was incorrectly repainted afterwards. The real A58-464 served with No. 8 OTU, RAAF and never saw operational service. Contemporary photographs suggest that the correct serial was A58-484.

Enter the Mk IX

Below: As Mk IXs were expected to fly longer distances over occupied Europe and lacked the extra wing leading-edge fuel tanks fitted to the Mk VIIs and VIIIs, attempts were made to improve range performance. Various trial installations, including wing-mounted tanks from a P-51, were flown. This Mk IXC, from an unidentified unit on an RAF station in the depths of winter, 1943/44, carries the chosen design – a 50-Imp gal (227-litre) belly tank. Late-production Mk IXs had extra fuselage tanks installed.

Right: Armourers prepare 20-mm ammunition for Mk IXs during spring/early summer 1944. 'US' codes were carried by No. 56 Squadron, equipped with Mk IXs for just three months (from April to June 1944) between relinquishing its Hawker Typhoons and re-equipping with Tempests in mid-June. The aircraft coded 'AH' was with No. 332 (Norwegian) Squadron, which was to join the Second Tactical Air Force (2nd TAF) and cover the Normandy landings just weeks after this scene was recorded. In August No. 332 moved to France, flying Mk IXs for the duration of the war.

Below: Mk IXs were first sent to North Africa in December 1942 to counter the threat posed by Luftwaffe Fw 190s deployed to the theatre the previous month. This is a Mk IX of No. 94 Squadron, which spent the war in North Africa and Mediterranean, receiving Mk Vs in August 1943. Mk IXCs were flown between February and August 1944 and, after a stint with Mk Vs again, between February and April 1945.

Above: One of the first units to re-equip with the Mk IX was No. 611 'West Lancashire' Squadron. These early production Mk IXCs are seen over south London in formation for RAF Biggin Hill's station photographer. Among roles added to the Spitfire's repertoire with the Mk IX were 'Diver' patrols to counter the German Fieseler Fi 103 (V-1) revenge weapon.

routes from Italy. Under Operation Flax, the Allied air forces concentrated their attention against the airlift carrying supplies to the Axis forces. Scores of transport planes were shot down, gravely reducing the carrying capacity of the airlift. From then, the days of the Axis forces in North Africa were numbered, and early in May 1943 they capitulated.

The Spitfire VII in service

Because of the continuing lack of a high-altitude threat to Great Britain, production of the Mk VII had only a moderate priority. It was May 1943 before No. 124 Squadron at North Weald became operational with the variant. In August 1943 three Mk VIIs were based at Skeabrae in the Orkney Islands, to engage high-altitude

reconnaissance aircraft attempting to photograph the fleet anchorage at Scapa Flow. Fighter squadrons based elsewhere in Great Britain were rotated through Skeabrae during their rest periods, and their pilots flew the Mk VIIs. There were few opportunities for them to go into action, but they served their purpose by acting as a deterrent.

In all, 140 Mk VIIs were built, the last being delivered in May 1944. In the spring of 1944, Nos 131 and 616 Squadrons converted to the Mk VII. During the preparations for the Normandy invasion their task was to prevent high-flying German reconnaissance aircraft from photographing the invasion ports.

During the days immediately following the invasion, the Mk VII units provided top cover over the beachhead area.

Above: When this photograph was taken, in October 1942, No. 340 'Ile de France' Squadron (a Free French unit) had just re-equipped with Mk IXBs, having flown Mk Vs. These it kept for just five months before being rested at Drem and Turnhouse in Scotland, where it reverted to Mk Vs.

First Mk IX victor

Spitfire Mk IXC
In BR600, Plt Off Donald Kingaby of No. 64 Squadron became the first pilot to score a kill in a Mk IX when, on 30 July 1942, he downed an Fw 190 over Boulogne. This was a turning point for RAF Fighter Command which was now able to engage the 'Butcher Bird' on equal terms.

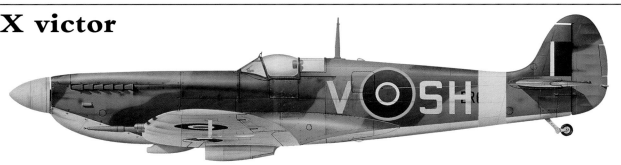

Above: Optimised for high-altitude operations, the HF.Mk IXC was powered by a Merlin 70, but lacked a pressurised cabin.

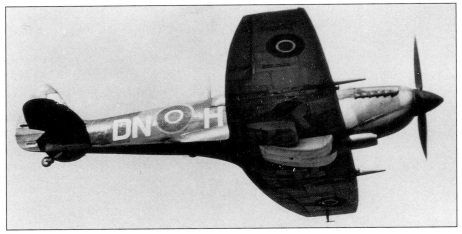

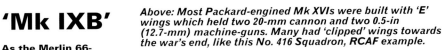

Above: Most Packard-engined Mk XVIs were built with 'E' wings which held two 20-mm cannon and two 0.5-in (12.7-mm) machine-guns. Many had 'clipped' wings towards the war's end, like this No. 416 Squadron, RCAF example.

Above: Though the 'LF' designation of the LF.Mk IXC implied that it was intended for low-level operations, this was misleading. These aircraft were fitted with the Merlin 66 engine, the supercharger of which was designed to cut in at lower altitudes to provide optimum performance for engaging Fw 190s.

'Mk IXB'

As the Merlin 66-engined Mk IXs entered service in spring 1943, an official designation for the variant simply did not exist. Wishing to differentiate between these aircraft and 'standard' Mk IXCs, squadrons devised their own designations, namely 'Mk IXA' for the Mk IXC and 'Mk IXB' for the Merlin 66-powered aircraft. Later in 1943 the Ministry of Aircraft Production allotted new official designations, under which the Mk IXC became the F.Mk IXC, while the 'Mk IXB' became the LF.Mk IXC. The later Merlin 70-engined high-altitude variant was to be the HF.Mk IXC. By the time squadrons were notified of the change, the unofficial designations were well established.

Peak deployment of Merlin-engined Spitfires, June 1944

(Unless otherwise stated, units operated in the fighter role. Units marked * operated a mixture of types that included Spitfires.)

Air Defence of Great Britain
No. 10 Group

Nos 1, 165 Sqns	Mk IX	Predannack
No. 126 Sqn	Mk IX	Culmhead
Nos 131, 616 Sqns	Mk VII	Culmhead

No. 11 Group

Nos 33, 74, 127 Sqns	Mk IX	Lympne
Nos 64, 234, 611 Sqns	Mk V	Deanland
Nos 80, 229, 274 Sqns	Mk IX	Detling
Nos 130, 303, 402 Sqns	Mk V	Horne
No. 345 Sqn	Mk V	Shoreham
No. 350 Sqn	Mk V	Friston
No. 501 Sqn	Mk IX	Friston

No. 12 Group

No. 504 Sqn	Mk V	Castletown, Digby, Acklington

No. 13 Group

No. 118 Sqn	Mk V	Skeabrae, Sumburgh

Second Tactical Air Force
No. 83 Group
(Mk IXs operated as fighters and fighter-bombers)

No. 125 Wing (Nos 132, 453, 602 Sqns)	Mk IX	Ford
No. 144 Wing (Nos 441, 442, 443 Sqns)	Mk IX	Ford
No. 126 Wing (Nos 401, 411, 412 Sqns)	Mk IX	Tangmere
No. 127 Wing (Nos 403, 416, 421 Sqns)	Mk IX	Tangmere

No. 84 Group
(Mk IXs operated as fighters and fighter-bombers)

No. 131 Wing (Nos 302, 308, 317 Sqns)	Mk IX	Chailey
No. 132 Wing (Nos 66, 331, 332 Sqns)	Mk IX	Bognor
No. 134 Wing (Nos 310, 312, 313 Sqns)	Mk IX	Appledram
No. 135 Wing (Nos 222, 349, 485 Sqns)	Mk IX	Selsey
No. 145 Wing (Nos 329, 340, 341 Sqns)	Mk IX	Merston

No. 85 Group
(Mk IXs operated as fighters and fighter-bombers)

No. 56 Sqn	Mk IX	Newchurch
No. 124 Sqn	Mk VII	Bradwell Bay

Air Spotting Pool

No. 26 Sqn	Mk V	Lee on Solent (gunfire spotting)
No. 63 Sqn	Mk V	Lee on Solent (GS)

Coastal Command

No. 275 Sqn	Mk V	Warmwell* (search and rescue)
No. 276 Sqn		Portreath* (SAR)
No. 277 Sqn	Mk V	Shoreham* (SAR)
No. 278 Sqn	Mk V	Bradwell Bay* (SAR)
No. 519 Sqn	Mk VI	Wick* (Met)

Army Co-operation Units

No. 288 Sqn	Mk V	Collyweston*

Mediterranean Air Command
Italy

Nos 32, 253 Sqns	Mk IX	Foggia
Nos 73, 87 Sqns	Mk V, IX	Foggia
No. 43 Sqn	Mk IX	Nettuno
Nos 72, 111	Mk IX	Largo
No. 145 Sqn	Mk VIII	Lago
No. 40 SAAF, 225 Sqns	Mk V, IX	Lago (Tac. Recon)
Nos 92, 417, 601 Sqns	Mk VIII	Venafro
No. 208 Sqn	Mk IX	Venafro (TacR)
No. 93 Sqn	Mk IX	Tre Canelli
Nos 249, 1435 Sqns	Mk IX	Grottaglie
No. 241 Sqn	Mk IX	Trigno (TacR)
No. 318 Sqn	Mk V	Trigno (TacR)

No. 7 SAAF Fighter Wing

Nos 1, 2, 4, 7 Sqns, SAAF	Mks V, IX	based in Italy

Corsica

Nos 154, 232, 242, 243 Sqns	Mk IX	Poretta
Nos 237, 238, 451 Sqns	Mk IX	Serragia
No. 328 Sqn	Mk IX	Borgo,

Malta

No. 185 Sqn	Mk IX	Hal Far

Middle East Command
Libya

No. 94 Sqn	Mk IX	Bu Amud
No. 335 Sqn	Mk V	Bersis

Egypt

No. 213 Sqn	Mk IX	Idku
No. 336 Sqn	Mk IX	Mersa Matruh

Aden

No. 3 Sqn SAAF	Mk V	Khormaksar

Air Command, Southeast Asia
No. 222 Group (Ceylon)

No. 17 Sqn	Mk VIII	Vavuyina
No. 273 Sqn	Mk VIII	Ratmalana

Eastern Air Command (India)

Nos 67, 155 Sqns	Mk VIII	Baigachi

No. 221 Group (India)

No. 81 Sqn	Mk VIII	Khumbirgram
No. 607 Sqn	Mk VIII	Imphal
No. 615 Sqn	Mk VIII	Palel

No. 224 Group (India)

No. 152 Sqn	Mk VIII	Palel
No. 136 Sqn	Mk VIII	Chittagong

No. 1 Fighter Wing (Australia)

Nos 54, 452, 457 Sqns	Mk VIII	Darwin area

Engine and propeller
Driving the four-bladed Rotol Jablo propeller in BS459 was a Merlin 61. Some F.Mk IXs were powered by either a Merlin 63 or 63A; different variants were fitted to LF.Mk IXs and HF.Mk IXs, optimised for Fw 190 engagement and high-altitude interception, respectively.

Late-production Mk IXs
As Mk IX production progressed, various improvements were introduced, including a 72-Imp gal (327-litre) fuel tank in the rear fuselage, a broad chord rudder and the 'rear-view fuselage' with a 'bubble' canopy. This latter change reduced fuselage tank capacity to 64 Imp gal (291 litres).

Spitfire Mk IX versus Fw 190
At Duxford, the Air Fighting Development Unit (AFDU) compared a captured Focke-Wulf Fw 190 with a fully operational Spitfire Mk IX for speed and manoeuvrability at heights up to 25,000 ft (7620 m). The Spitfire IX at most heights was slightly faster. During climbs at various heights up to 23,000 ft (7000 m), with both aircraft flying under maximum continuous climbing conditions, little difference was found between the aircraft, though on the whole the Spitfire was slightly better. The Fw 190 was faster than the Mk IX in a dive, had a superior roll rate and its initial acceleration was better than that of the Spitfire, except in level flight at such altitudes where the Spitfire has a speed advantage and then, providing the Spitfire was cruising at high speed, there was little to choose between the aircraft. The general impression gained by pilots taking part in the trials was that the Mk IX compared favourably with the Fw 190.

Camouflage
BS459 is finished in the standard RAF day fighter camouflage introduced in May 1942. Ocean Grey and Dark Green were the most commonly used upper surface colours; undersurfaces were Medium Sea Grey. The aircraft's spinner was Sky Blue, as were the Fighter Command recognition band on the rear fuselage and the unit codes. Additional markings include the Polish national insignia on the engine cowling and No. 306 Squadron's 'bird and bear' emblem.

Spitfire F.Mk IXC No. 306 Squadron Northolt, 1943

Part of the fifth order for Spitfire Mk IA/IBs placed in October 1940, BS459 was one of the earliest production Mk IXs. Completed at Supermarine's Eastleigh factory in September 1942, it was issued to No. 306 'Torunski' Squadron on 25 September. Based at Northolt, No. 306 was engaged in daylight sweeps over Europe in 1943. BS459 failed to return from operations on 26 January 1943 and is believed to have collided with sister aircraft BS241 over the English Channel.

Gun armament
Most Mk IXs were built with the six gun 'C' wing carried over from the Mk VC. (A few Mk IXs converted from Mk VCs carried four cannon.) Later production aircraft and the bulk of Mk XVI production had the 'E' wing, in which cannon were fitted in the outer cannon bays, each of the two inner bays being occupied by a 0.5-in (12.7-mm) US Browning.

Cooling systems
With Merlin 60-engined Spitfires came symmetrical underwing radiator intakes, first seen on the Spitfire Mk III. Merlin 60 series engines incorporated a supercharger intercooler with its own radiator under the port wing. The oil cooler, which had its own small intake on earlier marks, was incorporated in the same housing. The starboard intake fed the Merlin's cooling system.

Fighter-bombers
In the fighter-bomber role, which became increasingly important after D-Day, Spitfire Mk IXs were equipped to carry up to 1,000 lb (454 kg) of bombs. Wing racks were each able to hold a 250-lb (113-kg) bomb; a centreline rack had a 500-lb (227-kg) capacity. On Mk IXEs, wing buckling was an early problem, where the bomb rack was fitted directly below the cannon bay.

Receiving Mk IXs at the end of 1943, No. 241 Squadron saw out the war in Italy, engaged in tactical and shipping reconnaissance, escort and ground attack duties. Here two of its aircraft, finished in RAF temperate camouflage, are seen over Cassino, March 1944.

Above: This Mk IX was operated by the 309th Fighter Squadron, 31st Fighter Group of the US 12th Air Force and is pictured at Castel Volturno near Cassino, Italy in March 1944. Where more than 26 aircraft were assigned to a squadron – often the case after late 1943 – double code letters were assigned to the additional aircraft. The 309th's 'WZ-GG' is likely to have flown alongside an aircraft coded 'WZ-G'.

'Top cover' proved to be a relative term, however, for the Luftwaffe presented no credible high-altitude threat. The Spitfire VIIs flew the highest defensive patrols, though at altitudes of only about 20,000 ft (6100 m). After a few days, the Mk VIIs operated in the same way as other Spitfire variants, carrying out low-altitude patrols and going down to strafe road and rail targets. The fighters' pointed wingtips were replaced with the standard rounded tips to improve manoeuvrability at low altitude.

Soon after, the Mk VII's larger internal fuel tankage gave the variant a new lease of life, as a bomber escort. The longest such mission was on 11 August, when No. 131 Squadron escorted Lancasters making a daylight attack on the submarine pens at La Pallice. That 690-mile (1110-km) round trip was close to the Mk VII's maximum radius of action, leaving little fuel to go into action if enemy fighters engaged the force. The escorts flew above their charges throttled well back, hoping that by their mere presence they would deter enemy fighters. Fortunately for the Mk VII pilots, the stratagem succeeded.

In January 1945 the Spitfire VII passed out of front-line service, having had few chances to demonstrate its ability as a high-altitude interceptor.

With the Mk IX available in large numbers, there was reduced urgency to get the fully engineered Mk VIII into mass production. The first Mk VIIIs appeared in November 1942, but another seven months elapsed before production of this variant exceeded 50 per month. It was decided that the entire production of Mk VIIIs should be sent overseas, to units in the Mediterranean, Southeast Asia, southwest Pacific and Australia theatres. The need to ship the aircraft to those distant theatres further delayed the appearance of the variant in front-line service. The first unit to receive Mk VIIIs, No. 145 Squadron based in Malta, became operational only in June 1943.

In addition to the deliveries of Mk VIIIs to RAF units in Italy, the US Army Air Forces received 55 examples which operated with Mk Vs in the 308th Squadron of the 31st Fighter Group; the other squadrons in the group flew Mk IXs and Mk Vs.

Mk VIIIs in the Far East

In Southeast Asia the first Mk VIIIs arrived toward the end of 1943. Nos 81 and 152 Squadrons based at Alipore and Baigachi in eastern India converted to the new variant, soon followed by other fighter units in the theatre.

Below: Pictured at Appledram in June 1944, this LF.Mk IX of No. 310 (Czech) Squadron has been levelled off with a tail jack for the harmonisation of its gunsight and guns. Note the hastily applied 'D-Day' stripes and the serial number moved to a position on the fin.

D-Day Spitfires

Melsbroek, near Brussels, was the base in autumn 1944 for modified FR.Mk IXC armed reconnaissance aircraft operated by No. 16 Squadron. Painted pale pink, these aircraft were used for low-altitude photography. 'Invasion' stripes were painted under the rear fuselage and the undersurfaces of the wings. Oblique cameras were fitted and the 20-mm cannon were often removed. Fifteen Mk IXs were also converted to PR.Mk IX for unarmed high-altitude work, pending the arrival of the definitive Merlin-engined reconnaissance variant, the PR.Mk XI. First used operationally in November 1942, it was a PR.Mk IX that took the famous pictures of the Ruhr dams breached by No. 617 Squadron in May 1943.

Above: During the final year of the war, once air supremacy had been secured, the Merlin-engined Spitfires moved progressively to the fighter-bomber role. This German photograph shows a Spitfire strafing a ground target in Normandy in 1944.

Mk XVIs over Europe

Produced alongside Mk IXs at the Castle Bromwich Aircraft Factory, Packard Merlin-engined Mk XVIs carried the same modifications introduced in the Mk IX during production. The first examples entered service in September 1944 with No. 403 Squadron, RCAF, the variant staying in production until the end of the war and serving exclusively with RAF units in the north European theatre. Often referred to as 'LF.Mk XVIs' (as their Merlin 266s were simply US-built Merlin 66s), most had 'E' wing armament and many flew with 'clipped' wings.

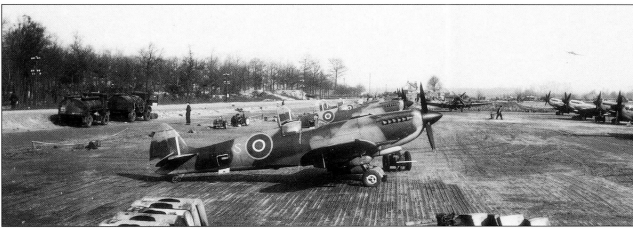

Above: Mk XVIEs of No. 443 Squadron, RCAF based at Diepholz in 1945, clearly show the effect of 'clipped' wings on the Spitfire's appearance. With the 'E' wing fitted, two Browning machine-guns were installed inboard of the cannon, which are discernible in this photograph. Also of note are the wing roundels, which have a non-standard yellow outer ring.

Initially, there was little air activity over the theatre. The Japanese Army Air Force was seriously overstretched and had to conserve its strength. The period of relative calm ended on 6 February 1944, when Japanese ground forces went on the offensive in the Arakan area. The attackers used their well-tried tactic of infiltrating forces through the jungle to get behind Allied positions, to sever their supply routes and force the troops to retreat. General William Slim, commander of the British 14th Army, had an effective answer to this enemy stratagem: he ordered the 5,000 troops

Above: Newly delivered 'clipped'-wing Mk XVIEs of No. 74 Squadron are parked on the PSP (pierced steel planking) at Schijndel in Holland in March 1945. Although they have yet to have the unit's '4D' code letters applied, a makeshift code appears to have been applied to the nearest aircraft, TB859. Some of the aircraft are bombed-up, ready for an operation with two 250-lb (113-kg) bombs under the wings and a 500-lb (227-kg) weapon under the fuselage, the maximum load it could carry against short-range targets. Stacked in the foreground ready for use are several 30-Imp gal (136-litre) drop tanks. Also in evidence are bowsers with fuel for the aircraft, and 'trolley accs' with which to start the Packard Merlins.

Notable RAF Nines

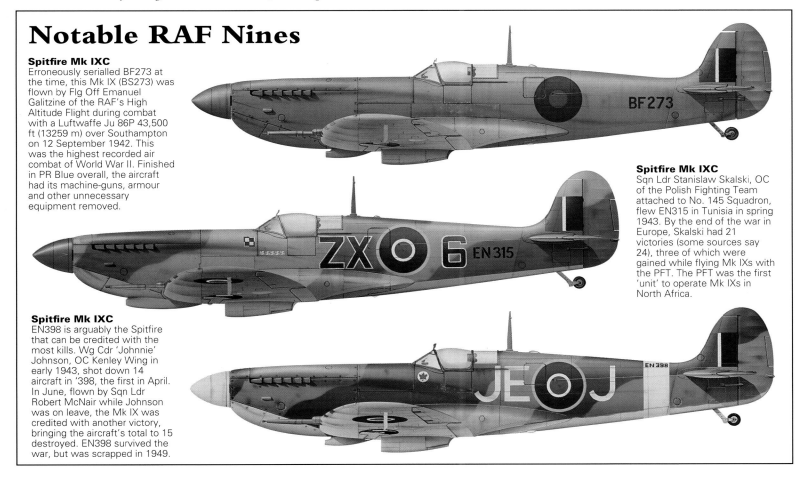

Spitfire Mk IXC
Erroneously serialled BF273 at the time, this Mk IX (BS273) was flown by Flg Off Emanuel Galitzine of the RAF's High Altitude Flight during combat with a Luftwaffe Ju 86P 43,500 ft (13259 m) over Southampton on 12 September 1942. This was the highest recorded air combat of World War II. Finished in PR Blue overall, the aircraft had its machine-guns, armour and other unnecessary equipment removed.

Spitfire Mk IXC
Sqn Ldr Stanislaw Skalski, OC of the Polish Fighting Team attached to No. 145 Squadron, flew EN315 in Tunisia in spring 1943. By the end of the war in Europe, Skalski had 21 victories (some sources say 24), three of which were gained while flying Mk IXs with the PFT. The PFT was the first 'unit' to operate Mk IXs in North Africa.

Spitfire Mk IXC
EN398 is arguably the Spitfire that can be credited with the most kills. Wg Cdr 'Johnnie' Johnson, OC Kenley Wing in early 1943, shot down 14 aircraft in '398, the first in April. In June, flown by Sqn Ldr Robert McNair while Johnson was on leave, the Mk IX was credited with another victory, bringing the aircraft's total to 15 destroyed. EN398 survived the war, but was scrapped in 1949.

Inside the Spitfire Mk IX

Left: Merlin IIIs were installed in late-production Spitfire Mk Is. Throughout the development of the Merlin-engined Spitfires, the cubic capacity of the engine remained unchanged. Power increases were gained largely through supercharger development.

Right: Although wooden and metal propellers were fitted to Spitfires, most had Jablo airscrews.

Spitfire F.Mk IXC cutaway

1 Starboard wingtip
2 Navigation light
3 Starboard aileron
4 Browning 0.303-in (7.7-mm) machine-guns
5 Machine-gun ports (patched)
6 Ammunition boxes (350 rounds per gun)
7 Aileron control rod
8 Bellcrank hinge control
9 Starboard split trailing-edge flap

19 Armoured spinner backplate
20 Coolant system header tank
21 Coolant filler cap
22 Rolls-Royce Merlin 61 liquid-cooled Vee 12-cylinder engine
23 Exhaust stubs
24 Forward engine mounting
25 Engine bottom cowling
26 Cowling integral oil tank, 5.6-Imp gal (25-litre) capacity

31 Two-stage supercharger
32 Engine bearer attachment
33 Suppressor
34 Engine accessories
35 Intercooler
36 Compressor air intake scoop
37 Hydraulic reservoir
38 Hydraulic system filter
39 Armoured firewall/fuel tank bulkhead
40 Fuel filler cap
41 Top main fuel tank, 48-Imp gal (218-litre) capacity
42 Back of instrument panel
43 Compass mounting
44 Fuel tank/longeron attachment fitting

45 Bottom main fuel tank, 37-Imp gal (168-litre) capacity
46 Rudder pedal bar
47 Sloping fuel tank bulkhead
48 Fuel cock control
49 Chart case
50 Trim control handwheel
51 Engine throttle and propeller controls
52 Control column handgrip
53 Radio controller
54 Bulletproof windscreen
55 Reflector gunsight
56 Pilot's rear view mirror
57 Canopy framing
58 Windscreen side panels
59 Sliding cockpit canopy cover
60 Headrest
61 Pilot's head armour
62 Safety harness
63 Pilot's seat
64 Side entry hatch

65 Back armour
66 Seat support frame
67 Pneumatic system air bottles
68 Fuselage main longeron
69 Auxiliary fuel tank, 29-Imp gal (132-litre) capacity, used only in conjunction with very-long-range slipper tank
70 Sliding canopy rail
71 Voltage regulator
72 Cockpit aft glazing
73 IFF radio equipment
74 HF aerial mast
75 Aerial cable lead-in
76 Radio transmitter/receiver
77 Radio compartment access hatch

78 Upper identification light
79 Rear fuselage frame construction
80 Fuselage skin plating
81 Oxygen bottle
82 Signal cartridge launcher
83 IFF aerial
84 Starboard tailplane
85 Starboard elevator

10 Aileron control cables
11 Cannon ammunition box (120 rounds)
12 Starboard 20-mm Hispano cannon
13 Ammunition feed drum
14 Cannon barrel
15 Rotol four-bladed constant speed propeller
16 Cannon barrel fairing
17 Spinner
18 Propeller hub pitch control mechanism

27 Extended carburettor air intake duct.
28 Engine bearer struts
29 Main engine mounting member
30 Oil filter

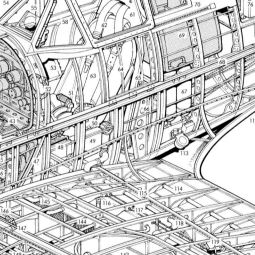

Above: The three main gun types fitted to Spitfires were, from the top: the 0.303-in (7.7-mm) Browning machine-gun (mounted in 'A', 'B' and 'C' wings); 0.5-in (12.7-mm) US Browning machine-gun ('E' wings); and two examples of the 20-mm Hispano cannon ('B', 'C' and 'E' wings).

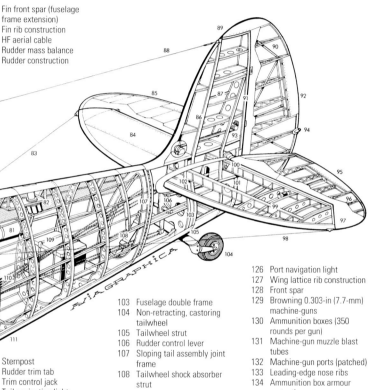

Fin front spar (fuselage frame extension)
Fin rib construction
HF aerial cable
Rudder mass balance
Rudder construction

Sternpost
Rudder trim tab
Trim control jack
Tail navigation light
Elevator tab
Port fabric-covered elevator construction
Elevator horn balance
IFF aerial cable
Tailplane rib construction
Elevator hinge control
Rudder control rod
Tailplane spar/fuselage frame attachment

103 Fuselage double frame
104 Non-retracting, castoring tailwheel
105 Tailwheel strut
106 Rudder control lever
107 Sloping tail assembly joint frame
108 Tailwheel shock absorber strut
109 Battery
110 Tail control cable runs
111 Fuselage bottom longeron
112 Wingroot trailing-edge fillet
113 Radio and electrical system ground socket
114 Trailing-edge flap shroud ribs
115 Rear wing spar
116 Radiator shutter jack
117 Aileron cable runs
118 Gun heater air duct
119 Flap hydraulic jack
120 Flap synchronising jack
121 Port split trailing-edge flap
122 Aileron control bellcrank
123 Aileron hinge control rod
124 Port aileron construction
125 Wingtip construction

126 Port navigation light
127 Wing lattice rib construction
128 Front spar
129 Browning 0.303-in (7.7-mm) machine-guns
130 Ammunition boxes (350 rounds per gun)
131 Machine-gun muzzle blast tubes
132 Machine-gun ports (patched)
133 Leading-edge nose ribs
134 Ammunition box armour protection
135 Cannon ammunition box (120 rounds)
136 Port 20-mm Hispano cannon
137 Ammunition feed drum
138 Cannon wing fairing
139 Cannon barrel
140 'C'-wing outboard cannon muzzle fairing (blanked-off)
141 Recoil spring
142 Inboard leading-edge lattice ribs
143 Main undercarriage wheel well
144 Oil radiator
145 Coolant radiator
146 Main undercarriage hydraulic jack
147 Retraction link
148 Wing spar/fuselage attachment joint
149 Oil pipe runs to radiator
150 Main undercarriage leg pivot fixing
151 Gun camera
152 Camera port
153 90-Imp gal (409-litre) jettisonable slipper tank
154 Mainwheel leg shock absorber
155 Undercarriage torque links
156 Port mainwheel
157 Mainwheel fairing door
158 Starboard mainwheel
159 Starboard wheel fairing door

Above: In this cockpit of an early production Spitfire Mk I, note the ring-and-bead gun sight and the absence of an armoured windscreen. The introduction of the reflector gunsight at the beginning of the war was a major advance. It, in turn, was superseded by the bulky but potentially very accurate gyro gunsight introduced in the Mk IX.

Left: Spitfires of Mks I, II and V shared a common cockpit. This example, equipped to a later standard than that above, has a new gun button and rudder pedals, the latter feature intended to improve rudder control during combat manoeuvres. The lever at the bottom of the picture controls the radiator intake flap.

Right: This is the right-hand side of the Spitfire cockpit illustrated above. Compared to those who flew the Messerschmitt Bf 109, the Spitfire's pilots enjoyed a relatively spacious cockpit. This was important during combat, for the pilots of these aircraft had enough space to apply more leverage to the control column during manoeuvres. By contrast, Bf 109 pilots had limited 'elbow room' in which to move.

Above: The Mk V was the first Spitfire variant to be equipped for air-to-ground roles, as illustrated in this photograph of a Mk VB carrying a 250-lb (113-kg) bomb under each wing.

Right and below right: Underwing 250-lb (113-kg) bomb installations on a Mk IXC aircraft.

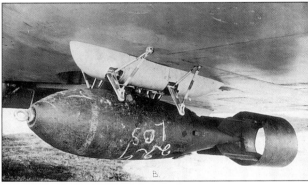

Among a number of air-to-ground weapons trialled on Spitfires was this rocket installation, using four on zero-length launchers, seen here fitted to a Mk IXC.

Above: This Spitfire Mk IX of No. 74 Squadron is fitted with a single launcher for a 60-lb (27-kg) rocket under each wing, of the type used by the RAF's Hawker Typhoons. This weapon was rather inaccurate, and most other fighter-bomber types ripple-fired eight or more to give a reasonable chance of hitting a small target. The two-rocket installation for the Spitfire appears to have been unique to this unit, and it saw little use.

cut off at Sinzweya to stand firm, and, relying on the Spitfires to maintain air superiority, transport planes supplied the outpost until it could be relieved. Nos 67, 81 and 152 Squadrons with Spitfire VIIIs moved to Ramu near the India/Burma border, from where they flew offensive patrols and escort missions. The airlift by heavily laden Dakota and Commando transport planes proceeded unhindered.

With the British and Commonwealth forces standing firm, it was the Japanese troops that now had problems. The latter had expected to live on food in the Allied stores they overran, but, supplied by air, the defenders held their ground and the food stores remained in their hands. Once

the Japanese soldiers had eaten what they carried in their backpacks, they went hungry. Lacking any effective means of resupply, they attempted to survive on the meagre fare they found in the jungle. When that proved insufficient, the starving infiltrators abandoned their positions and began the trudge to their own territory. The siege of Sinzweya ended on 23 February.

Spitfires rule the skies

The success achieved at Sinzweya served as a pattern to defeat the main Japanese offensive in Burma, launched in March 1944. Again the attackers infiltrated through the jungle, to cut off 55,000 Allied troops at Kohima and Imphal. Again the garrisons stood firm, supplied by a large-scale airlift. And, again, starvation forced the attackers to break off the action and retreat. Throughout, the Spitfires ruled the skies and during the 80 days of the airlift only three transport planes were lost to enemy action. It was a major victory for the Allies, and the Spitfire VIIIs had made it possible.

The Royal Australian Air Force received a total of 410 Mk VIIIs, with the first of them arriving at Melbourne in October 1943. Five squadrons in the south Pacific area were equipped with this variant. In the summer of 1945 No. 80 Wing, RAAF, commanded by fighter ace Group Captain Clive Caldwell, moved to New Guinea. By this time Japanese air activity over the southwest Pacific area had virtually ended, however. With little opportunity for air-to-air combat, the wing engaged mainly in ground attack operations.

The Mk XVI was a Mk IX airframe fitted with the Merlin 266 engine, a Merlin 66 manufactured under licence by the US Packard company. Externally the Mks IX and XVI were identical in appearance, and they were little different in performance. The Packard engine was manufactured to

American measurements, however, and servicing tools and spare parts were not interchangeable between the Rolls-Royce and Packard engines. To prevent confusion, therefore, the Packard-engined version was designated the Mk XVI.

Mk XVIs started to come off the production line at Castle Bromwich in October 1944. At the beginning of December, No. 403 Squadron based at Evère near Brussels was the first unit to exchange its Mk IXs for Mk XVIs. Other Mk IX units in the 2nd Tactical Air Force quickly followed and when the war in Europe ended, a total of 19 squadrons had re-equipped with this variant.

Four major improvements to the Mk IX and the Mk XVI

The Spitfire Mks IX and XVI were the last Merlin-engined fighter variants in production. To improve their combat capabilities, both had four major improvements incorporated: the gyro gunsight, the fitting of the 'E'-type wing and armament, the fitting of the bubble canopy, and the installation of additional fuel tanks.

1. The gyro gunsight

No matter how fast, how manoeuvrable or how heavily armed a fighter was, those factors counted for little if only a small proportion of the rounds it fired hit their target. With the fixed-graticule GM2 reflector sight previously fitted to

Late-war Spitfires

the Spitfire, the pilot had to judge the deflection angle when engaging a manoeuvring or crossing target. The ability to do this quickly and accurately was one of the main skills that separated the ace pilot from the also-ran.

After four years of development at the Royal Aircraft Establishment at Farnborough, the gyro gunsight Mk II went into large-scale production at the end of 1943. This sophisticated predictor sight calculated the correct point in

Above: Flaps down, a pair of Mk XVIEs of No. 74 Squadron is about to land at B.105/Droppe in western Germany after one of the unit's last missions of the war, in April 1945.

Left: Carrying a 45-Imp gal (204-litre) drop tank, this Mk XVIE of No. 403 Squadron, RCAF takes off from Soltau in Germany in July 1945. Though equipped with 'clipped' wings and the later-pattern broad-chord rudder, it is an early-build aircraft with the original-type cockpit.

Mk XVIs of 'B' Flight, No. 443 Squadron, RCAF are seen at Diepholz in April 1945. One of the last RCAF squadrons to be deployed to Europe, No. 443 flew its first sorties with No. 144 Wing just before D-Day. Mk XVIs replaced the unit's Mk IXs in January 1945.

'High back' Mk XVIEs of No. 74 Squadron are seen at their PSP (pierced steel planking) dispersal point at Schijndel in the spring of 1945.

Packard Merlin Spitfire

Spitfire LF.Mk XVIE
TB675 was one of No. 74 Squadron's Mk XVIs engaged in ground attack missions in the last days of the war in Europe. It exhibits most of the modifications made to Mk IX/XVI aircraft during production, including 'clipped' wings, a tropical filter, 'rear-view fuselage', broad-chord rudder and bomb racks.

Above: Before being dispatched to Australia as part of the wing sent to defend the Dominion from Japanese attacks, No. 457 Squadron, RAAF operated Spitfire Mk I, II and V aircraft from bases in England between mid-1941 and mid-1942. In Australia it flew tropicalised Mk Vs and Mk VIIIs.

Above: Three fighter squadrons, known collectively as the 'Eagle' squadrons, were manned by American volunteers before the US entered the war after Pearl Harbor. This Mk V carries the codes of No. 121 Squadron. With Nos 71 and 133 Squadrons, this unit became the 4th Fighter Group 'The Eagles', US 8th Air Force in September 1942.

Right: Spitfire Mk Vs of No. 401 Squadron, RCAF perform a flypast over Biggin Hill in September 1943. Of the foreign and Commonwealth countries that made personnel available to the RAF during the war, Canada contributed by far the largest number.

A Spitfire Mk VB of No. 312 (Czech) Squadron has the 'trolley acc' starter batteries plugged in, at its dispersal at Harrowbeer in the spring of 1942. No. 312 was one of two Czech RAF units to operate Spitfires, the other being No. 313 Squadron.

the sky ahead of the target, at which the pilot needed to aim his guns in order to score hits. It took time for pilots to learn the foibles of the new sight. However, once the average squadron pilot had done so, the accuracy of his deflection shooting improved dramatically. During 1944 an analysis of 130 combats by Spitfire IXs fitted with fixed-graticule sights showed there had been 34 kills – 26 per cent of the total. During the same period, a squadron operating the same variant with the new gunsight fought 38 combats and secured 19 kills – 50 per cent of the total. In other words, the use of the new gunsight had virtually doubled the effectiveness of a unit's air-to-air gunnery. With the new sight pilots, could hit evading targets at deflection angles of up to 50°, at ranges as great as 1,800 ft (548 m).

Many fighter aces refused to have the new gunsight in their aircraft, however. It was necessary to track the target for a few seconds while the mechanism calculated the deflection angle, and that was an unwanted inconvenience to those pilots who could judge the angle at a glance. For the rest of the Allied fighter force, however, the new gunsight brought a considerable and one-sided advantage in combat (the German equivalent, the EZ 42, came too late and saw little use in combat).

During the final months of the war, the Spitfire and other Allied piston-engined fighters had to battle with the much faster German jet types. The improvement in air-to-air gunnery brought about by the new sight helped compensate for their inferior performance, and assisted them to maintain air superiority in what might otherwise have been a difficult period.

2. 'E'-type wing and revised armament

From the spring of 1941 until the summer of 1944, the great majority of Spitfire fighter variants carried the standard armament of two 20-mm Hispano cannon and four 0.303-in Browning machine-guns. In air-to-air combat the four Browning machine-guns were of questionable value, however. By the latter stages of the war, nearly all combat aircraft had their vital areas armoured to protect them against hits with rifle-calibre rounds. Moreover, the Spitfire's 0.303-in weapons were mounted in the outer wings, which flexed when the pilot pulled *g*. When the machine-guns were fired under those conditions, the rounds went in a direction rather different from that in which the gunsight was pointing.

Above: A Mk VB of No. 302 (Polish) Squadron sports the four white nose stripes worn by many Spitfire units during the Dieppe landing operations of 19 August 1942. The aircraft was flown on that day by Wg Cdr Stefan Witorzenc, commanding the 1st Polish Fighter Wing.

Below: Coded '3W', this 'clipped'-wing aircraft was one of a number of Spitfires of Mks V, IX, XIV and XVI flown by Dutch pilots.

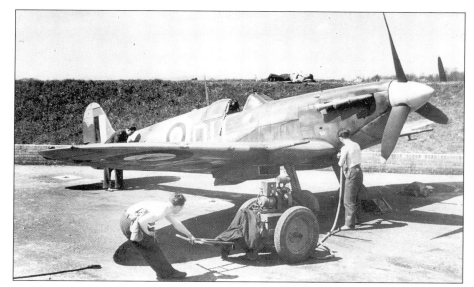

Neutral Spitfires

Neutral governments in Turkey, Portugal and Egypt were supplied with Spitfires at various stages during World War II, largely as a way of maintaining the favourable disposition of these states towards the Allies. Aircraft were supplied in large numbers to the Soviet Union.

This is one of the 18 by-then-surplus Spitfire Mk IAs supplied to Portugal in 1942 to equip a unit at Tancos Aerial Base, later transferred to Ota. The Azores Agreement, signed in 1943, was followed by the delivery of 33 ex-RAF Mk VBs to equip two more squadrons. Others were supplied after 1945.

During 1944, the US Browning 0.5-in (12.7 mm) machine-gun became available to the RAF in quantity. The Spitfire's wings were redesigned to house two of these weapons and two 20-mm cannon, all of them in the stiffer inboard wing section. The two 20-mm weapons were moved to the outer cannon positions, while the 0.5-in machine-guns went into the spaces previously occupied by the inboard cannon. The 0.5-in weapon delivered a greater penetrative punch than the rifle-calibre weapons it replaced, and it was considerably more effective for both air-to-air and air-to-ground firing.

3. The bubble canopy

Most pilots shot down in fighter-versus-fighter combat never saw their assailant before their aircraft was hit. Most of the surprise attacks came from the fighter's blind zone, to the rear and below. Anything that reduced the size of that blind zone would reduce the chance of a successful surprise attack. And, obviously, anything that improved a fighter's chances of survival in action increased its effectiveness by a correspondingly amount.

As on several other late-war fighter types, the rearward view was greatly improved by cutting back the Spitfire's rear fuselage and fitting a bubble canopy. A Spitfire VIII modified in this way went to the Air Fighting Development Unit at Duxford for service evaluation in the summer of 1943. Several experienced service pilots flew the aircraft and were extremely impressed with the improvement in the field of view. Their report on the aircraft stated: "This is an enormous improvement over the standard Spitfire rear view. The pilot can see quite easily round to his fin and past it, almost to the further edge of the tailplane, i.e. if he looks over his left shoulder he can practically see to the starboard tip of the tail. By banking the aircraft slightly

Aircraft '01' was one of the two PR.Mk IVs handed over to the Soviet air force. It is believed to be one of four Spitfire Mk IVs originally detached to Vaenga in northern Russia in the autumn of 1942, to fly reconnaissance missions over northern Norway. Note the oblique camera fitted behind the fuselage. In all, 1,333 Spitfires were delivered to the Red air force.

during weaving action, the downward view to the rear is opened up well."

Spitfire Mk IXs and XVIs fitted with the new canopy began reaching the operational squadrons early in 1945, where they immediately became popular with pilots.

4. Additional fuel tanks in the rear fuselage

Throughout the war the Spitfire's short radius of action had been a source of embarrassment when it flew offensive operations over enemy territory. The drop tank was one answer, but it caused additional drag and had to be jettisoned before the aircraft went into action. The Mks VII and VIII had small additional tanks fitted in the wing, but there was room for even more fuel inside the airframe.

By repositioning some items of equipment that had been in the rear fuselage, there was room to install a couple of additional fuel tanks there. In Mk IXs and XVIs with the old-style canopy, these tanks had a total capacity of 72 Imp

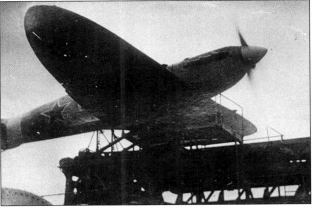

Above: Turkey remained neutral until 1 March 1945, when war was declared on Germany. Diplomatic efforts to curry favour with the Turkish government before this date included the supply of enough Spitfire Mk Vs to form a squadron in 1944. Eventually, 84 were supplied.

*Below left: One of the Spitfire Mk Vs delivered to the Soviet Union was used for catapult trials aboard the cruiser **Molotov** in 1946.*

Below: Spitfire Mk Vs en route to the Soviet air force await collection by Soviet pilots at Abadan, Iran early in 1943. These ex-RAF machines had, in many cases, seen considerable action. The nearest aircraft, BM185, had previously served with Nos 403 and 111 Squadrons, while the next aircraft, AD236, had flown with four squadrons and had received repairs after serious damage.

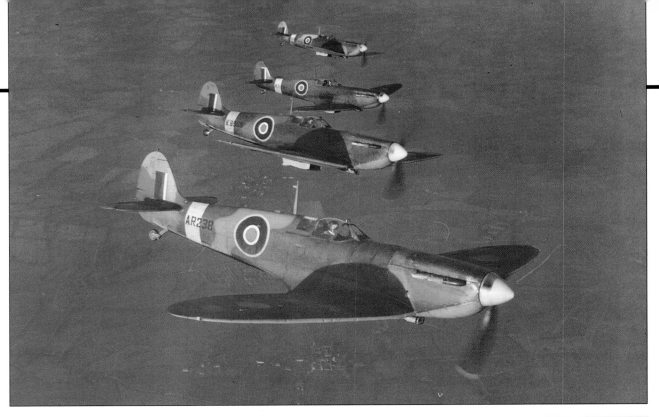

'Hooked' Spitfires

The Fleet Air Arm's first Seafires were converted Spitfire Mk VBs, a stopgap until production Seafire Mk IICs were available. FAA training units also flew around 100 unmodified Spitfires for training, some of which were fitted with arrester hooks to enable their use for deck landing training aboard carriers.

'Hooked' Spitfires (which retained their RAF serials) were used by the FAA for carrier training. Here, BL818, then of No. 768 Squadron, the Deck Landing Training School, is seen being hauled back on to the deck of HMS Ravager after a landing mishap on 10 August 1944.

gal (327 litres). In later production aircraft with bubble canopies, the total capacity of the extra tanks was reduced to 64 Imp gal (290 litres). The additional fuel gave a useful increase in the Spitfire's operational radius of action during the final months of the war.

Spitfire fighter-bomber

In 1944, following the large-scale introduction into service of the Griffon-powered Spitfires and other high-performance new Allied fighter types, the Merlin-powered Spitfire units moved progressively from air superiority to fighter-bomber operations.

Flying Officer David Green flew Mk IXs with No. 73 Squadron over Italy and Yugoslavia. He described the tactics employed during a typical dive-bombing attack by Spitfires: "Carrying two 250-lb [114-kg] bombs, the Spitfire made a very fine dive bomber. It could attack accurately and didn't need a fighter escort, because as soon as the bombs had been released it was a fighter. The briefing beforehand had to be good enough for us to be able to fly right up to the target even if we had never been there before, identify it and bomb it. Because the flak was often accurate, we didn't want to spend time circling in the target area before we went down to attack.

"We normally operated in sections of four, and would fly to the target at 10,000 ft [3050 m] in finger-four battle formation. We would make for an Initial Point decided at the briefing, a distinctive point on the ground in the target area with, ideally, a linear feature like a road, a river or a railway line leading to the target itself. By the time it reached the IP, the formation would have increased speed to 260 mph Indicated (about 305 mph/491 km/h, True) and we would be flying in loose echelon to starboard, ready to begin the dive. As the target came into view I would position it so that it appeared to be running down the line of my port cannon. As the target disappeared under the wing I would hold my heading, and when the target emerged from under the trailing edge I would pull the aircraft up to kill the forward speed, roll it over on its back and let the nose drop until the target was lined up in the gunsight graticule. That way one got the Spitfire to go down in the correct angle of dive of 60°. It is a pretty steep dive, it felt as if one was going down vertically. The other aircraft in the section, Nos 2, 3, and 4, would be following me down still in echelon.

"It was important to trim the aircraft nose-down, otherwise the pressure on the stick would become enormous as the speed built up and the Spitfire tried to pull itself out of

Second-line aircraft

As later Spitfire marks entered RAF service, earlier aircraft were transferred to advanced flying schools and operational training units. Here, a trainee fighter pilot takes his first solo in a No. 61 OTU aircraft.

Once they had been replaced in front-line units, Spitfires were employed in a host of second-line tasks. This LF.Mk VB served with No. 1688 Flight, Bomber Command, for target towing, fighter affiliation and other miscellaneous duties. Note the fixed towing hook mounted behind the tailwheel.

Left: The Air Fighting Development Unit (AFDU), which was based at Duxford and, later, Wittering, was equipped largely with Spitfires and Hurricanes. In the course of the war, the AFDU flew a number of types in its role as a tactical training school.

the dive. During the dive the speed built up rapidly and it was important to keep an eye on one's height, because the altimeter lag was considerable. When the altimeter read 5,000 ft (1524 m) above the target altitude, indicated, that meant the true altitude above the target was about 4,000 ft (1920 m). I would let my go my bombs and call 'Bombs gone!'; the other chaps in the section would then release theirs. At the time of release the aircraft would be doing about 420 mph Indicated (about 450 mph/724 km/h, True).

"If there had been little or no flak, the desire to see the results of the bombing was usually so great that I would pull hard on the stick to bring the aircraft out of the dive and into a slight climb, so that I could look over my shoulder to see where the bombs had gone. But if we were being fired at, we would use our high forward speed to get us down to ground level where there was cover."

The Mk IX, and the almost identical Mk XVI, marked the zenith of development of the Merlin-engined Spitfire fighter. Ironically, the stopgap variants of the Spitfire were built in the largest numbers. Large-scale production of the

Spitfires in Swastikas

A number of Spitfires are known to have been captured and flown by the Luftwaffe, including examples of Mks I, V and XI. As well as being evaluated against German types at the Luftwaffe's Rechlin test centre, some of these machines took part in propaganda films which were released as 'real footage' purporting to show RAF fighters being successfully engaged by the Luftwaffe.

Rare colour shots, from a German source, show the camouflage worn by RAF fighters during the Battle of Britain. Spitfire N3277 is seen (below) after it made a forced landing near Cherbourg on 15 August 1940, during the application of German markings. The same aircraft (above right) is seen after the application of markings is complete, being inspected by Luftwaffe pilots.

Above: At least one captured Spitfire was repainted in spurious British markings for propaganda photographs, which were later published in wartime German periodicals.

A remarkable modification was carried out by the Daimler-Benz company on a captured Mk VB (EN830) in the autumn of 1943. The British fighter had a DB.605 engine installed, and later it underwent flight testing in this condition. The reason for the change is unclear, however. Given the increasingly desperate military position facing Germany at the time, it appears to have been an extravagant waste of effort by highly skilled technicians.

Above: Stripped of its camouflage and carrying Flying Training Command codes, RW396 was with the Central Gunnery School at Leconfield when this photograph was taken, some time after 1946. Most of those Merlin-engined Spitfires that served with the RAF post-war were Mk XVIs, like this late-production Mk XVIE delivered in July 1945.

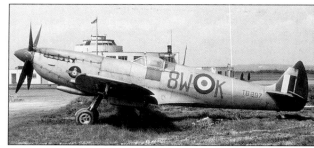

No. 612 'County of Aberdeen' Squadron, originally an army co-operation unit disbanded in 1945, reformed as an Auxiliary Air Force fighter squadron in 1946, equipped with Spitfire Mk XVIs. It flew them until 1951, the year in which the RAF retired its last Merlin-engined Spitfires.

Mk IX began in June 1942 and the last of more than 6,700 Mk IXs and Mk XVIs was delivered in June 1945.

The career of the Merlin-engined Spitfire fighter in front-line RAF units did not long survive the end of World War II. Large numbers of these aircraft were exported. They served with nearly a score of foreign air forces and saw action in half a dozen small-scale conflicts. The last service to employ Merlin-engined Spitfires in action was the Burmese air force. That service purchased 30 reconditioned Mk IXs from Israel in 1954, and used them in attacks on rebel troop positions during the long-running Burmese civil war.

Spitfires built for two

The two-seat Spitfire was first proposed in 1941, as a means of providing a transition trainer for future Spitfire pilots. Nothing came of the plan during the war, though a Mk V is known to have been fitted with a second seat by No. 261 Squadron, RAF in 1944 and a Mk IX was similarly converted by the Soviet air force. The plan was revived in 1946, when a Mk VIII was converted by Supermarine and demonstrated to RAF Reserve Command, which had a requirement for 20 examples. However, an RAF order never came. Overseas interest, on the other hand, led to 'production' conversions of 20 Mk IX aircraft for the air forces of Egypt, India, the Netherlands and the Republic of Ireland. Orders from Argentina (10 aircraft) and Iraq (six) were cancelled. Several of these aircraft, now privately owned, were airworthy in 1997.

Merlin-powered Spitfire development

Rolls-Royce provided the impetus for the long-running campaign to improve the Spitfire's performance, relying on the ability of its engineers to squeeze extra power from successive variants of the Merlin engine. The Merlin III fitted to the Spitfire I developed 1,030 hp (768 kW) at 16,250 ft (4950 m). With the same 27-litre capacity, the Merlin 61 fitted to the Spitfire IX gave 1,565 hp (1167 kW)

Above: This Spitfire Mk IX UTI was converted by the Soviet air force in 1944/45. The number so-treated is unknown. No. 261 Squadron, RAF's 1944 Mk V conversion differed in having a second open cockpit in front of the original cockpit.

Bearing the Class 'B' registration N32, this T.Mk 8 was the first of a number of two-seat trainer conversions made after 1946. Formerly Mk VIII MT818, N32 was later registered G-AIDN and sold. It remained airworthy in 1997.

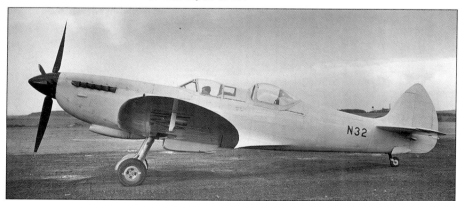

Above: Egypt took delivery of just one T.Mk 9, in 1950. Serialled 684, it had been used as Supermarine's demonstrator, registered G-ALJM.

H-99 (with its former RAF serial number BS147 on the fin) was one of three T.Mk 9s operated by the Royal Dutch Air Force between 1948 and the early 1950s. The others were serialled H-97 and H-98.

Above: The Irish Air Corps used six Spitfire trainers in the 1960s. Fitting a second cockpit to the Spitfire necessitated moving the original cockpit 13.5 in (34.3 cm) forward.

Spitfires at war post-1945

Significant numbers of ex-RAF Merlin-engined Spitfires were to see further service after 1945, principally in wars of self-determination in the Middle East and Far East. Perhaps the most famous of these were the Mk IXs flown by Israel's fledgling defence force. The first Israeli Spitfires were two aircraft assembled from abandoned RAF and captured Egyptian airframes; others were obtained from Czechoslovakia and, after 1949, Italy.

Above: This Spitfire Mk IX, 664 coded 'L', of No. 2 Squadron, Royal Egyptian Air Force was captured on 29 September 1948. It had come down, more or less intact, in Israeli territory and was promptly trucked to Tel Aviv and rebuilt for IAF service. During the fighting of 1948, a number of other downed REAF Mk IXs were cannibalised for parts to keep the IAF's hard-pressed aircraft in the air.

at 11,250 ft (3430 m) – an increase in power of more than 40 per cent.

In aircraft engineering one rarely gets something for nothing, however. With their greater power, the later Merlin engines were somewhat heavier than their predecessors. For example, the Merlin 61 installation, with the additional plumbing necessary for the intercooler, was about 300 lb (136 kg) heavier than the Merlin III installation.

Lead ballast

To convert the additional rotational power into thrust as efficiently as possible, it was necessary to fit a propeller with greater solidity. The Spitfire I entered service fitted with a fixed-pitch two-bladed propeller weighing 83 lb (37 kg). The Mk IX had a four-bladed constant speed airscrew weighing about 600 lb (272 kg). The addition of so much extra weight at the extreme nose would have made the aircraft too nose-heavy, so, to restore the centre of gravity to its normal place, the early Mk IXs carried 185 lb (84 kg) of lead ballast in rear fuselage.

Application of the hard-won lessons of air combat led to further increases in weight. The RAF demanded the installation of plate armour to protect the pilot and vulnerable parts of the structure. It also ordered the installation of additional equipment and more powerful (and therefore heavier) batteries of cannon and machine-guns.

Below: After World War II, France's Armée de l'Air became the largest foreign operator of Spitfires. It took delivery of about 500 Mk Vs, VIIIs, IXs and XVIs. This Mk IX belonged to the Groupe de Chasse 'La Fayette', based at Hanoi in December 1947, in what was then French Indo-China. Within a few months the unit would provide support for French ground forces during the opening stages of the war in Vietnam.

Above: The motley collection of Mk IXs gathered together by Israel's Heyl Ha'Avir (air force) in the late 1940s gave sterling service alongside P-51D Mustangs and Avia S.199s during the 1948 War of Independence, during which they were famously pitted against Egyptian Spitfire Mk Vs and IXs (used in the bombing role on several occasions) and Griffon-engined RAF examples. By 1956, the last IDF Spitfires had been retired.

Below: Having established an air force in the early 1950s with, among other types, a flight of Griffon-engined Mk XVIIIs, the Union of Burma took delivery of ex-Israeli Mk IXs in 1955. These aircraft and a number of Sea Furies supported Chinese and Burmese troops in attacks on CIA-supported Kuomintang (KMT) nationalists during 1960/61.

Armée de l'Air Mk IX fighter-bombers fly 'somewhere over French Indo-China'. The first French air force fighter unit in the region (GC II/7) was formed at Tan Son Nhut, near Saigon in December 1945, using Spitfire Mk VIIIs borrowed from the RAF pending the delivery of Mk IXs in January. Spitfires served with the French in the region until 1950.

Above: Former foes meet in the skies over Turkey. Having signed a non-aggression pact with Germany in 1941, only to declare war on the Nazis in 1945, Turkey had an air force of varied types by 1945. One hundred Fw 190As had been delivered in 1944, before Turkey had broken off diplomatic relations; an example is seen here with a Spitfire Mk V.

Below: Part of the 77-strong force of Spitfire Mk IXs supplied to the Czech air force after the war, these machines served with the 3rd Air Division at Brno in 1947.

Surplus Spitfires

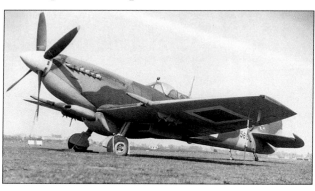

Above: Post-war, Turkey received a large amount of military equipment from Britain, including around 140 Spitfires, most of which were Mk IXs. This is a 'clipped'-wing Mk IXE, with bomb racks and a belly tank fitted.

Above: An ex-No. 318 Squadron Spitfire Mk IXE is seen shortly after being handed over to the Italian air force in August 1946. Italy took delivery of 99 Mk IXs after the war, some of which later served in Israel.

Above: A large collection of Spitfire Mk VCs of No. 335 Squadron, Royal Hellenic Air Force is seen at Elevsis in 1945. Mk Vs were retained by the RHAF for training purposes as late as 1951. Mk IXs were obtained in 1947.

Cumulatively, those increases in weight became significant. The Mk I in early production form had an all-up weight of 5,819 lb (2639 kg), while that of a late production Mk IX was 7,400 lb (3356 kg). That increase amounted to nearly 30 per cent. With the fighter sitting on the ground the difference was unimportant, but in combat it was a different matter. If a pilot pulled 6g in a turn, every part of the aircraft weighed six times more. If the structure was insufficiently strong to withstand the additional forces, it would collapse. To cope with the progressive increases in weight, the airframe of the Spitfire had to be strengthened

Above: Mk IXs of the JachtVlieg School (Fighter Training School) of the Royal Dutch Air Force based at Twenthe, Holland. After the war that service received 76 examples of the variant. This 'clipped'-wing example lands at Twenthe in August 1950.

Norwegian Nine

Spitfire F.Mk IXE
Having flown Spitfires in the RAF, Norwegian pilots continued to use the type post-war. Fifty Spitfires were purchased – 47 Mk IXs and three Mk XIs. They were operated until 1954. This aircraft few with the post-war No. 332 Squadron, RNAF, from Gardermoen in 1948.

Tugs and film stars

Above: Possibly the most spectacular use of Spitfires in a modern motion picture was during the filming of the epic Battle of Britain *production during 1968. Gp Capt T. G. 'Hamish' Mahaddie's company Film Aviation Services amassed this impressive collection of airworthy and static Spitfires of various marks, including a T.Mk 9. Here they are seen at RAF Henlow, with three Hawker Hurricanes.*

Below: Painted to represent a Battle of Britain period Spitfire Mk I for the film, this aircraft has a spurious serial number and code letters.

Above: For the film The Longest Day, *three ex-COGEA aircraft were painted in semi-accurate RAF markings of the mid-1944 period. Here OO-ARD (formerly MH415) poses with other COGEA aircraft, including OO-ARA (MH434). This latter aircraft was airworthy in 1997, owned by the Old Flying Machine Company at Duxford aerodrome, England.*

Above: Belgian company Compagnie Générale d'Exploitation Aérienne (COGEA) Nouvelle operated six Mk IXs in the gunnery target-towing and army co-operation roles from Ravensijde aerodrome, near Ostend. All were ex-Belgian air force aircraft purchased in 1956 and finally retired by COGEA in the early 1960s.

Below: Aircraft 'N3321' had another set of codes applied during the filming of Battle of Britain. Prepared to a common standard, all Spitfires used in the production were equipped with four-bladed propellers.

Left: Television series set during wartime have also utilised preserved Spitfires for flying sequences. At Charlton Park, England in February 1988 during the filming of Piece of Cake, the late 'Hoof' Proudfoot sweeps the set in The Fighter Collection's LF.Mk IX ML417 (refitted with standard wingtips). ML417 was one of 10 Mk IXs converted to T.Mk 9s for the Indian Air Force and was 'deconverted' during restoration.

from time to time to restore the safe load factor of the airframe. And, naturally, each such strengthening brought with it its own weight increase.

Standard wing

Apart from the high-altitude variants fitted with pointed wingtips, the Merlin-powered fighters had no increase in wing area. The early production Mk I had a wing loading of 24 lb/sq ft (1.01 kg/m²) while that of the Mk IX was 30.5 lb/sq ft (1.28 kg/m²). Each improvement in performance, fire power, range or capability added a further twist to the spiral of increased weight, causing a progressive deterioration in the fighter's handling characteristics. Alex Henshaw, chief test pilot at the Castle Bromwich factory, personally test flew more than 2,000 Spitfires. He summed up the changes in the fighter's handling characteristics in these words:

"I loved the Spitfire, in all of her many versions. But I have to admit that the later marks, although they were faster than the earlier ones, were also much heavier and so did not handle so well. You did not have such positive control over them. One test of manoeuvrability was to throw the Spitfire into a flick roll and see how many times she rolled. With the Mk II or the Mk V one got two and a half flick rolls, but the Mk IX was heavier and you got only one and a half. With the later and still heavier versions one got even less. The essence of aircraft design is compromise, and an improvement at one end of the performance envelope is rarely achieved without a deterioration somewhere else."

Dr Alfred Price

Spitfire Colours

Great Britain

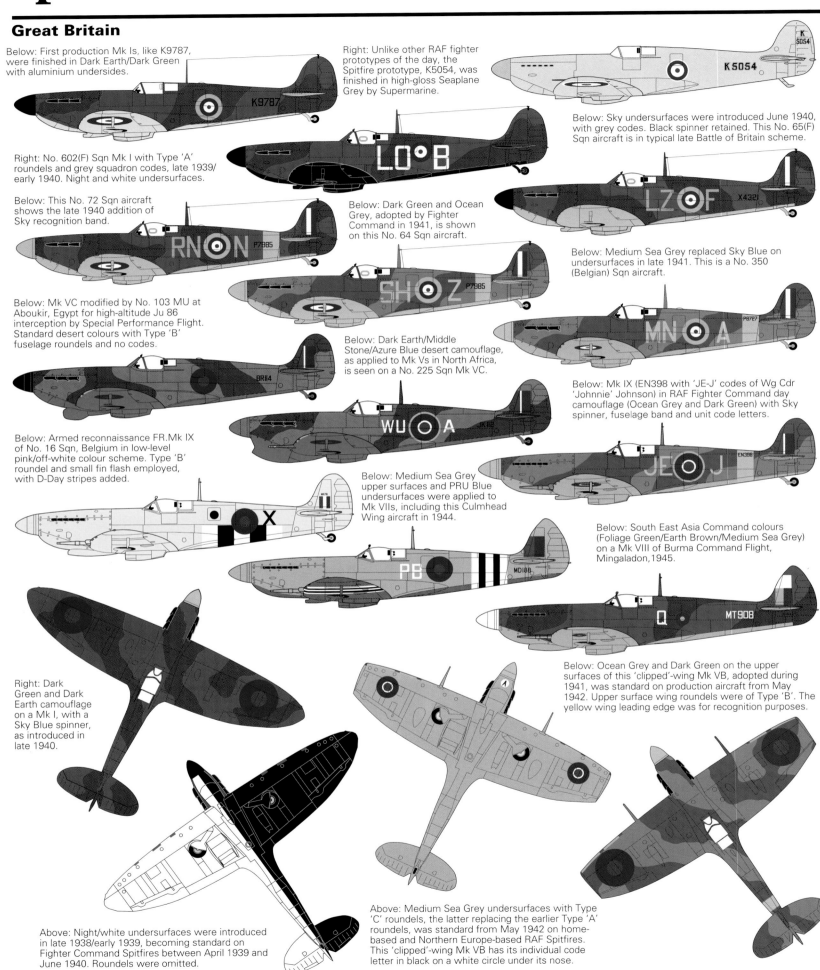

Below: First production Mk Is, like K9787, were finished in Dark Earth/Dark Green with aluminium undersides.

Right: Unlike other RAF fighter prototypes of the day, the Spitfire prototype, K5054, was finished in high-gloss Seaplane Grey by Supermarine.

Below: Sky undersurfaces were introduced June 1940, with grey codes. Black spinner retained. This No. 65(F) Sqn aircraft is in typical late Battle of Britain scheme.

Right: No. 602(F) Sqn Mk I with Type 'A' roundels and grey squadron codes, late 1939/early 1940. Night and white undersurfaces.

Below: This No. 72 Sqn aircraft shows the late 1940 addition of Sky recognition band.

Below: Dark Green and Ocean Grey, adopted by Fighter Command in 1941, is shown on this No. 64 Sqn aircraft.

Below: Medium Sea Grey replaced Sky Blue on undersurfaces in late 1941. This is a No. 350 (Belgian) Sqn aircraft.

Below: Mk VC modified by No. 103 MU at Aboukir, Egypt for high-altitude Ju 86 interception by Special Performance Flight. Standard desert colours with Type 'B' fuselage roundels and no codes.

Below: Dark Earth/Middle Stone/Azure Blue desert camouflage, as applied to Mk Vs in North Africa, is seen on a No. 225 Sqn Mk VC.

Below: Mk IX (EN398 with 'JE-J' codes of Wg Cdr 'Johnnie' Johnson) in RAF Fighter Command day camouflage (Ocean Grey and Dark Green) with Sky spinner, fuselage band and unit code letters.

Below: Armed reconnaissance FR.Mk IX of No. 16 Sqn, Belgium in low-level pink/off-white colour scheme. Type 'B' roundel and small fin flash employed, with D-Day stripes added.

Below: Medium Sea Grey upper surfaces and PRU Blue undersurfaces were applied to Mk VIIs, including this Culmhead Wing aircraft in 1944.

Below: South East Asia Command colours (Foliage Green/Earth Brown/Medium Sea Grey) on a Mk VIII of Burma Command Flight, Mingaladon, 1945.

Right: Dark Green and Dark Earth camouflage on a Mk I, with a Sky Blue spinner, as introduced in late 1940.

Above: Night/white undersurfaces were introduced in late 1938/early 1939, becoming standard on Fighter Command Spitfires between April 1939 and June 1940. Roundels were omitted.

Above: Medium Sea Grey undersurfaces with Type 'C' roundels, the latter replacing the earlier Type 'A' roundels, was standard from May 1942 on home-based and Northern Europe-based RAF Spitfires. This 'clipped'-wing Mk VB has its individual code letter in black on a white circle under its nose.

Below: Ocean Grey and Dark Green on the upper surfaces of this 'clipped'-wing Mk VB, adopted during 1941, was standard on production aircraft from May 1942. Upper surface wing roundels were of Type 'B'. The yellow wing leading edge was for recognition purposes.

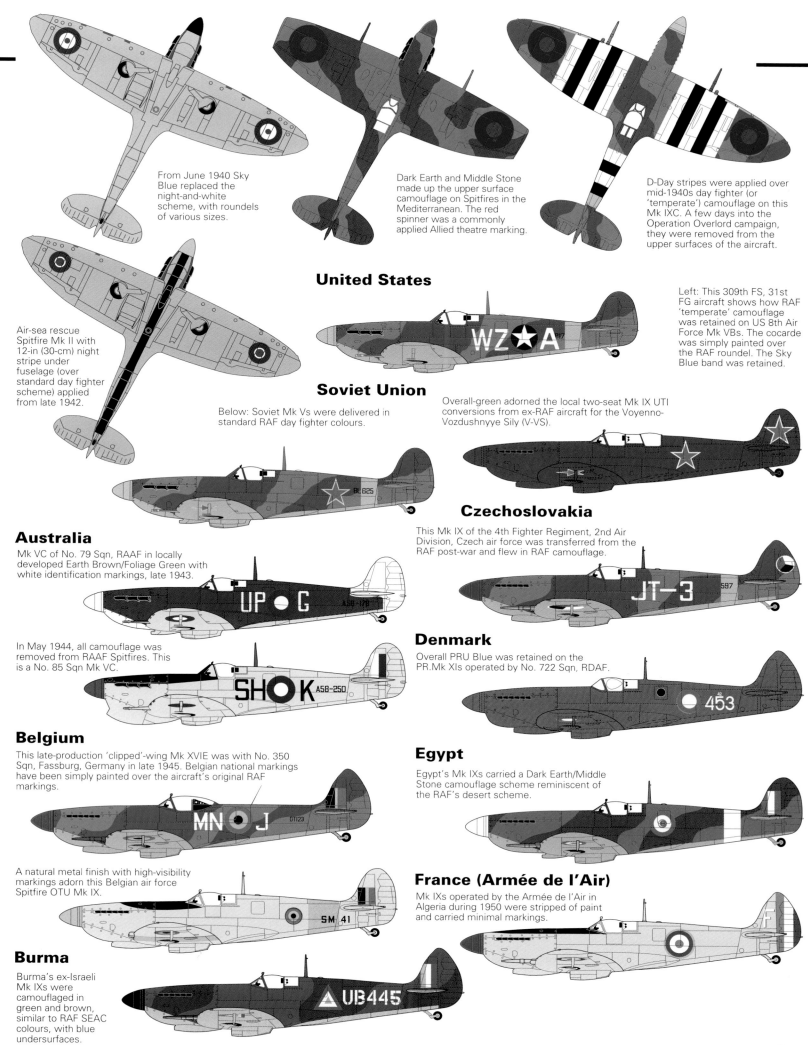

From June 1940 Sky Blue replaced the night-and-white scheme, with roundels of various sizes.

Dark Earth and Middle Stone made up the upper surface camouflage on Spitfires in the Mediterranean. The red spinner was a commonly applied Allied theatre marking.

D-Day stripes were applied over mid-1940s day fighter (or 'temperate') camouflage on this Mk IXC. A few days into the Operation Overlord campaign, they were removed from the upper surfaces of the aircraft.

Air-sea rescue Spitfire Mk II with 12-in (30-cm) night stripe under fuselage (over standard day fighter scheme) applied from late 1942.

United States

Left: This 309th FS, 31st FG aircraft shows how RAF 'temperate' camouflage was retained on US 8th Air Force Mk VBs. The cocarde was simply painted over the RAF roundel. The Sky Blue band was retained.

Soviet Union

Below: Soviet Mk Vs were delivered in standard RAF day fighter colours.

Overall-green adorned the local two-seat Mk IX UTI conversions from ex-RAF aircraft for the Voyenno-Vozdushnyye Sily (V-VS).

Czechoslovakia

This Mk IX of the 4th Fighter Regiment, 2nd Air Division, Czech air force was transferred from the RAF post-war and flew in RAF camouflage.

Australia

Mk VC of No. 79 Sqn, RAAF in locally developed Earth Brown/Foliage Green with white identification markings, late 1943.

In May 1944, all camouflage was removed from RAAF Spitfires. This is a No. 85 Sqn Mk VC.

Denmark

Overall PRU Blue was retained on the PR.Mk XIs operated by No. 722 Sqn, RDAF.

Belgium

This late-production 'clipped'-wing Mk XVIE was with No. 350 Sqn, Fassburg, Germany in late 1945. Belgian national markings have been simply painted over the aircraft's original RAF markings.

Egypt

Egypt's Mk IXs carried a Dark Earth/Middle Stone camouflage scheme reminiscent of the RAF's desert scheme.

A natural metal finish with high-visibility markings adorn this Belgian air force Spitfire OTU Mk IX.

France (Armée de l'Air)

Mk IXs operated by the Armée de l'Air in Algeria during 1950 were stripped of paint and carried minimal markings.

Burma

Burma's ex-Israeli Mk IXs were camouflaged in green and brown, similar to RAF SEAC colours, with blue undersurfaces.

Germany

In common with other captured Allied types, this Spitfire was finished in overall Olive Drab with solid yellow undersides.

Greece

Greece's Mk IXs delivered after the war were RAF aircraft already in the country. They carried RAF temperate camouflage.

India

Basic national markings were applied to India's Mk VIII aircraft. An anti-glare panel is painted in front of the cockpit, otherwise the aircraft is unpainted.

Ireland

T.Mk 9 number 161 of the Irish Air Corps wears overall green applied after delivery in 1951. Note the two-colour Celtic Boss.

The same aircraft in late 1950s guise features three-colour boss, natural metal finish and an anti-glare panel in front of the cockpit.

Israel

Mk IX 2002 'White 11' of No. 101 Sqn, Israeli air force, at Hatzor, mid-1949. Brown/green camouflage with grey undersurfaces.

[Image: Israeli Spitfire with Star of David marking and '11' — marked 2002]

Spitfire Mk IX 2001 'Black 10' of No. 101 Sqn, Israeli air force, late 1949, has a natural metal finish with rudder unit markings.

[Image: Israeli Spitfire '10' — marked 2001]

Italy

Italy's air force took delivery of ex-RAF Mk IXs already in Italy in 1945. Camouflage was removed and basic Italian serials applied.

[Image: Italian Spitfire A-32]

The Netherlands

Overall Green was applied to Mk IXCs employed by the Royal Netherlands East Indies Air Force Spitfires. This aircraft carries the markings of No. 322 Sqn, Semarang, 1949.

No. 322 flew this natural metal T.Mk 9 from Soesterberg.

Norway

Like Denmark, Norway operated ex-RAF PR.Mk XIs, which retained their wartime overall-PRU Blue scheme.

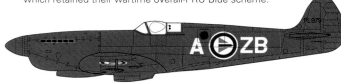

Flying this ex-RAF Mk IX in its 'as delivered' camouflage scheme, No. 331 Sqn was based at Vaernes in 1951.

Portugal

This Mk V was among the ex-RAF machines delivered to the Portuguese air force in standard RAF Ocean Grey and Dark Green camouflage.

South Africa

British standard Dark Green covered the upper surfaces of SAAF Mk IXs post-war. This No. 1 Sqn aircraft was based at Waterkloof in 1950.

Turkey

Mk Vs delivered to Turkey during the war were finished in RAF desert camouflage. Large serials were applied, with Turkish national marks.

Yugoslavia

Under the control of the RAF, No. 352 Sqn, Balkan air force flew tropicalised Mk Vs in standard RAF 'temperate' camouflage with Yugoslav markings.

Building the Spitfire

Left: Westland Aircraft built 685 Spitfire Mk Is and Vs, and was responsible for all Seafire development. Here, wing ribs are assembled in a fabrication shop at Sherborne.

Right: Two workers at the Castle Bromwich Aircraft Factory assemble a Spitfire fuselage.

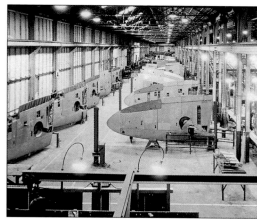

Left: Fitters at the CBAF introduce a Merlin 45 to its Mk V fuselage during final assembly. Below the front of the engine is its oil tank.

Right: Spitfire Mk VB wings undergo assembly at the Westland factory. The undercarriage is already installed so that it can be immediately lowered to support the airframe to which the wing will eventually be attached.

Below: This Mk VB is in the final stage of assembly. Engine cowlings and a propeller will be fitted, after which the hydraulics will be charged and the undercarriage lowered.

Right: Recently completed Rotol propeller-fitted Mk VBs await an air test after final assembly at Castle Bromwich in 1942. BL735 survived the war to be struck off in 1946; BL894 became a Seafire Mk IB in 1943.

Engine installation

Right: This Merlin 45 installation in a Mk VA features a Rotol propeller.

Above: The horseshoe-shaped cross-member was the key to the engine mount's strength.

Right: The open cowling of a Mk XVIE reveals the Packard Merlin 266. The power of the Merlin 60 series necessitated the use of a four-bladed propeller.

61

Merlin Spitfire Operators

United Kingdom

Royal Air Force

The following RAF operational squadrons used Merlin-engined fighter and reconnaissance variants of the Spitfire between 1938 and 1951.

Mk I: Nos 19, 41, 54, 64, 65, 66, 71, 72, 74, 92, 111, 122, 123, 124, 129, 131, 140, 152, 222, 234, 238, 249, 257, 266, 303, 308, 313, 411, 452, 457, 485, 501, 510, 602, 607, 609, 610, 611, 616

Mk II: Nos 19, 41, 54, 64, 65, 66, 71, 72, 74, 91, 111, 123, 124, 129, 130, 131, 132, 133, 134, 145, 152, 154, 222, 234, 266, 276, 277, 303, 306, 308, 309, 310, 312, 313, 315, 331, 340, 350, 352, 401, 403, 411, 412, 416, 417, 452, 457, 485, 501, 504, 602, 603, 609, 610, 611, 616

Mk IV: Nos 69, 140, 541, 542, 543, 544, 680, 681, 682, 683

Mk V: Nos 19, 26, 32, 33, 41, 43, 54, 63, 64, 65, 66, 71, 72, 73, 74, 80, 81, 87, 91, 92, 93, 94, 111, 118, 121, 122, 123, 124, 126, 127, 129, 130, 131, 132, 133, 134, 136, 145, 152, 154, 164, 165, 167, 184, 185, 186, 208, 213, 222, 225, 229, 232, 234, 237, 238, 241, 242, 243, 249, 253, 257, 266, 269, 274, 275, 276, 277, 278, 287, 288, 290, 302, 303, 306, 308, 310, 312, 313, 315, 316, 317, 318, 322, 326, 327, 328, 329, 331, 332, 335, 336, 340, 341, 345, 349, 350, 352, 401, 402, 403, 411, 412, 416, 417, 421, 441, 442, 443, 451, 453, 457, 485, 501, 504, 520, 521,

527, 541, 543, 567, 577, 595, 601, 602, 603, 607, 609, 610, 611, 615, 616, 680, 695, 1435

Mk VI: Nos 66, 124, 129, 234, 310, 313, 504, 519, 602, 616, 680

Mk VII: Nos 118, 124, 131, 154, 313, 519, 542, 611, 616

Mk VIII: Nos 17, 20, 28, 32, 43, 54, 67, 73, 81, 87, 92, 94, 131, 132, 136, 145, 152, 153, 154, 155, 185, 208, 238, 241, 253, 256, 273, 326, 327, 328, 417, 451, 452, 457, 548, 549, 601, 607, 615

Mk IX: Nos 1, 6, 16, 19, 28, 32, 33, 43, 56, 64, 65, 66, 72, 73, 74, 80, 81, 87, 91, 92, 93, 94, 111, 118, 122, 123, 124, 126, 127, 129, 130, 131, 132, 133, 145, 152, 153, 154, 164, 165, 183, 185, 208, 213, 222, 115, 229, 232, 234, 237, 238, 241, 242, 243, 249, 253, 256, 274, 283, 287, 288, 302, 303, 306, 308, 310, 312, 313, 315, 316, 317, 318, 322, 326, 327, 328, 329, 331,

332, 340, 341, 345, 349, 350, 400, 401, 402, 403, 411, 412, 414, 416, 417, 421, 441, 442, 443, 451, 453, 485, 501, 504, 518, 541, 544, 595, 601, 602, 611, 1435

Mk X: Nos 541, 542

Mk XI: Nos 2, 4, 16, 26, 28, 140, 253, 268, 400, 541, 542, 543, 680, 681, 682, 683, 684

Mk XVI: Nos 5, 16, 17, 19, 20, 33, 34, 63, 65, 66, 74, 126, 127, 164, 229, 287, 288, 289, 302, 303, 308, 317, 322, 329, 340, 341, 345, 349, 350, 401, 402, 403, 411, 412, 416, 421, 443, 451, 453, 485, 501, 567, 577, 587, 595, 601, 602, 603, 604, 609, 612, 614, 631, 667, 691, 695

In addition to the front-line squadrons,

there were several operational flights equipped with Merlin Spitfires, and many training units (mostly OTUs). Station flights and development units also made extensive use of Spitfires. The Royal Navy also employed 'hooked' as well as standard ex-RAF Merlin Spitfires for training purposes only, supplying aircrew for the Seafire units.

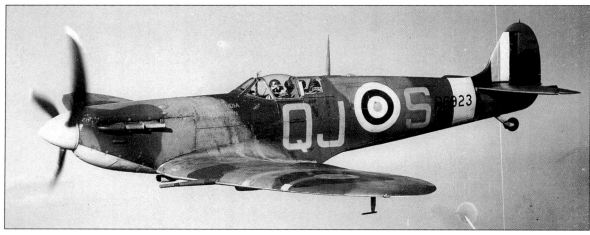

Above: No. 92 'East India' Squadron has a strong claim to being the RAF's senior Spitfire squadron. It converted to Mk Is in March 1940, and then flew Mk Vs (VB illustrated), Mk IXs and Mk VIIIs until late 1946. Through service on the home front, in North Africa and Italy, it became the highest-scoring RAF squadron of the war.

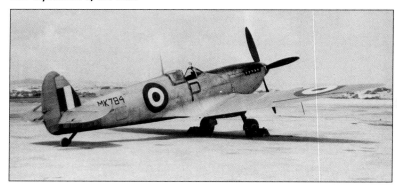

The Merlin Spitfire remained in the RAF for some time after the war. This Mk 9 is seen in the Middle East in 1948.

No. 74 Squadron was another famous Spitfire unit which flew the Mk I, II, V and IX (with a brief spell on Hurricanes in the Middle East). In March 1945 it transitioned to the Mk XVIE (illustrated) for fighter-bomber duties in the war's last months.

Argentina

At least three Spitfires arrived in Argentina after the war, including a Mk VIII, a IX and an XI. The Mk XI was delivered to Argentina for government photo-survey work in April 1947. The aircraft, PL972, was fitted with overload fuel tanks and flown by Captain J. Storey from Hurn to Buenos Aires via Gibraltar, Dakar and Natal. The aircraft was given the Argentine civil registration LV-NMZ. The Mk VIII, JF275, and the IX, PL194, were shipped out. An order for 10 T.Mk 9s was made but cancelled before delivery.

This is the PR.Mk XI which made the long self-ferry flight to Argentina. It was used by the government for photo-survey work.

Australia

Royal Australian Air Force

In all, 656 Spitfires were delivered to the Royal Australian Air Force between August 1942 and June 1945, comprising 246 Mk VCs, 251 Mk VIIIs and 159 HF.Mk VIIIs. At least another dozen were lost in transit. No. 1 Fighter Wing, RAAF formed with Mk VCs in 1942/43 for home defence. The three squadrons of the wing (Nos 54, 452 and 457 Squadrons) were re-equipped with Mk VIIIs in 1944, 420 of this mark (including F.Mk VIII and HF.Mk VIII sub-variants) entering service. Other squadrons were established to take the war to the New Guinea area and eventually seven front-line squadrons used the Spitfire in the Australian/Southwest Pacific theatre at some point, the others being Nos 79, 85 Squadrons, RAAF and Nos 54, 548 and 549 Squadrons, RAF. Replaced by CAC-built Mustangs from 1945, the Spitfire fleet was disposed of between 1946 and 1952.

Serials were: A58-1/185, A58-200/259, EE731 (Mk VCs); A58-300/550 (Mk VIIIs); A58-600/758 (HF.Mk VIIIs).

The delightful Mk VIII was numerically the most important RAAF version. In Australian hands it compiled a useful war record, notably as a ground attack platform during the 'mopping-up' operations in New Guinea and Morotai.

Belgium
Force Aérienne Belge/ Belgische Luchtmacht

In addition to 11 aircraft loaned by the RAF for training in 1946, the Belgian Air Force received 28 ex-RAF Merlin Spitfires in 1947-48. They were mostly Mk IXs with a few Mk XVIs among them. In 1952-53, the force also gained 15 Mk IXs formerly used by the

Spitfire Mk IXs formed the basis of the Belgian Air Force's rebirth in the late 1940s.

Dutch in the East Indies and refurbished by Fokker. The Merlin Spitfires were used by Nos 349 and 350 Smaldeel and the Jacht school; the two operational units traded in Spitfires for Meteors in 1949, while the fighter school continued to use the Spitfires (alongside Griffon-engined Mk XIVs), with the last being retired in 1956.

Burma
Union of Burma Air Force

The Union of Burma Air Force was formed following independence in 1948. The new force's air strength was built up with help from the RAF during a period of revolt by Communists and Karen ethnic groups. British assistance included 20 Seafire XVs

delivered in 1952, which were supplemented in 1954-55 by a batch of about 30 Spitfire IXs purchased from Israel. In 1958-59 the Spitfires were replaced by new Hawker Sea Furies. The Burmese Spitfires wore serials in the UB400 range.

Burma operated Spitfire Mk IXs alongside Seafires in the late 1950s. This aircraft has rocket launchers.

Czechoslovakia
Ceskoslovenske Vojenske Letectvo

At the end of the war, the Czech-manned Spitfire squadrons of the RAF (Nos 310, 311 and 313) returned to their homeland and formed the nucleus of the reborn

Czech Air Force. The Spitfire squadrons were organised within air divisions into fighter regiments from August 1945. 1st, 2nd and 3rd Divisions, 1st, 4th and 10th Regiments. The aircraft were sold to Israel in 1948.

The Czech air force flew ex-RAF Mk IXs briefly after the war, before the aircraft were sold to Israel.

Denmark
Flyvevabnet

Thirty-eight Spitfire Mk IXs and three Mk XIs were purchased together with non-flying instructional airframes in 1947 as part of the post-war re-equipment programme. Initially they equipped the Spitfireskolen at Karup. This unit was absorbed into No. 5 Eskadrille. In 1950 the Royal Danish Air Force was established as a separate entity, with Spitfires and Meteors in the fighter role.

725 Eskadrille (formerly the PR Flight of No. 4 Esk.) based at Karup operated Mk IXs, and No. 722 Esk. at Vaerlose operated Mk IXs as unarmed trainers. The Spitfire fighters were given the type number 41 in Danish service with serials in the range 401-436; the PR.Mk IXs were Type 42 and numbered 451-453. The Spitfire was retired in May 1955.

Mk IXEs were used as fighters and as trainers, serving until 1955. Denmark also used Mk IXs in the photo-reconnaissance role.

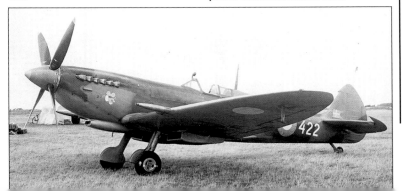

Egypt
Royal Egyptian Air Force

One squadron of Spitfire Mk VCs (15 aircraft) was received by the Royal Egyptian Air Force before the war's end and Mk IXs were delivered from surplus RAF stocks after the war. In total, 62 Merlin Spitfires were operated by the REAF, comprising 20 Mk Vs, 41 Mk IXs and one Tr.Mk IX. In the opening battles of the Israeli War of Independence, Egyptian Spitfires fought

RAF Spitfire Mk XVIIIs over Ramat David. During the war REAF Spitfires undertook many ground attack sorties. One shot-down example was recovered by the Israelis and put into service with the IDF/AF. Egyptian Spitfire operators included No. 2 Sqn at El Arish, with Mk IXs.

This No. 2 Sqn Mk IX crash-landed on 5 November 1948 and was stripped by Israeli technicians. Several more fell to Israeli Spitfires and Avia S.199s.

France
Armée de l'Air

One Spitfire Mk I was delivered to France before the war and evaluated by the Armée de l'Air. In 1941, the first Free French Spitfire Squadron (No. 340) was formed in the UK, followed by Nos 341 and 345. Each of these units was briefly part of the Allied occupation forces in Germany before being transferred to the Armée de l'Air in November 1945 as Groupes de Chasse IV/2, II/2 and II/2, respectively. Nos 326, 327 and 328 Squadrons were formed in Corsica

in December 1943 and No. 329 at Ayr in January 1944, transferring to the Armée de l'Air in November 1945 as GC II/7, GC I/3, GC I/7 and GC I/2, respectively.

With increasing attacks on French forces in Indochina in late 1946, GC II/7 was established at Tan Son Nhut with Spitfire VIIIs borrowed from the RAF. They were replaced by a delivery of Mk IXs of GC I/7 in January 1947, bringing the total strength to 30 aircraft. The Spitfires served on ground attack duties in the theatre until November 1950.

The Aéronavale also used 20 Mk IXs as trainers for Seafire pilots at Cuers.

Above: Mk IXs of GC I/3 'Navarre' and GC II/3 'Champagne' line up at Nha Trang in 1950. Spitfires left Indo-China in November.

Below: Aéronavale Seafires are well-remembered, but the service also used 20 Spitfire Mk IXs as land-based trainers.

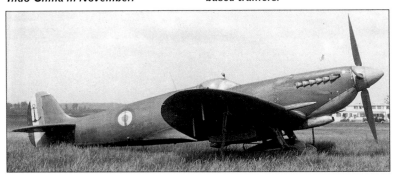

Merlin Spitfire Operators

Greece
Royal Hellenic Air Force

The Spitfire Mk VBs and VCs flown by the Greek-manned Nos 335 and 336 Squadrons, RAF were integrated into the Greek Air Force upon their return to Greece in late 1944. A total of 106 Mk Vs served, ultimately with the Advanced Training Squadron of the Scholi Icaron at Tatoi, as late as 1951. In 1947, 110 Spitfire LF and HF.Mk IXs were obtained by the reformed Royal Hellenic Air Force, mainly through the transfer of RAF aircraft already in the country. They were supplemented by 66 Mk XVIs in 1949. Aircraft of both marks were used against Communist targets in Athens and elsewhere during the 1948-49 campaign of the civil war. The active units were Nos 335, 336 and 337 Squadrons based at Hassani and Sedes. The last Greek Spitfires serving with the Scholi Icaron were retired in 1953. All Greek Spitfires retained RAF serials.

Greek Spitfires saw action during the civil war. Seen in 1949, this is a Mk XVI of No. 335 Squadron.

India
(Royal) Indian Air Force

Nos 4, 8, 9 and 10 Squadrons were all equipped with Spitfire Mk VIIIs by the end of the war, although the first two of these units had briefly operated the Mk VC. The aircraft were mainly employed in the fighter-bomber role, hampering the Japanese retreat. Griffon-engined marks had replaced the earlier aircraft in most units by the time of partition of the country in 1947, when most fighter units converted to the transport role, leaving only No. 2 Squadron with Spitfires. With growing tensions in the Kashmir region, Spitfires of various marks that had been left behind at Karachi docks by the RAF were uncrated and put into service. The Mk VIIIs were used for ground attack in Kashmir. Additionally, about a dozen Tr.Mk IXs were operated by the IAF from 1947 until the mid-1950s in the advanced/operational training role.

The Indian Air Force used the unarmed Mk IX for advanced training of future fighter pilots at Hakimpet.

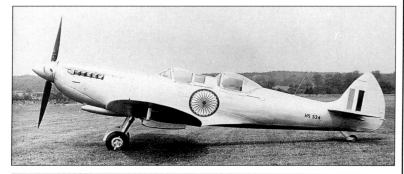

Ireland
Aer Chor na h-Eireann

In 1947 the Irish Air Corps replaced the Hurricane Mk IIs of No. 1 Fighter Squadron with 12 'de-navalised' Seafire LF.Mk IIIs. Six two-seat Spitfire T.Mk 9s (which had originally been built as LF.Mk IXs by Vickers-Armstrongs) were acquired for pilot training, all arriving on 5 June 1951. All had seen service with the RAF and several had recorded kills against the Luftwaffe. The aircraft (serials 158-163) were delivered in an overall pale green paint scheme, which was later replaced by a natural metal finish. The last operational aircraft was withdrawn from service in 1961, making Ireland probably the final military Spitfire operator in the world.

163 was the Irish Air Corps' last operational Spitfire. Of the six delivered one crashed but the other five are still flying, now as warbirds.

Israel
Heyl Ha'Avir

Approximately 59 Spitfires were bought from the Czechs during the 1948 war for $23,000 each, although the first two Israeli Spitfires were built from parts of scrapped RAF Mk IXs and a shot-down Egyptian aircraft. A number of the ex-Czech (and ex-RAF) aircraft were flown to Israel but the majority were shipped out. The main user was No. 101 Squadron, which saw much combat with the Spitfire. No. 105 Squadron was the main training unit, and No. 107 Squadron briefly used Spitfires. Another 30

A pair of No. 101 Sqn Spitfire Mk IXs is seen in January 1949 during an escort mission for No. 69 Sqn B-17s operating over the Faluja pocket. Israeli Spitfires scored several notable successes over Egyptian and RAF aircraft, including the destruction of a four-ship flight of RAF Spitfire FR.Mk 18s and the routing of a follow-up flight of Tempest Mk VIs.

Mk IXs were supplied from Italian surplus in 1953. The Spitfire was retired from IAF service in April 1956.

Italy
Aeronautica Cobelligerante del Sud/ Aeronautica Militare Italiana (AMI)

Following the Italian surrender, 53 RAF Spitfires (of which 33 were made airworthy) were transferred from RAF stocks to form the complement of 20º Gruppo, 51º Stormo. The unit became operational as part of the Co-Belligerent Air Force in October 1944. All but a few examples were withdrawn at the end of the European war. In June 1947, following the withdrawal of Allied forces, a large number of aircraft, including Spitfire IXs, were left behind, and they were taken on strength by the Aeronautica Militare Italiana (AMI). Some 145 of these aircraft received AMI serials, although initially the aircraft operated under their previous RAF identities. The last aircraft were retired from the 3º Gruppo Scuola Volo at Lecce in 1952.

This Mk V was one of the original 20º Gruppo aircraft (note the 51º Stormo badge of a black cat chasing three mice on the fin). This was the Co-Belligerent Spitfire unit, which later re-equipped with Mk IXs.

Netherlands
Luchtstridkrachten

No. 322 Sqn was formed in the RAF in June 1943 as the Dutch-manned fighter squadron, equipped with Spitfires. It was revived in the post-war Dutch air force, which did not gain autonomy from the army until 1953. Over 100 Mk VBs, XVICs and XIVEs, and 55 Mk IXs, were delivered between 1946 and 1948, with an additional three Tr.Mk IX two-seaters arriving during 1948. These aircraft equipped No. 322 Squadron, which was working up for transfer to the Far East. The aircraft were transferred to the JachtVlieg School (JVS) when the squadron ground echelon shipped out. A batch of 20 Mk IXs was delivered from RAF stocks directly to No. 322 Squadron based at Kalidjati in Indonesia in 1947, where they were used on ground attack missions against nationalist insurgents. The squadron reacquired its original aircraft on return to Twenthe in late 1949. In 1950, the 18 survivors of the East Indies force were returned to the Netherlands, and 15 were transferred to Belgium. The last Spitfires were withdrawn in 1954.

The homebased aircraft were serialled in the H-1 to H-35 range and the Far East aircraft H-101 to H-120, the survivors being reserialled H-50 to H-69.

Spitfire Mk IXs of No. 322 Squadron are seen at Twenthe in 1951. Earlier the squadron had used borrowed RAF Spitfires on counter-insurgency work in Indonesia.

Norway
Kongelige Norske Flyvapen

The two Norwegian Spitfire squadrons in the RAF, Nos 331 and 332, were transferred to the Royal Norwegian Air Force in November 1945. In 1947 Norway purchased a large package of defence equipment from Britain, including 47 Spitfire Mk IXs and three PR.Mk XIs. The Spitfires,

Norwegian squadrons used RAF-style two-letter codes. This LF.Mk IXE wears the 'CI' of No. 331 Sqn.

which were well-worn ex-RAF examples, served with 331 and 332 Skvadron at Gardermoen, Vaernes and Bardufoss. In total, 74 Spitfires served with the RNoAF. Twenty-five were lost in accidents before the type was retired in 1954. RAF serials were retained for at least the first part of their service.

Portugal
Aeronautica Militar/ Força Aérea Portuguesa

The Portuguese had ordered 15 Spitfire Mk Is prior to the outbreak of war but delivery was cancelled following the German assault of May 1940. In 1942, 18 Mk IAs were delivered, these aircraft forming Esc. XZ at Tancos (Base Aérea 3), then moving to BA 2 (Ota). Under the Azores Agreement, the British government agreed to supply 34 Mk Vs delivered from October 1943, these becoming operational at Ota with Escuadrilhas MR and RL. Some of the VBs went to Esc. ZE at BA 2 (serving

alongside Blenheims). An additional 60 Mk Vs were delivered in 1947-48. In January 1951, the surviving VBs were concentrated into Escuadrãos 20 and 21. Both units had given up the Spitfire some time before they were reformed with F-84Gs in late 1952/early 1953.

Spitfire Mk Vs from Escuadrilhas XZ, RL and MR are seen at Ota.

South Africa
South African Air Force

Nos 1, 2, 3, 4, 7, 9, 10, 11, 40 and 41 Squadrons, SAAF flew Spitfires Vs and IXs as part of the Desert Air Force in North Africa and Italy. No. 1 Squadron also flew Mk VIIIs and No. 40 some PR.Mk XIs. No. 11 Squadron re-equipped too late to see action with Spitfires. These aircraft remained on RAF charge and had RAF serials. After the war, Nos 1, 2 and 4 Squadrons were reformed in South Africa as the Fighter Wing at Waterkloof, using

136 Mk IXs donated by the British government. No. 60 Squadron also used Spitfires for reconnaissance and other roles. No. 2 Squadron personnel trained on Spitfires of the Bombing, Gunnery and Air Navigation School before going to Korea to fly P-51s in 1950. The Spitfires of the Fighter Wing were replaced from 1952 by Vampires.

Spitfires in South Africa carried a four-digit serial in the 5000 range.

This No. 60 Sqn Mk IX has an oblique camera fitted for the reconnaissance role.

Turkey
Türk Hava Kuvvetleri

Turkey received a pair of Spitfire Mk Is from an order for 15 in 1940. During the war, 84 tropicalised Mk VBs and VCs followed, equipping two Boluks (Companies) of the 6nci Alay (Regiment) at Gaziemir, four Boluks of the 7nci Alay at Kutahya and one Boluk of the 8nci at Erzincan. After the war, Turkey received a substantial amount of British war-surplus equipment including 207

Spitfires, 203 Mk IXs and four PR.Mk XIXs. Users of the Mk IX included the 7nci Alay (four Boluks), the 6nci Alay (two Boluks), and the 4nci Alay (four Boluks). In 1951, the Turkish Air Force was re-established along Western lines and the basic unit became the Filo (Squadron). Filos that operated Spitfire IXs until the last were retired and scrapped in 1954 included Nos 141-143, 161-163, and 171-173.

This group of Turkish Spitfires includes Mk Vs and Mk IXs.

USSR
Voenno Vozdushnyye Sily

The Soviet Union took delivery of 1,188 Spitfire Mk IXs, 143 Mk Vs and two PR.Mk IVs from early 1943, most of them delivered through Iran. Many were rebuilt

and reserialled ex-RAF aircraft. A number were converted in Russia into two-seat trainers with a locally-designed rear canopy. It is possible that a small number were transferred to China.

This is one of the 143 Mk Vs delivered to the VVS in April 1943. The aircraft has the locally fitted RPK 10M loop antenna.

United States
United States Army Air Forces

The three 'Eagle' squadrons of the RAF (Nos 71, 121 and 133) were equipped with Spitfire VBs at the time they were transferred to USAAF control in October 1942 as the 334th, 335th and 336th Pursuit Squadrons of the 4th FG respectively. The Spitfires were replaced by P-47s in March 1943, but another 600 aircraft had become available under 'reverse Lend-Lease' and

began to equip two groups of the Eighth Air Force (the 31st and 52nd FGs) in mid-1942. These units transferred to the 12th Air Force to take part in Operation Torch in November 1942, later equipping with Mk IXs and some VIIIs. Other Spitfire units within the 8th Air Force included the 350th FG (for training only), and the 67th Observation Group, both initially with Mk Vs, and the 14th Photo Squadron with PR.Mk XIs.

A Spitfire Mk V of either the 31st or 52nd FG is seen in England prior to its move to North Africa.

Yugoslavia
Jugoslovensko Ratno Vazduhoplovstvo

No. 352 Squadron, a Yugoslav-manned Spitfire squadron operating as part of the Tactical Wing of the Balkan Air Force, became operational in August 1944, flying ground-attack and bomber escort missions. The squadron's aircraft wore Yugoslav insignia with RAF serials. The squadron was

disbanded as an RAF unit on 15 June 1945 and became part of the Yugoslav Air Force. Eighteen Mk Vs and three Mk IXs served with the JRV until August 1952. The aircraft were serialled 9476-9503.

Complete with Yugoslav national markings, this tropicalised Mk VC served with the RAF's No. 352 Sqn, which was manned by Yugoslavs and later formed the basis of the reborn JRV.

Spitfire Spyplanes

The PR Specials

Today, the idea of sending a fast, high-flying unarmed reconnaissance aircraft to photograph targets, using its high performance to avoid the enemy defences, will not raise a single eyebrow. The notion is firmly accepted as a sound tactical method. In 1939, however, the conversion of a couple of Spitfire fighters to the reconnaissance role represented a radical departure from conventional military thinking. Thus modified, the aircraft quickly demonstrated their prowess in the new role. For the rest of World War II successive variants of the Spitfire ranged far and wide across enemy territory and returned with the precious photographs of their targets. Finally, almost at the end of its service career, a reconnaissance Spitfire making an inadvertent dive probably reached the greatest speed ever attained by a propeller-driven aircraft.

In August 1939, a few days before the outbreak of World War II, a junior Royal Air Force officer submitted a memorandum on the future of strategic aerial reconnaissance. In it Flying Officer Maurice 'Shorty' Longbottom stated: ". . . this type of reconnaissance must be done in such a manner as to avoid the enemy fighters and AA defences as completely as possible. The best method of doing this appears to be the use of a single small machine, relying solely on its speed, climb and ceiling to avoid detection."

Longbottom's paper called for a lone, unarmed, high-speed high-flying reconnaissance aircraft that could dart into enemy territory, take the photographs and dart out, with a minimum of fuss and avoiding the defences whenever possible. In 1939 most long-range reconnaissance was flown by converted bomber aircraft equipped with a full defensive armament to fight their way to and from their targets. Yet, as Longbottom pointed out, the weight and drag penalty from the guns and turrets reduced the aircraft's performance and brought it within reach of the very defences it had to avoid to perform the mission effectively.

High-speed platform

Longbottom's proposal for a long-range reconnaissance aircraft centred on a high-speed single-seat fighter like the Spitfire, stripped of its armament and fitted with cameras and additional fuel tanks. He argued that the removal of the guns and ammunition boxes, the radio and other unnecessary equipment would reduce weight by 450 lb (204 kg). Since a reconnaissance Spitfire would not need a high rate of climb, it could take off weighing 480 lb (218

Conceived by a young flying officer as the most survivable means of getting photo-intelligence from within the enemy's heartland, the photo-reconnaissance Spitfire emerged as the most important strategic camera platform in the European theatre. It was born at a time when every Spitfire was desperately needed to defend Britain, yet through perseverance and persuasion the embryonic programme was allocated some precious aircraft. After the results of the first few missions, there were no more doubts.

Illustrating the advances made in cameras in a short time, the photo above shows the city of Hamburg taken from a PR.Mk IF at about 30,000 ft in September 1940 with an 8-in (203-mm) lens, while that below shows the same area taken in July 1942 using a 36-in (70-mm) lens, revealing much greater detail. To confuse RAF bomb aimers part of the Alster Lake has been covered with rafts painted with streets and houses, and there is a fake railway bridge a few hundred yards north of the real one, which can be seen clearly in the earlier photograph.

Best-known of the wartime photo-reconnaissance Spitfire variants was the PR.Mk XI, which was based on the Mk IX airframe with a 60-series (later 70-series) Merlin giving it outstanding speed and altitude performance. The aircraft was designed as a dedicated PR platform with fully interchangeable camera installations, leading-edge fuel tanks and deep cowling for extra oil. Most aircraft had the broad-chord rudder with characteristic pointed tip but a few early machines, like this one, retained the original-style fin.

kg) more than the fighter version. Thus, the aircraft had more than 900 lb (408 kg) of spare lifting capacity for the carriage of cameras and additional fuel. Longbottom calculated that a reconnaissance version of the Spitfire could carry three times more fuel than the fighter and it would have a range of 1,500 miles (2414 km).

The Air Ministry in London received Longbottom's paper with polite interest, although at first nothing was done to confirm or refute his arguments. The RAF was desperately short of modern fighters and, in particular, Spitfires. Every one of these precious machines was allocated to Fighter Command for the defence of the homeland. It would take more than a discussion paper from a junior officer, however persuasive its arguments, to get Air Chief Marshal Dowding to part with any.

In the meantime the war had begun, and it immediately became clear that the RAF photographic reconnaissance units were ill-equipped for operations over enemy territory. The slow Bristol Blenheims suffered severe losses from flak and fighters, even during shallow penetration missions.

Secret unit

Following strong representations from the Air Ministry, Air Chief Marshal Dowding reluctantly agreed to release a pair of Spitfires for modification as reconnaissance aircraft. Two Mk I fighters straight off the production line, N3069 and N3071, went to Heston Aircraft Ltd for modification. Also at this airfield, Commander Sidney Cotton was forming his highly secret reconnaissance unit with the cover name of 'The Heston Flight'. Appropriately, one of the first officers posted to assist with its

formation was 'Shorty' Longbottom himself.

In the workshops at Heston the Spitfires had their armament and radios removed, and a vertically-mounted camera with a 5-in focal length lens was fitted in the empty gun bay in each wing. The airframes were cleaned up to give the last ounce of speed: the empty gun ports were sealed with metal plates, then all joints were filled with plaster of Paris and rubbed down to give a smooth exterior finish.

Cotton devised a novel colour scheme for the Spitfires. He had noticed that an aircraft observed from a distance and from below invariably appeared as a dark silhouette against the lighter sky background. He therefore reasoned that a light-coloured aircraft would be less visible than a dark one. Cotton had the Spitfires painted in a shade of pale green, which he called 'Camotint' and which he thought

Above: Taken at Seclin in France on 18 November 1939, this historic photograph shows the Spitfire PR.Mk IA being run up on the ground prior to the first reconnaissance mission by one of these aircraft. The aircraft was painted pale green to make it as inconspicuous as possible when viewed from below.

Left: Two of the personalities of the early PR Spitfire programme share a joke. On the left is Flying Officer Alistair Taylor, who flew the first low-level 'dicing' mission, while on the right is Flight Lieutenant Maurice 'Shorty' Longbottom, at whose initial suggestion the Spitfire was converted for the PR role.

would make them as inconspicuous as possible.

The initial reconnaissance Spitfires carried no additional fuel tank, and the other changes were kept to a bare minimum. The priority was to get the aircraft into the air on photographic missions as soon as possible. On paper, Longbottom's proposals seemed the best available, but only the acid test of war would prove whether they really were workable.

Operational trials

For a brief period in autumn 1939 Cotton's unit was renamed the 'Special Survey Flight'. Then, early in November 1939, the title changed yet again and to explain the odd colouring of its aircraft it became 'No. 2 Camouflage Unit'. Soon afterwards, one of the Spitfires flew to Seclin near Lille in France to commence operational trials. On 18 November, Longbottom, now a flight lieutenant, took off for the first-ever Spitfire reconnaissance mission. His target was the German city of Aachen and

the fortifications around it. Cruising through the area at 33,000 ft (10058 m), Longbottom found the navigation more difficult than expected, however. After his return to Seclin his strips of photographs showed the Belgian side of the frontier south of Aachen. Longbottom quickly discovered where he had gone wrong, and four days later he carried out successful photographic runs as briefed over the Belgian-German border area to the east of Liège.

Throughout the six weeks following those initial flights, cloud cover prevented high-altitude photography of enemy territory. Then at the end of December the skies cleared, and both Spitfires took part in the next series of operations. The modified fighters returned with photographs of Aachen, Cologne, Kaiserslautern, Wiesbaden, Mainz and parts of the Ruhr industrial area.

These initial flights demonstrated that as a vehicle for photographing enemy territory, the Spitfire was the best type available to the RAF. Between the start of the war and the end of 1939, Blenheims had flown 89 reconnaissance sorties into German airspace, and 16 (18 per cent) had failed to return. Because of these losses, and the frequent harassment from defensive guns and fighters, only 45 of the Blenheim sorties (about half) had yielded useful photographs. In contrast, by the end of the year the two Spitfires had flown 15 sorties without a single loss, and 10 (two-thirds) of the sorties had yielded useful photographs. Of the five abortive Spitfire sorties, four were due to cloud cover at the target and only one was due to fighter interference. The flights proved the soundness of Longbottom's concept for high-performance unarmed reconnaissance operations, and ACM Dowding agreed to release a dozen more Spitfires for the new role.

These early reconnaissance flights showed that the Spitfire's high-altitude performance exceeded that of the available cameras.

Very few examples of the PR.Mk IB were produced, and photos are rare. This aircraft, P9331 operated by No. 212 Sqn in 1940, was captured by German forces after the Dunkirk evacuation.

Above and right: The PR.Mk IC introduced a further increase in range by adding a 30-Imp gal (136-litre) tank under the port wing in addition to the PR.Mk IB's extra 29-Imp gal (132-litre) tank in the rear fuselage. The wing tank counterbalanced two 8-in (203-mm) lens cameras in the flattened blister under the starboard wing.

Photographs taken from 33,000 ft (10058 m) using 5-in focal length cameras produced small-scale pictures of limited military value. Interpreters could pick out roads, railways, villages and major fortifications. Yet even when prints were enlarged to the limits of the grain of the film, troop positions and individual vehicles were invisible. For the Spitfire to exploit its full capabilities, better cameras were needed.

In January 1940 the first of the improved photographic reconnaissance Spitfires was ready

Unusually for a PR.Mk IC, this aircraft has the deepened engine cowling indicating fitment of an enlarged oil tank. It is seen with the front-hinging camera blister open under the wing. Pilot Officer Gordon Green flew this aircraft during his first reconnaissance mission, to St Nazaire, on 13 February 1941.

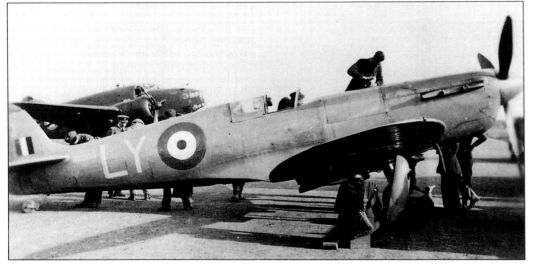

for operations. It was designated the PR.Mk IB, and to distinguish it the earlier variant was renamed the PR.Mk IA. The new variant carried one 8-in (20.3-cm) focal lens camera in each wing, giving a one-third improvement in the scale of the photographs. Also, to increase its range, the PR.Mk IB carried an extra 29-Imp gal (132-litre) fuel tank in the rear fuselage. During the operations with PR.Mk IAs, Cotton's light green camouflage scheme was found unsuitable for operations at high altitude. Accordingly, the new Spitfires were painted in

a medium-blue scheme later called 'PRU Blue'. In February 1940 'Shorty' Longbottom demonstrated the effectiveness of the new variant when, taking off from Debden in Essex, he returned with photographs of the important German naval bases at Wilhelmshaven and Emden.

Also at this time Cotton's unit was renamed the Photographic Development Unit (PDU), the first title to reveal the true nature of its role. Early in 1940 the operations in France were reorganised and a new unit, No. 212 Squadron, was formed at Seclin to fly reconnaissance missions from there.

Greater range

In March 1940 a so-called 'long-range' reconnaissance version of the Spitfire appeared. Designated the PR.Mk IC, it had a 30-Imp gal (137-litre) blister tank under the port wing counterbalanced by a pair of 8-in (20.3-cm) lens cameras in a similar blister under the starboard wing. With a 29-Imp gal (132-litre) tank in the fuselage, this version carried 59 Imp gal (269 litres) more fuel than the fighter version.

On 7 April Longbottom took the prototype PR.Mk IC to Kiel, and brought back the first photographs of the port taken since the outbreak of war. The pictures showed numerous ships in harbour, and lines of Junkers 52 transport planes drawn up on the nearby airfield at Holtenau. Ignorant of the normal level of activity in the area, RAF photo interpreters could

The PR.Mk IG was a low-altitude version intended to be used just underneath the cloud base. Most wore the pale pink scheme for the 'dicing' missions, although this could be highly conspicuous when there was no cloud cover.

Above: A pink Spitfire PR.Mk IG is prepared for a low-altitude 'dicing' mission from St Eval in Cornwall in 1941, this base being used as it was close to the major harbour at Brest.

PR.Mk ID, became known as the 'extra-super-long-range' version. With a 29-Imp gal (132-litre) tank in the rear fuselage, it had a total internal fuel capacity of 228 Imp gal (1037 litres) – two and a half times more than the Mk I fighter. In the rear fuselage the PR.Mk ID carried two 8-in (20.3-cm) or two 20-in (50.8-cm) focal length cameras.

The additional tankage gave a dramatic increase in the area of German-held territory where the reconnaissance Spitfires could operate. On 29 October 1940 a PR.Mk ID photographed the port of Stettin on the Baltic (now Sczecin in Poland) and returned after five hours and 20 minutes airborne. Other remarkable missions followed in rapid succession: to

A few PR.Mk IGs operated in standard fighter camouflage, this example serving with No. 140 Sqn in 1941. The squadron had been formed at Benson in September 1941 out of 1416 Flt. An unusual feature of the G was that the oblique camera was angled slightly backwards to reduce blur as the aircraft flew past targets at high speed. This necessitated the bulged camera blister on the side of the fuselage.

Marseilles and Toulon in the south of France, and to Trondheim in Norway.

When carrying its full load of fuel, the PR.Mk ID was difficult to handle. Flight Lieutenant Niel Wheeler explained: "You could not fly it straight and level for the first half hour or hour after take-off. Until you had emptied the rear tank, the aircraft hunted the whole time. The centre of gravity was so far back that you couldn't control it. It was the sort of thing that would never have got in during peacetime, but war is another matter." Once its rear tank was empty, however, the Spitfire's pleasant handling characteristics returned.

Cloud base special

The final reconnaissance variant based on the Spitfire Mk I was the Type G which, like the PR.Mk IE, was optimised for the low-altitude photographic role. This version retained the fighter's normal armament of eight 0.303-in machine-guns, to provide a self-defence capability if it encountered enemy fighters. The PR.Mk IG carried a 29-Imp gal (132-litre) fuel tank behind the pilot. The three-camera installation in the rear fuselage comprised one obliquely mounted camera, and a 14-in (35.6-cm) and a 5-in (12.7-cm) lens camera both mounted vertically. The Type G was intended

to photograph targets from just below the cloud base, wherever that happened to be. The oblique camera was for photography below 2,000 ft (610 m), the 5-in (12.7-cm) lens vertical camera was for use between 2,000 and 10,000 ft (610 and 3050 m) and the 14-in (35.6 cm) lens was for photography from above 10,000 ft. A few PR.Mk IGs were painted in normal fighter camouflage, but the majority

A close-up of a pink PR.Mk IG shows the oblique camera installation and the side bulges on the canopy fitted as standard to early PR Spitfires.

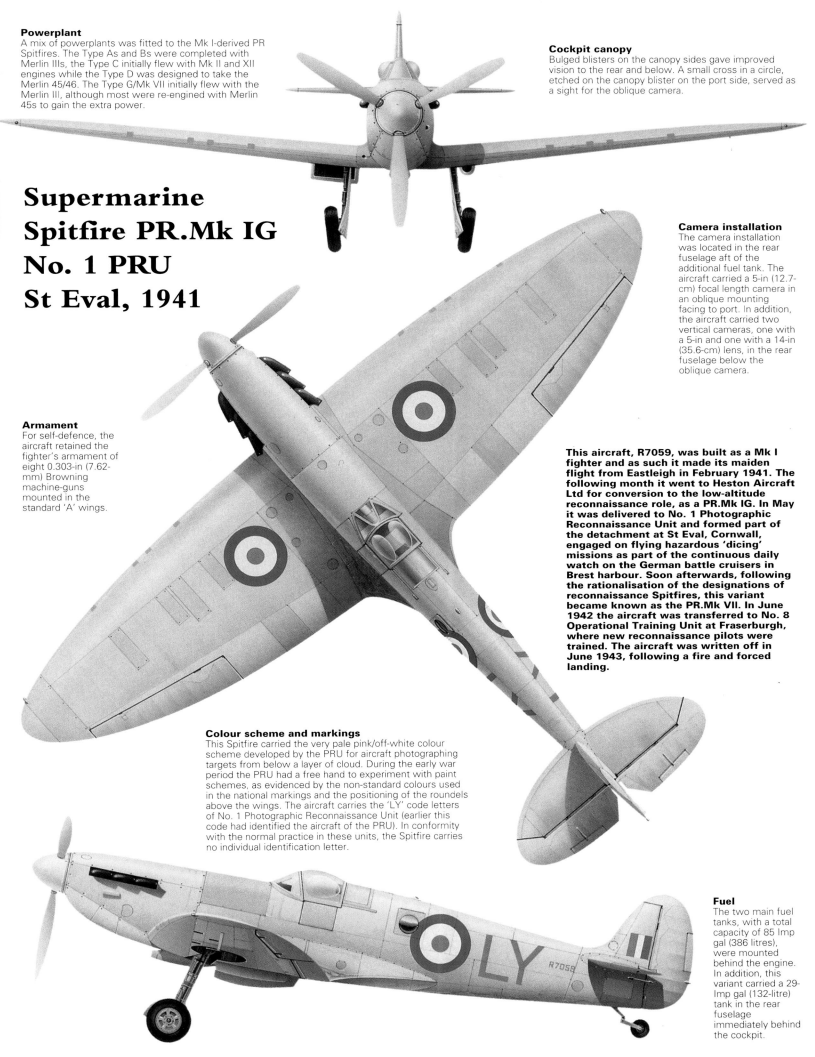

Powerplant
A mix of powerplants was fitted to the Mk I-derived PR Spitfires. The Type As and Bs were completed with Merlin IIIs, the Type C initially flew with Mk II and XII engines while the Type D was designed to take the Merlin 45/46. The Type G/Mk VII initially flew with the Merlin III, although most were re-engined with Merlin 45s to gain the extra power.

Cockpit canopy
Bulged blisters on the canopy sides gave improved vision to the rear and below. A small cross in a circle, etched on the canopy blister on the port side, served as a sight for the oblique camera.

Supermarine Spitfire PR.Mk IG No. 1 PRU St Eval, 1941

Camera installation
The camera installation was located in the rear fuselage aft of the additional fuel tank. The aircraft carried a 5-in (12.7-cm) focal length camera in an oblique mounting facing to port. In addition, the aircraft carried two vertical cameras, one with a 5-in and one with a 14-in (35.6-cm) lens, in the rear fuselage below the oblique camera.

Armament
For self-defence, the aircraft retained the fighter's armament of eight 0.303-in (7.62-mm) Browning machine-guns mounted in the standard 'A' wings.

This aircraft, R7059, was built as a Mk I fighter and as such it made its maiden flight from Eastleigh in February 1941. The following month it went to Heston Aircraft Ltd for conversion to the low-altitude reconnaissance role, as a PR.Mk IG. In May it was delivered to No. 1 Photographic Reconnaissance Unit and formed part of the detachment at St Eval, Cornwall, engaged on flying hazardous 'dicing' missions as part of the continuous daily watch on the German battle cruisers in Brest harbour. Soon afterwards, following the rationalisation of the designations of reconnaissance Spitfires, this variant became known as the PR.Mk VII. In June 1942 the aircraft was transferred to No. 8 Operational Training Unit at Fraserburgh, where new reconnaissance pilots were trained. The aircraft was written off in June 1943, following a fire and forced landing.

Colour scheme and markings
This Spitfire carried the very pale pink/off-white colour scheme developed by the PRU for aircraft photographing targets from below a layer of cloud. During the early war period the PRU had a free hand to experiment with paint schemes, as evidenced by the non-standard colours used in the national markings and the positioning of the roundels above the wings. The aircraft carries the 'LY' code letters of No. 1 Photographic Reconnaissance Unit (earlier this code had identified the aircraft of the PRU). In conformity with the normal practice in these units, the Spitfire carries no individual identification letter.

Fuel
The two main fuel tanks, with a total capacity of 85 Imp gal (386 litres), were mounted behind the engine. In addition, this variant carried a 29-Imp gal (132-litre) tank in the rear fuselage immediately behind the cockpit.

Radar sets were typical targets for the Spitfire's oblique cameras, close-up shots being required to determine the antenna arrangements. This image depicts the Würzburg radar station at St Bruneval near Le Havre, photographed by Tony Hill on 4 December 1941. The picture led to a raid by British paratroops who captured the radar and returned to England with vital parts from it.

Another famous photograph taken by Tony Hill shows the Giant Würzburg night-fighter control radar at Domberg on the Dutch island of Walcheren, taken on 2 May 1942. One of the operators stands helplessly by the ladder to the cabin, providing a ready-made human yardstick for British intelligence officers when they came to analyse the picture.

Flight Lieutenant Tony Hill was one of the most distinguished 'dicing' pilots of No. 1 Photographic Reconnaissance Unit. After promotion to squadron leader, he was killed in October 1942 during a hazardous mission deep inside France.

were painted overall in a very pale shade of pink, barely off-white, to conceal them when seen against a cloud background. If there was insufficient cloud the almost-white aircraft was vulnerable to fighter attack from above, and pilots had orders to abandon the mission if conditions were unsuitable.

In November 1940 the Photographic

Above: Another distinguished PR pilot was Flight Lieutenant Eric le Mesurier. Visible on the canopy bulge is the sighting cross for the starboard-facing oblique camera.

Reconnaissance Unit was redesignated No. 1 Photographic Reconnaissance Unit, to distinguish it from No. 2 Photographic Reconnaissance Unit then forming in the Mediterranean theatre. Soon afterwards, No. 1 PRU moved from Heston to Benson near Oxford, a permanent RAF airfield that would remain its base for the rest of the war.

Spitfire pilots engaged in lone flights deep into enemy territory had to contend with a range of problems that went with their specialised role. Pilot Officer Gordon Green flew operations with the PRU from February 1941 and he recalled: "During the early [photographic reconnaissance] missions there was no such thing as cockpit heating in our Spitfires. For the high-altitude missions we wore thick suits with electrical heating. Trussed up in our Mae West and parachute, one could scarcely move in the narrow cockpit of the Spitfire. When flying over enemy territory one had to be searching the sky the whole time for enemy fighters. On more than one occasion I started violent evasive action to shake off a suspected enemy fighter, only to discover that it was a small speck of dirt on the inside of my perspex canopy!

"A big worry over enemy territory was that one might start leaving a condensation trail without knowing it, thus pointing out one's position to the enemy. To avoid that we had small mirrors fitted in the blisters on each side of the canopy, so that one could see the trail as soon as it started to form. When that happened one could either climb or descend until the trail

ceased. If possible, we liked to climb above the trail's layer because then fighters trying to intercept us had first to climb through the trail's layer and could be seen in good time."

During 1941 the *ad hoc* system of designations for reconnaissance Spitfires underwent a rationalisation. The Type C was redesignated the PR.Mk III; the Type D became the PR.Mk IV; the Type E became the PR.Mk V; the Type F became the PR.Mk VI; and the Type G became the PR.Mk VII. By then the surviving Type As and the Type Bs had all been modified into later variants. Also during the year the reconnaissance Spitfires were fitted or retrofitted with the Merlin 45 series engine as fitted to the Mk V fighter variant. No change in designation followed this change, however.

Watching the German fleet

Early in 1941 the German battle cruisers *Scharnhorst* and *Gneisenau* and the heavy cruiser *Admiral Hipper* put into harbour at Brest in western France, after a destructive foray against convoys in the north Atlantic. If these warships put to sea the Admiralty needed to know as soon as possible, so it could position naval forces to meet the threat. As a result, No. 1 PRU received a top-priority task to photograph the port three times each day. To provide the best chance of meeting this requirement, whatever the weather, pairs of Spitfires took off from St Eval in Cornwall and flew to Brest independently: a blue-painted Type C or Type F at high altitude to photograph the port if the skies were sufficiently clear, and a pale pink aircraft to photograph it if there was cloud cover. On this assignment, six-tenths' cloud was termed the 'no-man's land' figure. It was too much to allow much chance of successful photography

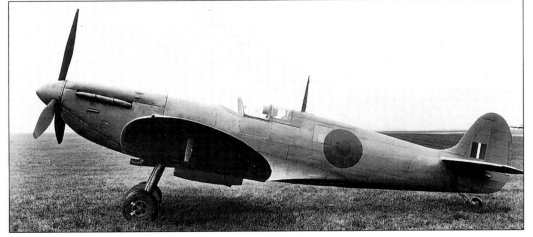

The PR.Mk IV was built in some numbers. There were three standard camera installations: the 'W' had two F8 20-in (508-mm) cameras in a split-vertical arrangement, the 'X' had two F24 14-in (356-mm) cameras in a split vertical with a single F24 8-in (203-mm) or 14-in oblique camera, while the 'Y' had a single F52 36-in (914-mm) camera mounted vertically. The 'W' and 'Y' installations had hot air heating, while the 'X' was heated electrically.

from high altitude, and too little to conceal a Spitfire at low altitude.

The fighter units and flak batteries defending Brest quickly became aware that regular flights were being made to photograph the harbour. Several Spitfires were lost and those who survived had to employ every possible stratagem. Gordon Green explained: "During the early [photographic reconnaissance] missions to cover Brest we lost about five pilots fairly quickly. After the first couple had failed to return the Flight Commander, Flight Lieutenant Keith Arnold, asked Benson to send some reserve pilots. They duly arrived. Both took off for Brest that evening and neither came back. That was a very sobering incident.

Get back at all costs

"The important thing with any photographic mission was to take the photos if one could, and get them back to base. As the 'boss' of PRU, Wing Commander Geoffrey Tuttle, often used to say, 'I want you to get home safely not just because I like your faces, but because if you don't the whole sortie will be a waste of time!' So it was no use trying to play hide and seek with the Luftwaffe. If one had lost surprise during the approach to a heavily defended target, the best thing was to abandon the mission. One could go back another time when things might be better.

"Looking back at my time with the PRU I get a lot of satisfaction from the knowledge that although I played my part in the war, I never had to fire a shot in anger. In one sense we in the reconnaissance business had things easy. All the time it was impressed on us: bring back the photographs or, if you can't, bring back the aeroplane. An infantryman taking part in the Battle of Alamein could not suddenly decide, 'This is ridiculous, I'm going home!' He just had to go on. But if we thought we had lost the element of surprise we were not only permitted to turn back, we were expected to do so. On the other hand, there were times when I knew real fear. When one was 15 minutes out from Brest on a low-altitude sortie, one's heart was beating away and as the target got nearer one's mouth got completely dry. Anyone who was not frightened at the thought of going in to photograph one of the most heavily defended targets in Europe was not human.

Spitfire PR.Mk IVs served with distinction in North Africa. The example above is on detachment to the theatre with No. 542 Sqn, while the aircraft below is from No. 2 PRU, which was formed in June 1941 at Heliopolis in Egypt. Both have the cumbersome tropical filters fitted.

"Whenever it was possible to photograph a target, flak could engage us: if we could see to photograph they could see to open up at us. But throughout my time as a reconnaissance pilot my luck held. I never once saw an enemy fighter, nor was my aircraft ever hit by flak. Indeed, only once during the time we were flying those missions over Brest did one of our aircraft come back with any damage, and that was minor. It was all rather like a fox hunt – either the fox got away unscathed or else it was caught and killed. There was rarely anything in between."

As the war progressed, the RAF reconnaissance force faced increasing demands to provide photographs of targets deep inside occupied Europe. To meet these requirements, No. 1 PRU underwent a steady increase in size. By May 1942 the unit had six flights of Spitfires with a total of 53 aircraft, and two flights of Mosquitos with 12 aircraft. In the following October the Spitfire and Mosquito flights of No. 1 PRU were reorganised into four squadrons. The two flights of Mosquitos were incorporated into No. 540 Squadron, while the six flights of Spitfires were divided between Nos 541, 542 and 543 Squadrons.

High-performance Spitfire

Also during 1942, the German air defences steadily improved with the deployment of the latest Bf 109G and Fw 190A fighters. As a result, the reconnaissance Spitfire units suffered mounting losses. The obvious answer was to produce a higher-performance reconnaissance aircraft powered by the Merlin 61 engine fitted to the Mk IX fighter. The new variant, the

This is another tropicalised Spitfire PR.Mk IV, incorporating the neater 'Aboukir' filter developed by 103 Maintenance Unit. The aircraft was dispatched to the Middle East on board the Amot Elkerk, disembarking at Takoradi on the Gold Coast for reassembly and onward flight to Egypt.

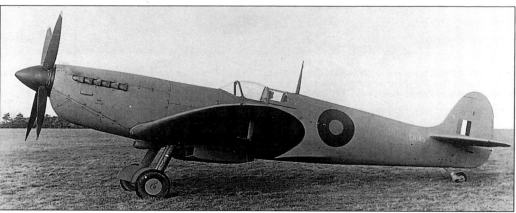

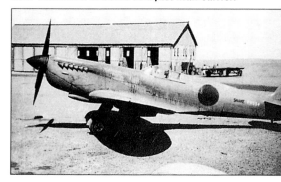

Fifteen Mk IX fighters became PR.Mk IXs to fill an urgent need for high-performance camera platforms before the Mk XI became available. The aircraft had guns removed and cameras fitted, but retained the fighter's standard fuel tankage, relying instead on a 90-Imp gal (409-litre) drop tank for extra range.

Spitfire PR.Mk XI, combined the strengthened airframe of the Mk VIII fighter with the wing fuel tank of the PR.Mk IV.

As an interim measure until the PR.Mk XI became available, 15 Mk IX fighters underwent modification for the reconnaissance role. Designated PR.Mk IXs, these aircraft had the armament removed and a pair of vertical cameras installed in the rear fuselage. The version had no extra internal fuel tankage, and during operations it usually flew with a 90-Imp gal

(409-litre) drop tank under the fuselage. No. 541 Squadron at Benson received the first PR.Mk IXs in November 1942. Although the PR.Mk IX was limited to operations over western Europe, it restored to the force the ability to photograph defended targets without incurring serious losses. In December 1942 the first Spitfire PR.Mk XIs began coming off the production line. The new variant could reach altitudes above 40,000 ft (12190 m), 10,000 ft (3058 m) higher than any previous reconnaissance version. The Mk XI replaced all other unarmed versions of the Spitfire in front-line reconnaissance units, and 471 examples were built. For more than a year after the variant entered service, it was almost immune to fighter interception while it was flying at high altitude.

Pictured in Egypt during transit to Southeast Asia is PR.Mk XI PA934. The 'Snake' designation indicates that the aircraft has been modified for operations in the humid Far East.

If one of these aircraft was lost, it was usually after it had descended either due to a technical failure or because of the pilot needed to go below cloud to take his photographs.

With the 8th Air Force to Berlin

During the autumn of 1943 the US 8th Air Force in Great Britain received a dozen Mk XIs. These formed the equipment of the 14th Photo Squadron, 7th Photographic Group, based at Mount Farm near Oxford. The unit's role was to take pre-strike and post-strike photographs of targets for US heavy bombers. Major Walt Weitner, commander of the 14th, flew his most memorable mission on 6 March 1944, following the first large-scale USAAF attack on Berlin. From Mount Farm that distant target was beyond the Spitfire's effective radius of action, so Weitner made an intermediate stop at Bradwell Bay in Essex to top off his tanks. For this mission the aircraft carried its maximum fuel load: 84 Imp gal (374 litres) in the two main tanks in front of the cockpit, 132 Imp gal (588 litres) in the integral tanks built into the leading edge of each wing, and 90 Imp gal (400 litres) in the 'slipper' drop tank under the fuselage. Carrying 306 Imp gal (1362 litres) of fuel the Spitfire was at maximum take-off weight, and it did not handle well on the ground.

Weitner recalled: "With a full load of fuel and that narrow undercarriage, the Spit would 'lean' disconcertingly during turns when one taxied. But once you got off the ground and got a little speed she really perked up, she would

My Darling Dorothy was one of the Spitfire PR.Mk XIs assigned to the 14th Photo Squadron, 7th Photographic Group. The unit was based at Mount Farm, just a few miles from the RAF's main PR base at Benson.

Right and below right: PR.Mk XIs of the 14th PS are seen during operations from Mount Farm. The Oxfordshire airfield, situated on the Thames plain, was more prone to flooding than Benson. The red band, seen on the aircraft right, was introduced in the winter of 1944/45 as a group marking.

leap away. Once the gear was up and you pulled up the nose, boy, would she climb! I took the direct route for Berlin, heading out on 086° over the North Sea towards Holland. Thirty-nine minutes after take-off I passed my first check-point, The Hague, at 39,000 ft. There was five-tenths' cloud cover below, through which I could make out the Zuider Zee. The Spitfire was easy to handle at very high altitude. This one was well trimmed and stayed pretty level. One had always to have hold of the stick, but it needed hardly any pressure. In the reconnaissance business you do not fly straight and level for long, you are continually banking to search the sky all around for enemy fighters and check the navigation.

"With all the extra clothing, the parachute, dinghy, life jacket, and oxygen mask, the narrow cockpit of a Spitfire was no place for the claustrophobic! The heavy flying clothing kept me pretty warm, though my extremities did begin to get a bit cold. The temperature outside was about -60°F, and from time to time I would stamp my feet to get the circulation going.

"Throughout the flight at high altitude my Spitfire left a long condensation trail. I could have avoided it by descending below 22,000 ft (6700 m), but I did not think that was the thing to do on a deep penetration like this. I thought the best bet was to cruise near to the ceiling of a Messerschmitt 109; then, if I had to go up, I had a little margin of altitude I could use. The Germans must have known I was up there but

This is the cockpit of the Spitfire PR.Mk XI, with the camera control unit mounted just below the windscreen. The cockpit could get very cramped when the pilot was wearing full cold-weather flying gear for high-altitude missions.

nobody was paying any attention to me. I thought that if enemy fighters did come after me they would have to leave trails, too, and I would get plenty of warning."

The reason for the lack of interest in the progress of the lone Spitfire is not hard to fathom: almost every available Luftwaffe fighter in the area was in action against the force of more than 600 Flying Fortresses and Liberators and their escorts battling their way westwards to their bases in England, after the attack on Berlin. As the Spitfire neared Berlin, however, defenders finally reacted to the high-flying intruder. A glance in one of the side mirrors told Weitner he had company in the form of three enemy fighters about a mile behind and a little below.

Crisis point

The discovery came at a particularly bad time for the American pilot. His engine was running on the fuel from the drop tank which, on his calculations, was almost empty. There was no gauge to measure the fuel left, however. The only indication that it was dry would be when the engine started to splutter and lose power. And that might happen at a critical time in the chase. Weitner thought of switching to one of the wing tanks and releasing the slipper tank; but this mission required every drop of fuel aboard the Spitfire. If he released the tank before it was empty, it would confuse his fuel calculations. More importantly, it might force him to abandon the mission before he reached the target. Nor could he switch the engine to one of the wing tanks for the time and return to the slipper tank later. If he did that, there was a good chance that the drop tank might not resume feeding if he reselected it. With no good alternative available, Weitner chose what he thought was the least bad: he would try to outrun the enemy fighters using the last of the fuel in the drop tank. When the fuel ran out, he

would try to switch to a wing tank before the engine died.

"I pushed the throttle forward as far as it would go without selecting emergency power, eased up the nose and began to climb. The whole time I nervously held the tank selector valve, ready to switch to one of the internal wing tanks the moment the engine faltered. As I climbed through 40,000 ft I could see that the German fighters behind me had split: one went on my right and two on my left, to box me in. And at that moment the engine coughed. I immediately selected internal fuel and the engine caught right away. At 41,500 ft [12500 m] I levelled off and my indicated airspeed increased to 178 mph [286 km/h, a true airspeed of about 360 mph/580 km/h]. After what seemed forever, but was probably only two to three minutes, the German fighters began to fall back and slid out of sight. Had they come any closer I should have gone to emergency boost, but it never got that desperate."

The pursuing fighters never came close enough for Weitner to identify them, but

Major Walt Weiner was commander of the 14th Photo Squadron. High Lady was the PR.Mk XI he flew to Berlin on 6 March 1944.

Three photos show 14th PS Spitfires, complete with the invasion stripes added in June 1944. The 7th PG had four squadrons: the 13th, 22nd and 27th PS flying the F-4/F-5 Lightning, and the 14th with Spitfires. The latter had received Mk Vs for training in the late summer of 1943 before receiving its PR.Mk XI operational equipment. P-51Ds and Ks were received from January 1945.

This is one of the photographs of Berlin taken by Major Weitner on 6 March 1944, showing fires burning in the Zehlendorf district of the city. The sensor used was the 36-in (914-mm) focal length F52 camera, the usual choice for bomb damage assessment missions.

almost certainly they were Bf 109Gs fitted with nitrous oxide power boosting to enhance their high-altitude performance.

Still keeping a wary eye for the fighters, Weitner checked his navigation. To the north he could make out the huge Lake Moritz, some 50 miles north-northwest of Berlin. He could not see the city itself, however, because it was hidden under a layer of industrial haze. The Spitfire lacked a pressurised cabin and Weitner had no wish to remain at maximum altitude longer than necessary, so he eased the aircraft down to 38,000 ft (11580 m). Then, suddenly, he saw the sprawling enemy capital laid out beneath him.

"There was quite a lot of haze, but I could see the sun glinting off the red brick and tile houses. If the German fighters reappeared I might be able to make only one photographic run so I planned to make the first from almost due north, down wind, to get a good line of photos without drifting off the target. I rolled the Spitfire on its side to line up the string of lakes I was using as check points, levelled out using the artificial horizon and switched on the cameras."

In the rear fuselage of the Spitfire the two vertically-mounted F.52 cameras, each with a 36-in lens, clicked at five-second intervals to photograph a 3-mile (4.8-km) wide strip of ground beneath the aircraft. During a photographic run accurate flying was essential: even a small amount of bank could cause gaps in the cover. Any correction to the aircraft's flight path had to be made in the five-second intervals between photographs.

"My orders were to photograph the bombers' targets and I had been given aerial photos of the city taken previously by the RAF,

with the targets marked on them. But I could see smoke rising from places other than my assigned targets so I decided to photograph the sources of the smoke also. The whole time I kept checking the sky behind my tail, as I expected further interference from the enemy fighters. But none showed up. There was some flak, I could see the smoke bursts mushrooming, but none of it was close. I spent about 25 minutes over Berlin, during which I made runs from different directions and took about 70 photographs. Then a solid layer of cloud began moving over the city from the east, and as fuel was beginning to run low I set a course of 297° for home."

On the return flight Weitner had another drama with the fuel. The order of using the Spitfire XI's fuel was, first, that in the drop tank; next the fuel in the wing leading-edge tanks, alternating between them at 15-minute intervals so the aircraft did not get out of trim; then the lower main tank and finally the upper main tank. As the last of the wing tanks emptied, the Merlin coughed briefly. Weitner switched to the lower main tank and the engine's even roar resumed. How long it would continue to do so was a moot point, however, for the American pilot was disconcerted to see the needle of the fuel gauge pushed hard against the zero mark. Could there have been a fuel leak, leaving the aircraft with insufficient fuel to regain friendly territory? Or might the gauge have frozen up?

"I discovered why I had toiled over maths for so long without learning its true value! Some

Powerplant

Power for the PR.Mk XI initially came from the Merlin 60 series engines (first 61, then 63). From PL768 onwards (after one installation in PL763) the Mk XI was fitted with the Merlin 70. This developed 1,475 hp (1100 kW) at high altitude, and drove a Rotol R12/4F5/4 four-bladed propeller. The enlarged oil tank under the nose, which caused the pronounced bulge to the cowling lines, held 14.4 Imp gal (65.5 litres).

Fuel

The two main fuel tanks, with a total capacity of 85 Imp gal, were mounted behind the engine. In addition, this variant carried 132 Imp gal (588 litres) in integral tanks built into the leading edge of each wing. Also, for the longer range missions, it could carry a 90-Imp gal (400-litre) 'slipper' drop tank under the fuselage.

Wing cameras

Later production PR.Mk XIs had provision to carry a vertical F24 5-in (12.7-cm) focal length camera in a blister mid-way along each wing.

Supermarine Spitfire PR.Mk XI
14th Photo Squadron
7th Photo Group
Mount Farm
1944

This aircraft, PL914, first flew in August 1944. After a brief period at Royal Air Force Benson, it was transferred to the US 8th Air Force and was assigned to the 14th Photo Squadron, 7th Photographic Group, based at Mount Farm near Oxford. The unarmed aircraft flew pre-strike and post-strike photographic missions with this unit almost until the end of the war in Europe. In April 1945 the Spitfire returned to 71 MU, RAF and went into storage. It was scrapped in April 1946.

Camera heating

On the PR.Mk XI the cameras were heated by hot air, ducts running from the cabin heating system (itself fed directly from the radiator) back to a box covering the magazines and shutters of the cameras.

Colour scheme and markings

The Spitfire wore the medium blue colour scheme that was standard for RAF high-altitude reconnaissance planes throughout most of World War II, known as 'PRU Blue'. The RAF serial number was painted in white on the rear fuselage and repeated in larger characters on the fin and rudder. The Spitfire carried invasion stripes under the fuselage. Later the 7th PG adopted red stripes on the forward fuselage as a group marking.

Main camera installation

The 'U', or Universal, camera installation was located in the rear fuselage. On aircraft operated by this unit it usually comprised two 36-in (91.44-cm) focal length cameras in a 'split pair' installation, the forward camera pointed just starboard of the vertical and the rear camera pointed slightly to port. These were located between frames 13 and 15 of the fuselage structure. If shorter focal length vertical cameras were carried in the rear fuselage, aircraft could carry an oblique camera facing either to port or to starboard.

Performance

The PR.Mk XI had a top speed of 417 mph (671 km/h) at 24,200 ft (7376 m) and a ceiling of 44,000 ft (13411 m). Endurance was 5.4 hours, and range was 2,300 miles (3700 km).

Undercarriage

All three wheels and tyres were made by Dunlop, the mainwheels being AH2061 units and the tailwheel an AH2184/IX. The first 45 PR.Mk XIs had fixed tailwheels, retractable wheels being fitted from MB794 onwards.

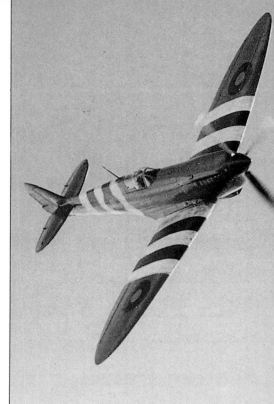

Wearing full invasion stripes, a PR.Mk XI of No. 541 Sqn from Benson cavorts for the camera. Noteworthy are the two camera windows in the underside of the fuselage. PR.Mk XIs had the 'U' (Universal) camera installation allowing a variety of sensors to be fitted.

Ground crew service the camera systems of a PR.Mk XI of No. 16 Sqn. The oblique camera window hatch is open, and an F52 camera lies on the grass.

rapid calculations almost proved the main tanks had to be full. During these reveries nothing of a threatening nature showed itself except a few far-off trails to the east. Soon the cloud covering the English coast was within gliding distance, and all was well again. Over the North Sea I descended to 30,000 ft and called 'Gangplank' [Bradwell Bay] on the VHF for a homing. Over the coast of East Anglia the gas gauge suddenly came to life showing about 20 Imp gal [89 litres]. At my altitude I knew I had enough fuel to reach Mount Farm without having to land at the coast to take on more."

Weitner descended to Mount Farm with the engine throttled back, made a low pass over the airfield, pulled round hard into finals, lowered his flaps and undercarriage and landed. He had been airborne for four hours and 18 minutes.

"On entering the dispersal area the gas and the maths ran out simultaneously, leaving a spluttering and dead engine on my hands just a few feet short of 'according to plan'."

The unpopular Mk X

The system of allocating Spitfire numbers was anything but methodical, and the PR.Mk X entered service more than a year later than the PR.Mk XI. The two variants were similar except that the Mk X was fitted with a pressurised cabin. Only sixteen examples were built and these entered service with Nos 541 and 542 Squadrons in May 1944. The commander of the latter unit, Squadron Leader Alfred Ball, remembered the PR.Mk X without any great affection.

"I flew the PR.Mk X a few times on operations. They were not popular because of the poor visibility out of the very thick perspex canopy. Outside everything looked a slightly discoloured yellow, the perspex was not as clear as on an ordinary Spitfire. Also, with the extra weight of the pressure cabin, the Mk X felt much heavier than the Mk XI. We preferred the unpressurised Mk XI to the Mk X."

The near-immunity of these versions from fighter interception lasted until the spring of 1944. Then the Luftwaffe deployed its first jet fighter types, the rocket-propelled Messerschmitt Me 163 and the turbojet-powered Me 262. High-flying Allied reconnaissance aircraft, unarmed and alone, offered perfect targets on which the German pilots converting to the jets could make practice interceptions.

PR.Mk 19 – The Master Spy

To overcome the threat of interception from German jet fighters, Supermarine designed a long-range unarmed reconnaissance variant of the Spitfire powered by the Rolls-Royce Griffon engine. This, the PR.Mk 19, had integral wing tanks as fitted to the PR.Mk IV and the PR.Mk XI. (Note, in 1943 the RAF changed from Roman to Arabic mark numbers for its aircraft.)

The new variant entered service in May 1944 and provided a huge advance in performance over the PR.Mk XI. Later production PR.Mk 19s were fitted with a pressurised cabin of improved design which overcame the shortcomings of that fitted to the PR.Mk X. With the power from the Griffon engine, the extra weight of the pressurised cabin caused no noticeable deterioration in performance. Comfortably ensconced in their pressurised cabins, pilots often took this variant above 45,000 ft (13716 m).

If the Spitfire PR.Mk 19 pilot saw an intercepting jet fighter in time, he had little difficulty in outmanoeuvring it. Alfred Ball recalled: "I encountered Messerschmitt 262s on a couple of occasions. Unless your eyes were shut when they jumped you, you could usually get away from them. They had a long climb to reach us, and they could not stay with us for very long. I would wait until the 262 pilot was about to open fire, then pull into a tight turn. You had to judge the turn correctly – if you turned too soon it was not difficult for him to pull enough

With a Hurricane and Mosquitoes in the background, this PR.Mk XI of No. 681 Squadron was photographed at Monywa, Burma in 1944. The aircraft sports the light blue/dark blue national insignia worn in the theatre to avoid any confusion with Japanese aircraft.

Right: The PR.Mk X was very similar to the PR.Mk XI. The major external difference was the intake scoop on the starboard side of the cowling, this providing air for the blower feeding the pressurised cabin. Due to problems with the pressurisation, the Mk X entered service more than a year after the Mk XI, and was never popular with its pilots.

Below: This PR.Mk XI was captured intact and flown by the Luftwaffe. It wears over-sized national insignia to prevent engagement by 'friendly' fighters or flak.

What it lacks in clarity this photo makes up for in rarity: it depicts a PR.Mk XIII in the markings of No. 718 Sqn, Fleet Air Arm. Only 26 of this variant were produced, and after their front-line service with the RAF was over, they were transferred to the Navy unit at Henstridge, for use in the army co-operation training role.

deflection and you were a sitting duck. Provided you handled your aircraft properly, it was very difficult for them to shoot you down."

Altogether, 225 examples of the PR.Mk 19 were built, before production of this version ended in the spring of 1946.

New low-level reconnaissance variants

As stated earlier, the Spitfire PR.Mk VII (aka PR.Mk IG) armed reconnaissance unit served successfully during the early war years in the low-altitude 'dicing' role. Early in 1943 these were replaced by the PR.Mk XIII, with a low-altitude rated Merlin 32 developing 1,645 hp (1227 kW) at 2,500 ft (792 m). The new variant had a maximum speed of 349 mph (562 km/h) at 5,400 ft (1650 m). The camera installation and fuel tankage was the same as the earlier variant. The defensive armament was reduced to four 0.303-in machine-guns in the outer wing positions. Only 26 PR.Mk XIIIs were built, all converted from PR.Mk VIIs or Mk I or Mk V fighters. The type saw service with Nos 4, 400, 541 and 542 Squadrons. Later,

after replacement in front-line units, some Mk XIIIs served with No. 718 Squadron, a Fleet Air Arm army co-operation training unit. In November 1944 a fighter-reconnaissance version of the Griffon-powered Spitfire XIV entered service, fitted with an oblique camera in the rear fuselage and designated the FR.Mk XIV. This variant retained the fighter's armament of two 20-mm cannon and four machine-guns, and was a considerable improvement over the PR.Mk XIII that it replaced.

Fastest dive by a piston-engined aircraft – ever

After the war Spitfire PR.Mk 19s made some truly remarkable high-altitude flights. In the RAF the term 'service ceiling' was defined as the altitude where the aircraft's rate of climb fell below 100 ft (30 m) per minute. In the case of

the PR.Mk 19 the service ceiling was officially recorded as 42,600 ft (12990 m). Yet that figure gave no indication of the altitude an aircraft could reach in a long cruise climb to a distant target. During the post-war air defence exercises in the United Kingdom, Spitfire PR.Mk 19s sometimes overflew their targets at 49,000 ft (14940 m).

Even that magnificent performance was eclipsed early in 1952 by a PR.Mk 19 of No. 81 Squadron based in Hong Kong. On 5 February Flight Lieutenant Ted Powles took off from Kai Tak for a meteorological height climb to 50,000 ft (15240 m). His briefing was to record the outside air temperature at various altitudes and report on any clear air turbulence and high wind speeds he encountered. The purpose of the sortie was to collect data on high-altitude meteorological conditions, to assist with a proposed air service through the area by the new Comet jet airliner.

At this point a few words of explanation are necessary concerning the effect of the height of the stratosphere on Powles' sortie. Over Great Britain the height of the stratosphere is around 36,000 ft (10973 m) and above that the air temperature remains steady at about -54°C (-65°F). Approaching the Equator, the height of the stratosphere gradually increases. In tropical latitudes (Hong Kong lies just south of the Tropic of Cancer), the stratosphere begins at about 50,000 ft (15240 m). Above that altitude the air temperature is steady at about -72°C (-97°F).

The lower the temperature of the air entering the carburettor air intake of the Spitfire, the

This was an early production example of the Spitfire PR.Mk 19, the ultimate PR version. It served with No. 541 Sqn, which received its first aircraft in June 1944. Early PR.Mk 19s lacked cabin pressurisation.

Fighter Reconnaissance Spitfires

No. 16 Squadron operated this Spitfire FR.Mk IX in the tactical reconnaissance role over Normandy following the June 1944 invasion. The aircraft had full armament options, although this aircraft has had the 20-mm cannon removed. A single oblique camera was mounted in the port side of the fuselage, and the aircraft wore pale pink scheme for below-cloud photography.

The Spitfire FR.Mk XIV took over much of the low-level tactical reconnaissance role from dedicated PR Spitfires. These are with No. 11 Squadron, seen in 1947 at Miho, Japan.

The similar FR.Mk 18 was the final fighter-recce version, with strengthened wing. This example served with No. 28 Sqn, based at Seletar in Singapore.

greater its density and therefore the greater the power developed by the engine. Thus, due to the increased height of the stratosphere, in the tropics the Griffon engine developed more power at altitude than it would have over Europe.

Powles flew his sortie methodically, levelling at each 5,000 ft (1524 m) step to collect and record the required readings. Then he resumed his climb to the next step. As he neared the final part of the ascent, about 1.5 hours after take-off, the Spitfire's rate of climb fell to a few tens of feet per minute. Finally he reached 48,500 ft (14785 m) indicated on his altimeter, which represented a true altitude of 50,000 ft (15240 m).

Perfect conditions

There, Powles found the Spitfire's controls extremely sensitive although the aircraft still had some performance in hand. He recalled: "I had been up to 48,500 ft indicated, that was 50,000 ft true, at least half a dozen times during earlier sorties. But on that particular day the conditions were perfect, the aeroplane was flying beautifully, I had the time and I had the fuel, so I decided to see if I could get her to 50,000 ft indicated."

Carefully he nudged the aircraft higher until eventually the altimeter read 50,000 ft – a true altitude of 51,550 (15715 m). The airspeed indicator read 108 kt (124 mph, 200 km/h, equating to a true airspeed of 275 mph, 443 km/h).

"I was flying on the very edge of the Spitfire's performance envelope and I felt exhilarated. It felt as if I was trying to balance on top of a ball. I had to fly on instruments, because if I looked over the side a wing would start to drop. I was flying almost on the stall, and if a wing did drop I had to pick it up using opposite rudder; if the starboard wing dropped I eased on left rudder, so that wing moved through the air a little faster and slowly rose."

He could not use the ailerons to hold the wings level, because lowering the surface would stall the wing on that side and cause the Spitfire to flip on its back.

Suddenly the red cabin pressurisation warning light illuminated, indicating that cabin pressure had fallen below a safe level. Now Powles had to make a rapid descent below 43,000 ft (13106 m), or the reduction in pressure would cause the nitrogen in his blood to expand and bring on the painful condition known as 'the bends'. He pushed the control column forward, throttled back and moved the pitch lever to 2,200 rpm to prevent the propeller from over-speeding the engine.

"While I was checking to see if the pressuri-sation seal around the canopy had burst, the aircraft started to shake and when I again looked at my flying instruments, I was shocked to see the needle on the airspeed indicator just passing the 280 kt [322 mph; 519 km/h] mark (the Pilot's Notes state that 260 kt should not be exceeded above 40,000 ft!).

"I immediately pulled back on the control column, but the more I pulled the steeper the aircraft dived. It was now shaking so violently that I could not read the instruments. The Spitfire was in a vertical dive and I was standing on the rudder bars. The control column was immovable and I was afraid if I pulled any harder something would break. Beside the vibration, the aircraft started to yaw from side to side. I felt as though a giant hand was shaking it."

High-Mach mist

The pilot's first thought was to try to ease up the nose using the elevator trim tabs. Glancing out over the wings he noticed that they were covered in a strange mist (caused, we now know, by the shock waves that form at high Mach numbers). Fearing the elevators might be torn off by the airflow if he moved the trim tabs, Powles decided to leave them alone.

"Eventually, after the longest few seconds of my life, the vibration and yawing stopped, the mist was clearing from the wings and the nose started to lift. I was still pushing on the unyielding control column and when I felt the resistance lessen the nose dropped again, so I quickly reversed the pressure and started to pull out of the dive. I placed my feet in the top stirrups of the rudder bar and pulled hard on the control column until I started to black out. I then eased the pressure. I could not afford to lose control at this point."

When Powles next scanned his instruments he saw the airspeed indicator unwinding rapidly through 500 kt (575 mph; 926 km/h), and the altimeter steady at 3,300 ft (1006 m). As the

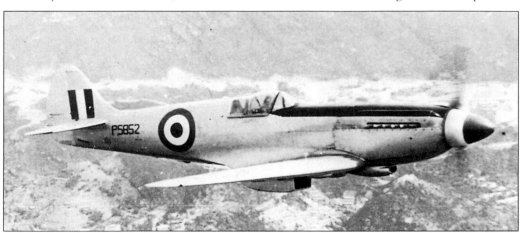

Shown above is Flight Lieutenant E. C. 'Ted' Powles of No. 81 Squadron, whose account of a hair-raising high-speed dive is given above. PS852 (left) was the aircraft involved in the 5 February 1952 incident.

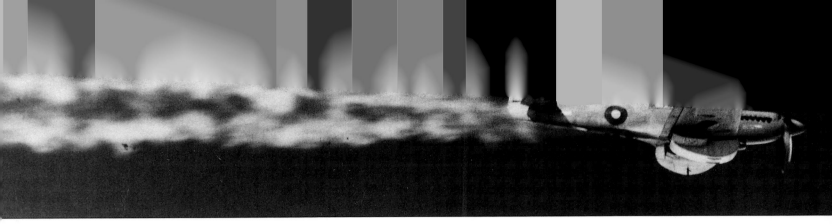

This PR.Mk 19 was photographed during high-altitude trials of the 180-Imp gal (818-litre) ferry tank which was fitted to the belly between the main undercarriage legs and radiators. On operational missions PR Spitfire pilots would try almost anything to avoid leaving a vapour trail.

Right: Seen post-war, this PR.Mk 19 wears the '6C' codes of the Photographic Reconnaissance Development Unit.

super-cooled aircraft entered the moist warm air low down, condensation froze on the inside of the canopy, preventing the pilot seeing outside. He then tried to open the canopy, but it was frozen shut and resisted his efforts to budge it.

Powles collected his thoughts and realised he was still not safe. Unable to see outside the aircraft, he had little idea of his position. And there were mountain peaks in the area extending above 5,000 ft (1524 m). He initiated a climb on instruments, heading southeast towards the sea.

"When I pulled out of the dive and levelled out, the altimeter indicated 3,300 ft. I started a climb with about 1,750 ft per min [8.89 m/sec] showing on the vertical speed indicator, but the altimeter stayed at 3,300 ft for quite some time before it started to rise."

Lagging altimeter

It was chillingly obvious that during the dive the altimeter had 'lagged' considerably in the reading it gave. When the Spitfire bottomed out of the dive must have been a good deal lower than the 3,300 ft shown on the instrument. Ted Powles had been very lucky indeed to pull out of the dive before the aircraft plunged into the ground or the sea.

Then matters began to sort themselves out. A call to Hong Kong Approach Control produced a radio bearing which showed that the Spitfire was safely over the sea. Then the canopy unfroze, allowing the pilot to slide it back. The inrush of warm air quickly cleared the frosting off the perspex and normality returned.

After he landed, Powles asked that Spitfire be given a thorough examination to see if the airframe had been overstressed. Surprisingly, the aircraft emerged from its torturous experience without any discernible harm.

Safely on the ground, Powles now tried to establish just what had happened during the dive. He had noted the times when he initiated the rapid descent, when he passed through 44,000 ft just before the vibration started, and again after the pull-out. He had taken nine seconds to descend from 50,000 ft (15244 m) to 44,000 ft (14432 m) indicated, and 47 seconds to descend from 44,000 ft until he levelled out at 3,300 ft indicated (which, due to altimeter lag, was probably well below 2,000 ft/610 m). The descent through about 42,000 ft (12800 m) and the subsequent pull-out had taken 47 seconds, which meant that at some time in the dive the Spitfire must have exceeded 1,000 ft per second, or over 680 mph (1095 km/h). The

aircraft had no Mach meter, but Powles had recorded the outside air temperatures at 5,000 ft (1524 m) intervals during the climb so it was a simple matter to work out the speed of sound for each altitude. After applying corrections for compressibility and other factors he calculated that the Spitfire had reached a speed of at least Mach 0.94 when it passed 15,000 ft (4573 m) in the dive, equivalent to 690 mph (1111 km/h).

Powles had considered using the elevator trim to raise the nose of the aircraft during the dive, but it is as well he did not try it. Later Jeffrey Quill, one-time chief test pilot at Supermarine, looked over the figures and expressed the view that use of the trim tabs in those circumstances might have caused a high-speed stall after which the aircraft would probably have disintegrated. As it was, when the aircraft reached the denser air below 15,000 ft its speed started to decay. Thereafter, the Spitfire exerted its natural tendency to pull itself out of the dive.

In the absence of any serious counter-claim, it appears likely that on 5 February 1952 Ted Powles achieved the highest altitude ever attained by a Spitfire, 51,550 ft (true). And during that subsequent hair-raising dive he reached the highest Mach number, Mach 0.94, and the greatest speed, 690 mph, ever attained by a

Spitfire – or any other piston-engined aircraft for that matter. In each case, those figures provide resounding endorsements of both the soundness of Reginald Mitchell's original design and of the structural improvements made to the aircraft during its lengthy development life.

Dr Alfred Price

Above: PR.Mk 19s remained on secondary duties with the RAF for some time after retirement from the front line. PS915 was one of the last three Spitfires in regular RAF use, flown by the Meteorological Flight at Woodvale until 1957.

Below: PS888 occupies a special place in RAF history, for it flew the last operational sortie by a Spitfire. Suitably adorned, the aircraft was launched out of Seletar by No. 81 Sqn on 1 April 1954 on a mission to photograph areas thought to harbour Communist guerrillas during the Malayan campaign. The unit also flew the last operational RAF Mosquito mission.

When it entered service in 1942, the Seafire Mk IB, the first variant of this naval derivative of the Spitfire, was the fastest naval fighter in the world. Developed to urgently fill a requirement for a Sea Hurricane replacement, it was far from suitable for the carrierborne role, but nonetheless went on to give a good account of itself in combat, particularly in the Mediterranean and Far East. Meanwhile, as the Seafire was about to make its debut, the Spitfire was undergoing its own transformation. Reworked to take a new, more powerful engine, the Rolls-Royce Griffon, the Spitfire was able to maintain its position as one of the Allies' most potent interceptors – a position held by the type until the dawn of the jet age.

Supermarine SPITFIRE (Griffon-engined variants) and SEAFIRE

Inset: Seafire Mk IICs of No. 880 Sqn are seen aboard HMS Indomitable in mid-1943. No. 880 Sqn was one of the first FAA units to re-equip with Seafires in late 1942, operating Mk IIs and IIIs in both hemispheres for the duration of the war.

Main picture: Spitfire development was coming to an end when this formation was photographed by Charles E. Brown in 1945/46. Flanking the Spitfire Mk 22 prototype, PK312, are Mk 21s LA217 and LA232.

Spitfires at sea

Deck suitability trials with Spitfire Mk VB BL676 began during Christmas week 1941 aboard HMS *Illustrious* in the Clyde. The urgency of the trials programme was such that the carrier was pressed into service despite sustaining damage some 10 days before in a collision in the mid-Atlantic. A sizeable part of its flight deck was unusable as a result. In early 1942 the somewhat clumsy 'Sea Spitfire' name first proposed for the new type was abandoned and the compressed Seafire name officially adopted.

Left and below: Vokes filter-equipped Spitfire Mk VB BL676 Bondowoso was the first of the so-called 'hooked' Spitfires. Converted for deck landing acceptance trials it was followed by 166 further conversions to Seafire Mk IB standard. New serials were issued; BL676 became MB328.

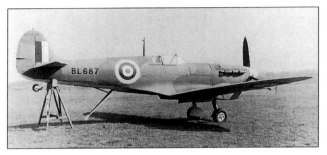

Right: The A-frame arrester hook fitted to 'hooked' Spitfires and early Seafires (up to Mk XV) is here seen in the deployed position. BL687 was the first 'production' conversion from Spitfire Mk VB standard carried out by Air Service Training Ltd at Hamble, becoming Seafire Mk IB MB329.

'Hooked' Spitfire Mk IIB P8537 lifts its tail as it roars down the deck of a carrier during trials.

Below: Seen aboard HMS Furious, the first carrier to take the Seafire into action, is a Mk IB of No. 801 Sqn (note the winged trident emblem beneath the cockpit). The lack of catapult spools on the Mk I was of little consequence as Furious, in which the squadron was embarked from October 1942, had no catapult.

Throughout the early years of World War II the Royal Navy had suffered from the lack of a high-performance carrier-based fighter. Following successful deck operating trials with Hurricanes during 1941, it was only to be expected that the Spitfire would also be considered for the role. A key to the Spitfire's success as a fighter was the mating of the most powerful engine available and a cleverly designed lightweight airframe; this made for an excellent land-based fighter, but not one that would be robust enough to withstand the rough-and-tumble of carrier operations. The entire service career of the navalised version of the fighter, the Seafire, was dogged by that fundamental problem.

The initial trials to test the suitability of the Spitfire for deck operations took place in December 1941. Commander

H. Bramwell DSC RN, Commanding Officer of the RN Fighter School, made a series of landings on HMS *Illustrious* in a Spitfire Mk V fitted with an A-frame hook mounted under the fuselage. The carrier was available for only a short time and the trials were in no way comprehensive. However, they did show that the idea of adapting the Spitfire to operate from aircraft-carriers was worth pursuing. As a result, the Royal Navy initiated a programme to modify a batch of Mk V Spitfires for this purpose.

Seafire F.Mk IB and F.Mk IIC

The initial navalised variant of the Spitfire, the Seafire Mk IB, was an existing Mk VB aircraft modified for the task. The B referred to the type of wing and the armament of two 20-mm cannon and four 0.303-in (7.7-mm) machine-guns; there was no Seafire Mk IA. In addition to the arrester hook, the navalised variant was fitted with slinging points for hoisting it on and off decks. It also carried specialised naval radio equipment in the shape of a high frequency R/T set, a homing beacon receiver and naval IFF equipment. For training purposes another batch of Spitfire Mk VBs was modified to a lower standard, with the arrester hook, navy R/T set and IFF equipment but without the slinging points or beacon receiver. To differentiate these aircraft from those fully equipped for carrier operations, the latter were known as 'hooked Spitfires'.

Meanwhile, work advanced rapidly on a batch of new-build Seafires, Mk IICs. This variant was based on the Spitfire Mk VC, which had a redesigned and more robust wing

Into service, 1942

23 June 1942 saw the first Seafire Mk IICs reach an operational FAA squadron, No. 807 at Lee-on-Solent. Four other squadrons followed suit in the second half of 1942, all receiving Mk IICs, except No. 801 Sqn, which acquired Mk IBs and was to be the only front-line unit to be equipped with a full complement of the early Seafire variant. The next front-line unit to receive the Mk I (for operational use, rather than training) did not do so until the summer of 1943, when torpedo-bomber/reconnaissance squadron, No. 842, acquired six examples with which to form a fighter flight. With most of the FAA's Seafire Mk IIs earmarked for use during the Salerno landings, Operation Avalanche, No. 842 Sqn was provided with Mk IBs withdrawn from training units in July, undertaking trade protection duties during the occupation of the Azores. No. 894 continued to operate Mk IBs until March 1944.

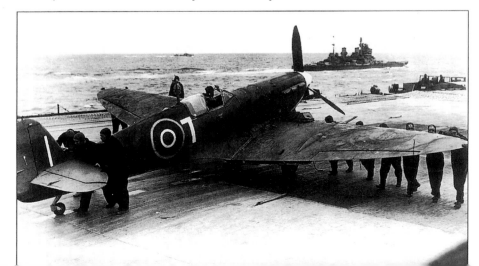

New build Mk IIs

As derivatives of the Spitfire Mk V, both the Seafire Mk I and II were powered by a Merlin 45 or 46, though in naval service their superchargers were modified to produce +14 lb boost at low level, instead of the standard +12 lb. Later, as it was found that Seafires had difficulty in overtaking fleet shadowers at low level, further modifications were made to allow +16-lb boost. Both Seafire Mk Is and IIs were modified, but in terms of outright performance the F.Mk IIC was inferior to the Mk IB. In the latter, airframe strengthening increased empty weight by six per cent, while catapult spools and the revised shape of the 'C' wing increased drag. Altogether, these changes took 15 mph (24 km/h) off the aircraft's top speed at all altitudes. Ultimately, the need to improve the Mk II's low-level performance led to a major re-engining programme, a large number of F.Mk IICs being fitted with a new Merlin 32 engine, of the type being installed in FAA's Fairey Barracuda Mk IIs and already in use by the RAF in their Spitfire Mk XIII low-level PR variant. L.Mk IICs, as these aircraft were designated, could be distinguished by their four-bladed propellers and entered service in May 1943, remaining in use until late 1944. Finally, from the L.Mk IIC was derived a camera-equipped variant – the LR.Mk IIC – effectively a naval equivalent to the Spitfire Mk XIII. Around 30 were converted and served with No. 4 Fighter Wing from late 1943.

Above: A Mk IIC, newly converted from Spitfire Mk VC standard, is readied for its first flight after weighing and CofG determination at Vickers-Supermarine's Worthy Down airfield.

Left: The first production Mk IIC, MA970, made its maiden flight on 28 May 1942 and served as a trials aircraft until a take-off collision with a Westland Welkin at Farnborough in 1944 brought about its destruction. Here it stands on a catapult rig at Farnborough in June 1942.

Below left: By September 1942 MA970 had been fitted with a four-bladed propeller of the type that would equip the Merlin 32-powered L.Mk IIC.

Below: Mk IIC MB293 was converted to L.Mk IIC standard shortly after completion in November 1942. Here it is seen during trials in 1944 of the Mk III light universal carrier with small bombs and reconnaissance flares.

structure. As well as the naval modifications applied to the Seafire Mk IB, it had catapult spools and some strengthening of the fuselage to accommodate the stresses of deck landing. Again, the C referred to the type of wing fitted, and there was no Seafire Mk IIA or Mk IIB.

At the start of the naval fighter programme, Supermarine engineers began design work on a wing-folding mechanism for the Seafire. While this was highly desirable for carrier operations, it was not indispensable, and to hasten the entry of the Seafire into front-line service, both the initial variants lacked wing folding.

The first Seafire Mk IBs and Mk IICs were taken on Royal Navy charge in June 1942. In the weeks to follow, five fighter squadrons re-equipped with the Seafires and began working up. No. 801 Squadron received Mk IBs, while Nos 807, 880, 884 and 885 Squadrons received Mk IICs.

In action during Torch

A total of 54 Seafires in five squadrons was embarked on carriers taking part in Operation Torch, the invasion of Morocco and Algeria. Nos 801 and 807 Squadrons embarked in HMS *Furious*, No. 880 in *Argus*, No. 884 in *Victorious*, and No. 885 Squadron in *Formidable*. For this operation the Seafires, like other Royal Navy aircraft involved, wore US national markings: since the Royal Navy attack on the French fleet at Oran in 1940, the latter service was known to be hostile to the Royal Navy and it was believed the French defenders would be less likely to fire at aircraft bearing US markings.

The Seafire first went into action on 27 October 1942, when Lieutenant S. Hall of No. 800 Squadron claimed hits on a Junkers Ju 88 that had been shadowing *Furious*.

On 8 November 1942, the first day of the landings, all Seafire units flew in support of British troops going ashore

Many Seafire L.Mk IICs operated with clipped wings to improve roll rate at low level. LR691 is a No. 808 Sqn aircraft precariously positioned on the port catwalk after a landing mishap aboard escort carrier HMS Hunter early in 1944, during exercises prior to the D-Day landings.

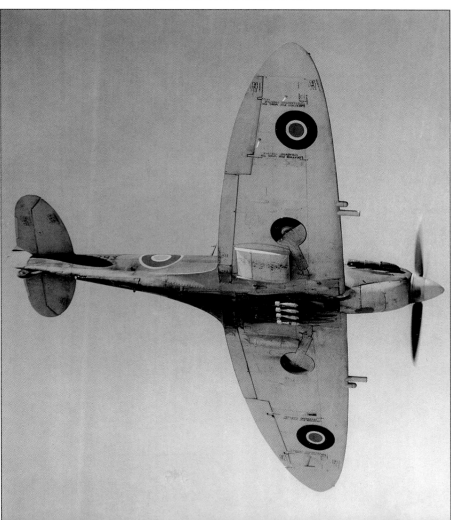

Training with the Seafire

Operating from an aircraft-carrier, the Seafire novice needed to get to grips with an aircraft that had a long nose, finely balanced controls and an approach speed that was little more than its stall speed – all features inconducive to safe operation at sea! The bulk of Seafire Mk I production was allocated to training units, in particular Nos 1 and 2 Naval Fighter Schools, at Yeovilton and Henstridge respectively, and the School of Naval Air Warfare at St Merryn.

Below: Seafire Mk IB NX890 'AC-C' formates with a pair of similar aircraft from No. 736 Sqn, the School of Air Combat. Established in May 1943, the unit took over from the RAF Fighter Leaders' School the task of training naval fighter leaders, and operated Seafires and Spitfires until late 1944.

Top: This photograph by Charles E. Brown shows a formation of No. 760 Sqn aircraft (including Seafire Mk IICs MB217 and MB264) in November 1942, when the unit formed part of the Fleet Fighter School.

Above: Student pilots familiarise themselves with a No. 760 Sqn Mk IIC at Yeovilton, November 1942.

Below: A Seafire Mk IB of No. 760 Sqn makes a successful landing aboard Ravager, an escort carrier employed for deck landing training from 1943.

in Algeria. In addition to the 54 Seafires, the Royal Navy fighter force in the area comprised some 80 Sea Hurricanes and Martlets. The main Vichy French air threat to the landings in Algeria comprised 75 Dewoitine D.520 fighters and 54 LeO 451 and Douglas DB-7 bombers. In addition, there was a potentially dangerous torpedo bomber unit equipped with 13 Latécoère 298s.

The Seafire Mk IICs of No. 807 Squadron, operating from *Furious*, were particularly active. Early that morning the unit sent 10 aircraft to strafe the airfield at Tafaraoui, causing the destruction of four LeO 451 bombers. On their way back to their carrier they passed La Senia airfield, then under attack from Albacores and Sea Hurricanes. French D.520s then appeared on the scene and, after a brief fight, Sub-Lieutenant G. Baldwin shot down one, to gain the Seafire's first confirmed aerial victory.

After the first day, French resistance in the air came to a virtual end. As invading troops seized airfields ashore and land-based fighter units flew in from Gibraltar, the dependence on the aircraft-carriers to provide fighter cover waned. At dusk on 9 November *Furious* and two escort carriers were withdrawn. The last of the Seafires departed from the area in *Victorious* and *Formidable* on 13 November.

During Torch the Seafires flew about 180 combat sorties. They destroyed three enemy aircraft and damaged three more in the air, and destroyed four on the ground in strafing attacks. During the operation 21 Seafires were destroyed, more than one-third of the force engaged. Three fell to enemy action, while nine more were wrecked in deck landing accidents. Of the rest, most ditched or made forced landings ashore after running out of fuel. Several pilots became lost in the haze, which was particularly severe on the first day. Two pilots were killed during the operation.

It would be misleading to judge the Seafire's performance during Torch solely on its kill-to-loss ratio. The Vichy French combat units in the area possessed enough modern aircraft to cause serious damage and disruption to the troops coming ashore. The only fighters able to prevent this, during the initial phase of the invasion, had been those operating from the carriers. In flying conditions that were far from ideal, the Royal Navy pilots ensured that the landings went ahead without any serious interference from the air.

Once the invaders were established ashore, the Seafires and other Royal Navy aircraft reverted to British national markings.

In action during Avalanche

The next major action involving the Seafire was Operation Avalanche, the landings at Salerno near Naples, Italy in September 1943. This time the beachhead was some 230 miles (370 km) from the newly captured airfields in Sicily, close to the maximum effective radius of action of the available Allied land-based fighter types. Spitfires could spend only 20 minutes on patrol at such a distance, while the twin-engined P-38 Lightning could spend 40 minutes over the landing area. However, if enemy aircraft approached the beachhead in force, there could be no rapid reinforcement of the beachhead patrols from land-based fighters. Until the invaders were able to capture an airfield ashore and bring it into use, the main source of fighter cover for the landings would be provided by carrier-based fighters. The Seafires operating from carriers close to the beachhead would be able to spend 60 minutes on patrol.

Left: No. 880 Sqn re-equipped with Seafire Mk IICs in September 1942 and covered the Torch landings as part of Force 'H' in November. Here squadron aircraft are seen aboard HMS Indomitable in mid-1943. In July the unit flew fighter patrols for the fleet during the landings on Sicily.

Right: '7-B' is MB240, an early production, Supermarine-built F.Mk IIC, with two Hispano 20-mm cannon and four Browning 0.303-in machine-guns fitted. The FAA had hoped to take advantage of the capacity of the 'C' wing to carry four cannon, but the weight penalty and its effect on take-off performance were too great. As service experience was gained in the Mediterranean, a number of Mk IIC aircraft were fitted with the ungainly Vokes air filters carried by Spitfires in the theatre. However, their use was short-lived as the extra drag and weight reduced climb rate to less than that of the Grumman Martlet Mk IV.

Moreover, reinforcements were readily available should a large enemy force be detected arriving.

The Royal Navy Force assigned Force V, with the small carrier *Unicorn* and the smaller escort carriers *Attacker*, *Battler*, *Hunter* and *Stalker*, to provide air cover for the Avalanche beachhead area. The five ships carried a total of 106 Seafire L.Mk IICs. From dawn on the first day of the landings, 8 September, until dawn on 14 September, the Seafires flew a total of 713 combat sorties from carriers and 56 more from airstrips established ashore. German bombers and fighter-bombers made several attempts to hit targets ashore, but most of their attacks were broken up or otherwise disrupted. The raiders inflicted no serious damage on the troops moving ashore. Seafires shot down two enemy aircraft and claimed to have inflicted damage on four others, for none lost to enemy action.

On the negative side, no fewer than 83 of these Seafires were wrecked or damaged beyond immediate repair in a succession of landing accidents during the operation. On average, one deck landing in nine resulted in the loss of, or serious damage to, a Seafire. Seven pilots were killed and three injured. Thirty-two Seafires were wrecked in catastrophic deck landing accidents, an average of one in every 22 sorties. The primary cause of the crashes was the light winds present in the area throughout much of the

Hook down, a Seafire F.Mk IIC prepares to touch-down aboard Indomitable during mid-1943.

Operation Torch

Operation Torch, the Allied landings in North Africa, was the first such invasion by an amphibious force to benefit from large-scale carrierborne co-operation. The FAA contributed seven carriers from Force 'H' to the operation, four of which were equipped with Seafires from five squadrons. No. 880 Sqn, in HMS *Argus*, had 18 Seafire Mk IICs, No. 885 Sqn aboard *Formidable* had six Mk IICs, while Nos 801 and 807 Sqns (12 aircraft each) joined *Furious*, the former with a handful of Seafire Mk IBs. Finally, No. 884 Sqn joined the second fleet carrier, HMS *Victorious*, also with six Mk IIs. It proved to be an auspicious start to the Seafire's combat career; three enemy aircraft were shot down and another seven damaged, three of these in the air. In all, 160 sorties were launched, many in the Tac/R role, during which 21 Seafires (40 per cent of those available on 8 November) were lost. Only three of these were due to enemy action; most of the result of very poor visibility off the coast.

Deck crewmen hold down a Seafire as it is run up before a sortie from HMS Formidable. MB156/'Ø-6G', an F.Mk IIC of No. 885 Sqn, was flown by Sub-Lt J. D. Buchanan during one of the type's first combats of Operation Torch on 8 November 1942. In this aircraft, Buchanan shared, with another of No. 885's pilots, in the destruction of a Vichy French bomber (sources differ as to the exact type) thus claiming one of the first Seafire kills of the war.

In North African skies

MB113/'6H-B'
Though it does not carry a known unit code, official records show that this Seafire Mk IIC was on strength with No. 885 Sqn (HMS *Formidable*) at the time of Operation Torch. As information regarding the codes used by aircraft of No. 884 Sqn during the action has not survived, it is possible that MB113 was in fact with the latter squadron aboard HMS *Victorious*. Of note are the 'U. S. NAVY' legend, painted over the fuselage band, and stars.

Such was the fragility of the Seafire and the inexperience of many FAA pilots, that many sorties ended like this, with the hapless aircraft damaged, often seriously. This is a No. 807 Sqn L.Mk IIC aboard HMS Battler during the Italian landings in 1943.

operation. When they landed on the slow escort carriers, the Seafires approached the deck at a relative speed somewhat higher than normal, compounded by many pilots having only limited deck landing experience in Seafires. In the resultant heavy landings, many Seafires suffered damage to the undercarriage or wrinkling of the skin of the rear fuselage, or both. Either fault was enough to keep a fighter out of action until it could be brought to a shore base for overhaul.

As in the case of Torch, the Seafire operations during Avalanche need to be viewed in a wider context than simply the victory-to-loss ratio they achieved. Working with Allied land-based fighters flying from Sicily, the

Seafires established a high degree of air superiority over the landing area. A few warships off the coast suffered serious bomb damage and had to withdraw, but the unloading operation went ahead with relatively little interference. In the grim arithmetic of combat attrition, the loss of seven pilots and the write-off of 30 or so relatively cheap Seafires – for whatever reason – was a small price to pay for safeguarding a major landing operation involving 200,000 men and 35,000 vehicles.

Despite that overall success, Avalanche established an unfortunate reputation for the Seafire that remained with it for the rest of its service career. The converted landplane had a fine turn of speed and was a match for any likely opponent in combat. Against this, it was obviously too fragile to survive long in the rough-and-tumble of prolonged deck operations. For repeated safe landings the Seafire required a reasonably good wind speed over the deck, which meant either a fast carrier or a strong wind, or preferably both. Most important of all, it required a pilot familiar with the Seafire's traits during a deck landing. The purpose-built American F4U Corsair and the F6F Hellcat were stronger, faster and altogether better aircraft for naval operations than the Seafire. The Royal Navy had placed large orders for both types but, until they arrived in quantity, the Seafire, for

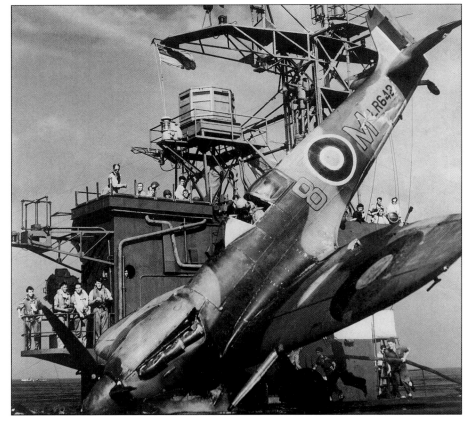

Husky and Avalanche

Operation Husky, the invasion of Sicily, again involved elements of Force 'H', including HMS *Indomitable* (with 28 Mk IICs of Nos 880 and 899 Sqns, and 12 L.Mk IICs of No. 807 Sqn) and *Formidable*, with five No. 885 Sqn Mk IICs in addition to 28 Martlet Mk IVs. The operation began on 10 July 1943, aircraft of Force 'H' flying daytime defensive patrols over its own ships and others passing through the area until the 15th. Sicily fell quickly and by 21 August Force 'H' was ready for its next task – the invasion of the Italian mainland, codenamed Avalanche. During this action *Formidable* and *Illustrious* (which had replaced the damaged *Indomitable*, and had No. 894 Sqn aboard, with 10 Seafire Mk IICs) were to provide protection for an inshore carrier force made up of *Unicorn* and four escort carriers (*Attacker*, *Battler*, *Hunter* and *Stalker*), all with Seafire L.Mk IICs aboard. D-Day was 9 September.

Below: Long-range escort HMS Venomous changes course astern of HMS Formidable. Most of No. 885's aircraft at this time appear to have been converted from Spitfire Mk Vs fitted with the much-maligned Vokes filter.

Right: Weatherbeaten No. 885 Sqn F.Mk IICs are seen aboard HMS Formidable in the Ionian Sea immediately prior to Operation Husky. In the background are other vessels of Force 'H', including the battleships Rodney and Nelson. The carrier to the right is almost certainly Formidable's sister ship, Indomitable.

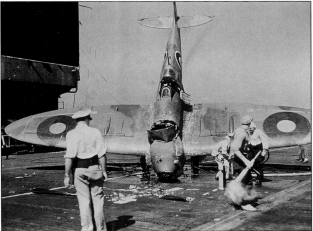

Far left: HMS Hunter *was one of the four US-built 'Attacker'-class escort carriers (supplied under Lend-Lease) in Force 'V' during Operation Avalanche. All were equipped with between 17 and 20 Seafire L.Mk IICs.*

Left: *This sequence of photographs, taken aboard* Hunter *during Avalanche, shows the serious damage that could be done to a Seafire in a landing mishap – an all too common occurance during the Salerno landings. This Seafire L.Mk IIC has nosed over, damaging the engine in its mountings and shattering its propeller. The damage is so severe, in fact, that the decision is made to salvage the engine and cut the airframe into managable pieces before shoving these over the side.*

all its limitations, would have to hold the line.

The next variant of the Seafire to appear, the Mk III, entered service with No. 894 Squadron in November 1943. This, the first Seafire to have folding wings, was powered by a Merlin 55 engine. The wing-folding operation was performed manually and each wing had two folds, the first immediately outboard of the main undercarriage legs, where the wing was hinged upwards past the vertical position. The second fold, necessary for the fighter to fit within the 16-ft (4.9-m) ceiling limit of British carriers' hangars, was achieved by folding the wingtip outwards and downwards. Thus, viewed from the front, the folded starboard wing looked like a letter 'Z' and the port wing looked like a reversed 'Z'. A jury strut on each side locked the folded wing in position. With the necessary locks, hinges and the additional strengthening of the wing, the folding mechanism imposed a weight penalty of 125 lb (57 kg). The modification reduced the wing's torsional rigidity by about 10 per cent.

Operation Dragoon and on to the Pacific

The final Allied invasion operation in the Mediterranean was Operation Dragoon, the landings on the south coast of France which began on 15 August 1944. Seven Royal Navy escort carriers supported the operation, HMS *Emperor*, *Pursuer*, *Searcher*, *Attacker*, *Khedive*, *Hunter* and *Stalker*. In addition to 75 Hellcat and Wildcat fighters, the carriers bore 97 Seafires L.Mk IICs, LR.Mk IICs and L.Mk IIIs.

On the first day the Seafires were employed principally on defensive patrols over the landing area. It quickly became clear that the Luftwaffe was in no position to mount any sort of strong reaction against the landings. As a result, from the second day, the Seafire and other units reverted to flying armed reconnaissance missions ahead of the advancing Allied troops. Targets of opportunity, mainly road and rail traffic, were bombed and strafed. By 19 August the first airstrips were completed ashore, enabling land-based fighters to take over the air defence task.

Despite low winds and occasional spells of poor visibility, the Seafire units suffered a relatively low accident rate during Dragoon.

The F.Mk III and the L.Mk III equipped several squadrons which deployed to the Far East with the British Pacific Fleet in the spring of 1945. During operations from escort carriers, the fighter continued to suffer serious losses in deck landing accidents. Only during the final two months of the war against Japan, when experienced pilots operated the fighter from the large fleet carriers, was the Seafire at last able to demonstrate its real worth. Nos 887 and 894 Squadrons in *Indefatigable*, and Nos 801 and 880 Squadrons in *Implacable*, performed particularly successfully during this period.

The most successful action in the Seafire's entire service career took place on 15 August 1945, the very day when hostilities ended in the Pacific. Eight aircraft from Nos 887 and 894 Squadrons escorted six Avengers to attack a coastal target in Japan. Between 12 and 14 A6M5 'Zeke' fighters

Seafire Mk III

The Seafire F.Mk III, with its folding wings, Merlin 55 engine (with automatic boost control and a barometric governor), four-bladed propeller and 'cleaned up' wing enjoyed a speed advantage of some 20 mph (32 km/h) at all altitudes over the Mk IIC and had a corresponding improvement in climb rate. However, its low-level performance was still inferior to that of the L.Mk IIC and after 103 F.Mk IIIs had been completed, production switched to the L.Mk III, with a Merlin 55M powerplant and a redesigned exhaust system. The first of these entered service five months after the F.Mk III, in February 1944 mainly in the low-level short-range defence role, the FAA by then being able to deploy Lend-Lease Corsairs and Hellcats at medium and high levels. The L.Mk III was followed later in the year by a small number of FR.Mk IIIs equipped with cameras and intended to replace the LR.Mk IIC. This variant was confined to service in the Far East and Pacific.

Above: Once again we see MA970, the first production Seafire Mk IIC, now reworked as the Mk III prototype.

Right: LR765 was the first production Seafire Mk III and, along with the 25 aircraft that followed it off the production line, lacked folding wings. In fact, this aircraft was later redesignated a Mk IIC, as it also had a non-standard Merlin 50 engine and a three-bladed propeller. Most of these early production aircraft were later brought up to full Mk III specification.

Right: The L.Mk III, distinguished by its Merlin 55M (with a cropped supercharger impeller for peak power at low altitude), was produced in larger numbers than any of the Merlin-engined Seafires. NF545 was completed by Westland in March 1944 and, after a spell at A&AEE Boscombe Down, joined No. 899 Sqn.

Below: A Seafire Mk III of No. 887 Sqn lands on HMS Indefatigable, *in the Far East in 1945/46. Having caught No. 5 wire it is brought to a halt and is soon surrounded by a deck party. As the hook is disengaged, other men work to fold the wings, before the aircraft is struck below.*

(8.08 Imp gal), one-third greater than that of the Merlin. Based on the design of the Rolls-Royce 'R' that had powered the Schneider Trophy racing seaplanes, the new engine was named the Griffon. The initial production version, the Griffon IIB, was fitted with a single-stage supercharger and developed 1,735 hp (1294 kW) for take-off. By cleverly positioning the components, the designers kept the length of the new engine within 3 in (7.6 cm) and its weight within 600 lb (272 kg) of the equivalent figures for the Merlin. Moreover, since the Griffon's frontal area was little greater than that of its predecessor, it was an obvious candidate to power a high-performance variant of the Spitfire.

The designations given to Spitfire variants were anything but logical. Nowhere was this more noticeable than with the first Griffon-powered aircraft, DP845. Essentially, the aircraft was a Mk III airframe, with revised and strengthened bearers to hold the larger engine. This aircraft initially had been designated the Mk IV. Soon after its maiden flight, in November 1941, the Ministry of Aircraft Production issued a directive to rationalise the growing profusion of Spitfire mark numbers. As a result, and with no significant changes, DP845 was redesignated as the Mk XX. Finally, in April 1942, still with no significant change to the aircraft, there was a further change of mark numbers and the Griffon-powered prototype became the Mk XII.

Powered by a 1,735-hp Griffon II engine fitted with a single-stage two-speed supercharger, DP845 had a maximum speed of 372 mph (599 km/h) at 5,700 ft (1737 m), increasing to 397 mph (639 km/h) at 18,000 ft (5487 m). The prototype was remembered with particular affection by Jeffrey Quill, chief test pilot at the Supermarine company: "DP845 was my favourite Spitfire. It had a wonderful performance at low altitude; it had a low full throttle height and a lot of power on the deck."

Early in 1942 the Luftwaffe introduced a new phase in its bombardment of the United Kingdom, with fighter-bomber attacks on coastal targets. The Messerschmitt Bf 109s and Focke-Wulf Fw 190s approached their targets at low altitude and high speed. There was little or no radar warning and by the time defending fighters reached the target the raiders were usually well clear.

The new threat led the RAF to issue a requirement for an interceptor optimised to counter these low-altitude high-speed raiders. In the summer of 1942 it was decided to run a comparative speed trial at low altitude, pitting the newest British fighter types against a captured Fw 190 fighter.

ran in to intercept the force and a dogfight developed. In the ensuing action the Seafires claimed eight enemy fighters destroyed, one probably destroyed and two damaged. One Seafire was shot down and another suffered damage. For their part, the Avengers delivered their attack and withdrew without loss.

Griffon-engined Spitfires

Meanwhile, as the Seafire entered service, the RAF was preparing to receive the first examples of a new Spitfire variant powered by a new and considerably more powerful engine than the Merlin.

In 1939 Rolls-Royce began development of a new combat aircraft engine with a cubic capacity of 36.75 litres

The event took take place at Farnborough, watched by a VIP audience. The Hawker Typhoon was considered to have the best performance at low altitude against the German fighter, but the Supermarine company was asked to send a Spitfire – any Spitfire – to make up the numbers. Jeffrey Quill decided to take DP845; the famous pilot described what happened next.

"On 20 July we all took off from Farnborough and flew to a point near Odiham, where we moved into line abreast formation. On the command 'Go!' we all opened our throttles and accelerated towards Farnborough, where an assortment of dignitaries had assembled to see which aircraft was the fastest. It was generally expected that the Fw 190 would come in first, the Typhoon second, and the poor old Spitfire would come limping in some way behind the other two. Well, I won the race easily in DP845, the Typhoon

East of Suez

East of Suez, the Seafire's lack of range was to prove an even greater handicap. Many fighter units re-equipped with American-built aircraft, but as insufficient numbers were available, the Seafire continued to serve. A small number of Seafires (Mk IICs equipping a flight of No. 834 Sqn aboard HMS *Battler*) were on trade protection duty in the Indian Ocean from October 1943 and towards the end of the year another squadron was added (No. 889 Sqn in *Atheling* with Mk IIIs). However, it was not until the beginning of 1945 that the FAA's striking power was concentrated in the Far East, with the Seafire Mk III eventually equipping eight squadrons east of Suez, aboard the escort carriers of the 21st Aircraft Carrier Squadron and the fleet carriers *Implacable* and *Indefatigable*. Notable actions for which the Seafires provided fighter cover included the the attacks on Japanese oil refineries in Sumatra in January and the occupation of Rangoon and Penang in May and August. In the Pacific during March/April, meanwhile, British Pacific Fleet Seafires (Nos 887 and 894 Sqns in *Indefatigable*) were in action over the Sakishima Islands. It was during this action that Seafires made their first combat claims in the Pacific and Sub-Lt Richard Reynolds of No. 894 Sqn became the FAA's first (and only) Seafire ace, downing three 'Zeros' to add to two BV 138s claimed off Norway. With the arrival of HMS *Implacable* (No. 38 Wing – Nos 801 and 880 Sqns), operations over Truk in the Caroline Islands in June saw Seafires in action once again and by August Seafires were flying over the Japanese mainland.

Below: Taken using the oblique camera in Seafire FR.Mk III NN612 on the last day of operations over Japan, this photograph shows a No. 880 Sqn Mk III sporting one of the non-standard drop tanks used by the squadron. Unhappy with the unreliability of the Seafire's standard 45- and 90-Imp gal (205- and 410-litre) slipper tanks, No. 880 Sqn modified 60 surplus 90-Imp gal (410-litre) tear-drop tanks, originally intended for use on RAAF P-40s and obtained via USAAF personnel from a base in New Guinea. No. 880 Sqn supplied two crates of whiskey in payment!

Operations in 1944

Seafire deployments during 1944 were diverse, encompassing land-based as well as carrier operations. Seafire units provided part of the escort for anti-shipping strikes off the Norwegian coast, in particular the well-known attacks on the German battleship *Tirpitz* mid-year, while in June a detachment from No. 879 Sqn with Seafire Mk IIIs had provided shore-based tactical reconnaissance for the Desert Air Force in Italy. Prior to the Normandy landings (Operation Overlord) Seafire Mk IIIs of Nos 887 and 894 Sqns based at Culmhead provided a fighter escort for RAF Typhoons on cross-Channel fighter-bomber sorties and during the landings in June four FAA units, with shore-based Seafires and Spitfires, carried out gunnery spotting for naval guns offshore. During Operation Dragoon, the invasion of southern France in August, of nine American and British carriers taking part, four of the latter had Seafire units aboard. As well as combat air patrols, Seafires also made tactical reconnaissance and bombing sorties over the beachhead. The latter were performed by aircraft of No. 4 Fighter Wing, this being the first major use of the Seafire in the fighter-bomber role.

Top left: One of No. 807 Sqn's L.Mk IIIs rests, firmly tied down on an outrigger, aboard HMS Hunter in the Aegean Sea, October 1944.

Left: With a 500-lb bomb under its fuselage, a Seafire L.Mk III of No. 899 Sqn, No. 4 Fighter Wing, gets airborne from HMS Khedive during Operation Dragoon in August 1944. With a bomb on board, a Seafire could not be catapulted. Thus, only two Seafire wings flew bombing missions – No. 4 Wing from American-built assault carriers (whose catapults were incompatible with the Seafire anyway), and No. 38 Fighter Wing in the fleet carrier Implacable. The latter had a sufficiently long deck to allow a fully laden Seafire to get airborne without the use of a catapult.

Below: No. 899 Sqn was designated a Seafire Operational Training Unit, converting RAAF pilots to form the nucleus of a planned Australian FAA. Two courses were held, the first aboard HMS Indomitable, in Australia at the time. Here a No. 899 Sqn Seafire Mk II comes to grief with a RANVR pilot aboard. Note the mixture of Pacific Fleet markings on the aircraft's fuselage and Type 'C' roundels on the upper wings.

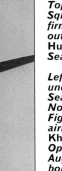

Below: A No. 801 Sqn Seafire Mk III loses a propeller blade in a typical example of 'pecking', as 'N/147' noses over slightly after catching the wire on landing aboard Implacable around the the time of VJ-Day.

Seafire versus 'Zeke'

Testing of a captured Mitsubishi A6M6 Model 52 yielded the following results in comparison with a Seafire L.Mk IIC.

Peak speeds: Seafire L.Mk IIC: 338 mph (544 km/h) at 5,500 ft (1677 m); Zeke 52: 335 mph (539 km/h) at 18,000 ft (5488 m) The comparative speeds in miles per hour are:

Height	Seafire L.Mk IIC	Zeke 52
sea level	316 mph (508 km/h)	292 mph (470 km/h)
5,000 ft (1525 m)	337 mph (542 km/h)	313 mph (504 km/h)
10,000 ft (3050 m)	337 mph (542 km/h)	319 mph (513 km/h)
15,000 ft (4575 m)	335 mph (539 km/h)	327 mph (526 km/h)
20,000 ft (6100 m)	328 mph (528 km/h)	333 mph (536 km/h)
25,000 ft (7625 m)	317 mph (510 km/h)	327 mph (526 km/h)
30,000 ft (9150 m)		317 mph (510 km/h)

Climb: The 'Zeke 52' climbs at a very steep angle and gives the impression of a very high rate of climb. The Seafire L.Mk IIC, however, has a much better initial climb and remains slightly superior up to 25,000 ft (7625 m). The climb of the Seafire is at a higher speed, but at a more shallow angle. The best indicated climbing speeds of the 'Zeke' and the Seafire are 120 and 160 mph (193 and 257 km/h) respectively.

Manoeuvrability, turning plane: The 'Zeke 52' can turn inside the Seafire L.Mk IIC at all heights. The 'Zeke 52' turns tighter to the left than to the right.

Manoeuvrability, rolling plane: The rate of roll of the two aircraft is similar at speeds below 180 mph IAS (290 km/h), but above that the aileron stick forces of the 'Zeke' increase tremendously, and the Seafire becomes progressively superior.

Dive: The Seafire is superior in the dive although initial acceleration is similar. The 'Zeke' is a most unpleasant aircraft in a dive, due to heavy stick forces and excessive vibration.

Tactics: Never dogfight with the 'Zeke 52' – it is too manoeuvrable. At low altitudes where the Seafire is at its best, it should make use of its superior rate of climb and speed to obtain a height advantage before attacking. If jumped, the Seafire should evade by using its superior rate of roll. The 'Zeke' cannot follow high speed rolls and aileron turns.

Conclusions: The Seafire L.Mk IIC is 24 mph (38 km/h) faster at sea level, this difference decreasing to parity between 15,000 and 20,000 ft (4575 m and 6100 m). The 'Zeke 52' is 10 mph (16 km/h) faster at 25,000 ft (7625 m). The 'Zeke' is very manoeuvrable and can turn inside the Seafire at all altitudes. The 'Zeke' fights best between 115 and 180 mph IAS (185 and 290 km/h). The rate of roll of the Seafire is better than that of the 'Zeke' above 180 mph IAS (290 km/h).

A Seafire Mk III lands after a strike on the Sumatran oil refineries in early 1945. The aircraft, of No. 894 Sqn, has ploughed into the barrier, its starboard undercarriage leg forced backwards and into the radiator, and its propeller blades disintegrating.

Far right and far right bottom: Here the results of the landing accident suffered by PP479 'D-5X' of No. 889 Sqn (the subject of the artwork opposite) are seen, the aircraft having lost all three undercarriage legs after missing the arrester wire and been caught in the barrier.

Below: Though frequent, and often spectacular, deck landing accidents cost comparatively few lives. However, this horrific example not only proved fatal, but indirectly led to the disbandment of the squadron. On 29 June 1944, aboard HMS Atheling in the Indian Ocean, this No. 889 Sqn Seafire missed the arrester wire on landing, crashed over the barrier and ploughed into an aircraft parked ahead of it. Two pilots and three members of the deck party were killed. The carrier had arrived in the Bay of Bengal in May, but after several accidents that cost the lives of a number of its pilots, including the CO, No. 889 Sqn was disbanded on 11 July.

came second and the Focke-Wulf was third, which was absolutely the wrong result!"

Following this trial the Spitfire XII was selected as the RAF's new low-altitude fighter. Production began in the summer of 1942, against an order for 100, and the first was delivered that November. Production Mk XIIs had wings clipped to 32 ft 8 in (9.96 m), to increase speed at low altitude and improve their rate of roll. Compared with the Mk IX, the main production variant of the Spitfire at this time, the Mk XII was 14 mph (22 km/h) faster at sea level and 8 mph (13 km/h) faster at 10,000 ft (3050 m); at altitudes above 20,000 ft (6100 m), however, the performance of the Mk XII fell away rapidly and it was slower than the Mk IX.

The report on the aircraft, written by the Air Fighting Development Unit at Duxford in December 1942, stated: "In the air the handling of both EN223 and another production Spitfire Mk XII which was made available by Supermarine for one day, were felt to be far superior to the normal Spitfire Mk IX or Mk VB, being exceptionally good in the lateral control which is crisper and light due to the clipped wings. The longitudinal stability is much better than that of the Spitfire Mk V, and in the dive it was particularly noticed that when trimmed for cruising flight, it stays in easily at 400 mph [644 km/h] IAS and does not recover fiercely. In turns the stick load is always positive and the control very comfortable. The rudder, however, is most sensitive to changes in engine settings and needs retrimming for most alterations of flight as it is too heavy to be held by the feet for long periods. The Spitfire Mk XII has the usual Spitfire stall characteristics. The engine runs noticeably more roughly than a Merlin."

In order to provide increased rudder authority to counter the greater engine torque of the Griffon engine, early in its career the Mk XII was fitted with a broad-chord rudder with a pointed tip.

Mk XII in service

In February 1943 No. 41 Squadron moved to High Ercall in Shropshire to re-equip with the Mk XII. In April the only other unit to receive the new variant, No. 91 Squadron, began its conversion. Both squadrons had previously operated the Spitfire Mk VB. As far as pilots were concerned, the main difference between the Mk XII and the previous version of the Spitfire was that the Griffon

Written off
Piloted by Sub-Lt F. Logie, this aircraft met its end after a landing accident in June 1945. In light winds, the aircraft floated over arrester wires, snagging the barrier and losing all three undercarriage legs. Beyond repair aboard the carrier, it was dismantled and stowed below decks until *Hunter* next reached Trincomalee, Ceylon where it was off-loaded, pronounced 'beyond repair' and scrapped.

Folding wings
The main improvement introduced in the Seafire Mk III was the folding wing, allowing the armoured carriers *Illustrious*, *Formidable* and *Victorious* to at last stow their Seafires below decks. Each wing folded in two places, just inboard of the inboard cannon bay, and between mainplane and wingtip. Power-assisted folding was rejected as imposing too great a weight penalty.

Supermarine Seafire F.Mk III No. 807 Sqn, 4th Fighter Wing HMS *Hunter* June 1945

With No. 807 Sqn aboard, 'Attacker'-class escort carrier HMS *Hunter* participated in Operation Dragoon in August 1944, and after a short short spell in the Aegean underwent a refit at Alexandria before departing for the Eastern Fleet. During April and May 1945, No. 807 Sqn provided fighter support for the re-occupation of Rangoon and by June was covering anti-shipping strikes in the Andaman Sea. PP479 was delivered to the FAA in late September 1944, issued to No. 807 Sqn and subsequently written off in mid-1945.

Improved performance
The Seafire Mk III gained a 20 mph (32 km/h) advantage over the Mk II at all heights thanks to its new engine (with multi-stack exhausts) and four-bladed propeller and other measures, including the removal of redundant cannon stubs and the fitting of smaller cannon belt feed fairings on the top surface of the wing. The Mk III remained inferior at low level, though this was of little importance given its role as medium- to high-level fighter.

Propeller 'pecking'
The greatest cause of Seafire unserviceability due to deck landing damage was propeller 'pecking', the result of failing to make a 'three point' touch-down at the instant the arrester hook took the weight of the aircraft. If the landing was less than perfect the aircraft tended to rotate forward, thanks to the positioning of the A-frame hook so close to the aircraft's CofG, with the result that the propeller blade tips struck the deck. Generally damage was confined to the blades (which were then simply sawn off), though damage to the engine and bearers by shock-loading could result. Often more serious damage was done as the aircraft fell back on its tailwheel.

Merlin powerplants
The standard Seafire F.Mk III was powered by a Merlin 55, of the type fitted to some Spitfire Mk Vs. This produced the same output as the Seafire Mk II's Merlin 45 or 46 – 1,470 hp (1096 kW) at 9,250 ft (2819 m) – but benefitted from an automatic supercharger boost control, with barometric governing of 'full throttle height'. A four-bladed propeller, as introduced on the L.Mk IIC, was standard. Produced in greater numbers than any of the Merlin-engined Seafires, the L.Mk III had a Merlin 55M installed, capable of producing 1,585 hp (1182 kW) at 2,750 ft (838 m).

Finish
Slate Grey and Extra Dark Sea Grey formed the basis for the finish applied to FAA fighters in the British Pacific and Far Eastern Fleets. The undersides of the aircraft were Sky Type 'S', the propeller spinner Sky Type 'S' or Light Grey. This aircraft also sports white SEAC bands and small Roundel Blue/White roundels.

Tailhook
All Merlin-engined Seafires were equipped with an A-frame hook, as fitted to the so-called 'hooked Spitfires' during the earliest deck landing experiments. From the Mk XV, a 'stinger'-type hook was fitted, hinged at the foot of the rudder post.

Below: Seafire Mk IIIs, with a mixture of Pacific Fleet and temperate markings, are seen leaving Brisbane harbour in August 1945.

Bottom: In the US towards the end of the war, trials were flown to compare the relative merits of the Seafire Mk III, Grumman F6F Hellcat and Mitsubishi J2M2 Raiden (Allied code name 'Jack') in combat. The programme was conducted by the US Navy from its Patuxent River airfield.

engine rotated in the opposite direction to the earlier Merlin, so instead of a mild tendency to swing to the left on take off, the new version tried to swing more strongly to the right. If the pilot was aware of the difference and applied sufficient rudder trim to compensate for the swing before it developed, he could cope with the change, but those who failed to do so were in for an exciting ride. There are authenticated cases of pilots making their first flight in a Griffon-powered Spitfire, and giving a firm push on the throttle on take-off without sufficient rudder trim or none at all. The fighter would swing viciously to the right, sometimes leaving the runway and careering across the grass. In extreme cases, where the rudder trim was set to the left (as on Merlin-powered Spitfires), the aircraft finally got airborne heading in a direction almost 90° to the intended direction of take-off. Provided the pilot was aware of the difference and applied sufficient rudder trim to counteract for the swing before it developed, however, the take-off in the Mk XII was simple enough. Squadron Leader Tom Neil, commander of No. 41 Squadron when the first of the new fighters arrived, later commented:

"As the Mk XII was reputedly faster than the Typhoon low down it was regarded as something of a 'hot ship' and there was a painful air of smugness abroad at dispersal. Our collective ego, however, was knocked sideways when the first XII was delivered by a pretty, pink-cheeked young thing in ATA [Air Transport Auxiliary] uniform, who taxied in with a flourish and stepped out as though she had been flying nothing more vicious than a Tiger Moth."

First Mk XII victory

In April 1943, No. 41 Squadron was declared operational and the unit moved to Hawkinge near Folkestone. From there it flew standing patrols in an attempt to catch enemy fighter-bombers making tip-and-run attacks on coastal targets. Initially, these operations had little success. The Spitfire Mk XII fired its guns in anger for the first time on 17 April, when Flying Officer C. Birbeck strafed an enemy patrol boat. Later that day, Flight Lieutenant R. Hogarth encountered a Junkers Ju 88 near Calais and shot it down.

Although the Mk XIIs had few encounters with enemy aircraft at this time, their sorties were not devoid of excitement, as Tom Neil explained:

"One of our early problems was to convince the Typhoons at Lympne and Manston that we were on their side. Our clipped wings gave us the appearance of 109s and there were several ugly encounters between the Typhoons and ourselves, with us on the receiving end. Fortunately, we could just out-distance a Typhoon provided we saw it in time, otherwise blood would have been spilled."

No. 91 Squadron joined its sister unit at Hawkinge in May 1943 and it, too, began operations, demonstrating its effectiveness with the Mk XII on the evening of 25 May. A small force of Fw 190s fighter-bombers from Schnellkampfgeschwader 10 was detected on radar running in at low altitude to attack Folkestone. The two Spitfires at readiness were scrambled, as were two more that had just landed after a patrol. These Spitfires engaged the Focke-Wulfs before the latter reached their target, forcing several to jettison their bombs into the sea. Only one bomb fell on the town, and that caused minor damage. Meanwhile, four other Mk XIIs had scrambled. In the ensuing chase across the channel the fighters claimed the destruction of six enemy aircraft, two of which were credited to the unit's commander, Squadron Leader Raymond Harries.

Just over a week later, on the morning of 4 June, No. 41 Squadron broke up another attack on Eastbourne by enemy fighter-bombers. Again, most of the Germans were forced to jettison their bombs. Flying Officer Solack was credited with the destruction of one Focke-Wulf, and ground gunners claimed three others. Soon afterwards, the daylight tip-and-run fighter-bomber attacks came to an end, as Schnellkampfgeschwader 10 shifted to night raids.

With the lifting of the requirement to counter the fighter-bomber attacks, the two Mk XII units shifted to

Mks IV, XX & XII

On 27 November 1941, Jeffrey Quill took the first Spitfire Mk IV prototype into the air from Worthy Down. Powered by a Rolls-Royce Griffon IIB, the Mk IV was essentially a re-engined derivative of the stillborn Mk III, and represented a considerable improvement over the Mk V in terms of performance. When, soon after its maiden flight, the Ministry of Aircraft Production rationalised Spitfire designations, the Mk IV became the Mk XX, this appellation applying to the second Griffon-powered aircraft, DP851 (flown in August 1942) from the outset. Meanwhile, by mid-1942 concern regarding the threat posed by Focke-Wulf Fw 190 making fighter-bomber raid across the Channel forced a rethink. Orders placed with Supermarine as far back as August 1941, for the construction of 750 Mk IVs (to be built at the Castle Bromwich Aircraft Factory) were cancelled and DP845 was reworked as the prototype of a low-altitude fighter, the Mk XII.

Above: The large Rotol propeller spinner and revised cowling contours were the only clue that an engine considerably larger than the Merlin was installed in DP845. Note that by this time the aircraft was close to production Mk XII standard, with clipped wingtips and a 'C' wing/armament fit.

Left: By spring/summer 1942, DP845 was known as a Mk XII and had gained a broad-chord rudder and Mk VC wing, with two cannon and four machine-guns installed.

Far left: DP845 is seen here in its original configuration as the first Spitfire Mk IV, mocked-up with six Hispano 20-mm cannon and still equipped with a narrow-chord rudder. Note the retractable tailwheel.

fighter sweeps and escort missions over enemy territory.

The Spitfire Mk XII's performance at low or medium altitude was unmatched by any opposing fighter type, and, during offensive patrols over France, pilots found it difficult to lure enemy fighters into turning fights low down. The German fighters' usual tactic, when they encountered Spitfires or other Allied fighters below them, was to make a diving attack from above and then zoom back to altitude and position themselves for a re-attack if necessary. From previous hard-won experience, they knew it was unwise to enter a turning fight with any variant of the Spitfire lower down.

Throughout the rest of the year the two squadrons flew sweeps and escort missions over enemy territory. The most successful action involving Mk XIIs took place on 20 October 1943, during the fighter sweep Operation Rodeo 263. Both squadrons took part in the sweep, flying as a wing under the command of Group Captain Grisham. As the force crossed the French coast it came under fire from accurate flak; one Spitfire suffered damage, and another was detached to escort it home. The rest of the force continued inland, climbing to 18,000 ft (5484 m) and heading for the Tricqueville-Bernay-Beaumont area. Near Rouen a pack of about 25 Bf 109s and Fw 190s dived on the Spitfires from the sun. The Mk XIIs turned to port and climbed, to face their attackers head on. The action developed into a fierce dogfight, and for once the German pilots did not dive away. That proved an unwise move, and during the ensuing mêlée the two Spitfire squadrons claimed the destruction of nine

enemy fighters without loss to themselves.

During the months that followed the pattern of operations continued, though never again did the Mk XIIs encounter an enemy force as aggressive as that on 20 October.

The last Mk XII in the batch of 100 had left the production line at Eastleigh in September 1943, and no further order was placed for the variant. Early in 1944, No. 91 Squadron was withdrawn from operations to become the first unit to re-equip with the Spitfire Mk XIV. No. 41 Squadron soldiered on with the Mk XII for a few more months before it also received the new variant at the end of the summer.

Spitfire Mk XIV

An obvious next step for the Griffon Spitfire was for it to be fitted with an engine that had a two-stage supercharger to give improved performance at high altitude. The new engine, the Griffon 61, appeared in the spring of 1943 and developed an impressive 1,540 hp (1148 kW) for take-off and 2,035 hp (1517 kW) at 7,000 ft (2134 m). Six Spitfire Mk VIIIs were modified to take the new engine, to become prototypes for the Spitfire Mk XIV. To absorb the additional engine power, the new variant featured a five-bladed propeller, and to cancel out the greater torque from larger engine and propeller, it had a larger fin and rudder. The Mk XIV had small additional fuel tanks fitted in each wing leading edge close to the fuselage, holding a total of 25 Imp gal (116 litres). This helped compensate for the higher rate of consumption of the more-powerful Griffon engine.

Flight tests with the initial Mk XIV conversions revealed this variant to be an extremely effective fighter. Its performance was a huge improvement over the Mk IX and

Below left: In this view of an early Mk XII, the resemblence of the aircraft's underside to that of the Mk V, from which the production Mk XII was derived, is clearly evident.

Below: EN221, the first production Mk XII, was extensively test flown by the manufacturer, initially with standard wingtips and a fixed tailwheel.

Mk XII in service

The first production Mk XII, EN221, appeared in October 1942 and in December the third aircraft was despatched to the Air Fighting Development Unit at Duxford. Such was the urgency of the requirement for a low-level interceptor that No. 41 Squadron received its first aircraft in February, at High Ercall. Production ceased in September, with 100 completed. The type's success against the low-level raiders making 'tip and run' attacks on English coastal targets was limited, given the lack of adequate radar warning of fast, low-level targets. Towards the end of their short service careers, the Mk XIIs joined the fight against the V-1 flying bomb menace launched against London from June 1944. Large numbers of 'Divers' were shot down before the Mk XII left the front-line RAF in September.

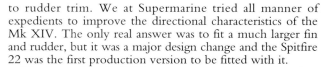

Above right: MB882, the last Mk XII built, is seen here in its element, at low level.

Right: MB858 first flew in July 1943, and was delivered to No. 41 Sqn in September. No. 91 Sqn was the only other Mk XII unit.

Below: MB882, coded 'EB-B', was flown by Flt Lt Don Smith in April 1944. An Australian, Smith first saw action in mid-1942, claiming three kills while flying Spitfire Mk Vs on Malta. Posted to No. 41 Sqn in 1943, he added another victory in a Mk XII, before becoming CO of No. 453 Sqn (Spitfire Mk IXBs) in 1944 and scoring a final victory.

the Mk XII. Jeffrey Quill said that in his view the Mk XIV had the best fighting ability of any of the Spitfire variants. That did not mean it was an easy machine to fly, however.

"... the Mk XIV, with its tremendous power, increased propeller solidity and increased all-up weight and moments of inertia, was a good deal more of a handful for the pilot and so required more attention to 'flying' than its predecessors. Directional stability was a problem and the aircraft was apt to shear about a lot with coarse use of the throttle; large changes in speed required prompt attention

to rudder trim. We at Supermarine tried all manner of expedients to improve the directional characteristics of the Mk XIV. The only real answer was to fit a much larger fin and rudder, but it was a major design change and the Spitfire 22 was the first production version to be fitted with it.

"So far as the Mk XIV was concerned, I took the view that performance was paramount; and if the pilots had to work a bit harder and concentrate a bit more on their flying, that was better than sending them to war in an aircraft of inferior performance."

Comparative air fighting trials against a captured Fw 190A and a Bf 109G confirmed Quill's view: the Spitfire Mk XIV showed itself to be superior to the German fighters in almost every respect.

The new variant went into production in the autumn of 1943 and by the following spring Nos 91, 322 and 610 Squadrons had converted to the Mk XIV. All three units were fully operational in June 1944, when the Luftwaffe commenced its attack on London with the first of its 'secret weapons'.

Griffon-Spitfires versus V-1 flying bombs

Early on the morning darkness of 13 June 1944, the Luftwaffe opened a new phase in the bombardment on London, employing the V-1 flying bomb. In Britain the new weapons was immediately nicknamed the 'Doodlebug'. By the end of the month German ground launching sites had fired just under 2,500 of these weapons at the capital; roughly one-third reached the Greater London area, causing just under 2,500 deaths and more than 7,000 cases of serious injury. The remaining missiles missed the city, or were brought down by fighters, guns or barrage balloons before reaching it.

The defenders quickly took the measure of the new German weapon. The V-1s were not manufactured to normal aircraft tolerances, so there were large variations in their performance. The majority flew at speeds around 350 mph (563 km/h), though the fastest were tracked at 420 mph (676 km/h) and the slowest came in at around 230 mph (370 km/h). There were similar variations in altitude; most crossed the coast at between 3,000 and 4,000 ft (915 and 1220 m), but the highest was recorded coming in at 8,000 ft (2440 m) and the lowest flew at tree-top height,

Hawkinge-based Mk XII

EN237/'EB-V'
Sqn Ldr Thomas Neil flew EN237 while OC of No. 41 Sqn at Hawkinge, spring 1943. Neil was a Battle of Britain veteran who scored all of his 12 victories during 1940/41. Mk XIIs generally flew in standard Fighter Command day fighter camouflage (Ocean Grey/Dark Green over Medium Sea Grey); EN237 was one of the first delivered to the squadron.

Another stop-gap: Mk XIV

The Spitfire Mk XII had been optimised for low-altitude operations. Further evolution resulted in the Mk XIV, a development of the Mk VIII fitted with a two-stage Griffon and intended as a high-altitude interceptor. Six Mk VIIIs were converted as prototypes. They were JF316 (fitted with a Griffon III of the type installed in late production Spitfire Mk XIIs, with single-stage supercharging), JF317 (the first to fly; fitted with a two-stage Griffon 61), JF318 (Griffon 61), JF319 (Griffon 65), JF320 (Griffon 61) and JF321 (Griffon 61). The last named went to Rotol at Staverton, where it was employed as a contra-rotating propeller trials airframe. The Mk XIV was to be the most numerous Griffon-engined Spitfire variant to see wartime RAF service, production ending in late 1945 after 957 had been completed.

which usually led to their early demise. The missile's time in the air, from the launching site to London, was about 25 minutes.

After some changes, the defenders put together a reasonably effective system to counter the flying bombs. Four belts of defences protected the capital. The first belt, running from mid-Channel to about 10 miles (16 km) short of the coast, was the Outer Fighter Patrol Area where fighters could be vectored in to engage the flying bombs. At the coast was the Gun Belt, with about 800 heavy AA

Far left: JF321 is seen here with a contra-prop fitted and an enlarged tailfin, with a straight leading-edge, of an interim design.

Above: JF318, the third Mk XIV, is seen here in its original configuration, with a Mk VIII tailfin and 'C' wing.

Left: Production FR.Mk XIV TZ138 was sent to Manitoba, Canada for cold weather trials in the winter of 1946/47. Adapted from a design intended for the de Havilland Tiger Moth, the skis fitted to this aircraft assisted only during taxying and take-off and were designed to fall away from the aircraft as it left the ground.

AFDU trials, Duxford 1944

Early in 1944 the Air Fighting Development Unit at Duxford flew a Spitfire Mk XIV in a comparative trial against captured examples of the Fw 190A and Bf 109G-6. Excerpts from the official trials reports are given below:

SPITFIRE XIV versus Fw 190A
Maximum Speeds: From 0-5,000 ft (0-1525 m) and 15,000-20,000 ft (4573-6100 m) the Spitfire XIV is only 20 mph (32 km/h) faster; at all other heights it is up to 60 mph (97 km/h) faster than the Fw 190A.
Maximum Climb: The Spitfire XIV has a considerably greater rate of climb than the Fw 190A at all altitudes.
Dive: After the initial part of the dive, during which the Fw 190 gains slightly, the Spitfire XIV has a slight advantage.
Turning Circle: The Spitfire XIV can easily turn inside the Fw 190. Though in the case of a right-hand turn, this difference is not quite so pronounced.
Rate of Roll: The Fw 190 is very much better.
Conclusions: In defence, the Spitfire XIV should use its remarkable maximum climb and turning circle against any enemy aircraft. In the attack it can afford to 'mix it' but should beware of the quick roll and dive. If this manoeuvre is used by an Fw 190 and the Spitfire XIV follows, it will probably not be able to close the range until the Fw 190 has pulled out of its dive.

SPITFIRE XIV versus Bf 109G
Maximum Speed: The Spitfire XIV is 40 mph (64 km/h) faster at all heights except near 16,000 ft (4878 m), where it is only 10 mph (16 km/h) faster.
Maximum Climb: The same result: at 16,000 ft the two aircraft are identical, otherwise the Spitfire XIV out-climbs the Bf 109G. The zoom climb is practically identical when the climb is made without opening the throttle. Climbing at full throttle, the Spitfire XIV draws away from the Bf 109G quite easily.
Dive: During the initial part of the dive, the Bf 109G pulls away slightly, but when a speed of 380 mph (611 km/h) is reached, the Spitfire XIV begins to gain on the Bf 109G.
Turning Circle: The Spitfire XIV easily out-turns the Bf 109G in either direction.
Rate of Roll: The Spitfire XIV rolls much more quickly.
Conclusion: The Spitfire XIV is superior to the Bf 109G in every respect.

guns and 1,800 lighter weapons positioned between Beachy Head and Dover; fighters had strict orders to keep out of this zone, thus allowing the gunners freedom to engage any airborne target that came within range without having to worry about identification. The belt from 10 miles inland to 10 miles short of London was the Inner Fighter Patrol Area, where more fighters could engage the V-1s. The fourth belt ran from the edge of the Greater London to 10 miles in front of it. There, about 1,000 barrage balloons were deployed to ensnare as many as possible of the missiles which had passed through the other defensive belts.

Left and below: From autumn 1944, Mk XIVs were completed to FR.Mk XIVE standard, with a bubble canopy and cut-down rear fuselage (containing an extra 33-Imp gal/150-litre fuel tank), camera ports and the 'E' wing. MV247 (left), is an early example, seen here with a 90-Imp gal (409-litre) external fuel tank.

Above: Resting on the PSP, possibly on an airfield in Belgium in early 1945, RN119, a mid-production F.Mk XIVC carries the 'AE' codes of No. 402 Sqn, RCAF, a 2nd TAF unit engaged in fighter-bomber, bomber escort and defensive duties in the final months before VE-Day.

ADGB and 2nd TAF

Air Defence of Great Britain squadrons were the first recipients of the Mk XIV, Nos 610, 91 and 322 (Dutch) Sqns re-equipping in early 1944. All were operational by June, when the V-1 flying bomb offensive began, becoming the most successful Spitfire units engaged in anti-'Diver' operations. Some aircraft were modified to run on 150-octane fuel and at +25 lb boost in order to wring an extra 30 mph (48 km/h) out of the aircraft at low level. This gave a modified aircraft a top speed of 400 mph (644 km/h) at 2,000 ft (609 m). When the main V-1 bombardment ended in September (as the Allied armies overran their launch sites in France), Mk XIV squadrons, of which there were seven by the end of the month, were transferred to the 2nd Tactical Air Force. From then until the end of the war in Europe, the Mk XIV was 2nd TAF's main air superiority type. By the end of the year, camera-equipped FR.Mk XIVs were in service and equipped four squadrons, including two tactical reconnaissance units – Nos II (AC) and 430 Sqns.

Initially, the Spitfires engaging the V-1s belonged to No. 150 Wing based at Lympne, comprising Nos 1 and 165 Squadrons with Mk IXs and No. 41 Squadron with Mk XIIs. Neither version had enough speed at low altitude to engage the faster V-1s, so, to alleviate this deficiency, Nos 91, 322 and 610 Squadrons – the first three units with the Mk XIVs – were ordered to assist in the defence of the capital. For these operations some Spitfire Mk XIVs had their engines modified to run on 150 octane petrol allowing

Right: 2nd TAF fighter-reconnaissance units Nos II (AC) and 268 Sqns operated camera-equipped FR.Mk XIVEs. This aircraft, based at Twente in the Netherlands in the final weeks of the war, is a No. 268 Sqn aircraft, notable for its lack of unit code letters.

CFE Mk XIV/Vampire trials

The F.Mk XIV was one of the fastest Spitfire variants. For a piston-engined aircraft it was certainly no slouch, and at the end of World War II it was acknowledged as one of the most effective air superiority fighters in service, yet it was outclassed in almost every significant aspect of air combat by the de Havilland Vampire Mk I. The comparative trial took place at the Central Fighter Establishment at West Raynham in the summer of 1946. The report on that trial, excerpts of which are reproduced below, puts figures to the superiority achieved by the first-generation jet fighter. In making a comparison, the properties of their different types of engines needs to be appreciated. The piston engine maintained power throughout the speed range, whereas the jet engine produced maximum power only at the top end of the speed range, which gave the Spitfire an advantage over a jet aircraft at low speeds. The Spitfire XIV used in the trial was a fully operational aircraft fitted with a Griffon 65 engine giving 2,015 hp (1503 kW) at 7,500 ft (2286 m).

Maximum Level Speeds: The Vampire (Goblin II engine) greatly superior in speed to the Spitfire XIV at all heights as shown below:

Approximate speed advantage over Spitfire XIVE:

Altitude	Speed
sea level	140 (225 km/h)
5,000 ft (1525 m)	120 mph (193 km/h)
10,000 ft (3050 m)	110 mph (177 km/h)
15,000 ft (4575 m)	110 mph (177 km/h)
20,000 ft (6100 m)	105 mph (169 km/h)
25,000 ft (7625 m)	85 mph (136 km/h)
30,000 ft (9150 m)	70 mph (112 km/h)
35,000 ft (10675 m)	70 mph (112 km/h)
40,000 ft (12200 m)	90 mph (145 km/h)

Acceleration and Deceleration: With both aircraft in line-abreast formation at a speed of 200 A.S.I. (322 km/h), on the word 'Go' both engines were opened up to a maximum power simultaneously. The Spitfire initially drew ahead, but after a period of approximately 25 seconds the Vampire gradually caught up and quickly accelerated past the Spitfire.
The rate of deceleration for the Spitfire is faster than the Vampire even when the Vampire uses its dive brakes. Once again this shows that the Vampire's dive brakes are not as effective as they should be. ·
Dive: The two aircraft were put into a 40° dive in line-abreast formation with set throttles at a speed of 250 mph (402 km/h) IAS. The Vampire rapidly drew ahead and kept gaining on the Spitfire.
Zoom Climb: The Vampire and Spitfire XIV in line-abreast formation were put into a 45° dive. When a speed of 400 IAS (644 km/h) had been reached, a zoom climb at fixed throttle settings was carried out at approximately 50°. The Vampire showed itself vastly superior and reached a height 1,000 ft (300 m) in excess of the altitude of the Spitfire in a few seconds, and quickly increased its lead as the zoom climb continued. The same procedure was carried out at full throttle settings and the Vampire's advantage was outstandingly marked.
Climb: The Spitfire XIV climbs approximately 1,000 ft (300 m) per minute faster than the Vampire up to 20,000 ft (6100 m).
Turning Circles: The Vampire is superior to the Spitfire XIV at all heights. The two aircraft were flown in line-astern formation. The Spitfire was positioned on the Vampire's tail. Both aircraft tightened up to the minimum turning circle with maximum power. It became apparent that the Vampire was just able to keep inside the Spitfire's turning circles. After four or five turns the Vampire was able to position itself on the Spitfire's tail so that a deflection shot was possible. The wing loading of the Vampire is 33.1 lb per sq ft (1.3 kg/m²). compared with the Spitfire XIV's 35.1 lb per sq ft (1.47 kg/m²).
Rates of Roll: The Spitfire XIV has a faster rate of roll at all speeds. The higher the speed the faster the Spitfire rolls in comparison with the Vampire. As previously mentioned, at speeds of 500 IAS (805 km/h) there is a feeling of overbalance and aileron snatch when attempting to roll the Vampire.
Combat Manoeuvrability: The Vampire will out-manoeuvre the Spitfire type of aircraft at all heights, except for initial acceleration at low speeds and in rolling. Due to the Vampire's much higher speed and superior zoom climb, the Spitfire can gain no advantage by using its superior rate of climb in combat.

Left: The well-known F.Mk XIVCs of No. 610 'County of Chester' Sqn formate for an official photographer shortly after the unit re-equipped with the type in January 1944. Based at Exeter and then Culmhead, No. 610 moved to West Malling in June to help combat the V-1 offensive. Fifty V-1 kills were claimed by the squadron.

SEAC service

As the war in Europe came to an end, Spitfire Mk XIVs were made available to squadrons in the Far East. In June 1945 No. 11 Sqn, stationed in India, was the first unit outside Europe to receive examples of the variant, but the war ended before they became operational. Nos 17 and 132 Sqns followed suit shortly afterwards, and in late 1945/early 1946 further units in the region were re-equipped, namely Nos 20, 28, 136 (renumbered No. 152 Sqn in May) and 273 Sqns. After the Japanese surrender, the British Commonwealth Air Forces of Occupation (Japan) was established and included Spitfire units Nos 11 and 17 Sqns between April 1946 and 1948 (the former also operating Mk XVIIIs).

a maximum of +25 lb boost to be used; this increased the fighter's speed by about 30 mph (48 km/h) at low altitude, to about 400 mph (644 km/h) at 2,000 ft (610 m).

About 90 per cent of the V-1s shot down by fighters fell out of control and detonated upon hitting the ground; the rest detonated in mid-air. Provided the fighter was more than 150 yd (137 m) from the explosion, there was little risk of serious damage. Sometimes fighters suffered minor damage if they flew through a cloud of burning petrol from the missile's fuel tank, after the detonation, or were hit by small pieces of wreckage hurled great distances by the force of the explosion. It could be hazardous if fighter pilots engaged flying bombs from within 150 yd, however. On 3 August Captain Jean Marie Maridor, a French pilot flying Spitfire Mk XIVs with No. 91 Squadron, was in hot pursuit of a flying bomb heading towards the military hospital at Benenden. Maridor closed to short range to ensure the destruction of the missile, but when he opened fire the warhead detonated. The Spitfire was wrecked and its pilot was killed. In total, Maridor was credited with the destruction of 11 flying bombs, but the last of them took him with it.

Dicing with 'Divers'

The V-1 was controlled by elevators and a rudder, having no ailerons. As a result, the missile was particularly vulnerable to any interference in the rolling plane. Fighter pilots developed the technique of flying alongside the missile, placing a wingtip under that of the flying bomb and then banking steeply to flip the missile out of control. On 20 August Flight Sergeant Paul Leva, a Belgian with No. 350 Squadron based at Hawkinge, was operating in the inner Fighter Patrol Area. Flying one of his unit's recently acquired Spitfire Mk XIVs, he employed this technique to bring down a V-1. Later, he wrote:

"... the bomb went unscathed through the two first

A Spitfire Mk IX-equipped fighter-bomber unit within 2nd TAF during 1944, No. 132 Sqn was transferred to the Far East in early 1945, re-equipping with Mk VIIIs in Ceylon. Preparations for the expected Allied invasion of Malaya coincided with the receipt of Mk XIVs in May, the squadrom embarking in HMS Smiter. However, with the Japanese surrender No. 132 was transferred to Hong Kong, sailing into Hong Kong harbour in September (above). The squadron was based at Kai Tak (left) for seven months, engaged in air defence and anti-piracy patrols before disbandment in April 1946.

Far left: No. 136 Sqn moved to India in November 1941, equipped with Hurricanes. From December 1943 the unit operated Spitfire Mk Vs, Mk VIIIs from 1944 and finally Mk XIVs from February 1946. This Mk XIV was probably photographed in Kuala Lumpur.

Below left: Spitfire FR.Mk XIVEs of No. 11 Sqn, RAF are seen at Miho, Japan in about 1946, as part of the Commonwealth occupation force.

Below: No. 273's Sqn's FR.Mk XIVEs were based in Thailand and Indo-China in 1945/46.

Griffon-engined Spitfire deployment, May 1945

When the war in Europe came to an end, two squadrons of Air Defence of Great Britain were operational with the Spitfire Mk 21. Four squadrons in No. 83 Group in Germany operated the F.Mk XIV and two more operated the FR.Mk XIV. One squadron in No. 84 Group in Holland operated the FR.Mk XIV. In Ceylon one squadron was in the process of equipping with F.Mk XIVs, and several other units in that theatre were scheduled to re-equip with this variant.

ROYAL AIR FORCE
Fighter Command
No. 11 Group

No. 91 Sqn	F.Mk 21	Ludham
No. 1 Sqn	F.Mk 21	Ludham

2nd Tactical Air Force
No. 83 Group (Germany)

Nos 414, 430 Sqns	FR.Mk XIV	Schneverdingen
Nos 41, 130, 350 Sqns	F.Mk XIV	Celle
No. 402 Sqn	F.Mk XIV	Wunstorf

No. 84 Group (Holland)

No. 2 Sqn	FR.Mk XIV	Twente

No. 222 Group (Ceylon)

No. 132 Sqn	F.Mk XIV	Vavuniya

Mk XIVs at home and abroad

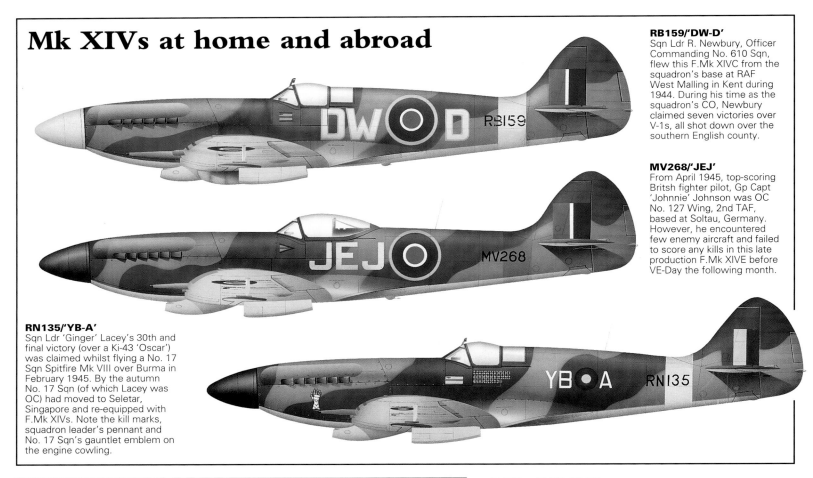

RB159/'DW-D'
Sqn Ldr R. Newbury, Officer Commanding No. 610 Sqn, flew this F.Mk XIVC from the squadron's base at RAF West Malling in Kent during 1944. During his time as the squadron's CO, Newbury claimed seven victories over V-1s, all shot down over the southern English county.

MV268/'JEJ'
From April 1945, top-scoring Britsh fighter pilot, Gp Capt 'Johnnie' Johnson was OC No. 127 Wing, 2nd TAF, based at Soltau, Germany. However, he encountered few enemy aircraft and failed to score any kills in this late production F.Mk XIVE before VE-Day the following month.

RN135/'YB-A'
Sqn Ldr 'Ginger' Lacey's 30th and final victory (over a Ki-43 'Oscar') was claimed whilst flying a No. 17 Sqn Spitfire Mk VIII over Burma in February 1945. By the autumn No. 17 Sqn (of which Lacey was OC) had moved to Seletar, Singapore and re-equipped with F.Mk XIVs. Note the kill marks, squadron leader's pennant and No. 17 Sqn's gauntlet emblem on the engine cowling.

Mk XVIII

Virtually indistinguishable from a late-production FR.Mk XIV, with its 'E' wing and bubble canopy, the Spitfire Mk XVIII differed primarily from the former in having a strengthened wing structure and undercarriage. Performance was very similar to that of the Mk XIV, power coming from the same Griffon 65 engine. The first prototype, NH872, flew in June 1945, too late for the variant to see wartime service. However, six RAF squadrons would eventually fly the type, all of them stationed overseas. The first to re-equip was No. 60 Sqn in Singapore, in January 1947, followed by Nos 11, 28 and 81 Sqns, also in the Far East, and Nos 32 and 208 Sqns in the Middle East. The Mk XVIII production run (mainly to FR.Mk XVIII standard) was comparatively short, 300 being completed before production ended in early 1946.

Above: SM843 was the Mk XVIII production prototype and, although ordered as an F.Mk XVIII, was completed to 'FR' standard, with vertical and oblique camera fittings. '843 became a trials airframe and was sold for scrap in 1953.

Right: A No. 32 Sqn FR.Mk XVIIIE, flown by Flt Lt F. E. Dymond, commander of 'A' Flight, taxis at its dusty base in Palestine during October 1947.

defence lines and, directed by the controller, I duly spotted the ugly little brute with the glowing tail below me. I banked to enter a steep dive, gathering speed and getting nearer and nearer to my target.

"Alas, though, I was not near enough. Soon, with my speed dropping after levelling off, I could see that the distance separating us did not diminish any more and even began to increase.

"Utterly disappointed, I nevertheless opened fire, aiming high to compensate for the distance. I had the happy surprise to see some impacts and bits flying off the wings. I fired burst after burst, damaging the bomb still more.

FEAF and MEAF actions

Operating in an environment where there was no effective opposition to air power, the post-war FEAF was required to fly obsolete types like the Spitfire, while the RAF in Europe was equipped with modern machines. Thus, it was in the Far East that the last operational Spitfire sorties took place. Spitfire Mk 14s and 18s of No. 28 Sqn and Mk 18s of Nos 60 and 81 Sqns took part in the opening actions of Operation Firedog, the British campaign against Communist guerrillas on the Malay Peninsula. Spitfires flew ground attack and fighter-reconnaissance sorties in the region until 1951, when No. 60 Sqn became the last RAF unit to use the 'Spit' in an offensive capacity, when it launched a strike against terrorists in the Kota Tinggi area of Johore on 1 January 1951. In the Middle East, Nos 32 and 208 Sqns, equipped with Spitfire Mk Vs and IXs, were deployed to police Palestine in the transition from UN mandate to the State of Israel. Both units re-equipped with Mk 18s, in 1947 and 1946 respectively, their main role being the provision of air support for army units. With the creation of Israel, in May 1948, came attacks by neighbouring Arab states. On 22 May, Ramat David airfield was bombed by Egyptian Spitfire Mk 9s, two of No. 208's Mk 18s being destroyed. A further attack later that day was met with swift resistance, four REAF Spitfires being downed – two by No. 208 Sqn and two by RAF Regiment AA fire. As related elsewhere, No. 208 Squadron also became embroiled in a skirmish with Israeli Spitfires in January 1949, losing four aircraft to IAF pilots.

Although no vital part was hit, its speed diminished and it entered a shallow dive.

"My hopes went soaring again, I was now approaching my target so fast that I had to throttle back. Ready for the kill, I positioned myself at what I estimated was the right distance. I depressed the trigger, but instead of the staccato of firing bullets I heard only the whistling sound of escaping compressed air.

"The voice of the controller came on again: 'Any luck?'

"'No,' I said forlornly. 'I damaged it, but have no ammunition left. It's very slow now and losing height. I am practically flying in formation with it.'

"'Tough luck,' said the controller. 'Time to turn back now – you are getting very near the balloon barrage.'

"It was then that suddenly, spurred no doubt by my frustration, I remembered the briefing of the intelligence officer [who earlier had spoken of sending V-1s out of control by tipping up one wing].

"'Wait,' I said. 'I think I can try something.' Adjusting the throttle I eased myself forward until I came abreast the bomb. What a sight it was at close range! The wings were so ragged with the impact of the bullets that I wondered how it could still fly almost straight and level.

"Positioning myself slightly underneath, I placed my starboard wingtip under the port wing of the bomb. I came up slowly, made contact with it as softly as I could, and then moved the stick violently back and to the left.

"This made me enter a steep climbing turn and I lost

sight of the bomb. I continued turning fast through 360°. Then I saw it – well below me, going down steeply, hitting the ground and exploding with a blinding flash."

The wingtip of the Spitfire made a poor battering ram. When Leva landed at Hawkinge he found that his fighter's wingtip was badly bent where it had come into contact with the V-1. The wing tip had to be replaced.

Above: No. 208 Sqn's Mk 18s saw considerable action in the Middle East, with the mixed fortunes of victory over REAF Spitfires, and somewhat humiliating overwhelming defeat at the hands of IDF Spitfires.

Left: Spitfire FR.Mk 18 TZ240 taxis past a guard post sandbagged against terrorist attack at Ein Shemar airfield, Palestine in 1948. When No. 208 Sqn repainted its aircraft with Type 'D' roundels and fin flashes, the squadron's 'RG' code letters were abandoned. Single aircraft letters were retained.

Above: No. 60 Sqn's Mk 18s were equipped as fighter-bombers, their cameras replaced with extra internal fuel capacity. This line-up, including TP197 nearest the camera, was photographed at Kuala Lumpur in 1950.

Left: During the Korean War, Spitfire Mk 18s of No. 28 Sqn, FEAF carried recognition stripes, though the unit was not involved in the conflict. This aircraft was photographed at Kai Tak in late 1950.

Supermarine Spitfire FR.Mk 18E No. 28 Squadron, Far East Air Force Kai Tak, Hong Kong late 1950

Markings

This aircraft, 'H' (serial unknown) of No. 28 Sqn, RAF, is finished in the standard RAF fighter scheme of the day – Dark Green/Dark Sea Grey upper surfaces over Medium Sea Grey undersurfaces. National insignia consisted of Type D roundels of the type introduced in 1947. Squadron marks included a red spinner and a unit badge on the fin. The latter featured a demi-Pegasus, representing the white horse on the downs near Yatesbury, Wiltshire, where the squadron received its fighters (Sopwith Camels) in 1917, after a period as a training unit. For the duration of the Korean War, Spitfires based in Hong Kong carried black and white recognition stripes on the rear fuselage (covering the serial number on the port side of this aircraft) and on both the upper and lower surfaces of each wing.

Air-to-ground armament

As originally conceived, the Spitfire was never intended to have an air-to-ground role, and was therefore not designed with underslung loads in mind. However, the need for a bomb-carrying capability in the Mediterranean led to the modification, from 1942, of Spitfire Mk VBs and VCs to carry a 500-lb (227-kg) bomb under the fuselage or a 250-lb (113-kg) bomb under each wing. Such was the success of these changes that Mk IX and XVI aircraft were similarly equipped, both variants equipping 2nd TAF units in the fighter-bomber role during the invasion of occupied Europe in June 1944. Rocket projectiles (RPs) were also tested on Mk IXs, but saw little use in combat.

Of the Griffon-engined Spitfire variants, the Mk XII was confined to an interception role, as was the Mk XIV in wartime RAF service. However, the latter variant was able to carry both the 500-lb (227-kg) bomb under the fuselage and the 250-lb (113-kg) underwing bombs, as well as six RPs (or 12 in pairs). The FR.Mk 18, effectively a strengthened late-production Mk XIV, was able to carry similar loads. Maximum loads quoted for the Mk 21, 22 and 24 appear to have been three 500-lb (227-kg) bombs or four 300-lb (136-kg) RPs, though in RAF service, the Mk 21 and 22 were confined to a fighter role. However, RPs were commonly seen fitted to Mk 24s, rocket firing forming part of the training programme for No. 80 Sqn at Kai Tak.

Hong Kong's Spitfires

Immediately after VJ-Day the British government set about re-occupying Hong Kong and re-establishing civilian control of the colony. Twelve days after re-occupation (on 1 September), ships of the Royal Navy arrived in Hong Kong, including HMS *Smiter*, with Spitfire Mk XIVs of No. 132 Sqn aboard. The squadron flew off the carrier and landed safely at Kai Tak, its base for the next seven months as it flew anti-piracy patrols over the waters around the colony. The squadron disbanded on 15 April 1946, after which patrols were made by RAF Sunderlands. Hong Kong was without a Spitfire presence for three years.

However, civil war in China and an increase in nationalist movements in the Far East (often supported by Communist elements) brought a need for renewed fighter reinforcement, and in May 1949 Spitfire FR.Mk 18s of No. 28 Sqn were deployed to Kai Tak from Malaya. At the same time, No. 80 Sqn with Spitfire F.Mk 24s left Germany for Hong Kong aboard HMS *Ocean* (with Tempest Mk 2s of No. 33 Sqn, bound for Malaya), arriving in August. Operational from September, No. 80 Sqn assumed daytime ground-attack and high- and low-level interception roles, No. 28 Sqn covering medium-level interceptions. Other tasks included Navy and Army co-operation and anti-piracy patrols. Though each unit had its assigned role, training covered all aspects of both the air-to-air and air-to-ground taskings. Low-level and dive-bombing, air-to-ground firing (cannon and rocket projectiles), mock attacks, practice interceptions, fighter affiliation and the like were all practised, along with the special skills required to operate from a busy airport like Kai Tak (the third busiest in the world in 1949), with its strong crosswinds, and over the mountainous country of the colony.

With the outbreak of war in Korea, No. 80 Sqn expected to be deployed to Korea, but the only changes were the painting of recognition stripes on both units' aircraft, and the issue of sidearms to their pilots. In fact, the two squadrons' pilots were forbidden from volunteering for service in Korea – though some took leave and made for Japan anyway, in the hope that they would find an obliging RAAF or USAAF Mustang unit.

Specifications (Griffon-engined aircraft)

	Spitfire F.Mk XII	Spitfire F.Mk XIV	Spitfire F.Mk 22
span	32 ft 7 in (9.93 m), clipped	36 ft 10 in (10.98 m), full span 32 ft 7 in (9.93 m), clipped	36 ft 11 in (11.25 m)
length	30 ft 9 in (9.37 m)	32 ft 8 in (9.96 m)	32 ft 11 in (10.03 m)
height	11 ft (3.35 m)	11 ft (3.35 m)	11 ft (3.35 m)
wing area	242 sq ft (22.45 m²)	242 sq ft (22.45 m²)	243.6 sq ft (22.59 m²
maximum loaded weight	7,400 lb (3356 kg)	10,065 lb (4565 kg)	10,086 lb (4574 kg)
maximum speed	389 mph at 12,500 ft (626 km/h @ 3810 m)	439 mph @ 24,500 ft (707 km/h @ 7468 m)	449 mph @ 25,000 ft (723 km/h @ 7622 m)
service ceiling	37,350 ft (11387 m)	43,000 ft (13110 m)	45,500 ft (13872 m)

	Seafire F.Mk XV	Seafire F.Mk 45	Seafire FR.Mk 47
span	36 ft 10 in (10.98 m)	36 ft 11 in (11.25 m)	36 ft 11 in (11.25 m)
length	32 ft 3 in (9.83 m)	34 ft 4 in (10.46 m)	32 ft 11 in (10.03 m)
height	11 ft (3.35 m)	12 ft 9 in (3.88 m)	12 ft 9 in (3.73 m)
wing area	242 sq ft (22.45 m²)	243.6 sq ft (22.59 m²)	243.6 sq ft (22.59 m²)
normal loaded weight	7,960 lb (3610 kg)*	9,357 lb (4243 kg)*	10,209 lb (4631 kg)*
maximum speed	383 mph @ 13,500 ft (616 km/h @ 4116 m)	446 mph @ 43,000 ft (718 km/h @ 13110 m)	451 mph @ 20,500 ft (726 km/h @ 6248 m)
ceiling	32,000 ft (9756 m)	40,000 ft (12195 m)	43,100 ft (13140 m)

Notes: * no external load

The Spitfire Mk XVIII in RAF service

The first Spitfire Mk XVIII (NH872) flew in June 1945, the new mark being externally identical to a late-production Mk XIV, with its bubble canopy and 'E' wing armament. Internally, the Mk XVIII had a stronger wing spar structure and two 31-Imp gal (141-litre) fuel tanks in the rear fuselage. Like the Mk XIV, there was a fighter-reconnaissance variant, the FR.Mk XVIII, with a single fuselage fuel tank and three cameras – two vertical and one oblique – behind the cockpit.

The Mk XVIII (known as the Mk 18 from 1947, when the RAF adopted arabic numerals for aircraft mark numbers) was too late to see service during World War II. The first examples did not join RAF squadrons until August 1946, when fighter-reconnaissance unit No. 208 Sqn re-equipped in Palestine. Deliveries began in earnest in 1947; in January No. 60 Sqn re-equipped at its base at Seletar, Singapore, followed by Nos 11 (with whom Mk 18s operated alongside Mk 14s), 28 (from February 1947) and 81 Sqns (from August, to augment the unit's PR.Mk 19s and Mosquito PR.Mk 34s). In the Middle East, No. 32 Sqn joined No. 208 Sqn in operating the new variant from April 1947.

No. 208 Sqn's Mk 18s became involved in an 'incident' with Israeli Air Force Spitfires in January 1949; an incident which, for 20 years, the British government would not acknowledge ever took place. During Operation Chorev, the final offensive of the 1948/49 Israeli War of Independence, which began with Israeli attempts to clear Egyptian forces from its territory, the IAF had gained air superiority beyond its borders. The British applied pressure on Israel to withdraw to its border with Egypt and transferred Spitfire FR.Mk 18s of No. 208 Sqn and Tempest Mk 6s of No. 213 Sqn from Cyprus to the Arab state to back its demands.

The RAF had already lost a No. 13 Sqn Mosquito PR.Mk 34 to an IAF Mustang on 20 November, photo-reconnaissance flights over Israel ceasing as a result. However, in order to monitor the Israeli withdrawal, the PR flights resumed and continued until the ceasefire of 7 January 1949. That morning four No. 208 Sqn Spitfire Mk 18s began a patrol of the Al Auja-Rafah road and soon found the remains of an Israeli armoured column recently attacked by Spitfire Mk 9s of No. 2 Sqn, Royal Egyptian Air Force. Expecting another attack, the Israeli army unit opened fire, damaging one of the RAF aircraft, causing it to crash land. Its pilot, P/O Frank Close, was captured. Meanwhile, two IAF Spitfires (flown by 'Slick' Goodlin and John McElroy), attracted by radio chatter after Close's loss, arrived on the scene. Spotting what were regarded as legitimate targets, McElroy quickly shot down another two Mk 18s (killing P/O Ron Sayers; F/O Tim McElhaw bailed out). Goodlin went after the last of the four RAF aircraft and caught and shot down F/O Cooper's machine (Cooper bailed out and managed to evade capture and return to his unit).

It would appear that none of the four Mk 18 pilots had managed to radio their base at Fayid before being downed, for a search was soon mounted with another four No. 208 Sqn Spitfires escorted by 15 Tempests from Nos 6 and 213 Sqns – all apparently unaware of the morning's events. Expecting retaliation from the RAF, the IAF put up continuous patrols over the area of the skirmish. Four Spitfire Mk 9s of No. 101 Sqn, IAF, spotted the 19-strong RAF formation and promptly attacked, Bill 'Sure Shot' Schroeder claiming one of the Tempests, killing its pilot (P/O David Tattersfield). Another Tempest and one of the IAF Spitfires were damaged before the Israelis broke off.

Though any acknowledgement of the incident took time to emerge, there were immediate ramifications at Fayid. Tempest pilots reported having mistaken the red spinners on No. 208's Spitfires for those of the IAF machines. No. 208 Sqn immediately repainted the spinners of its aircraft white and added a white band to the rear fuselage of its aircraft.

Camera fit

Unlike that of its predecessor, the Mk 14, Spitfire Mk 18 production was entirely of the FR.Mk 18 fighter-reconnaissance variant, characterised by its cut-down rear fuselage, bubble canopy and oblique camera ports behind the cockpit, either side of the fuselage. The standard camera fit for the type consisted of three F.24 cameras with lenses of varying focal lengths – usually one 14-in (35.6-cm) and two 20-in (50.8-cm). One of these was fitted to look obliquely through one of the two oblique ports, while the other pair was positioned to look downwards through the lower fuselage. An alternate load was a single F.52 vertical camera in the same position.

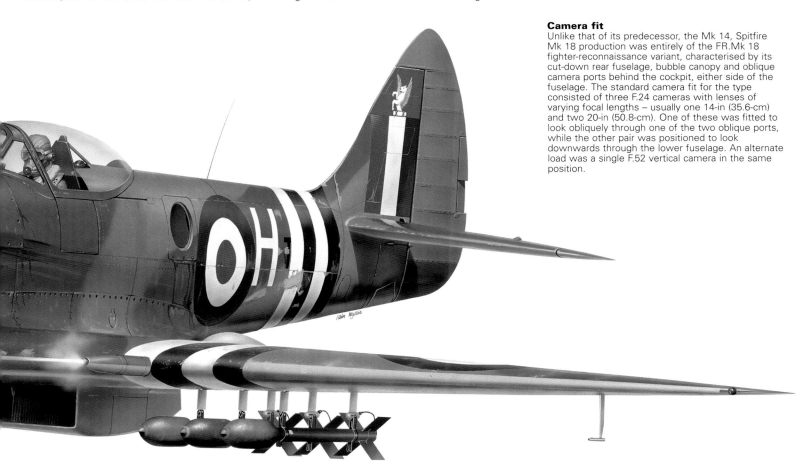

Pattern of development of the Griffon-powered Spitfire

The Rolls-Royce Griffon was a 12-cylinder, 60° Vee engine, with a bore and stroke of 6 in (15.24 cm) and 6.6 in (16.764 cm), respectively. This equated to a swept volume of 2,240 cu in (36.7 litres), some 35 per cent greater than that of the Merlin. Developed from the Buzzard via the 'R' racing engine (as fitted to the S.6 Schneider Trophy floatplanes), the Griffon was otherwise very much like an enlarged Merlin, incorporating many of the latter's features but rotating in the opposite direction (anti-clockwise, from the pilot's point of view).

A derated 'R' engine, known as the Griffon I, first ran in 1933 but was destined never to fly. Under pressure to develop a smaller engine (the Merlin), Rolls suspended Griffon development until 1939 and then carried out an extensive redesign to make the Griffon II a far more compact powerplant. As it was necessary to keep the engine's size and weight length within limits imposed by the configurations of existing fighter aircraft, much work went into keeping the Griffon's length to a minimum (centring on a redesign of the engine's supercharger drive system). Such was the success of these measures that the overall length of the Griffon was in the range 72-81 in (183-206 cm). For comparison, a Merlin with a single-speed supercharger measured 69 in (175 cm) in length, while a two-speed, two-stage Merlin was 88.7 in (225 cm) long.

The development of the Rolls-Royce Griffon did not produce such far-reaching improvements in engine power as those obtained from the Merlin. The Griffon Mks II, III and IV engines, with single-stage supercharging, developed 1,735 hp (1295 kW) for take-off. They powered the Spitfire XII at various stages of production. The next major development of the Griffon, the Mk 61, was the fitting of a two-stage supercharger to give improved performance at high altitude. This engine developed 2,035 hp (1518 kW) for take-off and powered Spitfire XIVs, 18s and early Mk 21s and 22s. The later Griffon 64, fitted to late-production Mk 21s, 22s and 24s, developed 2,375 hp (1771 kW) for take-off. The increase of 640 hp (477 kW) in take-off power from the Griffon 64, compared with the early versions of the engine, was significant, but proportionally it was much less than that achieved with the Merlin.

The airframe of the early production F.Mk XII was essentially that of the F.Mk VC, while that of the late production aircraft was a modification of that of the Spitfire F.Mk VIII. The airframe of the F.Mk XIV was essentially similar to the F.Mk VIII, but with a slightly larger fin and rudder to counteract the extra torque from the more powerful engine.

The enlarged fin and rudder of the F.Mk XIV was the first major move away from the 'classic' outline of the original Spitfires. The next major change, fitted to late production Spitfire F. and FR.Mk XIVs, took the form of a cut-back rear fuselage and bubble canopy. The Spitfire F.Mk 18, whose external appearance closely resembled the late production F.Mk XIV, was the first Griffon-powered variant with an airframe restressed to take the heavier engine.

With the next major variant, the Spitfire F.Mk 21, the fighter lost its original elliptical wing shape. Compared with that of the F.Mk 18, the new wing was further redesigned and strengthened. The F.Mk 21 retained the original faired canopy, however.

The Spitfire F.Mk 22 was essentially an F.Mk 21 with the cut-back rear fuselage and bubble canopy. On production Spitfire F.Mk 22s, the original tail and F.Mk XIV fin and rudder were replaced by the larger broad-chord tail unit which provided improved control authority to counteract the great engine torque. With the bubble canopy and reshaped wing and tail, the last remnants of the Spitfire's original outline were lost, though the aircraft was somehow still recognisable as a Spitfire. The Spitfire F.Mk 24, the final variant, was externally similar to the F.Mk 22 but was modified for the fighter-bomber role.

Built to replace the PR.Mk XI as the RAF's primary single-engined reconnaissance type, the Spitfire Mk XIX entered service with No. 542 Sqn in May 1944. Equipping seven PR squadrons by war's end, the bulk of Mk XIXs was flown in the European theatre, though a number also served in the Middle and Far East.

Above left: The seventh production Mk XIX, RM632 was built without a pressure cabin. Delivered to RAF Benson on 6 May 1945, it had reached No. 542 Sqn by 4 June. RM632 failed to return from a PR sortie on 6 January 1945 – one of the RAF's last Spitfire losses of the war.

Above: No. 681 Sqn, formed in 1943 from No. 3 PRU at Dum Dum, near Calcutta, operated PR.Mk XIXs from July 1945, these aircraft supplementing and eventually replacing Spitfire Mk XIs. By then based at Palam, the unit was renumbered No. 34 Sqn on 1 August 1946, and survived another 12 months before disbanding. Here five of the squadron's aircraft, including PM545/'A', are seen at Palam in 1946/47.

Later, pilots developed a more elegant method of disposing of V-1s if they could move into a position alongside it. The fighter's wing was placed over the top of that of the V-1, thus destroying the lift on that side of the flying bomb and forcing the V-1 into a steep bank from which it was unable to recover. The great advantage of this method was that there was no physical contact between the two aircraft, so the fighter suffered no damage.

'Wing tipping'

The 'wing tipping' tactic could be used only against V-1s flying relatively slowly, which explains why the method accounted for only a very small proportion of the missiles brought down. The great majority of V-1s destroyed by fighters fell to cannon fire. Three days after Leva sent his V-1 down out of control, Flight Lieutenant T. Spencer of No. 41 Squadron achieved the rare feat of destroying two missiles in a single sortie. The facts that he was flying the Spitfire Mk XII – which was slower than the Mk XIV – and the weather conditions were far from perfect, made his accomplishment all the more remarkable. The report on the action stated:

"Red Section [2 aircraft] airborne 0805 to 0915 from Lympne, under Kingsley 11 Control on Ashford [area] Patrol, was informed that flying bomb was approaching East of Folkestone. Seeing AA fire F/Lt T. Spencer dived from 9000' to 2000' and saw Diver [codename for V-1] at 10 o'clock 1000' above, over a point some 2 miles south of Mersham in hazy visibility. The Diver at 3000' on course

Top and above: Though completed in early 1945, PS858 did not reach an operational unit until the following year, having been flown by A&AEE Boscombe Down during trials of 90- and 170-Imp gal (409- and 773-litre) drop tanks. The latter is depicted in these views of the aircraft. Visible below the aircraft's exhausts is the air intake for the Griffon 66 engine's cabin pressurisation blower.

310° was travelling at 240 mph.

"Climbing, F/Lt Spencer opened fire with one- and two- second bursts. Closing from 250 yards to 80 yards from astern and slightly below, seeing strikes on the jet. He overshot the Diver and saw it go down near railway line at approximately R 5056 at 0820 hours.

"On the same patrol and under Kingsley 11 Control from Ashford F/Lt Spencer was informed that Diver would pass 4 miles due W of Ashford. Seeing flares [fired from Observer Corps posts on the ground to indicate the passage of a V-1 overhead] he dived from 10,000' and saw Diver at 2 o'clock. Closed and saw no strikes from 4-second burst. A second burst of 2 seconds obtained strikes on port side of fuselage and port wing root. The petrol tank exploded with black smoke and Diver flicked to port and went in north of railway line near Harrietsham R 3171 at 0907 hours. Diver was at 2500' on 340° doing 360 mph. Weather hazy."

In total, Spencer shot down six flying bombs, all while flying the Spitfire Mk XII. The top-scoring Spitfire pilots against the V-1s all flew Mk XIVs, however. Flying Officer R. Burgwal of No. 322 Squadron, a Dutchman, was credited with 21 of the missiles destroyed. Squadron Leader N. Kynaston and Flight Lieutenant R. Nash, both of No. 91 Squadron, were credited with 17 and 16 flying bombs, respectively.

The first phase of the V-1 bombardment on London came to an end in September 1944. Following the end of that commitment, in October the first three Spitfire Mk XIV squadrons redeployed to airfields in France and Belgium. In following weeks, four more squadrons

Below: PM655 carries the '6C' code of the Photo-Reconnaissance Development Unit at RAF Benson around 1950.

Performance

The Mk 19 had a top speed close to that of the Mk XIV fighter, though with a full fuel load its climb performance was rather worse. Cruising speeds of 370 mph (595 km/h) at 40,000 ft (12192 m) were generally sufficient to keep it out of reach of German wartime jets. During exercises after the war, Mk 19s were regularly flown at heights of 49,000 ft (14935 m) during PR sorties; not until the introduction of swept-wing jet fighters was the Spitfire Mk 19 seriously threatened.

Mk XI/XIV hybrid

The Spitfire Mk 19 effectively combined the wing tankage and camera installation of the Merlin-engined Mk XI with the Griffon power of the Mk XIV. With the range of the former and the performance of the latter, the Mk 19 was an outstanding reconnaissance aircraft that was destined to serve the RAF for 10 years in the absence of a jet-powered replacement with sufficient range.

Fuel capacity

The first 25 production Mk 19s had larger leading-edge fuel tanks than later aircraft, with a capacity of 86 Imp gal (391 litres) each. Total internal fuel capacity was increased to 256 gal (1164 litres), some 3½ times greater than that of the Spitfire prototype. Mk 19s frequently flew with external fuel, carried in a 90-Imp gal (409-litre) centreline slipper tank.

Supermarine
Spitfire PR.Mk 19
No. 81 Squadron,
RAF Seletar
March 1954

Delivered to No. 6 Maintenance Unit on 30 March 1945, PS888 moved to RAF Benson in April before being issued to No. 542 Sqn (the first unit to operate the type) on 17 June. Two days before Christmas 1950 the aircraft was shipped to the Far East where, on 1 April 1954, '888 (suitably named *The Last!*) had the distinction of flying the last sortie by an operational RAF Spitfire.

Colours and markings

During wartime service, Spitfire Mk 19s were finished, like most of the RAF's high-altitude PR assets, in PRU Blue, with low-visibility Type 'B' roundels and a standard three-colour fin flash. Post-war aircraft differed in having Type 'D' roundels applied over a modified PRU Blue paint scheme, with grey upper fuselage surfaces.

Griffon 65/66

The first 25 Mk 19s were completed without cabin pressurisation and therefore without the need for a cabin blower drive. The addition of this feature to the Griffon 65 (which powered these early aircraft) resulted in the Griffon 66, this variant powering the other 200 examples completed.

Last sortie

On 9 July 1957, PS853 brought 19 years of continuous RAF service by the Spitfire to a close when, in the hands of Flight Lieutenant J. Formby, it made the last operational flight by an RAF Spitfire. The meteorological sortie began at RAF Woodvale, Lancashire, base of the Temperature and Humidity Flight, and concluded at the same station at 1118 hours that day.

PS888

'Super Spitfire'

In order to fully exploit the power of the Griffon 60-series engine, Supermarine knew that a new Spitfire variant, with a considerably stiffer wing, would be needed. Spitfire Mk 21 was the designation given to the project, though consideration was allocating an entirely new name to the aircraft – Victor. The first aircraft modified was Mk XX DP851. This 'interim Mk 21' aircraft was fitted with a Griffon 61 and modified wings with a revised internal structure, thicker gauge skinning and pointed tips. A broad-chord rudder and redesigned cockpit windscreen and curved canopy were other features and, although it initially flew with a four-bladed propeller, a five-bladed example was soon substituted. Flight tests were promising, but the aircraft was written-off in a landing accident in May 1943. The true 'F.Mk 21 Victor' prototype (as it was briefly known), was PP139. This aircraft flew in July and differed from DP851 in a number of respects. It had bigger ailerons which gave the wing a straighter leading edge – the first change to basic outline of the Spitfire's wing since the Mk I. It also had pointed wingtips (later removed), increased wing tankage, four 20-mm cannon (no machine-guns) and redesigned undercarriage to improve ground handling and increase clearance for its 11-ft (3.35-m) propeller. The first production Mk 21 (LA187) flew in March 1944, though the solution of handling problems postponed the issue of aircraft to No. 91 Sqn until January 1945.

The second Griffon-engined Spitfire (the Mk XX), DP851, is seen here (top right) in original 'Victor' guise, re-engined with a Griffon 61 driving a four-bladed propeller. The latter was later replaced with a five-bladed unit (middle right).

Right: In this view of PP139 its revised windscreen, cockpit canopy, pointed wingtips and four-cannon armament are readily discernible.

Far right: LA235 was one of a number of Mk 21s tested with a Griffon 85 engine and contra-prop. Though popular with pilots at the CFE and AFDU, its unreliability, extra weight and expense counted against it.

Below: No. 91 Sqn's Spitfire Mk 21s, based at RAF Ludham in Norfolk, carried 'DL' unit codes.

equipped with the new variant joined them: Nos 41, 130, 350 and 403 Squadrons.

For the remainder of the war, the Spitfire Mk XIV was the RAF's primary high-altitude air superiority fighter type operating over northern Europe. During their initial operations over Europe, the Mk XIV units were constrained by bad weather and the poor condition of the newly captured airfields. The units spent most their time on armed reconnaissance missions, strafing vehicles and railway rolling stock when they could be found. There were few encounters with enemy aircraft, especially the sought-after jet types. Mk XIV pilots had fleeting encounters with the latter, before Flight Lieutenant Fredrick Gaze of No. 610 Squadron shot down a Messerschmitt Me 262 fighter-bomber near Munster on 14 February. On 12 April Gaze had another success, when he was credited with a half share of the

destruction of an Arado Ar 234. On 19 April Pilot Officer 'Blackie' MacConnell of No. 402 (Canadian) Squadron caught an Arado Ar 234 jet bomber on the landing approach for Lübeck/Blankensee airfield and shot it down.

During the final weeks of the war, as the Allied forces

Mk 21s at war – briefly

Though over 3,000 Mk 21s were ordered (almost all to be built by CBAF), mass cancellations meant that only 120 were completed. No. 91 Sqn's modified aircraft were finally operational by April 1945, and by VE-Day in May, No. 1 Sqn was working-up on the type. The only other front-line RAF units to fly the Mk 21 were Nos 122 and 41 Sqns, from February and April 1946, respectively.

No. 41 Sqn F.Mk 21s bask in the summer sun at Lübeck, Germany, shortly after VE-Day.

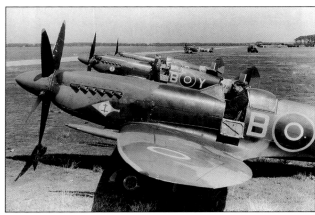

First with Mk 21s

LA224/'DL-V'
Delivered to No. 91 Squadron on 9 March 1945, LA224 was the 38th production Mk 21 and among the unit's operational aircraft based at Ludham at the end of the war. The variant's front-line career was to be rather short, No. 91 Sqn re-equipping with Meteor F.Mk 3s in October 1946. LA224 was finally struck off charge on 22 August 1947.

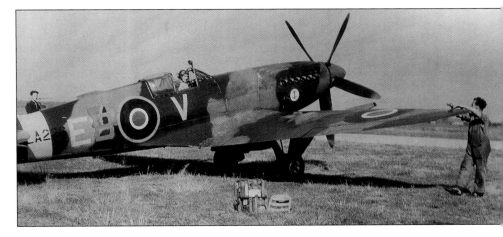

advanced deeper into Germany, the Spitfire Mk XIV units had more opportunities to engage. Typical of the hectic days was 20 April, when Nos 41, 130, 350 and 402 Squadrons all saw action. The units' total claims were 14 Fw 190s, two Bf 109s and an Me 262. The period of heavy fighting continued until the first week in May, then it petered out. On the morning of 5 May, No. 130 Squadron sent a pair of Mk XIVs to patrol the Hamburg area. Flight Lieutenant Gibbins and W/O Seymore sighted a Siebel Si 204 light transport and shot it down, the final victory claimed by the Royal Air Force over Europe during World War II.

Production of the Mk XIV came to an end late in 1945, with a total 957 fighter and fighter reconnaissance versions (reconnaissance variants of the Spitfire were described in detail in *Wings of Fame* Volume 5).

Throughout the Mk XIV's production run, the variant underwent continual changes, as a result of which the final aircraft off the line were considerably more effective fighting machines than those which had appeared early in 1944. The first improvement was the introduction of the Mk II Gyro gunsight. This device calculated automatically the deflection angle, that is to say, the distance ahead of the target that a pilot needed to aim to hit an enemy aircraft. The system worked on the principal that if a pilot followed an enemy aircraft into the turn and held his gunsight on the aircraft, the rate of turn was proportional to the deflection angle required to hit the enemy. A gyroscope measured the rate of turn, and tilted a mirror which moved the position of the sighting graticule to show the required deflection angle. The deflection angle increased with range, however, so the gunsight incorporated a simple optical system for measuring range. Before the engagement the pilot set on the sight the approximate wingspan of the enemy aircraft. As he closed on the enemy aircraft, he operated a control mounted on the throttle arm to adjust the diameter of the sighting graticule so that it appeared the same size as the

enemy plane's wingspan. Since the wingspan of the target aircraft had been set on the sight, the adjustment of the graticule 'told' the gunsight the range of the target. An analog computer in the gunsight worked out the correct point ahead of the target at which the pilot should aim in order to score hits. Once fighter pilots got used to the new sight, the general accuracy of air-to-air deflection shooting improved dramatically.

Early production Mk XIV aircraft were fitted with the 'C' type wing, with the standard armament of two 20-mm Hispano cannon with 120 rounds of ammunition each, and four 0.303-in machine-guns, with 350 rounds each. Later production aircraft featured the 'E' type wing, with two Browning 0.5-in machine-guns with 250 rounds each, instead of the four 0.303-in weapons. The 0.5-in machine-gun delivered a heavier penetrative punch than the smaller weapon it replaced, and was far more effective against air-to-air and air-to-ground targets. Aircraft fitted with the 'E' type wing were readily identifiable because the 20-mm

The first Griffon-Spitfire operator, No. 41 Sqn, was also an early recipient of the F.Mk 21. These photographs were taken at Lübeck shortly after the end of the war. LA226 (above) was one of the few Mk 21 airframes still extant in 1999. It was stored at the RAF Museum Restoration & Storage Centre at RAF Cardington. Other known survivors are LA198, under restoration in Scotland for eventual display in Glasgow, and LA255, owned by the No. 1 Sqn Association and stored at RAF Wittering.

The same, but different

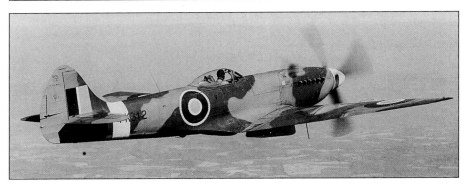

The only differences between the Mk 21 and its successor, the Mk 22, were the latter's cut-down rear fuselage and bubble canopy, changes that in the past had not resulted in the issue of a new mark number. The first example, PK312, was delivered in March 1945. Handling problems that plagued the new Spitfire designs were finally addressed towards the end of 1945, when enlarged tail surfaces, to the same design as those fitted to the Supermarine Spiteful, were incorporated in the Mk 22. Production totalled 278, though only one regular RAF squadron flew this variant – No. 73 Sqn – which converted to the type from Spitfire Mk IXs while based on Malta in 1947. Within a year, however, they had been replaced by de Havilland Vampires; the bulk of Mk 22 production was delivered to the RAuxAF, equipping 12 squadrons.

bubble-type canopies. The change brought an enormous improvement in rear view compared with the earlier canopy. With this modification, the pilot could see around the fin and past it as far as the tip of the tailplane on the opposite side. By banking the aircraft slightly during weaving action, the view into the danger area behind and below the fighter was also much improved. Production aircraft fitted with bubble canopies began reaching the operational squadrons early in 1945 and they immediately became popular with pilots.

The Mk 18

The Spitfire Mk XIV had been a hasty improvisation, combining the airframe of the Mk VIII with the Griffon 61 engine. The fighter proved a success, despite pilots having to be careful not to overstress the aircraft in combat. The 'definitive' Spitfire variant, the Mk 21 (described below), had a redesigned wing built to cope with much higher stress factors, but there would be delays in bringing it into front-line service. As an interim measure, the Spitfire Mk 18 was produced. Externally, this variant resembled the late production Mk XIV fitted with the 'E' type wing and armament, bubble canopy and additional fuel tanks in the rear fuselage. The Mk 18 featured a strengthened wing, which restored the fighter's strength factors, and incorporated a strengthened undercarriage to cope with greater take-off weights. The Mk 18 made its maiden flight in June 1945, too late to play any part in World War II; however, it later played an important part in the Royal Air Force's post-war overseas deployment.

Had the war continued into 1946, this definitive fighter variant of the Spitfire was set to become the RAF's main air superiority type. Powered by the Griffon 65 engine, it featured a completely redesigned wing with a much-strengthened internal structure. The new variant carried the four 20-mm cannon armament as standard. The first production prototype of the Mk 21, PP139, made its maiden flight in July 1943.

The new variant differed from its predecessors in several respects. To improve rolling performance, the ailerons were 5 per cent larger in area than those of early Spitfires. Instead of the Frise balance type used earlier, the ailerons were attached with piano-type hinges pivoting on the upper surface. As another innovation, balance was achieved using balance tabs. To improve ground handling, the track of the main undercarriage was widened by 7¾ in (19.7 cm). The five-bladed propeller was 11 ft (3.34 m) in diameter, 7 in (17.8 cm) larger than that of the Mk XIV. To provide the necessary ground clearance, the length of the main wheel oleo legs was increased by 4½ in (11.4 cm). Initially, PP139 was fitted with a revised, curved windscreen, and a fin with a straight leading edge; later, however, the shapes of these

Top: This colour view of a Mk 22 shows well the revised planform of the Mk 20-series Spitfires, with a straighter leading edge.

Above: Mk 22 prototype PK312 is seen here in its original configuration, with its Mk 21-type tailfin. Its performance was on a par with that of the Mk 21.

Above right: Towards the end of 1945, PK312 was fitted with an enlarged tailfin and tailplane of the type first flown on the 3rd Spiteful prototype in June 1945. Note also the outer set of undercarriage doors, introduced on the Mk 21.

cannon were moved from the inboard to the outboard cannon positions, about 12 in (30 cm) further out. On each side, the 0.5-in machine-gun occupied the vacant inboard cannon position.

To improve the view in the all-important rear sector, towards the end of 1944 Mk XIVs began coming off the production line fitted with cut-back rear fuselages and

Like the Mk 21 before it, the Mk 22 was tested with a Griffon 85 and contra-prop. Prototype PK312 was so-equipped from September 1946, while late-production example and ex-No. 615 Sqn, RAuxAF aircraft PK664 (left) followed suit after its sale to Vickers in 1954. This aircraft was stored at RAF Museum Restoration & Storage Centre at RAF Cardington in 1999.

Post-war RAuxAF ops

Large numbers of Spitfires served with Royal Auxiliary Air Force fighter units between 1946 and 1951. As well as Merlin-engined Mk IXs and XVIs, Griffon-engined Mk 14s, 21s and 22s were operated by 12 RAuxAF squadrons at different times.

features reverted to those of the Mk XIV.

The first production Mk 21, LA187, made its maiden flight in March 1944. It featured the new wing, with extended-span pointed tips, and Mk XIV-type fin and rudder. In November 1944 the prototype Mk 21 underwent a brief trial at Boscombe Down, where service pilots were unanimous in condemning the fighter's unpleasant handling characteristics:

"The rudder trimmer tab was very sensitive and required a very delicate touch to trim the aircraft for flight without yawing. This latter characteristic was accentuated by the large change of directional trim with speed, power and applied acceleration, rendering it necessary for the pilot to retrim the aircraft frequently during manoeuvres in order to avoid what appeared to be dangerous angles of sideslip.

"The directional qualities of the aircraft deteriorated markedly with altitude and also noticeably with aft movement of the cg. The bad directional qualities, linked with their effect on the longitudinal control, gave rise to very peculiar corkscrew behaviour of the aircraft, particularly at high Mach numbers, and at none of the loadings tested did the pilot feel comfortable when carrying out combat manoeuvres in the region of the aircraft's optimum performance altitude [25,000 ft/7620 m]."

For a fighter aircraft, these were serious shortcomings. Good directional handling qualities over a wide range of speeds and altitudes are an important attribute for an air superiority fighter, since during operations its success depended on its stability as a gun platform.

While the Boscombe Down trials were in progress, pilots at the Air Fighting Development Unit conducted tests to assess the Mk 21's value as a fighting aircraft. Their comments on the fighter's handling were even more scathing than those stated above:

"Whilst this aircraft is not unstable in pitch, above

25,000 ft the instability in yaw makes it behave as if it were unstable about all three axes. Because of its higher wing loading the high-speed stall comes in earlier than with other marks of Spitfire and in a steep turn the general feeling of instability, combined with its critical trimming qualities, is unpleasant. The control characteristics are such that this aircraft is most difficult to fly accurately and compares most unfavourably with other modern fighters."

The AFDU report concluded with a list of recommendations that could not have been more damning

Above and below: No. 600 'City of London' Sqn reformed at Biggin Hill on 10 May 1946, as a Royal Auxiliary Air Force unit. Initial equipment consisted of Spitfire Mk XIVEs (one of eight RAuxAF squadrons so-equipped), to which were added Mk 21s in March 1947.

Left: No. 602 'City of Glasgow' Sqn had the longest association with Spitfires of any RAF squadron, stretching as it did over 12 almost continuous years. The squadron first re-equipped with Spitfire Mk Is in May 1939 and later flew aircraft of Marks II, V, VI, IX, XVI, XIV, 21 (seen here) and 22. The unit's last Mk 22 was retired in early 1951.

Top: RAuxAF squadrons were allocated codes in the 'RAx' range, 'RAT' being that of No. 613 'City of Manchester'. This unit reformed as an auxiliary unit at Ringway in 1946, initially with Spitfire Mk 14s. They were replaced with Mk 22s in late 1948. Note that the aircraft retain the wartime ADGB camouflage applied before they left the factory.

Above: Eventually RAuxAF aircraft lost their camouflage, gained Type 'D' roundels and, in some cases, unit bars either side of the fuselage roundel, in the style of some regular squadrons. PK570/'F' is a Mk 22 of No. 603 'City of Edinburgh' Sqn.

to this latest Spitfire variant:

"It is recommended that the Spitfire Mk 21 be withdrawn from operations until the instability in the yawing plane has been removed and that it be replaced by the Spitfire XIV or Tempest until this can be done. If this is not possible then it must be emphasised that, although the Spitfire Mk 21 is not a dangerous aircraft to fly, pilots must be warned of its handling qualities and in its present state it is not likely to prove a satisfactory fighter.

"No further attempts should be made to perpetuate the Spitfire family."

The highly critical comments could not have come at a more embarrassing stage in the production programme. The Ministry of Aircraft Production had issued contracts for nearly 3,000 Spitfire Mk 21s. At the huge Castle Bromwich complex outside Birmingham, work was in full swing to retool the works to begin mass production of the new variant. Moreover, with each day that passed, more aircraft from the initial batch were coming off the line – all with the same poor handling characteristics as their predecessors.

Commenting on this unpleasant situation from his viewpoint as Supermarine's chief test pilot, Jeffrey Quill said:

"From the time I first flew the Spitfire 21 it was clear that we had a hot potato. There was too much power for the aeroplane and what was needed were much larger tail surfaces, both horizontal and vertical. The work to design and build these was already in hand, but would take several months to complete. In the meantime the great production 'sausage machine' was already rolling. So the immediate problem was to make the handling of the Mk 21 in the air reasonably tolerable, so that the aeroplane would be operationally viable pending the happy day when the much larger tail did become available … The AFDU were quite right to criticise the handling of the Mk 21, although in my opinion their report overdid it a bit. Where they went terribly wrong was to recommend that all further development of the Spitfire family should cease. They were quite unqualified to make such a judgement, and later events would prove them totally wrong."

The root cause of the fighter's problem was over-control, and in each case modifications to the controls provided a cure. Supermarine experimented with several expedients: different types of tabs, anti-balance tabs, changes to the horn-balanced area, etc. In the end, the over-control in the rudder sense was cured by removing the balance action of the rudder trim tab. The over-control in the elevator sense was cured by reducing the gearing to the elevator trim tab by half, and by fitting metal-covered elevators with rounded horn balances of reduced area.

It took three months to select and develop the various changes and incorporate them in a Mk 21, LA215. In March 1945 pilots at the AFDU flew the modified Spitfire, and commented on its suitability as a sighting platform:

"There has been considerable improvement in the qualities of the aircraft as a sighting platform and it is considered that the average pilot should be able to hold his sight on the target throughout all combat manoeuvres. The rudder was noticeably heavier than on the production aircraft and this reduced the amount of unintentional side-slip, except at speeds in excess of 400 mph [644 km/h] Indicated when the pilot is liable to over-correct."

Their report on the modified Mk 21 concluded by giving the variant a clean bill of health:

"The critical trimming characteristics reported on the production Spitfire 21 have been largely eliminated by the modifications carried out on this aircraft. Its handling qualities have benefited to a corresponding extent and it is now considered suitable both for instrument flying and low flying.

"It is considered that the modifications carried out on the Spitfire 21 make it a satisfactory combat aircraft for the average pilot."

The modifications to the controls were rapidly incorporated into aircraft on the production line. By then, No. 91 Squadron based at Manston had already begun to re-equip with unmodified Spitfire 21s; as modified aircraft became available, they were delivered to the unit and the unmodified machines were sent away for modification. By

One of a number of Spitfire Mk 22s known to have participated in air races during the late 1940s/early 1950s, this No. 607 'County of Durham' Sqn aircraft displays a prominent race number on the occasion of 1948 Cooper Trophy air race.

Mk 23 – a Valiant attempt

The Valiant, as it was to have been named, was a Spitfire Mk 21 derivative with which engineers attempted to make use of the latest research into wing aerodynamics, research that ultimately led to the laminar flow wing and its adoption for the Supermarine Type 371 Spiteful. In the interim, Supermarine proposed the 'Type 372 Spitfire F.Mk 23', which used a normal Mk 21 wing raised by 2 in (5.08 cm) at the leading-edge in order to improve the pilot's view and increase speed without increasing drag or pitching movement appreciably. The new wing was tested on Spitfire Mk VIII JG204, but results were disappointing. Mk 21 PP139 was then modified as an 'F.Mk 23', incorporating the revised wing and a new tailfin with a straight leading edge (right). Testing began in 1944, a contract for 438 'laminar flow wing LF.Mk VIII (F.Mk 23)' aircraft having been placed. However, by this time the F.1/43 (Spiteful) prototype had flown, leaving the Valiant dead in the water. PP139 reverted to Mk 21 standard and was eventually scrapped at Eastleigh.

the early part of April 1945, the squadron had received its full complement of 18 modified aircraft. On 8 April the unit was declared operational, and it moved to Ludham in Norfolk.

On the morning of 10 April the new variant flew its first combat sorties, when two aircraft carried out an uneventful armed reconnaissance of The Hague in Holland looking for V-2 launching activity. That afternoon the Mk 21 fired its guns in anger for the first time, when a flight of four aircraft strafed shipping off the Dutch coast. In the ensuing fire-fight two of the new Spitfires were shot down, but in each case the pilot was rescued.

Following this inauspicious start to the career of the Mk 21, the squadron settled into its operational routine. The main fare was armed reconnaissance missions over Holland, combined with patrols off the coast looking for German midget submarines operating in that area. These missions bore fruit on the morning 26 April, when Flight Lieutenants W. Marshall and J. Draper caught a Biber-type one-man submarine on the surface off The Hook. Each Spitfire carried out two strafing runs on the boat with

cannon. Following the last attack run, the submarine was seen to be sinking and stationary; as it disappeared, it left a large patch of oil and wreckage on the surface.

During its four weeks of operations before the war came to an end, No. 91 Squadron flew a total of 154 operational sorties with the Mk 21. Combat losses amounted to two of the new fighters, both of them on the first day.

The Seafire F.Mk XV and F.Mk 17

The Seafire Mk XV was essentially a navalised version of the Spitfire Mk XII, but without the latter's clipped wings. The new naval fighter was powered by the same Griffon IV engine with single-stage supercharger, developing 1,735 hp (1294 kW). The Mk XV had a maximum speed 383 mph (616 km/h) at 13,500 ft (4115 m), giving a useful improvement in performance over the earlier marks. The variant went into production in the winter of 1944, but it entered service too late to see action.

Production Mk XV and later Seafire variants were fitted with a 'sting'-type arrester hook, which extended from the

Post-war 'Spits'

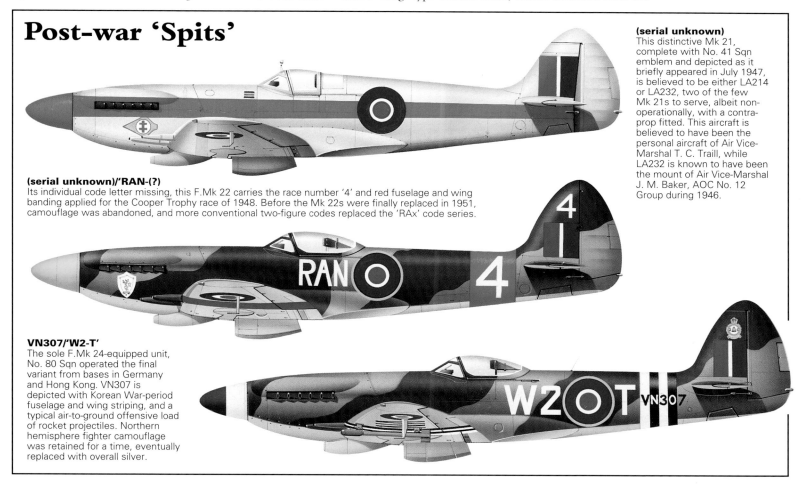

(serial unknown)
This distinctive Mk 21, complete with No. 41 Sqn emblem and depicted as it briefly appeared in July 1947, is believed to be either LA214 or LA232, two of the few Mk 21s to serve, albeit non-operationally, with a contra-prop fitted. This aircraft is believed to have been the personal aircraft of Air Vice-Marshal T. C. Traill, while LA232 is known to have been the mount of Air Vice-Marshal J. M. Baker, AOC No. 12 Group during 1946.

(serial unknown)/'RAN-(?)
Its individual code letter missing, this F.Mk 22 carries the race number '4' and red fuselage and wing banding applied for the Cooper Trophy race of 1948. Before the Mk 22s were finally replaced in 1951, camouflage was abandoned, and more conventional two-figure codes replaced the 'RAx' code series.

VN307/'W2-T'
The sole F.Mk 24-equipped unit, No. 80 Sqn operated the final variant from bases in Germany and Hong Kong. VN307 is depicted with Korean War-period fuselage and wing striping, and a typical air-to-ground offensive load of rocket projectiles. Northern hemisphere fighter camouflage was retained for a time, eventually replaced with overall silver.

Not only the last word in piston-engined fighter design, but one of the last such aircraft to enter service as the jet age dawned, the Mk 24 brought the development of the land-based variants of Reginald Mitchell's interceptor to a close. Though recognisable as a Spitfire, the Mk 24 was far removed from and bore little relation to the Mk I of 1938. Its engine (a Griffon 61) produced over twice the power of the Merlin 'C', the airframe was considerably larger and weighed in at just over 10,000 lb (4536 kg) all up – a loaded Mk I topped 5,800 lb (2631 kg) – and its 20-mm cannon armament packed considerably more punch than the Mk I's eight 0.303-in machine-guns. In fact, the Mk 24 differed little from the Mk 22. The main differences were the addition of two small fuselage fuel tanks and fittings for the carriage of underwing rocket projectiles. Late production examples had Hispano Mk V cannon, with shorter barrels than those fitted to the earlier example. Supermarine built 54 Mk 24s to which were added a further 27, converted from Mk 22s.

Above: Completed in February 1946 as the 14th production F.Mk 24, PK713 saw no service use and was eventually scrapped in 1956.

extreme tail of the aircraft and gave it a better chance of picking up one of the arrester wires. A few late production Seafire Mk XVs, and all F.Mk 17s, featured a cut-back rear fuselage and bubble canopy. The F.Mk 17 featured several detailed improvements over its predecessor, including the fitting of extended-stroke oleo legs to the undercarriage to give useful additional clearance for the propeller during deck landings. The Mk 17 also had provision to carry more fuel in underwing tanks stressed for combat.

The Seafire F.Mk XV equipped nine first-line units. The F.Mk 17 replaced it in three units, and equipped two others, before it passed out of first-line service in 1949.

The Seafire 45 was a navalised version of the Spitfire F.Mk 21. The prototype appeared in October 1944, fitted with a sting-type arrester hook, naval radio equipment and

slinging points. Flight tests revealed that the modified Mk 21 was unsuitable for deck operations, however. The powerful Griffon 61 engine, driving a five-bladed propeller, produced an uncomfortable twisting moment when the aircraft flew at high power settings at low airspeeds. This manifested itself in a marked tendency for the fighter to 'crab' during take-off or when it climbed away after a missed approach. Moreover, the revised wing fitted to the F.Mk 45 had to undergo a lengthy redesign if it was to fold. As a result, the 50 F.Mk 45s built were all confined to trials and second-line tasks.

The Seafire F.Mk 46, the penultimate step on the Seafire's evolutionary ladder, featured the cut-back rear fuselage, bubble canopy and broad-chord fin and rudder fitted to production Spitfire F.Mk 22s. Also, and more importantly for the Seafire's continued life as a naval fighter, the Griffon 87 engine drove a Rotol six-bladed contra-rotating propeller. The latter gave torque-free

Hong Kong's Mk 24s

Just one RAF unit operated Spitfire Mk 24s – No. 80 Sqn – based at Gütersloh, Germany. The first examples reached the squadron in January 1948, but in July 1949 the squadron moved to Kai Tak, Hong Kong to reinforce the colony in the face of the Communist threat from mainland China. In Hong Kong its complement of aircraft was eventually to include VN496, the last production Spitfire of all, completed at the South Marston factory in February 1948. No. 80 Sqn operated its Spitfires until January 1952, when they were replaced with de Havilland Hornets, bringing the front-line service of the Spitfire fighter in the RAF to an end.

Right: Upon arrival in Hong Kong harbour, No. 80 Sqn Spitfire VN314 is craned from the carrier HMS Ocean on to a lighter for transfer ashore.

Below and below right: Kai Tak airfield and the mountainous terrain around the colony were home to No. 80 Sqn's 'W2'-coded F.Mk 24s for 2½ years, the squadron eventually operating at least 40 of the 54 production examples.

power at all speeds, bringing about a vast improvement in deck handling characteristics compared with those of its predecessor. The F.Mk 46 still lacked wing-folding, however, so this variant was also unsuitable for first-line embarked operations. Only 24 examples were built.

The definitive Seafire

Externally, the F.Mk 47, the definitive Seafire variant, looked little different from the F.Mk 46. The most significant change was the installation of a completely new type of folding wing, with only one fold on each side. To keep within the 16-ft (4.9-m) hangar ceiling limit, the hinge line was moved farther outboard from the main wheel legs than it had been with the earlier system. Production versions of the Seafire 47 were fitted with a hydraulically-powered wing-folding system operated from the cockpit. This innovation greatly reduced the demands on the overworked deck handling teams. Other changes to the Mk 47 included an extension of the carburettor air intake to a position under the extreme nose, 20 per cent greater flap area, and long-stroke oleo legs to absorb the shock of landing at higher weights than previously. Production aircraft were built as FR.Mk 47s, able to carry one vertical and one oblique camera in the rear fuselage. The variant also had a fighter-bomber capability, with provision to carry a load of up to 1,500 lb (680 kg) of bombs or eight rockets.

The Royal Navy placed an order for 90 Seafire FR.Mk 47s, but following the end of World War II the urgency went out of the production programme. The aircraft were built at a rate of only about three per month, with the result that it took until January 1948 to amass enough fighters to form the first operational unit. No. 804 Squadron exchanged its F.Mk XVs for FR.Mk 47s, and later that year it took its new aircraft to sea aboard the light fleet carrier *Ocean*.

In April 1949 No. 800 Squadron became the second

Above: Eight of No. 80 Sqn's Mk 24s were passed to the Hong Kong Auxiliary Air Force, which flew them until 1955. The only external change made to the aircraft was the removal of No. 80 Sqn's codes.

Left: Shortly before their replacement, No. 80 Sqn's aircraft flew in an overall silver finish.

Exported aircraft

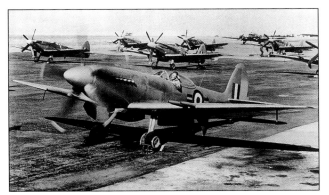

Above: These FR.Mk 14Es of the Force Aérienne Belge/ Belgische Luchtmacht carry the 'IQ' codes of the Ecole de Chasse at Coxyde, which operated the variant between 1948 and 1954.

Far left: The Southern Rhodesian Air Force's Mk 22s were operated by No. 1 Sqn.

Left: Sweden operated a sizeable fleet of some 50 ex-RAF PR.Mk 19s.

Spitfire Colours

Great Britain

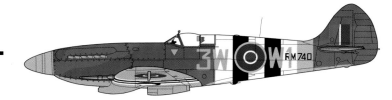

Above: No. 322 (Dutch) Sqn flew Spitfire Mk XIVs briefly during 1944. This aircraft carries 'invasion stripes' (as worn during Operation Overlord) and a Dutch orange triangle marking.

Above: In the Far East, Dark Earth/Dark Green camouflage was applied to Spitfire Mk XIVs initially. 'SEAC bands' and codes/serials were white; the 15-in (38.1-cm) roundels and fin flashes, roundel and light blue.

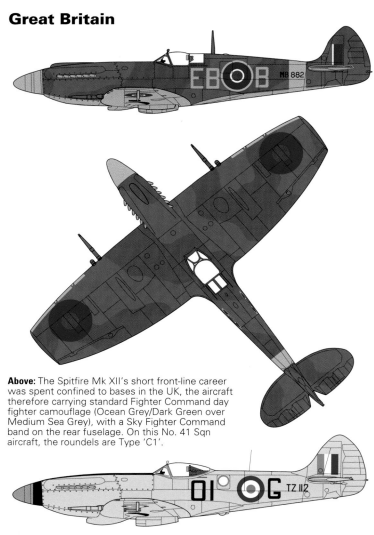

Above: The Spitfire Mk XII's short front-line career was spent confined to bases in the UK, the aircraft therefore carrying standard Fighter Command day fighter camouflage (Ocean Grey/Dark Green over Medium Sea Grey), with a Sky Fighter Command band on the rear fuselage. On this No. 41 Sqn aircraft, the roundels are Type 'C1'.

Above: Towards the end of the war, Dark Grey replaced Dark Earth in SEAC colour schemes and 'SEAC bands' gave way to a white band on the rear fuselage. This is a No. 132 Sqn aircraft based in India in August 1945.

Above: No. 60 Sqn, the last RAF Spitfire fighter unit to see active service, flew FR.Mk 18s in Malaya during the 'emergency'. Its aircraft were Dark Green/Dark Sea Grey over Medium Sea Grey, with a distinctive yellow/black nose marking.

Above: Post-war, camouflage was often removed, the aircraft finished in all-over silver and serial numbers applied on the lower surface of the wing. After 1947 Type 'D' roundels and a new fin flash were applied. This is a No. II (AC) Sqn, FR.Mk XIVE.

Above: In the Middle East, the camouflage applied to No. 208 Sqn's Mk 18s followed the FEAF pattern with white unit/aircraft codes and Type 'D' roundels.

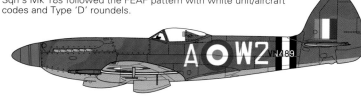

Above: No. 600 Sqn, RAuxAF received Spitfire Mk 21s in 1947, initially operating the aircraft in wartime camouflage and markings. RAuxAF aircraft wore three-letter 'RAx' codes from 1946.

Above: Based at Kai Tak, Hong Kong No. 80 Sqn's Spitfire F.Mk 24s carried recognition markings in the Korean War, though they were not actively engaged. Otherwise standard FEAF markings were applied.

Above: Squadron markings made a reappearance in the peacetime RAF, from 1948. On some aircraft they replaced unit codes (as on this No. 603 Sqn, RAuxAF Spitfire Mk 22), the aircraft code moving to the tailfin.

Above: PM655 displays standard wartime overall PRU Blue colours, with toned down national markings. In post-war PRDU service, codes were added.

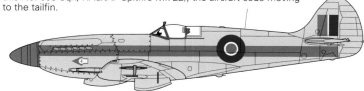

Above: This distinctive one-off, silver and red colour scheme, with No. 41 Sqn badge, was applied to a Mk 21 at the behest of an air vice marshal in the late 1940s.

Above: In the Far East during the 1950s, PR.Mk 19s mostly flew in PRU Blue (seen here on PS888, with grey fuselage upper surfaces) or in natural metal finish, with Type 'D' roundels.

Sweden

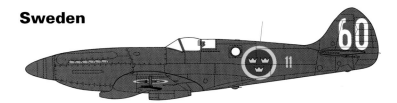

Above: Sweden operated its 50 Spitfire Mk 19s (S.31s) in PRU Blue, with a two-digit code on the fin. The '11' marking on the fuselage refers to the aircraft's unit – Flottilj 11.

Hong Kong AAF

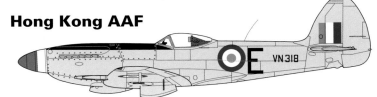

Above and right: Upon taking over No. 80 Sqn, RAF's Mk 24s, the HKAAF removed all camouflage, adopted an overall silver finish but otherwise retained standard RAF markings. A single-letter aircraft code was added.

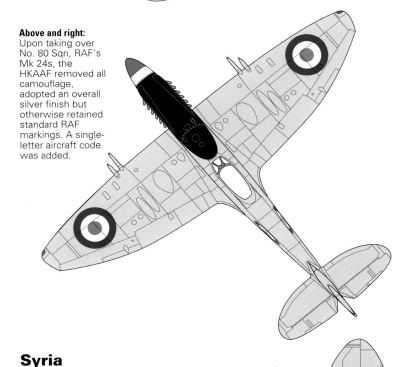

Syria

Above: Little is known of Syria's Mk 22s. When delivered they were finished in overall silver, with a black anti-glare panel, national markings and a serial or code number in Arabic on the fin.

India

Above: Initially flown in RAF SEAC camouflage and markings, many of the IAF's large fleet of Spitfire Mk XIVs later flew in natural metal with Indian national markings. RAF serials were retained.

Turkey

Above: Turkey's small batch of PR.Mk 19s are believed to have been camouflaged, with national markings and a three-figure serial. The '133' figure shown here would appear to be an aircraft code; the Mk 19s were serialled 6551-6554.

Belgium

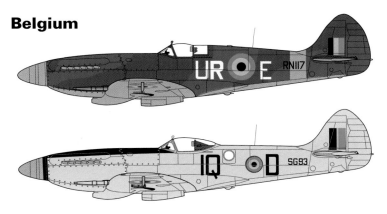

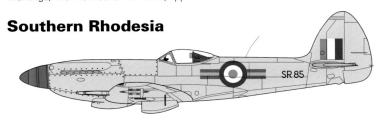

Above: Belgium's first Mk XIVs were delivered in standard RAF camouflage, over which were applied Belgian national marks and new unit codes. Later, camouflage was stripped off, an anti-glare panel painted forward of the cockpit and modified markings, with new serial numbers, applied.

Southern Rhodesia

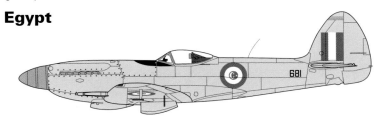

Above: This No. 1 Sqn, SRAF F.Mk 22 is finished in overall gloss light grey with a red spinner. Standard RAF Type 'D' roundels are carried in six locations, all flanked by green/yellow bars.

Egypt

Above: Like similar aircraft operated by Syria, little is known of Egypt's Mk 22s. On delivery they were similarly finished in overall silver, with national markings and new serial numbers applied.

Thailand

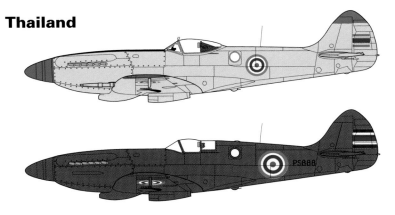

Above: Thailand's Spitfire Mk XIVs were flown in overall silver, with minimal markings other than national insignia. Their PR.Mk 19s included ex-FEAF aircraft, which were simply given Thai markings and retained their PRU Blue colours.

Canadian civil racer

Above: CF-GMZ was formerly FR.Mk XIVE TZ138, shipped to Canada in late 1945 for cold weather testing. Struck off charge in March 1949, the aircraft was sold and is depicted here as it was when participating in the 1949 Cleveland Air Races. Placed third in the Tinnerman Trophy Race, the aircraft was clocked at 359.565 mph (578.662 km/h). Then owned by Imperial Oil Ltd. of Edmonton, the aircraft had a polished natural metal finish, with red striping.

Seafire Colours

Great Britain

Above: Despite its US Navy markings, this Seafire Mk IIC is a Fleet Air Arm machine (possibly of No. 807 Sqn aboard HMS *Furious*) shown as it was marked for Operation Torch, the invasion of North Africa, November 1942.

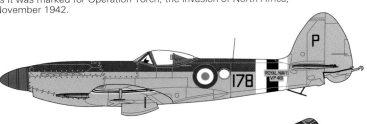

Above: As a recognition aid for American forces, black and white striping was applied over the Extra Dark Sea Grey/Sky scheme on Seafire FR.Mk 47s in action over Korea in 1951. This a No. 800 Sqn aircraft, carrying the deck letter of its ship, HMS *Triumph*.

Burma

Above: Burma's Seafire Mk XVs flew in 'natural metal', with an anti-glare panel over the nose and national markings on the fuselage tail and under the wings. Some aircraft are known to have carried single letter codes; this machine is depicted with British civil Class-B marks for delivery purposes.

France

Above: Shortly after delivery, the Aéronavale's Seafire Mk IIIs flew in standard FAA colours, with French roundels, unit marks (in this case, for 1.Flotille) and aircraft identity ('22') applied over the existing British markings.

Below: Seafire Mk XVs were due to be delivered to FAA units in the Pacific as World War II drew to a close. These deployments eventually took place in 1946/47, the aircraft involved being finished in the, by then, standard Extra Dark Sea Grey/Slate Grey camouflage, with Sky undersurfaces. '141-7/T' is a No. 804 Sqn aircraft based aboard HMS *Theseus* in late 1946.

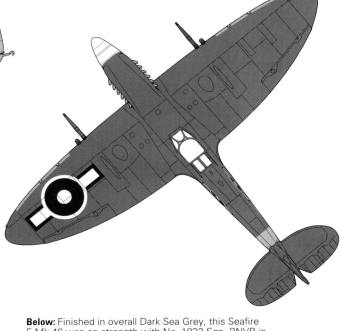

Below: Finished in overall Dark Sea Grey, this Seafire F.Mk 46 was on strength with No. 1832 Sqn, RNVR in 1947. Note the Type 'C1' roundel, three-digit aircraft code and 'CH' station code (for Culham).

Ireland

Below: Ireland's Seafire Mk IIIs were finished, like its T.Mk 9s, in overall green, with a two-colour Celtic Boss and three-colour wing stripes.

Canada

Below: RCN Seafire MK XVs were eventually finished in standard FAA Extra Dark Sea Grey over Sky colours, but with Canadian 'maple leaf' roundels. The 'TG' code on this aircraft referred to Training Air Group Number 1, the last operators of the type in 1948/49. This machine was the Commander Air's aircraft at HMCS *Shearwater* in 1946.

Seafire weapons

Given the limited bomb load-carrying capability of the Merlin-engined Seafire, the rocket projectile (R/P) was a far more suitable weapon. It could be aimed with the aircraft's existing gunsight and afforded the pilot a higher degree of immunity against light flak, as R/Ps were usually fired out of their range. As early as October 1943, theoretical tactics for the use of R/Ps were formulated, but as the heavy Universal launcher proved incompatible with the Seafire, R/P use was delayed until the lightweight zero-length Mk VIII launcher (seen on Seafire Mk III PP921, below left) was developed. When HMS Implacable sailed for the Far East in May 1945 it had sets of launchers aboard, but clearance for operational use was not given until after hostilities had ceased. Four launchers for 110-lb R/Ps (each with a 60-lb HE head) would have been the standard fit, though there was a considerable drag penalty. Unsurprisingly, though tandem R/Ps were trialled (below), they were not proceeded with.

Above: The standard load for a Seafire fighter-bomber was a 500-lb bomb (Medium Capacity or Semi-Armour Piercing), seen here suspended beneath a Mk III taking-off from HMS Khedive during Operation Dragoon, or a 250-lb GP bomb. With the weight and drag penalty imposed by the former, the Seafire Mk III's range was reduced to less than 100 miles (161 km). Given the aircraft's lack of air brakes, a glide-bombing technique was used and dive angle limited to 40° so as to avoid overstressing the aircraft's airframe.

Above: A number of alternative loads were trialled at A&AEE Boscombe Down in March 1945, including 500-lb bombs, the A Mk VIII mine (seen here), smoke floats and 250-lb bombs, the last on wing racks.

Production

Production Seafire Mk IIIs were built by Westland and Cunliffe-Owen. These two scenes, from Westland's Yeovil factory in January 1944, show Mk III production in full swing. Note the Welkin high-altitude fighters in the background (below). Seafire NF482 (below, left foreground) eventually served with the Aéronavale.

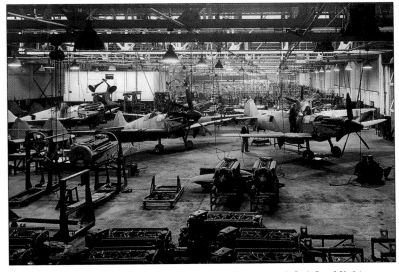

Above: With a 'sea' of Griffon engines in the foreground, Spitfire Mk 21s undergo final assembly at Supermarine's South Marston plant in 1945.

Below: Staff temporarily 'down tools' as the photographer records the final assembly of Mk XVIIIs at High Post in 1946.

Mk XV – the first 'Griffon-Seafire'

Above and right: Had the war in the Far East continued, Seafire Mk XVs would have replaced Mk IIIs. No. 806 Sqn reformed in August 1945, sailing for the region in April 1946, joining HMS Glory in September with F.Mk XVs. After a tour of Australia, the squadron returned home and disbanded. These examples of No. 806 Sqn aircraft (in wartime camouflage and sporting Glory's 'Y' deck code) were photographed around this time.

Potential difficulties in the adaptation of the Spitfire Mk VIII and IX for naval use centred around the need to strengthen its airframe for carrierborne use to such an extent that an unacceptable weight penalty would have resulted. Impressed with the potential of the Griffon/Spitfire marriage, the FAA therefore ordered that development of the next Seafire variant be based on the Spitfire Mk XII. In fact, the resulting Seafire Mk XV was, like the Spitfire Mk XII, a Mk V derivative, with the folding wings from the Seafire Mk III and the enlarged tail and retractable tailwheel of the Spitfire Mk VIII plus, of course, the engine installation of the Mk XII. Production began in the winter of 1944, but was not until September 1945 that the first squadron (No. 801 Sqn, in Australia) was able to re-equip with the variant. By the middle of 1946, the Mk III had been completely replaced. The Mk XV's Griffon VI engine, a derivative of the Griffon IIB fitted to the Spitfire Mk XII, gave the new Seafire an excellent low-level performance, but was to be the source of considerable problems during the first months of operation. The engine's M-ratio supercharger clutch was prone to slipping at high rpm settings, resulting in a power loss at crucial times, like take-off. Giving the potential dangers that this presented, embarked flying was prohibited from August 1946 – at a time when the Seafire Mk XV was the FAA's only front-line shipboard fighter. It was not until early 1947 that a modified clutch was developed. Mk XV production totalled 434, all by Westland and Cunliffe-Owen, the variant equipping nine front-line squadrons.

Right: The second Mk XV prototype, NS490, was photographed during flight trials carried out during 1944 by the manufacturers, A&AEE and RAE Farnborough.

Lower right: SR449 is a standard production Mk XV completed in October 1944. Note the bulged trim tab on the rudder, a feature of the first 384 Mk XVs introduced to compensate for the increased torque produced by the Griffon engine. When the 'stinger' hook was introduced, the entire rudder was redesigned.

Below and below right: No. 804 Sqn Mk XVs are seen during operations from HMS Theseus in early 1947.

(and last) front-line unit to re-equip with the Seafire FR.Mk 47. Lieutenant 'Tommy' Handley joined the unit as senior pilot (deputy commander) when it was based at Royal Naval Air Station Sembawang, Singapore. He had flown several variants of the Seafire, and found the FR.Mk 47 the nicest of them all.

"The Seafire 47 was a superb aeroplane in the air. It was a better fighter than previous marks, could carry a greater weapon load and had a better range and endurance. The Rolls-Royce Griffon fitted with the injector pump was a most reliable engine, and the squadron experienced no engine failures of any kind. The contra-rotating propellers were a big advance, and even at full throttle on take-off there was no tendency to swing. Also, there was no change of rudder trim in a dive, which helped considerably when operating in the ground attack role."

In February 1950 Handley's squadron, together with No. 827 operating Fireflies, embarked in HMS *Triumph* for a tour of the Far East. At each British naval base along the route, the carrier's air group flew ashore and continued its training programme from there. With the Seafire's earlier reputation in mind, those in authority sought to keep the FR.Mk 47's deck operations to a minimum.

Handley remembered: "Seafires were not easy to deck land. The Mk 47 was a much heavier aircraft than the previous marks, and heavy landings often resulted in damaged oleo legs. Also, the fuselage aft of the cockpit was not sufficiently strengthened to withstand anything but a near-perfect deck landing. The long sting hook made catching a wire reasonably easy, but if the landing was much off-centre or made with any skid or slip on, then the wire would shake the aircraft rather like a terrier shakes a rat. The result could be a wrinkling of the after fuselage section."

During April, May and June 1950 Handley made only 26 deck landings, an average of about two per week. Most of his take-offs were unassisted runs off the deck, but he also made some catapult launches. The catapult was used in light winds, or when a large number of aircraft were on deck and those at the front had insufficient room to make a full take-off run.

Triumph's enjoyable jaunt round the west Pacific came to a sudden and unexpected end on the morning of 25 June 1950, when North Korean troops stormed south and began

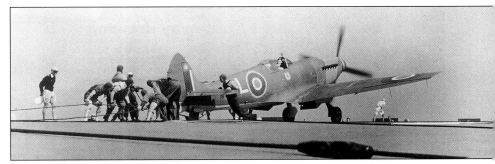

Seafire Mk XV operations aboard HMS Warrior (on loan to the Royal Canadian Navy) off Nova Scotia in March 1946, are seen here. Note that PR504/'B' (lower left) is a late-production aircraft with a 'stinger' hook and has underwing pylons fitted. The Mk XV was able to carry the same air-to-ground load as a Mk III, namely a single 500-lb bomb on the centreline, or four R/Ps.

advancing into South Korea. On the next day the US Navy was ordered to provide support for South Korean forces. On 27 June the Royal Navy placed its forces in Japanese waters under the operational control of the US Navy, for the same purpose. Escorted by a cruiser and two destroyers, *Triumph* left Japan and arrived off the west coast of Korea on 2 July. There it joined US Navy Task Force 77 which included the carrier *Valley Forge*.

First strike by Mk 47s

On the following morning the two carriers launched a joint strike against airfields in the Pyongyang area. It was the Seafire Mk 47's first operational mission from a carrier and, as Handley explained, some of these fighters needed to use RATOG (rocket-assisted take-off gear) to get airborne.

"For the strike we had a big range of aircraft on deck. On a small carrier like *Triumph* that meant the aircraft at the head of the range did not get a full take-off run, so the four Seafires at the front were fitted with RATOG. RATOG was not popular − carrier operations were hazardous enough, without having to rely on cordite and more electric circuitry. The technique was to fire the rockets late in the take-off run, as the aircraft passed a mark on the deck. Firing the rockets gave quite a push, though not as much as going off the catapult. Once airborne, the pilot would jettison the rocket packs. With free take-offs or using RATOG we could launch at 15-second intervals (catapulting was a much slower business, with about one launch per minute)."

The raiders found no enemy aircraft on the airfield, so they attacked the hangars with rockets and cannon fire. There was some return fire and one Seafire was hit by a machine-gun round. Another suffered minor radiator damage after it flew through debris thrown up by the explosions of its rocket projectiles.

On the next day, 4 July, *Triumph* launched seven Seafires and 12 Fireflies to attack rail targets. Following these initial strikes Task Force 77 withdrew from the combat zone.

When the carriers returned to the area, on 18 July, it was agreed that *Triumph*'s aircraft would fly combat air patrols (CAPs) and anti-submarine patrols to cover the Task Force, leaving the more-capable US Navy aircraft free to strike at targets ashore. Handley described the defensive operations:

"Usually we carried a 50-gal [Imperial] 'torpedo' tank under the fuselage. In addition we could carry a 22-gal combat tank under each wing. The combat tanks were stressed for combat manoeuvres, but we did not like them because they reduced our maximum speed by about 20 kt. They could be jettisoned, but as there were few spares we were ordered not to drop them except in a dire emergency. Shortage of range was never a problem for the Seafire 47s during the Korean conflict. All my flights were two hours or thereabouts and we always returned to the carrier with stacks of fuel."

The problem of wrinkling of the Seafire Mk 47's rear fuselage, which earlier would have prevented these fighters from flying, was solved by simply ignoring it.

Above: Another of No. 803 Sqn's aircraft is disengaged from an arrester wire on **Warrior**. Note the unit badge below the cockpit, maple leaf on the fin and camouflaged engine cowlings, presumably 'borrowed' from another aircraft.

Aéronavale Mk XV

SR520/'54.S-26'
Escadrille 54S was one of seven Escadrilles de Servitude to operate Seafire Mk XVs alongside 1 Flottille and 12 Flottille until 1951. Note the retention of the FAA colour scheme and serial number, to which was added Aéronavale roundels, codes and 'tricouleur' rudder striping.

Mk 17 – last of the first

The last of the 'first-generation' Seafires, the FR.Mk 17 first entered service in 1946. Generally similar to the Mk XV, the new variant differed primarily from the latter in having a bubble canopy and enlarged rudder, as fitted to the last 30 Mk XVs. The other useful change was the fitting of strengthened undercarriage with longer-travel oleos to reduce the risk of propeller 'pecking'. While the Mk XV had been unable to carry cameras, the Mk 17 had provision for a pair of F.24 cameras, or a small fuel tank in the lower fuselage behind the cockpit. The Mk 17's strengthened wings were also plumbed to allow the carriage of two small slipper-type 'combat tanks' of 22½-Imp gal (102-litre) each, or two 250-lb (114-kg) bombs. With the end of the war, production was cut back considerably to 233 and the variant spent less than two years in front-line service.

Above: NS493 was the third Seafire Mk XV prototype and was fitted with a bubble canopy during 1945. In the event, the last 30 Mk XVs were completed with the new canopy design.

Right: This profile of SX194 shows well the revised lines of the FR.Mk 17. '194 was a No. 781 Sqn aircraft based at RNAS Lee-on-Solent, as indicated by the 'LP' tailcode.

Right: Seafire Mk 17s remained in service until the final days of FAA Seafire operation. No. 764 Sqn, a fighter training unit equipped with Mk 17s at RNAS Yeovilton, was the last unit to fly Seafires of any variant, finally disbanding in late 1954.

Above: With his cockpit canopy open to facilitate his escape in the event of a ditching a No. 800 Sqn pilot is catapulted from HMS Triumph. The aircraft carries a 50-Imp gal (227-litre) 'torpedo' drop tank as introduced on the Mk XV, which proved more reliable than the 'slipper' tanks used on earlier Seafires.

Right: The busy deck of HMS Triumph plays host to No. 800 Sqn Seafires and No. 827 Sqn Firefly Mk 1s. The Seafires each carry four R/P launchers and are finished in the overall Extra Dark Sea Grey that was standard before 1948.

"Soon after we began operations nearly all the Seafires had wrinkled rear fuselages. The wrinkling was not really visible to the human eye, but if you ran a hand over the skin you could detect the trouble spots. The worry was that the structure was less strong than it should have been. The engineer officer said they were outside the limits for peace-time flying – but he let them fly on operational sorties!

"We found that we had far fewer deck landing accidents once we started flying more. Flying on operations nearly every day, we became better at deck landings and aircraft were damaged less frequently."

Throughout this period no enemy aircraft were encountered, and the CAP missions became a matter of routine. The only spell of excitement was on 28 July, when a pair of Seafires intercepted a B-29. Commissioned Pilot White was closing on the bomber when the latter's nervous gunners opened up at the unfamiliar fighter approaching them; an accurate burst struck the Seafire, which caught fire. White baled out and was picked up from the sea by a US destroyer. Suffering from burns, he was returned to *Triumph*.

Following this brief spell of operations, *Triumph* put into Kure dockyard for maintenance. On 11 August the carrier rejoined the blockade of the west coast of Korea, and the Seafires resumed operations. On 29 August No. 800 Squadron lost its commander, Lieutenant Commander Ian MacLachlan, in a tragic accident aboard *Triumph*. A Firefly ran into the crash barrier, shattering its wooden propeller and, in a million-to-one chance, a piece of blade flew through an open scuttle and struck him on the head, inflicting fatal injuries. Handley was promoted to lieutenant commander and assumed command of the Squadron.

Throughout most of September the Seafires flew operations against rail targets, and on 20 September Handley led an armed reconnaissance of the Chinnampo

The FAA's Spitfire 21 – Seafire 45

Never intended for squadron service, the Seafire Mk 45 represented the first step on the road to a second generation Griffon-Seafire. A Seafire Mk 21 airframe was fitted with a 'stinger' hook, slinging points and a naval radio set, while its undercarriage wheel fairings were cut back to increase clearance over arrester wires (the outer wheel bay doors being correspondingly enlarged). Serialled TM379, the aircraft flew in August 1944, but flight testing showed it displayed considerable instability (as had the Spitfire Mk 21) and proved to be somewhat maintenance heavy. Fifty Mk 45s were built, the last in late 1945. The variant saw limited second-line service, having been judged unsuitable for operational flying.

Above: TM379 is seen in its original form, effectively a Spitfire Mk 21 with essential naval equipment installed.

Top left: TM379 was later fitted with a Griffon 87 and contra-prop and an enlarged tailfin and rudder, the latter to correct the type's instability problems.

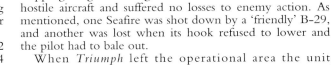

Left: This view of the second production Mk 45 (LA429) clearly shows the cut back undercarriage fairings introduced on this variant.

area. That uneventful mission turned out to be the last one flown by Seafires in Royal Navy service. On the following day the carrier put in to Sasebo, Japan, and a few days later set sail for the United Kingdom.

No. 800 Squadron had started the conflict with 12 Seafires, and during its course the unit received 14 replacements for aircraft lost or damaged. The squadron flew 360 operational sorties, of which 115 were against

shipping or ground targets. The Seafires encountered no hostile aircraft and suffered no losses to enemy action. As mentioned, one Seafire was shot down by a 'friendly' B–29, and another was lost when its hook refused to lower and the pilot had to bale out.

When *Triumph* left the operational area the unit possessed nine flyable FR.Mk 47s, but with the pressure of war removed, peacetime rules came into play. The unit's

Stage two – the Mk 46

TM383, originally intended to be the second Mk 45 prototype, was actually completed as the first Mk 46. It boasted several important changes over the earlier mark, namely a contra-rotating propeller (and associated Griffon 87 engine) and a Spiteful-type empennage. These features transformed the aircraft's performance to that of "a delightful pilot's aeroplane". Plumbing for wing 'combat tanks' was included; the total fuel capacity of the Mk 46 was some 228 Imp gal (1036 litres), almost double that of the Mk IB – 115 Imp gal (523 litres). Only 24 were built before production switched to the Mk 47.

Left: A handful of second-line units flew Mk 46s. This No. 778 Sqn aircraft was based at RNAS Ford sometime between 1946 and 1948. At this time No. 778 was a Service and Carrier Trials Unit.

Below: LA542, the second of just 24 Mk 46s, flew in December 1945. A few served with No. 1832 Sqn, RNVR.

The RNVR squadrons

The Royal Naval Volunteer Reserve was established in 1947, in parallel to the long-established RNVR for seamen, to provide an economical reserve of air and ground crews that could be called upon in an emergency. The RNVR squadrons soon became major Seafire operators, in the same way that Royal Auxiliary Air Force units operated a large number of Spitfires. Aircraft of Mks XV, 17, 46 and 47 equipped four different squadrons until 1954.

Above: This No. 1833 Sqn, RNVR Seafire Mk 17 came to grief while operating from HMS Triumph during annual training exercises in the English Channel in June 1952.

Right: SX311 '167/BR' prepares to leave Triumph. The aircraft's 'BR' tailcode indicates that its shore base was Bramcote.

Right centre: Seafire Mk 17 SX165 '115/JA' of No. 1831 Sqn, RNVR is caught by the barrier aboard HMS Illustrious on 22 September 1949. Note the two propeller blades that have become separated after striking the deck.

Right bottom: No. 1833 Sqn, RNVR was the only reserve unit to receive Mk 47s, flying the variant for just under two years from 1952 to 1954.

engineer officer immediately declared six of the survivors to be unserviceable due to wrinkling of the rear fuselages. At the end of 11 weeks of operations, of 26 Seafires originally on strength or received as replacements, No. 800 Squadron was reduced to three flyable aircraft. Upon its return to the United Kingdom, the unit disbanded; it would reform in the following year with Attacker jet fighters. So the Seafire ended its first-line career in the Royal Navy.

Seafire in retrospect

From start to finish the Seafire was an improvisation, an attempt to modify a successful land-based fighter into one that could operate from a carrier. Aircraft design is a matter of compromise, and any improvement made in one area is usually at the expense of capability in others. To wring the highest possible performance from his fighter design, Reginald Mitchell had kept its structural weight as low as possible; he had not designed the aircraft to take the shock of repeated heavy landings on heaving carrier decks. Despite the addition of some local strengthening, the Seafire's airframe was simply not robust enough to accept such treatment. This was reflected in the rate at which Seafires were wrecked or seriously damaged in deck operations, whenever they flew in conditions that were anything less than perfect.

Yet, in the absence of any serious competitor, the Seafire was by far the most effective British-built carrier fighter of the World War II period. It played a major role in establishing air superiority over the beachhead during the initial stages of the Torch and Avalanche landings, contributing materially to the success of those important operations. For that alone, the effort and expense of modifying the Spitfire into a naval fighter and bringing it into service were fully justified.

After the war there was a rapid rundown of the Spitfire force as the RAF reduced its strength and many units converted to jet fighters. During the early post-war period the Spitfire Mk 18 became the main type equipping fighter and fighter reconnaissance units in the Middle East and the

Below: No. 1832 Sqn, RNVR was the only unit, regular or reserve, to fly Seafire FR.Mk 46s. Based at Culham, the aircraft arrived in August 1947 and were retired in January 1950.

Far East. Production ran to some 300 aircraft and the variant equipped five first-line squadrons.

The Mk 18 saw some action with Nos 32 and 208 Squadrons based in the Suez Canal zone, when these units inadvertently became involved in clashes during the Arab-Israeli conflict at the time of the establishment of the Israeli state. It also saw action with Nos 28 and 60 Squadrons, both based at Sembawang on Singapore Island, which carried out attacks against Communist guerrillas in Malaya. Flying Officer John Nicholls of No. 28 Squadron described his unit's first combat mission against guerrillas on 2 July 1948:

"I went off with my squadron commander, Squadron Leader Bob Yule, to a target just across the causeway from Singapore, in South Johore. We took off at first light so that we could get in our dive attacks before the usual mid-morning layer of cumulus cloud developed. When we reached the target area we cruised round for more than half an hour, looking for something resembling our briefed objective, before eventually we did attack. Diving from 12,000 ft we dropped our 500 pounders, two from each aircraft, then we carried out a series of strafing runs with cannon and machine-guns. There was nobody firing back; it was really like being on the range – except that the target was far less distinct.

Top and above: These two views of Mk 47 prototype PS944 illustrate the wing-fold incorporated in the final Seafire variant. The first 14 aircraft had manually folding wings; the remaining 76 were fitted with hydraulic jacks and locks.

Last of the line – Mk 47

Few production piston-engined fighters were as fast or could climb as quickly as a Seafire Mk 47. RN trials between a Mk 47 and three of its contemporaries – the Sea Fury, Sea Hornet and Sea Vampire – showed that while each had its own area of superiority, the Seafire had the highest dive speed and climb rate at altitudes above 25,000 ft (7620 m). Though outwardly similar to the Mk 46, the Mk 47 differed from it in important respects. It had folding wings, which finally allowed the new-generation Seafire to be deployed aboard RN carriers. The wings were also strengthened to carry a 500-lb bomb each and electrical gun-firing was also fitted. Early production aircraft had the Griffon 87 engine, but most were fitted with the Griffon 88, which benefitted from a petrol injection system to ensure steady fuel flow under all *g* conditions. In all, just 90 were built, the last in March 1949.

Above: PS947, the fourth Mk 47, is seen landing during carrier trials, possibly aboard HMS Illustrious. Note that this aircraft has a production standard chin supercharger intake.

Below: This fully loaded Mk 47 carries a pair of 500-lb bombs and 135 Imp gal (614 litres) of external fuel, the latter in a pair of 22½-Imp gal (102-litre) underwing 'combat tanks' and a centreline 90-Imp gal (409-litre) drop tank. With external tankage the Mk 47 had a genuine range of 1,000 miles (1609 km).

"During the months that followed we flew several similar strikes. Most of the targets were in deep jungle, and sometimes half a dozen of us would circle for up to an hour looking for the hut or whatever it was we were supposed to hit. Then the first pilot who reckoned he had found it would bomb, and the rest of us would follow and aim at his bursts; after that we would strafe the area until we had used up our ammunition. At that time our intelligence on the whereabouts of the enemy was poor. Moreover, only rarely could our troops go in and find out what the air strikes had achieved. Sometimes a week or so after the attack we might hear a report that the target basha hut had been hit by cannon shells, but by the time the ground forces reached it there was rarely any sign of the actual terrorists.

"In the beginning it was a rather hit and miss affair, with one far more likely to miss than to hit."

The Spitfire attacks against supposed guerrilla positions in the jungle was one of the few roles in which the famous fighter failed to perform well.

Although the Mk 21 had been intended as the definitive fighter variant of the Spitfire, production ended after just 120 aircraft had been built. They formed the equipment of only four regular first-line squadrons. The rest of the production order, which at its peak stood at nearly 3,000 aircraft, was either cancelled or transferred to other variants of the Spitfire.

The next major production fighter variant, the Spitfire Mk 22, was essentially a Mk 21 with a bubble canopy and the new broad-chord tail assembly. The latter gave greatly improved control authority, and cured most of the Mk 21's remaining unfortunate traits. The majority of Mk 22s went to Royal Auxiliary Air Force squadrons, reserve units manned by the so-called 'weekend pilots'. During 1948 12 of the 20 Auxiliary squadrons received Spitfire Mk 22s.

Seafires abroad

The navies of both Canada and France obtained ex-RN aircraft-carriers in the years immediately after World War II, acquiring Seafire Mk IIIs as interim fighter equipment. These were later replaced by Mk XVs, the Griffon-engined variant also serving in the Burmese air force, though strictly as a land-based aircraft. The Irish Air Corps was the fourth foreign Seafire operator, using land-based Mk IIIs.

These Aéronavale Seafire Mk IIIs of 1 Flottille and Escadrille 54S are aboard Arromanches. The Escadrille 54S aircraft in the foreground is interesting as it appears to be a recent delivery, retaining its FAA colour scheme, roundels and codes, with Aéronavale overpainted.

One of No. 800 Sqn's Mk 47s makes a low pass with 'everything down' over HMS Triumph, after a missed approach. Fixed 22½-Imp gal (102-litre) 'combat' fuel tanks under each wing were a common fit during operations in Korean waters, given the distances involved when on offensive sorties.

Griffon-engined Spitfire and Seafire deployment, January 1950

Although the Spitfire had been replaced by jet fighters in many home defence squadrons and the re-equipment of others was proceeding apace, even at this late date the Spitfire still made up a substantial part of the service's order of battle. Squadrons in the 500 and the 600 series were Royal Auxiliary Air Force units, manned by part-time volunteers. In the Royal Navy the Seafire had largely been replaced by the Sea Fury and only No. 800 Squadron, with Seafire FR.Mk 47s, continued to operate the type.

ROYAL AIR FORCE

No. 11 Group

No. 600 Sqn	F.Mks 21, 22	Biggin Hill
No. 614 Sqn	F.Mk 22	Llandow
No. 615 Sqn	F.Mks 21,22	Biggin Hill

No. 12 Group

No. 502 Sqn	F.Mk 22	Aldergrove
No. 504 Sqn	F.Mk 22	Wymeswold
No. 602 Sqn	F.Mk 22	Abbotsinch
No. 603 Sqn	F.Mk 22	Turnhouse
No. 607 Sqn	F.Mk 22	Ouston
No. 608 Sqn	F.Mk 22	Thornaby
No. 610 Sqn	F.Mk 22	Hooton Park
No. 611 Sqn	F.Mk 22	Woodvale
No. 612 Sqn	F.Mk XIV	Dyce
No. 613 Sqn	F.Mk 22	Ringway

British Air Force of Occupation (Germany)

No. II Sqn	FR.Mk XIV	Wunstorf

Middle East Air Force
No. 205 Group (Egypt)

No. 208 Sqn	FR.Mk 18	Fayid

Far East Air Force
Air Headquarters Hong Kong

No. 28 Sqn	FR.Mk 18	Kai Tak
No. 80 Sqn	F.Mk 24	Kai Tak

Air Headquarters Malaya

No. 60 Sqn	FR.Mk 18	Kuala Lumpur

ROYAL NAVY
13th Carrier Air Group

No. 800 Sqn	Seafire FR.Mk 47	HMS *Triumph*

Above: The lack of recognition stripes on these 800 NAS Seafires and 827 NAS Firefly FR.Mk 1s aboard Triumph, suggests that the photograph was taken early on in Korean operations. Having joined ships of the US 7th Fleet in Task Force 77 off the Korean coast, the 13th CAG initially flew offensive sorties using both aircraft types. However, the Firefly's limited endurance led to increased use of No. 800 Sqn's Seafires in an offensive role, often armed with R/Ps.

Left: Its wings folded, this No. 800 Sqn Mk 47 has been struck below and is seen being pushed off one of Triumph's two lifts and into the hangar. The Mk 47's wings folded through 90° just outboard of the cannon bays, reducing its folded span to just over 19 ft (5.79 m). Overall height was 16 ft (4.88 m), just within the limit imposed by RN carrier design. By the time Triumph had been withdrawn from operations off Korea, in September 1950 (after eight operational patrols over 35 days), the squadron had just four serviceable Seafires, only one of which was fit for combat.

Below: FR.Mk 47 '180/P' lifts its tail wheel moments before getting airborne from Triumph in Korean waters, July 1950. Note the use of rocket-assisted take-off gear (RATOG), a necessity with a full load and light winds.

Far Eastern swansong

By July 1949, the FAA had just one operational Seafire squadron remaining. The first of the two Mk 47 units, No. 804 Sqn in HMS *Ocean*, had converted to the Sea Fury in Malta, passing the best of its Seafires to No. 800 Sqn aboard *Triumph*. In early August *Triumph* sailed for the Far East and by the beginning of October had reached Singapore, where the 13th CAG was put ashore and began operations from Sembawang, in co-operation with RAF aircraft, against Communist terrorists in Malaya. These continued until re-embarkation in February 1950. Exercises off the Philippines, a refit in Singapore and a cruise to Australia and Japan followed and on 24 June, *Triumph* sailed for Hong Kong. The following day, North Korean troops crossed the 38th parallel and the British Far East Fleet was put at the immediate disposal of the United Nations. Seafire operations in Korea ran from 1 July until 20 September, the carrier then returning to UK, where No. 800 Sqn disbanded on 10 November, bringing FAA Seafire operations to a close.

**Supermarine
Seafire FR.Mk 47
No. 800 Sqn, FAA
HMS *Triumph*
1951**

VP461 ('178/P') was delivered to the FAA in April 1948 and was among No. 800 Sqn's aircraft serving with the 13th CAG aboard HMS *Triumph* during offensive operations with the US 7th Fleet over North Korea. Seafire operations in the Korean theatre began on 1 July 1950 and continued until 20 September.

Wing folding
The Mk 47 was the first Seafire built with power-operated wing-folding (a system of hydraulic jacks and locks), though it was omitted from the first 14 aircraft.

Markings
VP461 sports the standard FAA colour scheme for carrier-based aircraft of the day – Extra Dark Sea Grey over Sky. Serials and codes are in black, the latter consisting of a three-digit code between '171' and '182', plus *Triumph's* deck letter, 'P'. Black and white stripes were applied to FAA aircraft in Korea as a recognition aid for American forces, unfamiliar with RN aircraft. The problem had come to a head on 28 July 1950, when a USAF B-29 fired on a No. 800 Sqn Seafire, the latter's pilot having to abandon the aircraft after it caught fire.

Air-to-ground role
This aircraft is equipped for the air-to-ground role given to No. 800 Sqn while in Korean waters. A 500-lb bomb and 22½-Imp gal (102-litre) 'combat' fuel tank are carried under each mainplane, while on the centreline is a 50-Imp gal (227-litre).

Powerplant
Griffon 80-series engines were equipped with the geared drive necessary to turn a contra-rotating propeller. In early production Seafire Mk 47s the Griffon 87 was installed; from the 15th aircraft the Griffon 88 was substituted. This had a fuel injection pump fitted in place of the 87's carburettor.

RATOG
Tested on Seafire Mk IIIs but never used operationally during World War II, the ability to use rocket-assisted take-off gear (RATOG) became standard on all Seafires from Mk XV, and was something of a necessity with a full load in light winds.

Keith Fretwell

The RAF's last Spitfires

Such was their usefulness, and in the absence of a PR version of the Meteor, Spitfire PR.Mk 19s were not only the last Spitfires in the operational RAF, but were destined to be the last active RAF Spitfires of all. No. 81 Sqn, operating from Seletar, flew the last Spitfire sortie on 1 April 1954. Back in the UK, Mk 19s remained on secondary duties until 1957, while a single example was flown again briefly, by the Central Fighter Establishment, in 1963. Two remain 'on the books' 40 years later, though purely as show aircraft, with the Battle of Britain Memorial Flight at RAF Coningsby.

Right: At the height of Operation Firedog, Spitfire PR.Mk 19 PS888 taxis as it begins the last sortie by an operational Spitfire on 1 April 1954. This routine flight, of a type soon to be taken over by Meteor PR.Mk 10s like the example in the background, was tasked with photographing suspected Communist guerrilla positions in the Malayan jungle.

Far right: Operated under contract by Short Brothers and Harland Ltd, the Temperature and Humidity (THUM) Flight at Woodvale retired its three Mk 19s in 1957. One was reactivated by the CFE at Binbrook in 1963, to assist in the training of Lightning pilots, pending deployment to Indonesia where fighter opposition was expected to include P-51s!

Above: One of No. 81 Sqn's Mk 19s dashes across Malayan jungle, on a PR sortie during the Malayan 'emergency'.

The final Spitfire variant, the Mk 24, looked little different from the Mk 22. The main changes were two additional fuel tanks fitted in the rear fuselage, and wing fittings to carry six 60-lb rockets. Supermarine built 54 Mk 24s, and converted 27 Mk 22s still on the production line to this configuration. The final Mk 24, the last of more than 20,000 Spitfires built, left the factory at South Marston near Swindon in February 1948.

Only one first-line Spitfire unit received the Mk 24 – No. 80 Squadron in January 1948, then based in Germany. In July 1949 the unit moved to Hong Kong to provide limited air defence for that colony. The last RAF unit to operate the Spitfire in the fighter role, No. 80 Squadron re-equipped with Hornets in January 1952.

Griffon-powered Spitfires in retrospect

Considering that the cubic capacity of the Rolls-Royce Griffon was one-third greater than that of the Merlin it replaced, the relative ease with which the larger engine fitted into the Spitfire was remarkable. The first Griffon-powered variant, the Mk XII, was optimised for the low-altitude air superiority role. It had only limited utility and did not remain long in first-line service. The Mk XIV that replaced it was a much more formidable fighter, with considerably enhanced high-altitude performance. That variant ensured that the RAF possessed a piston-engined fighter as good as any in existence at the end of the war. Had the Griffon not been available, the Spitfire's tenure in first-line service might well have ended some time around 1947. With the Griffon, the fighter's useful life continued for five more years.

Following the end of the war, the RAF's regular home defence fighter units rapidly re-equipped with jet aircraft. The early jets did not take kindly to having to operate from short airfields in hot and dusty areas, however; as a result, the Spitfire FR.Mk 18 and later the F.Mk 24 continued to perform usefully in the Middle East and the Far East until the last of them was replaced in 1952. In the Auxiliary Air Force the Spitfire F.Mk 22 equipped several units during the immediate post-war period, until the last of them re-equipped with jet fighters in 1951.

Dr Alfred Price

Above: This scene at RAF Lyneham in the immediate post-war period, showing withdrawn Spitfires awaiting disposal, was typical of a number of RAF stations.

Right: Partially broken up Spitfire Mk 24s await their final appointment with the cutting torch, which came in June 1956, when most of these airframes were sold to Enfield Rolling Mills. Very few Mk 24s survived the wholesale scrapping of late-mark aircraft that accompanied the arrival of jets in large numbers. Aircraft stationed overseas at the time of their withdrawal were usually scrapped locally; of the Hong Kong-based Mk 24s, VN485 was fortunately spared. As the HKAAF's last operational Mk 24, '485 was displayed in Hong Kong for some years before being repatriated to the UK in 1989 and placed in the care of the Imperial War Museum.

Griffon-powered Spitfire warbirds

Of the 49 Spitfires in airworthy condition in mid-1999, 10 (pictured here) were Griffon-powered aircraft of Mks XIV, XVIII and XIX, reflecting the fact that these marks were the late-production Spitfires built in the greatest numbers and were among the large numbers of Spitfires exported as they became surplus to RAF requirements; five of the airworthy warbirds are former Indian Air Force aircraft. Five of these aircraft were based in the UK, with four registered in the US and a single example in France. One machine, PM631 of the Battle of Britain Memorial Flight (BBMF) has been in continuous service with the RAF since 1945.

Compiled with the assistance of Peter R. Arnold

MV293 (G-SPIT)

Above: Owned by The Fighter Collection, Duxford, this FR.Mk XIVE originally served with the IAF. Its first post-restoration flight was in 1992.

NH749 (NX749DP)

Above: David Price operates this FR.Mk XIVE (another ex-IAF aircraft, flown in 1983) from the Museum of Flying at Santa Monica, Calif.

NH904 (N114BP)

Above: This FR.Mk XIVC is owned by Bob Pond of Palm Springs, Calif. and served with the RAF and Belgian air force. Restoration came in 1981.

PM631

Above: Completed after the end of World War II, this Mk XIX was among the last Spitfires in RAF service in 1957 and continues to fly with the BBMF.

PS853 (G-RRGN)

Above: Purchased by Rolls-Royce plc in 1996, this ex-BBMF Mk XIX entered RAF service in early 1945 and is a veteran of the THUM Flight.

PS915

Above: This Mk XIX joined the BBMF briefly in 1957, but was grounded soon afterwards. Restored to fly in 1986, it has rejoined the BBMF.

SM832 (F-AZSJ)

Above: Another airframe recovered from India, this F.Mk XIVE flew in 1995 after restoration and was owned by Christophe Jacquard of Dijon in 1999.

SM969 (G-BRAF)

Above: Owned by the late Doug Arnold's Warbirds of GB, this ex-IAF FR.Mk XVIIIE last flew in 1992, but has since been stored at Bournemouth.

Soon to fly?

Above: Of a number of Griffon-engined Spitfires in the throes of restoration, one of the closest to completion in 1999 was FR.Mk XVIIIE SM845 (G-BUOS), formerly HS687 of the IAF.

Below: One of the more interesting Spitfire restoration projects of recent years must be that of former No. 81 Sqn, RAF and RThaiAF Mk XIX PS890, photographed at the Planes of Fame Museum, Chino, California in June 1999. As may be seen, the aircraft has been fitted with the Griffon 50-series engine and contra-prop from an Avro Shackleton. It is believed that the aircraft, which was expected to fly in the latter half of 1999, would be used in a series of attempts to break time-to-height records for piston-engined aircraft.

TP280 (N280TP)

Above: Flown after restoration in 1992, this FR.Mk XVIIIE flew with the IAF as HS654 and was owned by Rudy Frasca of Urbana, Illinois in 1999.

TZ138 (N5505A)

Above: This FR.Mk XIVE (the former Imperial Oil racer, CF-GMZ) was restored by Pete Regina of Van Nuys, Calif and flown in 1999.

Seafires

Seafire L.Mk IIIC PP972, a veteran of Aéronavale operations, spent many years as an instructional airframe before being rescued from a scrapyard and restored for static exhibition in France in the early 1980s. Purchased by Precious Metals Ltd of Bournemouth in 1992 and registered G-BUAR, the aircraft was nearing the end of a restoration to flying standard in 1999. Its first flight was expected in 2000/01.

While there were, in 1999, no airworthy Seafires in existence, a number of long-term restoration projects were in various stages of completion. Of these, PP972 was perhaps the closest to its first flight when photographed in January 1999.

Griffon-Spitfire Operators

With large numbers of surplus Spitfires available after the end of World War II, a brisk trade in ex-RAF aircraft was done. Most of those exported were Merlin-engined Mk IXs and XVIs, though a handful of countries picked up Griffon-powered aircraft, mainly of Mks 14 and 22. Belgium and India amassed the largest fleets. Such was their usefulness, photo-reconnaissance Mk 19s were also a popular choice and were among the last Spitfires to see service anywhere.

Dr Alfred Price, with additional material by John Heathcott

United Kingdom
Royal Air Force

Continuous RAF front-line use of Griffon-engined Spitfires spanned 14 years from early 1943 (when the first Mk XIIs were delivered to No. 41 Sqn), to 1957, when the THUM Flight retired its last PR.Mk XIX.

Wartime units

The following front-line RAF squadrons (fighter units unless noted otherwise), operated Griffon-engined Spitfires from 1943 until the end of World War II:

Mk XII: Nos 41, 91, 595 (anti-aircraft co-operation)
F./FR.Mk XIV: Nos II (fighter-reconnaissance), 11, 41, 91, 130, 268 (fighter-reconnaissance), 322, 350, 402, 430, 610
PR.Mk XIX: (photo-reconnaissance units, except where noted) Nos II (fighter-reconnaissance), 16, 541, 542, 681, 682, 683, 684
F.Mk 21: No. 91

Post-war units

The following units became operational with 'Griffon-Spitfires' (in a few cases, for a second time) after the end of World War II. No. 541 Sqn, a wartime PR unit that operated Mk XIXs at the time of disbandment in 1945, reformed in 1947 within Bomber Command, with Mk 19s. Again, all are fighter units unless stated:

F./FR.Mk XIV: Nos 16 (fighter-reconnaissance), 17, 20, 26, 28, 132, 136, 152, 268 (fighter-reconnaissance), 273,
FR.Mk XVIII: Nos 11, 28, 32, 60, 81 (reconnaissance), 208 (reconnaissance)
PR.Mk XIX: (photo-reconnaissance units, except where noted) Nos 16 (fighter-reconnaissance), 34, 60, 81, 82, 268, 541
F.Mk 21: No. 1, 41, 122
F.Mk 22: No. 73
F.Mk 24: No. 80

RAuxAF units

The Auxiliary Air Force was re-established in June 1946 (becoming 'Royal' in December the following year and finally disbanding in March 1957) as a territorial force made up of part-time volunteer pilots and a nucleus of ground personnel from the regular air force. Of the 20 squadrons formed, a dozen were equipped with Griffon-engined Spitfires at some point before the last Mk 22s were replaced by Meteors in July 1951.

F./FR.Mk XIV: Nos 600, 602, 607, 610, 611, 612, 613, 615
F.Mk 21: Nos 600, 602, 615
F.Mk 22: Nos 502, 504, 600, 602, 603, 607, 608, 610, 611, 613, 614, 615

Numerous second-line units operated Spitfires, including Griffon-engined aircraft. These included the various Operational Conversion and Training Units, tactical trials establishments (like the Central Fighter Establishment and Photographic Reconnaissance Development Unit), Civilian Anti-Aircraft Co-operation Units (especially Nos 2 and 4 CAACUs – both notable operators of the Spitfire Mk 21) and, as related elsewhere, the Temperature and Humidity Flight at Woodvale.

In 1999, the RAF's Battle of Britain Memorial Flight operated, among other types, two PR.Mk XIXs (PM631 and PS915).

No. 208 Sqn was first equipped with Spitfires in December 1943, when Mk VCs were acquired for service in the Western Desert. Mk IXs and Mk VIIIs followed, the unit acquiring FR.Mk XVIIIs post-war. Wartime codes 'RG' (above) were soon abandoned and by 1948, Type 'D' roundels had been applied, as seen on TZ233 (left), up on trestles for gun repairs and harmonisation at Fayid, Egypt.

Right: No. 32 Sqn flew Spitfire Mk 18s for just under two years between 1947 and 1949. TP373 is seen at Ein Shemar, Palestine in 1948.

Below: RAF's last three PR.Mk 19s (from the front, PS386, '888 and '890 of No. 81 Sqn) are seen at Seletar in early 1954, the RAF's operational Spitfires' last year of service.

Above: Carrying recognition stripes at the time of the Korean War, a No. 28 Sqn Spitfire FR.Mk 18E lands at Kai Tak, Hong Kong in about 1950.

Below: PR.Mk XIX PS925 carries the '6C' code of the Photo-Reconnaissance Development Unit at RAF Benson in the late 1940s/early 1950s.

Photographed in 1990, when it was still in RAF service as one of three Mk XIXs with the battle of Britain Memorial Flight, PS853 formates with a No. 229 OCU Tornado F.Mk 3. The Spitfire has since been sold to fund the rebuilding of BBMF Hurricane LF363 and was owned by Rolls-Royce plc in 1999, registered G-RRGN.

Right: FR.Mk XIV NH803 was among a number of examples of this mark to serve in the Far East. Pictured post-war, the aircraft has been stripped of its wartime camouflage and has Type 'C1' fuselage roundels of a smaller-than-standard pattern not uncommon post-war.

Hong Kong Auxiliary Air Force

No. 80 Sqn, RAF began re-equipping with de Havilland Hornets in December 1951, passing eight of its Spitfire F.Mk 24s (PK687, PK719, PK720, VN308, VN313, VN318, VN482 and VN485) to the Hong Kong Auxiliary Air Force. These were operated until 1955, Flt Lt Adrian Rowe-Evans taking part in the Queen's Birthday Flypast on 21 April, the type's last day of operation. By then the HKAAF had just four Spitfires – two Mk 24s (VN318 and VN485) and two PR.Mk 19s, both ex-No. 81 Sqn aircraft (PS852 and PS854).

VN485 was put on display at Kai Tak the following July and remained there until 1989, when it was obtained by the Imperial War Museum. It is displayed at the Museum's Duxford site.

HKAAF F.Mk 24 VN482/'N', clearly no longer in airworthy condition, is seen at Kai Tak after its withdrawal from use.

Belgium
Force Aérienne Belge/Belgische Luchtmacht

In 1947 the Royal Belgian Air Force purchased 134 F/FR.Mk XIVs. Of these, 132 were delivered and equipped the 1st Fighter Wing (Nos 349 and 350 Sqns) at Beauvechain and the 2nd Fighter Wing (Nos 1, 2 and 3 Sqns) at Florennes. Later, some of these aircraft went to the 10th Wing at Chièvres (Nos 23, 27, 31 Sqns) which was designated a fighter-bomber unit in 1952. The Mk XIV remained in first-line service until December 1952, when several of the surviving aircraft were transferred to the Fighter School at Coxijde. The type finally passed out of service in 1954.

'Clipped-wing' F.Mk XIVE 'UR-S' carries the 'shooting star' emblem of No. 2 Sqn, 2nd Fighter Wing. Belgian Mk XIVs were serialled SG1-SG132, the prefix standing for 'Spitfire-Griffon'. Similarly, the serials of FAB Mk IXs were prefixed 'SM' – 'Spitfire-Merlin'.

Egypt
(Royal) Egyptian Air Force

In 1949 the Egyptian government placed an order for 20 Spitfire F.Mk 22s, an agreement being signed between Vickers and the Egyptian Government on 1 May 1950 for their supply. All were ex-RAF aircraft, bought and refurbished by Vickers for a total cost of £239,000. Nineteen were delivered, the last in late 1950. Little is known of the subsequent use of these aircraft; all served with No. 2 Sqn at Helwan until about 1953. Their serial numbers were possibly 680-699.

Above: An REAF Spitfire Mk 22, complete with national markings and a new serial number, is run up at the beginning of its delivery flight.

Spitfire FR.Mk XIVs of No. 4 Sqn, Royal Indian Air Force are seen at Iwakuni, Japan soon after their arrival to join the British Commonwealth Occupation Force. Nineteen aircraft were ferried to Japan aboard the RN carrier HMS Vengeance. After a week these machines moved to Miho where they remained for just over a year, flying surveillance patrols over the coastal areas of Shimane and Tottori prefectures, in conjunction with 268 Indian Brigade, to prevent illegal immigration. Note the retention of SEAC markings and, on at least one aircraft, a wartime camouflage scheme.

India
(Royal) Indian Air Force

The wartime Indian Air Force became the Royal Indian Air Force in March 1945, and by the end of the war totalled nine squadrons, equipped with Spitfires and Hurricanes of various marks. In August 1947, the RIAF disbanded and the force split between India and the newly formed Pakistan, the 'new' RIAF becoming the IAF once more in 1950.

During the two-year transition period, the following RIAF units operated Spitfire Mk XIVs: No.1 Sqn (March-August 1947), No. 4 Sqn (October 1945-mid-1947), No. 6 Sqn (November 1945-May 1947), No. 7 Sqn (December 1945-July 1947), No. 8 Sqn (December 1945-May 1947), No. 9 Sqn (January-June 1946) and No. 14 Sqn (1950-1951).

By mid-1946, all RIAF fighter units were equipped with Spitfires (including Mk VIIIs), No. 4 Sqn taking 19 Mk XIVs to Japan in April as part of the British Commonwealth Occupation Force.

The exact number of Mk XIVs operated by the RIAF is unclear, though it is known that a batch 20 was delivered in 1947, along with 58 Mk 18s. The latter equipped Nos 2, 9 and 14 Sqns. A further 42 Mk 18s and 13 PR.Mk 19s followed in 1949, the Mk 19s equipping No. 101 PR Flight (No. 101 PR Sqn from 1950) at Ambala and Palam until 1956.

After the partition of India, two years of fighting on the North-West Frontier and in Kashmir saw Spitfire Mk XIVs and 18s (based at Cawnpore, Poona and Srinagar) join the RIAF's Tempest Mk II force in attacking ground targets. No. 101 Flight's PR.Mk 19s were also employed.

By the mid-1950s the Spitfire had all but disappeared from IAF service, No. 14 Sqn dispensing with its last Mk 18s in 1957.

A handful of Mk XIVs and 18s also equipped the Central Flying School (at Jodhpur) and the Advanced Flying School (at Ambala) in the early 1950s.

Below: A No. 4 Sqn, RIAF, F.Mk XIV is craned aboard RN carrier HMS Vengeance for the trip to Japan as part of the BCOF. On the lighter below are two FR.Mk XIVEs, one of which carries a serial number in the MV2xx range. Note the way in which lifting gear was attached at a point near the engine bearers and that this necessitated removal of the engine's upper cowl.

Southern Rhodesia
Southern Rhodesian Air Force

In March 1951, 11 Spitfire F.Mk 22s, serialled SR58-68 were delivered to the SRAF. A second batch of 11 followed in December, two of which (SR79 and SR89) crashed during, or shortly after, delivery. The remaining nine machines were serialled SR80-88. SR84 was written-off in December 1953. The Mk 22s equipped Nos 1 and 2 Squadrons until the early 1954.

In 1955, the SRAF having received de Havilland Vampire FB.Mk 9s , 10 of the remaining Spitfires were sold on to Syria.

Spitfire F.Mk 22 SR65 of No. 1 Sqn rests in the east African in the sun at New Sarum airfield, Salisbury in June 1953.

Sweden
Flygvapnet

Sweden received 50 ex-RAF Spitfire PR.Mk XIXs in 1948, these equipping Divisions 1, 2, 3 and 5 of reconnaissance unit Flottilj 11 at Nyköping until August 1955. In Flygvapnet service the aircraft were designated S.31 and serialled 31001-31050.

Though initially earmarked for transfer to the Indian air force, PS935 was refurbished as 31001 – the first Mk XIX for the Flygvapnet. Here the aircraft poses for the camera prior to delivery in October 1948.

Syria
Syrian Air Force

In 1953 the Syrian government placed an order for 20 Spitfire F.Mk 22s, and deliveries began in the following year. Though it is known that the aircraft were serailled 501-520, little is known of their subsequent use.

This rather sorry-looking aircraft was among the Mk 22s operated by the Syrian air force and was one of four photographed near Damascus prior to the Six Day War in 1967.

Thailand
Royal Thai Air Force

In 1950 the Thai government purchased 30 reconditioned Spitfire F/FR.Mk XIVs for the Royal Thai Air Force. These carried the serials U14-1/93 to U14-30/93 and equipped No. 1 Sqn of No. 1 Wing and No. 1 Sqn of No. 4 Wing between 1951 and 1954. A handful were then passed to No. 12 Sqn and flown for about a year.

Three PR.Mk 19s are also known to have been sold to the Thai air force in mid-1954.

All were ex-FEAF aircraft and were PS888, the RAF's last operational Spitfire, PM630 and PS836, the latter becoming U14-27/97 in Thai service.

An RTAF FR.Mk XIV with clipped wings and six zero-length rocket rails fitted , is seen in pre-delivery guise with an overall silver finish.

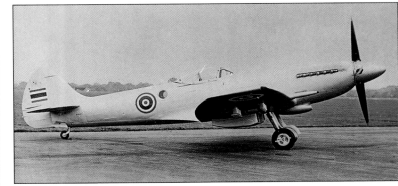

Right: PS888, the aircraft which flew the last operatonal RAF Spitfire sortie in 1954, was then sold to the RTAF and is seen here in service. Note the retention of its RAF serial number.

Turkey

Türk Hava Kuvvetleri

Among the 207 Spitfires received by the THK after World War II were four Spitfire PR.Mk 19s from ex-RAF stocks – PM548, '654, '656, and '657. After reconditioning in the UK the aircraft were delivered in 1947/48 and serialled 6551-6554 (not necessarily in that order), and were operated until at least 1954 by three reconnaissance units at different times, including 3 Bolük (Company), 10 Kesif Alay (Regiment). Bases included Afyon, in western Turkey, and Merzifon to the north.

Seafire Operators

Foreign use of the Seafire was naturally less than that of the Spitfire, given that the latter were more plentiful and there was little call for a carrier-capable aircraft outside the major powers. That said, both Canada and France operated the type from ex-RN carriers, as stop-gaps until more suitable aircraft became available. Burma and Ireland purchased 'denavalised' Seafires for land-based operations.

Dr Alfred Price, with additional material by John Heathcott

HMS Indefatigable, with No. 887 Sqn Mk IIIs aboard, made a goodwill visit to New Zealand in November 1945 before returning to the UK. Here the ship is seen in Wellington harbour.

United Kingdom
Fleet Air Arm
Wartime units

While Seafire Mk Is and IIs were the sole equipment in some FAA fighter units, only No. 801 Sqn was equipped completely with Seafire Mk Is; in other front-line units these early Seafires generally operated alongside Seafire Mk IIs. Units with Seafire Mk IIs and IIIs were either fighter units equipped exclusively with Seafires, or attack squadrons (e.g. torpedo-bomber/reconnaissance units with Swordfish) with a fighter flight of Seafires. The following units operated Merlin-engined Seafires during World War II and in the early post-war years.

Mk IB: Nos 801, 807, 809, 816, 842, 879, 885, 887, 894, 897 Sqns
F./L./LR.Mk IIC: Nos 801, 807, 808, 809, 816, 833, 834, 842, 879, 880, 884, 885, 886, 887, 889, 894, 895, 897, 899 Sqns
F./L.Mk III: Nos 802, 803, 805, 806, 807, 808, 809, 879, 880, 883, 885, 886, 887, 889, 894, 899 Sqns

Post-war units

When No. 801 Sqn disbanded in mid-1946, the front-line career of the Merlin-engined Seafire came to an end. This squadron had already received the first operational Griffon-engined Mk XVs, this variant going on to serve with nine front-line units. The following units operated Griffon-engined Seafires post-war.

F.Mk XV: Nos 800, 801, 802, 803, 804, 805, 806, 809, 883 Sqns
FR.Mk 17: Nos 800, 805, 807, 809, 879 Sqns
FR.Mk 47: Nos 800, 804 Sqns

RNVR units

The first Royal Naval Volunteer Reserve squadrons were established in 1947, four of them operating Seafires at different times. No. 1833 Sqn operated both generations of 'Griffon-Seafire', though not the Mk 46.

F.Mk XV: Nos 1831, 1832, 1833 Sqns
FR.Mk 17: Nos 1830, 1831, 1832, 1833 Sqns
FR.Mk 46: No. 1832 Sqn
FR.Mk 47: No. 1833 Sqn

Non-operational units

These comprised a myriad of different squadrons and flights, often operating a variety of types concurrently. Those employing Seafires, during wartime and post-war, were engaged in a variety of tasks, including training, trials and evaluation and communications.

Secondline squadrons that, at one time or other, are known to have operated Seafire(s) were: Nos 700, 703, 706, 708, 709, 715, 718, 719, 721, 727, 728, 731, 733, 736, 736B, 737, 738, 740, 744, 746, 748, 751, 757, 759, 760, 761, 764, 766, 767, 768, 770, 771, 772, 773, 775, 776, 777, 778, 779, 780, 781, 782, 787, 787Y, 790, 791 794, 798, 799 Sqns

Right: A Seafire Mk 17 of No. 1833 Sqn, RNVR prepares to land at a shore base. The Mk 17 saw less than two years of frontline service, but went on to equip four Reserve squadrons.

Below: No. 801 Sqn L.Mk IIIs are seen ashore, possibly at Skeabrae, in late 1944/early 1945, prior to sailing into action in the Far East.

Below: The Station Flight at RNAS Lossiemouth operated Seafire Mk 46 LA546 '900/LM' during early 1948. It was the personal mount of Capt. (later Admiral Sir) Caspar John.

Above: Seafire F.Mk IIIs of No. 880 Sqn visited Australia after VJ-Day. Here they are seen at Hobart on the Australian island state of Tasmania. Note the Seafires' P-40-type centreline drop tanks, unique to this squadron.

Burma
Union of Burma Air Force

Burma's Seafires were interesting hybrids, essentially 'denavalised' Mk XVs fitted with Spitfire Mk XVIII wings. Refurbished by Airwork Ltd, the 20 aircraft were delivered in 1951 to serve alongside Spitfire Mk XVIIIs in the counter-insurgency role.

Serialled UB401-420, these aircraft served with No. 1 Squadron for at least three years (at least one source suggests as long as 10 years), flying sorties against Burmese separatists, but were finally replaced by Sea Furies, possibly as early as 1954, bringing the Seafire's front-line service to an end.

Below: UB415 has had a single letter 'O' code applied, presumably while serving with No. 1 Sqn.

Seen shortly after delivery, Burma's Mk XVs were equipped with centreline drop tanks and underwing bomb racks.

Canada
Royal Canadian Navy

No. 803 Sqn, FAA equipped with Sea Hurricanes and Fulmars and after operations in and around the Indian Ocean, disbanded in August 1943. Upon its reformation in June 1945, it received 25 Seafire L.Mk IIIs and was to join the 19th CAG for service aboard an 'Implacable'-class carrier. However, VJ-Day brought a change of plan, the unit re-equipping with 12 Spitfire Mk XVs in August.

Within six months No. 803 Sqn had been transferred, with 35 Seafires, to the RCN to equip the 19th CAG aboard HMCS *Warrior*, on loan to the Canadian government. Based at Dartmouth, Nova Scotia when not embarked (and while problems with the Seafires' supercharger clutches were rectified), No. 803 returned, with *Warrior* to the UK in mid-1947, re-equipping with Hawker Sea Furies for service aboard HMCS *Magnificent*. The Seafire Mk XVs were passed to No. 883 Sqn.

This unit, like No. 803 Sqn, had been allocated to the RCN, reforming at Arbroath in September 1945 with Seafire Mk IIIs. The intention had been that this unit would join the British Pacific Fleet as part of the new 10th CAG but, again, VJ-Day made this

unnecessary. No. 883 moved instead to Nutts Corner in November, picking up No. 803's Mk XVs as it did so. Manning difficulties had meanwhile prevented its transfer to the RCN, and it disbanded at Machrihanish the following February.

Reformed in May 1947, No. 883 Sqn was again earmarked for transfer to the RCN, initially flying Seafire Mk XVs from Dartmouth and HMCS *Warrior* with the 18th CAG. In September 1948 it relinquished its Seafires for Sea Fury FB.Mk 11s and was renumbered No. 871 Sqn (later VF-871).

The Seafires were then relegated to second-line use, with Training Air Group Number 1. Their swansong came in 1949, when a flight of 10 Seafires was formed for a display at the Canadian National Exhibition. Though two of its pilots, including the flight's CO, Lt-Cmdr (P) C. G. Watson, were killed in a training accident, the display by 'Watson's Circus' went ahead to considerable acclaim.

Above: Though it carries the 'AA' codes of No. 883 Sqn, this Mk XV landing at an RCAF base at River, Manitoba in September 1948 had, by then, been handed over to Training Air Group No. 1.

Right: Mk XV PR434 'AA-J' is seen on its shore base at Dartmouth, Nova Scotia in 1947/48.

France
Aéronautique Navale

From March 1946, the French navy was supplied with 48 refurbished late-production Seafire L.Mk IIIs for use by 1 Flottille (1F) at its Hyères base. After working up 1F embarked in the light fleet carrier *Arromanches* (ex-HMS *Colossus*), then on loan from the RN, for carrier training.

Between January and June 1948, an additional 65 Mk IIIs were delivered, these consisting of 30 flyable aircraft and 35 for component recovery. This allowed the

formation of a second Seafire squadron – 12 Flottille – by splitting 1F in August 1948.

Meanwhile, with the activities of Communist insurgents in Indo-China reaching serious levels, *Arromanches* sailed for the region, to relieve *Dixmude* (ex-HMS *Biter*), on 30 October 1948, with 24 of 1F's Seafires and 12 SBD-5 Dauntlesses of 4F aboard. Arriving off Saigon on 29 November, the carrier disembarked most of its aircraft to Bien Hoa from where they immediately

began operational missions (mainly Tac/R and strafing) under the direction of the Armée de l'Air. Both squadrons rejoined *Arromanches* on 10 December and began operations against targets further north from the Gulf of Tonkin. By mid-January 1949, a lack of spares and losses due to light winds had reduced the strengths of both units to such an extent that their continued presence off Indo-China was pointless.

Arromanches returned to the northern hemisphere, 1F and 12F re-equipping with 15 Seafire ex-FAA Mk XVs, delivered in

June 1949. However, with an attrition rate similar to that of the RN, the Aéronavale had insufficient serviceable aircraft with which to maintain a squadron aboard *Arromanches* in the Mediterranean, and in 1950 F6F-5 Hellcats arrived to replace the remaining Seafires.

Training and communications units based ashore also flew both Seafire marks until about 1949. These were Escadrilles de Servitude 1S, 2S, 3S, 4S, 10S, 11S and 54S. The last named of these operated Mk IIIs and XVs until 1951.

Above and right: Seafire L.Mk IIIs (including '1.F-22') of 1F are seen during operations from Arromanches *in about 1948. Apart from a short spell off Indo-China, deployments were confined to the Mediterranean and Atlantic.*

Ireland
Aer Chor nah-Eireann/Irish Air Corps

The Irish Air Corps took delivery of 12 'denavalised' Seafire L.Mk IIIs in February 1947 to re-equip No. 1 (Fighter) Squadron at Gormanston, then flying Hurricane Mk IIs. The aircraft had been refurbished by Supermarine at Long Marston and were finished in an overall grey/green scheme, with red spinners.

The unit operated these aircraft for two years, though the last of the aircraft – 155 (ex-PR237) – was not finally withdrawn until June 1954. It was thus the last Merlin-engined Seafire in service anywhere.

Seven of the IAC's dozen Seafire L.Mk IIIs are seen here together, sometime shortly after their delivery. Note the black panther badge of No. 1 Sqn, painted on the nose of 149. Though the Seafires were withdrawn in 1954, the IAC's two-seat Spitfire T.Mk 9s lasted another seven years.

United States
US Navy

During and after World War II, the USN received 12 Seafire Mk IBs, 49 Mk IICs, and single examples of Mks XV and 47. All flew with second-line units or test establishments.

The Mk I and Mk II aircraft are believed to have received the USN designation FS-1 (Fighter, Supermarine, first variant), though some sources suggest that this designation was reserved for a batch of ex-RAF Spitfire Mk Vs that, in the event, were not delivered.

A handful of Seafire L.Mk IICs were transferred to the USN in August 1944 and allocated to the Liberator Wing based at Dunkeswell, Devon. Fitted with American VHF radios, these aircraft provided air combat training for the Liberator crews, in order to familiarise them with the tactics employed by fighter pilots in the skies over Europe.

US Spitfire operations
Part 1: Northern Europe

Many published US Air Force histories ignore the record of America's use of the Supermarine Spitfire in World War II, only presenting accounts of US-built types. Such treatment is a disservice to the pilots and mechanics who flew and serviced the large number of Spitfires which saw combat operations.

American air units first saw combat in Europe during World War I, flying, in the main, foreign-built types due to the logistical difficulties of transporting aircraft across the Atlantic Ocean, and the inferiority of US-built aircraft compared to their British and French contemporaries. In the aftermath of the conflict, US authorities vowed to ensure that this situation would not arise again, stating the intention to only supply its men based on foreign soil with the finest American aircraft, sent by whatever means necessary. This initiative was advanced in the early 1930s by the need to resuscitate America's decreased industrial productivity, following the great economic depression, using mass-production techniques and the new materials which were becoming available for industry.

When the UK entered World War II in September 1939, it was almost as unprepared to fight Germany, as the USA was to fight any country. Throughout the depression the US Army Air Corps had lobbied hard for every aircraft it could get its hands on. With very few

operational units, the service turned down thousands of applications, taking only a handful of the most qualified men for aircrew training.

At this time, Germany was beginning to threaten neighbouring countries with annexation and invasion or occupation, and although the UK began to put into place its re-arming programme, the political climate of appeasement prevented full-scale preparations. However, in late 1938, before Winston Churchill became Prime Minister, the UK had dispatched a number of purchasing commissions to the USA to explore the possibility of utilising the country's expanding aircraft mass-production facilities, situated far beyond the range of German bombers, and to determine if America could offer any combat-suitable aircraft for sale. A number of European nations, including Great Britain and France, placed initial orders, and these arms sales greatly benefited the American economy, providing a huge expansion of aircraft production and related military capability.

Production of several types of US aircraft was earmarked for the Royal Air Force,

Top: Spitfire Mk Vs from the 12th (coded 'ZM') and 109th TRS ('VX'), formate together during a publicity sortie for the 67th Reconnaissance Group in 1943. Although tasked in the tactical reconnaissance role, 67th RG Spitfires retained their armament for self defence and attacking 'soft' enemy targets of opportunity.

Above: Unlike regular RAF squadrons, the American-manned 'Eagle' squadrons adorned many of their aircraft with personal artworks. Many of them carried variations of the eagle symbol, including 'Little Joe', a No. 71 Sqn Spitfire flown by Pilot Officer Joseph Kelly.

Above: The aircraft in which the first 'American volunteer' squadron went to war was the Hawker Hurricane. Initially operating Mk Is from November 1940 until April 1941, No 71 Squadron replaced them with Mk IIs in the early summer of 1941. Here a pair of Mk Is returns to its base at Kirton-in-Lindsey in the spring of 1941.

Below: One of a famous sequence of photographs taken of Spitfire Mk VB, BM590, of No. 121 Squadron in September 1942, just days before the unit changed its identity to 335th Fighter Squadron of the 4th Fighter Group, USAAF.

Volunteer 'Eagle' ace

Spitfire Mk IIA
Flying this aircraft (P7308), Pilot Officer William R. Dunn of No. 71 Squadron, RAF, became the first American air ace of the war. He claimed his fourth and fifth victims on 27 August 1941, and remained the sole 'Eagle' ace until November of that year. According to USAAF records, Dunn only scored one 'kill', as they refused to include victories scored by its pilots in RAF service.

commencing in 1939. At this time the Curtiss P-36 and P-40 were the most capable fighter types in the US inventory and, with both Britain and France desperate for additional fighters, these aircraft entered priority production for both nations. When France fell in June 1940, the UK took the undelivered aircraft, adding them to its own orders.

To achieve a fair exchange for sales of American aircraft to the UK, an agreement, initially termed Defense Aid (later Lend-Lease), provided the organisational method by which the two English-speaking countries assisted each other in obtaining the best military equipment – including aircraft – available in either country. Supply of aircraft for, and from the UK was not always paid for in Dollars or Sterling, with much equipment being exchanged in tit-for-tat agreements.

Gathering of the 'Eagles'

From the outbreak of World War II, many US pilots had expressed a wish to fight the Germans alongside the British and French. Days after Germany invaded Poland, an American in Canada named Col Charles Sweeny (who was a mercenary soldier, achieving his rank during service with the French Foreign Legion) began recruiting US personnel for service with the French air force. His plans were supplemented

by his nephew in London, also named Charles Sweeny, who presented a formal suggestion to the authorities to recruit Americans in England to fight in the war. In May 1940, Col Sweeny sent his first 32 pilots to France, however, within weeks France was defeated and the surviving volunteers made their way to the UK to be absorbed into RAF squadrons.

At about the same time as the two Sweenys' efforts began, a Royal Canadian Air Force representative tasked an American named Clayton Knight, who had flown with the British Royal Flying Corps in World War I, to screen US pilots who might volunteer for military flying in Canada. Forming the Clayton Knight Committee, advertisements were placed in magazines and newspapers and some 50,000 responses poured in, of which some 6,000 pilots were selected for service with the RCAF, RAF and US Ferry Service.

Other US citizens, who eventually joined the 'Eagle' squadrons, enlisted in the RCAF and British Army, using this roundabout way to eventually receive pilot training and ultimately transfer into RAF squadrons. The motivation was certainly not pay, which was minimal, but a combination of the lure of combat flying, combined with a political desire to assist the UK and France in the struggle against Hitler's expansion plans.

On 19 September 1940, No. 71 Squadron

became the first of the 'Eagle' squadrons to form, and was initially based at Church Fenton. Manned by US pilots, but commanded by an RAF officer, initial equipment comprised the obsolete Brewster Buffalo Mk I, which was used for training purposes, before the unit received the Hurricane Mk I in November, coinciding with a move to Kirton-in-Lindsey. Operational sorties commenced on 5 February 1941, consisting mainly of defensive fighter sweeps, with the squadron re-equipping with Hurricane Mk IIs in April 1941. A number of the Hurricane Mk Is were passed to No. 121 Squadron, which became the second of the trio of 'Eagle' squadrons, forming on 14 May, before it too received the Mk II and commenced combat operations. In August, No. 71 Sqn received the first examples of the aircraft with which it, and the other 'Eagle' squadrons, would be forever associated – the Supermarine Spitfire. Two months later No. 121 Squadron also converted to the type, with both units initially working up using the Mk II/IIA, before receiving the cannon-armed Mk V for offensive fighter sweep operations over northern France. At the end of September, No. 133 Squadron, which had formed as the third and final 'Eagle' squadron on 1 August, began operations, initially with Hurricane Mk IIs, before receiving Mk IIA and Mk V Spitfires in October 1941 and January 1942, respectively.

Left: It was a proud moment for the 'Eagle' pilots when they were finally integrated into the USAAF, on 29 September 1942, as the 4th Fighter Group. Here the 'Stars and Stripes' is officially raised at the home base for the first time, as a flight of resident Spitfire Mk Vs passes overhead.

Below: The 4th Fighter Group remained proud of its 'Eagle' heritage throughout the war, as evidenced by these mementoes on the crewroom wall in 1944.

Combat Colours

The 52nd Fighter Group saw little action in the skies of northern Europe before its hasty departure to the Mediterranean theatre in November 1942. Having previously operated the tricycle-landing gear P-39 Airacobra, the Spitfire Mk V, with its narrow-track tailwheel undercarriage, took some getting used to. This 4th Fighter Squadron example was one of a number that suffered training accidents in August 1942 before operations began in earnest in September.

As the USA became increasingly aware of its citizens fighting a war in foreign uniform, concerns grew regarding the effect on the country's position of neutrality. The chief of the USAAC, Major General H. H. Arnold, was determined to regain control of all US military personnel whatever uniform they wore.

In June 1941, Arnold sent a memorandum to Robert Lovett, Assistant Secretary of War for Air, outlining "Directions in which the United States can render the British the greatest assistance in air matters". The memo suggested sending "units on a volunteer basis, with the purpose of taking part in RAF guise in operations against the enemy". This measure would allow the airmen to fight as British personnel, while remaining under Arnold's control. The plan also envisaged the testing of American aircraft in combat conditions, with the ultimate intention of the units flying only US-built types. Although the scheme was never implemented, as the US entered the war months later in the wake of the attack at Pearl Harbor, it highlighted the displeasure that politicians and high-ranking officers felt at US citizens fighting beyond their control.

In complete contrast, the British were grateful to have the services of these volunteers, and a great deal of publicity was afforded to the 'Eagles'. A movie, portraying the airmen as heroes, was shown in cinemas throughout the country. As the squadrons at this time were only just getting used to combat operations, and had achieved nothing to compare to this overblown star quality treatment, it caused great embarrassment among the pilots.

A memo to Arnold, dated 31 January 1941 and bearing the comments of Brig. Gen. M. J. Scanlon, stated that he was not pleased that a British officer led the 'Eagles' and that "certain elements of the squadron (No. 71) are of the publicity seeking, promoter type" which in his mind did not compare favourably with the exploits of the Lafayette Escadrille, an American unit which served during World War I. Lovett responded, saying "there will always be a certain number of wild men and grandstanders in any such group of so-called soldiers of fortune". He wanted the the RAF to "maintain discipline" and for the US government to "deny to this outfit the right to use any emblem, symbol, or other badges or identification marks" used by the Air Corps. It was clear from this time onwards that the USAAC wanted nothing whatsoever to do with the 'Eagles'. When the USA declared war, other US Fighter Groups were selected to join the soon-to-be mighty Eighth Air Force, and the 'Eagles' were completely overlooked.

'Eagle' aces

The 'Eagles'' reputation of being unruly and cavalier is, however, a great injustice to the pilots who flew with the squadrons. No. 71 Squadron pilot, William R. Dunn, became America's first ace of World War II, claiming his fourth and fifth 'kills' on 27 August 1941. In November, two more 'Eagles' became aces and the squadrons began establishing an excellent reputation in combat. A number of the USAAF's more famous pilots gained their first victories while flying Spitfires with the 'Eagles' including triple ace Don Blakeslee (later to command the 4th FG) and the war's most famous P-51 Mustang ace, Don Gentile, who downed three enemy aircraft in his Spitfire during the disastrous Allied landings at Dieppe on 19 August 1942. On this day, the three 'Eagle' units were among the 76 squadrons assigned to cover the landings, and a number of the pilots flew four missions during the day. By this time, plans were being drawn up to transfer the three squadrons to USAAF control to became the 4th Fighter Group, Eighth Air Force. The date set for the transfer was 29 September 1942, but three days before a disastrous conclusion to the 'Eagle' squadron operations occurred.

In late August, the RAF had honoured the contribution made by the 'Eagle' volunteers by appointing No. 133 Squadron as one of the first three combat units to receive the new Spitfire Mk IX. Commanded by Carroll 'Mac' McColpin, who had claimed No. 133's first kill on 26 April 1942, the unit was tasked with escorting Eighth Air Force B-17s on a raid over France on, or after, 7 September. Weather delayed the mission day after day, and during this time the pilots were going, a few at a time, from their forward base at Great Stampford, near Debden, to London to fill in paperwork and be fitted for uniforms, prior to their acceptance into the USAAF. On 26 September the weather cleared and the order was given for the raid to proceed, however, McColpin was away in London. The mission was led instead by an RAF officer, Flt Lt E. G. Brettell. With France under a blanket of cloud, Brettell proceeded to the rendezvous point but could not locate the bombers. Unwittingly, a miscalculation of high level tailwinds had driven the squadron deep over France and, after a period of searching, the squadron began the return to base. At the time that time-aloft and fuel-expended levels suggested the formation was over southern England, Brettell spied a hole in the cloud and descended. The squadron was still, however, over northern France and found itself on top of German artillery and a Staffel of Focke-Wulf Fw 190s. Within minutes, 12 of the new Spitfire Mk IXs had been shot down with little chance of defending themselves. The RAF did not replace the Mk IXs , the squadron instead reverting back to the Mk V, after the three 'Eagle' squadrons were officially inducted into the USAAF on 29 September.

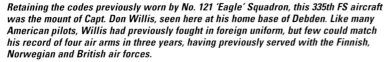

Retaining the codes previously worn by No. 121 'Eagle' Squadron, this 335th FS aircraft was the mount of Capt. Don Willis, seen here at his home base of Debden. Like many American pilots, Willis had previously fought in foreign uniform, but few could match his record of four air arms in three years, having previously served with the Finnish, Norwegian and British air forces.

Above: Learning to operate an unfamiliar type was not only a swift learning process for the pilots, but also for the mechanics. Here, a 336th FS, 4th FG Spitfire Mk VB has its engine removed for overhaul in April 1943. This example, like a number of US Spitfires, underwent major overhaul in the workshops at Audley End.

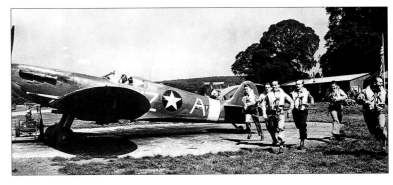

One of the USAAF's most famous Spitfire aces, Capt. Frank Hill, is seen on patrol over the English Channel in the summer of 1942. Flying with the 308th FS, Hill eventually became the 31st Group's top scoring Spitfire pilot with seven victories, most of which were accumulated in the Mediterranean theatre.

Allied plans to invade North Africa had been agreed early in 1942, and required the stripping of aircraft units from the newly-formed 8th Air Force in the UK, to enable the 12th Air Force to be established. All of the 8th Air Force fighter groups, of which there were four in mid-1942 – two Spitfire Mk V (31st and 52nd FGs) and two P-38 Lightning – were to be transferred, leaving the 8th Air Force without a single fighter group. With little enthusiasm, the USAAF requested the RAF to hand its 'Eagle' squadrons over to the USAAF. It was widely acknowledged that the USAAF 'top brass' was more proud of its own squadrons than it was, what it termed, a group of 'soldiers of fortune' who had bent neutrality laws to fight in a foreign uniform.

Formation of the 4th FG

Six weeks before the Allies launched their offensive in North Africa, Nos 71, 121, and 133 Squadrons became the 334th, 335th and 336th Fighter Squadrons of the famed 4th Fighter Group, respectively. Quickly dubbed the 'Debden Wing', the 4th FG's first C.O. was Col Edward W. Andersen, however, operational control remained in RAF hands, and an RAF Wing Commander led the 'Debden Wing' on missions. With the Spitfire Mk V suffering from relatively short range, operations comprised mainly convoy patrols in the English Channel, fighter sweeps and coastline patrols. The aircraft themselves received USAAF insignia, but retained the same code letters allocated to their predecessors. Standard RAF Day Fighter Scheme of dark green and ocean grey upper surfaces and sky blue undersurfaces were also retained as standard.

Despite its best efforts the 4th FG did not find itself engaged with enemy aircraft frequently, and 'kills' were few and far between. One of the group's most productive days occurred on 22 January 1943, when two Luftwaffe fighters were shot down. A month later the 334th FS began the transition to the longer-range P-47 Thunderbolt, acting as a training unit for the group. On 10 March the squadron flew the P-47's first ever combat mission, led by one of the 4th FG's Spitfire aces Lt Col Peterson. The first 'kill' by the P-47s was made by Blakeslee on 15 April, and the unit continued to operate the Thunderbolt until early 1944 when they were replaced by the P-51 Mustang.

Fighter squadrons from the US

Two months before the 'Eagle' squadrons transferred to the USAAF, two other fighter groups began Spitfire operations in the UK as part of the 8th Air Force. The decision to equip these units with British aircraft was highly contentious and involved a number of U-turns in policy during the first six months of 1942. Shortly after US entry into the war the Anglo-American agreement to conquer Germany first was formulated. The 8th Air Force would be formed to operate against the Axis from the UK, and the 12th Air Force would support the massive invasion of North Africa – planned for by the Allies for November 1942. From January

Below: The 31st Fighter Group saw the most combat action of the two USAAF groups which arrived in the summer of 1942. Involved in the disastrous raid on Dieppe, the group claimed a number of enemy aircraft during its brief period of operations. Here, the pilot of 'Lima Challenger', a 307th FS aircraft presented by a resident of the Peruvian capital, straps in to his parachute at the unit's home base at Merston. Note the small RAF serial number, EN851, at the top of the fin.

Above: One of the 31st FG's, most famous pilots was Major Harrison Thyng, who is seen here in the cockpit of his 309th FS Spitfire Mk V as his fellow squadron pilots sprint for their aircraft during a (probably staged) scramble. The aircraft were received straight from RAF Maintenance Units, and hastily had USAAF cocardes and unit codes applied, but retained the standard RAF day fighter scheme which had been introduced in August 1941.

Spitfires of the 8th Air Force

Spitfire Mk VB, 335th FS

The 4th Fighter Group only operated the Mk V version of the Spitfire, using the aircraft for fighter sweeps and coastal patrols in the English Channel region. The aircraft wore the standard RAF dark green and ocean grey colour scheme with medium sea grey undersides. Sky coloured fuselage bands and spinners were added as standard before delivery.

AV D LN853

Spitfire Mk VB, 309th FS

The 31st Fighter Squadron received its Spitfire Mk Vs straight from RAF storage on arrival in the UK. The aircraft had the US national markings applied over the top of the RAF roundel and the appropriate unit codes added. On departing for North Africa, a number of the 31st's Spitfires were passed-on to the 15th TRS.

WZ Y BM

Below: Robert 'Fat Boy' Kraft exits his Spitfire at Membury in November 1942. A large number of the Spitfires operated by the 15th TRS were those left behind by the 31st FG on its departure to North Africa. This example was previously operated by the 309th FS.

Above: Pilots from the 12th TRS, 67th Reconnaissance Group, line-up in front of their aircraft during a visit by Brig. Gen. R. C. Candee at RAF Membury on 20 April 1943. Despite being outclassed by the Focke-Wulf Fw 190, the 8th Air Force fighter and Tac-R groups only received the Mk V, the RAF retaining the more capable Mk IXs for their own squadrons.

1942 General Arnold began to prepare the, as yet, inadequately trained USAAF pilots to fly heavy bomber and pursuit units across the Atlantic, to begin combat operations under the command of the 8th Air Force. The British had urged the US to provide fighter support for their troops in North Africa, and had asked that the units destined to arrive in the UK undergo training to acquaint them with RAF methods, before transfer to North Africa. The British were fully aware that the Bell P-39 and Lockheed P-38 fighters were unsuitable for combat in Europe, and were likely to suffer heavy losses at the hands of the German *experten*. In April 1942 Air Chief Marshall Sir Charles Portal sent a letter to Gen. Arnold suggesting "therefore why not equip US pursuit squadrons with British aircraft … and correspondingly increase US liabilities to Russia and (the) Eastern Theatre". These liabilities were part of the allied commitment to supply equipment to any country in the anti-Axis pool – resulting in the delivery of large numbers of P-39s to Russia and P-40s to the Far East and north Africa for the AVG 'Flying Tigers' and the RAF. On 20 April, Col H. A. Craig of the US War Department suggested that Arnold approve "a proposal of the British to furnish our pursuit units with Spitfires, provided we can furnish light numbers of American pursuit aircraft to the Middle East, India and Russia". He later added that he preferred the option of ferrying US aircraft to the UK, despite US production barely meeting current demands. He also found it undesirable to force US units to be "wholly dependent upon the British supply system", and the "morale factor" in Americans flying Spitfires would be adverse. In the event the opposite was true, with the pilots quickly learning to appreciate the Spitfire's abilities.

Arnold was, however, determined to stick to the US aircraft-only policy, and on 23 April named the units that were to deploy with their aircraft across the Atlantic during the summer months. These were to include the 31st PG flying the P-39 and the 1st PG with the P-38. On 14 May the 52nd PG was added to the list of units, again equipped with the P-39.

The 31st Pursuit Group (Fighter Group after May 1942) had been formed from the personnel of the 1st PG in February 1940. After its initial squadrons (39th, 40th and 41st FS) were assigned to the 35th PG for operations in the south west Pacific region following the attack on Pearl Harbor, the 307th, 308th and 309th squadrons were formed to return the 31st PG to complete status. Bell P-39s were allocated in late 1941 and from May 1942 training for the trans-oceanic crossing began.

The second P-39 unit, the 52nd PG, was activated in January 1941 and its constituent 2nd, 4th and 5th PS received outdated Seversky P-35s, Curtiss P-36s and Republic P-43 Lancers, before re-equipping with the Airacobra in late 1941. In May, the unit moved to northeastern USA to prepare to fly its aircraft to England.

In early June 1941, following a number of training accidents and the realisation that the P-39 was not suitable for combat in northern Europe, the USAAF's plan to take its own fighters to the UK was abandoned as unworkable – the units would travel to the UK by sea under the name Operation Bolero, and on arrival be allocated Spitfire Mk Vs. On 10 June, the 31st FG embarked on a troop ship for Scotland followed by the 52nd FG on 1 July destined for Liverpool. On arrival, both units entered a period of familiarisation and training well away from the combat arena. The UK's often adverse weather conditions and non-geometrical countryside posed navigational problems not previously encountered in the USA, causing a number of forced landings away from base. Additionally the tailwheel landing gear and hand-brake lever of the Spitfire were to cause difficulties for those accustomed to the tricycle landing gear and rudder pedal brakes on the P-39. These teething problems were, however, quickly overcome and the pilots rapidly built up an affinity with the aircraft. On 26 July 1942, pilots of the 31st FG flew their first practice

sweep over the Channel alongside a Canadian squadron. Deemed ready for combat, the 31st's three squadrons moved to forward airfields in England in early August, with the 307th FS going to Biggin Hill, the 308th to Kenley and the 309th deploying to Westhampnett.

As the only USAAF group selected for participation in the raid on Dieppe, the three squadrons underwent intensive training with experienced RAF squadrons to prepare them for combat. The group's combat debut duly arrived over the beaches of Dieppe on 19 August. Lt Samuel F. Junkin, Jr, of the 309th FS, claimed a Focke-Wulf Fw 190 and Lt John White scored another victory. However, the illusion that the USAAF squadrons were invincible was shattered on that day, as four Spitfires were lost to enemy fighters.

The 52nd FG squadrons remained in Northern Ireland, completing their training in late August 1942. By early September the 2nd and 4th FS had commenced combat fighter sweeps over France from Biggin Hill and Kenley, respectively. But these operations were curtailed when the order came for both the 31st and 52nd FG to prepare for deployment to the Mediterranean theatre, for the Allied invasion of

496th Fighter Training Group

To provide the 8th Air Force Groups with air-to-air gunnery training in the UK, the 496th Fighter Training Group was established at Goxhill. A number of types were used from 1943 as gunnery target tugs, including USAAF-marked Spitfire Mk Vs, P-47 Thunderbolts and P-51 Mustangs. In February, the group moved to Halesworth and remained there for the duration of the war in Europe.

Left: The coding system adopted by the Tac-R units, and in particular by the 15th TRS, caused some confusion. MX was not only previously used by 307th FS, 31st FG, but also by another UK based unit – the 78th FG.

Below: Known as the 109th Observation Squadron on its arrival at RAF Membury in September 1942, the unit was later redesignated 109th Tactical Reconnaissance Squadron. It eventually ran up a total of 11 victories, although all were achieved in the P-51, which replaced the Spitfire Mk V in early 1944.

north Africa. In October, the newly created 12th Air Force took control of the 8th Air Force's fighter assets, and the 12th Fighter Command absorbed the 31st and 52nd Fighter Groups. Shortly after, the pilots of the two groups were sent by train to Greenock, Scotland to board a transport ship. Destined to see more combat than they could have imagined, the 31st and 52nd FGs deployment to the Mediterranean commenced at Gibraltar, with a briefing from Maj. Gen James Doolittle.

Tactical reconnaissance

At the outbreak of World War II observation and reconnaissance within the USAAC had changed little from World War I. Slow and obsolete high- or mid-wing aircraft equipped the few observation squadrons in existence, with a crewman holding a camera in an open cockpit shooting vertically downwards. With the USA's entry into the war in Europe, it was quickly apparent that aircraft such as these would not survive over enemy territory. The US was busy developing a photographic reconnaissance version of the P-38 Lightning, known as the F-4 (later versions F-5), but additional assets were needed to monitor German activities and provide target information in France and the low countries. The mission was defined as tactical reconnaissance (Tac-R), and the main unit assigned to the task in Europe was the 67th Reconnaissance Group. Arriving in England in September 1942, the units were initially assigned to the 8th Air Force and its constituent squadrons, comprising the 12th, 107th and 109th Reconnaissance Squadrons and the 153rd Liaison Squadron, were all-equipped in part, or wholly with, the Spitfire Mk V. A number of these aircraft had previously been used by the departing 31st and 52nd FGs. Initially based at Membury, Wiltshire, the aircraft retained their armament but did not carry cameras, the pilots instead undergoing intensive training in visual observation of enemy targets, strafing tactics and local familiarisation flying. In late 1943, the 9th Air Force relocated from the Mediterranean to the UK and the 67th Reconnaissance Group was

absorbed into 9th Fighter Command. At this time a fifth unit, the 15th TRS, joined the other Spitfire Mk V squadrons, although it was initially based at nearby Aldermaston. In 1944, camera-equipped Tac-R versions of the Mustang, designated F-6, began replacing the war-weary Spitfires, and the final example had been withdrawn by the time the 67th RG moved into France in July 1944. Although never claiming an air-to-air victory, the 67th Group's Spitfires provided valuable information during their often hazardous low-level operations over enemy territory, and also can lay claim to the destruction of many enemy targets during strafing attacks on 'targets of opportunity'.

Spitfires in blue

As the bombers of the 8th Air Force markedly increased the scope and scale of their daylight bombing offensive against targets in northern Europe in 1943, the need for accurate photo-reconnaissance of targets both before and after a strike became of paramount importance. The RAF had already established an extensive photographic reconnaissance operations centre at RAF Benson, Oxfordshire, and, on arrival in the UK in November 1942 the C.O. of the 7th PRG requested that his unit be based nearby. His wish was duly obliged, and in January 1943 the 13th PS received its first F-5A (photographic reconnaissance version of the P-38G Lightning)

Above: High Lady was the 14th PS Spitfire PR.Mk XI in which Major Walter Weitner made the USAAF's first photographic reconnaissance flight over the German capital on 6 March 1944. Three Luftwaffe fighters attempted to intercept Weitner, but could not catch him at his operating altitude of some 41,500 ft (12500 m). The flight took Weitner 4 hours 18 minutes, and to the very limit of his fuel reserves.

Left: A 14th PS Spitfire Mk XI undergoes an engine test, complete with groundcrew preventing the tail from lifting, at Mount Farm some time after the D-Day invasion in June 1944. The majority of the Spitfires were painted with yellow spinners, although some examples were coloured dark blue or white.

Left: Seen with the upper half of the invasion stripes removed, dating the photograph as post June-1944, a 14th PS Spitfire PR.Mk XI roars in over the airfield at Mount Farm at the end of another sortie. The more rounded nose profile of the Mk XI held the additional oil needed for long endurance operations.

Below: Three views of the same aircraft (PA944) show the three colour schemes carried between June 1944 and March 1945. For the majority of its service life, the aircraft was flown by 14th PS pilot John Blyth. The first photo shows Blyth getting airborne at around the time of D-Day, with invasion stripes circling the entire fuselage. The second view shows the upper section of the stripes removed, leaving the aircraft rather untidy and with the 'P' of its serial number missing on the fuselage. The third view shows PA944 as one of the 14th PS Spitfires which had their RAF PR blue scheme replaced by bare metal, with a red cowl rectangle and green squadron rudder.

at their adopted base of Mount Farm, some five miles from Benson.

Flying the squadron's first PR mission on 28 March 1943, the 13th PS was, at the time, the only unit of the 7th Photographic Reconnaissance Group (PRG) and was assigned directly to the 8th Air Force. Over the next eight months, the three other constituent squadrons of the 7th PRG joined the 13th PS at Mount Farm, starting with the 14th and 22nd PSs in June, followed by the 27th PS in November. All four squadrons were initially equipped with versions of the F-5, although from July 1943 the 13th and 14th PS were allocated five war-weary Spitfire Mk Vs, to be used for the sole purpose of navigation training.

Initial operations with the F-5 raised a number of concerns. The aircraft suffered problems at the low temperatures encountered above 30,000 ft (9144 m), which was the preferred operating level for the majority of the missions. The freezing temperatures affected the engines and turbo-superchargers, and a lack of cockpit heating caused additional discomfort for the pilot. A less reported prob-

lem was that, in a dive, the F-5 entered compressibility at a lower Mach number than other equivalent types. The problems prompted the USAAF to impose a 300-mile (483-km) radius restriction on operations from July 1943.

From late 1943, the build up to the invasion of France called on the 8th Air Force to strike at targets deeper inside Germany, and although the F-5s performed extremely well on low-level 'dicing' missions, the USAAF Generals became increasingly concerned at the 7th PRG's inability to fulfil a growing number of operations. It fell too one man to solve the problem.

Col Homer Sanders became Group C.O. in September 1943 and, on learning on the capabilities of the Spitfire PR.Mk XI operated by the RAF from nearby Benson, began to lobby 8th Air Force Headquarters for their acquisition. At the time the 7th PRG was not subordinated to a Wing organisation, instead reporting directly to HQ 8th Air Force. It is stated that it was over a game of poker with the commander of the 8th Air Force, Maj. Gen. Ira Eaker, that Sanders persuaded Eaker that the only way that the 7th PRG could fulfil its longer range tasking was to

'Bluebirds' of the 7th PRG

Spitfire Mk IX
14th PS, 7th PRG
Mount Farm, Oxfordshire
Nov 1943-May 1945

The Spitfire PR.Mk XIs of the 7th PRG were specially requested by the USAAF to provide the unit with a long-range platform capable of avoiding interception by Luftwaffe aircraft while operating deep inside enemy airspace. Along with the larger fuel tank, other features included a heated camera bay fed with hot air from ducts running from the cabin heating system. The bay itself housed the Universal camera installation, usually comprising two 36-in (91.4-cm) focal length cameras in a 'split pair' configuration.

Seen in the colours worn by by the unit in the late summer of 1944, PL914 carries the twin serial number arrangement and underside invasion stripes of the period. The PRU blue was the same colour as worn by their RAF equivalents.

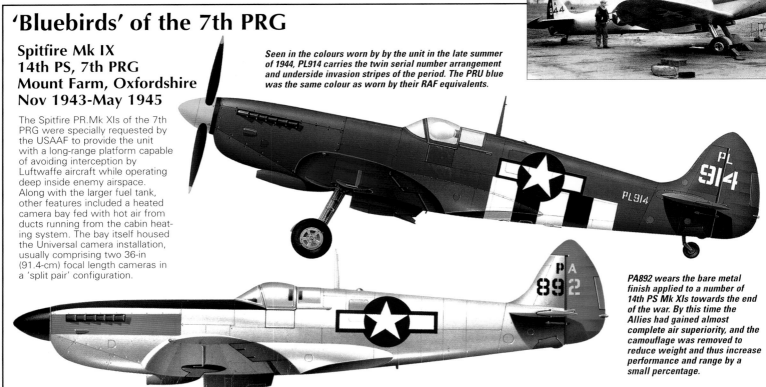

PA892 wears the bare metal finish applied to a number of 14th PS Mk XIs towards the end of the war. By this time the Allies had gained almost complete air superiority, and the camouflage was removed to reduce weight and thus increase performance and range by a small percentage.

Above: With three of the four squadrons assigned to the 7th PRG flying the F-5 Lightning, it was a matter of coincidence that the 4,000th mission happened to be flown by a 14th PS Spitfire PR.Mk XI. Col George Humbrecht, C.O. of the 7th PRG congratulates Lt Jack H. Roberts as he exits the cockpit, while in front of the aircraft Maj. Gerald M. Adams, C.O. of the 14th PS, celebrates with another 14th PS pilot, Lt Robert E. Sanford. Note the late-war bare-metal finish and the anti-glare panel forward of the cockpit.

Right: The mount of Lt Robert Kraft, Spitfire PR.Mk IX 'Dorothy' poses for the camera in the autumn of 1944. The sorties were usually flown at altitudes in excess of 40,000 ft (12192 m), and were generally invulnerable to interception by Luftwaffe fighters until the introduction of the Messerschmitt Me 262.

use the Spitfire Mk XI. Eaker duly obliged, and in November the first of the new aircraft was accepted by the 14th PS. This unit was to become the sole Spitfire operator within the Group, passing its F-5s to the other three squadrons. The aircraft itself was a far cry from its short-legged fighter brethren. To enable missions to be flown as far as Berlin, Vickers Supermarine crammed in 218 gallons (991 litres) of fuel, compared with just 85 gallons (386 litres) carried by earlier fighter versions, and a larger oil tank was fitted beneath the nose, giving the aircraft its distinctive profile. The additional fuel raised its range to 1,360 miles (2189 km), and this could be further increased by the carriage of drop tanks, for targets such as Berlin. The aircraft

could comfortably operate at heights up to 44,000 ft (13411 m) and had a maximum speed well in excess of 400 mph (644 km/h).

By early 1944, the tempo of aerial reconnaissance had increased significantly, and with plans for the invasion being formalised the 7th PRG was tasked with photographing German coastal defences from Spain to Norway. Additionally, the usual strategic targets were covered, along with the search for new menaces such as the V-1 flying bomb launch sites. On 6 March 1944, Capt. Walter Weitner made the USAAF's first photo-recce sortie to Berlin in Spitfire Mk XI *High Lady*. Two days later Lt Charles Parker repeated the mission, with both pilots having spent the majority of the mission at heights in

excess of 38,000 ft (11582 m) in an unpressurised cockpit – a remarkable tribute to their stamina and endurance. In the build-up to D-Day, the 7th PRG was absorbed into the 8th Reconnaissance Wing, which itself was re-designated the 325th Wing of the 9th Air Force in March 1944. The Spitfires continued to operated alongside the F-5-equipped squadrons throughout 1944, and by February 1945 the group had flown its 4,000th operational mission. Three months later the war in Europe was over. A number of reconnaissance pilots and aircraft were earmarked for transfer to the Pacific for the continuing war against Japan, however, US policy dictated that only US aircraft were to be used in the theatre so the 7th PRG quietly handed its Spitfires back to Britain, bringing to an end the US operations of this most famous fighter aircraft.

Paul Ludwig

VCS-7, US Navy Spitfire operations

Among the massive offensive forces to be utilised during the D-Day landings in Normandy were US Navy battleships and cruisers, which were tasked with pounding the German coastal defences. A key role during the bombardment would be that of the spotter aircraft, which were tasked with accurately directing the fire. However, the ships' resident Curtiss SOC Seagulls and Vought OS2U Kingfishers were deemed too slow and vulnerable to enemy aircraft and ground defences. In April 1944, the ship's aircraft were catapulted off and flown ashore to be placed into short-term open storage. The pilots were then temporarily assigned to a new unit designated VCS-7, to be trained by the 15th TRS to fly the Spitfire Mk V. Pilots from six ships were transported to RAF Middle Wallop and, after training, went to RNAS Lee-on-Solent to be placed under the command of the Third Naval Fighter Wing of the Fleet Air Arm. For the invasion period, two RAF and four Fleet Air Arm squadrons, plus the Spitfires of VCS-7, were tasked with the gunnery spotting role. On D-Day itself, the VCS-7 pilots flew in pairs, completing some 34 sorties. One pilot was downed but returned after the invasion. After four days of intensive flying the taskings decreased, and VCS-7 was disbanded on 26 June – its pilots returning with their aircraft to their host ships.

US Spitfire unit codes in Europe

Unit	Type	Code
Eagle Squadrons		
71 Sqn, RAF	Spitfire Mk II, IIA, V	XR-
121 Sqn, RAF	Spitfire Mk II, IIA, V	AV-
133 Sqn, RAF	Spitfire Mk IIA, V, IX	MD-
4th Fighter Group		
334th FS	Spitfire Mk V	XR-
335th FS	Spitfire Mk V	AV-
336th FS	Spitfire Mk V	MD-
31st Fighter Group		
307th FS	Spitfire Mk V	MX-
308th FS	Spitfire Mk V	HL-
309th FS	Spitfire Mk V	WZ-
52nd Fighter Group		
2nd FS	Spitfire Mk V	QP-
4th FS	Spitfire Mk V	WD-
5th FS	Spitfire Mk V	VF-
67th Reconnaissance Group		
12th TRS	Spitfire Mk V	ZM-
15th TRS	Spitfire Mk V	MX-/WZ-
107th TRS	Spitfire Mk V	AX-
109th TRS	Spitfire Mk V	VX-
153rd LS	Spitfire Mk V	mixed
7th Photo-Reconnaissance Group		
13th PS	Spitfire Mk V	none
14th PS	Spitfire Mk V, XI	none/large serial on tail
496th Fighter Training Group		
–	Spitfire Mk V	C7-
US Navy		
VCS-7	Spitfire Mk V	4?*

*4 followed by a letter (eg. 4X)

US Spitfire operations

Part 2: The Mediterranean theatre

Both the 31st and 52nd Fighter Groups left the Eighth Air Force in England in late 1942, bound for North Africa and a new assignment with the Twelfth Air Force supporting the Allied invasion of North Africa. Still equipped with Spitfires, in the absence of suitable American aircraft, the two groups fought their way eastwards and across the Mediterranean to Corsica and the Italian mainland.

The invasion of North Africa, some 11 months after the Japanese attack on Pearl Harbor, was intended to wrest control of the African continent from German and Italian forces. American President Franklin D. Roosevelt and British Prime Minister Winston Churchill had quickly agreed to defeat Germany and Italy first, before turning to the Japanese. However, any clash of arms and troops between American and German ground forces would require massive and secret sea transportation to support a land invasion, and preparations for such a huge invasion took time.

Codenamed Operation Torch, the invasion began on 8 November 1942 and marked the first clash between American ground forces and German and Italian forces (although, initially,

Above: The Spitfire Mk Vs of the 31st and 52nd Groups served along side such American types as the Curtiss P-40 and Bell P-39. It was not unusual for Allied aircraft in North Africa to be without unit code letters, though this practice appears to have been less common in the USAAF than in the RAF. ES264 'V' is a 52nd FG machine.

Top: A 308th FS Spitfire Mk VIII meets its replacement – a newly delivered olive drab P-51B Mustang – at Castel Volturno, March 1944.

the Americans were to face resistance from Vichy French forces).

The two American Spitfire fighter groups operating in England – the 31st and 52nd – were among the major portion of US Army Air Forces units stripped from the Eighth Air Force and added to the newly-created Twelfth Air Force for the invasion. Lieutenant General Dwight D. Eisenhower, until then in charge of US forces in England, was given command of the North African invasion.

Under reverse Lend-Lease, the Twelfth Air Force received 274 Spitfire Mk Vs for use by the 31st and 52nd Fighter Groups. This well known view shows aircraft assembled at North Front airfield on Gibraltar, awaiting issue to squadrons on the front line. Crude US markings have been applied over RAF roundels; though RAF fin flashes remain in place these were soon removed and remained a rarity on Twelfth Air Force aircraft.

When the air echelons of the two US Spitfire groups disembarked from transport ships at Gibraltar, they found the tiny airfield at North Front crowded with aircraft. The inexperienced American Spitfire groups were to fly into battle on equal terms, at least in terms of their equipment, with the combat-experienced RAF. Spitfire Mk VCs reserved for the two US groups were installed with Vokes desert filters, which not only changed the graceful shape of the Spitfire, but produced considerable drag. A Spitfire Mk VC was some 14 mph (22.5 km/h) slower than a Mk VB without the filter. Nevertheless, the Americans were eager to join the battle.

At Gibraltar, pilots were briefed by General James Doolittle's Twelfth Air Force staff for Operation Torch. German and Italian ground forces in Egypt and Libya were being pushed to the west by the British Eighth Army, and the eastward push by the Americans forced Axis forces into a closing vice in Tunisia.

Winter had begun by this time and rain often turned unprepared desert airfields and tent areas into muddy quagmires. The Spitfires' short range necessitated being near the front, and advances of American forces resulted in 15 to 20 base changes for the two groups in the 18 months the men operated Spitfires in the Mediterranean theatre.

Even with the arrival of Spitfire Mk VIIIs and IXs in 1943, tropicalised Spitfire Mk Vs remained in service with both the 31st and 52nd Fighter Groups until just before the Spitfires were replaced by Mustangs in 1944. ES306 of the 308th FS was photographed on the unprepared airstrip at Thelepte, Tunisia, in February/March 1943.

The initial task of the 31st and 52nd FGs on 8 November 1942 was to protect invasion forces landing at Meirs el Kabir, the port for Oran, Algeria. In addition, one squadron of the 52nd FG was ordered to escort General Doolittle's B-17 across the strait, to an airfield where he would set up his HQ. Tafaraoui and La Senia, major French airfields near Oran, had been liberated by US paratroopers by the time the two US fighter groups arrived.

On the day of the invasion, Royal Navy carriers sent their Hawker Sea Hurricanes to fight, and US carriers sent their Grumman Wildcats to gain air superiority over Oran's harbour. Unfortunately, total air superiority was not achieved and Vichy French fighters lay in wait. Runways at La Senia were reported to be holed by bombs or cannon shell fire, and Colonel John Hawkins, CO of the 31st FG, led his 307th, 308th and 309th Squadrons' aircraft to

New aircraft – Spitfire Mk IXs

Beginning in April 1943 the 31st FG (307th and 309th Fighter Sqns) began to receive its first Spitfire Mk IXs, introduced by the RAF in the Mediterranean the previous December to counter the threat posed by newly deployed Luftwaffe Fw 190s. The 52nd FG was issued with Mk IXs at about the same time, the new variant (powered by the new 'two-stage' Merlin 61 which offered much improved performance at altitude) serving alongside Spitfire Mk Vs in the 2nd, 4th and 5th Fighter Sqns. Pictured are EN354 *Doris June II* (part of an order for Spitfire Mk Vs converted to Mk IX standard by Rolls-Royce before delivery) of the 4th FS at La Sebala in June 1943 (above) and an unidentified aircraft of the 307th FS in Sicily. Early Mk IX deliveries were in RAF desert camouflage.

'HL-AA', a Spitfire Mk VC of the 308th FS, is pictured during a patrol over the Mediterranean in mid-1943. Interestingly, JK226 survived the war and was passed to the Greek air force in 1946.

Tafaraoui. Runways were pitted but Hawkins and some of his pilots landed. As the last Spitfires were landing, Vichy French artillery shelled the field and French Dewoitine D.520 fighters shot down one US aircraft, killing the pilot. Major Harrison Thyng, Lieutenant Carl Payne and First Lieutenant Charles C. Kenworthy, Jr, all from the 309th FS, each downed a Dewoitine D.520. Harrison Thyng became an ace, with five victories in Spitfires.

In the meantime Doolittle's B-17 transport had taken off ahead of its escort, and 12 Spitfires of the 2nd FS, led by Lieutenant Colonel Graham 'Windy' West, Deputy Commander of the 52nd FG, raced ahead to make the rendezvous. The pilots struggled through thick cloud to keep Doolittle's transport in sight. A few pilots of the 4th FS had navigation problems and landed in outlying areas, but soon returned to Tafaraoui. The 5th FS did not fly in combat that day as it was scheduled to arrive later.

The next day, the French shelled Tafaraoui. The Allies also encountered resistance at

The dusty, unprepared strip at Thelepte, Tunusia was typical of many in North Africa. The need for the cumbersome Vokes tropical filters to protect engines from excessive wear is immediately apparent.

Casablanca and Algiers, the two other Torch invasion points. When it was reported that an armoured column of French Foreign Legion forces was moving north from its base at nearby Sidi Bel Abbes towards Oran, pilots scrounged fuel abandoned by the French, used 5-US gal (19-litre) cans to load it into their Spitfires, and took off. The 31st FG and the two available squadrons of the 52nd FG flew several strafing missions and halted the column, driving it southward, then silenced French artillery around La Senia and Tafaraoui.

Ground personnel were landed on the day of the invasion but were forced to march a considerable distance inland to Tafaraoui. Men and equipment necessary to service and fuel aircraft were slow in coming. The ground echelon of the 52nd FG sailed from Scotland on the day of the invasion and was not ashore at Meirs el

Commanding Officers' aircraft – 31st Fighter Group

Below: Colonel Fred M. Dean (standing on the wing of his Spitfire Mk VC, coded 'F-MD') took command of the 31st FG one month after Opeation Torch. The group had advanced as far as Sicily when, on 15 July 1943, he was replaced by Lieutenant-Colonel Frank A. Hill (with right foot on wing).

Colonel Charles M. McCorkle
'Sandy' McCorkle replaced Frank Hill and oversaw the Group's transition from Spitfire to Mustang in March 1944. McCorkle finished the war with 11 aerial victories, all claimed while CO of the 31st FG – five while flying Spitfire Mk VIIIs and IXs and six on P-51B and D Mustangs. *Betty Jane* was a Spitfire Mk VIII, serial unknown.

Lieutenant-Colonel Frank A. Hill's tenure as CO of the 31st FG was comparatively brief, lasting until the conclusion of the Sicilian campaign in mid-August 1943. Here Hill is pictured with his personal Spitfire Mk IX, appropriately carrying his initials 'FA-H'. The use of initials in place of code letters was an RAF custom, accorded officers of Wing Commander rank or higher, and adopted by USAAF group COs.

31st Fighter Group – 'Return with Honor'

307th Fighter Squadron
Sharkmouth markings were not a common sight on Spitfire Mk Vs in any theatre; this aircraft is one of at least two examples in the 307th FS that were so-adorned. Its camouflage follows the standard desert RAF scheme, comprising dark earth and middle stone, with azure blue undersurfaces.

308th Fighter Squadron
Fargo Express was the well-known mount of Captain Leland P. Molland, CO of the 308th FS at Castel Volturno in early 1944. Molland scored 10½ kills, including 4½ while flying Spitfire Mk VIIIs. This aircraft, a late-production Mk VIII with an enlarged rudder, is often (incorrectly) depicted with the codes 'HL-X'. The standard RAF desert camouflage scheme is applied.

309th Fighter Squadron
From the end of 1943 replacement Spitfire Mk IXs were delivered in RAF temperate day fighter colours of the period, i.e. dark green/ocean grey camouflage over medium sea grey undersurfaces. Note also the red-bordered national insignia, adopted for two months during mid-1943. *Thurla Mae III* was flown by Lieutenant Robert Belmont.

Kabir until 11 November. The 2nd and 4th Squadrons of the 52nd FG were in combat right away, but the men of the 5th FS arrived by ship on 12 November.

The 31st FG transferred to the bombed French main air base at La Senia on 14 November followed by the 52nd FG three days later. Following negotiations between General Eisenhower's staff and leaders of the Vichy French in North Africa, resistance ended in Morocco and Algeria on 13 November, and by 18 November in Tunisia. Northern Tunisia, however, was soon to become an armed German camp: German forces were defeated at El Alamein in late October 1942 and Tobruk fell to British forces on 13 November, forcing the Germans to head for Tunisia. The Luftwaffe was far to the east in late November and it mounted only a few raids against American forces at Oran. Excepting losses and victories on the first day of the invasion, the 31st and 52nd Groups saw little air action and did not achieve another credited victory until 30 November. (The 57th FG had been operating in the Middle East since August, scoring victories. The 1st, 14th, 33rd and other US fighter groups took the lion's share of aerial victories from November.)

The large influx of aircraft meant any airfield used in North Africa was crowded by a great number and variety of Allied aircraft. The 31st

and 52nd Groups were never the sole occupants of airfields, and were often based apart from each other. Individual squadrons were frequently separated from their group.

The 31st FG began flying patrols and on 20 December the 307th FS moved east to Maison Blanche, Algeria, from where pilots flew transport-escort missions. Spitfires carried external 'slipper' tanks to improve range. The 309th FS remained at La Senia while the 308th FS flew to Casablanca in January 1943, where it was given the honour of flying cover for the (now famous) strategy conference between Roosevelt and Churchill and the top generals and admirals of both countries. Bad weather set in, lasting intermittently through the winter.

Severe air fighting lay farther to the east, and the 2nd FS was given the choicest assignment

of those offered to the two Spitfire groups: on 25 November it flew to a muddy field at Algiers and two days later it moved on to Bône in Algeria, just west of Tunisia, where it joined No. 81 Squadron of No. 322 Wing, RAF.

Allied harbour defence at Bône was a key aspect of maintaining the Americans' eastward push, and the Luftwaffe defended its own shore and harbour areas around Bizerte and Cape Bon in Tunisia. Bône and Cape Bon were not far apart, and pilots of the 2nd FS soon achieved success. Luftwaffe strength in North Africa was supplemented by air units based on nearby Sicily, just across the water from Bizerte. The 2nd FS engaged the Luftwaffe as it harassed defences at Bône, and the Luftwaffe fought when Allied air units raided Bizerte, finding itself in the thick of combat three weeks

This 307th FS Spitfire Mk V fell to 'friendly' AA fire near Salerno in September 1943. Misidentification was not confined to AA gunners; the caption to this USAAF photograph describes the aircraft as a "Curtiss P-40". In the background vehicles of the 817th Engineer Aviation Battalion roll off an LST and onto Italian soil.

1st Lieutenant William Skinner inspects the damage caused to his 308th FS Spitfire Mk V by an 88-mm flak shell, Monte Corvino, 1 October 1943. By this time the 308th was re-equipping with Mk VIIIs

The 52nd FG moved to Sbeitla, Tunisia, on 6 April and then to La Sers, Tunisia, six days afterward. The war in North Africa was nearing its end, as Allied air superiority prevented the Luftwaffe from resupplying ground forces. The 31st FG moved closer to the front lines, going to Djilma at about the same time that the 52nd Group moved to La Sers.

The fight for Tunisia

German forces were bottled up in Tunisia, but Hitler wanted Tunisia held, and he ordered fleets of poorly-escorted, slow-flying Ju 52/3m and gigantic six-engined Me 323 transports to fly from Sicily to Tunisia at low altitude in clear weather to maintain his forces in North Africa. Those transport aircraft were sitting ducks to fast Allied fighters. Allied high command knew ahead of time of the massive effort and on 5 April 1943 it sent its fighter groups on a 'killing spree'. Under Operation Flax RAF, SAAF and AAF fighter pilots inflicted heavy losses on the Luftwaffe.

Flax lasted for a fortnight from 5 April. The interception and massive destruction of Luftwaffe aircraft attempting to supply and/or evacuate German forces in Tunisia resulted in 48 German aircraft being downed on 5 April,

Lt Jerome C. Simpson and 1st Lt John F. Pope each got two. Captain McDonald downed three Ju 87s. On 9 April Butler downed two aircraft and 1st Lt Fred Ohr got his first, a Ju 88, north of Kairouan. Ohr's next kill came on 31 May 1944 in a P-51B, and later he became an ace with a total of six victories. Ohr, whose original name was Oh, is the only Korean-American ace. He later was CO of the 2nd FS. Also on 9 April, 1st Lt Victor Cabas of the 4th FS downed 1½ Ju 88s northeast of Kairouan. Cabas was later an ace with five victories, including his first, an Fw 190 over Dieppe when he was flying with No. 403 Sqn, RCAF.

USAAF Spitfire aces of the Mediterranean theatre

Nine 31st FG pilots and five from the 52nd FG 'made ace' in the MTO on Spitfires, while a number of pilots who later claimed five or more victories, on types such as the Mustang, scored at least one kill while flying Spitfires.

Above: Pictured at Termini on Sicily in August 1943, Lieutenant-Colonel Frank Hill, CO 31st FG (right), chats with Wing Commander Brian Kingcome in front of the latter's Spitfire Mk VIII. Hill had joined the 31st FG shortly before it left the US for England in 1942 and finished the war with seven confirmed kills, all achieved while flying Spitfires. Battle of Britain ace Kingcome, who led No. 244 Wing, RAF, during the invasion of Sicily, was no stranger to the 31st; he had led the 308th FS on its first combat missions over Europe in 1942.

Above: The honour of top-scoring USAAF Spitfire pilot went to Sylvan Feld, who scored nine kills as a 1st Lieutenant with the 4th FS between late March and early June 1943, flying Spitfire Mk Vs and IXs. At the end of his tour Feld transferred to the 373rd FG, based in England and equipped with P-47Ds, his second tour commencing in September 1943. On 13 August 1944 he survived being shot down by flak over France, only to be killed the following week in an Allied bombing raid.

Left: Pictured in RAF flying gear in the cockpit of his 307th FS Spitfire Mk V at RAF Biggin Hill, Lieutenant J. D. 'Jerry' Collinsworth scored six kills on Spitfire Mk Vs and IXs, all in the Mediterranean during 1943. Wounded in Sicily, Collinsworth returned to the US in September 1943.

In mid-October the 308th FS moved to Pomigliano, a former Regia Aeronautica facility with a concrete runway and permanent buildings. The airfield was frequently strafed by the Luftwaffe; here 1st Lieutenant Harold 'Dutchy' Holland (right) chats with his crew chief while on alert with his Spitfire Mk VIII.

the same number on 10 April, and 31 on 11 April. Some 76 enemy aircraft were shot down on 18 April, in what has been called 'The Palm Sunday Massacre'; in all 400 transports were downed, plus a large number of their German and Italian escorts.

However, despite the huge numbers of Allied aircraft involved, the USAAF Spitfire groups played little part in the operation. By this time Spitfire Mk VIIIs and IXs were beginning to supplement Mk VCs in the two US groups and there has been considerable speculation as to why these aircraft were not called into battle during Flax.

It is known that the USAAF was unhappy that it had been forced to equip the 31st and 52nd FGs with foreign aircraft to begin with, even if they were Spitfires. Though a proven fighting machine, the Spitfire was not ideal for some of the roles it was asked to perform, thanks largely to its lack of range. It was recognised that, as soon as suitable American aircraft were available, both groups would be re-equipped.

Thus, while other US fighter groups in the Mediterranean, equipped with US-built aircraft, were asked to perform a full range of tasks,

including an air combat role, the 31st and 52nd FGs seemed to be viewed as of secondary importance as an air combat force, even though they had often been first into battle with the invasion forces and, by the time of Operation Flax, were partially equipped with new Spitfire Mk IXs.

North Africa finally fell to the Allies on 13 May 1943; on 23 May the 52nd FG was transferred to the RAF's Mediterranean Allied Coastal Air Force (MACAF). On that day, the 52nd FG moved to La Sebala near the Cape Bon peninsula in Tunisia, where the group remained until 30 July, past the time when Pantelleria was taken and long after the invasion of Sicily. The

Above: Well known as a Korean War ace, Harrison Thyng 'cut his teeth' on the Spitfire, joining the 309th FS as its CO prior to the unit's move to England with the 31st FG. His first confirmed kill (a Vichy French Dewoitine D.520) came during the Torch landings and four more followed over the next six months. Spitfire Mk V Mary and James *was his personal aircraft.*

Above: Major Fred Ohr scored five of his six kills on Mustangs, after claiming an all-important first victory while flying a Spitfire. The only American ace of Korean ancestry, Ohr (original surname 'Oh') scored his first kill – a Junkers Ju 88 – on 9 April 1943 and went on to command the 2nd FS during 1944. His second kill came over a year after the first; by then the 52nd FG had converted to Mustangs.

Left: CO of the 307th FS from October 1943 until his death the following February, Major Virgil Fields had joined the 31st FG from the 388th FG earlier in the year. His first kill (a Bf 109) came on 6 April 1943 and was followed by five more, the last just eight days before he fell to enemy aircraft over Anzio on 6 February 1944.

Right: Little is known of the USAAF career of 1st Lieutenant Richard F. Hurd, other than that he scored six victories flying Spitfire Mk VIIIs with the 308th FS during 1943/44. Here he is pictured with his aircraft at Castel Volturno, Italy during January 1944, at which point he had just a single kill to his name. Five more followed between 20 February and 21 March.

Spitfire HF.Mk VIIIs of the 308th Fighter Squadron

While the other squadrons in the group received Spitfire Mk IXs, the 308th was re-equipped entirely with Spitfire Mk VIIIs, beginning in August 1943. Among those delivered to the 31st Fighter Group were a number of HF.Mk VIIIs, equipped with Merlin 70 engines and extended wingtips for high-altitude operation. This example is pictured at Pomigliano, Italy, in October 1943.

52nd FG remained far behind the front lines. US forces worked closely with the British, and the 52nd FG was subordinated to the RAF. It ceased to be a fighter group in all but name, flying reconnaissance and convoy protection patrols and harbour patrol for almost one year. US Spitfire pilots grew discouraged at being kept from the aerial front in the war. The 52nd FG was not employed again as an air superiority fighter group until it was transferred in early 1944 to the newly-created US 15th Air Force after receiving P-51 Mustangs.

Pantelleria

The brief campaign to take the isolated and poorly defended island of Pantelleria began on 14 May and ended on 11 June. On 9 June, the 308th FS was credited with eight victories. Captain Thomas B. Fleming and First Lieutenant Walter J. Overend downed two aircraft each. On the next day, the 31st FG got 12. First Lieutenant Robert O. Rahn of the 309th

FS downed one. Rahn became a well-known test pilot with the Douglas Aircraft Company after the war. First Lieutenant Dale E. Shafer, Jr, of the same squadron downed an MC.202 over Pantelleria. Shafer's war total was seven, four in Spitfires and three in Mustangs, including a twin-jet Arado Ar 234B in April 1945 when he was with the 503rd FS. First Lieutenant John White also scored two on 10 June, an Fw 190 and a Bf 109 over Pantelleria. 31st FG pilots did well on 11 June over or near Pantelleria. First Lieutenant Charles R. Fischette of the 307th FS shot down two Bf 109s 10 miles (16 km) northwest of the island, making him an ace in Spitfires.

Disaster struck the 52nd FG at La Sebala on 22 June. A small grass fire on the airstrip spread to one of a number of abandoned German aircraft and turned into a major blaze. Alerted to the conflagration, Colonel West, First Lieutenant Howard H. Brians and Sergeant Bernard Schreiber ran to attempt to put the fire

out. However, the flames set off a heavy-calibre shell in the wrecked Luftwaffe aircraft, killing Brians and Schreiber, and injuring West's legs so badly they had to be amputated. Colonel James S. Coward became Group CO.

On 30 June the 31st FG was moved to the island of Gozo, to the north of Malta and only 60 miles (97 km) from Sicily, which put that group at the forefront of air action as the day of the invasion of Sicily approached – 10 July.

On 11 July, pilots of all three squadrons downed seven aircraft. Captain Carl Payne of the 309th FS damaged a Do 217 with a Spitfire Mk VB on one sortie and downed an Fw 190 with a Spitfire Mk VIII later that same day. On 8 August, Second Lieutenant Richard F. Hurd of the 308th FS shot down his first aircraft, an Fw 190. He scored all of his six victories in a Spitfire Mk VIII.

Sicily falls

On 30 July the 52nd FG's long stay at La Sebala ended when the 2nd FS flew into Bocca di Falco, near Palermo, Sicily. Ground crew and the other squadrons followed. The group was needed for dive-bombing missions in Italy.

At about the same time the 31st FG flew into Ponte Olivo near Gela, Sicily, and by 2 August was at Termini, a few miles from the Italian coastline. It was here, three weeks later, that the group witnessed the arrival of an Italian delegation that signed the armistice at Termini on 17 August.

On 31 August Italy signed an armistice with the Allies. Although some Italian forces now joined the Allies in the war against Germany, German forces remained in the north of the country and on the islands of Corsica and Sardinia. The latter was abandoned and Corsica reinforced, but the Allies launched a ground campaign and, by 4 October, Corsica was in Allied hands. It became an Allied staging area and forward island air base.

In the meantime the 31st FG had moved forward to Milazzo, Sicily, to continue combat operations over Italy. Colonel Charles McCorkle had by now taken command of the 31st and on 30 September, in a Spitfire Mk IX, downed an Me 210 – the first of five victories in Spitfires.

In November, Colonel Marvin McNickle took command of the 52nd FG, and the 2nd and 5th Squadrons flew into Borgo, Corsica, and the 4th FS moved to Calvi, Corsica. Ground personnel moved by sea to Corsica on 1 December.

The first of many Spitfire dive-bombing missions was flown by the 52nd FG on 28 December at San Vincenzo, Italy, led by Major Robert Levine. These continued to be part of the 52nd's repertoire until the group received Mustangs. On 23 January 1944, one such mission encountered Luftwaffe twin-engined bombers heading for Allied ships; the Spitfire pilots jettisoned their bombs and waded into the enemy. Second Lieutenant Mike Encinias and First Lieutenant James W. Bickford of the 2nd FS downed two aircraft each, and two other pilots got one apiece. Lieutenant Colonel Levine replaced McNickle as Group CO at the end of February 1944.

Air actions over Italy began before the invasion of Salerno on 9 September 1943. On 11 August, pilots of the 307th FS scored well. Captain Royal N. Baker, 308th FS, downed an Fw 190 with his Spitfire Mk VIII. Baker had three victories in Spitfires, a half kill in a P-47

Above: **Mk VIIIs of the 308th FS, equipped with 45-Imp gal (205-litre) slipper tanks, taxi prior to take-off from Castel Volturno in early 1944. Behind the aircraft coded 'HL-G' is a machine with an RAF roundel and no unit codes – presumably a newly delivered replacement aircraft.**

Right: **Lady Ellen III was Spitfire Mk IX MH894 of the 309th FS, finished in RAF temperate day fighter colours. It later served with No. 326 (Free French) Sqn, RAF.**

10 March 1944 saw the first P-51B Mustangs for the 31st FG ferried to Castel Volturno, Italy, from Algiers; on 1 April the Group joined the 15th Air Force. These views show aircraft from each of the Group's squadrons at the time of the Mustangs' arrival. The 309th FS aircraft (above) include newer Mk IXs delivered in late 1943 in RAF temperate camouflage, though the squadron commander's aircraft ('WZ-VV', with the red wing stripe, nearest the camera) is an earlier machine in a faded desert scheme. Mk VIIIs (as flown by the 308th FS, right) continued to be delivered in RAF desert camouflage until the end; this view shows a newly arrived P-51B being run-up in the background. The 307th FS (below) also possessed a mixture of both 'temperate' and 'desert' Mk IXs.

and, later, 13 kills in F-86s in the Korean War. (He went on to fly 140 missions in Vietnam during 1968/69, retiring as a Lieutenant General in 1975.)

No US Spitfire pilot scored for an entire month after Baker's victory, and then single victories were recorded on various days. Not until 7 December 1943 was there a flurry of kills on a single day, when five pilots of the 309th FS were credited with six aircraft. Among them was First Lieutenant James O. Tyler of the 4th FS, who claimed an Me 210 in his Spitfire Mk IX. Tyler went on to score six in P-51Bs and Cs, for a final total of eight.

On 20 January 1944, the 31st FG downed four. Second Lieutenant Leland Molland, 308th FS, got his first, a Bf 109, in his Spitfire VIII. Molland eventually had four kills in Spitfires and six in Mustangs. The next day, Molland and three others in his squadron scored one each.

The landings at Anzio took place on 22 January 1944. On 28 January, Second Lieutenant Frank J. Haberle, 307th FS, got three, and others did well. Molland downed two on 22 February and others were credited. On 18 March, pilots of the 31st FG scored six. Second Lieutenant N. H. Youngblood Ricks of the 308th FS downed one.

Mustangs

In early March 1944, men of the 31st FG were told they would be re-equipping with Mustangs. On 10 March, Mustangs were ferried from Algiers to Castel Volturno, Italy, where the group was, by then, based. The group then

moved to San Severo. The final mass flight of 31st FG Spitfires took place on 29 March. From 1 April, the 31st FG was transferred from the XII Air Support Command to the US Fifteenth Air Force. On 16 April 1944, 52 P-51Bs and Cs escorted B-17s and B-24s on a 400-mile trip (644-km) to Romania and back. No Spitfire mission had gone as far.

The 52nd FG was transferred from MACAF to the 15th AF. At Aghione, Corsica, where it had received and trained on Mustangs, it flew its first Mustang bomber escort mission on 10 May 1944. The group moved to Madna, north of Foggia, Italy, on 13 May 1944.

The importance and success of the 52nd FG changed almost overnight when it received Mustangs and became part of the strategic 15th AF, flying bomber escort missions over Germany. In two months – May and June 1944 – the group shot down more aircraft than it had while flying Spitfires for 20 months. It set a

record in June 1944 for the MTO, being credited with 102 kills, and earned two Unit Citations for extremely successful escort missions on 9 June and 31 August 1944. Spitfire credits were 164⅓, and for Mustangs, 257, for a total of 421⅓.

The 31st FG was officially credited with 570½ victories, of which approximately 192 were scored in Spitfires.

Thus the USAAF's association with the Spitfire in a combat role came to an end. For whatever reason the exploits and successes of the 31st and 52nd Fighter Groups over those 18 months from late 1942 received scant coverage. Most histories of the US Air Force compiled since virtually ignore the use of Spitfires in World War II, even though these Groups, and others based in the UK, operated Spitfires exclusively for most of the war and made a major contribution in the theatres in which they served.

Paul Ludwig

The 31st FG kept a number of their beloved Spitfires as 'hacks'. Clipped-wing, late production Spitfire Mk VIII JF470 was retained by the 308th FS well into 1945. It was finished in an unusual overall grey with azure blue undersurfaces.

Bertha, Clara, Dora and Emil
Messerschmitt Bf 109
The First Generation

Flying low over the Mediterranean from its base at Ain-el-Gazala in Libya, a Bf 109E-7/Trop of JG 27 displays an exotic camouflage which proved remarkably effective over the arid scrub of the western desert, particularly near the coast where there were pockets of vegetation. By the time the Bf 109 reached North Africa in April 1941 it was past the zenith of its career, but it nevertheless turned the tables in the desert air war.

There will always be long arguments over which really was the greatest fighter of all time, yet to even be considered in the running any contender would have to match the incredible combat record of the Bf 109, in particular the Bf 109E, which was undoubtedly the most successful of the variants. Technically way out in front of its rivals at the time of its debut, the Bf 109 was only really matched in the early days by the Spitfire, and, when the two met head-on over Britain in the late summer of 1940, it was the first and only occasion where the Bf 109E truly met a worthy opponent.

The greatest exponent of the Messerschmitt Bf 109, indeed probably the finest fighter pilot ever, was Werner Mölders, seen here climbing from his cannon-armed Bf 109E-3. Having been top Luftwaffe scorer in the Spanish Civil War, he repeated the feat during the Battle of Britain. He then went to the Russian Front in mid-1941, and had soon passed von Richthofen's 80-kill score., He then became the first ace to pass the magical 100-kill mark on 15 July. After downing his 100th and 101st kills, he was regarded as too valuable to risk losing in combat and was recalled to Germany to take up the post of General der Jagdflieger. Mölders was killed in November, riding as a passenger in an He 111 bomber while on his way to attend the funeral of Ernst Udet, one of Germany's leading aces of World War I.

At the proving centre at Rechlin, the Bf 109 V1 impressed all those who saw it, although Heinkel's He 112 was considered more likely to get the RLM nod as the first monoplane fighter in the new Luftwaffe.

Below right: The Bf 109a (later designated 109 V1) was the first of more than 30,000 Messerschmitt Bf 109s to be built in a period of just under 10 years. Despite many improvements, and a number of different powerplants, the basic outline of the prototype remained recognisable throughout the series.

Right: D-IABI was the only 109 to have an upright (as opposed to inverted) engine. Ironically, this was a Rolls-Royce Kestrel, as used in contemporary RAF fighters such as the Hawker Fury. One perceived advantage of the inverted configuration was improved forward view for the pilot, but in fact all 109s (and all tail-dragger fighters of the era, virtually regardless of engine type) were poor in this respect.

Below: The third B-series aircraft, the Bf 109 V6 D-IHHB, was used to study the stalling characteristics of the design. A pitot tube was mounted on a pole above the cowl so as to be outside the surface airflow, and a ciné camera was attached to the fin.

It has often been said that no war can be won solely in the air: to achieve final victory ground troops must occupy the objective. However, the seizure of total air superiority can make the task of the ground forces much easier by removing the threat of harassment from the air. In recent times, the 1991 Gulf War vividly demonstrated this, but in no conflict was air superiority more vital than in the German Blitzkrieg campaigns that swept through northern Europe in 1939/40. Providing mastery of the air over Poland and France was the Messerschmitt Bf 109, the most enduring image of Hitler's Luftwaffe and in its day the most advanced fighter in the world.

In the early days of the Third Reich, Germany was preparing for war under a veil of secrecy, yet its engineers and scientists were advancing technology far more rapidly than in any other nation. World War I had shown that the aircraft was quickly becoming the major weapon of war, and during the mid-1930s the German aviation industry produced a number of highly advanced world-leading designs. Much of the rush of technological advance of this decade was squandered by internecine politics within the upper echelons of the Reich, but the 1930s laid the foundations for the aircraft that would sweep German forces across virtually all of Europe and part of Africa in just two years. Of these types, none was more crucial than the Bf 109.

Design of the Bf 109 began in March 1934 at the BFW works at Augsburg. The Bayerische Flugzeugwerke had a long history of aircraft manufacture behind it, having taken over the work of the Udet company. Banned from producing military aircraft under the terms of the 1919 Treaty of Versailles, the German aircraft industry produced airliners and mailplanes. Another Bavarian company, Messerschmitt Flugzeugbau, established by Dipl.-Ing. Willy Messerschmitt, was also producing designs, notably the M.18. The Bavarian state government ordained a merger, with Messerschmitt assuming design control while BFW at Augsburg-Haunsletten became the production facility.

Work on the Bf 109 started in answer to an early 1934 requirement for a new fighter issued by the Luftwaffenführungsstab. Arado, Focke-Wulf and Heinkel were the main contenders, as they were established as the principal fighter manufacturers for the new Luftwaffe. Messerschmitt had no experience in designing high-speed aircraft, and he was personally disliked by several Reichsluftfahrtministerium (RLM) officials, notably Erhard Milch. Nevertheless, BFW was allowed to compete for the fighter competition, and was also instructed to produce an aircraft to take part in an international tourist aircraft competition.

Lightplane predecessor

The latter emerged as the Bf 108A, a highly advanced design incorporating fully enclosed cabin, cantilevered monoplane wings with slots and flaps, flush-riveted stressed-skin construction, retractable undercarriage and an excellent performance. Messerschmitt was aided in the design by Dipl.-Ing. Robert Lusser, who had arrived from Heinkel, and Hubert Bauer, both of whom would be highly influential in the design of the Bf 109, as was Ing. Walter Rethel, who joined Messerschmitt from Heinkel. The Bf 108 was not successful in the competition, held in 1934, but it had proved to be the fastest aircraft at the meet. It was subsequently reworked as the four-seat Bf 108B Taifun, which became a standard utility/trainer type for the Luftwaffe and was built in large quantities. More importantly, it provided important spin-off technology for the fighter.

Messerschmitt was painfully aware of the antagonism towards his project, and seemed resigned to the fact that he would not win a production contract. He saw the emerging fighter as a means to incorporate the most modern features available in one airframe rather than address the individual requirements of the customer. Consequently, the design embodied all of the features of the Bf 108, the single spar wings having automatic slots on the outer leading-edge panels and flaps on the trailing edge. The undercarriage was fully retractable and the pilot sat under a hinged canopy. The fuselage was made of light metal, a monocoque structure of roughly oval section, made in two halves joined along the centreline. None of these features was in itself novel, but the Bf 109 was the first to combine all in one fighter design.

From the start, power was intended to come from one of the powerful inverted-Vee 12-cylinder engines under development at Junkers and Daimler-Benz (although a mock-up installation of the BMW 116 was tested). In the event, the Junkers Jumo 210 was selected in the autumn of 1934, with the Daimler-Benz DB 600 as a potential for the future. At a similar time construction of the first prototype, the Bf 109a, began. By May 1935 the aircraft was essentially complete, and the aircraft rechristened Bf 109 V1 (Versuchs) in line with newly adopted German policy. Delivery of the Jumo 210 was delayed so, in a twist of fate to be fully realised five years later, the V1 was hastily fitted with a Rolls-Royce Kestrel VI engine rated at 695 hp (519 kW) for take-off.

With the civil registration D-IABI, the V1 first underwent taxiing trials with the undercarriage locked

Development and training

This aircraft was used as a trials airframe for the DB 600 installation. The unusual tunnel-type supercharger air intake was not adopted. Photographs of aircraft like this were used for propaganda.

Many of the Jumo-powered 'Berthas', 'Claras' and 'Doras' ended their days with fighter training schools. This Bf 109C was assigned to such an establishment at Zagreb in Yugoslavia.

together by means of a horizontal bar. Near the end of May 1935, the exact date unknown, senior test pilot Hans-Dietrich 'Bubi' Knoetzsch lifted the Bf 109 from the Haunstetten runway for the first time. After initial factory trials the aircraft was ferried to the Erprobungsstelle at Rechlin for service trials. These started inauspiciously, for the aircraft suffered an undercarriage collapse on arrival, and was immediately the focus of much criticism on account of its novel configuration. At the time, most fighter pilots still believed in open cockpits and the manoeuvrability of the biplane. However, flight trials soon dispelled any doubts that the test pilots may have harboured, the V1 proving to be considerably faster and better handling than the rival Heinkel He 112 V1 which was also at Rechlin.

Jumo power

At that point, the He 112 was still favourite to win the fighter contract. Its outward-retracting undercarriage gave it much better stability and its lower wing loading was regarded with less suspicion than the faster Bf 109. Nevertheless, the Rechlin trials had made the first inroads into the official antagonism towards the Messerschmitt design. Construction of the next two prototypes proceeded through late 1935, and the Jumo 210A engine became available in October 1935 for fitment to the V2. Wearing civil registration D-IUDE, the V2 joined the flight trials programme in January 1936.

Apart from the Jumo engine, which gave 680 hp (507 kW) for take-off, the V2 differed in only minor detail from the V1, although it was fitted with armament in the form of two 7.9-mm MG 17 machine-guns in the fuselage upper decking, each weapon having 500 rounds. The V3 (D-IOQY) first flew in June, this aircraft having provision for a 20-mm MG FF/M engine-mounted cannon, with corresponding cropped propeller spinner. By this time the Bf 109 was being viewed with increasing favour within the RLM. Across the English Channel the roughly comparable Supermarine Spitfire had been ordered into production, despite having first flown nine months after the Messerschmitt. Continuing trials further eroded the inertia concerning the Bf 109. Both the Bf 109 and rival He 112 were awarded contracts for 10 pre-production aircraft pending the outcome of the official trials.

Any remaining intransigence towards the Bf 109 was virtually wiped away at the official trials held at Travemünde in the autumn of 1936. A remarkable flight demonstration involving flick rolls, tailslides, 21-turn spins, terminal dives and tight turns could not fail to impress the onlookers, and, after the official figures had been pored over, the Bf 109 was announced the winner. Marginally faster in level speed and in the climb, the Bf 109 could outdive the He 112 with ease, and its aerobatic handling

was superb. The leading-edge slots, once viewed with great apprehension, functioned perfectly, giving the Bf 109 the ability to turn much tighter than the Heinkel. Roll rate was also significantly higher. There remained much argument and dissent from various political factions which supported the Heinkel programme, and indeed the He 112 was further developed for export and entered limited Luftwaffe service at the time of the Sudeten crisis.

There were, of course, other competitors in the fighter competition, but these were viewed mainly as back-up designs should both of the main contenders fail to meet specifications. The Arado Ar 80 was a low-wing monoplane which suffered from high drag and too much weight to be a serious contender, while the Focke-Wulf Fw 159 parasol monoplane suffered from undercarriage problems, and was lacking in performance anyway. Thus the field was left clear for the Bf 109, and by the autumn of 1936 some urgency was being attached to the programme as Germany's expansionist plans began to crystallise.

Development proceeded with the 10 pre-production aircraft, which were designated Bf 109B-0. All of these were assigned Versuchs numbers in the range V4 to V13, and were individually known as the Bf 109B-01, B-02 *et seq.* The V4 (D-IALY) took to the air in November 1936, armed with two MG 17 machine-guns and powered by a Jumo 210B providing 640 hp (477 kW) for five minutes

The third prototype was the first to be fitted with armament, the muzzles of the cowl-mounted MG 17s and spinner-mounted MG FF being visible here. This aircraft and its immediate successors, the V4 and V5, were sent to Spain in December 1936 for semi-operational evaluation.

Throughout its career, the Bf 109 was known for its crashworthiness in that the cockpit usually protected its occupant from all but the worst accidents. The V17, fifth of the E-series prototypes, came to grief while wearing Yugoslav fighter codes under its civil registration of D-IWKU.

Messerschmitt Bf 109

The fourth International Flying Meeting held at Zurich-Dubendorf in Switzerland between 23 July and 1 August 1937 provided the Luftwaffe with an opportunity to publicise their new capabilities, which they took with both hands. A variety of types were displayed at Zurich, including the Do 17 V8 bomber, like the Bf 109 a type also in service with the less easily publicised Legion Condor. The five Messerschmitts present came away with four of the trophies on offer in the military aircraft category, although one aircraft (the V14) was written off in the course of the competitions. The Propaganda Ministry made great claims for the Bf 109 on the strength of the performance of these unrepresentative pre-production examples, but the rest of Europe was alerted to the threat posed by the resurgent Luftwaffe and its new fighter aircraft.

D-IPKY (above) was one of two DB-powered aircraft at Zürich, immediately distinguishable from the Jumo-powered aircraft (right) by having a three-bladed propeller. The V9 (below) attended in warlike camouflage as a timely warning to the rest of Europe.

Above: The Bf 109 V7, V8 and V13 were displayed at Zurich in a high-gloss grey civilian scheme, with the swastika national insignia of the time. The V8 won two trophies – that for fastest individual circuit of the Alps, and for the best time around four laps of a 31-mile (50-km) circuit. The V13, fitted with the DB 600Aa, took the Climb and Dive trophy.

Although it was the DB 600-powered aircraft which were the main attractions at Zürich, the three Jumo aircraft won the team trophy. All three had the 210Ga engine, which had fuel injection in place of a float carburettor. The benefits of this system in combat were proven by the few Bf 109Cs which fought in Spain.

and 540 hp (403 kW) in continuous running. Both the V5 (D-IIGO) and V6 (D-IHHB) had three MG 17s, these aircraft flying in December. The third gun was mounted inside the engine block, firing through the spinner. They differed further by having variable-pitch VDM-Hamilton propellers in place of the Schwarz fixed unit of the early aircraft, and had revised nose contours with three gun cooling slots behind the spinner instead of the single opening, resulting in a marked step.

As a prelude of events to come, the V3, V4 and V5 were dispatched to Spain in December 1936 for an evaluation under operational conditions. These trials were dogged with problems, not least of which was the damage caused to the V3 by an inexperienced pilot during its first post-reassembly test flight. It was not until 14 January 1937 that Leutnant Hannes Trautloft flew the V4 up to the front line. In the ensuing days Trautloft flew the fighter on its first ever combat sorties. Although it achieved no significant success, much operational experience was gained which would smooth the full entry into service a few weeks later

of the production Bf 109Bs. At the end of January, the prototypes returned to Germany.

As soon as the fighter competition had been won, BFW began tooling up at Haunstetten for Bf 109 production, the Bf 109B being the production version (the designations Bf 109B-1 and B-2 appear to have been retrospectively applied erroneously to aircraft fitted with the Schwarz and VDM propellers, respectively). The phonetic nickname 'Bertha' was given to the first production version. BFW was also involved in the licence-manufacture of other types, and with the potential of a major fighter contract it had already become obvious that the Haunstetten facilities were not adequate. Accordingly, the Messerschmitt GmbH company was established with a factory at Regensburg, and production of the Bf 109B was soon transferred there. The design offices remained at Augsburg.

First deliveries

Production Bf 109Bs began leaving Augsburg in February 1937, with the famous Richthofen Geschwader, JG 132, earmarked as the first service recipient. However, events in the Civil War in Spain, where the nimble Russian Polikarpov I-15s and I-16s were enjoying superiority over the Heinkel He 51s of the Legion Condor, dictated that the new fighters were needed desperately overseas. A short conversion course completed, II/JG 132 personnel were immediately dispatched to Tablada, near Seville. Sixteen Bf 109Bs were shipped to Spain and reassembled in March 1937.

These 'Berthas' were powered by the uprated Jumo 210Da engine of 720 hp (537 kW), driving the original Schwarz fixed-pitch propeller. Armament was restricted to the two MG 17s with 500 rounds each, aimed using a Carl Zeiss Reflexvisier C/12C reflector sight. A 55-Imp gal (250-litre) fuel tank was fitted behind the pilot's seat, and there was provision for a short-range FuG 7 radio, although this was rarely fitted to aircraft operating in Spain.

2. Staffel der Jagdgruppe 88 was the first unit to get the Bf 109 under the command of Oberleutnant Günther Lützow, who was to achieve ace status in Spain and eventually lose his life in a Me 262 jet in April 1945 with 108 kills to his credit. Conversion to the Bf 109 progressed

remarkably smoothly, despite the considerable differences between the Messerschmitt and the He 51 biplane flown previously. By late April the Staffel was to all intents operational, but it was not until the fighting around Brunete began in July that 2./J 88 got into action.

Assigned to provide escort to Ju 52 bombers and reconnaissance aircraft, the Bf 109Bs soon became entangled with the Polikarpov fighters on the Republican side. Below about 10,000 ft (3050 m) there was little to choose between them, the I-16s enjoying greater manoeuvrability and the Bf 109s better speed and dive performance. At higher altitudes, the Bf 109s were virtually invincible, and it was swiftly learned that the large formations of Republican aircraft could be easily attacked from above and behind, picking off the rear echelons in uncatchable dives. The only recourse available to the Republicans was to lure the Bf 109s down low, but this was far from easy, and the Bf 109 immediately assumed an enviable reputation.

Combat successes

Although the Republicans claimed a Bf 109 kill as early as 8 July (almost impossible, as 2./J 88 was still many miles from the war zone), there were some losses, but there were far more victories, one of the first being credited to Leutnant Rolf Pingel, later commander of I/JG 26. The

Messerschmitt's base at Avila became the subject of increasing Republican bombing raids, so that the Staffel had to mount standing patrols and keep aircraft on alert to meet the intruders. No aircraft were lost on the ground, and by the end of July the battle of Brunete ended, allowing 2./J 88 to return to its previous base at Herrera.

In August 1937 the Nationalists launched an assault on the Santander front, accompanied by the Bf 109Bs which moved almost daily from small strip to small strip. Almost total superiority was enjoyed through this campaign, and this was further heightened by the arrival of more aircraft in September, deliveries of Bf 109Bs eventually totalling 45. Jagdgruppe 88's 1. Staffel converted to the Bf 109 in September with Lützow transferring as commander. The Gruppe itself was commanded by the Olympic gold medal pentathlete Hauptmann Gotthardt Handrick, whose personal Bf 109 wore the Olympic rings on its spinner. The end of the Santander campaign allowed the Nationalists to concentrate on the southern front, with Madrid the eventual prize, and the two Bf 109 units headed south for a period of rest before turning on Guadalajara. Oberleutnant

Above: With the Bf 109B, the Luftwaffe threw off the shackles of the past and began to develop the tactics of Blitzkrieg. This relied on technical superiority to wipe out superior numbers in a short time.

Above left: At the end of 1938, the Swiss government took delivery of the first 10 of what was to become a large number of Bf 109s in service with the Fliegertruppe. These were D models and were accepted pending the delivery of 109Es. Armament and equipment was fitted in Switzerland.

Early Luftwaffe service

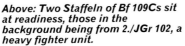

Below: Less than 30 Bf 109Bs were produced with the Schwarz fixed-pitch propeller before the VDM-Hamilton was introduced.

Above: Two Staffeln of Bf 109Cs sit at readiness, those in the background being from 2./JGr 102, a heavy fighter unit.

Below: This Bf 109C served with 1./JG 137 at Bernburg. Note the small oil cooler intake under the wing.

Above: Photographs of the Bf 109Bs used for engine development, and fitted with three-bladed propellers were distributed for propaganda.

Below: This line-up shows Bf 109Ds fresh from the Focke-Wulf factory at Bremen. The D was built in parallel with the C during 1938.

Spanish warrior

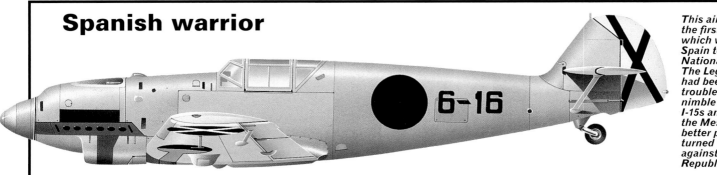

This aircraft is one of the first Bf 109Bs which were sent to Spain to join the Nationalist cause. The Legion Condor had been having trouble with the nimble Polikarpov I-15s and I-16s until the Messerschmitt's better performance turned the tables against the Republicans.

Wolfgang Schellmann arrived to take command of 2./J 88, his tally from Spain eventually totalling 12 kills.

Back in Germany, development of the Bf 109 continued. The V3 was fitted with an engine-mounted MG FF/M cannon, but the installation posed vibration problems. In March 1937 the V7 (D-IJHA) first flew, featuring a VDM-Hamilton variable-pitch propeller and a Jumo 210G direct fuel injection engine with two-stage supercharger. The VDM propeller was introduced during the Bf 109B production run, but the fuel injection engine, with the obvious benefits of maintaining full power with the aircraft in any attitude, was not available until the Bf 109C, for which the V7 and V8 (D-IPLU) served effectively as prototypes. Both of these aircraft had repositioned oil cooler intakes, although in the event the C model emerged with a deeper, redesigned radiator bath and oil cooler position as originally fitted to the B. The V8 also tested wing-mounted MG 17 guns, as the fuselage-mounted weapons had proved troublesome. These guns were to become standard on the Bf 109C-1. Both V7 and V8 were subsequently fitted with the Jumo 210Ga engine.

Daimler-Benz into the air

The V10 had started life with a Jumo 210Ga, but in June 1937 had been fitted with a Daimler-Benz DB 600Aa giving 960 hp (716 kW) for take-off and 775 hp (578 kW) in continuous running. This engine also powered the next four pre-production aircraft (V11 to V14). The Benz engine was much longer and heavier, which caused a shift in centre of gravity. This was offset by the redesign of the cooling system, which had a shallow radiator bath under the nose and two underwing radiators behind the centre of gravity. A three-bladed VDM propeller was fitted, and the aircraft had considerable local strengthening, including the undercarriage, to handle the higher weights and loads. The supercharger was aspirated through a prominent port-side intake.

Initial operations in Spain had more than proven the capabilities of the new fighter, and it had come through a

stern test with flying colours, especially given the intensity of operations during the major campaigns and the extremely hot and dusty conditions encountered by ground crews. However, such achievements could not be publicised for political reasons, and so further propaganda opportunities were sought. The 4th International Flying Meeting, held at Zürich-Dübendorf between 23 July and 1 August 1937, was the perfect answer.

Five Bf 109s were dispatched to Dübendorf, comprising three Jumo 210Ga-powered aircraft – the V7, V8 and V9 – and two with the new Daimler-Benz DB 600A, V13 (D-IPKY) and V14 (D-ISLU). Ernst Udet flew the V14 in the 'Circuit of the Alps' race but suffered an engine failure. The event was won by Major Hans Seidemann in the V8, covering the 228-mile (367-km) circuit in 56 minutes 47 seconds at 241 mph (388 km/h). The three Jumo-engined aircraft took the team prize for the fastest trio of aircraft round the same course, while Dipl.-Ing. Carl Francke won the dive and climb competition in the V13 and a four-lap 31-mile (50-km) circuit race in the V8. So impressive were the figures that several competitors dropped out part way through. As a propaganda exercise, Zürich was a total success, the Germans also stating that the fighter was in large-scale service. The name Messerschmitt and the designation Bf 109 were now on the lips of air staff planners the world over.

Of course the aircraft was only in limited service at the time of Zürich. Apart from 1./J 88 (and imminently 2./J 88), the Bf 109B was only in service with I/JG 132 at Döberitz, II/JG 132 at Jüterbog-Damm and I/JG 234 'Schlageter' at Cologne, although none of these was at full strength. In November 1937 II/JG 234 at Düsseldorf began converting to the aircraft, and at the end of the year the first aircraft from a second source – Gerhard Fieseler Werke at Kassel – was delivered. The B model was not built in great quantities and was soon replaced in service by later variants. A few lingered on in Luftwaffe service until the early part of 1940, flying with the fighter schools.

Following the Zürich triumph, the BFW management

This Bf 109B with the Olympic rings symbol on the spinner was the personal aircraft of Oberleutnant Gotthardt Handrick, Gruppenkommandeur of J 88. Handrick was the Modern Pentathlon champion at the 1936 Berlin Olympics, and later went on to command JG 26. In front of the cockpit is the starting handle for the Jumo 210Da engine.

Right: On 4 December 1937 one of the first production Bf 109Bs which had been sent to the Legion Condor (6-15) force-landed out of fuel behind Republican lines. The aircraft was evaluated in Spain by a French mission, and flown by test pilot Capitaine Vladimir Rozanoff. Unfortunately, the (very favourable) report was suppressed for diplomatic reasons and this windfall proved of little practical significance.

strove for further international glory and on 11 November 1937 Dr.-Ing. Hermann Wurster flew the V13 to the world landplane speed record, setting a mark of 379.38 mph (611 km/h) in four runs along a 1.86-mile (3-km) straight course at low level. The aircraft had been specially prepared with a boosted version of the Daimler-Benz DB 601 engine and featured an elongated, streamlined spinner, strengthened cockpit canopy and a polished skin to minimise friction. To capitalise on the successes of the speed record and Zürich, the directors of BFW agreed on 11 July 1938 to the formal renaming of the company as Messerschmitt AG, with by then Dr.-Ing. Willy Messerschmitt as Chairman and Managing Director.

Development after Zürich concentrated on the next production model, the Bf 109C 'Clara'. The V9 was fitted with 20-mm MG FF cannon in the wings in place of the MG 17s. The cannon were mounted further outboard than the MG 17s, and had 60-round drums inboard of the weapons. The breeches were covered by a blister fairing on the lower side of the wing. This armament was not adopted initially for the Bf 109C-1, which had two nose-mounted MG 17s with 500 rounds each, and two in the wings with 420 rounds each. The engine was the Jumo 210Ga with revised exhaust slots and the 'Clara' had the deeper radiator bath. The C-2 was a projected model with a fifth MG 17 mounted in the engine but was not proceeded with. The C-3 was the designation of C-1s retrofitted at the factory with the wing-mounted MG FF cannon originally tested on the V9.

Deliveries began in the early spring of 1938, with I/JG 132 converting during the summer. A small number of C-1s was shipped to Spain, but production was very limited,

the majority of the aircraft produced at the time being the Bf 109D 'Dora', which was built in parallel. This version entered service in early 1938 with I/JG 131 at Jesau, and many served subsequently with the heavy fighter units.

If anything, the 'Dora' was a retrograde step, for it reverted to the Jumo 210Da engine with carburettor. It did, however, have four-gun armament. For many years, the Bf 109D designation was thought to apply to aircraft powered by the DB 600, but no production aircraft had this powerplant. The myth has been perpetuated in many publications to this day, and many photographs which have appeared as being Bf 109Ds were actually early Bf 109Es, while many labelled as 'Claras' were really 'Doras'.

Production Bf 109D-1s were also built at Erla Maschinenwerk in Leipzig and by Focke-Wulf Flugzeugbau at Bremen, second-source production kicking in during early 1938. In August 1938 a batch of five was sent to 3./J 88 in Spain, and the D-1 also attracted export orders from Hungary for three, to be used for evaluation purposes. Most potential customers were far more excited by the prospect of the forthcoming Daimler-Benz-powered version, although Switzerland took delivery of 10 Bf 109Ds for familiarisation prior to receiving the DB-powered Bf 109E. The first of the Swiss 'Doras' was delivered on 17 December 1938, and the batch was fitted with locally-supplied 7.45-mm machine-guns (480 rounds for fuselage guns; 418 for wing guns). The Swiss 'Doras' served alongside the Bf 109Es until finally scrapped in 1949.

Captured in Spain

This account had left the Bf 109Bs of 1. and 2./J 88 having headed south from the Nationalist victories in the north for a recuperation period before the next major phase of the Spanish Civil War. During the late summer and autumn of 1937 there was little activity in the air save for a few bombing raids which were escorted by the Bf 109Bs. This situation lasted until 15 December. However, on 4 December, a significant event occurred. During a raid on a Republican airfield, one Bf 109B, piloted by Feldwebel Polenz, ran out of fuel and had to land on a road behind Republican lines. The aircraft was still fitted with the original Schwarz fixed-pitch propeller, but the Republicans had nevertheless acquired an intact example of the fighter which was causing them so much anguish in the air. At a similar time the Republican forces had also acquired an intact Heinkel He 111 bomber.

Hearing of the Messerschmitt's capture, the French air

Above: Bf 109s were given the type number 6 and numbered consecutively in Nationalist service. 6-52, one of five Ds in Spain, wears the famous 'Zylinder Hut' (top hat) insignia of 3./J 88, subsequently worn on the unit's Bf 109Es, and later adopted by a number of Condor veterans as a personal insignia.

Top left: In order to counter improved versions of the Polikarpov I-16 then entering service, 3./J 88 was re-equipped with Bf 109Cs in April 1938. One of the five aircraft that arrived at that time, marked Luchs *(Lynx) is seen here sporting three kill markings.*

Above left: Four members of the Legion Condor pose with one of the Bf 109Ds.

Under the nom de guerre *of the Legion Condor, the Luftwaffe honed the men, equipment and tactics that were to prove so effective in the wider European conflict to come. The Bf 109D was not vastly superior to the contemporary Republican fighters, but better tactics and formations, such as the four-aircraft* Schwarm, *meant that the German pilots would usually gain the upper hand against the enthusiastic, but less disciplined government pilots.*

Original plans for the acquisition of the 109 by the Luftwaffe called for production interchangeability between the Jumo 210 and DB 600. In fact, only three machines (including the V11 seen here) were to be DB 600 powered as initial production was slated for bombers. By the time the DB 600 had proved its suitability as a fighter engine, the improved DB 601 was almost available.

The German press made the most of the V13's achievement, the first speed record to be held by a German landplane, and grand claims were made for potential higher speeds at altitude.

attaché signalled Paris and clandestine overtures were made to the Republican forces to seek permission to evaluate the two captured aircraft. As the French had recently sealed the Franco-Spanish border, preventing the flow of Soviet war materiel into Spain, it was in the interests of the Republicans to appease the French in order to reopen the border, so approval was granted.

Arriving in Barcelona on 31 January 1938, the French mission, which included the chief test pilot of the Centre d'Essais en Vol, Capitaine Rozanoff, travelled to Sabadell airfield where an exhaustive study was made of the two types, Rozanoff undertaking many flights. The ensuing reports were very detailed, but were labelled top secret, and were not distributed to the French aviation industry. As would be seen during the Battle of France, the industry had indeed a lot to learn from the Messerschmitt Bf 109.

At the time of Polenz's loss, the Nationalists were preparing for a major offensive, but the Republicans surprised them by opening the battle for Teruél on 15 December. The town was not recaptured by Nationalist forces until 21 February 1938, and the battle involved much air activity. Jagdgruppe 88 deployed from the Guadalajara front to Calamocha, where night-time temperatures were so low that the engines had to be started regularly through the night to prevent them seizing.

In the air, the Bf 109s continued to prove their mastery. On 7 February, a group of J 88 aircraft, led by

Gruppenkommandeur Handrick, waded into an unprotected formation of 22 Tupolev SB bombers. Although a few Polikarpov I-16s arrived later, the rout was completed in five minutes with Bf 109s shooting down 10 bombers and two I-16s for no loss. Also that day, Leutnant Wilhelm Balthasar (later to command JG 2 'Richthofen') was scrambled from Calamocha to intercept a group of SBs attempting to bomb his base. Three bombers and a fighter fell to his guns in just six minutes, the greatest individual success of the conflict. By the end of the Teruél battle, Jagdgruppe 88 had scored 30 kills with no losses.

Soon after, on 9 March, the Nationalists opened their long-planned offensive, which eventually succeeded in cutting Spain in two when ground echelons reached the Mediterranean on 15 April. The Messerschmitts moved with the ground forces but encountered increasingly stiff opposition. The He 51s could hardly operate at all, and the ravages of constant operations in primitive conditions and woeful spares shortages combined to sap considerably the might of the Legion Condor as a whole. Deliveries of fresh aircraft from Germany were small and sporadic.

Battle of the Ebro
In June, 3./J 88 was eventually withdrawn from the battle to begin its re-equipment with the Bf 109. Its commander, Oberleutnant Adolf Galland, returned home after his tour of duty and was replaced by one of the finest fighter pilots of all time: Oberleutnant Werner Mölders. Allowing partial re-equipment for the Staffel was the arrival in April of five Bf 109Cs, with four-gun armament. This coincided with the delivery to the Republicans of the four-gun I-16 Type 10. The air war continued, and, although the Bf 109 still had the upper hand, losses mounted. In early July, 3./J 88 returned to the fray, Mölders scoring his first kill, an I-16, on 15 July. At the end of the month the second Ebro campaign opened, heralding some of the fiercest fighting of the war. The Messerschmitts were heavily tasked with bomber support, the targets in the main being the bridges across the Ebro river which were usually repaired again the night following their daytime destruction.

In early August five Bf 109D-1s arrived, allowing 3./J 88

V13 record-breaker

The Bf 109 V13, which had appeared at Zürich in 1937 with a Jumo engine, was later that year fitted with a special sprint version of the DB 601 for an assault on the world speed record for landplanes. In addition to the new powerplant, which was rated at around 1,700 hp (1270 kW), the aircraft had a number of aerodynamic refinements, including a streamlined canopy, no pitot tube and all gaps taped over. The aircraft was stripped of paint and the skin was highly polished in preparation for the record attempt in November of 1937. On 11 November Dr.-Ing. Hermann Wurster made six timed runs along a 3-km (1.86-mile) stretch of the Augsburg-Kaufbeuren railway line at an average speed of 610.95 km/h (379.6 mph), breaking the previous record by 44 km/h (27 mph).

'Emil' on the eve of war

Left: This Bf 109E-3 was operated by II/JG 54 on the outbreak of war. The Bf 109 entered the war with no armour and a lightweight windshield, despite the lessons of Spain.

Right: Upon the outbreak of war, many units were redesignated. 2./JG 20's black cat was transferred to 8./JG 51.

Left: III/JG 51 was one of the units involved in the Polish campaign and moved to eastern Germany just prior to the outbreak of hostilities.

Above: Frequent exercises were undertaken in preparation for fast-moving campaigns. Aircraft were regularly serviced in portable canvas hangars.

to reach full strength. The second Ebro campaign lasted through to mid-November, and the Legion Condor had largely achieved air supremacy in early September, although a few losses were still incurred. It was during the second Ebro campaign that Mölders introduced the *vierfingerschwarm* formation. Until this point the Legion had employed a two-ship *rotte* as its main formation, the two aircraft roughly 200 yards apart. By doubling up the formation and adding longitudinal spacing, Mölders at a stroke vastly increased the flexibility of the formation. This was of inestimable value during fighter sweeps, and the 'finger four' became the basic formation of fighter tactics, used to this day.

Mölders had scored his 14th and final kill on 3 November, having shot down 10 I-16s and four I-15s to become the Legion Condor's leading pilot of the war. Wolfgang Schellmann was in second place with 12 and Harro Harder was in third with 11. After the second Ebro campaign there was a period of rest, but the successful outcome had pushed the war irrevocably in favour of the Nationalists. Nevertheless, one more major offensive was required, and the Legion was exhausted and depleted to the point where it could no longer be expected to fight on without fresh supplies of equipment. This was to arrive in the form of the Bf 109E, but too late, as recounted later.

Throughout the year of 1938, the Luftwaffe had undergone a massive expansion in its home forces. On 13 March 1938, the date of the Austrian Anschluss, the following Gruppen had converted or were converting to

the Bf 109: I/JG 131 at Jesau, I/JG 132 at Döberitz, II/JG 132 at Jüterbog-Damm, I/JG 234 at Cologne, II/JG 234 at Düsseldorf and I/JG 334 at Wiesbaden. With the planned annexation of the Sudetenland, after which the Germans feared action from France and Britain, there was a pressing need to boost the domestic air forces. Large numbers of new Gruppen were formed, equipped largely with obsolescent types, and production of the Bf 109 was stepped up. However, the results of this increased production, which now included Arado at Warnemünde in addition to Messerschmitt, Erla, Focke-Wulf and Fieseler, could not be absorbed by the Luftwaffe's operational units. By way of illustration, the Luftwaffe possessed fewer than 300 Bf 109s on 1 August 1938, but by 19 September no fewer than 583 were on strength, although many were not with operational units. All were of the Jumo-powered B, C or D variants, for delays with the Daimler-Benz engine had dented plans for the rapid fielding of the Bf 109E.

On 1 August 1938 a naval Bf 109 unit was also established at Kiel-Holtenau. Equipped with Bf 109Bs, 6. Trägerstaffel/186 was formed to begin the training of pilots destined to serve on the Reich's first aircraft-carrier, the *Graf Zeppelin*, which was launched on 8 December 1938. In mid-1939, 5. Trägerstaffel/186 was formed on the Bf 109B, and both units were to have eventually re-equipped

Above: As war approached, the tempo of exercises and their realism increased. Here an NCO shouts orders and a 'dead' mechanic lies beneath a Bf 109E-1, as his colleagues carry out field repairs. The devil marking is a personal symbol of a type popular up until the early months of the war.

Below left: Yugoslavia was one of the few pre-war export customers of the Bf 109. The 6th Fighter Regiment of the Yugoslav Royal Air Force received its first 109E-3s in late 1939.

Below: A pair of JG 51 Bf 109Cs makes a scramble take-off. The dark camouflages of the time were primarily for concealment on the ground.

Above: Two aircraft of JG 27 are seen at Boenninghard, near Wesel, before the battle for France. The mottling was not common until the latter part of the Battle of Britain.

Below: Ground crew reload the wing- and engine-mounted machine-guns on a Bf 109C of III/JG 51. Scrupulous cleanliness was needed for this task.

Above: An early war picture of a JG 27 Bf 109E. The oversized wing markings were a recognition aid for German forces, following a number of unfortunate incidents early in the war.

Left: As the war approached and then began, individual markings flourished on the predominantly dark green Bf 109s of the Luftwaffe. This E-3 seen in Poland during early September 1939, wore the cartoon character 'Max' of the strip 'Max and Moritz' on the starboard cowl, with 'Moritz' on the other side.

with a specialist carrier variant, of which more later. Trägergruppe 186, which also included Ju 87s, was to have been the first of two carrier air groups, the second being earmarked for the carrier *Peter Strasser*.

A major reorganisation of the Luftwaffe took place on 1 November 1938, with the fighter force being divided into *leichten* (light) and *schwere* (heavy) fighter groups, although the latter were rechristened Zerstörergruppen on 1 January 1939. Virtually all of the 14 light groups were flying the Bf 109B or C, although I/JG 130 now also had Bf 109Ds. The seven heavy groups had Bf 109Bs, Cs and Ds, although many subsequently converted to the main Zerstörer type, the Messerschmitt Bf 110.

Enter 'Emil'

At the beginning of 1939 the first Bf 109E 'Emils' began rolling from the production lines with Daimler-Benz engines. The original Luftwaffe requirements that had spawned the Bf 109 had strongly recommended the ability of its new fighter to be powered by either the Jumo or DB 600 engine, and Messerschmitt had designed the Bf 109 accordingly. With the promise of greater power than the Jumo, the DB 600 was always the favoured engine in the early days, but it was at a later stage of development, and could not have been ready by the time that Bf 109 production started.

Daimler-Benz had started work on the DB 600 as far back as 1932, but it was not until June 1937 that one of the DB 600Aa engines had been fitted to a Bf 109. As

The first of 40 Bf 109Es to arrive in Spain before the end of the Civil War arrived at the beginning of 1939. 6-91 was the first of these aircraft, whose arrival allowed the Spanish to inherit the older 109s still in service.

recounted earlier, this was the B-07/V10 airframe, which had originally flown under Jumo power. With its new powerplant, it effectively became the prototype for the Bf 109E production series. Subsequent development aircraft were also powered by Daimler-Benz engines, the V11, V12, V13 and V14 all being powered by the DB 600Aa, although a special DB 601 was subsequently fitted to V13 for the speed record attempt.

DB 601s powered the next development aircraft, starting with the V15 (D-IPHR) and V16 (D-IPGS). The DB 601 was very similar to the DB 600 apart from a few vital characteristics. The main one was that it had fuel injection instead of a float carburettor, allowing negative *g* flight and also improving fuel economy. Compression ratio was raised slightly, and there were improvements made to the supercharger. Power output was increased slightly, the engine being rated at 1,175 hp (877 kW) for take-off and 990 hp (739 kW) at 12,140 ft (3700 m). The improvements did themselves throw up some difficulties, which deferred quantity production until late in 1938. This delay consequently postponed production of the Bf 109E, resulting in the much larger than anticipated number of Jumo-powered Bf 109Ds being produced.

Bomber priority

DB 600s could have powered Bf 109s much earlier, but there were three main reasons why this did not occur, the principle reason being that bomber production was accorded priority in the mid-1930s, and the DB 600s were mainly produced for Heinkel He 111 production. When, in 1938, priority moved to fighter aircraft, the DB 601 was nearing maturity, so production of the DB 600 was geared down to concentrate efforts on the DB 601. Lastly, the benefits of the fuel injection system of the DB 601 were seen as great enough to be worth the extra delay. With overall dimensions virtually unchanged, the DB 601 posed no mounting problems in the Bf 109, the hard work of rearranging the cooling system to maintain centre of gravity position having already been undertaken for the DB 600-powered pre-production aircraft.

With the DB 601 fitted, the Bf 109E-1 gained an

The 'Emil' arrived just too late to see action in the Spanish Civil War, although 2. Staffel der Jagdgruppe 88 had just converted when the war ended.

immediate improvement in performance, maintaining its position as the world's most advanced fighter. The extra performance was offset by a degradation in turning circle and high-speed handling caused by the extra wing loading, but in general the Bf 109E retained the superb handling and manoeuvrability of its Jumo-engined predecessors. Take-off and climb performance was exhilarating and, although the stall speed was relatively high, the characteristics were benign, with ample buffet warning of the impending stall. Spin characteristics were exemplary.

The performance of the Bf 109E-1 was outstanding. Company test data compiled in early 1939 revealed a maximum speed of 311 mph (500 km/h) at sea level rising to 354 mph (570 km/h) at 16,405 ft (5000 m). At 19,685 ft (6000 m), the Bf 109's 88-Imp gal (400-litre) tank gave an endurance of over an hour at maximum continuous power. A climb to 3,280 ft (1000 m) could be made in just 60 seconds, while 19,685 ft (6000 m) could be reached in 6.3

minutes. The ceiling was set at 36,090 ft (11 000 m). Take-off run to clear a 66-ft (20-m) obstacle was 1,050 ft (320 m), and landing from the same altitude could be achieved in 2,250 ft (685 m). The fuel injection allowed the Bf 109E-1 to capitalise on the aircraft's already legendary dive performance by making rapid transitions from level to diving flight with no interruption of power.

An unusual feature was the drooping ailerons, which were interconnected with the flaps. When the latter were lowered, the ailerons drooped 20°, with the corresponding pitch change being offset by a change in tailplane incidence.

While the Bf 109 was frequently used in the ground-attack role in Spain, bombs were not carried by the fighter in this war, despite the impression given by this photo which shows bombs awaiting loading into He 111Bs. Bomber and fighter units frequently shared airfields in Spain.

Battle of France

Most of the Bf 109-equipped Jagdgruppen were assembled for the Western Campaign, which swept through much of France and the Low Countries. The Bf 109s maintained air superiority over the defenders with some ease, although attrition was high and fresh supplies of aircraft were virtually non-existent.

Above: These are 'Emils' of III/JG 26 pictured at Villacoublay near Paris, where the Gruppe's rapid advance halted in late June as resistance collapsed.

Below: The Jagdgruppen withdrew from France to make good their losses before the next battle. Here a France-based E-3 awaits the High Command's next move.

The rapid advance across the Low Countries implied operations from airfields with few or damaged facilities. These Bf 109Es of 6./JG 27 were parked in the open, but under camouflage nets, at St Trond in Belgium in May 1940.

Messerschmitt Bf 109

Above: With the RAF on the defensive, the threat of attack on the Luftwaffe bases in the Pas de Calais was limited. Nevertheless, these ground crew are building blast pens for their charges, and thinking of the day soon to come when the war will be over.

Right: Typical early Battle of Britain colours are displayed on these II/JG 27 Bf 109E-3s. At this time, the unit was based at Crepon in western France as part of Luftflotte 3.

Werner Mölders (below) was given command of JG 51 during the Battle, and he became one of only three pilots to be awarded the Oakleaves to the Knights Cross during this period. Note the head armour fitted to the canopy of Mölders' 'Emil'.

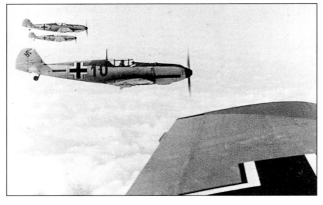

Landing speed was 78 mph (125 km/h).

Armament of the E-1 was the same as that of the D-1, comprising two synchronised MG 17 machine-guns in the fuselage upper decking, staggered slightly to accommodate the ammunition feed chutes, and two unsynchronised MG 17s in the wings. The latter each had 500 rounds, while the fuselage guns had 1,000 rounds each. The same Revi C/12C sight was fitted, and the FuG 7 radio was standard, this having a range of about 40 miles (65 km).

Following closely behind the E-1 on the production line was the Bf 109E-3, which retained the fuselage MG 17s but replaced the wing guns with the 20-mm MG FF cannon, each weapon having 60 rounds. Following satisfactory trials with the Bf 109C-3, the Luftwaffe came to favour the heavy throw weight and destructive power of this weapon

Above: This is one of a number of pictures, widely published in Germany, of Luftwaffe aircraft purportedly operating off the coast of England. In fact the scene was more likely in France. The 'finger four' developed in Spain was superior to the RAF formations of the early part of the battle.

despite its slow rate of fire. Dubbed the 'Kanonenmaschine', the E-3 was generally regarded as the best of the early generation Bf 109s – no other variant was to enjoy such a great margin of superiority over its rivals. The E-2 designation was applied to an E-1 with a hub-mounted gun, but this variant was not produced.

Bf 109E deliveries

With the delivery of the first DB 601s in late 1938, production of the Bf 109E-1 got under way. Due to pressing military needs and the political situation, some of the first 'Emils' went to Spain. The Nationalists still urgently required new equipment following the second Ebro campaign. Aircraft such as the Bf 109 had been in short supply as the Luftwaffe needed to build up its home strength in preparation for the Sudeten annexation. However, the urgent needs of the Nationalists could be exploited by Germany to its own advantage, with the Spaniards paying for the re-equipment of the Legion Condor while also securing the supply of strategic materials such as iron ore to fuel the German industries.

The Spaniards themselves also wished to re-equip their fighter units, which had been using the Fiat CR.32 biplane, and to that end they received 17 Heinkel He 112Bs and a promise for the delivery of Bf 109s. In October 1938 three Spanish pilots joined 3./J 88 to gain experience on the

Aces of the Battle of Britain

Below left: Highest-scoring ace of the Battle of France, Wilhelm Balthasar (centre) chats with two other notable pilots, JG 3 Kommandeur Gunther Lutzow (left) and Egon Troha, the Staffelkapitan of 9./JG 3. Balthasar's aircraft, probably an E-4, sports 39 victory bars, 14 of them with downward-pointing arrows, indicating kills achieved against aircraft on the ground.

Horst Tietzen (below) was the Staffelkapitan of 5./JG 51 during the Battle of Britain and had brought his personal score to 18 (including seven victories in Spain) by the time this picture was taken. He had added two further 'kills' by 18 August 1940 when he was shot down into the English Channel by Hurricane Mk Is of No. 501 Squadron and killed.

Adolf Galland (below) was one of the most brilliant fighter leaders of the war, and rose rapidly through the ranks until his differences with Göring finally put a cap on his career. His Bf 109s often had non-standard additions such as a telescopic gunsight and a cigar lighter. During the battle he was promoted from leading III/JG 26 to commanding the Geschwader.

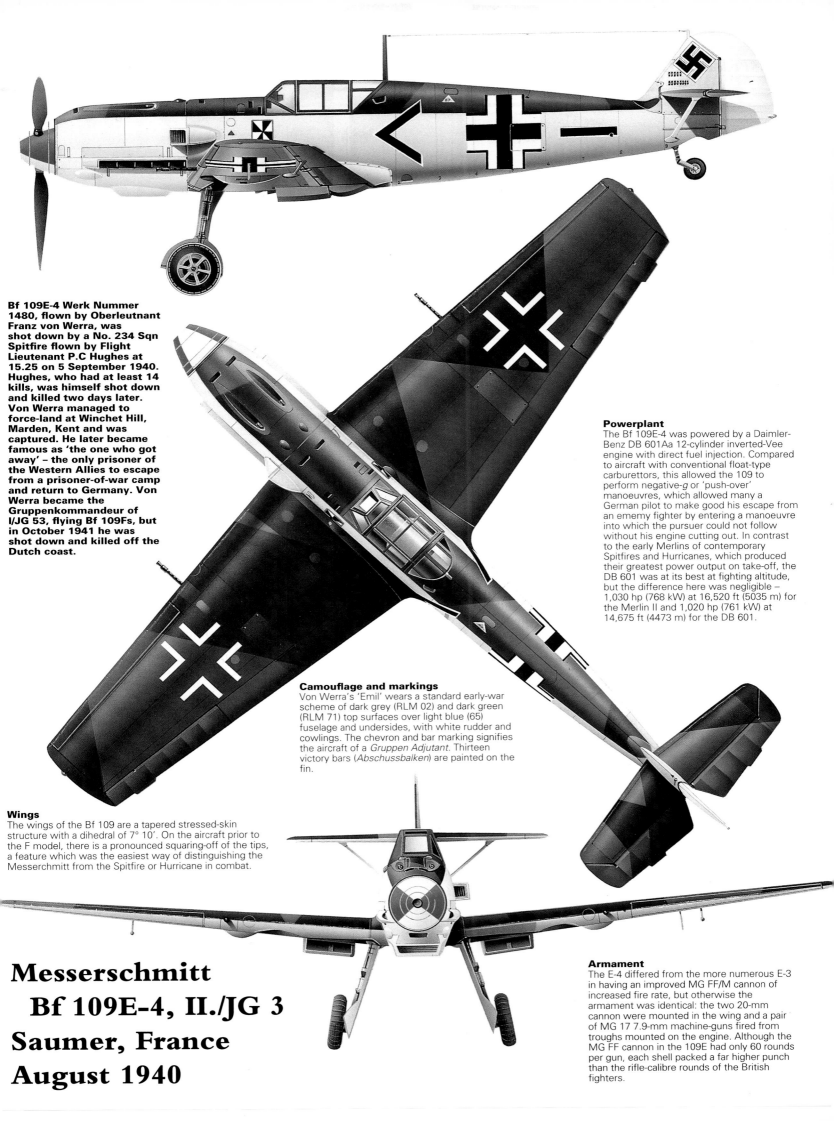

Bf 109E-4 Werk Nummer 1480, flown by Oberleutnant Franz von Werra, was shot down by a No. 234 Sqn Spitfire flown by Flight Lieutenant P.C Hughes at 15.25 on 5 September 1940. Hughes, who had at least 14 kills, was himself shot down and killed two days later. Von Werra managed to force-land at Winchet Hill, Marden, Kent and was captured. He later became famous as 'the one who got away' – the only prisoner of the Western Allies to escape from a prisoner-of-war camp and return to Germany. Von Werra became the Gruppenkommandeur of I/JG 53, flying Bf 109Fs, but in October 1941 he was shot down and killed off the Dutch coast.

Powerplant
The Bf 109E-4 was powered by a Daimler-Benz DB 601Aa 12-cylinder inverted-Vee engine with direct fuel injection. Compared to aircraft with conventional float-type carburettors, this allowed the 109 to perform negative-*g* or 'push-over' manoeuvres, which allowed many a German pilot to make good his escape from an ememy fighter by entering a manoeuvre into which the pursuer could not follow without his engine cutting out. In contrast to the early Merlins of contemporary Spitfires and Hurricanes, which produced their greatest power output on take-off, the DB 601 was at its best at fighting altitude, but the difference here was negligible – 1,030 hp (768 kW) at 16,520 ft (5035 m) for the Merlin II and 1,020 hp (761 kW) at 14,675 ft (4473 m) for the DB 601.

Camouflage and markings
Von Werra's 'Emil' wears a standard early-war scheme of dark grey (RLM 02) and dark green (RLM 71) top surfaces over light blue (65) fuselage and undersides, with white rudder and cowlings. The chevron and bar marking signifies the aircraft of a *Gruppen Adjutant*. Thirteen victory bars (*Abschussbalken*) are painted on the fin.

Wings
The wings of the Bf 109 are a tapered stressed-skin structure with a dihedral of 7° 10'. On the aircraft prior to the F model, there is a pronounced squaring-off of the tips, a feature which was the easiest way of distinguishing the Messerschmitt from the Spitfire or Hurricane in combat.

Messerschmitt Bf 109E-4, II./JG 3 Saumer, France August 1940

Armament
The E-4 differed from the more numerous E-3 in having an improved MG FF/M cannon of increased fire rate, but otherwise the armament was identical: the two 20-mm cannon were mounted in the wing and a pair of MG 17 7.9-mm machine-guns fired from troughs mounted on the engine. Although the MG FF cannon in the 109E had only 60 rounds per gun, each shell packed a far higher punch than the rifle-calibre rounds of the British fighters.

Messerschmitt Bf 109E-4 Gruppenkommandeur's aircraft I. Gruppe, Jagdgeschwader 3 Grandvilliers, France, August 1940

Bf 109s in the Battle of Britain

After supporting the Wehrmacht in its Blitzkrieg through the Low Countries and France (to say nothing of the offensives in Poland and Norway), the Jagdflieger pilots were experienced, battle-hardened and confident. After the fall of France, Britain refused to make peace, and an aerial offensive against Britain became inevitable. Adlerangriff (the attack of the eagles) was to be launched on 10 August (Adlertag, or eagle day), although fierce attacks began even earlier, with a major air battle on 8 August. Adlertag itself was delayed until 13 August by bad weather. Thus started the Battle of Britain. While the RAF's Spitfire and Hurricane squadrons contained relatively few pilots with combat experience, the pilots were quick learners, and inadequate pre-war tactics were soon modified or abandoned. The Bf 109 squadrons started the battle below establishment, depleted by attrition. Furthermore, the RAF was equipped with Spitfires and Hurricanes, which were in many respects equal to or better than the Bf 109E, and enjoyed the great advantage of being controlled by radar. The Luftwaffe soon found itself confronting its most formidable foe to date. While the Luftwaffe's Bf 109Es were fighting at the very limit of their range, the RAF fighters had fuel to linger and fight, and even to pursue their retreating enemies. When a Bf 109 was shot down, its pilot was inevitably killed or captured, while downed RAF pilots were usually recovered to fly and fight again – sometimes the same day. The battle was closely fought until the Luftwaffe was ordered to switch from attacks against RAF airfields to attacks against Britain's cities, and until the Bf 109s were ordered to stick close to the bombers they were escorting. For the first time, the Luftwaffe's Bf 109Es were assigned what was essentially a strategic role (the destruction of the RAF) and, as the battle progressed, the Luftwaffe began to find itself getting the worst of it – an unfamiliar and alarming experience. The Luftwaffe lost 610 of its Bf 109s (and 235 Bf 110s) on operations, while the RAF lost 631 Hurricanes and 403 Spitfires (272 and 219 to the Bf 109, respectively). The honours in single-seat fighter combat were as near to even as made no difference; this represented an RAF victory, since it lost far fewer pilots, and since the British industry was able to make up attrition more rapidly than was the German.

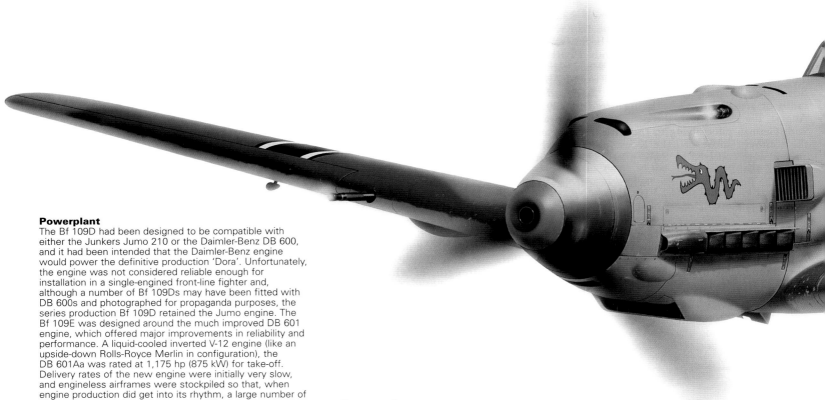

Powerplant

The Bf 109D had been designed to be compatible with either the Junkers Jumo 210 or the Daimler-Benz DB 600, and it had been intended that the Daimler-Benz engine would power the definitive production 'Dora'. Unfortunately, the engine was not considered reliable enough for installation in a single-engined front-line fighter and, although a number of Bf 109Ds may have been fitted with DB 600s and photographed for propaganda purposes, the series production Bf 109D retained the Jumo engine. The Bf 109E was designed around the much improved DB 601 engine, which offered major improvements in reliability and performance. A liquid-cooled inverted V-12 engine (like an upside-down Rolls-Royce Merlin in configuration), the DB 601Aa was rated at 1,175 hp (875 kW) for take-off. Delivery rates of the new engine were initially very slow, and engineless airframes were stockpiled so that, when engine production did get into its rhythm, a large number of Bf 109Es were delivered very quickly. Some of these aircraft went to the Legion Condor in Spain, and others were delivered to home-based Jagdgruppen. Thirty were delivered to the Swiss Fliegertruppen from 14 April 1939, providing the Reich with much-needed hard currency.

Although the Jumo 210Da-powered Bf 109D-1 retained a two-bladed VDM propeller (a licence-built Hamilton variable-pitch prop), the Bf 109E-1 introduced a new three-bladed prop. The spinner still had the hollow centre designed to allow carriage of the engine-mounted 20-mm cannon, but this was still far from being reliable enough to be adopted for use. Early Bf 109E-3s had the troublesome cannon fitted, but they again proved unsuccessful, and the Bf 109E-4 had no provision for the cannon, although the 'holed' spinner was often fitted. Some Bf 109Es even had a new spinner, in which case the former cannon port was faired over. The nose contours of the Bf 109E were completely changed, with the small oil cooler (fitted below the port inner wing of Jumo-powered '109s) moved to a position below the nose, while the much larger 'chin' radiator was replaced by a pair of underwing glycol radiators, just aft of the main undercarriage bays. Aft of the engine firewall, the Bf 109E was little different to the Bf 109D-1, which had been strengthened in anticipation of the higher weights which could have been possible with the DB 600 engine. When it first appeared, the Bf 109E enjoyed a marked performance advantage over the contemporary Spitfire Mk I, which at the time had a two-pitch, twin-bladed propeller. By the time the Bf 109E-4 was in service, Spitfires all had constant-speed three-bladed propellers and the performance advantage was eroded.

Armament

During the early part of its career, the Bf 109 was given progressively heavier armament. The prototype was originally specified with two cowling-mounted 7.92-mm MG 17 machine-guns (each with 500 rounds of ammunition), with a third later added between the banks of cylinders to fire through the propeller hub. This provided a useful concentration of fire, while the central gun did not need to be harmonised. Unfortunately, Messerschmitt were never able to make the centre-mounted gun work properly: it produced too much vibration for the engine, while the engine produced too much heat for the gun. The Russians and Americans produced more successful 'through-the-hub' cannon installations on the P-39 Airacobra and Yak-3/-9 series. A heavier 20-mm MG FF cannon was tested in the central position by the Bf 109C-1, but proved no more successful than the engine-mounted MG 17. The C-3 model instead received an extra pair of 7.92-mm MG 17 machine-guns in the wings, just outboard of each mainwheel bay, each with 420 rounds of ammunition. Accuracy was improved in the Bf 109D through the addition of a Revi C/12D gunsight. The Bf 109E-1 standardised on the armament of four MG 17s, while the E-2 and E-3 tried to re-introduce the engine-mounted cannon (with 200 rounds). Some E-3s were delivered with the cannon, but these were soon removed. Most E-3s had a revised armament wherein wing-mounted MG FF cannon (with 60 rpg) replaced the MG 17 machine-guns but the cowling-mounted pair of MG 17s was retained, albeit with ammunition capacity for these guns doubled. Aircraft with the wing-mounted cannon had small bulges on the underside of the wings, covering the weapon's larger breech blocks, and the cannon muzzles projected slightly from the leading edge. The Bf 109E-5 was a tactical reconnaissance version and had the wing cannon removed, with an RB 21/18 cannon in the fuselage adjacent to the trailing edge. The Bf 109E-6 was another recce version, with four MG 17s. The Bf 109E-4 was the first variant of the 109 to see service in the fighter-bomber (Jabo) role. The Bf 109E-4/B used a rudimentary ETC 500 bomb rack between the mainwheels, capable of carrying a single 250-kg or 500-kg bomb. Trials by Erprobungsgruppe 210's 3. Staffel proved very successful, and each Bf 109 Gruppe was ordered to convert some of its Staffeln to the Jabo role, while Lehrgeschwader 2's II. Gruppe traded its ageing Henschel 123s for Bf 109E-4/Bs. The /B designation suffix was applied to all Bf 109Es used as fighter-bombers, resulting in Bf 109E-1/Bs and Bf 109E-3/B designations. The Bf 109E-7 differed from earlier versions of the 'Emil' in that it could carry a 300-litre (66-Imp gal) fuel tank in place of the underfuselage bomb. The E-7/U2 had extra armour on the oil cooler, radiators and fuel pump. The Bf 109E-9 was a reconnaissance aircraft, based on the re-engined Bf 109E-8; it lacked wing cannon and but did have an Rb 50/30 camera in the rear fuselage.

Combat capability

Allied pilots who flew captured examples of the 'Emil' found the aircraft quite a culture shock, with its tiny, uncomfortable and cluttered cockpit, from which they found it hard to get a decent all-round view. The cockpit was so cramped that it even restricted the amount of stick force which the pilot could apply (especially in roll), so that the Spitfire pilot could apply 60 lb of force while the Bf 109 pilot could manage 40 lb at most. The situation was worsened by the more limited throw of the Bf 109's control column. The aircraft was faster in the climb than an early Spitfire (at least up to 20,000 ft) and its fuel injection system gave it an advantage in the entry into a dive – the Bf 109E pilot could simply push the aircraft into a negative *g* bunt, while the Spitfire pilot had to half-roll and pull through with positive *g* to avoid the float carburettors cutting off fuel from the engine. This was of little tactical significance except as an escape manoeuvre, and a high-speed dive was dangerous for the Bf 109 pilot since the aircraft was reluctant to pull out quickly without stalling, and since the aircraft could barely roll at high speed. The German aircraft had a poor turn radius due to its high wing loading and poor control responsiveness, and it stalled readily under *g*. At low speeds, the leading-edge slots could deploy without warning, causing aileron snatching. With the aircraft turning tightly, teetering on the brink of the stall, a Spitfire or Hurricane could follow with ease, without showing any sign of the approaching stall. If bounced by a Bf 109, the Spitfire or Hurricane could escape by making almost any hard manoeuvre, whereas, if the tables were turned, the Bf 109 pilot had little option but to climb fast and steep, or bunt into a very steep dive. As a gunnery platform, the Bf 109 pilot was hampered by not having a rudder trimmer. At anything but the most modest speeds he had to hold on a significant amount of rudder to avoid sideslipping, and this rapidly became tiring. Allied evaluation of the Bf 109E tended to considerably reduce Allied pilots' fear of the aircraft, which was revealed to be 'just another fighter', with its own unique advantages and disadvantages, but far from being the unbeatable machine once thought.

Camouflage

The Luftwaffe's Messerschmitt Bf 109s originally wore dark green upper surfaces with light blue-grey (Hellblau) undersides, but these colours were replaced by a disruptive two-tone green splinter camouflage on the top surfaces. The two shades of green were so close to one another in tone that they looked almost like a single colour, and weathering further reduced the differentiation between the shades. In the winter of 1939, the top surface colours were limited to the upper surfaces of the wings and tailplanes, plus the top decking of the fuselage. The fuselage sides and fin were painted Hellblau. On most aircraft the top surface camouflage was repainted, with 71 Dunkelgrün (the lighter of the two tones used previously) and 02 Grau (a pale grey-green). These had a greater tonal variation than the previous colours. The basic new camouflage scheme was modified at unit level during the Battle of Britain. Some aircraft had a neutral grey area painted along the wing leading edge to soften the demarcation between the dark topsides and light undersurfaces. Fuselage sides were often overpainted with a mottled 02 Grau, as seen on this aircraft.

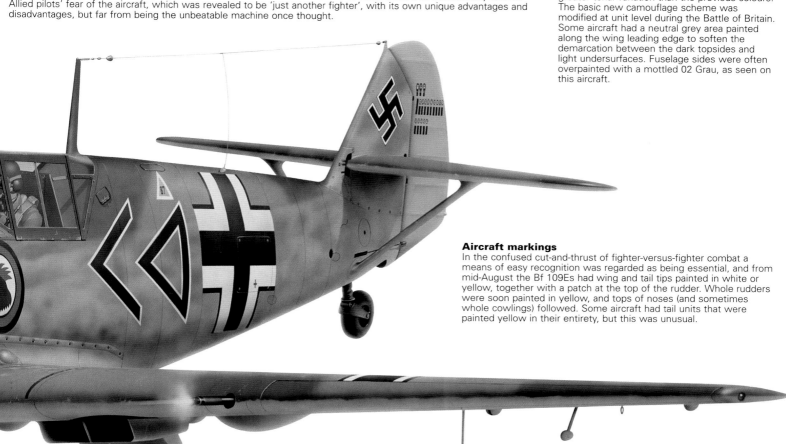

Aircraft markings

In the confused cut-and-thrust of fighter-versus-fighter combat a means of easy recognition was regarded as being essential, and from mid-August the Bf 109Es had wing and tail tips painted in white or yellow, together with a patch at the top of the rudder. Whole rudders were soon painted in yellow, and tops of noses (and sometimes whole cowlings) followed. Some aircraft had tail units that were painted yellow in their entirety, but this was unusual.

Personal markings

As Gruppenkommandeur of JG 3's I. Gruppe, Hans 'Vadder' ('Daddy') von Hahn's aircraft carried his own distinctive version of the standard double chevron (Winkel) or 'triangle in chevron' Gruppenkommandeur's marking. Under the cockpit was a cockerel's head, a play on his name (Hahn meaning cockerel in German), an insignia also used by his better known namesake, Hans 'Assi' Hahn. Von Hahn began the war as the adjutant of JG 53, later becoming the Staffelkapitän of 8./JG 53 under Werner Mölders during the Battle of France. At the height of the Battle of Britain, when Herman Göring replaced his older fighter leaders (many of whom, like Theo Osterkamp and Dr Mix, had fought and even become aces in World War I) von Hahn was promoted to become the Gruppenkommandeur of I./JG 3, replacing Gunther Lützow, who was in turn promoted to become Geschwaderkommodore. Von Hahn took the Tatzelwurm Gruppe to Russia in June 1941 and returned with the Gruppe in January 1942, having added 17 kills to his tally to bring his total to 34 in 300 missions. The Gruppe redesignated as II./JG 1 and began converting to the Fw 190, and von Hahn began the first of a succession of staff and training appointments, ending the war as Jafü (fighter leader) Oberitalinen (Upper Italy). He died in Frankfurt in 1957, aged 53.

Up-engined 'Emils'

The Bf 109E-4/N was powered by a DB 601N engine, whose flattened (instead of concave) piston heads gave a higher compression ratio, and which used higher octane fuel. The Bf 109E-7 was similarly powered, and the Bf 109E-7/Z introduced a nitrous oxide (GM1) supercharger injection system, which boosted altitude performance and was known as the 'Ha-Ha' system. A similar performance increase was provided in the Bf 109E-8 and the recce-roled Bf 109E-9 by the new DB 601E engine, with increased maximum rpm, improved supercharging and take-off power of 1,350 hp 1006 kW). The down side was that the new engine was considerably less economical, and even with a 100-litre (22-Imp gal) increase in fuel capacity (to 400 litres/88 Imp gal) the Bf 109E's already inadequate reach was not greatly improved.

Anatomy

The Bf 109 was built as a semi-monocoque fuselage, constructed in two halves and joined at the centreline. The undercarriage was attached directly to the fuselage, allowing the wing to be easily removed without the need for assembling jacks. The wing itself was a single-spar construction, the cannon-armed variants having a strengthened cut-out in the spar to accommodate the weapon. Similarly, the tail and tailplanes were simple single-spar structures, the tailplanes being externally braced by a single strut. The incidence of the tailplane could be altered via a torque tube in landing configuration to offset the effects of deploying both the flaps and the drooping ailerons. The wing slots, flaps and ailerons were actuated by rods, but the tail surfaces had cable runs through the rear fuselage, the rudder having a simple left/right pivoting arm. A tube was located transversely across the fuselage just forward of the tail unit, through which a rod could be inserted for lifting the aircraft's tail. The rear fuselage was largely empty but did provide housing for the two oxygen bottles and the FuG 7 radio equipment, which was supported on brackets attached to both the upper and lower fuselage frames. In the forward fuselage the engine was cantilevered on A-frame engine bearers, above which were mounted the guns. The ammunition tanks were located below and behind the engine, feeding upwards into the weapons. The glycol coolant was held in a header tank just aft of the propeller.

When the Germans invaded Yugoslavia, the 6th Fighter Regiment lost all but seven of its 46 serviceable Bf 109Es in the first two days of fighting, although a reasonable amount of damage was done to the attackers in the process. These pilots of the 6th are seen at Zemun prior to the invasion.

Unit	Variant	Number	Serviceable
Luftflotte 1			
I/JG 1	Bf 109E	54	54
I/JG 2	Bf 109E	42	39
10. (Nacht)/JG 2	Bf 109C	9	9
Stab and I/JG 3	Bf 109E	51	45
I/JG 20	Bf 109E	21	20
I/JG 21	Bf 109C/E	29	28
JGr 101 (II/ZG 1)	Bf 109B	36	36
JGr 102 (I/ZG 2)	Bf 109D	44	40
Luftflotte 2			
Stab and I/JG 26	Bf 109E	51	51
II/JG 26	Bf 109E	48	44
10. (Nacht)/JG 26	Bf 109C	10	8
I and II/ZG 26	Bf 109B/D	96	92
JGr 126 (III/ZG 26)	Bf 109B/C	48	44
Luftflotte 3			
I/JG 51	Bf 109E	47	39
I/JG 52	Bf 109E	39	34
JGr 152 (I/ZG 52)	Bf 109B	44	43
I/JG 53	Bf 109E	51	39
II/JG 53	Bf 109E	43	41
1. and 2./JG 70	Bf 109E	24	24
1. and 2./JG 71	Bf 109C/E	39	18
Luftflotte 4			
I/JG 76	Bf 109E	49	45
I/JG 77	Bf 109E	50	43
II/JG 77	Bf 109E	50	36
JGr 176 (II/ZG 76)	Bf 109B/C	40	39
Luftwaffe-Lehrdivision			
Stab and I (Jagd)/LG 2	Bf 109E	39	37
11. (Nacht)/LG 2	Bf 109E	10	9
Oberkommando der Marine			
II/JG 186	Bf 109B	24	24

As can be seen, many of the Zerstörergruppen were temporarily given Jagdgruppen titles, and there were also night-fighter units mainly operating the Bf 109C. The Lehrdivision was an organisation involved in the development of operational tactics, but also had an operational tasking. The naval unit comprised two Staffeln of Bf 109s which were training crews for the forthcoming carrier force.

Polish campaign

Despite this good strength, the Bf 109 was employed in only small numbers during the Polish campaign. This was due in part to a reluctance by the German high command to commit large numbers of aircraft to the campaign in case the attack brought about instant military reaction from Britain and France. Indeed, the whole Polish invasion was a big risk, for the Luftwaffe had insufficient reserves of fuel and ammunition to undertake any major action in the West should the occasion arise. Of course, the British and French were no more prepared for major war than were the Germans, and a mutual lack of intelligence prevented any escalation in the West until the following year.

At the start of the campaign, Bf 109 units assigned to the fighting comprised JGr 101 with Bf 109Bs, I/JG 21 flying Bf 109Cs, JGr 102 with Bf 109Ds, and Bf 109Es flying with I (Jagd)/LG 2, I/JG 1 and I/JG 21. In the air the Poles put up little resistance, and what was provided by the hopelessly outclassed PZL P.7 and P.11 fighters was easily quashed by the Bf 109s. The immediate establishment of aerial supremacy allowed two of the Gruppen, I/JG 1 and I/JG 21, to be withdrawn back to the West soon after the start of the fighting, while the remaining Bf 109s largely turned to

Right: This Bf 109E-1 of JG 77 was brought down during the Balkans Campaign. In Yugoslavia, 'Emil' faced 'Emil' for a few days of fighting, and a number of defending aircraft were brought down by 'friendly' anti-aircraft fire.

ground-strafing missions. There were a few losses to fighters, but the majority of the 67 losses recorded between 1 and 28 September were to groundfire.

Owing to the numerical state of the Jagdgruppen, this was serious, but due to the relative inactivity of the next few months, this attrition was easily remedied. Activity by the RAF in the West was largely confined to tentative coastal reconnaissance and bombing missions, and the Bf 109s were on alert to intercept such attempts. The first kill in the West was a Wellington of No. 9 Squadron, downed on 4 September by a Bf 109E-1 of II/JG 77. On the last day of the month JG 53 Messerschmitts dispatched four out of five Fairey Battles engaged on a daylight mission, relegating the light bomber to nocturnal missions thereafter. The largest air battle of 1939 was played out on 18 December, when Bf 109Bs, Cs and Es, together with Bf 110s, from a variety of units took on 24 Wellingtons near Wilhelmshaven. Twelve of the bombers were shot down, and another three crash-landed back in England. Two Bf 109s were lost, but RAF Bomber Command had suffered a severe blow, one which was to change its future tactics.

Phoney War

These early months of the war, known in England as the 'Phoney War' and in Germany as the 'Sitzkrieg', provided few opportunities for fighter versus fighter combat, but on the few occasions that the Bf 109E met either M.S.406s or the Hurricanes of the advanced RAF force in France, the Messerschmitt proved far superior. Conversion to the Bf 109E from the earlier models continued, with Bs and Cs passing mainly to Jagdfliegerschulen. The 'Doras' were mainly passed to the hastily-formed night-fighter force.

The first element of this force had been established in the summer of 1939 as 10. (Nacht)/JG 26, under the command of Oberleutnant Johannes Steinhof. The unit was tasked with developing night-fighting tactics, and was initially equipped with Arado Ar 68s and Bf 109Bs. These gave way to Bf 109Cs, and a second C night unit was formed, 10. (Nacht)/JG 2. A third unit, 11. (Nacht)/JG 2, formed in late 1939 with Bf 109D-1s, and this took up residence in the Helgoland region, where it was joined by the other two Staffeln to form IV/JG 2. By now all three units were operating the 'Dora', and continued in service defending northern Germany at night until the summer of 1940, when the last Jumo-powered Bf 109s were finally phased out of the Luftwaffe front line.

During the 'Sitzkrieg' the Allies were presented with two golden opportunities to study the Bf 109 exhaustively. The first occurred as early as 24 September 1939, when an aircraft of II/JG 51 landed at Strasbourg-Neuhof airfield. After only limited test flying, a French pilot damaged the aircraft during a heavy landing at Nancy on 6 September. Following repair, the 'Emil' was flown again, but on 28 November it was lost in a mid-air collision with a Curtiss Hawk 75A being flown by Capitaine Rozanoff, the pilot who had originally evaluated the Bf 109 captured in Spain.

The fighters of 7./JG 52 are seen lined up on a former civil airfied during the Balkans campaign. The yellow nose, wingtips, rudder and fuselage band on these Bf 109E-1s were theatre markings.

Just days before, another 'Emil' (of I/JG 76) had landed by mistake on the wrong side of the Franco-German border. Promptly ferried by road to the Centre d'Essais en Vol at Orléans-Bricy, the Bf 109 was tested by several pilots before being flown to Boscombe Down in England on 4 May 1940. On 14 May it transferred to the Royal Aircraft Establishment at Farnborough and, assigned RAF serial AE479, was thoroughly assessed by the Aerodynamic Flight.

These flights confirmed that the Bf 109 was superior in almost all respects to the Hurricane, except for low-altitude manoeuvrability and turning circle. Dependent on the type of propeller fitted, the Spitfire Mk I fared much better. The Bf 109 was in most respects superior to the Spitfire fitted with the two-pitch propeller then in widespread service with RAF squadrons, but with the Rotol three-bladed variable-pitch propeller, the Spitfire was faster. Above 20,000 ft (6096 m) the Spitfire was untouchable, but the Bf 109 could outclimb the RAF aircraft to that height. Nothing could out-dive the Messerschmitt, and the benefits of the fuel injection engine in such a manoeuvre were not lost on the British pilots.

Staged fighting

Mock combats were staged between the Bf 109 and the Hurricane and Spitfire. In low-speed turns the RAF fighters had no trouble staying with the Messerschmitt, and at high speeds aileron forces became too heavy for rapid manoeuvres. An interesting point was that the cockpit of the Bf 109 was so cramped that the pilot could only apply two-thirds of the sideways pressure on the stick achievable in the Spitfire.

In conclusion, the RAF pilots judged that the best escape manoeuvres for the Bf 109 were a steep-angle climb, which the Hurricane and Spitfire could not match, and a bunt manoeuvre which utilised the dive prowess and fuel

The two-bladed propellers immediately identify these aircraft as Jumo-powered. They are 'Claras', seen in the service of one of several Jagdfliegerschulen which operated the older types into 1941.

injection of the Bf 109 to increase spacing. On the other hand, both Hurricane and Spitfire could evade a pursuing Messerschmitt using any number of violent manoeuvres, such as a half-roll followed by a rapid pull-out of the ensuing dive. If the Messerschmitt attempted to follow these it would either encounter too-heavy control forces at high speeds or stall out at lower speeds. In either case, around 2,000 to 3,000 ft (600 to 900 m) of altitude would be lost, fatal when fighting near the ground. Indeed, several Messerschmitts were noted to have been downed in this way without a shot having been fired.

AE479 was transferred to the Air Fighting Development Unit at Northolt on 20 September 1940, with whom it flew until being damaged in a crash landing on 5 January 1941. It was then flown by No. 1426 (Enemy Aircraft) Flight at Duxford until being crated and shipped to Wright Field, Ohio, in April 1942 for evaluation by the US Army Air Forces. Another Bf 109E was assembled out of parts from various aircraft and was flown by the RAF on 25 February 1941. With registration DG200, this aircraft was used for calibration trials by Rolls-Royce, and was later

Bf 109 in Greece

Although it still wears the badge of JG 52, this aircraft served with I (Jagd)/LG 2 during the Greece campaign. The pilot was the Gruppen-kommandeur, Hauptmann Herbert Ihlefeld, who had already scored seven kills in Spain when the war started. Ihlefeld became the Kommodore of several Geschwaders, surviving the war with 130 victories.

Messerschmitt Bf 109

Far right: Despite their activities in the arid conditions of the Mediterranean, the Bf 109Es of 7./JG 26 retained their north-European colour scheme of mottled greys and yellow extremities. This is the E-7 of Ernst Laube at Gela, Sicily.

Right: Only about a dozen pilots served on JG 26's Mediterranean sojourn. Their undoubted star was their Kommandeur, Joachim Müncheberg, who added a number of RAF aircraft to his eventual tally of 135 during this period. This could be Müncheberg's Bf 109E-7 'white 12'.

something of a celebrity with several public appearances. Today the aircraft resides in the RAF Museum at Hendon, returned to Luftwaffe camouflage.

Bf 109s played little part in Operation Weserübung, the invasion of Denmark and Norway, where there was little fighter opposition and the ranges too great to be covered by the Bf 109. The main unit involved was II/JG 77, which occupied several bases in Denmark during April. The main effort in early 1940 was to gear up for the assault in the West, Operation Fall Gelb, which abruptly brought to an end the 'Sitzkrieg' on 10 May. To say the French were unprepared for the shock of meeting the Bf 109 in combat is an understatement: despite the bad weather in the winter of 1939-40, there had been sufficient aerial skirmishes for the French to see just how inferior their aircraft were. The margin of superiority could not be bridged by the acknowledged skill and bravery of the French pilots. Indeed, in many ways the Germans were better trained and flew with far superior tactics thanks to the experiences of the Spanish Civil War.

The assault in the West was as much a gamble as that on Poland, for the Luftwaffe still did not have sufficient depth of spares and supplies to sustain a long campaign. Production of aircraft had barely risen during the early

months of 1940, so that just over 1,000 Bf 109s were available to the vast majority of the Jagdgruppen which prepared for the attack. A greater determination in production was later to take hold, especially as it was realised that a successful French campaign did not automatically mean the end of the war.

Air superiority

From the outset, the Bf 109E fighters of JGs 1, 2, 3, 21, 26, 27, 51, 52, 53 and 54 established total air superiority over the Dutch, Belgian, British and French air forces, allowing the Stukagruppen and Kampfgruppen to devastate the Allied forces. Only the Dewoitine D.520, available in small numbers, posed any serious threat to the Bf 109. Holland capitulated on 14 May, and on 21 May the RAF pulled its tattered British Expeditionary Force Air Component out of France and Belgium, and the British AASF (Advanced Air Strike Force) moved way back into France. The Bf 109s followed closely on the heels of the rapidly advancing Wehrmacht, moving bases often. On the other side of the lines, the constant retreat of Allied air units and the continuous bombing their fields received turned maintenance and spares supply into a nightmare. Many Allied fighters were destroyed on the ground, and those

Sicily and Malta

In February 1941 the first German single-seat fighter unit arrived in Sicily to help the Italian forces who were unable to subdue the Allied units defending Malta. This was 7./JG 26 who detached from the parent unit on the

Channel Front, and under Oberleutnant Joachim Müncheberg. They sorely tested the RAF on and around Malta until late May when the Staffel was ordered to Greece, and then Libya, returning to France in August.

These three photos depict E-4/Bs of 9./JG 27 bombing up for a mission over Malta. Of note is the presentation of tactical numbers on the cowls of the Messerschmitts peculiar to this unit. The aircraft flying a metal pennant from the radio mast is that of Staffelkapitan Erbo Graf von Kageneck who was JG 27's highest-scoring pilot at the time of his death from wounds in January 1942.

Aces in Sicily

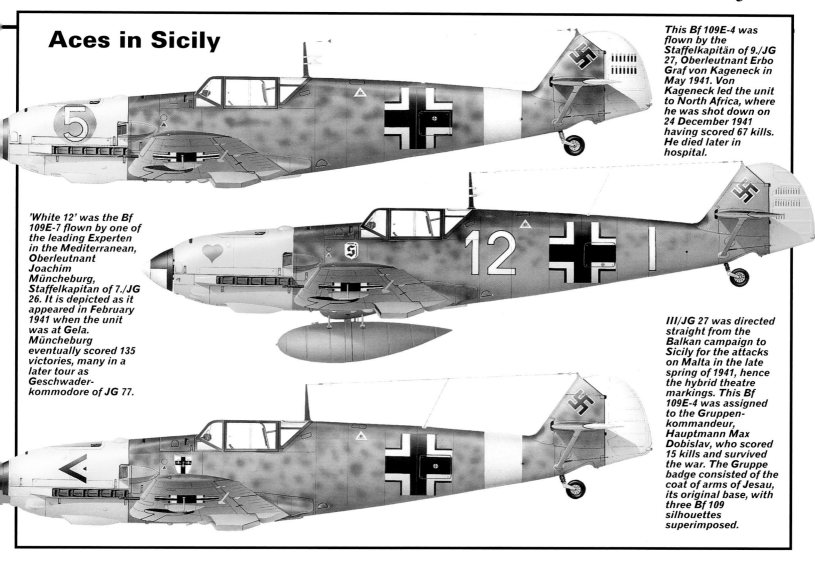

This Bf 109E-4 was flown by the Staffelkapitän of 9./JG 27, Oberleutnant Erbo Graf von Kageneck in May 1941. Von Kageneck led the unit to North Africa, where he was shot down on 24 December 1941 having scored 67 kills. He died later in hospital.

'White 12' was the Bf 109E-7 flown by one of the leading Experten in the Mediterranean, Oberleutnant Joachim Müncheburg, Staffelkapitan of 7./JG 26. It is depicted as it appeared in February 1941 when the unit was at Gela. Müncheburg eventually scored 135 victories, many in a later tour as Geschwaderkommodore of JG 77.

III/JG 27 was directed straight from the Balkan campaign to Sicily for the attacks on Malta in the late spring of 1941, hence the hybrid theatre markings. This Bf 109E-4 was assigned to the Gruppenkommandeur, Hauptmann Max Dobislav, who scored 15 kills and survived the war. The Gruppe badge consisted of the coat of arms of Jesau, its original base, with three Bf 109 silhouettes superimposed.

that did engage the enemy made little impact on the air battle.

The major enemy of the Jagdgruppen was the speed of the advance itself, which lengthened supply lines to almost breaking point. The light attrition suffered by the force throughout May and June nevertheless proved difficult to atone given the parlous state of the reserves back in Germany. The final evacuation of the Allies from Dunkirk was not quite the military disaster that it is often painted, for it was the Germans' intention to prevent any such evacuation to Britain. That they failed to do so was largely due to the long distances the Bf 109s had to fly to cover the bombers attacking the Allies, which in turn meant they suffered heavy losses. Another factor which was to have much greater bearing a few weeks later was the first encounters with the Supermarine Spitfire, which began to

cover Allied forces from bases in England.

From 3 June, the Western campaign took less than three weeks to complete, ending in a French armistice. During this time the Bf 109s had little trouble against the French, despite the depleted numbers within the Jagdgruppen. Units were progressively withdrawn to Germany for re-equipment and recuperation, although this process was exacerbated by the low rate of production and the fact that export contracts were still being fulfilled. Among these was the delivery to the Soviet Union of five Bf 109E-3s for evaluation purposes in return for raw materials. Like the French earlier, the Soviets concluded that they had nothing to learn from the Bf 109 – how expensive that conclusion was to become the following year!

Sights on Britain

Militarily, the campaigns of early 1940 were an outstanding success for the Germans: all of mainland Europe was now either under their control or neutral. Only Britain remained. While the German forces were in no state to tackle Albion just yet, the German High Command's sights were set firmly across the Channel. Following a month's lull in activity, during which only the three Gruppen of JG 51 Bf 109s remained in France to face the RAF, a slow but deliberate build-up of forces began on 12 July with the return of III/JG 3. At the end of July, JGs 26, 27 and 52 returned to France. Other Gruppen followed.

Although the Bf 109s had enjoyed air superiority over France, combat losses were still high, and one of the chief concerns was the lack of armour protection. In the summer of 1940 Bf 109E-3s began to appear with a heavily-framed canopy and 8-mm seat armour. A further armour plate was

Left: The first Luftwaffe fighter unit to be sent as a Gruppe to the Middle East was I/JG 27. The pilots were all seasoned veterans of the western campaigns and in some cases, Spain. The officer at left with papers is Hauptmann Karl-Wolfgang Redlich, here briefing pilots of the Gruppe for the final Sicily-Libya leg of their journey to the war.

Inside the Bf 109

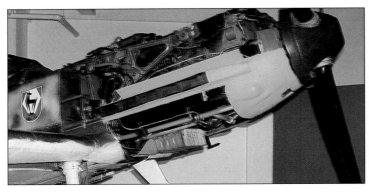

Above and right: Two views show the DB 601 engine of the Bf 109E on its cantilevered engine bearers. The supercharger was on the port side, its position marked by the louvred air intake on the exterior.

Messerschmitt Bf 109E-4

1. Hollow propeller hub
2. Spinner
3. Three-bladed VDM variable-pitch propeller
4. Propeller pitch-change mechanism
5. Spinner back plate
6. Glycol coolant header tank
7. Glycol filler cap
8. Cowling fastener
9. Chin intake
10. Coolant pipe fairing
11. Exhaust forward fairing
12. Additional (long-range) oil tank
13. Daimler-Benz DB 601A engine
14. Supplementary intakes
15. Fuselage machine-gun troughs
16. Anti-vibration engine mounting pads
17. Exhaust ejector stubs
18. Coolant pipes (to underwing radiators)
19. Oil cooler intake
20. Coolant radiator
21. Radiator outlet flap
22. Cowling frame
23. Engine mounting support strut
24. Spent cartridge collector compartment
25. Ammunition boxes (starboard loading)
26. Engine supercharger
27. Supercharger air intake fairing
28. Forged magnesium alloy cantilever engine mounting
29. Engine mounting/forward bulkhead attachment
30. Ammunition feed chutes
31. Engine accessories
32. Two fuselage-mounted MG17 machine-guns
33. Blast tube muzzles
34. Wing skinning
35. Starboard cannon access
36. 20-mm MG FF wing cannon
37. Leading-edge automatic slot
38. Slot tracks
39. Slot actuating linkage
40. Wing main spar
41. Intermediate rib station
42. Wing end rib
43. Starboard navigation light
44. Aileron outer hinge
45. Aileron metal trim tab
46. Starboard aileron
47. Aileron/flap link connection
48. Combined control linkage
49. Starboard flap frame
50. Cannon ammunition drum access
51. Fuselage machine-gun cooling slots
52. Gun mounting frame
53. Firewall/bulkhead
54. Instrument panel near face (fabric covered)
55. Oil dipstick cover
56. Control column
57. Oil filler cap (tank omitted for clarity)
58. Rudder pedal assembly
59. Aircraft identity data plate (external)
60. Mainspar centre-section carry-through
61. Underfloor control linkage
62. Oxygen regulator
63. Harness adjustment lever
64. Engine priming pump
65. Circuit breaker panel
66. Hood catch
67. Starboard-hinged cockpit canopy
68. Revi gunsight (offset to starboard)
69. Windscreen panel frame
70. Canopy section frame
71. Pilot's head armour
72. Pilot's back armour
73. Seat harness

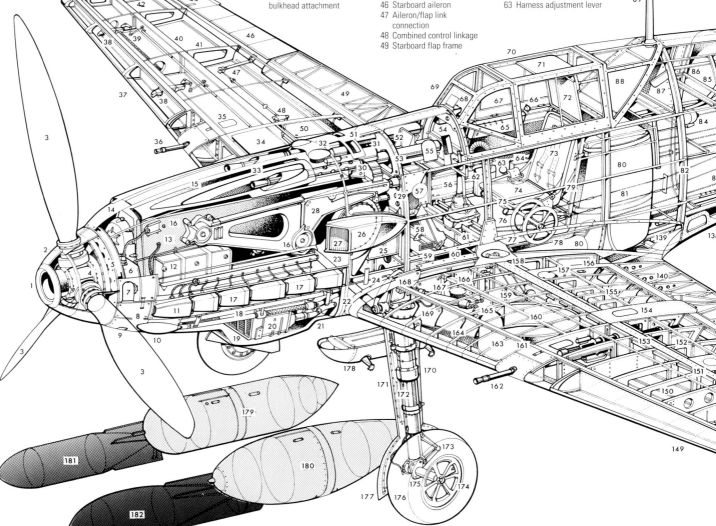

Messerschmitt Bf 109

The Jumo 210Da installation of the Bf 109B had a deep chin inlet with auxiliary ejector flap. Note the Schwarz fixed-pitch propeller.

The V7 and V8 were both powered by the Jumo 210Ga with VDM propeller, and uniquely had the oil cooler intake ahead of the radiator intake.

The DB 600 installation of the V10 to V13 tested the intake arrangement for the Bf 109E, the radiators being moved back under the wings.

This is the definitive installation of the DB 601 on a Bf 109E-3. The main undercowling intake fed the oil cooler, and there were additional cooling intake just behind the spinner, two on top and one underneath. The exhaust ejector stubs were partially sunk into a trough. The bulge just below the front of the exhaust fairing covered coolant pipes.

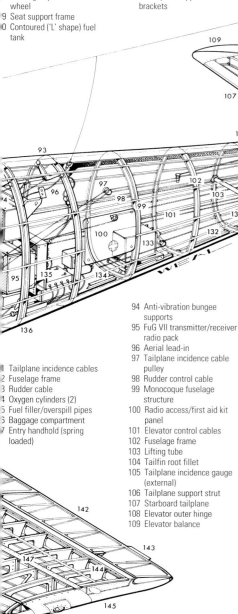

Above and below: Two views show the VDM three-bladed propeller of the Bf 109E. Most aircraft retained the hollow shaft for the engine-mounted cannon, but this was rarely fitted.

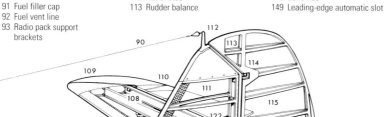

84 Pilot's seat
85 Seat adjustment lever
86 Tailplane incidence handwheel
87 Cockpit floor diaphragm
88 Landing flaps control hand wheel
89 Seat support frame
90 Contoured ('L' shape) fuel tank

88 Canopy fixed aft section
89 Aerial mast
90 Aerial
91 Fuel filler cap
92 Fuel vent line
93 Radio pack support brackets

110 Starboard elevator
111 Tailfin structure
112 Aerial stub
113 Rudder balance

146 Port navigation light
147 Wing main spar outer section
148 Solid ribs
149 Leading-edge automatic slot

94 Anti-vibration bungee supports
95 FuG VII transmitter/receiver radio pack
96 Aerial lead-in
97 Tailplane incidence cable pulley
98 Rudder control cable
99 Monocoque fuselage structure
100 Radio access/first aid kit panel
101 Elevator control cables
102 Fuselage frame
103 Lifting tube
104 Tailfin root fillet
105 Tailplane incidence gauge (external)
106 Tailplane support strut
107 Starboard tailplane
108 Elevator outer hinge
109 Elevator balance

91 Tailplane incidence cables
92 Fuselage frame
93 Rudder cable
94 Oxygen cylinders (2)
95 Fuel filler/overspill pipes
96 Baggage compartment
97 Entry handhold (spring loaded)

114 Rudder upper hinge
115 Rudder frame
116 Rudder trim tab
117 Tail navigation light
118 Port elevator frame
119 Elevator balance
120 Rudder control quadrant
121 Tailplane structure
122 Elevator torque tube sleeve
123 Tailplane end rib attachment
124 Fuselage end post
125 Elevator control rod
126 Port tailplane support strut
127 Non-retractable tailwheel
128 Tailwheel leg
129 Elevator control cable rod link
130 Tail wheel leg shock-absorber
131 Rudder control cable
132 Fuselage stringer
133 Accumulator
134 Fuselage half ventral join
135 Electrical leads
136 Fuselage panel
137 Radio pack lower support frames
138 Entry foothold (spring loaded)
139 Wingroot fillet
140 Flap profile
141 Port flap frame
142 Port aileron frame
143 Aileron metal trim tab
144 Rear spar
145 Port wingtip

150 Rib cut-outs
151 Control link access plate
152 Wing rib stations
153 Port wing 20-mm MG FF cannon installation
154 Ammunition drum access panel
155 Inboard rib cut-outs
156 Flap visual position indicator
157 Control access panel
158 Main spar/fuselage attachment fairing
159 Wing control surface cable pulleys
160 Port mainwheel well
161 Wheel well (zipped) fabric shield
162 20-mm MG FF wing cannon
163 Wing front spar
164 Undercarriage leg tunnel rib cut-outs
165 Undercarriage lock mechanism
166 Wing/fuselage end rib
167 Undercarriage actuating cylinder
168 Mainwheel leg/fuselage attachment bracket
169 Leg pivot point
170 Mainwheel oleo leg
171 Mainwheel leg door
172 Brake lines
173 Torque links
174 Mainwheel hub
175 Axle
176 Port main wheel
177 Mainwheel half-door
178 Ventral ETC centre-line stores pylon, possible loads include:
179 Early-type (wooden) drop tank
180 66-Imp gal (300-litre) (Junkers) metal drop tank
181 551-lb (250-kg) HE bomb, or
182 551-lb (250-kg) SAP bomb

Above: The desert imposed harsh conditions on man and machine. The inevitable sand storms whipped up by aircraft necessitated wide spacing on take-off. The first unit in the desert, I/JG 26, left all its aircraft behind when it left due to unservicabilty brought about by the dust and unforgiving landing strips.

The mission of the 'Emil' in the desert ranged from pure fighter interception to ground attack to long-range escort. Here, the E-7/Trop of I/JG 27's adjutant Oberleutnant Ludwig Franzisket escorts a Ju 87B Stuka with empty bomb cradle over Libya in April 1941.

Far right: The greatest ace of the desert was Hans-Joachim Marseille, who had only seven victories on arrival in Africa – relatively few compared to some of the Experten already serving with JG 27. Early in his career he had a lucky escape when his Bf 109E-4/Trop. suffered combat damage close to the engine, as seen here.

provided over the pilot's head, attached to the canopy. The Bf 109E-4 rapidly replaced the E-3 on the production line, this variant differing by having the MG FF/M cannon in the wings. Essentially similar to the first 20-mm weapon, the new gun had an improved rate of fire. Ikaria-Werke studied a belt-feed for the MG FF, but in the event the trial installation was not flown until early 1941, and was cancelled. The Bf 109 retained the capability for an engine-mounted weapon, although problems with cooling and vibration had meant they were not fitted. The hollow spinner was nevertheless retained in the fighter variants.

In late August 1940 the Bf 109E-7 began to arrive at fighter units. This differed from the Bf 109E-4 by having the capability to carry a 66-Imp gal (300-litre) jettisonable plywood fuel tank. The lack of range had been one of the main disadvantages of the Bf 109 during the French

campaign, and would further embarrass the Jagdgruppen over England, limiting combat time to just a few minutes. In practice, the tank was prone to terrible leaks and suspected of a tendency to ignite. It was rarely used in action due to the suspicions of the pilots. The rack could also carry a single SC 250 bomb.

Other more radical approaches were being made to address the range problem in the summer of 1940. The most novel involved the use of bombers literally towing the fighters to the target area before they were cast off and went about defending their erstwhile tugs. At Augsburg,

The perfect matching of camouflage with environment is rare in wartime, but the sand with brownish-green topsides of this I/JG 27 Bf 109E-4/Trop blends in perfectly with the scrubby terrain of North Africa, at least at low level.

Desert Experten

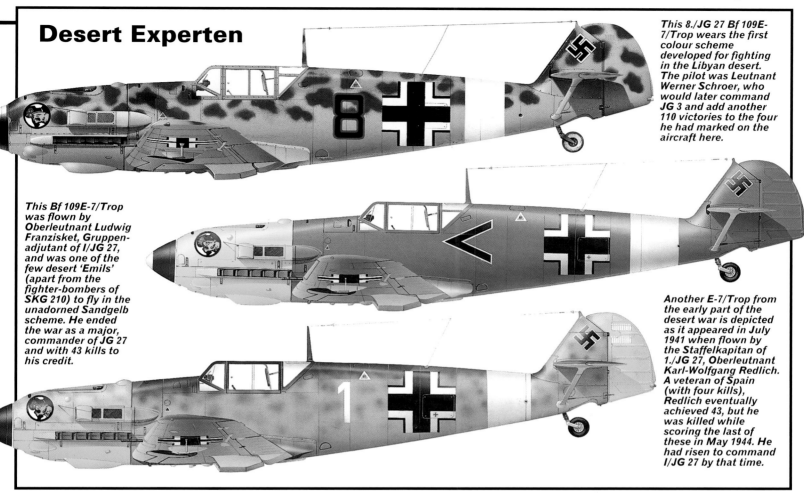

This 8./JG 27 Bf 109E-7/Trop wears the first colour scheme developed for fighting in the Libyan desert. The pilot was Leutnant Werner Schroer, who would later command JG 3 and add another 110 victories to the four he had marked on the aircraft here.

This Bf 109E-7/Trop was flown by Oberleutnant Ludwig Franzisket, Gruppen-adjutant of I/JG 27, and was one of the few desert 'Emils' (apart from the fighter-bombers of SKG 210) to fly in the unadorned Sandgelb scheme. He ended the war as a major, commander of JG 27 and with 43 kills to his credit.

Another E-7/Trop from the early part of the desert war is depicted as it appeared in July 1941 when flown by the Staffelkapitan of 1./JG 27, Oberleutnant Karl-Wolfgang Redlich. A veteran of Spain (with four kills), Redlich eventually achieved 43, but he was killed while scoring the last of these in May 1944. He had risen to command I/JG 27 by that time.

Karl Baur tested the concept using a Bf 110 towing a Bf 109, attaching the towline in the hollow spinner. Both aircraft took off under their own power, attached by the tow cable. Once at altitude, the 109's engine was cut and the propeller fully-feathered. The trials showed some promise, but the idea was not adopted.

With the benefits of experience from France, the summer months of 1940 saw a flurry of development activity, the most important being the development of the Bf 109 as a Jagdbomber, or Jabo, type. Under the command of Hauptmann Walter Rubensdörffer,

Left: The French obtained two examples of the Bf 109E before the end of 1939, both of which landed in error in French territory. The first was written off in a collision. The second aircraft shown here, an E-3 of I/JG 76, was flown by a number of test pilots and then sent to Britain at the start of the Battle of France.

Captured aircraft

The few intact Bf 109s that fell into Allied hands in the early part of the war were thoroughly evaluated to determine the strengths and weaknesses of the type. Flown against Allied fighters, the 109 was found to be about equal to the Spitfire, but superior to the Hurricane in most respects except low-altitude turning circle. The experienced operational pilots who flew the 'Emil' were impressed by its low-speed handling, high top speed and climb rate, and its fuel-injected engine that did not cut out when inverted. On the other hand, the heaviness of the controls at high speed was criticised, as was the high wing loading and consequent poor turning circle. Other faults were seen as the lack of a rudder trimmer and the cramped cockpit that prevented the pilot getting full movement from the controls in combat. Unfortunately, and partly due to a series of mishaps, the French were again unable to

make much use of the data from the captured Messerschmitts in time to counter them when they appeared in force in May 1940. The British evaluations of airworthy examples were of more benefit, although they were not completed in time to be of use during the Battle of Britain.

Below: The ex-French Bf 109E-3 was tested in the summer of 1940 at Farnborough and Boscombe Down with the RAF serial of AE479. It wore a standard RAF scheme of dark earth and dark green.

Above: The second Bf 109E to be flown in evaluations by the RAF was E-3/B Wk Nr 4101 of 2./JG 51, which crash-landed at Manston after combat with Spitfires on 27 November 1940. Refurbished by Rolls-Royce, the aircraft was given the serial DG200 and operated mainly from Hatfield, where the canopy was removed in order to accommodate test-pilot Harvey Heyworth who was over 6 ft (1.83 m) tall.

Above: With Russian air forces largely neutralised, the Luftwaffe fighter arm could concentrate on supporting the ground advance. One unit involved in this process was II./JG 54 on the Leningrad front. JG 54 was famous for its non-standard – even artistic – camouflage schemes, and the pattern on this Bf 109E-4/B lives up to that reputation.

Above right: The campaign against the Soviet Union was not expected to last into the winter but, when the snows fell, the Luftwaffe had to adopt concealment techniques. This 'Emil' of an unidentified unit is wearing a weathered coat of white distemper.

Below right: SKG 210, the Luftwaffe's 'hit and run' specialists, was sent from North Africa to the Eastern Front, where it adopted the wasp badge seen on this Bf 109E-7/B of the Gruppe staff flight.

Below: The Luftwaffe formed a number of units of volunteers from occupied and sympathetic countries, and these served primarily against the Soviet forces. One such unit was 13. (slowak)/JG 52, one of two such Staffeln serving with this Geschwader. The aircraft retained the blue Balkankreuz with red disc insignia of Slovakia.

Erprobungsgruppe 210 was established to evaluate fighter-bomber tactics, using Bf 109s equipped with a rudimentary centreline rack for a single bomb from 110 to 550 lb (50 to 250 kg) weight. The unit went into action against coastal shipping in July 1940.

No specialist bombing systems were added to these aircraft, but it was soon discovered that the Revi gunsight could be used with some accuracy for 45° diving attacks. To set up the attack, a line was painted at 45° on the cockpit glazing for alignment. Such were the successes of Rubensdorffer's unit that an immediate order was issued for each Jagdgeschwader to establish a Jabo unit. At first the Bf 109E-1 was hastily converted to Bf 109E-1/B status by the addition of a rack for a single SC 50 (110-lb/50-kg) bomb, although the Bf 109E-4/B was also introduced on the factory production line, this having a better rack capable of lifting a single SC 250 bomb or four SC 50s. The E-4/B finally dispensed with the hollow spinner in favour of a streamlined unit, and in later months the weapon repertoire of the Jabo variants grew considerably.

Reconnaissance

Small numbers were also produced in parallel with the E-4 of tactical reconnaissance aircraft. The Bf 109E-5 variant had the wing cannon removed, and a single vertical Rb 21/18 camera mounted in the rear fuselage immediately behind the cockpit. The Bf 109E-6 retained its wing cannon, but featured an Rb 50/30 camera. The final variant to reach the Luftwaffe before the launch of the attack on Britain was the Bf 109E-4/N. This aircraft had a DB 601N engine, which was a result of major tinkering with the DB 601A. By using 96 octane C3 fuel in place of

the standard 87 octane B4, and by raising the compression ratio considerably, the DB 601N could put out 1,200 hp (895 kW) for take-off and 1,270 hp (947 kW) at 16,400 ft (5000 m), although both output figures could only be maintained for a maximum of one minute.

Adlerangriff (attack of the eagles) was the grand name bestowed on the operation aimed at Britain, and 13 August was Adlertag (day of the eagles), the date of the major opening bombing assault. Prior to this there were a growing number of exploratory missions along the coast and several skirmishes ensued. The Jagdgruppen were still at about 80 per cent of their strength when they had launched the Western campaign, and on Adlertag their numbers comprised 805 serviceable Bf 109Es. They were divided between Luftflotte 2 in Belgium and the Netherlands, with the full Geschwaders JGs 3, 26, 51 and 52, together with the Stab and I./JG 54 fighter-bombers of 3./Erprobungsgruppe 210, and Luftflotte 3 in France, which boasted JGs 2, 27 and 53.

Tactical freedom

In the initial onslaught on Britain, the Bf 109s enjoyed great success, largely because they were entrusted with an anti-fighter role which allowed the 'Emil' to fight in its best environment. Complete tactical freedom in the *freie Jagd* role allowed the Luftwaffe to exploit the dive and climb characteristics in picking off RAF fighters almost at will, and the fluid tactical formations devised in Spain by Mölders proved to be so much better than the rigid and predictable tight formations based on three-ship vics flown by the RAF. Begrudgingly, the RAF began to adopt the finger-four formation, with dramatically improved results.

Where the Luftwaffe was at a real disadvantage was in the poor performance of the much-vaunted Messerschmitt Bf 110, which was supposed to be escorting the bombers. The Zerstörer forces were cut to ribbons, and it became painfully obvious to the Luftwaffe commanders that the Bf 110 could no longer provide adequate protection for the bombers. Accordingly, the Bf 109 was switched from its fighter sweep role to close escort around the beginning of September, immediately denying the tactical freedoms enjoyed by the Messerschmitt pilots during the opening weeks of the battle. With its limited range, the Bf 109 could reach no further than London, while combat over the southern coast of England could rarely be maintained

Jagdbomber

Production of the Bf 109E had been phased out by the summer of 1941, and the numbers in service dwindled until the type disappeared from the fighter role in the Luftwaffe altogether. In one role, however, that of ground attack, the 'Emil' lingered on until well into 1943 in the Middle East and particularly in Russia. The last units operating the 'Emil' in action were the Schlacht (literally: Slaughter) Gruppen, mainly with E-7/B aircraft.

for more than 20 minutes at the most.

This situation severely hampered the attempts of the Luftwaffe to defeat the RAF in the air, and, coupled with the decision to leave the bombing of RAF airfields and begin attacking the cities, marked a turning point in the battle. Hurricanes and Spitfires began to exploit the situation to the full, introducing more advanced tactics themselves to keep the rampant Bf 109s in check. Tied closely to the bombers, the Bf 109s could be easily out-turned by both Spitfires and Hurricanes, and, instead of being the hunters who struck at large formations in slashing manoeuvres from altitude, the German aircraft found themselves on the receiving end. Losses began to escalate.

Of course, the Bf 109 was still a most feared opponent, especially in the hands of experienced pilots of the Jagdgruppen who, under the tutelage of Spanish veterans such as Galland and Mölders, built upon their experiences over France to rack up impressive victory tallies. Mölders himself was the leading ace of the Battle of Britain, becoming the first pilot to pass 50 victories while serving with JG 51. Galland, flying with JG 26, was not far behind. Apart from its performance characteristics and experienced pilots, a key advantage enjoyed by the Bf 109E was the 20-mm MG FF cannon, which proved to be devastating against the British fighters.

Establishment of the Jabostaffeln

As the battle progressed, the Bf 109 units were reorganised to reflect their new-found encumberment. The fighter-bomber unit had been joined by I (Jagd)/Lehrgeschwader 2 with new Bf 109E-7s, and the Bf 109E-4/Bs of II (Schlacht)/LG 2. These units mounted several effective raids, although of little destructive effect.

31 October is recognised as the last day of the Battle of Britain. Since July the Luftwaffe had lost 610 Bf 109s, while RAF Fighter Command lost 631 Hurricanes and 403 Spitfires. Drained of energy by the bloody daytime battle of attrition, both sides withdrew from the fighter battle to attempt to recover their strengths, both in numbers of aircraft and from an emotional standpoint. Looked at from an objective, strategic standpoint, the battle ended inconclusively, although from the British perspective the fact that it, alone in Europe, had not succumbed to the might of the German military machine was seen as a great victory. From a German point of view, the fact that it had not completely crushed the RAF was conversely seen as defeat. A vitally important corner in the course of the war had been turned.

Two important lessons had been learned by the Luftwaffe. One was that the need to reverse the dwindling trend in fighter production was paramount, and the other was that the Bf 109E needed considerable development to stay ahead of its opponents. By February 1941 the decrease in production was turned around dramatically, a fact helped by the addition of the AGO Flugzeugwerke at Oschersleben to the Bf 109 manufacturing complex. The parent company also hastened the development of the next major variant, the Bf 109F 'Friedrich', although the 'Emil' stayed in production a while longer. There was still much fighting for it to do before later models completely replaced it in front-line service.

An interesting sideline was the Bf 109T 'Toni', the

carrier version of the Bf 109. As described earlier, the nucleus of a Trägergruppe (carrier air group) had been laid down in 1939 with the establishment of Ju 87 and Bf 109B squadrons at Kiel-Holtenau, and Messerschmitt had been asked to develop a special carrierborne version. The resulting Bf 109T was a simple modification of the Bf 109E-1 with each wing extended by a 21.25-in (0.54-m) panel and corresponding increases in leading-edge slot and ailerons. Flap travel was increased to further reduce landing speed. The wings were provided with a manual folding point although this required that the flaps be removed first. Folded span was 15 ft 0.75 in (4.59 m). Catapult points and an arrester hook were fitted to the fuselage with local strengthening. Armament remained the same at four MG 17s, although it was envisaged that production aircraft would have the MG FF cannon in the wings.

Fieseler was responsible for finalising the design and production, and a 10-aircraft batch of Bf 109T-0 pre-production aircraft was built. They were powered by the DB 601A and featured retractable spoilers on the upper wing surfaces to steepen the glide angle. A strengthened

Above: The introduction of the ETC 50/VIIID rack with capacity for four SC 50 bombs greatly increased the versatility of the Bf 109E as a ground attack platform. With a liquid-cooled engine and limited armour protection, the Messerschmitt was not an ideal aircraft in the close-support role.

Left: Ground crew load an SC 500 500-kg (1,100-lb) fragmentation bomb on a Bf 109E-4/B of II (schlacht)/LG 2. In addition to conventional bombs, the 109 could drop up to 96 SD-2 'butterfly bombs', which were devastating against troops or soft-skinned transport.

A Hauptmann of 15. (span)/JG 51 inspects the cannon of a Bf 109E/Trop somewhere on the central Eastern Front in August 1942. This unit was formed as the 'Blue Squadron' (Escuadron Azul) with Spanish volunteers in March 1942, and was rotated with new pilots from Spain every six months.

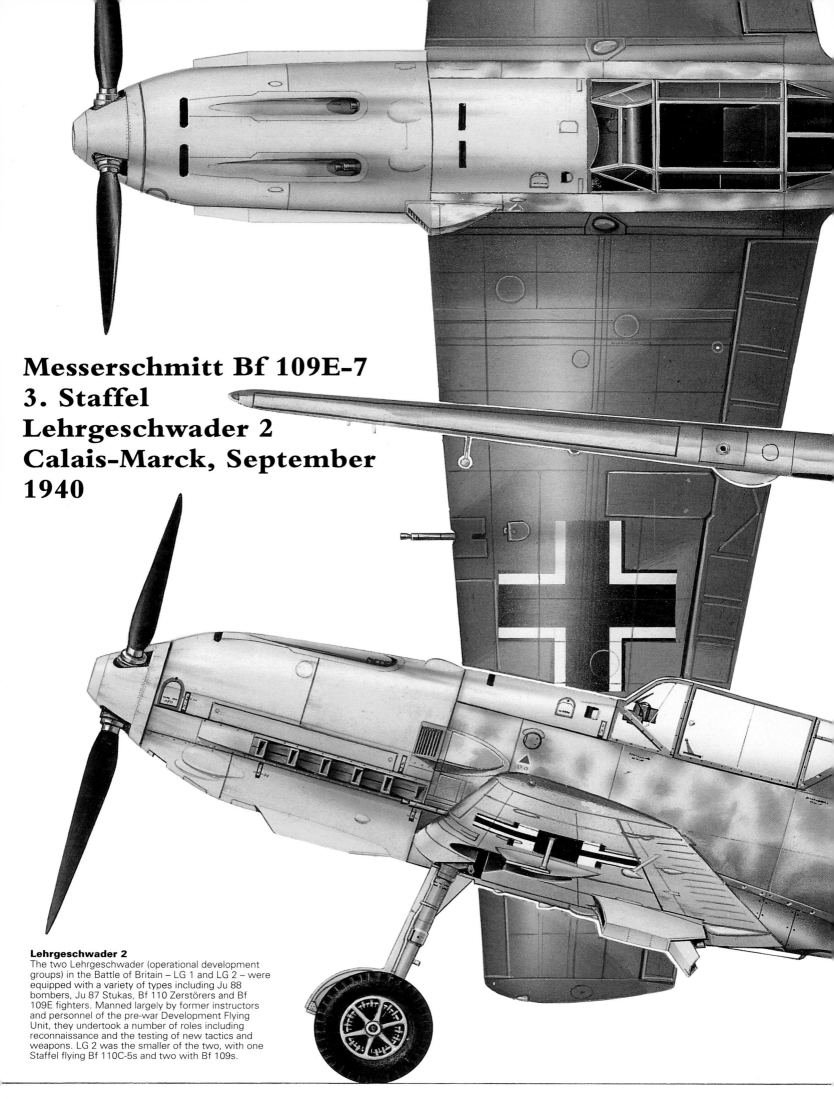

Messerschmitt Bf 109E-7
3. Staffel
Lehrgeschwader 2
Calais-Marck, September
1940

Lehrgeschwader 2
The two Lehrgeschwader (operational development groups) in the Battle of Britain – LG 1 and LG 2 – were equipped with a variety of types including Ju 88 bombers, Ju 87 Stukas, Bf 110 Zerstörers and Bf 109E fighters. Manned largely by former instructors and personnel of the pre-war Development Flying Unit, they undertook a number of roles including reconnaissance and the testing of new tactics and weapons. LG 2 was the smaller of the two, with one Staffel flying Bf 110C-5s and two with Bf 109s.

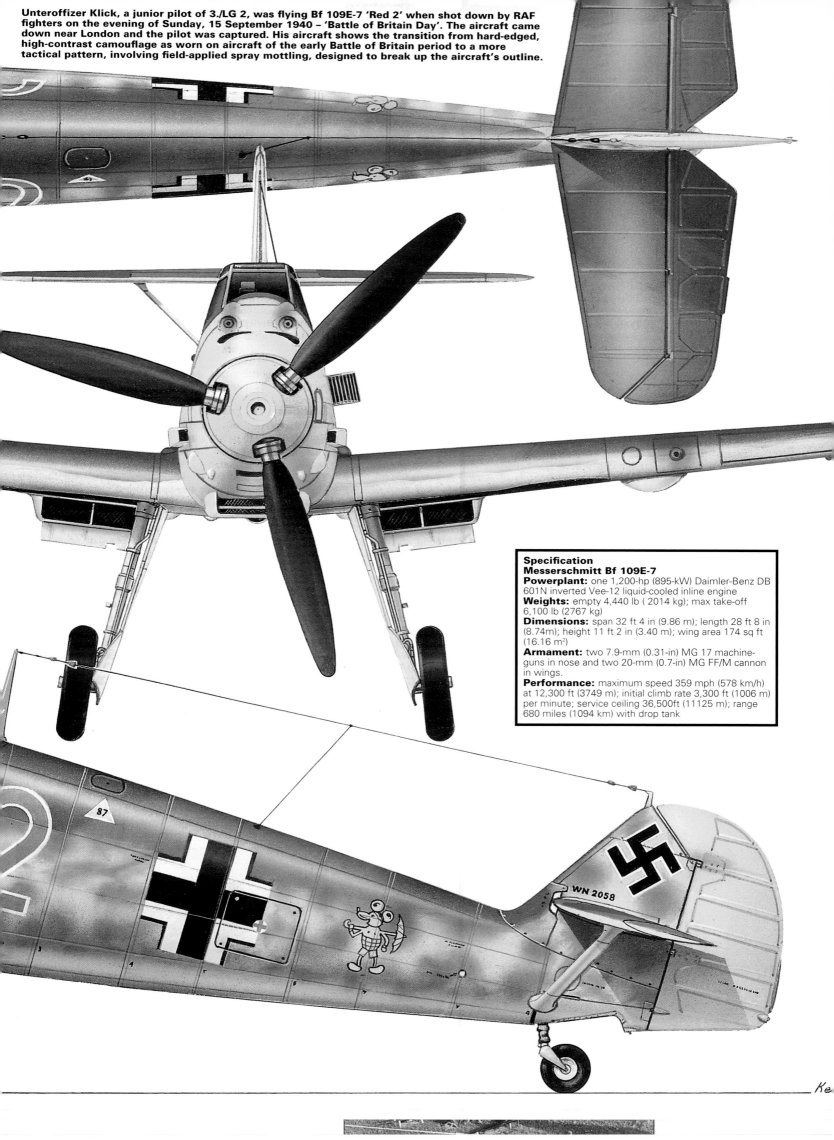

Unteroffizer Klick, a junior pilot of 3./LG 2, was flying Bf 109E-7 'Red 2' when shot down by RAF fighters on the evening of Sunday, 15 September 1940 – 'Battle of Britain Day'. The aircraft came down near London and the pilot was captured. His aircraft shows the transition from hard-edged, high-contrast camouflage as worn on aircraft of the early Battle of Britain period to a more tactical pattern, involving field-applied spray mottling, designed to break up the aircraft's outline.

Specification
Messerschmitt Bf 109E-7
Powerplant: one 1,200-hp (895-kW) Daimler-Benz DB 601N inverted Vee-12 liquid-cooled inline engine
Weights: empty 4,440 lb (2014 kg); max take-off 6,100 lb (2767 kg)
Dimensions: span 32 ft 4 in (9.86 m); length 28 ft 8 in (8.74m); height 11 ft 2 in (3.40 m); wing area 174 sq ft (16.16 m²)
Armament: two 7.9-mm (0.31-in) MG 17 machine-guns in nose and two 20-mm (0.7-in) MG FF/M cannon in wings.
Performance: maximum speed 359 mph (578 km/h) at 12,300 ft (3749 m); initial climb rate 3,300 ft (1006 m) per minute; service ceiling 36,500ft (11125 m); range 680 miles (1094 km) with drop tank

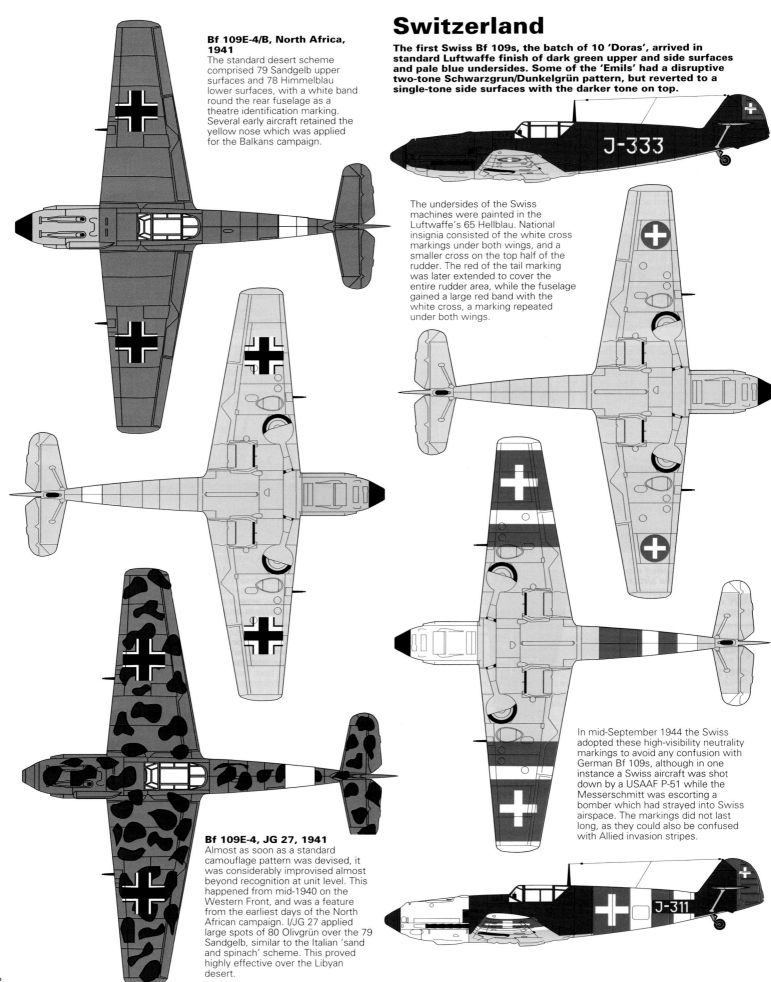

Bf 109E-4/B, North Africa, 1941
The standard desert scheme comprised 79 Sandgelb upper surfaces and 78 Himmelblau lower surfaces, with a white band round the rear fuselage as a theatre identification marking. Several early aircraft retained the yellow nose which was applied for the Balkans campaign.

Switzerland

The first Swiss Bf 109s, the batch of 10 'Doras', arrived in standard Luftwaffe finish of dark green upper and side surfaces and pale blue undersides. Some of the 'Emils' had a disruptive two-tone Schwarzgrun/Dunkelgrün pattern, but reverted to a single-tone side surfaces with the darker tone on top.

The undersides of the Swiss machines were painted in the Luftwaffe's 65 Hellblau. National insignia consisted of the white cross markings under both wings, and a smaller cross on the top half of the rudder. The red of the tail marking was later extended to cover the entire rudder area, while the fuselage gained a large red band with the white cross, a marking repeated under both wings.

Bf 109E-4, JG 27, 1941
Almost as soon as a standard camouflage pattern was devised, it was considerably improvised almost beyond recognition at unit level. This happened from mid-1940 on the Western Front, and was a feature from the earliest days of the North African campaign. I/JG 27 applied large spots of 80 Olivgrün over the 79 Sandgelb, similar to the Italian 'sand and spinach' scheme. This proved highly effective over the Libyan desert.

In mid-September 1944 the Swiss adopted these high-visibility neutrality markings to avoid any confusion with German Bf 109s, although in one instance a Swiss aircraft was shot down by a USAAF P-51 while the Messerschmitt was escorting a bomber which had strayed into Swiss airspace. The markings did not last long, as they could also be confused with Allied invasion stripes.

The upper and lower cowlings were easily removed for access to the engine for maintenance, while the propeller had a standard bevel fixing. The small tank immediately to port of the propeller shaft was the header tank for the glycol coolant.

The centre section of the heavily-framed canopy hinged to starboard for access. Noticeable inside is the armour plate around the pilot's head which was attached to the canopy itself.

The single-strut main undercarriage units were attached directly to the fuselage structure and had oleo suspension with a small scissors-type torque link at the bottom of the strut. The brake cables ran down the front of the strut.

Below: Owing to the single-spar wing construction, incorporation of the wheel well posed few structural problems. Visible behind is the wing-mounted radiator.

Above: Due to the Bf 109's narrow fuselage, the cockpit was very cramped compared to other wartime fighters. This, combined with the short length of the control column, made control inputs difficult to make. The dashboard was topped by the *Reflexvisier* reflecting sight, offset to starboard. A circuit breaker panel was on the starboard side of the cockpit.

Right: The Bf 109's tail control surfaces were aerodynamically balanced. A key omission was a rudder trimmer, which made gunnery and long-distance flying tiring. Note the strut-braced, variable-incidence tailplane and the lifting tube forward of the tailwheel.

Two underwing views show the DB 600-powered V13 (above) and the Bf 109E (right), providing details of the aileron linkages, radiator ejector flaps and the aileron horn balances, the latter differing between the two aircraft. The bulge under the wing of the 'Emil' housed the breech of the wing-mounted MG FF cannon.

Messerschmitt Bf 109

Part 2: The later variants

The 1940 exploits of the Bf 109E 'Emil' firmly established the Messerschmitt fighter as the world's best. Building on those successes, the Augsburg company developed the Bf 109F, which was arguably the best variant of them all, and the spearhead of the devastating opening attack on the Soviet Union. However, it was not until the Bf 109G that the aircraft came to be built in huge numbers and in a wide variety of versions. By mid-war, the Bf 109 was beginning to lose its supremacy, yet it remained the backbone of the Luftwaffe fighter forces for the remainder of the conflict, and in the final days of the Reich late-model Bf 109Gs and Bf 109Ks were putting up fierce resistance to the overwhelming Allied forces. Even the close of the war did not spell the end for the Bf 109: the airframe continued to be developed in Czechoslovakia and Spain, seeing action in two post-war conflicts and surviving as a front-line type until the mid-1960s.

From 1991 to 1997 the only genuine flying Messerschmitt Bf 109 was the Bf 109G-2/Trop WkNr 10639 'Black 6', operated by the Imperial War Museum at Duxford, England. Originally laid down as an F-3 by Erla at Leipzig, the aircraft was completed as a G-2 Trop and issued to 8./JG 77 at Gambut in Libya. Here it was found by No. 3 Sqn, RAAF after the Germans had retreated. After spending some time with the Australians, it was allocated to the RAF's No. 1426 Enemy Aircraft Flight at Collyweston and was used for demonstration and evaluation flights. Soon after the war an unsuccessful attempt was made to put it back in the air. The final restoration began at RAF Lyneham in 1972, subsequently moving to Northolt and then to Benson, from where the aircraft made its 'first' flight in the hands of Group Captain Reg Hallam on 17 March 1991. The RAF restoration team was aided by Rolls-Royce, which overhauled the DB 605 engine, and many individuals. The result is a 100 per cent genuine Bf 109. Unfortunately, at the end of the show season in 1997, the aircraft was badly damaged in a landing accident and its future is uncertain.

Above: Bf 109Gs of 7./JG 27 escort a bomber at low level over the Adriatic from their base at Kalamaki, in Greece. The two aircraft in the background are G-6/Trops, fitted with underwing gondolas for MG 151/20 cannon (Rüstsatz-6). The nearest aircraft is a G-6 without tropical filter or additional cannon. All three carry the 300-litre centreline tank (Rüstsatz-3) which was regularly fitted to the late-model Bf 109s.

Right: Huge numbers of Bf 109Gs were produced by three factories. These G-6 aircraft are seen on Messerschmitt's own Regensburg line.

Far right: A Luftwaffe experte adds another victory to the tail of his Bf 109. Despite some reports to the contrary, the Luftwaffe was rigorous in its examination and award of victory claims. The term experte referred to a pilot with 10 or more kills, this figure having been used by the Germans, British and French to designate an ace since World War I. It was the US which introduced the five-kill figure.

When the Battle of Britain ground to an indecisive halt in late 1940, the German military machine had faced its first reversal in fortune. Unable to wrest control of the skies over Britain from the Royal Air Force, the Luftwaffe had not been able to provide the security blanket which the Wehrmacht had enjoyed during its previous successful campaigns, and it had been impossible for the invasion of Britain to proceed. The failure to capture Britain was of crucial importance to the outcome of the war for many reasons: it provided a bastion from which Britain and its allies could continue to attack, and eventually destroy, German military production; it provided a ready-made jumping-off point for the Allied invasion of Europe; it allowed Britain to retain control of the Atlantic and Mediterranean approaches; and it hammered the first dent into the morale of a buoyant German populace. Initially, while fighting alone, Britain could do little more than harass the Germans in mainland Europe, although the cross-Channel war diverted valuable forces away from other theatres.

Without doubt, the key weapon in the British inventory during the Battle of Britain and subsequent cross-Channel operations was the Supermarine Spitfire; this fighter had

been the first to challenge the Messerschmitt Bf 109 for supremacy of the air. The Spitfire was aggressively developed throughout the remainder of the war, its airframe proving remarkably able to absorb ever greater power, loads and speeds. Furthermore, the Allies continued to develop new aircraft and bring them into service just as another type began to fade. It was forward planning and the full backing for rapid development that brought the P-47, P-51, Typhoon and Griffon Spitfire into the fray at a time when they could make a difference, and in more than sufficient numbers.

Left: It was on the Russian front where the late-model Bf 109s enjoyed their greatest successes, huge numbers of Soviet aircraft falling to the guns of the Luftwaffe experten. Always grossly outnumbered, the Jagdflieger continued their fight against growing odds, and against ever more capable opponents. Seen on a snowy airfield here are the Bf 109G-6s of I./JG 51, displaying a variety of winter finishes.

In Germany, things were different. The Focke-Wulf Fw 190 was essentially the only new fighter brought into widespread Luftwaffe service during the course of the war, and there were never enough to go around. Its own development problems also caused delays to its service introduction, giving the Luftwaffe something of a gap in capability during 1941/42. The otherwise excellent Jumo-powered Fw 190D arrived too late to make a difference, while the potentially war-winning jets were far too late and too few to make any impact. This failure to provide a seamless stream of new fighter types for the Luftwaffe occurred for a number of reasons, including the internecine way Germany itself was governed, internal friction in the RLM and a considerable amount of 'laurel-resting' in the first years of the war. Such was the scale and rapidity of the early military successes that few in Germany expected the war to last long enough to warrant the rapid development of follow-on weapons. Campaigns were expected to last weeks, not years.

When faced with the reality of the situation, the Luftwaffe and RLM had no choice other than to turn to its serving fighter, the Bf 109, to provide answers to many procurement questions. Only this aircraft could be made available in short order and in large numbers. Consequently, the Bf 109 was developed beyond its natural limit and at a pace forced by the exigencies of war. From the early G models onwards, the Bf 109 endured a slow and steady decline when compared with its enemies, gaining weight and speed but losing much of the fighting prowess with which the 'Emil' had been blessed. Yet huge numbers were built. In the right hands, of course, and in the right theatre, the late-model Bf 109s were still potent warplanes, but they never enjoyed the mastery of the skies achieved by their illustrious forebears. It would not be until the summer of 1941 that this fundamental planning weakness would begin to manifest itself.

Development of the 'Friedrich'

Eighteen months earlier, in early 1940, such a problem seemed to be impossible, and subsequent events would reinforce the delusion. Although numerically inferior and with woefully thin reserves, German forces swept through much of Europe with technologically superior weapons and superb tactics. Britain, the Soviet Union and the Balkans would surely follow.

In its Bf 109E, Messerschmitt had undoubtedly the finest fighter in the world, yet the company realised that a structured development would have to be implemented to protect that position. Daimler-Benz was promising developed versions of the DB 601, and Messerschmitt set about designing a new variant to harness the extra power in a way which would improve performance without losing the manoeuvrability and handling of the 'Emil'. The result would be the Bf 109F, arguably the finest version of all.

Compared to the Bf 109E, the F introduced a host of aerodynamic modifications, the structure remaining essen-

Above: This typical scene shows the pilots of II./JG 53 on Sicily in 1942, preparing to take their Bf 109G-2s to war in Tunisia. It would not be long before they would be back in Sicily, in full retreat from the Allied forces. In the Mediterranean theatre the Bf 109s were heavily employed in escorting the vulnerable Ju 52 transports.

Left: An increasingly common sight as the war progressed: a Bf 109G is caught by an RAF Spitfire. Although the Bf 109G was largely outperformed by Allied types in the last months of the war, it could still put up a more than credible fight in the right hands. Fortunately for the Allies, the once large number of experienced pilots had dwindled to just a handful, and the majority of Luftwaffe pilots were inexperienced and poorly trained.

Messerschmitt Bf 109

Bf 109F prototypes

Messerschmitt produced four Bf 109F prototypes (V21, V22, V23 and V24) in mid-1940. The first was powered by the DB 601A of the Bf 109E, albeit housed in the new, sleeker cowling. Subsequent aircraft all had the intended DB 601E.

Above: The most obvious new feature of the Bf 109F (fourth prototype V24 shown) was its streamlined cowling and enlarged spinner. The engine-mounted cannon, virtually never fitted to the Bf 109E, became a standard feature of all subsequent Bf 109s.

Below: The four prototype Bf 109Fs were fitted with short circular intakes for the supercharger. This aircraft is the V23 third prototype, which was the first to be fitted with the rounded wingtips which became standard.

Above: As originally designed, the Bf 109F had much shorter wings than the Bf 109E, as emphasised in this view of the V24. Although roll rate was significantly enhanced, the effect on handling was extremely detrimental, leading to the restoration of some wing area and span in the form of rounded wingtips.

The head-on view of the Bf 109F-0 highlights the shallow radiator configuration and the port-side supercharger intake. For the pre-production variant this had a square capture area, reverting to circular for production aircraft.

tially unchanged. Most noticeable at first glance was the redesigned engine cowling, which was deeper and more streamlined, and accompanied by a much larger, rounded spinner. The reduction in propeller diameter by a few inches further enhanced the visual effect of the new spinner.

Of more importance was the new wing design. Based on the E structure, the span was reduced by 2 ft (61 cm) and new ailerons were provided, of reduced span but greater chord. They were no longer interlinked to the flaps, and were changed from the slot to Frise type, with inset hinges and a bevelled upper leading edge. A new low-drag radiator was designed, which employed a boundary-layer removal system ahead of the intake, thereby allowing the radiator to project less far into the airstream, reducing drag. The boundary layer air was ejected through a duct above the flaps. The flaps themselves were split into two, the inboard sections being split horizontally. The upper and lower portions moved simultaneously to form a normal flap section for landing and take-off, but the upper and lower sections could move up and down independently, under control of a thermostat, to form a variable radiator ejector flap.

In the tail area, the Bf 109F introduced a semi-retractable tailwheel, while the tailplane was moved slightly forward of its position on the E. The bracing struts were removed. The rudder was reduced in size slightly, while the whole fin was given a cambered aerofoil section, as opposed to symmetrical, to reduce rudder inputs during take-off and climb. Following input from leading fighter pilots, the armament was changed to feature a single cannon firing through the engine hub, together with two MG 17 machine-guns in the upper fuselage decking. This concentration of firepower was thought to be entirely adequate, and the removal of the heavy cannon from the wings would have a beneficial effect on manoeuvrability and rate of roll.

Prototype construction

At about the time Bf 109Es were clearing the skies over France and the Low Countries, work began on Bf 109F construction, which consisted of four prototypes and a pre-production batch of 10 Bf 109F-0s. The first aircraft, Bf 109 V21, was fitted with the DB 601Aa engine which powered the Bf 109E-3 and E-4, offering 1,175 hp (876 kW) for take-off and 1,000 hp (746 kW) at 3700 m (12,140 ft). However, the second aircraft (V22) was powered by an early version of the Bf 109F's intended engine, the Daimler-Benz DB 601E. Both the third (V23) and fourth (V24) aircraft also had trials DB 601Es. The V22 was subsequently heavily employed in powerplant testing.

First flight (date not recorded) occurred in the summer of 1940, and immediately the F showed enormous promise, although the cut in wingspan severely hampered handling. Accordingly, the third aircraft was fitted with detachable rounded wingtips, which immediately restored the aircraft's

Bf 109F-0

Following on from the prototypes was a batch of 10 Bf 109F-0s, powered by the DB 601N pending delivery of the DB 601E. Similarly, the MG 151/15 cannon was not ready, so F-0s had the 20-mm MG FF/M installed in its place.

The rectangular supercharger air intake identifies this machine as one of the Bf 109F-0 pre-production aircraft. The armament consisted of only three weapons, as opposed to the four of the Bf 109E.

fine handling and were adopted as standard. The fourth aircraft had some minor changes applied, including a deeper oil cooler fairing under the nose, but it retained the short wings.

Bf 109F-0 pre-production aircraft left the factory in the late autumn, fitted with the rounded wingtips and deep oil cooler. The DB 601E engine was experiencing development problems, so the DB 601N (1,200 hp/895 kW for take-off and 1,270 hp/947 kW at 5000 m/16,400 ft) was employed instead, this engine having been used in the E-4/N and E-7 variants. Neither was the Mauser MG 151 engine-mounted cannon ready, so the trusty MG FF/M was substituted. Even with the E's engine, the Bf 109F showed a considerable advance over the 'Emil'. Performance and manoeuvrability were better in all respects, notably in terms of sustained turning and climb. The only retrograde step was the reduction of heavy-calibre firepower from two MG FFs to one, but the impending introduction of the MG 151 was expected to offset this.

In October 1940 the first Bf 109F-1 production aircraft left the assembly lines. It was similar to the F-0 except that it had a circular, as opposed to rectangular, supercharger air intake, as had been tested on the V24. DB 601Ns were fitted, burning high-octane (96) C3 fuel. Initially, they were for delivery to service evaluation units. A spate of crashes ensued, during which severe engine vibration was encountered. Naturally, attention was drawn to the powerplant, although, since it was the same engine which powered many Bf 109Es in service, it was not considered to be the cause. The Fs were grounded, but no cause could be found for the accidents. Flying resumed, whereupon another F-1 crashed. During the crash the engine sustained only minor damage, allowing it to be completely ruled out as the source of the problem. Instead, it was found that many of the rivets in the tail area were missing or loose. Further investigation revealed the true cause: the removal of the tailplane bracing struts had altered the rigidity of the tailplane, and at certain throttle settings an oscillation was set up in the spar. This overlapped that of the engine, causing resonance that eventually resulted in structural failure and a loss of control. The fix consisted of strengthening plates being attached externally.

'Friedrich' enters service

A handful of F-1s reached France as early as October 1940, to be flown by the most experienced pilots. The first production aircraft was used by Werner Mölders of Stab/JG 51, his first sortie being variously recorded as 6 or 25

October. Delay to the main issue of 'Friedrichs' was inevitable while the accidents were investigated and a cure devised. Therefore it was not until March 1941 that Bf 109F-1s entered service in any great numbers. Naturally, the first units to receive the type were the two Geschwaders of Luftflotte 3 remaining in France which, at the time, were the only Luftwaffe fighter units facing a real enemy. JG 2 'Richthofen' was the first to get the new fighter, closely followed by JG 26 'Schlageter', although II./JG 26 remained on the Bf 109E-7 pending the arrival of the first Focke-Wulf Fw 190A-1s in July. Several other units subsequently received F-1s, although none was ever fully equipped due to the small number produced.

Left: Werner Mölders is seen in the cockpit of an early Bf 109F-1. He was the first pilot to take the new variant into combat, flying it on the Channel front in October 1940. The following June, he led JG 51 into battle in the East, scoring rapidly in the first weeks of the campaign.

Left: Werner Mölders is seen in the cockpit of an early Bf 109F-1. He was the first pilot to take the new variant into combat, flying it on the Channel front in October 1940. The following June, he led JG 51 into battle in the East, scoring rapidly in the first weeks of the campaign.

Far left: An early Bf 109F displays the rounded wingtips and angular mainwheel cutouts of the type. The F was widely regarded as the best of the Bf 109s from a pilot's standpoint, retaining much of the fine handling of the 'Emil' while enjoying better performance. It was well-matched with the Spitfire Mk V, enjoying some notable advantages such as diving speed.

Above: The 'Friedrich' was welcomed at the front line, especially in France where the Luftwaffe was facing the well-equipped RAF. This early aircraft served with II./JG 2 'Richthofen'. In the early days on the Channel, the Bf 109Fs usually sported all-yellow cowlings.

The first production series of Bf 109Fs (F-1 to F-3) retained the DB 601N engine, requiring the use of high-octane fuel. The deeper oil cooler bath under the nose was introduced on the fourth prototype and applied to all subsequent machines.

Messerschmitt Bf 109

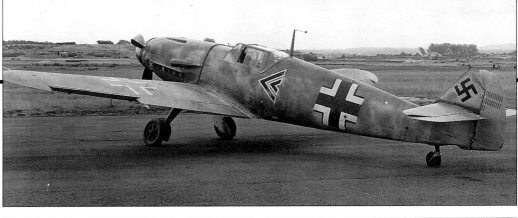

Stars and roundels

A number of Bf 109s were captured intact by the Allies and subsequently flown in evaluation trials. The first was the Bf 109F-2 of Major Rolf Pingel (right), of I./JG 26, who was forced to make a wheels-up landing at St Margaret's Bay, Kent, on 10 July 1941. The aircraft was damaged only slightly, and was flown by the RAF until it crashed on 20 October.

Many Bf 109s were abandoned during the reversals in the desert, and some were flown as squadron 'hacks'. This F-4/Trop previously flew with III./JG 53.

The USAAF acquired this Bf 109F-4 from the USSR as a goodwill gesture. It arrived at Wright Field in March 1943, subsequently moving to Eglin in Florida.

In the East the Russians acquired at least one flyable Bf 109F (W Nr 7640), which was then put through its paces by the NII VVS, the Red air force's principal test establishment.

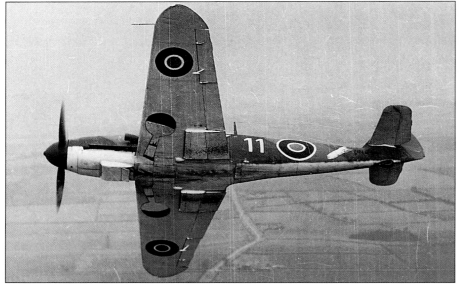

Deliveries of F-1s were undertaken alongside those of F-2s, which entered production in January 1941. They differed only by having the interim 15-mm MG 151/15 cannon (with 200 rounds) in place of the MG FF/M. The first few were built without the external stiffeners to the rear fuselage, but these were probably retrofitted.

At the same time, the RAF was introducing its first Spitfire Mk Vs on the Channel front, and, like the Spitfire Mk I/II and Bf 109E before them, the two proved to be remarkably well-matched. Just as its immediate predecessor had shown, the Spitfire Mk V could easily out-turn the Bf 109F, yet the 'Friedrich' still had the edge in diving and climbing. An early chance to fully evaluate the Bf 109F was handed to the RAF on 10 July 1941, when the aircraft flown by I./JG 26's Gruppenkommandeur, Hauptmann Rolf Pingel, was shot down near Dover and landed virtually intact. The damage to radiators and propeller was repaired, and the aircraft flew again (with RAF serial ES906) on 19 September at Farnborough. It was soon dispatched to Duxford for exhaustive testing against British fighters, but it crashed on 20 October, denying the chance for a quantitative test against the Spitfire Mk V.

Above: As 'White 11' of 10.(Jabo)/JG 26, this Bf 109F-4/B crash-landed at Beachy Head in Sussex on 20 May 1942. After repair, the aircraft flew again in October, assigned the RAF serial NN644 but retaining its Jabo markings. It was allocated to No. 1426 (Enemy Aircraft) Flight.

Although primarily day-fighters, Bf 109s were used in the nocturnal war, especially on the Eastern front during the early months of the campaign. Here they were employed against Soviet nuisance raiders. This Bf 109F of II./JG 54 displays 19 victory bars on the tail.

Fs in the East

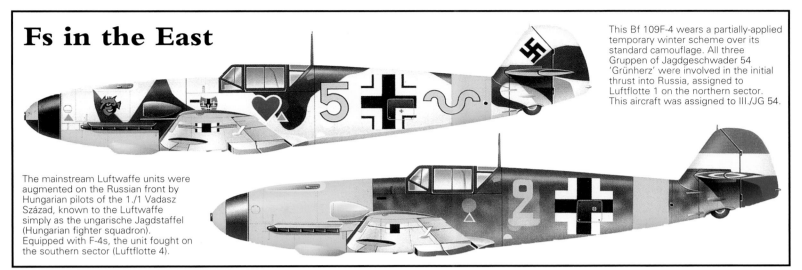

This Bf 109F-4 wears a partially-applied temporary winter scheme over its standard camouflage. All three Gruppen of Jagdgeschwader 54 'Grünherz' were involved in the initial thrust into Russia, assigned to Luftflotte 1 on the northern sector. This aircraft was assigned to III./JG 54.

The mainstream Luftwaffe units were augmented on the Russian front by Hungarian pilots of the 1./1 Vadasz Század, known to the Luftwaffe simply as the ungarische Jagdstaffel (Hungarian fighter squadron). Equipped with F-4s, the unit fought on the southern sector (Luftflotte 4).

After having equipped the Channel front units, the next priority was to re-equip the Jagdgruppen which had been pulled back to Germany to await the assault on the Soviet Union. Bf 109Fs took no part in Operations Bestrafung, Marita and Merkur, the invasions of Yugoslavia, Greece and Crete, which were covered by units still flying the Bf 109E. However, by 22 June 1941 the majority of the Jagdgruppen involved in the opening attack on the Soviet Union were flying the 'Friedrich'. On the northern sector, Luftflotte 1 had I., II. and III./JG 54 'Grünherz' flying the F and no E units; covering the central sector, Luftflotte 2 had I., II., III. and IV./JG 51 (later named 'Mölders') and I., II. and III/JG 53 'Pik As' flying Bf 109Fs and a further two Gruppen (II. and III./JG 27) on Bf 109Es; on the southern sector, Luftflotte 4 had five Gruppen with Bf 109Es and three with Fs (I., II. and III./JG 3 – later named 'Udet').

Blitzkrieg in the East

Barbarossa was savage. By midday on the first day, the VVS had lost 1,200 aircraft, of which around 320 had been shot down, almost all by Bf 109s and the majority of these by Fs. The Russian Polikarpovs had a few tricks up their sleeves, relying almost entirely on the astonishing agility of the nimble fighters, but they were so hopelessly outperformed, especially by the Bf 109F, that the defence was futile, if brave. Once the Luftwaffe pilots had relearned the lessons of the Spanish Civil War and avoided tangling with the I-153s and I-16s in a slow, close-in fight, there was little the Polikarpovs could do. The Bf 109 pilots scythed into the Soviet defences using the dive and climb tactics which had been so successful in Spain and every campaign since; and, if a pilot should find himself in trouble, opening

the taps and diving away would almost certainly guarantee safety. The early Fs swept away the Red air force during the early weeks of Barbarossa, paving the way for the lightning ground advance that took the Wehrmacht almost to the gates of Moscow.

On the Russian front, Bf 109F *experten* began compiling scores that even bettered those of their compatriots in

'Black 3' was a Bf 109F of 8./JG 54, seen during the long winter of 1941/42 in the Leningrad area. The aircraft has a temporary white finish applied, and carries the Geschwader's large 'Grünherz' marking. Note the damaged radio aerial mast and sagging aerial.

One of the least popular roles was escort for the Ju 87s, Bf 109s being tied to the slow bombers instead of ranging free over the front. This Bf 109 wears the buzzard badge of JG 51 'Mölders'.

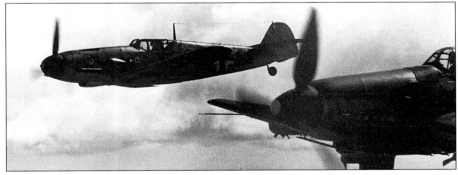

Operation Barbarossa

Barbarossa, the invasion of the Soviet Union, was delayed by the campaign in the Balkans, which was necessary to underpin the southern flank. This delay proved costly to the Germans, for the winter snows came early, stagnating the advance of the Wehrmacht tantalisingly close to Moscow. The 'Friedrich' spearheaded the German lunge into Russia, proving more than adequate for dealing with any Soviet fighters. A large proportion of the VVS had been destroyed in the opening blitz, either in the air or by strafing attacks. Those that survived the initial onslaught continued to fall in large numbers to the guns of the combat-hardened Jagdflieger.

A pilot brushes snow off his Bf 109F-2 during the winter of 1941/42. The harsh weather became a major factor in Luftwaffe operations. For all their lack of fighting capability, the Soviet aircraft of the time were able to operate in the coldest of weather, while the sophisticated Luftwaffe aircraft were often grounded. Note the fuel filler triangle, marked with 'C-3' to remind ground crew to only use 96-octane fuel.

Libya. Heading the list was Werner Mölders, the Geschwaderkommodore of JG 51, and the leading German pilot in both the Spanish Civil War and Battle of Britain. By the end of June he had passed von Richthofen's score of 80, and shot down his 101st aircraft on 16 July. Deemed to be too valuable to be risked further, he was recalled to

Berlin to take up the post of General der Jagdflieger. He was ironically killed while flying as a passenger in an He 111, on his way to Ernst Udet's funeral.

There were many candidates eager to take up the challenge, not that the Soviet air force represented much of an opposition in the last half of 1941. Several aces used the Bf 109F as the springboard to the 100-, 200- and even 300-kill marks, including Heinz Bär, Gerd Barkhorn, Gordon Gollob, Hermann Graf, Erich Hartmann and Joachim Müncheberg. Several élite units were subsequently transferred to the Mediterranean, and the Jagdgruppen operated at an alarmingly low level. In 1942 the VVS also began to represent a greater challenge: more competitive types entered service, and the Il-2 began to make its presence felt over the battlefield. Nevertheless, the Bf 109 held sway in the air war, although it was grossly outnumbered.

'Friedrich' heads south

As the Bf 109F was proving itself to be a worthy successor to the illustrious 'Emil' in the Russian summer, the variant began to reach another theatre where it would also make a considerable impact: the deserts of North Africa. Bf 109Es (of I./JG 27) had reached Libya in late April 1941, and had made an immediate impression on the air war in the theatre. In July the SAAF and RAF began to introduce the Kittyhawk Mk I into the theatre, and the Luftwaffe felt that it posed a threat to the Bf 109Es (erroneously, as it turned out). The consequence was an immediate request to convert JG 27 to the Bf 109F, a process initiated swiftly. In September, 'Friedrichs' arrived in Libya with II./JG 27, while the E-equipped Gruppe returned briefly to Germany to convert to the new variant. Their aircraft were designated Bf 109F-2/Trop and F-4/Z Trop, and they featured a dust/sand filter over the supercharger air intake (with a clamshell cover over the intake operated from the cockpit),

Tropical Fs

Desert wings

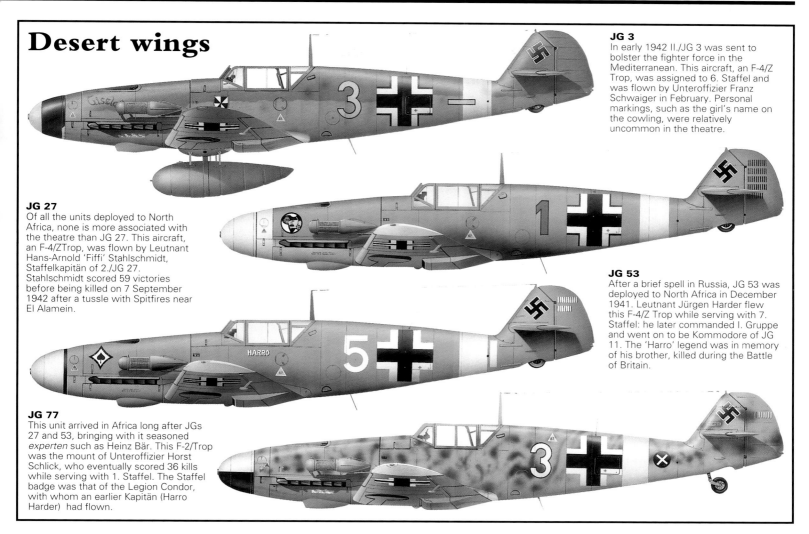

JG 3
In early 1942 II./JG 3 was sent to bolster the fighter force in the Mediterranean. This aircraft, an F-4/Z Trop, was assigned to 6. Staffel and was flown by Unteroffizier Franz Schwaiger in February. Personal markings, such as the girl's name on the cowling, were relatively uncommon in the theatre.

JG 27
Of all the units deployed to North Africa, none is more associated with the theatre than JG 27. This aircraft, an F-4/ZTrop, was flown by Leutnant Hans-Arnold 'Fiffi' Stahlschmidt, Staffelkapitän of 2./JG 27. Stahlschmidt scored 59 victories before being killed on 7 September 1942 after a tussle with Spitfires near El Alamein.

JG 53
After a brief spell in Russia, JG 53 was deployed to North Africa in December 1941. Leutnant Jürgen Harder flew this F-4/Z Trop while serving with 7. Staffel: he later commanded I. Gruppe and went on to be Kommodore of JG 11. The 'Harro' legend was in memory of his brother, killed during the Battle of Britain.

JG 77
This unit arrived in Africa long after JGs 27 and 53, bringing with it seasoned *experten* such as Heinz Bär. This F-2/Trop was the mount of Unteroffizier Horst Schlick, who eventually scored 36 kills while serving with 1. Staffel. The Staffel badge was that of the Legion Condor, with whom an earlier Kapitän (Harro Harder) had flown.

in addition to other desert modifications. It is not thought that any Trops were produced at the factory, aircraft being so altered in the field. Pitted against P-40s and Hurricanes, the Fs enjoyed a period of considerable ascendancy.

Despite the successes achieved in the opening months on the Russian front, there was still considerable attrition. Overall fighter production had been stepped up, but that of the Bf 109 was little increased. This was mainly due to the transition of three of the six factories which had hitherto built Bf 109s to the Fw 190 production effort. Fieseler was the first to go, in July 1941, followed by Arado and AGO before the end of the year. This left only Erla, WNF and the parent factory producing the Bf 109, although the latter contributed little in 1941.

Bf 109F developments

Nevertheless, new variants had been produced. A few F-2s had a centreline pylon for bomb carriage, being designated Bf 109F-2/B. At least one F-2/U1 is recorded as having seen combat (flown by none other than Oberstleutnant Adolf Galland of JG 26), this sub-variant featuring 13-mm MG 131 machine-guns in place of the MG 17s. The Bf 109F-2/Z was intended to introduce GM 1 nitrous oxide boosting, but probably never progressed further than test aircraft.

However, at the end of 1941 the intended engine, the DB 601E, finally became available. It had the advantage of running on low-octane (87) B4 fuel, which was easier to produce and more plentiful. The first DB 601E-powered variant was the Bf 109F-3, of which only a handful were built, closely followed by what was the definitive 'Friedrich': the Bf 109F-4. The latter differed in several respects from its forerunners, the most important change

being the installation of the 20-mm calibre MG 151/20 (with ammunition dropping to 150 rounds). At last, the originally intended Bf 109F armament and powerplant had been brought together. Other changes included revised self-sealing tanks and additional armouring, notably an angled plate above the pilot's head. Early F-4s retained the external stiffeners to the rear fuselage, but a more elegant solution of internal strengthening was applied to most of the batch.

This line-up is believed to be of the Bf 109F-3 variant, which was powered by the DB 601E. Only a few F-3s were built, differing in only minor detail (principally by retaining the MG 151/15 cannon) from the F-4 which followed.

Left: The Bf 109F-4 was the major production version of the 'Friedrich', and also represented the definitive standard with DB 601E engine and MG 151/20 cannon firing through the spinner. All F series aircraft retained the small quarterlight glazed panel, a useful recognition feature.

One of the success stories of the early cross-Channel operations were the 'hit-and-run' Bf 109E fighter-bombers, which caused considerable damage along the English coast. Some time after the fighter units had been re-equipped, the two Jabostaffeln transitioned to a dedicated version of the Bf 109F-4, fitted with an ETC 250 bomb rack under the centreline.

Above: 10.(Jabo)/JG 26 left the observer in no doubt as to the role of the Staffel. Clutching an SC 250 bomb to its belly, one of the unit's Bf 109F-4/Bs sets out for a mission across the Channel.

Above right: Partnering 10./JG 26 in the Jabo mission was 10./JG 2. The two Jabostaffeln specialised in anti-shipping attacks against coastal targets, and achieved a fair measure of success. Early warning of such attacks was often impossible, as the F-4/Bs operated in small formations (often just a pair) and crossed the Channel at very low level.

These Bf 109F-4/Trops are of I./JG 53, seen on Sicily. All carry the Rüstsatz-3 centreline drop tank.

On the Channel front, the F was used only briefly in the pure fighter role, as the Fw 190A-2/A-3 began arriving in numbers during the latter half of 1941. Only II./JG 26 operated the F-4, and that only briefly in the winter of 1941/42 while it gave up Fw 190As and waited for Bf 109Gs. However, at about this time, the Bf 109F-4/B was being introduced to Luftflotte 3's two fighter-bomber units. Both of the Channel front Geschwaders had a single Staffel assigned to hit-and-run duties, with shipping and coastal installations the main targets. Bf 109E-4/Bs had been used in this role throughout 1941, despite the re-equipment of the rest of JG 2 and JG 26 with Fw 190s. They were replaced in early 1942 with Jabo-roled Fs, which could carry a single 250-kg (551-lb) SC 250 bomb on a centreline ETC 250 rack. Bf 109F-4/Bs served with 10.(Jabo)/JG 2 at Beaumont-le-Roger and 10.(Jabo)/JG 26 at Poix, and achieved considerable success along the English coastline.

North African success

Events in the desert turned very much in the Bf 109F's favour. Facing opposition from Hurricanes, Tomahawks and Kittyhawks, the 'Friedrich' reigned supreme in the fighter v. fighter combat which dominated the air war. Several pilots began to amass large tallies, but no star shone more brightly than the 'Star of Afrika' himself – Leutnant Hans-Joachim Marseille of 3./JG 27. Marseille had already

scored five kills in the Battle of Britain (albeit with the loss of four Bf 109Es!), but it was when he arrived in the desert and began flying the Bf 109F-4Z Trop (at least four individual aircraft wore his famous 'Yellow 14') that his abundant skills began to show. An acknowledged master of deflection shooting, he astonished fellow pilots and ground crew by how few rounds he required to down his victims.

Marseille passed 50 kills on 22 February 1942, 75 on 6 June and reached 101 on 18 June, having been promoted

Above: A 'black man' catches up with his rest while the Bf 109F-4/Trops of 5./JG 27 sit at alert. The tropical filter was an Italian-designed unit.

Below: A group of 'Tommies' poses with a downed JG 27 Bf 109F. The desert was littered with aircraft from both sides – the recovery of downed pilots was a major problem.

Star of Afrika

This F-4/Z Trop is the aircraft used by Hauptmann Hans-Joachim Marseille after his return to Africa, and is seen as it appeared in September 1942, days before his death in a G-2/Trop. Marseille used at least four F-4/Z Trops during his reign in the desert, all coded 'Yellow 14'. The fin bears testament to 151 kills: he scored a total of 158 (all but seven in the desert). Marseille was a superb fighter pilot, but his high spirits ruined his chances for a meteoric rise to a plum command job. In June 1942 he was made Staffelkapitän of 3./JG 27.

'Pik As' in Sicily

Based at Comiso in May 1942, this Bf 109F-4 was one of the aircraft used by Oberstleutnant Günther Freiherr von Maltzahn, the Kommodore of JG 53. In addition to the Kommodore markings, the aircraft has its spinner tip painted blue, denoting the Geschwaderstab. Von Maltzahn scored 68 kills while with JG 53.

This F-4/Z wears typical Russian front summer camouflage, hastily applied with Mediterranean theatre bands for service with 5./JG 53 at Comiso in February 1942. The machine was the mount of Hauptmann Kurt Brändle, the Staffelkapitän, who went on to command II./JG 3, scoring 180 kills before being killed in November 1943.

to Oberleutnant and put in command of 3./JG 27. Days after, he was ordered back to Berlin to receive the Swords to his Ritterkreuz from Hitler himself. A two-month leave followed, after which Marseille returned to Libya, now promoted to Hauptmann. On 1 September, 'Jochen' achieved the near-impossible by downing 17 fighters in one day. More action in the month brought his total to 158. Having scored virtually all of his victories in a Bf 109F, Marseille was flying a G-2/Trop when he departed on a routine sortie on 30 September. Returning from a fruitless patrol, the DB 605 engine caught fire, leaving Marseille with no choice but to bail out. As he did so, his body struck the tailplane, and he fell to his death. He was just 22 years old.

Despite the arrival of the 'Gustav', the 'Friedrich' still reigned supreme in the Mediterranean theatre for some months, having been operated in North Africa by all of JG 27 (bar a Jagdkommando in Crete), III./JG 53 and the Jabo Staffel Afrika. The Stab. and II./JG 53 were in Sicily alongside I./JG 77. Reshuffling of units between Africa and Sicily, and between the theatre and the Russian front, was commonplace. By the time of Marseille's death, the Spitfire Mk V was being encountered in some numbers, considerably reducing the discrepancy between the two fighter forces, although the Spitfires were hampered by their cumbersome Vokes filters. Furthermore, the steady attrition among the *experten* was not being made good, new arrivals in Africa being almost universally 'green' pilots fresh out of fighter school. On 23 October, the landmark battle of El Alamein opened. The Luftwaffe was on its way out of Africa.

In the hands of a competent pilot, and against primarily fighter opposition, the Bf 109F's three-gun armament proved entirely adequate. The MG 151 was an excellent weapon for its time, with a higher rate of fire and faster muzzle velocity than the MG FF. The shells' trajectory closely matched that of the bullets from the MG 17s, providing a great concentration of fire. However, there were some disadvantages. In the desert the MG 151 was prone to jamming, leaving the Bf 109F with just its two MG 17s, hardly enough to down an aircraft. This problem was not attended to until the Bf 109G series. Another problem, and one which caused much debate, was that the three-gun armament was not sufficient against bomber-sized targets, and it also required a good pilot to employ it with effect.

Increased weight of fire

Accordingly, the first Rüstzustand (equipment condition) was developed for the Bf 109F, allowing for the addition of a pair of 20-mm MG 151/20s in gondolas under the wing, each provided with 120 rounds. This greatly increased the overall firepower, and enhanced the chances of a hit as the shells were more widely spread, but also adversely affected the handling. Not only did the extra weight and drag hamper performance, but the guns caused the Bf 109F to swing like a pendulum, requiring careful use of rudder to counteract the movement. This inevitably caused the Bf 109F-4/R1 to lose much of its effectiveness when used against

The Berlin bear badge identifies this Bf 109F as belonging to II./JG 27. It is seen sharing Martuba airfield with a Ju 88 of LG 1. Virtually all Bf 109s sent to North Africa wore a standard Sandbraun scheme, although the demarcation line along the fuselage varied considerably in position.

Far left: A Bf 109F-3 cavorts for the camera. Most Luftwaffe pilots agreed that the 'Friedrich' was the pinnacle of Bf 109 design from a handling point of view. The aircraft retained the fine handling of the Bf 109E, but rolled faster thanks to the new wingtips and was considerably better performing. The 'Gustav' was faster still, especially at altitude, but the extra weight eroded the handling considerably.

Tactical reconnaissance

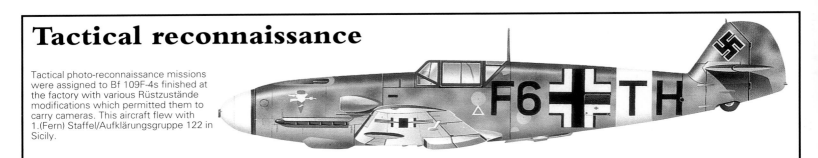

Tactical photo-reconnaissance missions were assigned to Bf 109F-4s finished at the factory with various Rüstzustände modifications which permitted them to carry cameras. This aircraft flew with 1.(Fern) Staffel/Aufklärungsgruppe 122 in Sicily.

Sunshades protect the pilots of these reconnaissance-configured Bf 109F-4s from the sun's rays as they prepare for a mission. The reconnaissance aircraft usually had small pipes which ducted excess oil back behind the camera window to avoid the latter being fouled.

Right: Last-minute preparations are undertaken prior to this Bf 109F leaving on a reconnaissance mission. In addition to the factory-installed modification which provided for camera installations, the reconnaissance Bf 109s occasionally had armament removed in the field to make them lighter and faster.

A group of 7./JG 54 Bf 109Fs taxis out for a mission across a snow-covered airfield on the Leningrad front in 1942. Once compacted, snow presented little problem to the Bf 109, but in the summer the mud caused severe wheel-clogging. Note the victory bars on the tail of the aircraft in the foreground.

fighters. Although not seen as such at the time, the Bf 109F-4/R1 was really the point where the rot set in as far as the fighter's ascendancy was concerned. Aircraft so-equipped were nicknamed 'Kanonenboote' ('gunboat'), a nickname which was also used throughout the G series.

A number of Rüstsätze were developed for the Bf 109F, but few reached the front line as the Bf 109G had already largely replaced the F by the time they were ready. One which did see some action was Rüstsatz-6, which added an ETC 250 bomb rack beneath the centreline, this being able to lift a single 250-kg (551-lb) SC 250 bomb, four SC 50 bombs (50-kg/110-lb) on an ER 4 adaptor, or a single 300-litre (66-Imp gal) drop tank. At this juncture it is worth pointing out that the term Rüstsatz covered a field modification kit only, and this in itself was not sufficient to alter an aircraft's designation. The 'R' suffixes in sub-variant designations apply to the Rüstzustand only, being applied at the factory and describing the configuration in which the aircraft left its makers. The 'U' suffix (Umbausatz) covered a factory conversion kit.

Fs with cameras

Additional versions were the F-4/Z with GM 1 boosting and several sub-variants of reconnaissance aircraft built in four Rüstzustände. Previously thought to be the Bf 109F-5 and F-6, the reconnaissance variants are now known to

have been designated Bf 109F-4/R2, R3, R4 and R8. The first three Rüstzustände designations covered aircraft with single vertically-mounted cameras (Rb 20/30, Rb 50/30 and Rb 75/30, respectively) immediately behind the cockpit, and no radios, while the single Bf 109F-4/R8 had either an Rb 50/30 or Rb 75/30 and radio. Available production figures for reconnaissance aircraft are very low, suggesting that they are either wrong, or that many aircraft were converted to the role after leaving the factory. Many had at least the cannon armament removed, and had a slight excrescence under the fuselage on which to mount the optically-flat glass through which the camera peered. As for the F-5 (an undescribed fighter variant), only one aircraft is believed to have been built, while the planned large batches of F-6s and F-8s were not fulfilled.

Foreign Fs

Luftwaffe service for the 'Friedrich' was relatively brief, as it was rapidly superseded by the Bf 109G on both the production lines and in the front line. By the end of 1942 it had largely disappeared from the day fighter forces, although a number were still being used as Jabos. Ex-Luftwaffe aircraft were supplied to other Axis or friendly nations, beginning in mid-1942 with Spain, which received 15 Bf 109F-4s. They were flown by 25 Grupo at Alcalá de Henares to prepare Spanish pilots for the volunteer unit flying on the Eastern Front. Known as the Escuadrón Azul, or more formally as 15.(span.)/JG 51, this Staffel converted from Bf 109Es to Bf 109F-4s in October 1942, and flew the 'Friedrich' until July 1943.

Second foreign recipient of the F was the Magyar Királyi Légierő (Royal Hungarian Air Force), which received Bf 109F-4s to replace the Reggiane Re.2000s of the 1./1 Vadasz Század (fighter squadron) which was serving on the Russian front, known simply as the ungarische Jagdstaffel

(Hungarian fighter squadron). In early 1943 the transfer of Bf 109F-4/R1s and F-4/Bs allowed the transition of two Italian units to the 'Friedrich', these being 3° and 150° Gruppo Caccia Terrestre.

As a test vehicle, the Bf 109F performed useful work, notably for the 'Gustav' which supplanted it on the production lines. One aircraft (V30) was employed to test the G-1's pressurised cabin. Surplus Bf 109Fs were involved in a number of other trials programme, including five assigned to different aspects of the Me 309 fighter project. Two were the third and fourth Bf 109F prototypes, modified with a fixed tricycle undercarriage and a ventral radiator bath, respectively. Other Fs tested the Me 309's inward-retracting undercarriage, air conditioning and cabin pressurisation systems.

Bf 109Fs were flown with both the BMW 801 radial engine and the Jumo 213 with its annular radiator (à la Fw

Above and top: The Hungarian air force received Bf 109Fs in 1942, and its aircraft were soon in action against the Russians in the East. The aircraft at top has the green/white/red Hungarian fin markings, but retains German national insignia. The aircraft above is in full Hungarian markings.

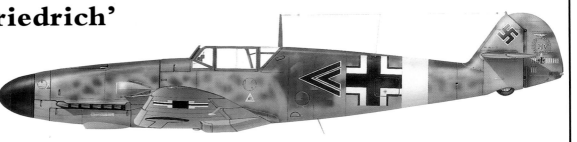

Italy-based 'Friedrich'

This F-4, the personal aircraft of Leutnant Heinz-Edgar Bär, Kommandeur of I./JG 77, is shown as it appeared while based in southern Italy in July 1942, prior to the move to North Africa. 'Pritzl' Bär had opened his account on 25 September 1939, and scored his last of 220 kills on 28 April 1945, flying an Me 262 jet with JV 44.

Bf 109Fs for research

When it came to research purposes, the Bf 109F was the major source of airframes, due mainly to their ready availability and general similarity to the 'Gustav'. In addition to powerplant and armament trials, F airframes were used to test aspects of the Me 309 programme, as the upper component of the Mistel combination, and as high-altitude fighter testbeds.

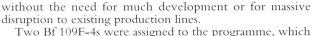

Above: Heavily retouched, this photograph shows the V23 after installation of the tricycle undercarriage intended for the Me 309.

Above right: Another Me 309 testbed was this aircraft, fitted with the wide-track undercarriage and retractable ventral radiator.

Left: This close-up shows the Bf 109F fitted with a BMW 801 radial (which powered the Fw 190A). Another F was fitted with a Jumo engine with an annular radiator.

Right: A Bf 109F-2 was tested at Tarnewitz with the RZ 65 rocket, housed singly in tubes faired into the leading edge. The weapon was tested for anti-bomber duties with both a contact and time-delay fuse, and with just a contact fuse for ground attack work.

190D), while one was tested with a butterfly tail. The latter aircraft first flew with its new empennage on 21 January 1943, with Karl Baur at the controls. The V-tail offered little advantage and plenty of problems, including decreased longitudinal stability and increased swing on landing. It was not adopted. Another F was assigned to Junkers for Mistel trials, acting as the upper component of the prototype.

Zwilling

Although it never flew, another project which initially involved the Bf 109F is worthy of mention – the Bf 109Z 'Zwilling' (twin). Originally proposed for (and carried out on) the Heinkel He 111, the 'Zwilling' concept married two standard fuselages of an existing type by a new centre-section and tailplane. In the Bf 109's case it was proposed as a means of producing a new Zerstörer-type heavy fighter

without the need for much development or for massive disruption to existing production lines.

Two Bf 109F-4s were assigned to the programme, which was initiated in earnest in late 1942. The two component aircraft retained their fuselages and one wing virtually unchanged, but a new straight-chord tailplane and centre-section joined the two halves. All four original radiators were retained, and all four main undercarriage units, although the latter were arranged in pairs under the centre of each fuselage, set much closer together than on the Bf 109F but still retracting outwards, away from the fuselage. A lower fuselage keel member was introduced to support them. There was still enough room between the legs for an ETC 250 bomb rack under each fuselage. The pilot flew the contraption from the left-hand fuselage, the cockpit of the right-hand fuselage being faired over. The prototype Bf

Below and below right: Werknummer 14001, bearing Stammkenn-zeichen (factory code) VJ+WA, was the first of three Bf 109G-0s. The aircraft displays the heavy cockpit framing and lack of quarterlight glazing of the production Gs, but does not have the two small airscoops aft of the spinner.

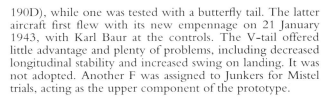

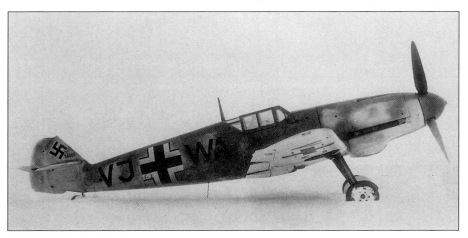

The first 'Gustavs'

Following tests with a Bf 109F fitted with a pressurised cockpit, Messerschmitt produced a batch of three pre-production Bf 109G-0s. Cockpit pressurisation was fitted, but the intended DB 605 engines were not ready in time. Accordingly, the Bf 109G-0s flew with the F's DB 601E powerplant.

Bf 109 replacements

Throughout the life of the Bf 109, Messerschmitt made three serious attempts to provide a follow-on fighter to replace its original masterpiece, these projects running alongside the ongoing work of steadily improving the existing design. All were doomed to failure.

Messerschmitt Me 209

In 1937/38 Messerschmitt had designed a special craft to capture the world speed record, designated Me 209. The second prototype eventually took the record at a speed of 469.22 mph on 26 April 1939, pipping the mark set by the Heinkel He 100 V8. The propaganda machine went into full swing, calling the aircraft an 'Me 109R' and inferring that it was a version of the service fighter. In fact, the Me 209 was much smaller, and bore no resemblance to the Bf 109 apart from having a DB 601 engine.

Spurred on by its success, Messerschmitt studied turning the record-breaking design into a service fighter. The result was the Me 209 V4 (D-IRND), which first flew on 12 May 1939. Initially outwardly similar to the racing aircraft, the V4 had provision for armament (two MG 17s and an engine-mounted MG FF/M), increased vertical fin area, shortened undercarriage and a new, larger wing. The surface evaporation cooling system of the racer was retained, but was soon found to be insufficient, and was replaced by two conventional underwing radiators after just eight flights. These, too, were inadequate, and were eventually replaced by a large single radiator under the centreline. Handling was distinctly unpleasant, leading to two successive increases in wing span.

By mid-1940 the V4's DB 601A had been replaced by a DB 601N, but this did not provide enough extra power to overcome the aircraft's increased weight and wing area, and certainly precluded plans to fit operational Me 209s with the MK 108 cannon in the engine, plus two further weapons underwing. Despite its racing origins, the Me 209 V4 was marginally slower than the Bf 109E then in widespread service, and its ground

The Me 209 V4 was finished with (just visible) provision for armament. It is seen here in its interim configuration with two shallow underwing radiators. The snake motif was purely for propaganda purposes.

and flight handling properties remained atrocious. The new Bf 109F then in development would have left the Me 209 standing, and development was abandoned.

Messerschmitt Me 309

In late 1940, while Bf 109F development was continuing, Messerschmitt began work on an all-new fighter which, it was hoped, would be the natural successor to the Bf 109. Designated Me 309, the new fighter employed many novel features, several of which were tested on Bf 109Fs. Among the most radical were a tricycle undercarriage with wide-track inward-retracting mainwheels, a variable, retractable central radiator bath, and reversible-pitch propeller.

When first proposed, RLM interest in the type was not great: at the time, no-one foresaw the need to develop a successor to the Bf 109. Development continued at a leisurely pace and the first prototype was not completed until June 1942. It first flew, with Karl Baur at the controls, on 18 July. Initially, problems with the cooling system were encountered, and the aircraft showed a lack of directional stability both on the ground and in the air. During the first test of the reverse-pitch in September, the aircraft braked so violently that it damaged the flaps and nosed over, breaking the nosewheel leg.

By November the Me 309 V1 was flying again with enlarged tail surfaces, in time to undergo mock combat trials with a Bf 109G. Although the Me 309 was faster than the 'Gustav', the Bf 109 could easily turn well inside the prototype fighter. On 29 November the V2 joined the test fleet, but not for long – its nosewheel collapsed on landing, the fuselage breaking in two in the ensuing crash. The V2 had the intended DB 605 engine installed, the first aircraft having hitherto flown with a DB 603A. In March 1943 the DB 605-powered V3

Messerschmitt engineers work on the Me 309 V1. The wide-track tricycle undercarriage made the Me 309 a tricky aircraft to taxi, and caused swerving on the runway.

flew, but by then the RLM had lost interest in the design, which it was felt would have been too difficult for the average pilot to operate, and which offered only a marginal speed increase as compensation for poor manoeuvrability when compared with the Bf 109.

Nevertheless, the V4 prototype did make it into the air in July 1943, equipped as the prototype for the Me 309A-2 heavy fighter. It was armed with a powerful battery of weapons for the anti-bomber role, consisting of four MG

131s, two MG 151/20s and two MK 108s, the latter in the overwing fairings developed for the Me 209 II. The V4 was destroyed in a bombing raid, while the V1 and V3 were used sporadically to test elements of the Me 262 programme and for undercarriage/reverse-pitch research. Proposed variants included the Me 309B dive-bomber and the Me 609 Zwilling, with two fuselages joined by a common centre-section.

The Me 309 V2 is seen in a sorry state at Lechfeld at the end of its one and only flight.

Messerschmitt Me 209 II

Although it carried the same designation as its racing predecessor, and the Versuchs (prototype) numbers continued sequentially from the earlier series, the aircraft referred to as the Me 209 II had nothing in common with the earlier machine. The original concept was to provide a fighter with some 65 per cent parts commonality with the Bf 109G but with considerably improved performance. Major changes compared to the Bf 109 consisted of an inward-retracting undercarriage (tested on a Bf 109F), taller fin and a DB 603 engine with annular radiator. Studies soon showed that the Bf 109G wing was impractical, so a new wing was designed. This could not accommodate the planned MK 108 wing guns, leading to a series of redesigns, most of which increased weight and consequently required a more sturdy structure. As a result, the Me 209 V5 emerged with little commonality with the Bf 109G, rendering its chances of being built, at a time when fighter production was being ramped up in the face of an ever more

desperate war situation, less likely.

Flugkapitän Fritz Wendel flew the Me 209 V5 for the first time on 3 November 1943. Initially flying with a DB 603A, the aircraft soon acquired a DB 603G, which necessitated an increase in fin size. The V5 was intended to serve as the prototype for the Me 209A-1 series, which had an armament of one engine-mounted MK 108 and two MG 131s in the wingroot. Various Umbausatz conversions added extra cannon in the wings, for which a streamlined fairing was developed (and tested on a Bf 109F) to house the feed system. The fairings extended back over the trailing edge, and were found to provide some hitherto-unexpected aerodynamic benefits – as 'Küchemann carrots', the fairings were later adopted in the jet age by several designs.

Following the V5 was a further prototype powered by a Jumo 213E, intended to serve as the development aircraft for the Me 209A-2. It was armed with the engine-mounted MK 108, but had MG 151/20s in the wingroots. A more radical derivative was the Me 209H, proposed as a specialised high-altitude fighter. It was to be produced by inserting an untapered centre-section to increase wing span and by using either

the special DB 628 engine or a turbo-supercharged DB 603E. In the event, the aircraft was completed with a standard DB 603G, pending the availability of the final choice of engine, the DB 627 (a DB 603 with two-stage supercharging). Proposed armament consisted of one MK 108 in the engine, two MG 131s in the forward fuselage and four MG 151/20s in the wings.

In the late spring of 1944 all Me 209 work was abandoned as it had become blatantly obvious that a new fighter type could not be introduced to the existing production lines; all the while, every last Bf 109G was urgently needed on the front line. Despite this, and damage caused during an air raid, the Me 209H V1 was completed in June 1944. No flight records have survived.

This is the DB 603G-powered Me 209 V5 (first prototype for the Me 209 II), seen with the tall vertical fin which accompanied the installation of this powerplant. The Me 209 V6 had a Jumo 213 engine, characterised by smoother lines under the cowling.

Messerschmitt Bf 109

Bf 109G-1

The first production variant of the 'Gustav' was the pressurised G-1, built in small numbers for the specialist high-altitude units based on the Channel Front. When USAAF bombers arrived in North Africa, the variant was dispatched to the region to oppose their operations.

Above: This is an early production Bf 109G-1. An additional airscoop was added behind and slightly below the gun muzzle trough.

Top right: G-1s gave the Luftwaffe a useful capability against high-flying bombers. Most G-1s and G-2s were fitted with retractable tailwheels, although they often flew with them extended.

109Z was believed to be complete when it was destroyed in an air raid.

Production Bf 109Zs would have been based on the Bf 109G airframe (as the Bf 109F had by then long been out of production), and would have been armed with one 30-mm MK 108 cannon firing through each propeller hub, plus a similar weapon in a gondola beneath each outer wing. The centre-section would have housed a 30-mm MK 103 cannon, and carried an ETC 500 bomb rack in addition to the two ETC 250s. As such, this five-cannon heavy fighter would have been formidable, and promised much better performance than other Zerstörer types. However, interest waned considerably after the loss of the

prototype, and the 'Zwilling' project was cancelled in early 1944. Soon Germany would have far more pressing matters with which to contend.

Enter the 'Gustav'

In mid-1941, as the Bf 109F was leading the German charge into Russia, development work was under way for a new version of the Bf 109, the G or 'Gustav', which would become the most numerous of the variants. Not that the Bf 109G was that good, but the circumstances of the mismanagement which had prevailed earlier required it to be built in huge numbers simply because there was nothing else. What should have been built was an entirely new successor, but such an aircraft (the Me 209) was far from ready. That the Bf 109G was in production from early 1942 until the end of the war is ample testament to the ineptitude of the Luftwaffe's overlords.

From the earliest days of Barbarossa it was becoming obvious that the Luftwaffe was suffering much higher attrition than had been envisaged. The German aviation industry had not been geared up sufficiently to cater for such attrition and, as the pressures on the Axis mounted daily from an increasing number of directions, never truly caught up to the demands of war, despite some desperate measures being taken. Similarly, the provision of new types was woeful – even the new Fw 190 was not available in sufficient numbers, and suffered its own share of development problems which delayed its mass appearance at the front lines.

Charged with limiting the damage, Messerschmitt's work on the Bf 109G was by necessity of great haste, with the result that the aircraft was a minimum-change version of the 'Friedrich' with improved basic performance. By 1941 the greatest emphasis was being placed on speed, with handling and manoeuvrability considered to be of lesser importance. Also, the air battle, especially in the west, had moved continuously upwards, and the ability to fight at higher altitudes carried increasing weight. Therefore, the Bf 109G was designed with a more powerful engine – the DB 605 – for greater speed, and cabin pressurisation.

Unfortunately, there was no time to develop the aerodynamic and structural modifications alongside the new equipment. The Bf 109E and F had represented harmony between installed power, aircraft weight and handling. The G, however, lost much of the fine handling at the expense of speed and greater weight. On the other side of the Channel, development of the Spitfire was following a similar line: the Mk IX was hastily being cobbled together by the marriage of the two-stage Merlin 60 series and the

Above: The clean cowling and small tailwheel identify this aircraft as Bf 109G-2. Although unpressurised, the G-2 was fitted with the heavily-framed canopy of the G-1.

This mixed bag of 'Gustavs' consists of a Bf 109G-3 (nearest the camera) fitted with the large, fixed tailwheel, a G-6 (centre) and an early machine (background) with retractable tailwheel, probably a G-2.

'Gustav' in the Med

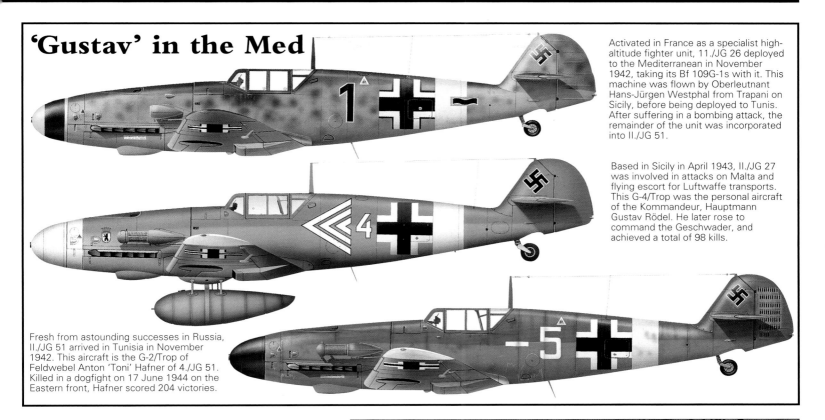

Activated in France as a specialist high-altitude fighter unit, 11./JG 26 deployed to the Mediterranean in November 1942, taking its Bf 109G-1s with it. This machine was flown by Oberleutnant Hans-Jürgen Westphal from Trapani on Sicily, before being deployed to Tunis. After suffering in a bombing attack, the remainder of the unit was incorporated into II./JG 51.

Based in Sicily in April 1943, II./JG 27 was involved in attacks on Malta and flying escort for Luftwaffe transports. This G-4/Trop was the personal aircraft of the Kommandeur, Hauptmann Gustav Rödel. He later rose to command the Geschwader, and achieved a total of 98 kills.

Fresh from astounding successes in Russia, II./JG 51 arrived in Tunisia in November 1942. This aircraft is the G-2/Trop of Feldwebel Anton 'Toni' Hafner of 4./JG 51. Killed in a dogfight on 17 June 1944 on the Eastern front, Hafner scored 204 victories.

existing Mk V airframe, to provide an expeditious means of countering the Fw 190A, which had demonstrated a striking superiority over the Mk V. To illustrate the fickle-ness of fate, the unmodified Spitfire airframe proved easily capable of absorbing the additional power and weight, and the Mk IX established itself as one of the outstanding fighters of the war. It, too, was also the most produced version (if one includes the nearly-identical Mk XVI with a US-built Merlin).

DB 605 power

Daimler-Benz's new DB 605A for the Bf 109G was closely based on the DB 601E, but introduced greater bore, higher permissible rpm and increased compression ratio. The result was an engine which produced 1,475 hp (1100 kW) for take-off. Although of similar overall dimensions, the engine was heavier, demanding a strengthening of the engine bearers and other parts of the fuselage structure. In turn, the extra weight required a beefing up of the main undercarriage. The engine installation required additional cooling, and the G featured an enlarged oil cooler and four small additional airscoops just aft of the spinner.

Above: Factory-fresh Bf 109G-2s await delivery to a front-line unit. The aircraft have undergone flight-testing, as evidenced by the oil streaks over the wingroot which characterised all Bf 109s.

Left: In November 1942 Bf 109G-1s were deployed from France to North Africa to provide high-altitude defence. This aircraft is seen serving with 3./JG 53 in Tunisia in early 1943, having been transferred from 11./JG 2. Note the silica pellets slotted into the sandwich of the canopy glazing.

Expert pair

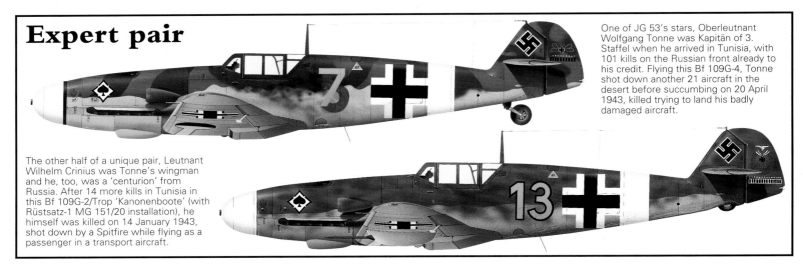

One of JG 53's stars, Oberleutnant Wolfgang Tonne was Kapitän of 3. Staffel when he arrived in Tunisia, with 101 kills on the Russian front already to his credit. Flying this Bf 109G-4, Tonne shot down another 21 aircraft in the desert before succumbing on 20 April 1943, killed trying to land his badly damaged aircraft.

The other half of a unique pair, Leutnant Wilhelm Crinius was Tonne's wingman and he, too, was a 'centurion' from Russia. After 14 more kills in Tunisia in this Bf 109G-2/Trop 'Kanonenboote' (with Rüstsatz-1 MG 151/20 installation), he himself was killed on 14 January 1943, shot down by a Spitfire while flying as a passenger in a transport aircraft.

A Bf 109G-2 of II./JG 54 is seen at rest on an airfield in northern Russia. Luftwaffe pilots on the Russian front led a somewhat nomadic existence, living in and operating from tents for much of the time, moving forward (and then retreating) through a series of grass airfields with no facilities. A large ground transport effort was required to move the accommodation, equipment, spares and supplies necessary to keep the aircraft flying.

Cabin pressurisation was provided by the expedient means of sealing the original Bf 109 cockpit enclosure without major redesign. The fore and aft bulkheads, walls and floor were all sealed, while the canopy and windshield incorporated rubber seals. The lower quarterlights which had characterised the earlier models were dispensed with, while the canopy had strengthened framing. The glazing was made of a sandwich, which incorporated a silica pellet to dry the air between the layers. The result was a pressure cabin able to withstand 4.4 lb/sq ft of overpressure. To further aid high-altitude operations, Bf 109Gs were built with provision for the GM-1 boost system from the outset,

Two views show the development aircraft for the Bf 109G-2/R1. This aircraft appears to be a G-1 airframe: it has the cockpit scoop and silica pellets in the cockpit glazing.

although this added yet more weight. The GM-1 system did provide welcome extra power at altitude, and the capacity of 115 litres (25.3 Imp gal) allowed its continued use for about 50 minutes.

Construction of the first pre-production batch of three Bf 109G-0s was undertaken at Regensurg in October 1941, but the DB 605A was not yet available. Accordingly, the G-0s were powered by the DB 601E, albeit with the G's revised cowling (minus the four small airscoops). The first production Bf 109G-1s introduced the DB 605A, and they began to leave the factories in the late spring of 1942, in parallel with the Bf 109G-2, which differed only by having the pressurisation equipment and GM-1 provision deleted. To confuse students of the Bf 109, many G-2s were built with some, or all, of the external airscoops which were associated with the G-1's pressurisation system. Identification between Fs and the early Gs is readily possible thanks to the heavier cockpit framing, deletion of quarterlights, the adoption of a deeper oil cooler bath and the addition of two small airscoops on either side the cowling just aft of the propeller.

'Gustav' enters service

Owing to its simpler construction, it was the Bf 109G-2 which entered service first, initial examples reaching the front line in June 1942. The G-1 was not far behind, being dispatched initially to JG 2, and then to JG 26, the two units which remained in the west facing the RAF across the Channel. Both Geschwaders established an 11. Staffel as a dedicated high-altitude unit. 11./JG 2 and 11./JG 26 both

Four-legged Messerschmitt

Under the designation FiSk 199, the Fieseler works modified a Bf 109G to an experimental long-range fighter-bomber configuration (Jabo-Rei). Quite apart from the problem of providing sufficient clearance for the underfuselage bomb, the FiSk 199, with two 300-litre tanks under the wings, was also extremely heavy. It is thought that 10 Bf 109G-2/R1s were built.

Left: After take-off, the extra undercarriage leg's usefulness had ended, and it was jettisoned. A chute was deployed to slow its return to earth, allowing it to be used again.

numbered a few Bf 109G-1/R2s in their complement, this Rüstzustand covering aircraft specially lightened for high-altitude work. The factory-undertaken modifications included deletion of unnecessary equipment and some armour, and fitment of GM-1. The two high-altitude Staffeln were transferred to the Mediterranean in November 1942, resulting in G-1s being subsequently reassigned to JGs 51 and 53 (and probably fitted with tropical filters), while JGs 1 and 5 also received the type. Rüstsätze noted on Bf 109G-1s were R3 (300-litre/65-Imp gal centreline tank) and R6 (gondola-mounted MG 151/20s).

Unpressurised fighter

The unpressurised Bf 109G-2 was built in much larger numbers, and was soon in evidence in all theatres, notably on the Russian front where the first examples arrived in June 1942. Two Rüstzustände were applied to this variant: the R1 and R2. One of the more unusual test programmes concerning the Bf 109 was that undertaken by Fieseler to provide a Jabo-Rei (Jagdbomber mit vergrösserter Reichweit – extended-range fighter-bomber) version of the Bf 109G-2. Quite apart from supporting the overload weight of 4080 kg (8,995 lb), the main problem was providing sufficient ground clearance for the carriage of the intended weapon: a single SC 500 500-kg (1,102-lb) bomb. The solution was an auxiliary undercarriage leg mounted halfway along the rear fuselage. Attached behind the fuel tank, the auxiliary leg was attached with explosive bolts, and after take-off was jettisoned by the pilot. The leg fell to earth

under a parachute for reuse. A single G-2 was modified by Skoda to the new design, being designated the Bf 109G-2/R1 or FiSk 199 (the latter being the Fieseler/Skoda designation). In addition to the extra leg, the FiSk 199 had strongpoints incorporated in the inner wings for the carriage of two 300-litre (66-Imp gal) drop tanks. Trials were successful, but the idea was not taken any further.

The second Rüstzustand was far more conservative, concerning the provision of aircraft for tactical reconnaissance. The Bf 109G-2/R2 had a similar camera installation to that in the F-4, but could change between camera fits. GM-1 was fitted as a matter of course.

Against the Spitfire Mk V, the Bf 109G-2 maintained some of the F's ascendancy in diving and climbing. Initially, the G retained the Bf 109's traditional advantage of being able to bunt away from a pursuing Spitfire, which still did

In summer the frozen ground rapidly turned to mud, proving as much of a hindrance to operations as the snow, with wheel-clogging becoming a real problem. In the summer of 1942 the Germans continued their push east, led by Bf 109s such as this G-2 of II./JG 54.

Above: These Bf 109G-2s are from the II. Gruppe (left) and Geschwaderstab (adjutant's aircraft, right) of Jagdgeschwader 54 'Grünherz'.

Left: The Bf 109G-4 differed only in minor detail from the G-2, the principal improvement being the adoption of FuG 16Z radio, externally distinguished by having the vertical wire on the radio antenna moved aft. Seen in Russia, these aircraft are from III./JG 3 'Udet', the aircraft in the foreground being assigned to the Gruppenkommandeur.

213

Eastern colours

This Bf 109G-6 was on the strength of IV./JG 5, based at Petsamo in the winter of 1943/44. The fourth Gruppe employed a spot as its badge behind the Balkankreuz. The aircraft sported an unusual winter dapple finish, applied over dark green, this proving very effective over the forested northern sector of the Russian front.

Sporting a garish summer camouflage, this is a Bf 109G-2 of II./JG 54 'Grünherz' at Siverskaya in 1942. JG 54 was heavily involved in the fighting in Russia, serving under Luftflotte I on the northern sector. Tans and greens were found to be highly effective camouflage, but the effect was somewhat ruined by the yellow theatre bands, cowling underside and wingtips.

A Bf 109G-2, probably of I./JG 77, rests on a Tunisian airfield in the spring of 1943, next to the remains of another G-2 and a Ju 52. In the background three Ju 52s can be seen arriving from Sicily. At this time, with the Allies closing in on the Germans in Tunisia, the perilous air bridge from Sicily was the only means of keeping the German forces supplied. In addition to fighting the massed Allied air forces supporting the land push, Bf 109s were heavily involved in attempting to escort the vulnerable transports.

Right: This Bf 109G-2/Trop was operated by 2.(H)/14, a reconnaissance unit. It was shot down in Tunisia on 7 April 1943.

Below: Pilots of 4./JG 53 are seen during a March 1943 'Alarmstart' in Tunisia. 'White 4' was the aircraft of Oberleutnant Fritz Dinger, who scored 67 kills.

not have a negative-*g* carburettor. The ability to employ the GM-1 boost in difficult circumstances saved the neck of many a Jagdflieger.

With the DB 605A, the Bf 109G-2 was slightly faster than the F-4 at high altitude, reaching 640 km/h (398 mph) at 6300 m (20,670 ft), compared with 624 km/h (388 mph) for the 'Friedrich'. At low altitude the F-4 was actually marginally quicker, the G gaining the ascendancy at about 1500 m (4,920 ft). Climb rate was also improved. However, normal loaded weight was raised from 2900 kg (6,393 lb) to 3100 kg (6,834 lb), and would grow even more as the G series developed.

Early 'Gustavs' were subjects of several test programmes, including the fitment of Messerschmitt-designed P6 variable-pitch propellers (Bf 109G-2/U1). A G-2/R2 photo-reconnaissance aircraft was flown with a Waffentropfen (WT) 17 pod underneath, containing two aft-firing MG 17 7.92-mm machine-guns. The WT 17 added too much weight and drag for service adoption.

Refined 'Gustav'

Chronologically, the next 'Gustav' variant was the G-4, which began to roll from the lines in October 1942. Like the G-2, it was an unpressurised multi-role fighter built in large numbers and equipping many units. Differences between it and its predecessor were small, the main one being the installation of a FuG 16Z radio in place of the FuG VIIa, with a resultant subtle change in antenna configuration. Early in the G-4 production run, larger mainwheels were introduced (as a result of the increasing weight of the 'Gustav'), which in turn led to the addition of bulges on the top of the wings. These bulges are believed to be the inspiration for the nickname 'Beule' ('bump') which stuck with the Bf 109G throughout its life, although it has

A Bf 109G comes in to land at a Tunisian airfield. It carries two Rüstätze modifications, the R3 centreline tank and the R6 MG 151/20 cannon pods. The latter were handed, and not interchangeable between wings. Visible are the case ejector chutes, which always faced towards the fuselage.

also been attributed to the gun fairings of the G-6. Not all G-4s had the wheel bulges, while several later and rewinged G-2s did. Like its immediate predecessor, the G-4 was regularly seen with Rüstsatz 3 fuel tanks and R6 wing gondolas, although some had the R1 and R2 bomb racks fitted.

Many G-4s were issued to reconnaissance units, some as Bf 109G-4/U3s with MW-50 water-methanol boosting. A specialist reconnaissance variant was the Bf 109G-4/R3, which was a long-range sub-variant with racks for two 300-litre tanks under the wings and a single Rb 50/30 or Rb 75/30 camera in the rear fuselage. The MG 17 machine-guns were removed and the muzzle troughs faired over. At least one G-4 was given a trials installation of three MG 151/20 cannon gondolas, with one mounted on the centreline.

Early Gs were sent to the Eastern Front, where they maintained the ascendancy established by the 'Friedrichs' a year before. However, on the ground the Wehrmacht was suffering and the advance into Russia stumbled to a halt at Stalingrad. Despite the best efforts of the Jagdflieger, the inevitable came on 2 February when the encircled 6th Army surrendered to the Soviets. The last fighter aircraft (Bf 109G-2s of JG 3) had left the Stalingrad pocket a few days earlier. Just as the Red army was finding success on the ground, so the VVS was clawing back the initiative in the air. By late 1942 the Yak-7 and Yak-9 fighters were beginning to make their presence felt, especially against the less experienced of the Luftwaffe pilots. Losses began to mount, but still the leading *experten* added to their scores. Among the new pilots finding their feet was the young Erich Hartmann of JG 52, who scored his first kill in November.

Bf 109G-6

The G-6 quickly followed the early variants on the production line, and remained in production until the end of 1944. More than 12,000 aircraft were built, although the last aircraft differed considerably from the first. All, however, featured 13-mm MG 131 machine-guns in place of the 7.92-mm MG 17s of earlier Bf 109s. These guns could not be fitted into the confines of the existing cowling, requiring bulged fairings just forward of the cockpit to house the spent belt chutes.

Sizeable numbers of both G-2s and G-4s were built as Trops, with dust filter and umbrella stand. The latter was vital to give the pilots some protection from the sun when sitting at cockpit alert, and consisted of two small metal attachments below the port cockpit rail. G-2/Trops appeared in North Africa at the end of June 1942, and G-4/Trops soon after. They were widespread by the time the momentous battle of El Alamein began on 23 October, although many aircraft were lost during the retreat which followed.

Some time after the G-4 had appeared, the Bf 109G-3 entered service, in March 1943. This was a high-altitude pressurised fighter like the G-1, but featured the improvements of the G-4. Only 50 were built, serving at first with the specialist high-altitude units 11./JG 2 and 11./JG 26, although later noted in use with JG 1 and 11./JG 54. The only sub-variant noted was the Bf 109G-3/U2, which had a GM-1 system that could be used for 20 minutes.

G-6 – the definitive variant

By mid-1942 the Bf 109G was being asked to perform an ever-increasing number of differing missions – no longer was it a pure fighter. To cater for this diversity of role without major disruption to the production lines, Messerschmitt

Bottom left: This Bf 109G-6 'Kanonenboote' is from the Gruppenstab of I./JG 27, wearing the chevron/triangle marking of the Gruppenkommendeur himself. Aircraft assigned to schwarm (a four-ship) leaders usually had white rudders. As well as R6 cannons, it appears to have Rüstsatz-1 for the carriage of a centreline bomb.

Left: A close-up of the cowling shows the bulged cowling fairings that characterised the Bf 109G-6. Also visible are the 'Beule' fairings on top of the wings, introduced in 1942 by late G-2s and early G-4s.

Below: A group of Bf 109G-6s undergo final checks outside the factory before delivery to the front. Most, if not all, have the Rüstsatz-6 underwing cannon installation.

Above: Bf 109G-6s occasionally flew close support missions, fitted with Rüstsatz-1 which added an ETC 500 IXb bombrack on the centreline. Shown preparing for a bombing mission is a G-6 of JG 3, the Geschwader badge being a stylised 'U' in memory of Ernst Udet.

Above: Between April 1942 and March 1944 Hauptmann Horst Carganico was Gruppenkommandeur of II./JG 5, operating against the Russians in the north. The giant Mickey Mouse replaced the usual chevron markings. Carganico's pet Scottie inspired the badge of his previous command, 6./JG 5.

Above right: Rüstsatz-3 was commonly seen on Bf 109G-6s, consisting of a 300-litre (66-Imp gal) drop tank. Here the carrier is a Stab/JG 54 aircraft.

introduced the Bf 109G-6, which was in many ways the definitive sub-variant of the 'Gustav'. It was also by far the most numerous, accounting for over 12,000 airframes. The principle behind the G-6 was to produce a basic fighter airframe which could accept any one of a number of conversion sets to equip it for its chosen mission. The aircraft could also accept a number of versions of the DB 605.

The cannon malfunction problems encountered by the Bf 109Fs in the desert mentioned earlier had given some cause for concern. While the MG 151/20 remained the cannon armament of the G-6, the MG 17 machine-guns were replaced with the 13-mm Rheinmetall-Borsig MG 131 machine-gun, with 300 instead of 500 rounds per gun. The new weapon provided the Bf 109G with a reasonable weight of fire even if the primary cannon jammed. The muzzle troughs were moved further back, but the most obvious difference was the addition of large fairings over the spent case return feeds of this much larger gun.

G-6s began to issue from the lines in late 1942 and were rapidly fielded in all theatres, although their arrival did not unduly upset the balance of power. Much later, the RAF got the chance to fully evaluate a G-6 when an R6-equipped 'Kanonenboote' landed by mistake at Manston, allowing the Air Fighter Development Squadron at Wittering to mount a series of comparisons with Allied fighters. Against the Spitfire Mks IX and XIV the Bf 109G's only real advantage was in the dive, for the Spitfire was able to outclimb and out-turn the Messerschmitt with ease, also being slightly faster (a marked advantage with the Griffon-powered Mk XIV) and possessing a much quicker roll rate. Against the P-51C (Mustang Mk III) the Bf 109G was

found to be much slower, but could generally outclimb the Mustang. In the dive the P-51 had the edge, and it could easily out-turn the German fighter. Roll rates were identical. Before tests could be performed with a Tempest Mk V, the Bf 109 was lost in a take-off accident.

Interspersed with the G-6 on the production lines were small numbers of Bf 109G-5s. They were essentially pressurised versions of the G-6 with one important external difference. Fitting the larger MG 131 machine-guns caused the pressurisation compressor to be moved to the starboard side of the engine, with the result that a small fairing had to be added to cover it. This adjoined the main bulge covering the MG 131s. The compressor intake scoop was mounted immediately beside it. Just to add further to the enormous confusion surrounding 'Gustav' models, many unpressurised aircraft (G-6s and G-14s) were built, inexplicably, with the extra fairing. G-5s entered service in September 1943, some time after the G-6, and virtually all were assigned to units in the West or on home defence duties.

Conversion kits

As befitted its initial design concept, the G-6 (and G-5) was subject to a bewildering array of conversions and modifications. Many aircraft were fitted with either the GM-1 (U2) or MW-50 (U3) boost systems. Initially, the engine cannon remained the Mauser MG 151/20 with 150 rounds, but increasingly became the Rheinmetall-Borsig MK 108 30-mm cannon with 60 rounds as production of the weapon ramped up from mid-1943 onwards. The heavier cannon was a lethal weapon, with one hit sufficient to bring down any fighter. Fitment of the MK 108 (most numerous among WNF-built aircraft) was covered by the Umbausatz-4 designation. Other U designations also concerned armament: the U5 was an MG 151/20-armed aircraft fitted with MK 108s in wing gondolas, while the U6 was an aircraft with three MK 108s. These latter two schemes remained in the test phase only, and were never deployed.

Rüstzustände designations for the G-6 included the R2 and R3 tactical reconnaissance platforms, with camera installations similar to those of the G-4, while the standard range of Rüstsätze was available, including R1 (centreline ETC 500 bomb rack), R3 (centreline drop tank) and R6 (underwing MG 151/20s). The suffix 'Y' was applied to aircraft fitted with FuG 16ZY radio (with a whip antenna

Captured 'Gustavs'

DB 605D-powered Bf 109G-10 in use with No. 318 'Gdanskski' Sqn (Spitfire Mk IXs) in Italy

Bf 109G-2/Trop, wearing No. 3 Sqn RAAF squadron codes after capture. Flown again in UK, 1991-97, after lengthy rebuild as 'Black 6'

Bf 109G-6/Trop under test by USAAF

Bf 109G-2, RAF serial HK849, used as hack in Italy

Bf 109G-6 (ex-JG 1), RAF serial TP814. Used for comparative trials with Spitfire and P-51

Bf 109G-14, one of two such aircraft tested by the RAF. Note Fw 190 in background

VVS Bf 109G-2 (ex-JG 3)

VVS Bf 109G-2 with Rüstsatz 6, near Leningrad

VVS Bf 109G-2 with Rüstsatz 6, NII trials

under the fuselage), this equipment allowing ground commands to control aircraft in the air. It was consequently usually fitted to the aircraft of unit leaders.

Mediterranean retreat

Following the victory at El Alamein, the Allied forces in the desert slowly steamrollered the Wehrmacht back into Tunisia. The following month, in November 1942, Operation Torch saw Allied forces landed on the Atlantic coast, and at once the German forces were split. Now equipped with Bf 109G-2s, -4s and -6s, the Jagdflieger were also divided as they attempted to prevent the jaws of the Allied pincers closing. Torch brought with it the first large-scale US involvement, and initially the experienced German pilots found the inexperienced and over-confident Americans easy game. However, the general improvement of Allied aircraft – large numbers of Spitfires and P-38s were now in theatre – together with the sheer weight of numbers combined to create an unstoppable force. By May 1943 the Axis was pushed out of Africa for good.

Post-Torch operations had seen the introduction of large numbers of medium and heavy bombers, and this set the pattern for the remainder of the war in the Mediterranean theatre which had, more than any other, hitherto been a

By necessity the evacuation from Sicily was conducted hastily, the fight being continued from Italian bases. Here British officers inspect a pair of apparently serviceable II./JG 53 Bf 109G-2/Trops left behind at Comiso airfield. The aircraft on the left is a Gruppenstab aircraft, while that on the right is a 'Kanonenboote'.

Sicilian defenders

As soon as Axis forces were ousted from North Africa on 13 May 1943, the Allies immediately turned their attentions to Sicily. For the next two months USAAF bombers pounded the island as a prelude to the invasion which began on 10 July. Bf 109s put up a stout resistance, but were ultimately overwhelmed by the sheer number of fighters which the Allies could muster. In addition to the fighting over the battlefront in the south of the island, the Jagdflieger were tasked with keeping open the escape route to Italy in the east.

Left: This group of Bf 109G-6s is seen at Sciacca airfield on Sicily in June 1943. They belong to 2./JG 77, which fought through to the end of the whole Italian campaign in June 1944. The aircraft exhibit a variety of camouflage patterns, and carry the small individual aircraft numerals common at the time among certain units.

Bf 109G in Italy

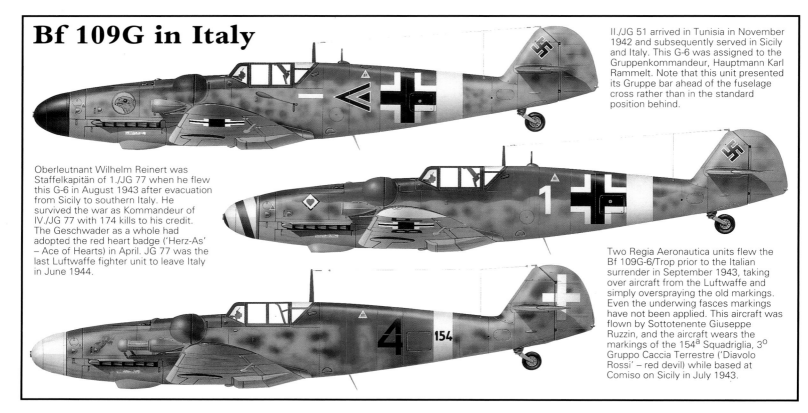

II./JG 51 arrived in Tunisia in November 1942 and subsequently served in Sicily and Italy. This G-6 was assigned to the Gruppenkommandeur, Hauptmann Karl Rammelt. Note that this unit presented its Gruppe bar ahead of the fuselage cross rather than in the standard position behind.

Oberleutnant Wilhelm Reinert was Staffelkapitän of 1./JG 77 when he flew this G-6 in August 1943 after evacuation from Sicily to southern Italy. He survived the war as Kommandeur of IV./JG 77 with 174 kills to his credit. The Geschwader as a whole had adopted the red heart badge ('Herz-As' – Ace of Hearts) in April. JG 77 was the last Luftwaffe fighter unit to leave Italy in June 1944.

Two Regia Aeronautica units flew the Bf 109G-6/Trop prior to the Italian surrender in September 1943, taking over aircraft from the Luftwaffe and simply overspraying the old markings. Even the underwing fasces markings have not been applied. This aircraft was flown by Sottotenente Giuseppe Ruzzin, and the aircraft wears the markings of the 154ª Squadriglia, 3º Gruppo Caccia Terrestre ('Diavolo Rossi' – red devil) while based at Comiso on Sicily in July 1943.

Below right: Having fought in North Africa, II./JG 51 was dispatched to Sardinia on 20 April 1943, where this aircraft is seen. Most of the Gruppe was destroyed on the ground, with the result that when it evacuated to Italy only four G-6/Trops could be mustered for the flight.

Bottom right: A small number of Regia Aeronautica units converted to the Bf 109G-6 in 1943. This aircraft belonged to the 363ª Squadriglia, 150º Gruppo, 53º Stormo.

Below: Partnering the 363ª in the 150º Gruppo was the 364ª Squadriglia. This aircraft wears the 'Gigi Trei Osei' badge of the Gruppo, worn in honour of Teniente Luigi 'Gigi' Caneppele.

fighter vs fighter contest. It did not take the greatest military strategist to work out the Allies' next move, for Sicily lay in all its temptation across the Sicilian Channel. Massed Allied air attacks meant that the Axis defence of the island was doomed to failure, and when Operation Husky, the invasion, was launched on 10 July, the defending Bf 109Gs of Stab and II./JG 27, II./JG 51 and II./JG 77 had just days left before evacuating to the Foggia airfield complex in southern Italy. The evacuation was completed before the end of the month.

September 1943 was a crucial month in the Italian campaign. Allied forces went ashore, to be followed almost immediately by the Italian surrender. This effectively cut the Regia Aeronautica in half; many units reformed and fought for the Allied cause as the Co-Belligerent Air Force, while those staying loyal to the Fascists formed the Aviazione Nazionale Repubblicana. By the end of September the Luftwaffe Bf 109 units had flown to safety to airfields around Rome, and several then continued north back to Germany or to the Eastern Front. The only new arrival was I./JG 4.

German withdrawal from Italy

At the start of 1944 the remaining Bf 109 units were faced with fighter-bombers, medium bombers and heavies in ever increasing numbers, always attended by swarms of escort fighters. Back in Berlin, the German High Command had largely lost interest in Italy, and it was felt that the fighters could be better employed defending Germany itself. Units were slowly withdrawn until only I./JG 4 and JG 77 were left. The fall of Rome on 5 June 1944, and the Allied landings in Normandy the following day, precipitated the final withdrawal, and the last Bf 109s left by the end of the month.

Not that the Germans left Italy entirely to its own fate, for it had nurtured the newly-formed ANR forces (flying Macchi MC.205s and Fiat G.55s) and subsequently

Left: I⁰ Gruppo Caccia was an ANR unit which flew the Bf 109G-10 from January to April 1945, disbanding at Gallarate.

Below: This Bf 109G-6 served with the ANR's 4ª Squadriglia, II⁰ Gruppo.

equipped two Gruppi with Bf 109Gs. The Regia Aeronautica had briefly operated the Bf 109G before the armistice, and this provided a nucleus of pilots who were dispatched to Germany to collect new aircraft. II⁰ Gruppo Caccia was the first to return with Messerschmitts, flying its first operation with the Bf 109G-6 in June 1944. I⁰ Gruppo came back to the front line in January 1945, bringing Bf 109G-10s with it. Both units operated strictly on defensive missions, attempting to hit unescorted bombers operating over northern Italy. Despite their small number and the ultimate futility of their efforts, the ANR Bf 109G units proved to be a constant thorn in the Allied side, and the Italian pilots revealed themselves as skilled and brave opponents.

In the east, the G-6 was continually embroiled in huge battles with massed formations of Soviet aircraft. There was certainly no shortage of trade for the Jagdflieger, although the quality of the opposition had changed out of all recognition compared with that which it had faced in 1941. Still, individual tallies began to mount, notably within Jagdgeschwader 52. In addition to standard G-6s, several

Trop models fought on the Russian front, especially in the south where the summer dust caused engine problems. Despite the fact that the G-6 entered service at a time when the Luftwaffe was in retreat from Africa, large numbers were built with provision for taking the tropical modifications. It was not uncommon to see aircraft in the harsh Soviet winter fitted with sunshade stands.

Anti-bomber operations

By the end of 1942, Germany was facing what was arguably its sternest test: the concerted bombing campaign launched from English soil, and later from southern Italy. Relentlessly, the day bombers of the US 8th Air Force and night bombers of RAF Bomber Command chipped away at Germany's industrial and military complex, while wearing the morale of its populace to the bone. Despite increasing losses in the east and in the Mediterranean, fighter forces had to be diverted to meet the growing threat, and large numbers of 'Gustavs' (mainly G-6s) were employed on home defence duties. Ideally, Bf 109s would put their good

Above: These G-6s equipped the II⁰ Gruppo of the ANR, which was also known as the Aviazione della Repubblica Sociale Italiano. The decision to equip the ANR with the Bf 109G was taken to reduce the identification problem between Macchis and Bf 109s, which had hitherto caused some fratricidal kills.

Top left: Along with I./JG 4, JG 77 was the last Luftwaffe fighter unit in Italy. Here a 4. Staffel aircraft flies in formation with a I⁰ Gruppo MC.205 prior to the Luftwaffe's withdrawal from Italy.

Aviazione Nazionale Repubblicana

After the Italian armistice, many Italian pilots continued flying with the Axis forces as part of the ANR. Two units were Bf 109G-equipped, and these flew missions defending northern Italy. This G-6 was the mount of Capitano Ugo Drago of 1⁰ Gruppo Caccia, the ANR's top scorer with 11 kills.

1⁰ Gruppo Caccia was the second ANR unit to convert to the Bf 109, arriving back in Italy in January 1945 with Bf 109G-10/AS fighters. This is the aircraft of the unit's commander, Maggiore Adriano Visconti, who scored seven kills with the ANR to add to the 19 achieved with the Regia Aeronautica. The badge is that of the RA's 153⁰ Gruppo.

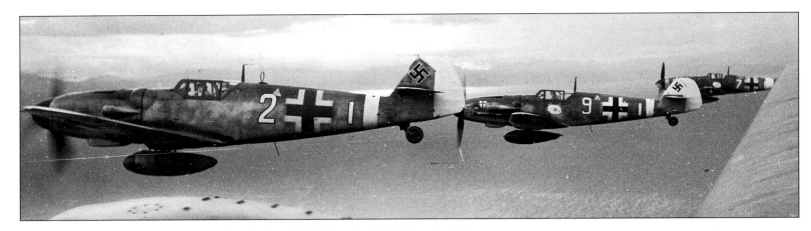

Above: 7./JG 27 Bf 109G-6s are seen escorting the He 111 bomber carrying Generals Fiebig and Holle during their inspection of forces on Crete on 1 December 1943. 'White 9' was the aircraft of Staffelkapitän Emil Clade, who survived the war with 26 kills to his credit. Within weeks of this picture being taken, III./JG 27 moved north to Vienna to join the Reich defence effort.

Above right: This unfortunate Bf 109G-6/Trop 'Kanonenboote' was also a 7./JG 27 aircraft, seen at Malemes on Crete after a crash-landing. The aircraft wears the III./JG 27 Gruppe badge on the engine cowling, and the 7. Staffel badge of a pierced apple below the cockpit.

high-altitude performance to use in tackling the escort fighters, while the more heavily-armed Fw 190s took on the bombers. In practice, this was rarely achievable. In recognition of this, the relatively light armament of the Bf 109 was usually augmented by the Rüstsatz-6 cannon installation so that it could attack the bombers.

Other more innovative methods of attacking bombers were introduced. In early 1943 5./JG 11 G-1s experimented with air-burst bombs, using a time-delay fuse to theoretically explode the bomb in the midst of a bomber formation. The USAAF 'heavies' relied on tight formation-keeping to maintain a withering wall of defensive fire against attack from any quarter. If the bombers could be split up, they would become much easier targets for follow-up cannon attacks. The idea persisted throughout the remainder of the war, but never proved worthwhile.

More successful was the use of air-to-air rockets. G-6s (and a few older variants) were modified to carry two launch tubes under the wings for the Werfergranate 210-mm rocket. This was little more than a mortar, but did

have a large 40-kg (88-lb) warhead. Known as *Pulk-Zerstörer* (formation-destroyer), the WGr 21-equipped Bf 109Gs served in specialist Staffeln within the Gruppen assigned to home defence duties, including those in northern Italy, and again the aim was principally to break up the formation. Their first major use came during the 14 October 1943 raid by 8th AF 'heavies' on Schweinfurt, resulting in catastrophic losses to the American formations.

Wilde Sau night-fighters

Bf 109Gs also played their part in the night defence of the Reich, especially between June 1943 and March 1944, when G-6s (and Fw 190s) equipped the specially created night-fighter units of 30. Jagddivision. The large-scale adoption of single-seat fighters for this role had come about following trials of a new tactic known as *wilde Sau* (wild boar), in which fighters roamed above the bombers, stalking them visually over their targets when they were silhouetted against target flares, searchlights and fires on the ground. *Wilde Sau* was the brainchild of Major Hajo Herrmann. To test his ideas, JG 300 had formed on Bf 109G-6s, and initial results were highly promising.

The nascent *wilde Sau* force suddenly gained great importance in July through the RAF's introduction of chaff, known to the RAF as 'Window' and to the Germans as 'Düppel'. It proved to be an effective blinding agent against German radars, rendering the traditional night-fighter force largely superfluous, tied as it was to the Himmelbett radar control system. Two further *wilde Sau* Geschwaders were hastily formed (JG 301 and 302) to form 30. Jagddivision under the control of promoted Oberstleutnant Herrmann. Each Geschwader had three Gruppen, but only one in each Geschwader had its own aircraft assigned. The other two Gruppen borrowed aircraft from co-located day-fighter units.

Greek 'Gustavs'

When JG 27 'Afrika' was ordered out of the continent in November 1942, the Gruppen dispersed to Crete and Greece. In February 1942, 8. Staffel was on Rhodes, from where this G-2/Trop was flown by the Kapitän, Hauptmann Werner Schroer. He survived the war, ending it as Kommodore of JG 3 and with 114 victories to his credit.

Fitted with tropical filter and R1 wing guns, this Bf 109G-6 was flown by Hauptmann Ernst Düllberg, Kommandeur of III./JG 27. It is depicted as it appeared when based at Argos in Greece, in October 1943. The following month, the Gruppe returned to Germany to defend the homeland.

Messerschmitt Bf 109G-6/R6
11. Staffel Jagdgeschwader 27 Kalamaki, Greece September 1943

'Red 13' was flown by Heinrich Bartels (then an Oberfeldwebel) during IV./JG 27's sojourn in the eastern Mediterranean from autumn 1943 to spring 1944. Bartels's rudder recorded 56 kills and the award of the Knight's Cross at this time. Bartels's final official tally was 99 victories, 47 of them scored against Russian pilots while flying with JG 5 in Norway. He disappeared during the furious air battles near Bonn on 23 December 1944 after downing a P-47. His victor was possibly Dave Schilling, CO of the 56th FG, who was credited with three Bf 109s destroyed in this area on that day. Bartels's body remained undiscovered until 1967.

Camouflage
'Red 13' was painted in the basic factory scheme for most G-6s. This consisted of RLM 74 light blue underside and lower fuselage with a pattern of RLM 75 mid-grey and RLM 76 dark grey top surfaces. A light mottle of RLM 76 was applied to the fuselage sides in the field. A variation on the basic scheme is that the upper surface camouflage stops short of the spinner.

Markings
The parallel bars painted across the white theatre band were a Gruppe marking unique to IV./JG 27 and were painted in the Staffel colour. This was fairly short-lived, however, and the unit had reverted to the more usual 'wavy line' marking by the time it began full combat operations in October. The name *Marga* was a personal marking and was also painted on Bartels's Bf 109G-10 at the time of his death.

'Beule'
The most distinctive recognition feature of the G-5, G-6 and G-8 versions was the pair of cowl protrusions which contained the spent-cartridge ejection chutes. The G-6 also had the bulges on the upper wing surfaces. Both of these features gave rise to the nickname 'Beule' (bulge).

Canopy
This G-6 has the standard three-piece canopy arrangement of early models and the so-called 'Galland-Panzer' head armour with armoured glass panel. The Erla-Haube clear-vision hood was introduced during G-6 production.

'Kanonenboote'
The MG 151 20-mm cannon in underwing gondolas were a field option (Rüstsatz) for all Bf 109Gs except the -12. Together with the single spinner-mounted cannon (usually an MG 151/20 but occasionally an MK 108) and pair of nose-mounted MG 131s, the G-6/R6 made the aircraft an effective bomber-destroyer, but the MG 151 installation had a deleterious effect on combat manoeuvrability and made the aircraft more vulnerable to escorting fighters.

Pulk-Zerstörer

Several units involved in anti-bomber operations employed Bf 109G-6s equipped with the WGr-21 rocket for breaking up bomber formations. Most were defending the homeland, but a few units were dispatched to northern Italy. Among them was the newly-formed IV./JG 3 which served in Italy from July to September 1943. This G-6/Trop was the aircraft of the Kommandeur, Major Franz Beyer.

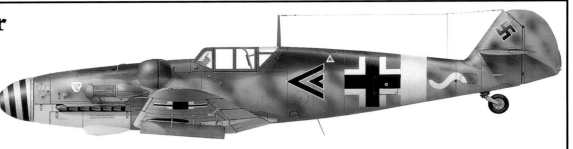

Two photographs show 'Pulk-Zerstörer' Bf 109G-6s armed with the Werfergranate 210-mm rocket. The tubes were more like mortars than rockets, lobbing a heavy warhead. The tubes were angled upwards to achieve adequate range. The projectiles were detonated by time delay, calculated to explode in the middle of a bomber formation. Even if the projectile did not hit a bomber, its effect would cause the tightly held formation to split up, reducing the effect of the mutual defensive fire.

The glazed dome on the spine identifies this aircraft as a Bf 109G-6/N, one of a small batch built with Naxos Z equipment to home on to the bombing radars used by RAF heavy bombers.

30. Jagddivision achieved a great deal of success in the late summer of 1943, by which time the Germans had begun to field airborne radars that could see through 'Window'. A dedicated night-fighter version of the Bf 109G-6 appeared from the factory in early 1944, designated Bf 109G-6/N. This version had Rüstsatz-6 armament, flame-damped exhausts, FuG 16ZY radio for tactical communications and direction-finding, FuG 25a beacon-homing equipment and FuG 350 Naxos Z. The latter was widely used night-fighter equipment, consisting of a receiver which picked up on the emissions from the H2S bombing radar carried by the RAF bombers. On the G-6/N, it was carried in a glass dome mounted on the spine behind the canopy.

Only a handful of G-6/Ns was built, and they were only used by a special cadre of experienced *wilde Sau* pilots within NJG 11. The reason for their non-adoption was the dissolution of 30. Jagddivision in March 1944 after a winter of appalling attrition. Whereas the single-seat fighters had been effective during good weather, many had been lost when the winter weather arrived. Without suitable radio aids (as carried by the traditional night-fighters), many were getting lost or finding landing at night in bad weather impossible. It was far from uncommon for pilots to bale out rather than risk a landing. JGs 300, 301 and 302 all retrained for the day-fighter role, still in defence of the homeland.

'Gustav' in foreign service

From mid-1942, the Bf 109G began appearing in the insignia of several air arms allied to the German cause (in addition to Italy, described above), beginning with Croatia. The fighter component of the Croatian legion fighting in Russia was 15.(kroat)/JG 52, and this unit had converted to the Bf 109G-2 as early as July 1942. By November it was flying the Bf 109G-6, although aircraft availability was very low. Two more Croatian squadrons were planned, the personnel having trained on Bf 109Gs, but in the event they were fielded flying Fiat G.50s and Macchi MC.202s. In the meantime, 15.(kroat)/JG 52, also referred to as simply the kroat. Jagdstaffel, had fought for much of the war in the Crimea, and had retreated with other Luftwaffe units. It converted to the Bf 109G-10 towards the end of the war.

In the Continuation War in the north, Finland found itself facing growing numbers of Lavochkin La-5 fighters, against which the Brewster Buffalo offered no real opposition. Accordingly, in January 1943, Germany delivered a batch of 16 Bf 109G-2s (dubbed 'Mersu' in Finnish air force parlance) with which HLeLv 34 was formed, followed by another similar-sized batch in May. The Finnish pilots immediately took to their new mounts, and began to rack up impressive scores. Highest-scoring was Eino Juutilainen, who achieved 94 kills, mostly in the Bf 109, to become the highest-scoring non-German ace of all time. Amazingly, his aircraft was never scratched by a single bullet from his opponents, a remarkable feat unmatched by any of the major German *experten* (Erich Hartmann, for example, survived 14 force-landings during his 352-kill career).

When the Soviets stepped up their campaign against Finland in 1944, further batches totalling 132 aircraft were supplied to Finland, including G-6s, G-8s, G-10s and G-14s, although the Finns referred to them all as Bf 109G-6s. Two additional units, HLeLv 24 and HLeLv 28, were formed, although their effectiveness was crippled by poor spares supply from Germany. On 4 September 1944 Finland accepted the terms of surrender offered by the Soviet Union, although the Bf 109s did not take part in the ensuing Finnish operation against German forces in Lappland. In December 1944 HLeLv 24 and 34 were redesignated as HLeLv 31 and 33, and with these two units the Finnish Bf 109s continued in service until 1954.

Hungary also acquired Bf 109G-2s in early 1943, these aircraft supplanting the F-4s delivered in October 1942. Two units were formed, 5/1 and 5/2 Vadasz Század, which

The Croatian Legion pilots were organised into 15.(kroat)/JG 52 and fought as part of the Luftwaffe on the Russian front. Aircraft usually wore standard Luftwaffe markings with the Croatian shield displayed prominently.

Left: *This is one of the Bf 109G-2s supplied to the Fortelor Regal de Aeriene Româna (Royal Romanian air force), initially as defence for the vital oilfields around Ploesti.*

Above: *These Bf 109G-6s are of the 102 Vadasz Osztaly (fighter group), administered by the Fliegerführer 102 Ungarn. This unit had two constituent squadrons.*

Below: *Bulgaria received 149 Bf 109Gs, this being a G-6. The aircraft is unusual in being fitted with the G-5 cowling, with additional fairing below the main bulge over the gun.*

This poor photograph, taken at Tri Duby, shows one of the two Bf 109Gs used by the Combined Squadron of the Slovakian Insurgent air force during the Slovakian uprising against the Germans in September 1944.

Allies in the East

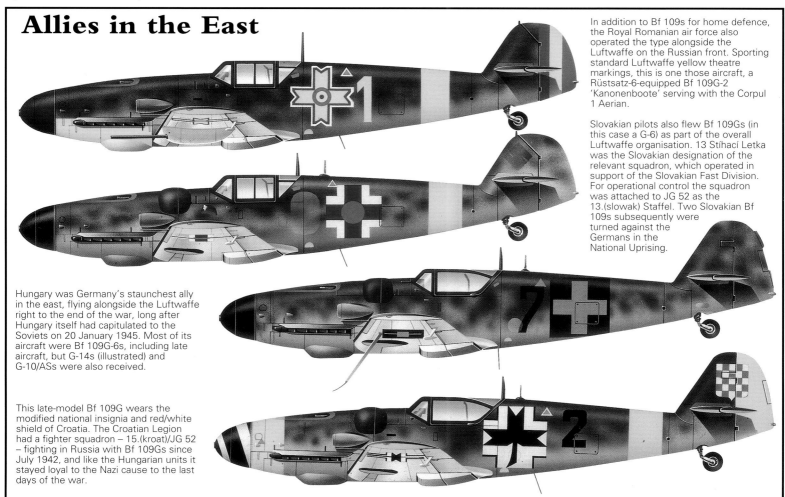

In addition to Bf 109s for home defence, the Royal Romanian air force also operated the type alongside the Luftwaffe on the Russian front. Sporting standard Luftwaffe yellow theatre markings, this is one those aircraft, a Rüstsatz-6-equipped Bf 109G-2 'Kanonenboote' serving with the Corpul 1 Aerian.

Slovakian pilots also flew Bf 109Gs (in this case a G-6) as part of the overall Luftwaffe organisation. 13 Stíhací Letka was the Slovakian designation of the relevant squadron, which operated in support of the Slovakian Fast Division. For operational control the squadron was attached to JG 52 as the 13.(slowak) Staffel. Two Slovakian Bf 109s subsequently were turned against the Germans in the National Uprising.

Hungary was Germany's staunchest ally in the east, flying alongside the Luftwaffe right to the end of the war, long after Hungary itself had capitulated to the Soviets on 20 January 1945. Most of its aircraft were Bf 109G-6s, including late aircraft, but G-14s (illustrated) and G-10/ASs were also received.

This late-model Bf 109G wears the modified national insignia and red/white shield of Croatia. The Croatian Legion had a fighter squadron – 15.(kroat)/JG 52 – fighting in Russia with Bf 109Gs since July 1942, and like the Hungarian units it stayed loyal to the Nazi cause to the last days of the war.

Above: 9./JG 3 was at Bad Wörishofen in September 1943, engaged on Reich defence duties. The Staffel marked its Bf 109G-6s with an eye on the gun fairing: 7. Staffel had a large comet marking in the same position.

Above: II./JG 26 operated this cannon-equipped Bf 109G-6 from France in early 1943. The two Channel-based Geschwaders became increasingly active in trying to take a toll of 8th AF bomber formations on their way to and from Germany.

Right: With the North African campaign behind it, most of JG 27 was pulled back for Defence of the Reich duties. These G-6s are of III. Gruppe, seen at Wiesbaden in 1944.

Bf 109G-6s taxi out for a mission from an airfield in Germany. The G-6 proved better able to tackle the fighters at high altitude than the Fw 190, although it was at a distinct disadvantage from the beginning of 1944 when the Merlin-powered Mustang arrived in service. At altitude the P-51 was much faster and more manoeuvrable than the Messerschmitt.

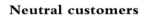

were engaged on mostly escort duties on the Russian front. In November 1943 they were withdrawn to Hungary and redesignated 102/1 and 102/2. In April 1944 US bombing operations over Hungary were greatly increased, leading to the supply of six squadrons of Bf 109G-6s for service with the 101 Vadasz Ezred (fighter regiment), which formed the main air defence of Hungary. 102/1 and 102/2 continued to support Luftwaffe operations at the front until pulled back to join their compatriots at home. Despite the Soviets overrunning their homeland and forcing an armistice on 20 January 1945, the 101 Vadasz Ezred fought on, ending the war near Linz in Austria.

Romania also began to receive Bf 109G-2s in early 1943, mainly to help the indigenous IAR 80 fighters defend the vital oilfields around Ploesti. On the Russian front the Corpul 1 Aerian (1st Air Corps) took delivery of Bf 109G-6s and G-8s for its operations within I Fliegerkorps, while further G-6s were delivered for use by home units. After the Soviet-forced coup on 23 August 1944, Romanian Bf 109Gs were turned on their erstwhile masters and used in support of Soviet offensives.

Slovakia, too, joined the Bf 109 club in early 1943, receiving 15 Bf 109G-6s to equip the 13.Stíhací Letka (fighter squadron), also known by its Luftwaffe titles of 13.(slowak)/JG 52 or slowak Jagdstaffel. Slovakian 'Gustavs' fought in the Crimea, while at home the 11. Stíhací Letka was also formed. Most of this unit was wiped out in one action with USAAF P-38s. At least two Bf 109G-6s changed sides and were used in the Slovakian uprising in July 1944. The Royal Bulgarian air force received its first 'Gustavs' in early 1944, a mixed bag of G-2s and G-6s for service with the 6 Polk. Principally acquired to defend the capital, Sofia, Bulgarian Bf 109s also fought in Romania, defending the Ploesti oilfields. Deliveries totalled 149, and most of the survivors were destroyed in late 1944 by a heavy RAF attack on the base at Karlovo.

Neutral customers

The final two Bf 109G customers were both neutral countries. The story of the supply of Bf 109G-2 airframes to Spain as a prelude to licence-production, and their subsequent emergence as HA-1109s, is recounted later. Switzerland, on the other hand, acquired its Bf 109G-6s in the most extraordinary manner. On the night of 28/29 April 1944, a lone Messerschmitt Bf 110G night-fighter, pursuing a Lancaster in Swiss airspace, encountered engine trouble and was forced to land at Dübendorf airfield, near Zürich. German officials were highly anxious that the FuG 220 radar and *schräge Musik* cannon installation of the night-fighter should not be examined by Allied agents, and struck a deal with the Swiss whereby the Bf 110 would be burned in return for the release to the Swiss of 12 Bf 109G-6s, which were required to make good attrition suffered by the Flugwaffe's 'Emil' force.

On 20 and 22 May 1944, the dozen 'Gustavs' arrived from Germany, joining a single example which had been interned earlier (and later joined by a further internee). Assigned to Fliegerkompagnie 7, the G-6s represented a considerable increase in the Flugwaffe's ability to defend

Operation Beethoven: the Mistels

By far the most unorthodox trials involving the Bf 109F actually led to an operational weapon: the Mistel. Known as Operation Beethoven, the Mistel (mistletoe) programme employed the use of a piloted fighter mounted on the back of an explosives-laden surplus bomber airframe in a combination nicknamed 'Vater und Sohn' (father and son). The pilot took off, flew the combination to its target, aimed the bomber airframe and then released the shackles holding his fighter to its carrier. He then returned to base. Strictly speaking, the term Mistel applied only to the lower component, but rapidly became the name by which these odd 'combos' were known.

Beethoven was originally inspired by a suggestion concerning the use of piggyback fighters to deliver explosives, but the first airborne tests, conducted in 1942 and termed 'Huckepack', were intended to provide a means of delivering a transport glider. The 'Huckepack' combination employed a Bf 109E mounted on a DFS 230. The idea of a weapon combination was pursued with renewed vigour in 1943, with Junkers providing the engineering and test team. A flying prototype was created using a Bf 109F-4 upper component, attached to a Ju 88A-4 lower component, which had two tripod supports for the fighter, running between the centre-sections of each aircraft. A single spring-loaded strut supported the tail of the fighter, this falling away when the fighter released its carrier.

Junkers received instructions to produce 15 Ju 88A-4 lower components in July 1943, and initial prototype trials (using the Bf 109F-4) proved the feasibility of the project. The initial combinations were called Mistel 1, and employed the Bf 109G-2 upper component. The first few Mistel lower components were completed with a standard Ju 88 bomber nose but with spartan equipment. Designated Mistel S1, these aircraft could be piloted and served as trainers. Standard Mistel 1s were also built with a bomber nose, but this was a quick release section which could rapidly be swapped for a 3800-kg (8,377-lb) hollow-charge warhead, which fired a steel core that could penetrate the heaviest ship armour or nearly 20 m (65 ft) of concrete.

This Mistel 1 (with Bf 109G-2 upper component) is seen shortly after delivery to the Einsatz-staffel of IV./KG 101. The bomber's nose was used for ferrying, and was attached by bolts. It could be rapidly replaced by the hollow-charge warhead.

Above: Operational Mistel 1s of II./KG 200 are seen at a Danish airfield in the winter of 1944/45, where they were gathered in preparation for a raid on the British Home Fleet. The only operational Mistel sorties involving the Bf 109 were the handful of attacks in late June 1944 against ships forming part of the invasion fleet.

Below: The prototype Mistel combination utilised a Bf 109F-4 mounted on a Ju 88A-4. The support struts were considerably strengthened in the operational Mistels, but the prototype suffered no serious problems during trials. Note the rear fuselage support strut, which fell under spring-load into a cradle.

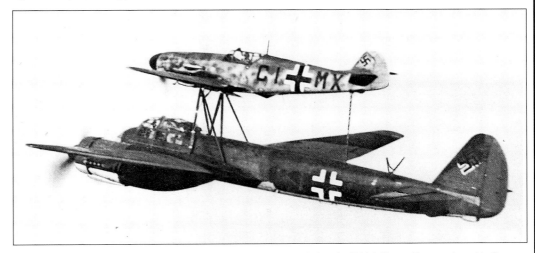

In the spring of 1944 crews began assembling with the Einsatz-staffel of IV./KG 101 at Nordhausen to begin training on the Bf 109G and the Mistel 1. In May the unit moved to St Dizier with five Mistel 1s in preparation for attacks on the Allied invasion fleet. The first operational mission was conducted by one Mistel on the night of 24 June 1944, but was cut short when a Mosquito night-fighter appeared, forcing the pilot to detach from the Ju 88 prematurely. Soon after, the remaining four Mistel 1s were released successfully against Allied ships off the coast of France. All four hit, but none of the ships was sunk.

In October 1944 the Einsatz-staffel of IV./KG 101 became the Einsatz-gruppe III./KG 66, and soon after was redesignated again as II./KG 200. Mistel production had been building up for a major strike, the chosen

target being the British Home Fleet anchored in Scapa Flow. Some 60 Mistel 1s were gathered at airfields in Denmark, but the operation could not be launched because of bad weather. When it cleared, bright moonlight kept the combinations on the ground, as they would have been very vulnerable to the fighters which defended the Orkneys and surrounding seas.

By January 1945 the operation had still not taken place, and further bad weather continued to keep the Mistels on the ground. At this juncture a new plan to launch an all-out strike was hatched, this time against Soviet armament production (Operation Eisenhammer). In early 1945, the Bf 109G was removed from the Mistel combination, its place as upper component being taken by the Fw 190A (as the Mistel 2 and 3). In the event, the mass raid never did take place.

Above: The Mistel 1 featured a long proboscis mounting the contact fuse. This was necessary to ensure the penetrating warhead worked correctly. Taxiing the combination required considerable skill from the Bf 109G pilot, a task made all the more difficult by the massive weights at which the Mistel took off.

225

Reich defenders

Jagdgeschwader 3 'Udet' (I. Gruppe shown) was one of the units on Reich defence duties, a Bf 109G-6 being depicted here. The black/white *Spiralschnauze* markings were applied to aircraft engaged primarily on anti-bomber interception duties. JG 3 contributed two Gruppen to Operation Bodenplatte in January 1945.

From the summer of 1944 the Bf 109G-14 began to arrive at fighter units. Most had the tall wooden tail and apparently all had the clear-view Erla hood. This aircraft is marked for the Gruppenadjutant of III./JG 27, the Geschwader being allocated a green fuselage band for its Defence of the Reich duties. The unit was assigned to Luftflotte 3, defending western Germany and Holland.

The black RV (Reichsverteidigung) band identified JG 53, this G-14 being assigned to III. Gruppe. The Geschwader had the Stab, II. and III. Gruppe all flying with Luftflotte 3, while I./JG 53 was with Luftflotte 4 in Hungary and Yugoslavia.

Virtually all Bf 109 'Kanonenboote' flew with the MG 151/20 cannon underwing, but a handful are believed to have received the harder-hitting 30-mm MK 108. This is a test aircraft, showing the much shorter barrel of the larger-calibre weapon.

A Bf 109G-14 of 1./JG 53 'Pik As' sits among Fw 190s at Bad Aibling at the end of the war. The Erla-Haube canopy was fitted to Bf 109s from late 1943, significantly improving visibility from the cockpit.

Swiss airspace, but the aircraft suffered from serious manufacturing defects, symptoms of the poor workmanship and production difficulties that were then facing the German production lines. The Fliegertruppe complained to Germany, and eventually recovered half of the purchase cost, while working hard to remedy the problems. They were never

fully solved, and the flying hours of the 'Gustavs' were limited. In 1947 the type was retired altogether, leaving the original Bf 109Es flying for another two years.

Production line changes

Throughout its production run the Bf 109G-6 was subject to several major modifications, with no resulting change in designation. The first was introduced in about August 1943, when aircraft began to appear with a direction-finding loop antenna on the spine and a corresponding reduction in height of the main radio mast. As with virtually all Bf 109G aircraft configurations, there were many variations, and many aircraft were built with the D/F loop, but had it removed at the front. Some even dispensed with the radio mast altogether, yet retained the D/F, the radio wire antenna passing through the loop.

A common complaint concerned the lack of visibility from the cockpit, and two modifications were incorporated into the G-6 to address this. The first, appearing in the summer of 1943, was the Galland-Panzer, the replacement of the all-metal head armour with armoured glass. More radical was the adoption of the Erla-Haube, a new lightly-framed canopy which replaced both the hinging and rear fixed portions of the old canopy. This appeared at the start of 1944, as did a new, taller vertical fin assembly, characterised by a straight rudder joint and a controllable Flettner tab. The rudder was covered with plywood, which was cheaper to produce, eased the strain on the supply of strategic materials, and utilised the skills of carpenters rather than

metalworkers. Right towards the end of G-6 production, aircraft appeared with a much longer, non-retractable tail-wheel leg which raised the tailplane into the propeller slipstream, improving take-off characteristics.

Experience with the Bf 109G had shown that the GM-1 and MW-50 systems, while useful, were less effective than the provision of extra supercharging, leading to the installation of the DB 605AS engine. This powerplant featured the supercharger which had been developed for the larger DB 603 and gave a maximum output of 1,200 hp (895 kW) at 8000 m (26,250 ft). The DB 605AS had a somewhat larger supercharger, requiring a complete redesign of the engine cowling. The result was a much cleaner cowling which dispensed with the characteristic bulges in favour of larger but more streamlined fairings. First appearing in the spring of 1944, G-6/AS aircraft were produced as both new-build machines and by conversion of older airframes. Most were assigned to home defence duties, where their increased altitude performance was welcome in the ongoing battle with the bombers. A few served with night-fighter units. A small number of Bf 109G-5s also received DB 605AS engines, although it is thought that at least some, if not all, lost their pressurisation capability in the process.

Bf 109G production had included many aircraft destined to serve in the reconnaissance role, but a dedicated variant was produced from August 1943 – the Bf 109G-8. Based on the G-6, the G-8 entered service in November, and swiftly became the standard equipment of the Nahauf-klärungsgruppen. The cameras were mounted further back in the fuselage than on previous reconnaissance Bf 109s, and usually comprised two Rb 12.5/7x9s or a single Rb 32/7x9. Some had a camera installation in the leading edge of the port wing, but this was removed when found to be unsuitable. The standard range of 'Us' and 'Rs' was applicable, but rarely employed. Indeed, many G-8s had the engine-mounted cannon removed to save precious weight. Among the G-8's achievements was taking the first photographs of the Allied invasion fleet on the morning of 6 June 1944, captured by two aircraft from 3./NAGr 13.

Foreign production and trainers

Limited production of the Bf 109G was undertaken in Romania and Hungary. IAR at Brasov assembled 30 Bf 109G-6s from Messerschmitt-supplied kits and constructed another 16 itself before US bombing raids brought a halt to production. In Hungary the production effort was more successful, being centred, initially, on the Györ factory. This built one G-2 (designated Ga-2) and three G/Ga-4s before production got under way with the G-6, engines being provided by Manfred Weiss. Over 600 G-6s and G-14s were delivered from Hungary, production being shifted to the Köbánya brewery in the summer of 1944 after Györ had been bombed.

From the very start of the Bf 109's service career in 1937, it had always been felt unnecessary to have a training version, but by late 1943 the calibre of the young pilots being sent for training had reached the point where they would be lucky to survive their conversion course, let alone

the rigours of combat. Accordingly, the RLM directed that around 500 surplus G airframes should be converted into two-seaters and issued to the Jagdschulen (JGs 101 to 110) to aid conversion to fighter types. G-2s, G-3s, G-4s and early G-6s were involved in the programme.

Designated Bf 109G-12, the two-seater entered service in early 1944. The original cockpit remained in its position, a second cockpit being added behind, cutting fuel capacity from 400 litres (88 Imp gal) to 240 litres (53 Imp gal). Rüstsatz-3 (300-litre/66-Imp gal tank) was regularly installed to boost the endurance of a training mission. The canopy of the front cockpit was essentially similar to that of the single-seater, except that it hinged from the top of the fixed (starboard) panel rather than at the bottom. A fixed glazed section separated it from the rear canopy, which was

Above: A late-model Bf 109, either a G-6 or a G-14, taxis out for a mission in 1944. By the end of the year the Bf 109 production system was in a confusing state, with aircraft being completed with either long or short tailwheels, tall or short fins, DB 605AM or AS engines and with large or small mainwheels.

Left: A Bf 109G-6 lands at a base in the west. The aircraft has the tall fin introduced in early 1944, which dispensed with the characteristic aerodynamic horn balance at the top of the rudder in favour of an inset balance.

Two photographs depict Bf 109G-12s, the aircraft at the bottom being hastily and rather ineffectively camouflaged with foliage.

Bf 109G-12 – two-seat trainer

Trainer versions appeared right towards the end of the war, and reflected the calibre of hopeful pilots rather than any aircraft problems. Based on a variety of G versions, the G-12s retained many of the individual features of the aircraft from which they had been converted.

Above: This Bf 109G-6 or G-14 taxis out at Merzhausen past a construction crew attempting to repair damage caused by Allied bombing. Aircraft of both production series were completed with the DB 605AS engine, distinguished by a larger but more streamlined fairing over the engine gun breeches.

Right: This late-production Bf 109G-6 carries both R3 fuel tank and R6 underwing cannon gondolas. From late 1943 units assigned to the defence of Germany (Reichsverteidigung – RV) applied coloured bands around the rear fuselage of their fighters. This plain band could denote JG 1 (red) or JG 54 (blue).

bulged slightly to give the instructor a measure of forward vision. A hood was fitted in the rear seat for instrument flying, requiring the student and instructor to swap seats for such missions. Although armament was scheduled to have been removed during the G-12 conversion, many retained at least one or both machine-guns, and were used as gunnery trainers. In the last desperate weeks of the Reich, several were used in combat.

High-altitude fighter

By the beginning of 1943, the requirement for a specialist high-altitude fighter had assumed ever-larger proportions, and throughout the year Messerschmitt was working on two Höhenjäger programmes which ran side-by-side. Of these, the most important was the Me 209H, which was intended to be the definitive high-altitude fighter, based on the Me 209 II fighter which was proposed as a replacement for the Bf 109. As it was obvious that no version of the Me 209 could be in production much before the end of 1944, Messerschmitt also worked in parallel on a high-altitude Bf 109 which could be fielded much earlier.

As initially envisaged, the resulting Bf 109H was a Bf 109F-4 with an uprated DB 601 engine and an additional taperless wing centre-section which raised span to 11.92 m (39 ft 1 in). The undercarriage was moved to the outer edges of the new section, which increased its track considerably. As detailed design was being undertaken, the ceiling

requirements were raised, and the F-based fighter could not achieve the new figures. The answer lay in adapting certain features of the parallel Me 209H programme to the Bf 109G.

Among the new aircraft's features was installation of the DB 628A engine, which had a two-stage supercharger. A mock-up of the new engine was tested in a Bf 109G-5, followed soon by a real engine, fitted into a Bf 109G-3 and flown for the first time on 18 May 1943. This aircraft, the V50, featured a ducted spinner and a paddle-blade propeller. The lengthening of the forward fuselage caused by the DB 628A installation upset the centre of gravity, so balance weights were installed in the rear fuselage as compensation. So equipped, the V50 underwent high-altitude trials which achieved 15500 m (50,850 ft), the engine delivering some 1,130 hp (843 kW) at 12000 m (39,370 ft).

Meanwhile, Messerschmitt had been converting a Bf 109G-5 airframe to the Bf 109H configuration, with DB 628A engine, extra centre-section and larger tail surfaces. As the V54, this aircraft first flew in June 1943. Messerschmitt was also producing a batch of Bf 109H-0 aircraft, based on the Bf 109F-4/Z (with DB 601E engines, GM-1 boosting and full armament). This batch was used only for evaluating the problems associated with operating high-altitude fighters.

Service test

The first Bf 109H-1 fighters followed, based on the Bf 109G-5 airframe and powered by a GM-1-boosted DB 605A. In addition to the standard three-gun armament, they had provision for the installation of reconnaissance cameras in the rear fuselage. In early 1944 several were sent to Guyancourt, near Paris, for a service evaluation. Generally found to be satisfactory, the Bf 109H-1 did show some wing flutter, which occasioned Messerschmitt to undertake a series of diving tests. In the course of one of them, a port wing parted company with the aircraft flown by Fritz Wendel.

This Bf 109G-6 was fitted with an experimental auxiliary fuel tank, known as the Irmer-Behälter. The tank had a small fin on the centreline to restore directional stability.

Found at Salzburg by US soldiers in 1945, this is a Bf 109G-10. It has the bulged cowling designed to house the DB 605D engine, although some G-10s with this cowling were fitted with the older DB 605AS.

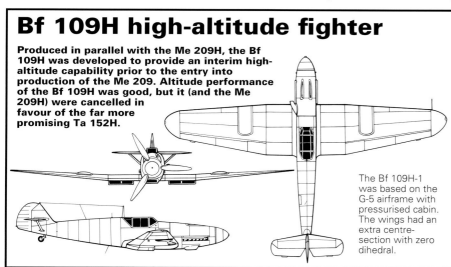

Bf 109H high-altitude fighter

Produced in parallel with the Me 209H, the Bf 109H was developed to provide an interim high-altitude capability prior to the entry into production of the Me 209. Altitude performance of the Bf 109H was good, but it (and the Me 209H) were cancelled in favour of the far more promising Ta 152H.

The Bf 109H-1 was based on the G-5 airframe with pressurised cabin. The wings had an extra centre-section with zero dihedral.

One other airframe took part in the Bf 109H test programme, the V55. Initially laid down as the Me 209 V6, it was transferred to the Bf 109H programme when the Me 209 was cancelled, and was completed with extra centre-section, lengthened forward fuselage, extended wingtips (total span 13.26 m/43 ft 6 in) and redesigned tail surfaces. First flying on 22 December 1943, the V55 was initially powered by a DB 605B, which was essentially a standard DB 605 fitted with the larger supercharger of the DB 603. When the DB 603G engine, for which the V55 had been designed, failed to materialise, the aircraft subsequently had a Jumo 213E installed. On 25 February 1944 the Bf 109H V55 was destroyed in an air attack, a similar fate befalling the V54 in August. By that time, however, the Bf 109H programme had long been cancelled in favour of development of the Focke-Wulf Ta 152H.

The final 'Gustavs'

Production of the Bf 109 had run at a surprisingly low level for the early part of the war, but in 1943 it began to pick up considerably, peaking in mid-1944. The constant attention of the Allied bombing efforts were met with a dispersal of production, although assembly remained the province of the three main factories: Messerschmitt at Regensburg, Erla at Leipzig and WNF at Wiener Neustadt. Some attempts were made to move engine production into disused mines, but the humidity caused corrosion of the tooling. The big push to increase production was administered by the newly created Jägerstab, which used the threat of imprisonment, or worse, to coerce the factories into producing more and more fighters. The result, inevitably, was bad workmanship, resulting in many aircraft being delivered with serious defects.

However, at the front line the numbers of serviceable Bf 109s did not rise appreciably, for two reasons. Firstly, Allied aircraft were shooting down Messerschmitts almost as fast as they were being built and, secondly, aircraft with relatively minor damage were not being repaired owing to a lack of

spare parts. The increased production drive concentrated almost exclusively on building new aircraft, with little thought to the provision of additional components for the field repair of aircraft. Large numbers of aircraft were left lying around airfields while awaiting new parts, a problem exacerbated by the differing configurations of the aircraft themselves.

In July 1944 the first of a new variant – the Bf 109G-14 – entered production, and it was soon active in the skies of western Europe, especially facing the US/Commonwealth forces which had landed in France the previous month. The concept behind the G-14 was to rationalise the production standard of the fighter and to incorporate all of

Above: This pair of late 'Gustavs' consists of a G-14 nearest the camera and a G-10 behind. The latter has the DB 605D engine fitted, with its characteristic small bulges low down on the sides just behind the propeller. It also has the FuG 16ZY radio antenna under the port wing.

Left: This Croatian Bf 109G-10 was surrendered at Falconara in April 1945. It cannot be seen whether it has the DB 605D engine, or whether it was fitted with the DB 605AS. Until surrender, the Croatian volunteer unit operated under Jagdfliegerführer Ostpreussen.

Left: Seen in May 1945 at Prague-Kbely, this DB 605AS-powered Bf 109G-10 wears the green/white/green RV bands of I./JG 51. The AS and D engines both replaced the engine gun fairings with a neater unit, seen here partially removed.

Below: This Bf 109G-10 was captured and tested by the USAAF. It is seen here in July 1946 at Patterson Field, where it was painted in an approximation of a mottled Luftwaffe scheme. Note that the aircraft has the two additional fixed rudder tabs seen on some aircraft.

Bf 109G-10

To maximise its assets, the Luftwaffe introduced the G-10 variant as a means of bringing older G airframes (G-6s and G-14s) up to the standard of the new-build K-4. However, not all of the K's improvements could be incorporated into all of the remanufactured G-10s, with the result that they were completed in many configurations. The G-10 became the most important variant (alongside the K-4) of the last months of the war, with about 2,600 upgrades completed.

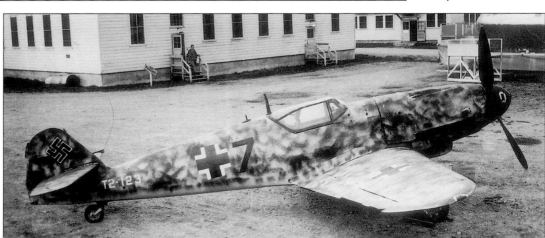

Bf 109 details

The aileron had a horn balance mounted underneath. Bf 109Ks introduced an aileron tab but this was usually locked in the neutral position.

Right: The direction-finding loop of the G-6 and later variants served the Peilrufanlage navigation aid. Some aircraft dispensed with the radio mast, the antenna passing through the loop.

The WGr 21 air-launched mortar installation consisted of a simple launch tube braced to the wing.

This is the late-standard tall wooden fin, as seen on Hans Dittes's Bf 109G/Buchón.

Bf 109G-14 cutaway

1 Starboard navigation light
2 Starboard wingtip
3 Fixed trim tab
4 Starboard Frise-type aileron
5 Flush-rivetted stressed wing skinning
6 Handley Page automatic leading-edge slot
7 Slot control linkage
8 Slot equaliser rod
9 Aileron control linkage
10 Fabric-covered flap section
11 Wheel fairing
12 Port fuselage machine-gun ammunition feed fairing
13 Port 13-mm Rheinmetall-Borsig MG 131 machine-gun
14 Engine accessories
15 Starboard machine-gun trough
16 Daimler-Benz DB 605AM 12-cylinder inverted-Vee liquid-cooled engine
17 Detachable cowling panel
18 Oil filter access
19 Oil tank
20 Propeller pitch-change mechanism
21 VDM electrically-operated constant-speed propeller
22 Spinner
23 Engine-mounted cannon muzzle
24 Blast tube
25 Propeller hub
26 Spinner back plate
27 Auxiliary cooling intakes
28 Coolant header tank
29 Anti-vibration rubber engine mounting pads
30 Elektron forged engine bearer
31 Engine bearer support strut attachment
32 Plug leads
33 Exhaust manifold fairing strip
34 Ejector exhausts
35 Cowling fasteners
36 Oil cooler
37 Oil cooler intake
38 Starboard mainwheel
39 Oil cooler outlet flap
40 Wingroot fillet
41 Wing/fuselage fairing
42 Firewall/bulkhead
43 Supercharger air intake
44 Supercharger assembly
45 20-mm cannon magazine drum
46 13-mm machine-gun ammunition feed
47 Engine bearer upper attachment
48 Ammunition feed fairing
49 13-mm Rheinmetall-Borsig MG 131 machine-gun breeches
50 Instrument panel
51 20-mm Mauser MG 151/20 cannon breech
52 Heelrests
53 Rudder pedals
54 Undercarriage emergency retraction cables
55 Fuselage frame
56 Wing/fuselage fairing
57 Undercarriage emergency retraction handwheel (outboard)
58 Tail trim handwheel (inboard)
59 Seat harness
60 Throttle lever
61 Control column
62 Cockpit ventilation inlet
63 Revi 16B reflector gunsight (folding)
64 Armoured windshield frame
65 Anti-glare gunsight screen
66 90-mm armourglass windscreen
67 Erla-Haube clear-vision hinged canopy
68 Galland-Panzer framed armourglass head/back panel
69 Canopy contoured frame
70 Canopy hinges (starboard)
71 Canopy release catch
72 Pilot's bucket-type seat (8-mm back armour)
73 Underfloor contoured fuel tank (400 litres/88 Imp gal of 87 octane B4)
74 Fuselage frame
75 Circular access panel
76 Tail trimming cable conduit
77 Wireless leads
78 MW-50 (methanol/water) tank (114-litre/25-Imp ga capacity)
79 Handhold
80 Fuselage decking
81 Aerial mast
82 D/F loop
83 Oxygen cylinders (three)

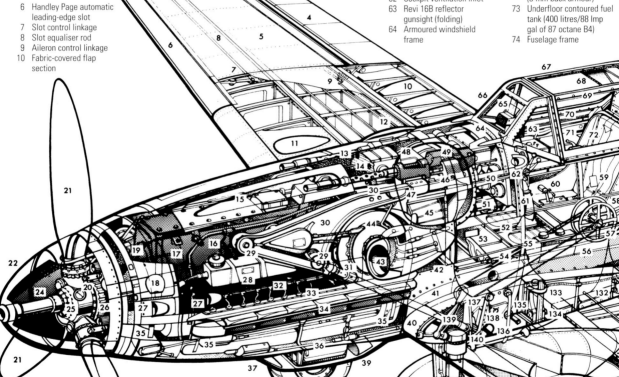

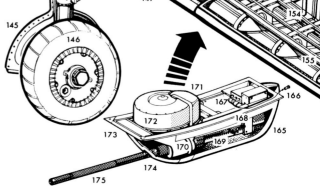

*bove: The Erla-Haube clear-view canopy
*nsiderably improved visibility from the cockpit,
*s did the Galland-Panzer armoured glass
ckrest and head protection.

*ight: The inboard flap section was split in two
*nd acted as a variable ejector for the radiator.
*he degree to which the two petals opened was
ntrolled by thermostat.

4 Filler pipe
5 Wireless equipment packs (FuG 16ZY communications and FuG 25 IFF)
6 Main fuel filler cap
7 Aerial
8 Fuselage top keel (connector stringer)

95 Starboard fixed tailplane
96 Elevator balance
97 Starboard elevator
98 Geared elevator tab

*This is the tall (non-retractable) tailwheel
introduced late in the G-6 production run, and
subsequently fitted to G-10s and G-14s.*

Aerial lead-in
Fuselage skin plating sections
'U' stringers
Fuselage frames (monocoque construction)
Tail trimming cables
Tailfin root fairing

99 All-wooden tailfin construction
100 Aerial attachment
101 Rudder upper hinge bracket
102 Rudder post
103 Fabric-covered wooden rudder structure
104 Geared rudder tab
105 Rear navigation light
106 Port elevator
107 Elevator geared tab
108 Tailplane structure
109 Rudder actuating linkage
110 Elevator control horn
111 Elevator connecting rod
112 Elevator control quadrant
113 Tailwheel leg cuff
114 Castoring non-retractable tailwheel
115 Lengthened tailwheel leg
116 Access panel
117 Tailwheel shock strut
118 Lifting point
119 Rudder cable
120 Elevator cables
121 First aid pack
122 Air bottles

123 Fuselage access panel
124 Bottom keel (connector stringer)
125 Ventral IFF aerial
126 Master compass
127 Elevator control linkage
128 Wingroot fillet
129 Camber changing flap
130 Ducted coolant radiator
131 Wing stringers
132 Wing rear pick-up point
133 Spar/fuselage upper pin joint (horizontal)
134 Spar/fuselage lower pin joint (vertical)
135 Flap equaliser rod
136 Rüstsatz-3 auxiliary fuel tank ventral rack
137 Undercarriage electrical interlock
138 Wing horizontal pin forward pick-up
139 Undercarriage retraction jack mechanism
140 Undercarriage pivot bevel
141 Auxiliary fuel tank (Rüstsatz-3) of 300-litre (66-Imp gal) capacity
142 Mainwheel leg fairing
143 Mainwheel oleo leg
144 Brake lines
145 Mainwheel fairing
146 Port mainwheel
147 Leading-edge skin
148 Port mainwheel well
149 Wing spar
150 Flap actuating linkage
151 Fabric-covered control surfaces
152 Slotted flap structure
153 Leading-edge slot-actuating mechanism
154 Slot equaliser rod
155 Handley Page automatic leading-edge slot
156 Wing stringers
157 Spar flange decrease

158 Wing ribs
159 Flush-rivetted stressed wing skinning
160 Metal framed Frise-type aileron
161 Fixed trim tab
162 Wingtip construction
163 Port navigation light
164 Angled pitot head
165 Rüstsatz-6 optional underwing cannon gondola
166 14-point plug connection
167 Electrical junction box
168 Cannon rear mounting bracket
169 20-mm Mauser MG 151/20 cannon
170 Cannon front mounting bracket
171 Ammunition feed chute
172 Ammunition magazine drum
173 Underwing panel
174 Gondola fairing
175 Cannon barrel

*The single-strut
mainwheel assembly
(right), retracted into a
well forward of the
wing spar (below). The
lower portion of the
wheel was left
uncovered when
retracted. Note the
shallow underwing
radiator.*

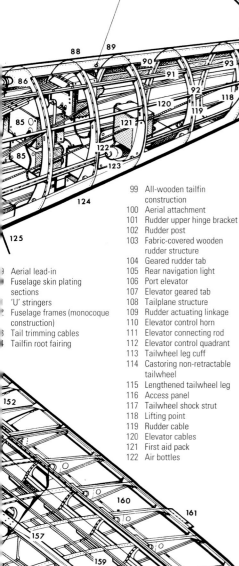

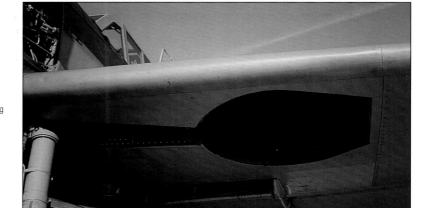

Right: A Bf 109K-4 displays the salient features of the variant: additional main undercarriage doors (rarely fitted in service), retractable long tailwheel, deep oil cooler bath and the relocation aft of the direction-finding loop antenna.

This close-up reveals the installation of the DB 605D in the Bf 109K-4, and how the main undercarriage leg was attached to the fuselage structure rather than the wing spar.

This is another view of the same aircraft. Large numbers of late-model 'Gustavs' and K-4s were found by the Allies in semi-derelict state.

As production continued, some minor improvements were incorporated to some aircraft. In addition to the Flettner rudder tabs, some G-14s were fitted with two fixed tabs above and below the moveable surface, projecting beyond the rudder line. A new rudder of subtly altered shape was introduced, this being fabric- instead of ply-wood-covered, and tapering to a more pronounced point at its aft-most corner. G-14/AS aircraft appeared with a new, larger oil cooler (although the old unit was inevitably fitted to some aircraft) with a correspondingly deeper chin intake and fairing. At the end of 1944, larger mainwheels were adopted, in turn requiring a wing redesign which dispensed with the characteristic rounded wing bulges in favour of larger, rectangular fairings. To maintain the confusion, many G-6s were refitted with these wings.

As a final twist in the convoluted tale of the 'Gustav', repairable G-6s and G-14s were reworked at the factories to become Bf 109G-10s, this version being roughly equivalent to the Bf 109K-4. The definitive engine for the K-4 was to be the DB 605DM, but apparently few such engines reached the G-10, most being completed as Bf 109G-10/AS aircraft with the DB 605AS. Production got under way in October 1944, and amounted to about 2,500 aircraft. As with the G-14, any attempt at standardisation failed, and the G-10s emerged in a bewildering array of configurations, although most had the tall tailwheel and tall, wooden tail.

One feature which was new to at least some G-10s was a revised cowling, introduced for the DB 605DM engine. The slightly larger size of the new engine required the addition of a small bulge on either side of the cowling just below the forward exhaust stub. The presence of these bulges did not necessarily mean the aircraft was powered by the new engine, for several were completed with the new cowling but retained the DB 605AS. G-10s remanufactured by WNF were known as Bf 109G-10/U4s, the Umbaustaz designation covering the installation of the MK 108 cannon in place of the MG 151/20. Various Rüstsätze were fitted, including R1 (bomb-rack), R3 (auxiliary fuel tank), R5 (gondola-mounted MG 151/20s), R6 (rudder-control autopilot) and R7 (WGr 21 rocket tubes).

Bf 109K

As might be gathered from the descriptions above, the late-model Bf 109Gs represented a minefield of confusion, and positive identification of exact models became virtually impossible without reference to Werknummern. While all this has become a fascinating subject for modern-day researchers, full of conflicting opinions, it represented a serious problem for the Luftwaffe. Of course, the principal problem lay in the massed Allied armies approaching the very Reich itself, preceded by thousands of aircraft flown by well-trained and confident crews. However, the desperate defence against the growing onslaught was not made easier by the wildly differing standards of equipment reaching the front line. The Bf 109K represented a last effort to rationalise the chaotic Bf 109 production programme.

Development of the Bf 109K was spurred by the DB 605DM engine, which offered 2,000 hp (1492 kW) for take-off and 1,800 hp (1343 kW) at 5000 m (16,400 ft). A small batch of Bf 109K-0s was built, featuring the DB 605DB engine, without the MW-50 boosting of the DM.

the modifications which had been developed for the G-6 during its long production. From the outset this aim failed abysmally, and G-14s appeared in almost as many combinations as their predecessors. As far as is known all had the Erla canopy, but they appeared with various antenna configurations, long or short tailwheels and tall or regular fins. Engine cannon armament was either the MG 151/20 or MK 108. The first aircraft were powered by the DB 605AM with MW-50 boosting, but were also followed by G-14/AS aircraft with the DB 605AS. One small difference between the G-6 and G-14 was the relocation of the FuG 16ZY antenna (when fitted) from the centreline to under the port wing.

Messerschmitt Bf 109K-4
III./Jagdgeschwader 53 'Pik As'
Kirrlach
Bavaria
March 1945

Last of the Bf 109s to enter quantity production under the original management, the Bf 109K-4 entered service with home-defence units in October 1944; by the end of November, a total of 534 had been delivered. The K-4 actually preceded the G-10 into service and both types (as well as G-14s) were often mixed within units. III./JG 53 was one of only four Gruppen to be solely equipped with the Bf 109K-4 at some point.

Wings and wheels
One of the improvements made to the basic Bf 109G airframe to make its ground handling more 'friendly' for inexperienced new pilots was the fitting of wider tyres during G-10 production and to all K models. In order to accommodate these wide (660x190 mm) wheels in the thin wing of the 109, large bulges were added to the top surface.

Markings and colours
This JG 53 aircraft wears the 'Pik As' (ace of spades) badge and this Geschwader's black 'defence of the Reich' band on the rear fuselage. On this bar is superimposed the vertical bar marking of the fourth Gruppe, and the yellow colour of the individual number further identifies it as an 11th Staffel machine.The national insignia are of the late-war outline type and the basic scheme is the less common 82 (dark green)/83 (bright mid-green)/76 (light blue) pattern.

Armament
Armament on the K-4 was all concentrated in the fuselage. The R6 gunpacks were a proposed field modification that was never fitted. The main weapon was the devastating MK 108 cannon mounted in the spinner, supplemented by two MG 131 13-mm machine-guns mounted above the engine.

...n and rudder
...he tall wooden tail first appeared on some G-5s and was ...troduced into G-6 production in early 1944, although by no ...eans was it seen on all late examples of this variant. It was ...andard on the G-10. The unit, which featured a vertical ...dder hinge line, was introduced to give a higher degree of ...ntrol during take-off. Being made of wood, it placed less ...rain on the supply of strategic materials. The horizontal ...abiliser was also wooden and had a metal sheath on the ...ading edge.

Last days of JG 53
Despite its nominal Reich defence (bomber interception) role, JG 53 flew mainly tactical support missions after its withdrawal to Bavaria in the last weeks of the war. The Geschwader's last kills (a B-26 and an Auster) were scored on 24 April and its last operation was flown on 2 May. That same day, the surviving aircraft were drained of valuable fuel and burnt at Prien, south-east of Munich, and the personnel dispersed.

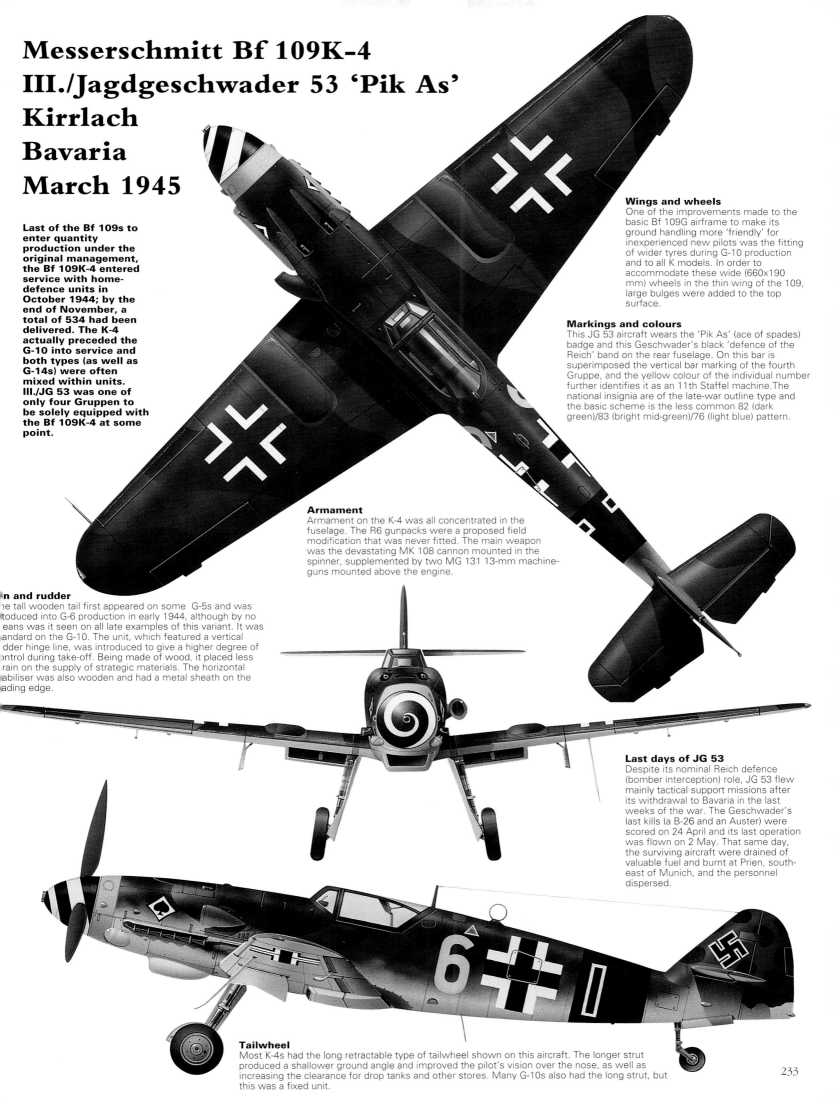

Tailwheel
Most K-4s had the long retractable type of tailwheel shown on this aircraft. The longer strut produced a shallower ground angle and improved the pilot's vision over the nose, as well as increasing the clearance for drop tanks and other stores. Many G-10s also had the long strut, but this was a fixed unit.

233

Reichsverteidigung Bf 109Ks

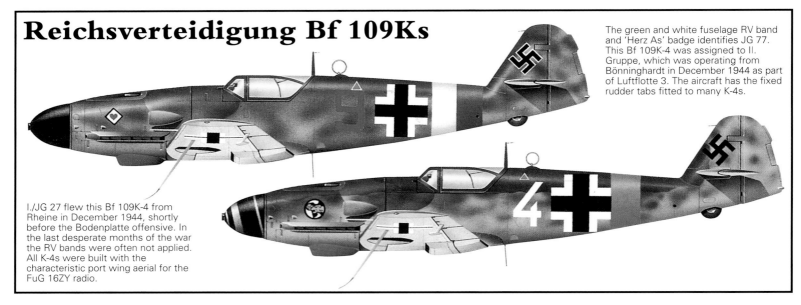

The green and white fuselage RV band and 'Herz As' badge identifies JG 77. This Bf 109K-4 was assigned to II. Gruppe, which was operating from Bönninghardt in December 1944 as part of Luftflotte 3. The aircraft has the fixed rudder tabs fitted to many K-4s.

I./JG 27 flew this Bf 109K-4 from Rheine in December 1944, shortly before the Bodenplatte offensive. In the last desperate months of the war the RV bands were often not applied. All K-4s were built with the characteristic port wing aerial for the FuG 16ZY radio.

Although some test aircraft were built, production of three early variants (the pressurised K-1, standard fighter K-2 and standard/reconnaissance fighter K-3) was cancelled at an early stage to make way for the K-4, which was to be the only mass-produced K variant, incorporating all of the 'standardisation' features of the similar G-10. Among these were DB 605DM engine with characteristic extra cowling bulges, tall fin, long tailwheel, deep oil cooler, wide-bladed propeller, rectangular wing fairings for the larger main-wheels and FuG 16ZY radio antenna under the port wing. The engine-mounted MK 108 was standard, although there are reports of Ks being fitted with the 30-mm MK 103.

Where the K-4 differed was in the relocation of the ADF loop antenna to further back on the spine, the addition of trim tabs for the ailerons (usually locked shut, as they caused a major discrepancy between the stick forces required to operate the tabbed ailerons and untabbed elevators) and the provision of additional undercarriage doors to cover the lower portion of the wheels which had traditionally been left open to the elements. The latter were usually removed by operational units. There were very small numbers of two Rüstzustände, R2 for reconnaissance and R6 with autopilot, while Rüstsätze applied included R1 (bomb), R3 (drop tanks), R4 (underwing cannon) and R6 (gun camera in the port wing).

Further development of the Bf 109K had largely ended by the beginning of 1945, and only the Bf 109K-6 can be ascertained, this being a heavy fighter with an MK 108 cannon installed in each wing (rather than in a gondola) in addition to the standard armament. A K-6 was certainly tested in late 1944, but it is not known if it was put into production. Various accounts mention Bf 109K-8 reconnaissance aircraft, while the K-10 and K-14 fighters may also have been built in small numbers. The last-mentioned was powered by the DB 605L high-altitude engine, allowing the aircraft to attain 727 km/h (452 mph) at 11500 m (37,730 ft), a very respectable performance for an aircraft originally designed 10 years earlier. The K-12 was a planned two-seat trainer.

Defence of the Reich

In the final year of the war the Reich was being squeezed from all sides, and on all fronts the Jagdflieger were very much on the defensive. Every Allied daylight operation was attended by huge numbers of escort fighters. During the early months of the daylight bombing campaign, the German day fighters had exacted a frighteningly heavy toll from the 8th AF heavy bombers, relatively unhindered. The arrival of the Merlin-engined P-51 Mustang at the start of 1944 changed all that, and anti-bomber missions became increasingly dangerous for Bf 109 pilots. The introduction of Bf 109G-10s and Bf 109K-4s could not in any way redress the balance, for even these advanced Bf 109s were no match for the P-51D or Spitfire Mk XIV.

Right: J-704 suffered a number of incidents during its Swiss carreer. After turning over in January 1945, its fin and rudder were replaced by the tall wooden unit. It was written off after a forced landing in November 1946.

Below: Like J-704, J-701 was one of the 12 Bf 109Gs delivered in May 1944. Two Luftwaffe Fs and two other Gs were interned during the war and put into service.

Right: Although heavily retouched, this photograph of an unfortunate Messerschmitt is noteworthy for depicting one of the Yugoslavian Bf 109G-12s, acquired as part of the large batch of aircraft supplied by Bulgaria as war reparations (in return, Yugoslavia also supplied the Bulgarians with much-needed Il-2 spares). The Yugoslavian aircraft differed from standard G-12s in being fitted with an Erla-Haube over the rear cockpit in place of the heavily-framed hood with bulged sides. This modification was almost certainly undertaken in Bulgaria.

The Finnish air force operated five sub-types of 'Gustav': the G-1, G-2, G-6, G-8 and G-10. The first appeared in 1943 and were swiftly thrown into the Continuation War with the Soviet Union. The 'Mersu' performed well in Finnish hands, although the numerically superior forces of the Red Army eventually overwhelmed the Finns.

Left: MT-201 was the first of the batch of Bf 109G-2s supplied to Finland in 1943.

On 1 January 1945 the Luftwaffe launched its last concerted offensive – Operation Bodenplatte. Over 800 fighters, including 17 Gruppen of Bf 109G/Ks from JGs 3, 4, 11, 27, 53 and 77, were launched on strafing attacks of 27 Allied airfields in France, Belgium and the Netherlands. Achieving almost complete surprise, Bodenplatte destroyed over 450 Allied aircraft, gaining a brief measure of respite for the ground forces facing the Allied ground attack onslaught. However, those aircraft were swiftly replaced, while the 150-plus pilots lost by the Luftwaffe during the course of the operation were not. These losses left the Jagdflieger reeling from a blow from which it was never to recover. To make matters worse, in the East, where most of the aerial fighting was conducted at low level, the Luftwaffe was facing large numbers of the excellent Lavochkin La-7 and Yakovlev Yak-3, both types which could leave the Bf 109 standing in terms of both speed and manoeuvrability.

As the Reich's territory shrunk by the day, the Luftwaffe found it easier to rapidly redeploy fighter forces to areas where they were most needed, and to the credit of the Germans they put up a savage defence against overwhelming odds on all fronts. Inevitably, the last weeks of war saw some desperate defence measures introduced, notably Operation Wehrwulf, which entailed stripped-down Bf 109s being deliberately rammed into USAAF bombers. A special unit was created for these attacks, the Sonderkommando Elbe. On 7 April 1945 it undertook its only ramming mission, hitting eight bombers for the loss of over 60 fighters.

The final account

Sizeable numbers of Bf 109s were still flying right up to the end, with around 800 on Luftwaffe charge at the end of the war. Many units had simply run out of fuel, while others were caught up in the rapid Allied advances. In early April 1945, the following units were still equipped with Bf 109Gs and Ks: II. and IV.(Einsatz)/JG 1, II. and III./JG 3, III./JG 4, III./JG 6, 1., 4. and 7./NJG 11, I., II. and III./JG 51, Stab, I., II. and III./JG 52, Stab., I., II., III. and IV./JG 53, Stab, I., II. and III./JG 77.

JGs 27, 52, 53 and 77 had flown the Bf 109 throughout the war, and between them had shot down an estimated 22,000-plus enemy aircraft. By far the most successful (and

the most successful fighter unit of all time) was Jagdgeschwader 52, which boasted a combat record of nearly 11,000 kills. Included in its personnel were 67 holders of the Ritterkreuz (Iron Cross), six of the 15 pilots to shoot down more than 200 aircraft, and the Luftwaffe's three top scorers (Erich Hartmann – 352 kills; Gerhard Barkhorn – 301 kills; Günther Rall – 275 kills). Given the

Seen at Erding in Bavaria in early 1943, this group of Finnish pilots relaxes before undertaking the delivery flight of the Bf 109G-2s in the background back to Finland.

After the war the Finns were restricted to 60 combat aircraft by the Allied powers. Of the 102 Bf 109Gs then in service, 42 were put into storage. The swastika insignia was replaced by the blue/white roundel after 1 April 1945. MT-504 'G' was a G-10 serving with HLeLv 31 in 1947.

Post-war operators

The Swiss Fliegertruppe operated a total of 14 Bf 109G-6s, 12 of which were purchased from Germany in a bizarre deal. The other two aircraft were Luftwaffe machines which landed in Switzerland and were interned. The 'Gustav' served with Fliegerkompagnie 7 from 1944 to 1947.

Finland's long association with the Bf 109G lasted until 1954 and encompassed several variants, this being a late-model G-6 with tall fin. The aircraft served with HLeLv 31 at Utti in 1948, and wears the post-armistice roundel markings which replaced the swastika device of the war years.

Above: This photograph is one of the very few to depict an S 99 (Bf 109G-14) in Czechoslovak AF service. The aircraft is marked with a red lightning flash on the fuselage.

Left: Carrying the civilian registration OK-BYH, this S 99 is one of the aircraft allocated to the Czechoslovak National Air Guard. The S 99 featured the standard armament of two MG 131 machine-guns and an engine-mounted MG 151/20 cannon.

Post-war Czechoslovak production

Faced with equipping its nascent air arm in the immediate post-war years, Czechoslovakia naturally turned to the Bf 109, which had been put into production at the Avia factory at Cakovice in the last months of World War II. No Bf 109s were finished during the war, but enough nearly-complete airframes had been built to assemble 20 Bf 109G-14s and a pair of Bf 109G-12s under the designations S 99 and CS 99, respectively. This paved the way for further production, which by circumstance was forced to turn to the Junkers Jumo engine.

Two airframes were completed as CS 99 two-seaters, these being similar to the Bf 109G-12. Both examples were believed to be unarmed, and provided a useful training capability for the young air arm. Although powered by the DB 605AS, the S/CS 99s were completed with the bulged cowling of the DB 605D.

amount of good fortune that must inevitably accompany fighting and flying skills in compiling a huge victory tally, it is perhaps not surprising that all three survived the war. 'Bubi' Hartmann had shot down his 352nd aircraft on the last day of the war, but was subsequently captured by the Russians and held captive for 10 years. Following his release, he returned to Germany, assuming command of the reborn Luftwaffe's premier fighter unit, JG 71 'Richthofen'. Both Barkhorn and Rall also served in the post-war Luftwaffe, the latter becoming the first German to solo in an F-104 Starfighter.

With the end of World War II came an abrupt end to the careers of many Luftwaffe aircraft types. The greatest exception was, of course, the Bf 109. For a start, four countries used the Bf 109 for some years after the end of

the war as front-line equipment. Switzerland had a single Fliegerkompagnie equipped with Bf 109G-6s until 1948, when P-51s arrived. Romania, too, flew the Bf 109G-6/ -10/-14 until 1948. Yugoslavia acquired several ex-Luftwaffe and Croatian aircraft at the end of the war, and was also presented with about 60 Bf 109Gs from Bulgaria, including some G-12 two-seaters. They served for some years. The longest-lived Messerschmitts were those of Finland, which kept its fleet of mixed Gs flying until 1954. However, the basic design was to fly and fight for a good deal longer thanks to two indigenous production efforts – in Czechoslovakia and Spain.

Production in Czechoslovakia

In 1944 Germany had established a Bf 109 manufacturing organisation in the vicinity of Prague, feeding a final assembly line in the Avia works at Cakovice. Bf 109G-12 two-seaters and G-14s were produced in small numbers before the German withdrawal. Almost unbelievably, the capacity for Bf 109 production was left almost intact by both the departing Germans and liberating Soviets. At the end of the war, the Czechoslovak government ordered that the assembly line be reopened, plus a second one at the Letov factory at Letnany, to produce Bf 109s for the National Air Guard. Completed components were rounded up and enough gathered to complete 20 Bf 109G-14s, christened S 99 in local service, and two Bf 109G-12 two-seaters, which were designated CS 99.

Plans were hatched for a major production of Bf 109Gs to equip the regular air force (Ceskoslovenske Vojenske Letectvo), utilising the many partly- or wholly-completed airframes then available and a large stock of DB 605AM engines being held in a sugar refinery warehouse. Unfortunately, the refinery burned to the ground in September 1945, taking with it all the precious DB 605AMs. Nevertheless, the idea was a sound one, promising a cheap and rapid way of providing an air force, so an alternative powerplant was sought. The only one available was the Junkers Jumo 211F (1000 kW/1,340 hp for take-off) and Jumo 211H (1060 kW/1,420 hp for take-off), intended for

Avia S 99 – the Czechoslovak G

The first equipment of the National Air Guard was the Avia S 99, powered by a DB 605AS. All had the tall tail associated with the Bf 109G-14, and were completed with the large mainwheels and corresponding rectangular wing fairings. The tailwheel, however, remained of the short variety. The Air Guard used a curved, triangular marking, later changed to a circular insignia for the Czechoslovak air force.

Avia S 199 – Jumo power

When the stock of DB 605s was destroyed in a fire, Avia had to look to the Junkers Jumo 211 to power its Bf 109 airframes. The result was an inelegant installation which retained the earlier bulges for the fuselage guns but which did not permit the installation of an engine cannon.

A pair of Czechoslovak air force S 199s is caught in flight. The 'Mezec' was armed with a pair of MG 131 machine-guns in the upper fuselage, and usually carried MG 151/20s under the wings in the standard Bf 109 gondolas.

CS 199

Right: CS 199 two-seater production reached 58 aircraft. Early production aircraft retained the original side-hinging canopy inherited from the CS 99/Bf 109G-12.

Below: Part way through the CS 199 production run a new aft-sliding canopy was introduced, greatly improving vision from both cockpits. The angle of the wheel axles was also changed during the production run.

He 111 bombers and by no means ideal, but available in quantity.

Adapting the Bf 109 airframe to take the Jumo was a relatively easy matter, and the first aircraft, designated S 199, first flew at Cakovice on 25 March 1947, with Petr Siroky at the controls. The S 199 was far from a good aircraft. The Jumo drove a VS 11 paddle-bladed propeller with vicious torque and, as soon as the tailwheel rose on take-off, the tail swung alarmingly, requiring an instant boot of rudder to counteract the swing. Handling the aircraft once airborne was demanding, and the performance was sluggish, the S 199 demonstrating a maximum speed of only 550 km/h (341 mph). In service, the S 199 quickly acquired the derisory nickname 'Mezec' (mule).

Deliveries to the CVL

Considerable numbers were built for the CVL, both Jumo 211F- and 211H-powered versions being on strength. First deliveries were made in 1948. Some of the original S 99s were re-engined and redelivered for service

as S 199s. Standard armament comprised two MG 131s in the upper fuselage and two MG 151/20 cannon in underwing gondolas, à la Rüstsatz-6. Some aircraft had MG 131s or MG 17s mounted in the wings in place of the gondola weapons. The 'Erla' hood with which the first aircraft were completed later gave way to an aft-sliding single-piece hood, which was bulged to give the pilot better visibility. To aid pilot conversion, Avia also produced 58 two-seaters, designated the CS 199 and first flying on 24 January 1949. They had armament removed, and initially flew with the standard Bf 109G-12-type side-hinging canopies. Later, a neater three-section aft-sliding canopy was developed and fitted.

S 199.185 was one of the aircraft rebuilt by Avia from a DB 605-engined S 99. The Vojenské Letectvo received its first S 199 in 1948, and the type served for some time into the 1950s before being replaced by modern Soviet jets (MiG-15 and Yak-23).

Large numbers of S 199s of the Czechoslovak air force are seen receiving maintenance. The original Erla-Haube canopy was soon exchanged for a new, bulged, aft-sliding Avia design.

Above: 101 Sqn was the first unit to form in the Chel Ha'Avir, and it flew the S 199 into action within days of the fighters arriving in the newly-proclaimed state of Israel. 101 Sqn marked its aircraft with the now-famous red and white stripes, the rear fuselage bearing identification bands to prevent any confusion with Israeli Spitfires.

Right: 101 Squadron's Chief Technical Officer, Harry Axelrod, poses in front of D-123. Among the unit's pilots was well-known Bell test pilot Chalmers 'Slick' Goodlin.

Far right: A small number of S 199s were completed with MG 131 machine-guns mounted internally in the wings (making a total of four), rather than featuring podded cannon.

Right: This S 199, number 54, is seen at Munich after having been flown in by a defecting Czech political refugee. The national insignia have been hastily taped over.

Although the S 199 served for some years with the CVL and Czechoslovak National Air Guard, it is best remembered for its exploits with the only export customer: Israel. It was not until 14 May 1948 that the Jewish state of Israel officially came into being, yet the fledgling Israeli air force had been created as early as March. It had money and volunteers in abundance, many of them experienced World War II veterans, but it lacked aircraft. An arms embargo had been placed on exports to the Middle East, preventing the Chel Ha'Avir from obtaining arms from the usual sources. Accordingly, the Israelis turned to Czechoslovakia, which was desperate for hard currency.

On 23 April 1948, a contract was signed covering the supply of 10 S 199s, at a unit price of US$190,000, this also including spares and ammunition. Under Operation Balak, Czechoslovakia was flying arms into Israel using a chartered Douglas DC-4, and it was by this means that the 10 S 199s, plus 15 more signed for in May, arrived, disassembled, in Israel. In the meantime, Israeli pilots had been training at a clandestine school in Rome, before spending two weeks on S 199 conversion in Czechoslovakia.

Within days of the declaration of the state of Israel, attacks came from its Arab neighbours. The rapid procurement and training effort had resulted in No. 101 Squadron at Ekron being made combat-ready on S 199s in time. The first operational sortie, a strafing attack by four aircraft, was mounted on 19 May. During the mission two of the aircraft were lost: one to ground fire and the other in a landing accident. This set the scene for the S 199's less than illustrious career in the Chel Ha'Avir. Disliked by Israeli pilots as much as it was by the Czechoslovaks, the S 199 suffered from an alarming accident rate, while it proved to be nearly useless in combat. Nevertheless, it did achieve a few kills, the first being the shooting-down of two bomb-carrying Egyptian C-47s on 3 June by No. 101 Squadron's commander, Mordechai 'Modi' Alon.

The 'Mule' at war

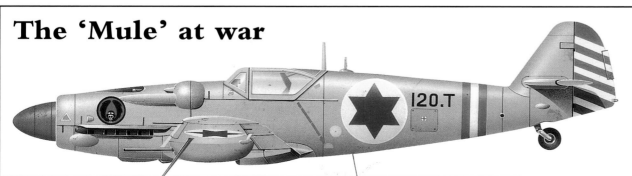

Desperate for fighters, the fledgling Israeli air force (Chel Ha'Avir) was in the market for anything that could get past the United Nations arms embargo. Czechoslovakia was desperate, too, for hard currency, and the Israelis were offering US dollars. A total of 25 early production aircraft was delivered. On 29 May 1948, the S 199 flew its first combat mission in Israeli hands.

HA-1109-J1L

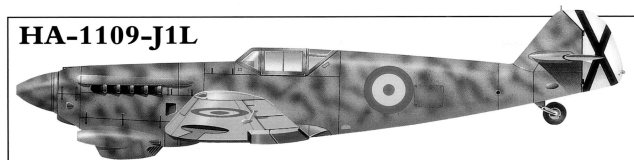

Twenty-five HA-1109-J1Ls were built up from Bf 109G-2 airframes originally supplied by Germany, with the Hispano-Suiza 12Z 89 engine installed. None was issued for service, although they underwent limited trials. This aircraft is seen as it appeared on trials with the Escuadrón de Experimentación en Vuelo at Cuatro Vientos.

Hispano power

Faced, like Czechoslovakia, with no suitable powerplant for its Bf 109G airframes, Spain turned to the Hispano-Suiza 12Z engine. The physical installation of the engine was painless, but the powerplant was not really suitable for the Bf 109, the resulting aircraft being underpowered and having some less than ideal handling characteristics.

Above: To test the Hispano-Suiza engine, a 12Z 89 was installed in a Bf 109E-1. It was tested by both Hispano and the Instituto Nacional de Técnica Aeronáutica.

Crippling the HA-1109-J1L in terms of drag was the inelegant and bulky carburettor and oil cooler installation under the engine. The fuel-injected 12Z 17 removed the need for a carburettor and cut drag by a large factor.

On 18 July two S 199s tackled two Egyptian Spitfires, probably the last time the two old warriors met head-to-head. Alon accounted for one of the Spitfires that day, but it was obvious that the 'Mule' was largely ineffective. It was the S 199 that killed Alon on 16 October 1948 in an accident. Thankfully for the Chel Ha'Avir, Spitfire Mk IXs and P-51Ds soon arrived to redress the balance and allowed the new air force to provide a meaningful defence. By the time the fighting ceased in January 1949, only about five S 199s were still airworthy, flying alongside Spitfires and Mustangs for a short while, but by the end of the year they had disappeared from service. Despite its failure, the S 199 had proved to be an invaluable morale booster at a time when Israel was desperately fighting for its very survival.

Spanish production

Bf 109s, albeit in a rather different guise, were still flying at the other end of the Mediterranean long after the S 199. Spain had made the first combat use of the Bf 109 back in 1937, and it was perhaps fitting that the old warrior should see out its operational days in the Iberian peninsula. The Ejército del Aire was no stranger to the Bf 109, having operated those left behind by the Legion Condor, and later

received Bf 109Fs. Anxious to maintain a modern fighter force, the Spaniards approached Germany in 1942 to acquire a licence to manufacture the Bf 109G-2, resulting in an agreement by which Hispano-Aviación (part of the newly created CASA concern) would undertake the work. Germany would provide 25 broken-down airframes, together with drawings, jigs and tools, followed by armament, propellers and engines for another 200 aircraft.

Delays dogged the establishment of the Hispano production line so that by the time it was ready, the worsening war situation meant that Germany only managed to supply the original 25 airframes (and these lacked tails) and incomplete drawings. Hispano was faced with a considerable struggle to produce a fighter, the major problem being the lack of a suitable engine. By late 1944 it was painfully obvious that the long-promised DB 605s would not appear,

Above: 6-119 was the Bf 109E-1 used for the trial engine installation. It had been delivered to the Legion Condor in 1939 and left behind for use by the Ejército del Aire.

Below: Fitting the fuel-injected Hispano-Suiza 12Z 17 engine to produce the HA-1109-K1L certainly improved both the looks and the performance of the Spanish '109, but it was still some way short of being a viable combat aircraft.

Armament trials

As it first appeared, the HA-1109-K1L was unarmed, and a series of trials was run to investigate possible armament options for the type. The originally intended weapons were two wing-mounted Breda-SAFAT 12.7-mm (0.50-in) machine-guns under the wings, but a role change from fighter to ground-attack saw the adoption of various rocket, gun and cannon options.

Above: The designation HA-1109-K3L covered this aircraft, which flew with no gun armament but with eight launchers for 80-mm Oerlikon rockets under the wings. The HA-1109-K2L was similar but had 12.7-mm machine-guns above the engine.

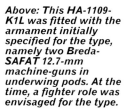

Above: This HA-1109-K1L was fitted with the armament initially specified for the type, namely two Breda-SAFAT 12.7-mm machine-guns in underwing pods. At the time, a fighter role was envisaged for the type.

Above right: The final choice of armament retained the Oerlikon rockets, but added a 20-mm Hispano-Suiza cannon in each wing, necessitating the addition of a prominent wing fence to smooth airflow. With this armament, aircraft were delivered as HA-1112-K1Ls.

Right: In its unarmed HA-1109-K1L form, the Spanish Bf 109 was a sleek aircraft. None was delivered to a service unit, all being used for trials pending delivery of the armed aircraft.

Below: Most of the armed HA-1112-K1Ls were delivered to the Escuela de Caza (fighter school) at Morón for use as advanced ground attack trainers.

and so, as in Czechoslovakia, the search was on for a new engine. The answer, initially, came in the form of the Hispano-Suiza 12Z 89, a 12-cylinder engine rated at 970 kW (1,300 hp) for take-off, which had just entered production. One example was tested in a Bf 109E-1 (6-119) by the Air Test and Development Centre at Cuatro Vientos, and although the results were merely satisfactory (the aircraft was at least faster than the Bf 109E), the 12Z 89 was adequate – and, besides, there was nothing else.

Assembly began on the 25 Bf 109 airframes supplied from Germany, followed by production of the 175 remaining airframes from entirely Spanish sources, the Hispano engineers having been able to reverse-engineer some of the parts for which accurate drawings had not been provided. With the designation HA-1109-J1L, the first 12Z 89-powered Messerschmitt flew from Tablada on 2 March 1945, initially fitted with a Hamilton-Standard (VDM) propeller, as the intended production propeller, the Swiss Escher-Wyss V71 L1, had not yet arrived.

Installing the Hispano-Suiza engine required considerable redesign of the cowling, fuel and oil systems and the engine bay, although the original Messerschmitt bearers were easily adapted to the new powerplant. The vertical tail surfaces were also modified to cater for the Hispano's propeller turning to the right, instead of the left as with the DB 605. The self-sealing tanks were replaced by metal units. With the Ejército del Aire designation of C.4J (C=Caza – fighter), the prototype went to the INTA (Instituto Nacional de Técnica Aeronáutica) for testing in January 1946 at Alcalá de Henares. Soon after the Escher-Wyss propeller was fitted. In 1947 the prototype was damaged at Morón.

Initial production variant

That year, the first of the 25 Bf 109Gs flew as a HA-1109-J1L, on 10 July. The remaining 24 aircraft were completed over a period of time, but none was issued to the EdA due to general dissatisfaction with the 12Z 89 engine. A replacement was found in the Hispano-Suiza 12Z 17, which provided a similar power output but was much improved in other areas, including having fuel injection. Both engine types were assembled in Barcelona using major components supplied from the French factory near Paris. The first six of these engines arrived in 1951 and were fitted to three of the original Bf 109Gs and three new-production aircraft, the first flight occurring in the spring. Two of these aircraft were fitted with de Havilland Hydromatic PD-63-335-1 propellers, with no provision for an engine-mounted cannon.

Designated HA-1109-K1L, but retaining the EdA C.4J appellation, the new variant was delivered to the air force from May 1952, initially to 11 Grupo de Experimentación

Below: Among the production of Hispano-engined aircraft was a pair of two-seaters, which remained devoid of armament throughout their lives. Designated HA-1110-K1L, the trainers featured a long, aft-sliding canopy. The first aircraft flew in 1953. Both were later re-engined with Merlins and both are still extant.

Merlin Messerschmitt

Alternative engines for the HA-1112 had been denied to the Spanish due to trade embargoes. In the early 1950s, relationships with the victorious Allied powers began to thaw, and trade sanctions lifted in 1952. This paved the way for an approach to the British for the Merlin in 1953, the Merlin 500-45 driving a four-bladed Rotol propeller being chosen. On 30 December 1954, the first HA-1109-M1L took to the air at San Pablo airport.

(later known as 11 Escuadrón) at Tablada. The first two aircraft were joined by a third in November, by which time the unit had moved to Morón. In 1952 another 19 HA-1109-K1Ls were taken on strength, most serving with the Escuela de Caza at Morón, although four were sent to INTA for tests and a solitary example served with Grupo 23 at Reus.

By the time the HA-1109-K1L entered service, it was obvious that the aircraft could not be used as a fighter, and the originally intended armament of two wing-mounted 12.7-mm (0.5-in) Breda-SAFAT machine-guns was only fitted to one aircraft. Instead, the aircraft was envisaged for ground attack duties, and a series armament trials ensued. One aircraft, designated the HA-1109-K2L, received two Breda-SAFAT guns above the engine and underwing launchers for eight 80-mm Oerlikon rockets. The HA-1109-K3L was a single aircraft with rockets but no guns. Finally, the last of the J1Ls, suitably re-engined with a 12Z 17, had been modified with rocket launchers and a pair of Hispano HS-404 20-mm cannon in the wings. This became the standard configuration, and most of the C.4Js were modified with the new armament, being redesignated as HA-1112-K1Ls in the process. Most were used for operational training.

Meanwhile, in 1951, work had begun on a two-seater version for type conversion, the HA-1110-K1L. Only the two prototypes of this variant were built, flying for the first time in October 1953. The aircraft represented a considerable internal rearrangement, as the normal seat was moved forward to make room for the instructor. The aircraft were unarmed, and the fuel tankage was redesigned and rearranged to bring the quantity (423 litres/93 Imp gal) above that of the 400 litres (88 Imp gal) of the single-seater. The two-seat cockpit was covered by an elegant aft-sliding canopy arrangement which dramatically improved the view compared to the single-seater.

Merlin power

Airframe production had outstripped the provision of powerplants, so that by the end of 1949 80 had left the factory, with more following. Soon after the service introduction of the C.4J it was apparent that the type was not only worthless as a fighter, but it had little combat potential

at all. Again, a new engine was needed to power the large number of completed airframes which were piling up at the factory. The only answer was the Rolls-Royce Merlin. Considering that way back in 1935 it was a Rolls-Royce engine which had taken the first ever Bf 109 aloft, and that the Merlin had powered the Spitfires that had been the Bf 109's main opposition throughout World War II, the choice was supremely ironic.

Earlier, the Merlin had been unavailable due to arms embargoes, but in the early 1950s these were dropped, and an order was placed in the summer of 1953 for the two-speed Merlin 500-45, which developed 1200 kW (1,610 hp) for take-off. A four-bladed Rotol R116/4F5/12 propeller was fitted. The first conversion was aircraft no. 197, and flew for the first time – unarmed – on 30 December 1954 at San Pablo with Fernando de Juan Valiente at the controls. Designated HA-1109-M1L, the aircraft was found to have much improved performance in all areas. It was never as fast as the late-model German aircraft, being capable of 674 km/h (419 mph) at 4000 m (13,125 ft), and in service the armament imposed severe drag penalties, but it was respectable for the task it was asked to perform. Problems in the original design which were never addressed concerned the weak undercarriage and poor brakes, which were to cause a relentless series of accidents throughout the aircraft's career.

Above left: The first and second Merlin-powered Messerschmitts were designated HA-1109-M1L, and were unarmed. Subsequent aircraft were the re-engined armament trials aircraft, resulting in the designations HA-1112-M1L, M2L and M3L. In the event, the original armament of the HA-1112-K1L was retained.

Left: The installation of the Merlin may not have been as elegant as that in the Spitfire, but it dramatically improved the HA-1109's performance. This remained some way short of that achieved by the late-model Bf 109Gs and Ks, but for an aircraft whose task was ground-attack it was nevertheless respectable.

Proudly wearing the badge of Ala 7 de Caza-bombardeo (a diving pelican superimposed on the numeral '7') on its nose, this HA-1112-M1L was assigned to 71 Escuadrón, the first unit to form on the type. When deliveries to the unit exceeded 100 examples, a second Escuadrón (72) was formed, and Ala 7 was created to administer both. A third front-line unit was 364 Escuadrón, part of Ala Mixta 36, whose aircraft wore a white eight-pointed star. Buchóns were initially painted in a dark blue scheme, with a stylish black panel to hide the soot deposits from the exhaust.

movie *Battle of Britain*, which was completed the following year. This was not the first time the Buchón had played before the cameras, as several had been used during the filming of *The Star of Africa*, a film about the life of Hans-Joachim Marseille. Of the 23 purchased for the British film, 15 were resurrected as fliers, including one of the HA-1112-M4L two-seaters, all painted in Luftwaffe colours to play the part of Bf 109s. The remaining eight were employed in static roles. Although the Merlin installation had irrevocably altered the distinctive lines of the original Bf 109, the sight of the Luftwaffe-marked Buchóns lined up next to CASA 2.111s, Spitfires and Hurricanes on the airfield at Duxford (first operational home of the Spitfire) was one which would have been thought impossible when the RAF and Luftwaffe had slugged it out in the skies of southern England nearly 30 years earlier. With filming concluded, the aircraft became available for preservation by collectors and museums, joined by others from EdA stocks.

Shooting for *Battle of Britain* was the swansong for the Messerschmitt Bf 109 as a useful tool, although, thankfully, a number of airframes continue to delight air show crowds

in the hands of warbird enthusiasts, with more set to join them. From 1937 to 1965, the Bf 109 was in full military service – an amazing feat given the pace of aircraft development during that period. The Bf 109 was also one of the most numerous aircraft ever, with around 33,000 built. A large percentage of this figure covered the later variants, notably the G-6, which accounted for over a third of this figure.

Although the later variants lost much of the fine handling and fighting ability of the thoroughbred Bf 109E, the huge numbers built ensured that the aircraft remained the backbone of the Luftwaffe throughout World War II, flying in every theatre and doggedly defending the Reich against ever more unfavourable odds, right to the end. Its combat record is unmatched by any other warplane, and it was, by a wide margin, the aircraft type with the most kills. In the event, the Allied industrial machine could always produce more aircraft than the Bf 109 could shoot down, one of the many factors which doomed Germany to its fate. For the reasons above, however, the Bf 109 remains a true classic in the history of air combat. **David Donald**

Filming *Battle of Britain*

Below: A single two-seat HA-1112-M4L was used in the making of Battle of Britain. *Registered G-AWHC, the aircraft has been stored by 'Connie' Edwards at Big Spring, Texas for nearly 30 years.*

Despite its deep-breasted appearance, the HA-1112-M1L made an acceptable Bf 109E for film purposes, and it was fortuitous that the Spanish air force was retiring the type when the producers of *Battle of Britain* were amassing the armada of vintage warplanes needed for the film. In all, 23 Buchóns were employed during filming, of which 15 were flown. Filming took place in Spain (for the 'France' scenes) and at Duxford, from where Buchóns, CASA 2.111s and RAF fighters operated for the aerial scenes.

Above: A Battle of Britain *Hispano 'Messerschmitt' is seen at Duxford together with a CASA 2.111-D (Heinkel He 111H-16). These were used as transports in the Spanish air force and were also Merlin 500-powered.*

Messerschmitt survivors

At least 58 post-Bf 109E Messerschmitts are known to exist in some form or other, with the likelihood of more appearing from the former Soviet Union, which has already yielded a number of airframes in recent years. Of the total, more than half are Spanish-built aircraft, including a unique HA-1109-K1L in the Spanish air force museum, which also has a Buchón. Of the 30 HA-1112-M1Ls Buchóns still extant, five remain in storage (along with the sole remaining M4L two-seater) at Big Springs in Texas, and other non-modified, non-flying examples are on display or under restoration to static condition in Canada, France, Germany (three), Spain and the USA (five). Another HA-1112-M1L is on display in the USAF Museum, masquerading as a Bf 109G with a DB 605 fitted. Three Buchóns are flying in the USA with the Confederate Air Force, Planes of Fame Museum and Erickson, while in Europe single airworthy Buchóns reside in Belgium and the UK (Old Flying Machine Company). The OFMC has an additional example being restored to fly, and another aircraft should fly in the USA.

More adventurous have been the projects which have married Buchóns to DB 605 engines for flying purposes. The first was undertaken by Messerschmitt-Bölkow-Blohm (now Daimler-Benz Aerospace) using much of the fuselage of a Bf 109G, DB 605 engine and Buchón parts to create an aircraft which flew again in 1983. The aircraft crashed, and was rebuilt using another airframe. The German Hans Dittes also produced a 'Bf 109G' by using a Buchón and DB 605, with some genuine 'Gustav' parts. This aircraft flies from the Imperial War Museum's airfield at Duxford in England, where it shared hangar space with the IWM's own Bf 109G. Three more Buchóns are being rebuilt to fly again with DB 605s, two in France and one in the USA.

Only three Avia-built aircraft are extant, an S 199 under restoration and a CS 199 on display with the Czech air force museum at Kbely, while the third aircraft, a CS 199, is on display at the Israeli air force museum at Hatzerim.

As far as genuine Messerschmitts are concerned, there are five 'Friedrichs' extant, including two being restored in the UK, one in France and another in Finland. At the time of writing the only example on public display is the immaculate Bf 109F-2/Trop in the South African Military Museum. 'Gustavs' are far more numerous, with at least 16 known to survive. Static examples are on display, in storage or under restoration in Australia, Canada, Finland (two), Italy, Norway, Russia, the USA (NASM and Planes of Fame) and Yugoslavia.

In recent years only one genuine Messerschmitt has been flying, that being the famous 'Black 6' of the IWM in the UK. Captured by the RAAF's No. 3 Sqn in Libya in November 1942, the Bf 109G-2/Trop was used for a series of trials in Egypt and the UK for the remainder of the war, and was subsequently used for static historical displays. In 1972 the painstaking restoration back to flying condition was started, culminating in a 'first' flight on 17 March 1991 at RAF Benson. Painted in its original JG 27 colours, the aircraft was due to fly for three years (subsequently extended to six) before being gracefully retired to static display. However, on 12 August 1997, at the end of what was to be its last ever flight, 'Black Six' was severely damaged in a landing accident at Duxford. Thankfully, the pilot, Air Chief Marshal Sir John Allison, CinC RAF Strike Command, escaped with minor injuries. The aircraft will be repaired back to at least ground display condition, but at the time of writing the world is without a genuine flying Bf 109. That may not be the case for long, for, in addition to a number of Bf 109E projects, two 'Gustavs' (a G-6 and a G-14) are being restored to airworthiness in Colorado.

Above: The Bf 109G-6 at the Finnish Air Force Museum was displayed outdoors at Utti Air Base for many years.

Above: This Bf 109G-6 is now displayed in the Yugoslavian Aviation Museum. A sister aircraft is being restored to fly in the USA.

Above: This CS 199 is now on display at the Czech air force museum at Kbely, near Prague. An incomplete single-seat S-99 is also in the museum.

Below: The Israeli Air Force Museum at Hatzerim displays an Avia S 199 marked as an aircraft of No. 101 Squadron. The aircraft was converted from a two-seat CS 199.

Right: The Bf 109F-2/Trop (31010) in the Saxonwold museum in South Africa was captured in Libya by No. 7 Sqn, SAAF in late 1942.

Above: This Buchón appeared in Battle of Britain, A Piece of Cake and Memphis Belle as a Luftwaffe Bf 109. It is now with the Cavanaugh Flight Museum in Texas.

Below: The only genuine Bf 109 to fly since the 1950s was G-2 'Black 6' (G-USTV), restored 1972-91 and flown 1991-97.

Above: Messerschmitt-Bölkow-Blohm converted a Buchón to DB engine power in the late 1970s. Despite two major accidents, it is currently airworthy.

Above: Hans Dittes owns this Bf 109G/HA-1112 composite (completed as a G-10), operating it from Duxford, from where it flew alongside the IWM's own 'Black 6'.

Bf 109 colours

Luftwaffe

As Bf 109F production was gearing up in 1941, Messerschmitt produced an official painting guide to incorporate camouflage experience gained in the war's early campaigns. This plan served as the basis for painting the G series from March 1942. By mid-1944, the more defensive nature of the air war and the need to optimise use of manpower and materials led to a new range of grey, green and violet shades and much less consistency in colour and markings application.

The white nose, fuselage band and wingtips were a Mediterranean theatre marking first introduced by I./JG 27 on its arrival in Libya in 1941. The normal marking for a Gruppenkommandeur was a double chevron, but the holder of that office in II./JG 27 during late 1941 sported a triple device on his Bf 109F-4, with the addition of a small tactical number. Such obvious displays of a pilot's rank were outlawed later in the war as they made it easier for the enemy to identify and eliminate the most experienced pilots in a formation.

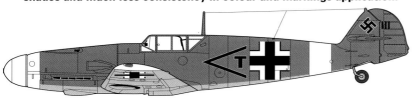

Unlike Bf 109Es in the North African theatre, Bf 109Fs and Gs were not given a topside heavy green mottle on delivery to the front. For the most part, they operated in factory-standard sand-yellow (Sandgelb) 79 over light blue (Hellblau) 78, although later deliveries were often in European theatre colours. On this Bf 109F-4/Z the 'T' within the chevron – indicating the Gruppe technical officer – was a non-regulation marking of a type common to JG 27. Normally this would be '< (chevron) IO' to the left of the fuselage cross.

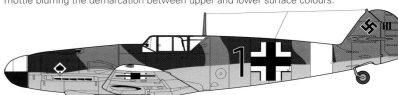

Another unit in the Mediterranean to use non-standard patterns was II./JG 53 on Sicily in early 1942. This aircraft belonging to 5. Staffel had the basic 79/78 colours oversprayed with a pattern of dark green (Dunkelgrün) 71. Other aircraft of this unit had variations of this, some with a hard-edged application of 71 and others with a mottle blurring the demarcation between upper and lower surface colours.

(above) The Bf 109F-2 of the I./JG 27 Gruppenkommandeur during late 1941 featured the higher fuselage colour demarcation common to later batches of 109F Trops. The yellow nose and rudder markings were a hangover from the Balkan campaign seen on desert-camouflaged Bf 109s only during 1941.

Application of the white wingtip markings varied greatly. It could be found above and below both wingtips, on the undersides only or not at all. Otherwise, upper surface colours varied little in North Africa. An exception is the 'scribble' pattern seen below which extended over the wings.

The Bf 109G-4 Trop of the Gruppenadjutant of I./JG 77 in southern Tunisia in early 1943 had 79 topsides with a mottle of olive green (Olivgrün) 80. The yellow panels under the nose remained on many Bf 109s in the theatre long after the full yellow nose marking was discarded.

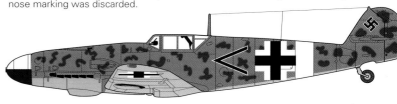

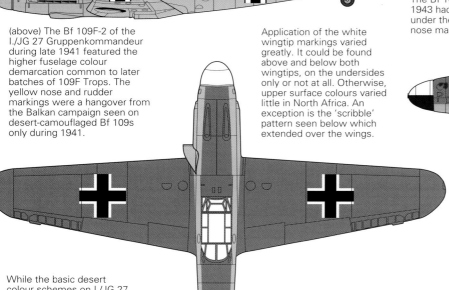

The standard grey camouflage pattern for the Bf 109F (and carried over to the G) was promulgated in August 1941. The colours were Graugrün (grey-green) 74, Grauviolett (grey-violet) 75 and Hellblau (light blue) 76. Although the colour separations appear hard, an overspray of 19 mm (0.75 in) was specified.

While the basic desert colour schemes on I./JG 27 Bf 109s generally conformed with regulation, local conditions in other parts of the Mediterranean led to variations such as this 'scribble' overspray of dark green (Dunkelgrün) 71 seen on this Bf 109G-2/Trop of 2./JG 77 in Tunisia 1943. The pattern was similar to those seen on Regia Aeronautica fighters and it is believed that the Italians supplied the paints for the first Luftwaffe fighters in the theatre. The sand yellow (Sandgelb) 79 on later fighters was a notably darker shade than that seen initially.

At the beginning of 1944, the RLM specified the use of a simplified form of national insignia consisting of an outline only – black against light-coloured aircraft undersides and white against dark backgrounds. Where a white cross was to be placed over a light area, the interior was to be filled with the darker camouflage. In practice, these rules were often not followed to the letter as seen on this example.

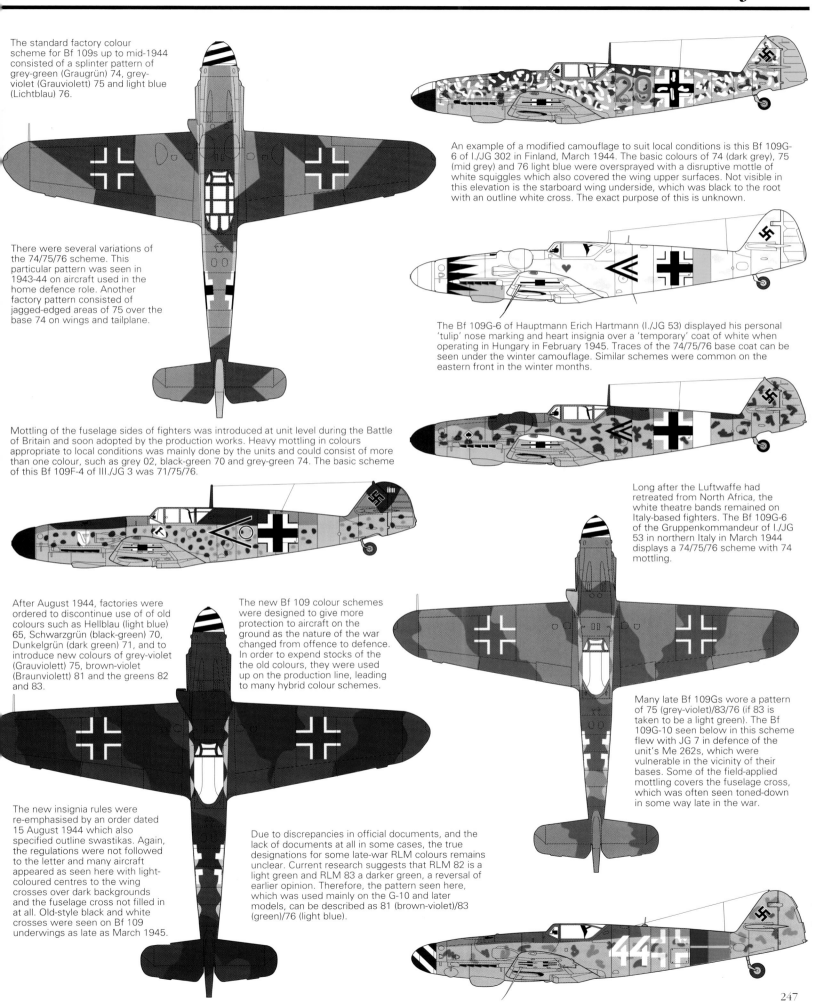

The standard factory colour scheme for Bf 109s up to mid-1944 consisted of a splinter pattern of grey-green (Graugrün) 74, grey-violet (Grauviolett) 75 and light blue (Lichtblau) 76.

There were several variations of the 74/75/76 scheme. This particular pattern was seen in 1943-44 on aircraft used in the home defence role. Another factory pattern consisted of jagged-edged areas of 75 over the base 74 on wings and tailplane.

Mottling of the fuselage sides of fighters was introduced at unit level during the Battle of Britain and soon adopted by the production works. Heavy mottling in colours appropriate to local conditions was mainly done by the units and could consist of more than one colour, such as grey 02, black-green 70 and grey-green 74. The basic scheme of this Bf 109F-4 of III./JG 3 was 71/75/76.

After August 1944, factories were ordered to discontinue use of of old colours such as Hellblau (light blue) 65, Schwarzgrün (black-green) 70, Dunkelgrün (dark green) 71, and to introduce new colours of grey-violet (Grauviolett) 75, brown-violet (Braunviolett) 81 and the greens 82 and 83.

The new insignia rules were re-emphasised by an order dated 15 August 1944 which also specified outline swastikas. Again, the regulations were not followed to the letter and many aircraft appeared as seen here with light-coloured centres to the wing crosses over dark backgrounds and the fuselage cross not filled in at all. Old-style black and white crosses were seen on Bf 109 underwings as late as March 1945.

The new Bf 109 colour schemes were designed to give more protection to aircraft on the ground as the nature of the war changed from offence to defence. In order to expend stocks of the old colours, they were used up on the production line, leading to many hybrid colour schemes.

Due to discrepancies in official documents, and the lack of documents at all in some cases, the true designations for some late-war RLM colours remains unclear. Current research suggests that RLM 82 is a light green and RLM 83 a darker green, a reversal of earlier opinion. Therefore, the pattern seen here, which was used mainly on the G-10 and later models, can be described as 81 (brown-violet)/83 (green)/76 (light blue).

An example of a modified camouflage to suit local conditions is this Bf 109G-6 of I./JG 302 in Finland, March 1944. The basic colours of 74 (dark grey), 75 (mid grey) and 76 light blue were oversprayed with a disruptive mottle of white squiggles which also covered the wing upper surfaces. Not visible in this elevation is the starboard wing underside, which was black to the root with an outline white cross. The exact purpose of this is unknown.

The Bf 109G-6 of Hauptmann Erich Hartmann (I./JG 53) displayed his personal 'tulip' nose marking and heart insignia over a 'temporary' coat of white when operating in Hungary in February 1945. Traces of the 74/75/76 base coat can be seen under the winter camouflage. Similar schemes were common on the eastern front in the winter months.

Long after the Luftwaffe had retreated from North Africa, the white theatre bands remained on Italy-based fighters. The Bf 109G-6 of the Gruppenkommandeur of I./JG 53 in northern Italy in March 1944 displays a 74/75/76 scheme with 74 mottling.

Many late Bf 109Gs wore a pattern of 75 (grey-violet)/83/76 (if 83 is taken to be a light green). The Bf 109G-10 seen below in this scheme flew with JG 7 in defence of the unit's Me 262s, which were vulnerable in the vicinity of their bases. Some of the field-applied mottling covers the fuselage cross, which was often seen toned-down in some way late in the war.

A variation on the 75/83/76 scheme more commonly seen on Bf 109G-14s is that shown here, the main difference being the distribution of colour on the fuselage spine. The actual hue of the late-war colours such as light green (83) and Braunviolett (81) varied greatly. Dispersed production and absence of explicit colour descriptions from the RLM led to much variation in these colours, which also suffered from staining, fading and wear in service, which especially effected 83 light green.

Below right: This Bf 109K-4 of 11./JG 53 in April 1945 wears 82/75/76. This was not a standard combination, but mixing of the older colours such as 75 with the new late-war greens was not unusual.

After a directive issued in August 1944 that forbade the use of four-letter factory codes, the last three digits of the Werk Nummer were frequently sprayed on the rear fuselage of Bf 109s as a 'book-keeping' measure. This Bf 109K-4 captured at Amberg, Germany has a non-standard pattern of 81/82 on the fuselage and a quartered (rather than spiral) spinner.

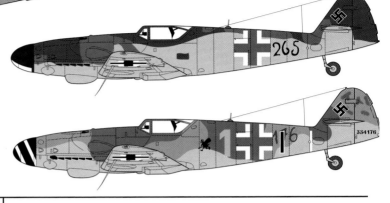

Foreign users

The allies of Germany that received late-model Bf 109s during the war took delivery of the aircraft in the camouflage specified for Luftwaffe aircraft of the time of manufacture. The majority of Bf 109s remained that way, with the addition of new national insignia, although some aircraft were later repainted in locally-devised schemes. Those aircraft fighting against Russian forces adopted the yellow theatre-identification markings worn by Luftwaffe aircraft. Post-war Messerschmitt operators tended to use whatever paints came to hand as the basis for their schemes.

Czechoslovakia

The S-99s (Czech-built Bf 109G-14) of the National Air Guard were predominantly light blue 76 (or possibly even an older colour such as 65), with red undersurfaces and nose.

In Czech air force service, the Mezec was usually painted in overall dark green (probably an RLM colour). Note the circular (rather than lozenge-shaped) insignia used by the regular air force.

Finland

Most Finnish Bf 109s appeared in standard Luftwaffe schemes such as this 74/75/76 pattern. Some aircraft wore a locally-devised green/black/light blue scheme.The background to the *hakaristi* (swastika) was white or light grey.

From 1945, the Finns adopted the blue/white roundel and removed the Axis yellow theatre markings used in the Continuation War. Both spiral and quartered spinners were seen on Ilmavoimat Bf 109s.

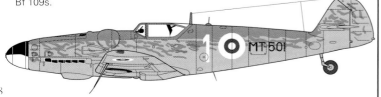

Hungary

The first batch of 80 Hungarian Bf 109Gs was numbered from V-310. Swastikas were uncommon on HAF aircraft, and this G-6 of 5/2 Fighter Squadron in 1943 has had the marking partly removed.

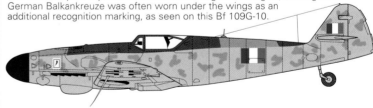

Israel

IAF Avias wore the same blue as used on Czech aircraft. The red/white rudder was the 101 Squadron marking and the black/white band was a recognition for all Israeli fighters in the 1948 war.
The code translates from Hebrew as 'D120'.

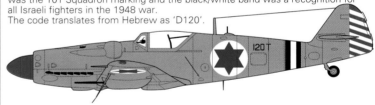

Italy Aviazione Nazionale Repubblicana

The ANR adopted a yellow-bordered Italian flag as its insignia, although the German Balkankreuze was often worn under the wings as an additional recognition marking, as seen on this Bf 109G-10.

Spain

Spanish HA-1112-M1Ls wore an overall coat of blue (similar to FS 35050) in the early part of their service. The area affected by exhaust staining was painted black.

Switzerland

The red and white neutrality markings adopted in mid-September 1944 were applied over the base camouflage, which varied considerably between aircraft. Some Gs wore the markings as late as the end of 1945.

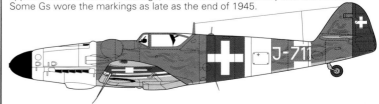

DB 605 installations seen on Black 6 (left) and D-FMBB (above) highlight the sturdy A-frame bearers from which the engine was suspended. Noticeable on the port side of the engine is the circular intake for the supercharger. The upper cowling leaves have apertures through which the fuselage machine-guns fired.

Bf 109 cockpit

Shown above is the cockpit of a Finnish Bf 109G-2, dominated by the Revi 16B sight and by the breech for the engine-mounted cannon, which projected back into the cockpit. Below is the cockpit of a Czech Avia S 199, showing some detail differences compared to the standard Bf 109G, notably the lack of cannon.

Bf 109G-6 cockpit

1. Undercarriage emergency lowering handwheel
2. Tailplane trim wheel
3. Seat height adjustment handle
4. Tailplane incidence indicator panel
5. Fuel injection primer pump
6. Fuel cock lever
7. Throttle
8. Throttle-mounted propeller pitch control thumbswitch
9. Dust filter handgrip
10. Canopy lever
11. Undercarriage switches
12. Undercarriage position indicators
13. Start plug cleansing switch
14. Starter switch
15. Panel light
16. Main line switch
17. Ignition switch
18. Frame struts
19. Armoured glass windscreen
20. Revi 16B reflector gunsight
21. Armament switch
22. Ammunition counters
23. Clock
24. Repeater compass
25. Artificial horizon/turn-and-bank indicator
26. Fine and coarse altimeter
27. Airspeed indicator
28. Gunsight padding
29. Manifold pressure gauge
30. Tachometer
31. AFN 2 homing indicator (FuG 16ZY)
32. Mechanical propeller pitch position indicator
33. Tumbler switch
34. Combined coolant exit and oil intake temperature indicator
35. Fuel warning lamp
36. 30-mm MK 108 cannon breech
37. Rudder pedals
38. Firing trigger
39. Gun charging knob
40. Control column
41. Pilot's seat
42. Undercarriage emergency release
43. Electric fuel contents gauge
44. Dual oil and fuel pressure gauge
45. Auxiliary fuel contents indicator
46. Panel light
47. Coolant radiator control
48. Oxygen supply indicator
49. Oxygen pressure gauge
50. Radio switch panel
51. Oxygen supply
52. Radio tuner panel

Bf 109 late-model operators

Luftwaffe

Production of all Bf 109 variants reached around 33,000 airframes, almost all of which were supplied to the Luftwaffe. Of this number, around 27,500 were late-model (Bf 109F, G and K) aircraft, this figure not including the large numbers of 'Gustavs' reworked as G-10s and G-12s. By far the lion's share of production was taken by the G-6, with over 12,000 produced. Throughout the early years of the war Bf 109 production was barely adequate to meet the demands of attrition, with the result that front-line units were spread extremely thinly as the war widened and more theatres of operations introduced. Continuing to offset this trend were the ongoing successes of the Jagdflieger themselves, although time was swiftly running out.

The first dramatic rise in production occurred at the start of 1943, and it is no coincidence that this occurred soon after the two pivotal reversals at El Alamein (October 1942) and Stalingrad (November 1942). Only when attack turned to defence did the question of fighter production achieve a position of priority. As the war situation worsened, production climbed rapidly, reaching a peak in July to September 1944. From July 1944 production of aircraft other than fighters was phased out to concentrate the efforts of the whole German aviation industry. After September 1944 the figure steadily declined as the effects of the Allied bombing campaign began to bite ever deeper.

Production figures for individual variants vary depending on source, and for some variants records are incomplete. The following figures, taken largely from the excellent reference work *Messerschmitt Bf 109F, G & K Series: An Illustrated Study* (Jochen Prien and Peter Rodeike, Schiffer Military History, ISBN: 0-88740-424-3), are considered to be the most accurate, and provide the best guide as to the numbers of late-model Bf 109s – **F-0**: 14, **F-1**: 208, **F-2**: c.1,830, **F-3**: c. 15, **F-4**: 1,841, **G-0**: 13, **G-1**: 167, **G-2**: 1,587, **G-3**: 50, **G-4**: 1,242, **G-5**: 475, **G-6**: 12,000 plus, **G-8**: 900 plus, **G-10**: c. 2,600 conversions, **G-12**: c. 500 conversions, **G-14**: c. 5,500, **K-4**: c. 1,700.

In October 1940 the Bf 109F-1 entered service with the Geschwaderstab (wing staff flight) of Jagdgeschwader 51 on the Channel coast. It was not until the following spring, however, that the 'Friedrich' got into widespread service. The 'Gustav' followed in June 1942. Deployment of new variants was made rapidly, with the result that the primary Bf 109 units re-equipped with a quick succession of the major variants (F-2, F-4, G-2, G-4, G-6, G-14). From October 1944 G-10s and K-4s began to be delivered, and these became the most important variants of the last months of the war, although only a few units fully converted to the K-4, most retaining various G models on strength alongside the new arrival.

Of the major fighter formations, JGs 3, 5, 27, 51, 52, 53 and 77 stayed largely loyal to the Messerschmitt fighter throughout the war, while others converted to the Fw 190 (JGs 1, 2, 26 and 54). New units were introduced to the Bf 109 during the course of the war (JGs 4, 76, 300, 301 and 302),

A Bf 109G-2 is seen at cockpit alert in the desert, the starting handle already in place.

In 1941 the Bf 109F units were staffed by highly experienced fighter pilots, many of whom would go on to compile huge personal tallies. This group of JG 2 pilots from the Stabsschwarm comprises (from left) Leutnant Egon Mayer (102 kills, first to achieve 100 on the Channel front), Oberleutnant Rudolf Pflanz (52 kills in West), Gescwhaderkommodore Walter Oesau (123 kills) and Oberleutnant Erich Leie (118 kills).

especially as the war situation got worse. In the final months more desperate measures were taken, leading to the hasty conversion of bomber units to a day fighter role with Kampfgeschwader (Jagd) designations. Bf 109s also served with a large number of operational trials, night-fighter, training and tactical reconnaissance units. The following list provides a guide to the units operating the late-model Bf 109s, together with the variants confirmed as having been on strength.

Principal fighter units (Jagdgeschwader)

Stab/JG 1	F-2
I./JG 1	F-1, F-2, F-4, G-1, G-3
II./JG 1	F-4
III./JG 1	F-2, F-4, G-4, G-5, G-6, G-10, G-14, K-4
IV./JG 1	F-1, F-2, F-4
Stab/JG 2	F-2, F-4
I./JG 2	F-2, F-4, G-1, G-4
II./JG 2	F-2, F-4, G-4, G-5, G-6, G-14, K-4
III./JG 2	F-1, F-2, F-4
10./JG 2	F-2, F-4
11./JG 2	G-1, G-3
12./JG 2	G-4
Stab/JG 3	F-1, F-2, F-4, G-2, G-4, G-6, G-14
I./JG 3	F-1, F-2, F-4, G-2, G-4, G-5, G-6, G-10, G-14
II./JG 3	F-2, F-4, G-2, G-4, G-5, G-6, G-14
III./JG 3	F-1, F-2, F-4, G-2, G-4, G-6, G-10, G-14, K-4
IV./JG 3	G-4, G-6
Stab/JG 4	G-6
I./JG 4	G-2, G-4, G-6, G-10, G-10, G-14, K-4
III./JG 4	G-6, G-10, G-14, K-4
IV./JG 4	G-6, G-10, G-14
Stab/JG 5	F-1, F-4, G-2, G-6, G-14
I./JG 5	F-2, F-4, G-1, G-2, G-6, G-14
II./JG 5	F-2, F-4, G-2, G-6, G-14
III./JG 5	F-2, F-4, G-2, G-6, G-14
IV./JG 5	F-2, F-4, G-2, G-6, G-14
III./JG 6	G-6, G-10, G-14
II./JG 11	G-3, G-4, G-5, G-6, G-14, K-4
III./JG 11	G-6
Alarmstaffel/JG 11	G-6
Stab/JG 26	F-1, F-2, F-4
I./JG 26	F-2, F-4, G-1
II./JG 26	F-1, F-2, G-4
III./JG 26	F-1, F-2, F-4, G-4, G-5, G-6, G-14
10./JG 26	F-2, F-4
11./JG 26	G-1, G-3, G-4
12./JG 26	G-4
Stab/JG 27	F-4, G-2, G-6, G-14
I./JG 27	F-4, G-2, G-4, G-6, G-10, G-14
II./JG 27	F-4, G-2, G-4, G-5, G-6, G-10, G-14, K-4
III./JG 27	F-4, G-2, G-4, G-6, G-14, K-4
IV./JG 27	G-2, G-6, G-10, G-14, K-4
10./JG 27	F-4
Stab/JG 51	F-1, F-2, F-3, F-4, G-6, G-14
I./JG 51	F-1, F-2, G-6, G-14
II./JG 51	F-1, F-2, G-1, G-2, G-4, G-6, G-10, G-14
III./JG 51	F-1, F-2, F-3, F-4, G-6, G-10, G-14
IV./JG 51	F-1, F-2, G-4, G-6, G-14
Stab/JG 52	F-2, F-4, G-2, G-4, G-6, G-14
I./JG 52	F-1, F-2, F-4, G-2, G-4, G-6, G-14
II./JG 52	F-2, F-4, G-2, G-4, G-6, G-10, G-14, G-14
III./JG 52	F-2, F-4, G-2, G-4, G-6, G-10, G-14, K-4
Stab/JG 53	F-1, F-2, F-4, G-1, G-2, G-4, G-6, G-14
I./JG 53	F-1, F-2, F-4, G-1, G-2, G-4, G-6, G-10, G-14
II./JG 53	F-1, F-2, F-4, G-2, G-4, G-6, G-14, K-4
III./JG 53	F-1, F-2, F-4, G-4, G-6, G-14, K-4
IV./JG 53	G-14
10./JG 53	F-4
Stab/JG 54	F-1, F-4, G-2
I./JG 54	F-1, F-2, F-4, G-2
II./JG 54	F-2, F-4, G-2, G-4
III./JG 54	F-2, F-4, G-2, G-4, G-6
IV./JG 54	G-6
11./JG 54	G-3
I./JG 76	G-6, G-14
III./JG 76	G-6, G-14
Stab/JG 77	F-4, G-2, G-4, G-6, G-14
I./JG 77	F-4, G-2, G-4, G-6, G-10, G-14, K-4
II./JG 77	F-4, G-2, G-4, G-6, G-10, G-14, K-4
III./JG 77	F-4, G-2, G-4, G-6, G-14, K-4
Stab/JG 300	G-6, G-14
I./JG 300	G-5, G-6, G-10, G-14
III./JG 300	G-6, G-10, G-14
IV./JG 300	G-10, G-14
Stab/JG 301	G-6
I./JG 301	G-6
II./JG 301	G-6
III./JG 301	G-6
IV./JG 301	G-6
Stab/JG 302	G-6
I./JG 302	G-6
II./JG 302	G-5, G-6
III./JG 302	G-6

Other fighter units

Jagdgruppe Nord	G-6, G-14
Jagdgruppe Sud	F-2, F-4, G-2, G-4, G-6
Jagdgruppe Ost	F-2, F-4, G-1, G-2, G-4, G-6, G-14
Jagdgruppe West	F-4, G-0, G-1, G-2, G-6, G-14
Jagdgruppe 25	G-6
Jagdgruppe 50	G-6
Jagdgruppe 200	G-6
Jabo-Gruppe Afrika	F-2, F-4
I./EJG 1	G-6, G-14
II./EJG 1	G-5, G-6, G-14
III./EJG 1	G-5, G-6, G-14
IV./EJG 1	G-6, G-14
I./EJG 2	G-5, G-6, G-14
I./NJG 10	G-6
I./NJG 11	G-5, K-4
II./NJG 11	G-5, G-6, G-10, G-14
III./NJG 11	G-14
I./KG(J) 6	G-6, G-10, G-14, K-4
I./KG(J) 27	G-10, G-14, K-4
II./KG(J) 27	G-10, K-4
II./KG(J) 30	G-14
I./KG(J) 55	G-14
II./KG(J) 55	G-6, G-14
Jagdgeschwader 101-112 (fighter schools) most variants up to and including G-6, G-12	
Sonderkommando Elbe	G-6, G-10 (ramming unit)

Reconnaissance units

Aufkl.ObdL	F-4
4.(H)/12	F-4, G-2
2.(H)/14	F-4, G-2, G-4, G-6
(F)/100	F-4
(F)/122	F-4, G-2, G-4
(F)/123	F-4, G-2, G-4, G-5, G-6
(F)/124	G-4, G-6
NAGr 1	G-6, G-8, G-14
NAGr 2	F-4, G-2, G-4, G-5, G-6, G-8, G-10, G-14
NAGr 3	G-6, G-8, G-14
NAGr 4	F-4, G-2, G-4, G-6, G-8, G-10, G-14
NAGr 5	G-6, G-8
NAGr 8	G-6, G-8
NAGr 9	G-4
NAGr 11	G-5, G-6, G-8
NAGr 12	G-4, G-5, G-6, G-8
NAGr 13	G-5, G-6, G-8
NAGr 14	G-6, G-8, G-10, G-14
NAGr 15	G-6, G-8, G-10
NAGr 32	G-8

Close up, these wooden dummies did not look much like Bf 109s, but from an attacking aircraft travelling at low level they would have been convincing.

JG 53 'Pik As' was a stalwart of the Bf 109, flying the type to the end of the war. It served on all fronts, including in the desert where this II. Gruppe G-6 is seen.

Bulgaria

The Vazdushnite na Negovo Velichestvo Voiski (Royal Bulgarian air force) had taken delivery of 19 Bf 109E-4s in 1940, but it was not until 1943 that more Messerschmitts were delivered, in the form of 25 Bf 109G-4s. Further deliveries of G-2s and G-6s brought the VNVV total to 149, allowing the VNVV to largely retire its obsolete fighters such as the Avia B.534. The Messerschmitts served with the two Orliaks (regiments) of the 6th Iztrebitelen Polk (fighter division) for the defence of Sofia, which was under constant attack from USAAF bombers in 1943-44. The two main bases were Bozhouriste and Vrazhdebna. Over 50 kills were claimed by VNVV Bf 109s. Many were destroyed on the ground by Allied bombing attacks.

On 9 September 1944 Bulgaria joined the Allied cause, and VNVV Bf 109s were used against German forces, although there is no record of them having met Luftwaffe Bf 109s in air combat. At the end of the war more than 100 Bf 109G-10/12/14s were handed to Bulgaria after having been found intact in an Austrian factory. Fifty-nine of

Above: Bulgaria received 149 Bf 109Gs, this being a G-2 seen at Bozhouriste. The Bulgarian Bf 109s scored 65 kills, before joining the Allied cause.

Far right: Ground crew turn the propeller of a Croatian Bf 109G-2. The aircraft is marked with the red/white check shield of Croatia, and a coloured spinner.

these were sent to Yugoslavia as war reparations. Bulgarian Bf 109s were withdrawn from service in 1946.

Croatia

Raised as a volunteer force to fight alongside the German forces on the Russian front, the Croatian Legion included a fighter component established with Bf 109E-7s as the 15.(kroat)/JG 52, or kroat.J.St. This unit converted to Bf 109G-2s as early as July 1942, later converting to G-6s. However, the number of serviceable aircraft dwindled so that, by February 1944, it had only four machines at its base at Karankut in the Crimea.

It had long been planned to form two further Croatian Legion fighter squadrons, and personnel had received training on the

Bf 109G-6 in France. However, there were not enough Bf 109s available, and so the 2nd and 3rd squadrons converted to the Fiat G.50 and Macchi MC.202. The original unit, now known as the 1st Fighter Squadron, re-equipped in late 1944 with the Bf 109G-10, operating the type from bases in Croatia and Italy until the end of the war.

Czechoslovakia

At the end of hostilities Czechoslovakia set about creating a new air arm, using the large number of Bf 109G airframes that had

been completed under a late-war licence-construction scheme. A few S 99s and two-seat CS 99s were completed using DB 605 engines, but the bulk were S 199s and CS 199s powered by the Jumo 211 engine.

S/CS 99s served with the National Air Guard while deliveries of the S/CS 199 to the regular air force (Ceskoslovenske Vojenské Letectvo) began in February 1948. Service life was brief, as Soviet-supplied jets

became available in the early 1950s, the S 199 flying on with the National Air Guard until 1954. A few continued in use afterwards as trainers, with armament removed.

Left: Nineteen S 199s can be discerned in this view of a Czech air base. A handful of aircraft continued in service into the mid-1950s.

Above: An S 199 leads out a section of Il-10s for an attack mission. The S 199 exhibited a vicious swing on take-off.

Finland

The Ilmavoimat established a squadron (HLeLv 34, under Lentorykmentii 3) to operate the Bf 109 on 23 January 1943, but it was not until 13 March that the initial batch of 16 Bf 109G-2s reached Finland. A dozen more were delivered in May to allow HLeLv 34 to reach its operational strength of 28 aircraft. The regiment was divided into three squadrons, 1/HLeLv 34 being based at Malmi for the defence of Helsinki, while 2 and 3/HLeLv 34 operated from Utti. Soon 1 squadron moved to Suulajärvi, 2 squadron and the HLeLv 34 headquarters moved to Kymi, and 3 squadron took over the Malmi base. Finnish Bf 109G-2s found immediate success against the Soviets, shooting down over 100 aircraft (for the loss of six) between May and mid-September.

In April 1944 a batch of 15 Bf 109G-6s arrived for service with HLeLv 34, some of the displaced G-2s going to form a new unit: HLeLv 24. Additional aircraft arrived in May and June, including three G-8s for reconnaissance and G-10s. These deliveries allowed a third unit, HLeLv 28 at Lappeenranta, to partially equip with the 'Gustav'. Spares shortages led to poor serviceability, however. HLeLv 34 moved to Lappeenranta in June, and then to Taipalsaari, while HLeLv 24 deployed to Utti.

A total of 150 'Mersus' were supplied to Finland. By the time of the armistice on 4 September 1944, Finnish Bf 109s had accounted for 270 Soviet aircraft for the loss of 22 aircraft and 11 pilots. Owing to their lack of range, they took no part in the Finnish operations against German forces in Lappland. In December 1944 the two operational units, HLeLv 24 and 34, were

Above: Bf 109G-6s arrived with HLeLv 34 from April 1944, along with some G-8s and G-10s.

Right: MT-216 was from the first batch of Bf 109G-2s supplied to HLeLv 34 in March 1943.

redesignated as HLeLv 31 and 33, respectively, operating from Utti under Lentorykmentit 3 (from 1952 Lennosto 3). Two new units, HLeLv 11 and 13, were established under Lentorykmentit 1 at Luonetjärvi, although by 1952 they had dwindled to a single Hävittäjälentu (fighter flight). HLeLv 31 and 33 continued to operate the Bf 109G from Utti until 1954.

Bf 109 Operators

Hungary

As one of Germany's closest allies in the East, the Magyar Királyi Légierö (Royal Hungarian air force) was supplied with Bf 109s from an early stage. Bf 109F-4s were acquired to replace Reggiane Re 2000s in October 1942 for the 1/1 Vadasz Század, which operated as the ungarische Jagdstaffel on the Russian front. In early 1943 1/1 became 5/1 Vadasz Század, and re-equipped with Bf 109G-2s. In May it was joined by 5/2 Vadasz Század. The two units together formed 5/1 Vadasz Osztaly which was operated as part of VIII Fliegerkorps. In November 1943 5/1 Vadasz Század was withdrawn from the Russian front, while 5/2 was redesignated as 102 Önálló Vadasz Század. This was subordinated to Fliegerführer 102 Ungarn, becoming 102/1 when a second Bf 109G squadron, 102/2, was formed in May 1944. 102/2 was formed on the G-6 variant.

By the spring of 1944 two units (101/1 and 101/2) had been formed in Hungary to defend against the growing number of raids mounted by USAAF bombers. In April a third squadron was added, followed by three more by July. The combined six-squadron regiment was known as the 101 Vadasz Ezred. As the Wehrmacht fell back through Hungary, the two squadrons of the 102 Vadasz Osztaly were added to the 101 Vadasz Ezred, which then formed a ninth squadron. Despite the establishment of a Soviet puppet government and Hungary's 'surrender' on 20 January 1945, the 101 Vadasz Ezred continued to fight alongside the Luftwaffe, seeing out the war at Austrian bases. Most aircraft were destroyed prior to surrender in the Linz area.

Hungary operated large numbers of Bf 109s, peaking at nine squadrons. National insignia varied in presentation, but usually featured a white cross on a black square.

Israel

The infant Chel Ha'Avir acquired a total of 25 Avia S 199s with which to equip its first fighter unit, 101 Squadron. While pilots trained in Italy before a brief S 199 conversion course in Czechoslovakia, the aircraft were delivered (air-freighted in a Douglas DC-4) from 20 May 1948. 101 Squadron was based at Ekron, and began combat operations against the Egyptians as soon as it had sufficient aircraft. The S 199 force moved to Herzlea, and flew combat missions until January 1949, when the fighting ceased. By that time only a handful of S 199s were left, the fleet having suffered drastically from accidents and poor serviceability. The type was retired at the end of the conflict, its role having been assumed by the far better Spitfire Mk IX and P-51D Mustang.

This S 199 was seen on display in 1973. Bombs were not carried during the type's brief months of service.

Three of 101 Sqn's pilots pose with an S 199. They are (from left) Chalmers 'Slick' Goodlin, Aaron 'Red' Finkel and Syd Cohen. The squadron badge was a winged skull wearing a flying helmet.

Italy

The Regia Aeronautica received its first Bf 109s in early 1943 when Bf 109F-4s were supplied to form two units. These were the 3° Gruppo Caccia Terrestre (154ª and 155ª Squadriglia) and the 150° Gruppo CT (363ª and 364ª Squadriglia). Bf 109G-6s were subsequently supplied, shortly before the air force was divided into the pro-Allies Co-Belligerent air force and the pro-Axis Aviazione Nazionale Repubblicana. The ANR had two fighter units, of which the II° Gruppo Caccia Terrestre became operational on the Bf 109G-6 in September 1944. I° Gruppo CT became operational on the Bf 109G-10 in January 1945, and both Gruppi flew until surrendering in April 1945 at Udine and Gallarate. A third Gruppo was away in Germany converting to Bf 109s when the war ended.

This is a Bf 109G-10/AS of the ANR's I° Gruppo CT.

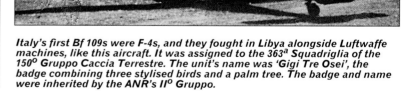

Italy's first Bf 109s were F-4s, and they fought in Libya alongside Luftwaffe machines, like this aircraft. It was assigned to the 363ª Squadriglia of the 150° Gruppo Caccia Terrestre. The unit's name was 'Gigi Tre Osei', the badge combining three stylised birds and a palm tree. The badge and name were inherited by the ANR's II° Gruppo.

Romania

Romania's air arm, the Fortelor Regal ale Aeriene Româna (Royal Romanian air force), had acquired 69 Bf 109E-4s from early 1942, and a year later began to receive Bf 109G-2s to equip the Grupul 1 Vinatoare, which was charged with the defence of the vital oilfields around Ploesti (along with earlier Bf 109s and IAR-80s). In mid-1943 Romania's air component on the Russian front, the Corpul 1 Aerian, also received Bf 109s in the form of G-6s and a few G-8s for reconnaissance. The fighter force was based at Zhdanov in the Ukraine, comprising 45, 46, 47 and 48 Escadrile. By the start of 1944 the Romanian contribution to I Fliegerkorps had been reduced to one squadron (rum 49. Jagdstaffel) based at Saki in the Crimea. Further Bf 109G-6 deliveries to units based at home swelled the numbers of the Corpul 1 Aerian, which had been retasked with home defence. 51 Escadrile was based at Tepes-Voda, while 52 Escadrile was at Mamaia. These units fought until the Romanian coup on 23 August 1944, after which they flew in support of the Red army, seeing action against German forces, notably during the battles around Klausenburg.

With the declaration of the People's Republic, the air force was retitled the Fortele Aeriene ale Republicii Populare Româna. In addition to its own aircraft, it took over Bf 109G-10s and G-14s from the Luftwaffe, and operated a mixed bag of 'Gustavs' until 1948.

These 'Gustavs' are two of the original Bf 109G-2s supplied to the home defence unit. The aircraft sport a heavily dappled camouflage.

Slovakia

Slovakia's air arm, the Slovenské Vzdusné Zbrane, had received Bf 109E-7s to equip its 11. Stíhací Letka at Piestany, and also the 13. Stíhací Letka on the Russian front, the latter operating as 13.(slowak)/JG 52 or slowak.J.St. In early 1943 this squadron received Bf 109G-6s, which it used against Russian forces, attached to the Slovak Fast

Division. In April 1944 it was transferred back to Piestany to join the 11. Stíhací Letka, which had by then also converted to Bf 109G-6s. By this time, the Slovaks were involved in clandestine discussions with the Allies, and fighting between Slovakian fighters and USAAF bombers was avoided. However, on 26 July 1944 all of 11. Stíhací Letka was wiped out after a fight started, inexplicably, with USAAF P-38s, which were escorting a

Above: This is one of the two Bf 109Gs which flew as part of the Combined Squadron, Slovak Insurgent air force. Note the revised national insignia under the wing.

Left: This Bf 109G Kanonenboote is from the 13. Stíhací Letka, or slowak Jagdstaffel, operating as part of JG 52 on the Russian front. The unit's aircraft wore standard Luftwaffe markings but with a white/blue/red spinner, the colours of the Slovak national flag.

B-24 raid. Two 13.Stíhací Letka Bf 109G aircraft (along with two Bf 109Es) were subsequently used during the Slovakian

National Uprising of late August 1944, operating from Tri Duby airfield in 'free' Slovakia.

Spain

Spain's Bf 109 association dates back to the Civil War, when large numbers of 'Emils' were left behind for use by the Ejército del Aire. In early 1942 some Bf 109F-4s were supplied for use by 25 Grupo/23 Regimiento based at Alcalá de Henares. These were principally employed to train pilots for the Spanish volunteer force on the Russian front, which converted from the Bf 109E-7 to the F-4 in October 1942. This unit was known as the Escuadrón Azul, or in Luftwaffe parlance 15.(span)/JG 51.

Spain negotiated in 1942 with Germany to licence-build 200 Bf 109G-2s, of which 25 were supplied in kit form from Germany, together with tooling, jigs, armament and engines for the remaining 175. In the event, the DB 605 engines were not supplied, leading to the development by Hispano-Aviación of the HA-1109/1112 series.

None of the initial batch of HA-1109-K1Ls was delivered to a regular air force unit, being retained for trials purposes. However, the HA-1112-K1L was delivered, although only used as a trainer by the Escuela de Caza at Morón. A single example was operated by Grupo 23 and a number served

The Hispano-engined HA-1112-K1L was the first service type, but it was used almost exclusively for advanced training.

with trials units. It was therefore left to the Merlin-powered HA-1112-M1L Buchón to become the principal service variant. Initial deliveries were made to Escuadrón 71 of Grupo 7 at Tablada, which was soon involved in the war in Spanish Sahara. As deliveries gathered pace, a second squadron was formed, Escuadrón 72, in turn requiring the establishment of Ala 7 to

Only two two-seaters were built, but they had long and productive careers, first with Hispano engines and then with Merlins (illustrated).

parent both Buchón units. For a brief time in 1963/64 Escuadrón 364 operated Buchóns in the Canary Islands as part of Ala Mixta 36. Right at the end of the aircraft's career, Ala 7 was renumbered as Ala 47, by which time the component squadrons numbered just one, this being rechristened 471 Escuadrón. The Buchón was retired in November 1965.

Switzerland

Switzerland's Fliegertruppe had operated the Bf 109D-1 since 1938, subsequently purchasing sizeable numbers of E-3s. During the course of the war it acquired four further Bf 109s (two Bf 109Fs and two Bf 109Gs) through internment of Luftwaffe aircraft, and also by the purchase of 12 Bf 109G-6s in 1944. In the normal course of events Switzerland could not have received the 'Gustavs' at this stage of the war, such was the demand of the Luftwaffe and its allies. However, the Swiss were presented with a powerful bargaining tool in April 1944 when a Bf 110 night-fighter landed at Dübendorf and was interned. Denied its immediate return, Germany was anxious to see it destroyed to prevent Allied agents gaining access to its radar and gun

installation, and so it was burned in return for early supply of the required 12 Bf 109s.

Deliveries were made to Dübendorf in two batches of six on 20 and 22 May 1944. The Bf 109Gs (together with the interned aircraft) were allocated to Fliegerkompagnie 7, replacing Bf 109Es. Unfortunately for the Swiss, the workmanship of the Gs was very poor, and their flying was severely curtailed, leading to their eventual retirement in 1946, by which time the Fliegertruppe had been reorganised as the Flugwaffe.

Swiss experience of the Bf 109G-6 was far from happy, as the aircraft showed many manufacturing defects and poor serviceability. Continuing complaints to Germany resulted in a 50 per cent refund of the initial purchase price.

Yugoslavia

Prior to its invasion by German forces in 1941, Yugoslavia had operated Bf 109E-3s, these serving with 32, 51 and 52 Lovácka Grupa. By the end of 1944 Yugoslav pilots were flying alongside liberation forces. Some used Bf 109Gs left behind by the retreating Luftwaffe, while several more 'Gustavs' were acquired when Croatian

pilots defected to the Yugoslav side. These aircraft undertook sporadic strafing and bomber-escort missions against the remnants of the Axis forces, flown by the Independent Headquarters Escadrille. By the end of the war 17 Bf 109Gs were still in service. These were stored until 1947 but were reactivated following the supply from Bulgaria of 59 aircraft. These were war reparations, although Yugoslavia supplied Bulgaria with Il-2 parts in return. The

nascent Jugoslovensko Ratno Vazduhoplovstvo (Yugoslav air force) established two fighter wings with Bf 109s, which were a mixed bag of 'Gustavs' (G-2, G-6, G-10 and G-12). Both the 83rd and 172nd Fighter Wings were based at Cerklje. Training began using three G-12 two-seaters, which were notable for having an Erla-Haube fitted over the rear cockpit. In November 1950 the 172nd Fighter Wing transferred to Zemunik airfield near Zadar.

Both wings were employed on coastal fighter patrols, and both flew sorties during the confrontation with Italy over the free port of Trieste. In JRV service the Bf 109 was operated successfully, the aircraft undergoing several minor modifications such as the installation of Soviet-style radio, gun cameras and new cameras for reconnaissance-configured machines. The aircraft began to fade from service in mid-1952 when new types were received.

Picture acknowledgments

The publishers would like to thank the following organisations and individuals for their help in supplying photographs for this book.

6-7: Charles E. Brown Collection/RAF Museum (two). **8:** Dr Alfred Price, Aerospace, MoD (two). **9:** Aerospace (three), RAF Museum. **10:** Vickers-Armstrongs via Dr Alfred Price, MoD (two), Vickers-Armstrongs. **11:** Vickers-Armstrongs, Vickers-Armstrongs via Dr Alfred Price. **12:** Vickers-Armstrongs, Aerospace (two), Vickers-Armstrongs via Dr Alfred Price. **13:** Vickers-Armstrongs via Dr Alfred Price, RAF Museum, Dr Alfred Price. **14:** MoD, Dr Alfred Price (three), Aerospace. **15:** Dr Alfred Price. **16:** Dr Alfred Price, RAF Museum. **17:** Aerospace (three). **18:** Dr Alfred Price (two), RAF Museum (two). **20:** Imperial War Museum (IWM) (two), Dr Alfred Price, RAF Museum. **21:** RAF Museum (two). **22:** Paul Lambermont via Dr Alfred Price, MoD, Vickers-Armstrongs via Dr Alfred Price. **23:** IWM, MoD, Larry Davis Collection. **24:** IWM (three), RAF Museum, Durnford via Dr Alfred Price. **25:** MoD (two), Aerospace (two), IWM. **26:** US Navy, US Navy via Dr Alfred Price (four). **27:** MoD, IWM (two), Andrew Thomas (two), RCAF via Andrew Thomas. **28:** IWM (four). **29:** Australian War Memorial via Dr Alfred Price (two), Aerospace, IWM, RAF Museum. **32:** USAF, IWM. **33:** Aerospace (four), Sissons via Dr Alfred Price. **34:** Vickers-Armstrongs, MoD (three), Aerospace. **35:** IWM (two), MoD (two), Westland (two). **36:** USAF, Nicholson via Dr Alfred Price (two), Aerospace. **38:** MoD (two), John Fawcett via Dr Alfred Price, Aerospace, RCAF via Dr Alfred Price, RAF Museum. **39:** Peter Arnold, MoD, Aerospace. **40:** USAF, Glaser via Dr Alfred Price, Dr Alfred Price. **41:** IWM (three), MoD, RAF Museum. **42:** RAF Musuem, MoD (two). **44:** MoD, Fawcett via Ethell via Dr Alfred Price, via Hurt via Dr Alfred Price, RAF Museum (two), Bundesarchiv via Dr Alfred Price. **45:** RAF Museum, Murland via Dr Alfred Price. **46:** Rolls-Royce, MoD. **47:** Tim Senior, Aerospace (three). **48:** IWM, Dr Alfred Price (two), Murland via Dr Alfred Price, MoD. **49:** Murland via Dr Alfred Price (two), RCAF, RAF Museum. **50:** Aerospace (two), IWM, RCAF via Dr Alfred Price, Sitensky via Dr Alfred Price, Dr Alfred Price. **51:** Aerospace (five). **52:** RAF Museum, MoD, Aerospace. **53:** IWM (two), Dr Alfred Price, via Trenkle via Dr Alfred Price (three), Hans Redemann via Dr Alfred Price. **54:** Aerospace (four), MoD, RAF Museum, Michael Stroud. **55:** Peter Arnold, Aerospace (two), ECPA, Goyat via Dr Alfred Price. **56:** Aerospace (two), RAF Museum, Andrew Thomas, Hurt via Dr Alfred Price, Van der Meer via Dr Alfred Price. **57:** Peter R. March (two), Jim Winchester, Aerospace, Michael Stroud, Simon Watson. **61:** Westland (two), MoD (three), Dr Alfred Price (two), Aerospace (two). **62:** MoD, RAF Museum (two), Peter Arnold, Vickers-Armstrongs. **63:** Aerospace (six), RDAF. **64:** Aerospace, Peter Arnold, Peter R. March, IDF/AF, Gregory Alegi via Peter Arnold, Dr Alfred Price. **65:** Dr Alfred Price (two), Peter Arnold, Andrew Thomas, Bruce Robertson, USAF, IWM. **66:** RAF Museum. **67:** Dr. Alfred Price (two). **68:** Dr. Alfred Price (two), Tuttle via Dr. Alfred Price. **69:** Dr. Alfred Price (three). **70:** Dr. Alfred Price (three), Tuttle via Dr. Alfred Price. **71:** Dr. Alfred Price (four). **72:** Green via Dr. Alfred Price (two), Dr. Alfred Price (two). **74:** Dr. Alfred Price (three), Tuttle via Dr. Alfred Price, Aerospace. **75:** AFM via Ethell via Dr. Alfred Price, Dr. Alfred Price, IWM. **76:** Aerospace, Dr. Alfred Price (two), Ethell via Dr. Alfred Price. **77:** Ethell via Dr. Alfred Price (two), Horsfal via Dr. Alfred Price, Dr. Alfred Price. **78:** Ethell via Dr. Alfred Price (three), Dr. Alfred Price. **80:** Dr. Alfred Price (two), Horsfal via Dr. Alfred Price, Redmond via Ethell via Dr. Alfred Price. **81:** Dr. Alfred Price, via Petrick via Dr. Alfred Price, Sturtivant via Dr. Alfred Price, Saffrey via Dr. Alfred Price. **82:** Horsfal via Dr. Alfred Price, Dr. Alfred Price (two), via P. Arnold via Dr. Alfred Price, Powles via Dr. Alfred Price. **83:** Dr. Alfred Price (three), H. Peck via Dr. Alfred Price. **84-85:** Charles E. Brown/RAF Museum. **85 (inset):** Aerospace. **86:** Ministry of Defence (MOD), via Dr Alfred Price (three), Aerospace. **87:** RAF Museum, via Dr Alfred Price (two), Aerospace, MOD. **88:** RAF Museum (two), via V. Flintham, Aerospace. **89:** RAF Museum (two), Aerospace (two). **90:** Aerospace (two), Imperial War Museum (IWM). **91:** RAF Museum, Aerospace (three). **92:** Aerospace, MOD (two), via Dr Alfred Price (four). **93:** RAF Museum, via Dr Alfred Price, Peter R. Arnold collection (two), via Andrew Thomas. **94:** IWM, via Dr Alfred Price (three). **96:** via Dr Alfred Price (three). **97:** Aerospace (two), via Dr Alfred Price (two), MOD. **98:** RAF Museum, via Dr Alfred Price (two). **99:** via Dr Alfred Price (two), MOD, Aerospace (two). **100:** Public Archives of Canada via Dr Alfred Price, Arthur Houston via Dr Alfred Price, IWM. **101:** IWM (three), Aerospace, via Dr Alfred Price. **102:** via Dr Alfred Price (two). **103:** via Dr Alfred Price (two), via Andrew Thomas, MOD. **106:** MOD (four), via Andrew Thomas. **108:** via Dr Alfred Price (five), MOD. **109:** via Dr Alfred Price (two). **110:** RAF Museum, Aerospace, via Dr Alfred Price, Vickers. **111:** Aerospace (two), MOD. **112:** via Dr Alfred Price (three). **113:** via Dr Alfred Price. **114:** MOD, via Dr Alfred Price (three). **115:** via Dr Alfred Price (four), Aerospace. **119:** via Dr Alfred Price (five), Aerospace, Westland (two). **120:** John Kenyon via Peter R. Arnold, Peter R. Arnold collection, via Dr Alfred Price (three), MOD. **121:** Public Archives of Canada via Dr Alfred Price (three). **122:** Aerospace (three). **123:** Rolls-Royce, via Dr Alfred Price (three), RAF Museum. **124:** MOD, via Dr Alfred Price, Aerospace (three). **125:** via Dr Alfred Price (two),

Aerospace, via V. Flintham, Charles E. Brown. **126:** Aerospace, via V. Flintham (two), via Andrew Thomas, Aerospace. **127:** Charles E. Brown, Vickers (two), Aerospace, Peter R. Arnold collection. **128:** via Dr Alfred Price (three), via Grant Race. **130:** MOD (two), Aerospace (two), via Dr Alfred Price. **131:** Peter R. Arnold (11), Peter R. Arnold collection, Peter R. March. **132:** via Andrew Thomas (three), via Dr Alfred Price. **133:** Aerospace, British Aerospace, MOD, via Andrew Thomas, Ian Peak via Peter R. Arnold. **134:** via Dr Alfred Price, Peter R. Arnold collection (two), via Andrew Thomas. **135:** via Andrew Thomas, via Peter R. Arnold (four). **136:** via Grant Race, Aerospace, via Dr Alfred Price (two), Peter R. Arnold collection, Ian Pedder via Peter R. Arnold. **137:** via Dr Alfred Price (three), via V. Flintham, Irish Air Corps via Robert Hewson. **138:** Bill Dyche Collection via Paul Ludwig, Smithsonian via Paul Ludwig, Paul Ludwig, IWM via Paul Ludwig. **139:** Smithsonian via Paul Ludwig, Paul Ludwig. **140:** Bill Dyche via Paul Ludwig, USAF via Paul Ludwig, USAF via Dr Alfred Price. **141:** Hill via Paul Ludwig, USAF, IWM via Paul Ludwig. **142:** Marsh via Paul Ludwig, USAF via Paul Ludwig, via Paul Ludwig. **143:** Marsh via Paul Ludwig, Bill Dyche via Paul Ludwig, Dr Alfred Price (two). **144:** Dr Alfred Price, Comanitsky via Paul Ludwig, Lombard via Paul Ludwig, Don Bilyard via Paul Ludwig. **145:** via Paul Ludwig, Bettin via Paul Ludwig, National Archives via Paul Ludwig. **146:** William Skinner via Paul Ludwig (two), via PL, via Dr Alfred Price. **147:** Frank Hill via PL, via PL, William Skinner via PL. **148:** Hagins via PL, IWM via PL, Frank Hill via PL (two). **149:** USAAF via Dr Alfred Price. **150:** via PL (two), USAAF via Dr Alfred Price, IWM via Dr Alfred Price. **151:** via PL, Frank Sherman via PL. **152:** William Skinner via PL, Frank Hill via PL, via PL (two). **153:** William Skinner via PL (two), via PL, John Fawcett via PL, USAAF via Dr Alfred Price. **154:** William Skinner via PL, John Fawcett via PL (two). **155:** John Fawcett via PL, Haings via PL, William Skinner via PL, Arthur Bleiler via PL. **156-157:** MBB via Michael Stroud, Dr A. Price. **158:** Aerospace (three), Bruce Robertson. **159:** Aerospace, Bruce Robertson. **160:** Aerospace (all). **161:** Aerospace (three), MBB via Michael Stroud (two), Bundesarchiv via Dr A. Price, Bruce Robertson. **162:** Aerospace (three). **163:** Aerospace (three), Patrick Laureau. **164:** Aerospace (all). **165:** Aerospace (six), Bundesarchiv via Dr A. Price. **166:** Dr A. Price (two), Aerospace (two), Bundesarchiv via Dr A. Price. **167:** Aerospace (two), Dr A. Price (two), MBB via Michael Stroud. **168:** Dr A. Price (four), Aerospace (two), Imperial War Museum. **170:** Aerospace, Dr A. Price (two), MAP. **171:** Aerospace (three), Dr A. Price. **174:** Dr A. Price, Bundesarchiv via Dr A. Price. **175:** Dr A. Price (two), Bundesarchiv via John Weal. **176:** Bundesarchiv (four), Aerospace. **177:** Dr A. Price. **178:** Jim Winchester (two). **179:** Aerospace (four), Jim Winchester. **180:** Aerospace (three), Bundesarchiv via John Weal. **181:** Aerospace, A&AEE, USAF. **182:** Dr A. Price, Bundesarchiv, Aerospace (two). **183:** Bundesarchiv (two), Aerospace. **186-188:** Aerospace. **189:** Werner W. Gysin (three), P.H.T. Green. **191:** P.H.T. Green Collection. **193:** Bundesarchiv, Jim Winchester (five), Aerospace (two). **194-195:** Peter R. March. **196:** Bundesarchiv via John Weal, MBB, MacClancy Collection. **197:** Bundesarchiv via John Weal, Bundesarchiv, Imperial War Museum. **198:** Aerospace (five). **199:** Aerospace (three), Bruce Robertson. **200:** MoD, Aerospace (two), USAF, Bruce Robertson, MBB. **201:** Bundesarchiv via John Weal, Bundesarchiv (two). **202:** Bundesarchiv via Dr Alfred Price, Dr Alfred price, Bundesarchiv, Aerospace. **203:** Aerospace (two). **204:** Aerospace, Bundesarchiv (three), Imperial War Museum via John Weal. **205:** Bundesarchiv via John Weal, Aerospace. **206:** Bundesarchiv (two), Aerospace. **207:** Bundesarchiv, Aerospace. **208:** Aerospace (six). **209:** Aerospace (four). **210:** Aerospace (three), MoD. **211:** Aerospace, Bundesarchiv via John Weal. **212:** Bundesarchiv, Aerospace (three). **213:** Bundesarchiv via Dr Alfred Price, Bundesarchiv (two). **214:** Bundesarchiv via John Weal (two), Imperial War Museum via John Weal. **215:** Bundesarchiv, Aerospace (three). **216:** Bruce Robertson, Bundesarchiv via John Weal (two). **217:** MAP (two), Imperial War Museum, USAF, Aerospace, MoD, Yefim Gordon Archive (three), Imperial War Museum via John Weal, Bundesarchiv via John Weal. **218:** Bundesarchiv, Carmine de Napoli and R. Mancini (two). **219:** Bundesarchiv via John Weal, Carmine de Napoli and R. Mancini (two), Aerospace. **220:** Bundesarchiv via John Weal (two). **222:** Aerospace (three). **223:** Dragisa Brasnovic, Aerospace (two), Bundesarchiv via Patrick Laureau, via Alexander Mladenov. **224:** Bundesarchiv, John Weal, via Dr Alfred Price, Bundesarchiv via John Weal. **225:** Aerospace (four). **226:** Aerospace, Imperial War Museum via John Weal. **227:** Bundesarchiv, Bundesarchiv via John Weal, Aerospace (two). **228:** Dr Alfred Price, Aerospace (two), Larry Davis Collection. **229:** Aerospace (four). **230:** Tim Senior (three), Aerospace). **231:** Tim Senior (five). **232:** Aerospace (three). **234:** Aerospace (three). **235:** Aerospace (two), Dr Alfred Price. **236:** Aerospace (three). **237:** Aerospace (five). **238:** Aerospace (three), Leon Frankel Collection via Shlomo Aloni. **239:** Aerospace (four). **240:** Aerospace (four), Hispano (two). **241:** Hispano, Aerospace, Bruce Robertson. **242:** Aerospace (three). **244:** Aerospace (four). **245:** Carmine de Napoli and R. Mancini (two), Aerospace (two). Jeremy Flack/API, Simon Watson, MBB, Photo Link, Peter R. March. **249:** Tim Senior, Aerospace (three). **250:** Aerospace (three), Bundesarchiv via John Weal. **251:** Alexander Mladenov, Aerospace (five). **252:** Aerospace (two), Israel Ben-Shachar Collection via Shlomo Aloni, Aaron Finkel Collection via Shlomo Aloni, Carmine de Napoli and R. Mancini (two). **253:** Aerospace (five).